The Extraordinary Book
of Native American Lists

The Extraordinary Book of Native American Lists

ARLENE HIRSCHFELDER
PAULETTE F. MOLIN

THE SCARECROW PRESS, INC.
Lanham · Toronto · Plymouth, UK
2012

Published by Scarecrow Press, Inc.
A wholly owned subsidary of The Rowman & Littlefield Publishing Group, Inc.
4501 Forbes Boulevard, Suite 200, Lanham, Maryland 20706
http://www.scarecrowpress.com

10 Thornbury Road, Plymouth PL6 7PP, United Kingdom

British Library Cataloguing in Publication Information Available

Library of Congress Cataloging-in-Publication Data

Hirschfelder, Arlene B.
 The extraordinary book of Native American lists / Arlene Hirschfelder, Paulette F. Molin.
  p. cm.
 Includes bibliographical references and index.
 ISBN 978-0-8108-7709-2 (cloth : alk. paper) — ISBN 978-0-8108-7710-8 (ebook)
 1. Indians of North America—History—Registers. 2. Indians of North America—
Social life and customs—Registers. I. Molin, Paulette Fairbanks. II. Title.
 E77.H586 2012
 970.004'97—dc23

                    2011026005

♾™ The paper used in this publication meets the minimum requirements of American
National Standard for Information Sciences—Permanence of Paper for Printed Library
Materials, ANSI/NISO Z39.48-1992.

Printed in the United States of America

Arlene Hirschfelder dedicates this book to Dennis Hirschfelder, researcher extraordinaire.

Paulette Molin dedicates this work to the memory of her brother, Jim, with wishes for fine Seabee days always. Love and thanks to him, Larry, and the rest of the family.

Contents

Acknowledgments

Thank you to all the individuals and organizations that assisted us:

Association for the Study of American Indian Literatures Listserv
Ginny Z. Berson, National Federation of Community Broadcasters
Tommy Cheng, Hawaiian culture and hula teacher
Lee Francis IV, Wordcraft Circle of Native Writers and Storytellers
Hampton (Virginia) Public Library, especially Inter-Library Loan service
Megan Minoka Hill, Harvard (University) Project on American Indian
    Economic Development
Geary Hobson, poet, novelist, literary scholar
Rima Ibrahim, Brooklyn Museum
Shawn Pensoneau, National Indian Gaming Commission
Joseph Procopio, Economic Policy Institute
Kimberly Roppolo, Wordcraft Circle of Native Writers
    and Storytellers
Brittany Sandefur, All Nations Skate Project
Beverly Singer, independent filmmaker
Mytia Smith, American Indian Film Institute
Loris Taylor, Native Public Media
Jack Trope, Association on American Indian Affairs

Stephen Ryan, senior editor, The Scarecrow Press, Inc.
Jayme Bartles Reed, production editor, Rowman & Littlefield
Christen Karniski, assistant editor, The Scarecrow Press, Inc.

Introduction

While Native groups are perhaps the most studied people in our society, they too often remain the least understood and, for too many, invisible, imaginary, or non-existent. Fictions and stereotypes (descriptions of war-bonneted, war-painted, tipi dwellers) predominate, obscuring substantive and fascinating facts about Native societies. As a 2008 Harvard study points out, such facts reveal that these societies are as varied "as the life and experience of the subsistence fisherman living in the Native Village of Quinhagak, Alaska, is from the life and experience of the Wall Street-savvy Mohegan Tribal Council member, as the Navajo veteran of World War II is from the Akimel O'odham teenager skateboarding on the Gila River reservation, and as the parliamentary Flathead democracy is from the traditional Cochiti theocracy" (Harvard Project on American Indian Economic Development, *The State of the Native Nations: Conditions Under U.S. Policies of Self-Determination*. New York: Oxford University Press, 2008, p. 1).

Since 1977, when *The Book of Lists* by David Wallechinsky and Amy Wallace first appeared, hundreds of list books have been published, covering countless subjects. Not one of them, however, has been devoted exclusively to Native Americans. *The Extraordinary Book of Native American Lists* seeks to address that gap, underscoring the centrality of tribal nations, histories, and cultures in North America.

The Extraordinary Book of Native American Lists, arranged into twenty-four chapters, communicates information about the rich histories and contemporary presence of Native peoples in the Lower 48, Alaska, and Hawaii. Readers will be introduced to United States senators, Medal of Freedom winners, Medal of Honor recipients, Major League baseball players, and Olympians, as well as a United States vice president, NASA astronaut, Pulitzer Prize winner, and National Book Award winner. Readers will learn about Native figures from a wide range of cultures and professions, including award-winning athletes, authors, filmmakers, musicians, and environmentalists. *The Extraordinary Book of Native American Lists* also features sidebars with fascinating facts, as well as print and Web resources and an index.

The following twelve points guided the authors in researching and compiling lists for *The Extraordinary Book of Native American Lists*:

1. The authors emphasize major themes, providing lists that include selected cultural events, firsts, films, legislation, organizations, and award honorees.

2. The terms *American Indians* and *Native Americans* are used interchangeably to refer collectively to Native peoples from hundreds of tribal nations in what is now the United States. In Canada, *Indians, Inuit,* and *Métis* refer to three separate groups of indigenous peoples. *First Nations* is a term that collectively refers to Indian peoples who live in Canada. These terms also encompass hundreds of Native cultures.

3. The lists have primarily a United States focus. At times, though, First Nations people of Canada are included, especially when considering individuals from tribal nations with lands, bands, and international relations on both sides of the U.S.–Canadian border. As much as the authors would have liked to incorporate additional First Nations lists, it was beyond the scope of this book to do so.

4. Generally speaking, *Indian Country* refers to the areas over which the federal government and tribes exercise primary jurisdiction, including land within Indian reservations and lands outside a reservation designated primarily for Indian use. The term, which is used primarily in legal and sociopolitical contexts, also refers to Native communities and areas.

5. In southwestern Alaska, many people prefer the name *Yupik* (or *Yupik Eskimo*) rather than *Eskimo*, and in northwestern Alaska, *Iñupiat* is preferred. In Canada, where the word *Eskimo* has practically disappeared, there is a preference for *Inuit*.

6. The word *Aleut*, whose meaning is unclear, was bestowed upon Native people living on the Aleutian and Pribilof Islands by the first Russian explorers to visit the area. Many present-day Native people from the Aleutians prefer to call themselves *Unangan* ("the people of the passes"), the original word they used to describe themselves.

7. Where possible, the authors have used tribal names and spellings preferred by tribal nations. In a number of cases, though, there are variations, such as those reflected in research materials as well as tribal or individual preferences or changes. Names such as *Ojibway* and *Ojibwe*, applied to Native peoples also called *Anishinaabe* and *Chippewa*, have varied spellings. The Winnebago of Wisconsin officially renamed themselves *Ho-Chunk*, but the Winnebago Tribe of Nebraska has not changed its name. *Sioux*, the popular name for Dakota and Lakota peoples, is often used in official documents, book titles, and other sources.

8. Names of some individuals appear with their specific band or reservation (as in Rosebud Sioux or Turtle Mountain Chippewa), others do not, depending upon source materials.

9. At times, spellings of personal names and tribal affiliations vary. For example, depending on the source, the name Maria Tallchief may appear as Maria Tall Chief. The authors generally adhere to the information provided

by organizations and other sources, but may include changes such as adding tribal affiliations.

10. Lists vary in length, depending on factors such as the state of published research on a given topic or the topic's popularity with authors and filmmakers. Again, they are selective, not comprehensive. In other words, not all awards could be cited, nor all individuals in particular areas of endeavor or expertise. Lists are also subject to change, especially those with time-sensitive material. Others will remain the same over time.

11. Lists throughout the book include awards granted by a range of organizations. Depending on the resource materials, identifying information varies. Some organizations cite tribal affiliations and professional titles for award recipients, others do not. Some identify a break in annual awards (years without awards being granted), others do not. Likewise, contact information for organizations varies, including some with office headquarters and others with Web site addresses.

12. *The Extraordinary Book of Native American Lists* is intended as an informational starting point. It is hoped that the lists will prompt readers to delve into research materials housed in libraries and resource centers, as well as accurate information available online through countless Internet sites, many of which are listed throughout the book.

1

History

ANCIENT AMERICA

Fourteen Books about Ancient America

1. *Ancient Cahokia and the Mississippians,* by Timothy R. Pauketat (2004).
2. *Ancient Hawaii,* by Herb Kawainui Kane (1998).
3. *Ancient North America,* by Brian M. Fagan (2005).
4. *Ancient Puebloan Southwest,* by John Kantner (2005).
5. *Ancient Ruins of the Southwest: An Archaeological Guide,* revised edition, by David Grant Noble (1991).
6. *Atlas of Ancient America,* by Michael Coe, Dean Snow, and Elizabeth Benson (1986).
7. *Exploring Ancient Native America: An Archaeological Guide,* by David Hurst Thomas (2000).
8. *The First Americans* (Time-Life Books: The American Indians), series edited by Henry Woodhead (1992).
9. *Guide to Ancient Native American Sites,* by Michael Durham (1994).
10. *Indian Mounds of the Middle Ohio Valley: A Guide to Mounds and Earthworks of the Adena, Hopewell, Cole, and Fort Ancient People,* by Susan L. Woodward and Jerry N. McDonald (2002).
11. *In Search of Ancient Alaska: Evidence of Mysteries of the Past,* by Ellen Bielawski (2006).
12. *Keepers of the Treasures: Protecting Historic Properties and Cultural Traditions on Indian Lands,* by Patricia Parker (1990).
13. *Native Americans before 1492: The Moundbuilding Centers of the Eastern Woodlands,* by Lynda Norene Shaffer (1992).
14. *The Rock Art of Eastern North America: Capturing Images and Insight,* edited by Carol Diaz-Granados and James R. Duncan (2000).

Ancient and Historic Sites

Many ancient and historic areas in the United States have played a significant role in the history of Native Americans. These include archaeological sites, mounds, parks, battlegrounds, treaty sites, tribal villages, trails, massacre sites, trading posts, churches, forts, and other cultural properties.

The National Park Service (NPS), which has numerous designations for these ancient and historic areas, is the agency that cares for these places. Listed below are the Web sites for NPS lists of nationally designated sites:

National Heritage Areas: http://www.cr.nps.gov/heritageareas/VST/INDEX.HTM

National Register of Historic Places: http://www.cr.nps.gov/nr

National Historic Landmarks Program: http://www.cr.nps.gov/nhl/designations/listsofNHLs.htm

TIMELINE: 1507 TO 1911

1507	The name "America" was used for the first time on a 1507 world map created by Martin Waldseemüller.
1540–42	Native peoples living in what is now Arizona, New Mexico, Texas, and Kansas encountered non-Indians for the first time when Spanish explorer Francisco Vásquez de Coronado and hundreds of his followers searched in vain for the Seven Cities of Gold.
1564–65	French artist Jacques Le Moyne drew some of the earliest known European pictorial representations of American Indians.
1565	The oldest permanent European settlement in what is now the United States was established in St. Augustine, present-day Florida, in the Timucuan homeland.
1585	Sir Walter Raleigh established the first English settlement in North America on Roanoke Island, present-day North Carolina. The colony lasted one year. Artist and cartographer John White accompanied a Raleigh-sponsored voyage to present-day Outer Banks of North Carolina, where he made numerous sketches of Native people.
1598	Spanish colonist Juan de Oñate took formal "possession" of an area encompassing Texas, New Mexico, Arizona, and lower California in the name of Spain and established the first Spanish capital near what is known today as Ohkay Owingeh (formerly San Juan Pueblo).

1603–15	Samuel de Champlain's voyages in the Northeast lead to extensive contacts with various Algonquian and Iroquois tribal nations.
1607	The British Virginia Company established a settlement at Jamestown (present-day Virginia) in the homeland of the Powhatan Chiefdom.
1609	The Spanish founded Santa Fe (present-day New Mexico) in the Pueblo homeland.
1620	English colonists arrived at Plymouth, Massachusetts. Barely surviving the first winter, they were assisted by Tisquantum (Squanto) (Wampanoag), who served as a cultural broker.
1624	Dutch colonists founded Fort Orange (Albany) in New Netherlands (New York) in Algonquian and Iroquoian territory.
1626	Carnarsee/Shinnecock/Manhattan Indians who occupied the southern end of the island of what is now Manhattan negotiated a land transaction with Peter Minuit, Dutch governor of New Amsterdam, now New York. The only account of the event was contained in a letter written by a Dutch official indicating that "they have bought the island of Manhattes from the Wild Men for the value of sixty guilders."
1638	English colonists in what is now New Haven, Connecticut, negotiated a land sale with Quinnipiac Indians and established what is called the first reservation in the United States.
1650	John Eliot, an English missionary known as the "Apostle to the Indians," established Natick, the first of fourteen "praying Indian" villages in Massachusetts Bay Colony. Indians were required to convert to Christianity and renounce their Native languages, ceremonies, beliefs, dress, and customs in the praying towns.
1680–92	During this period, Pueblo Indians in New Mexico remained free and independent after their religious leaders united and successfully expelled the Spanish from their homelands. In 1692, the Spanish returned and reconquered Pueblo villages.
1737	Delaware "Walking Purchase" The "Walking Purchase" refers to the means by which descendants of Pennsylvania founder William Penn and their agents acquired 1.2 million acres of Delaware (Lenape) land, an area about the size of Rhode Island. Claiming that an early deed ceded Delaware land "as far west as a man could walk in a day and a half," Pennsylvania's colonial administrators hired three of their fastest runners, who ran for sixty miles, cheating the Delawares, who were forced to give up their lands.

1751   Albany Plan of Union

Representing an early attempt to form a union of the British colonies in America, this plan was proposed by Benjamin Franklin. Franklin, who was familiar with the Haudenosaunee (Iroquois Confederacy, Six Nations), had written the year before:

> It would be a very strange Thing, if six Nations of ignorant Savages should be capable of forming a Scheme for such an Union, and be able to execute it in such a Manner, as that it has subsisted Ages, and appears indissoluble; and yet that a like Union should be impracticable for ten or a Dozen *English* Colonies, to whom it is more necessary, and must be more advantageous; and who cannot be supposed to want an equal Understanding of their Interests.

1763   Treaty of Paris

This treaty, signed by Great Britain, France, and Spain, ended the Seven Years' War (French and Indian War). The British gained substantial areas of land in North America, especially at the expense of both Indians and the French. The latter gave up New France and other claims to colonized territory. Indians, who were not mentioned in the treaty, played a large part in the war for both sides.

Royal Proclamation of 1763

This British ruling, issued by King George III, resulted in the Proclamation Line of 1763, which ran along the crest of the Appalachian Mountains. The proclamation designated the land west of the line, from the Appalachian Mountains to the Mississippi River, as Indian country, but the crown began negotiating treaties for lands in that region a short time later.

1774–75   Formation of the Indian Departments

During the First Continental Congress in 1774, delegates committed funds for Indian affairs and appointed a Committee on Indian Affairs to negotiate terms of neutrality or support from the Indians. In 1775, the First Continental Congress assumed control over Indian affairs, creating northern, southern, and middle Indian departments and appointing Benjamin Franklin, Patrick Henry, and James Wilson as their first commissioners.

1776   Declaration of Independence—excerpt concerning Indians:

"He [the king of Great Britain] has excited domestic insurrections amongst us, and has endeavoured to bring on the inhabitants of our frontiers, the merciless Indian Savages, whose known rule of warfare, is an undistinguished destruction of all ages, sexes and conditions."

1783   Confederation Congress Proclamation of 1783 (or Proclamation of the Continental Congress)
        This proclamation was enacted to prohibit unauthorized settlement or purchase of Indian lands. Suggested by George Washington, the act sought to promote peace between the United States and American Indians by preventing white encroachment on Indian lands.

1786   Ordinance for the Regulation of Indian Affairs
        Approved by the Continental Congress, this ordinance to govern trade with Indians proposed a licensing system administered by superintendents and agents. The policy was aimed at curbing actions of irresponsible traders and independent actions of states.

1787   Northwest Ordinance
        Passed by the Continental Congress, the Northwest Ordinance established the Northwest Territory and inaugurated the policy by which the United States would organize and govern the region west of the Appalachians. Concerning American Indians, the policy stated: "The utmost good faith shall always be observed towards the Indians."

1790   Trade and Intercourse Act
        The first of a series of laws passed by Congress "to regulate trade and intercourse with the Indians." The legislation sought to restrain frontier whites from invading tribal lands and violating United States treaties with Indian nations.

1796   Establishment of Government Trading Houses
        In response to George Washington's recommendation, Congress established a system of government trading houses to carry on trade "with the several Indian nations, within the limits of the United States." This measure, called the factory system, was designed to counteract the Spanish and British, ensure a good price for furs, and supply Indians with cheaper and better goods. The trading stores were abolished in 1822.

1802   Trade and Intercourse Act
        An act passed by Congress "to regulate trade and intercourse with the Indian tribes, and to preserve peace on the frontiers." It largely restated temporary measures passed in the 1790s and remained in force until 1834.

1819   Civilization Fund Act
        Enacted by Congress on March 3, 1819, this act provided for instruction in "the habits and arts of civilization" among the Indian tribes

vation, unless such a jurisdiction has been granted by Congress. The court enunciated a doctrine of plenary federal power that "it alone can enforce its laws on all the tribes."

1887   General Allotment Act (Dawes Act)

Named for Massachusetts senator Henry L. Dawes, the sponsor of the General Allotment Act of 1887, the Dawes Act provided for the breakup of collectively held landholdings of tribes by partitioning reservation lands into individually owned parcels, or allotments, and selling the "surplus."

1898   Curtis Act

This legislation extended the provisions of the General Allotment Act in Indian Territory (present-day Oklahoma), authorizing the allotment of Cherokee, Chickasaw, Choctaw, Creek, and Seminole lands, abolishing tribal courts, and prohibiting the enforcement of tribal laws in federal court. The act also abolished the constitutional governments of these tribal nations.

1903   Plenary Power Doctrine

In *Lone Wolf v. Hitchcock*, the Supreme Court gave Congress the authority to decide how to deal with and dispose of all Indian lands. Congress created the doctrine of plenary power in Indian affairs, which means there is no higher authority in deciding issues in Indian affairs.

1911   The Society of American Indians (SAI), considered the first pan-Indian political organization in the country, was organized and held its first annual conference on Columbus Day weekend in Columbus, Ohio. SAI's founders included Carlos Montezuma (Yavapai), Charles Eastman (Santee Sioux), Thomas L. Sloan (Omaha), Charles E. Dagenett (Peoria), Laura Cornelius (Oneida), and Henry Standing Bear (Lakota).

Ten Books of Timelines and Chronologies of Native American History

1. *The American Indian: 1492–1976,* by Henry C. Dennis (1977).
2. *Chronology of American Indian History,* by Liz Sonneborn (updated edition, 2006).
3. *Chronology of Native North American History: From Pre-Columbian Times to the Present,* edited by Duane Champagne (1994).
4. *Handbook of the American Frontier: Four Centuries of Indian-White Relationships,* vol. 5, *Chronology, Bibliography, Index,* by J. Norman Heard (1998).
5. *Native American History: A Chronology of a Culture's Vast Achievements and Their Links to World Events,* by Judith Nies (1996).
6. *Native Time: A Historical Time Line of Native America,* by Lee Francis (1996).

7. *This Day in Native American History: Important Dates in the History of North America's Native Peoples for Every Calendar Day*, by Phil Konstantin (2002).
8. *The Timeline of Native Americans: The Ultimate Guide to North America's Indigenous Peoples*, by Greg O'Brien (2008).
9. *Timelines of Native American History*, by Carl Waldman (1994).
10. *Timelines of Native American History: Through the Centuries with Mother Earth and Father Sky*, by Susan Hazen-Hammond (1997).

Images of Native Peoples by Jacques Le Moyne, 1564, and John White, 1585

In 1564, Jacques Le Moyne, a French artist, accompanied a French expedition in an ill-fated attempt to colonize northern Florida. He traveled through the area, depicting its landscape, flora, fauna, and, most importantly, the lives of the Timucua, who were Native inhabitants of present-day northern Florida. All but one of Le Moyne's original drawings were reportedly burned up in a Spanish attack on the French settlement. On his return to France, Le Moyne redrew the Florida scenes from memory. A Flemish master engraver, Theodor De Bry, reproduced the drawings and Le Moyne's descriptions, publishing them in 1591. The engraved drawings are reported to be the earliest images of Native people by European colonists.

In 1585, John White, an English artist and mapmaker, and Thomas Harriot, explorer and scientist, were among those who sailed with explorer Sir Richard Grenville to present-day Roanoke Island, North Carolina. During his time at Roanoke, White made a number of watercolor sketches of the surrounding landscape and the Native Algonkin (Algonquian) peoples. In 1588, Harriot published *A Briefe and True Report of the New Found Land of Virginia*, an account of the 1585 exploration, without illustrations. In 1590, Harriot's account was republished by Theodor De Bry in four languages, with the addition of engravings based on the watercolors White created in America.

Visual representations of Native peoples by Le Moyne and White became influential at a time when Europeans were first becoming aware of Native Americans and beginning to form ideas about them.

The Oldest Recorded Native American Map, 1602

The oldest recorded Native American map was made by Miguel, "an Indian, native of the provinces of New Mexico," who had been captured by the Spanish and taken to Mexico City, where he was interrogated and instructed to make a sketch of his homeland. The map covers a large area of the south central Plains, demonstrating Native networks and geographic knowledge. The map's existence also reflects Spanish interests in colonial expansion.

EXPLORERS AND COLONIZERS

Native Explorers and Interpreters of North America, 1526–1854

1526   Chicora (Shakori Indian?)
              Chicora guided Spanish explorer Lucas Vásquez de Ayllón to
              present-day South Carolina.

1535   Domagaya and Taidanoaguy (Huron)
              Domagaya and Taidanoaguy, two sons of Chief Donnacona
              (Huron), guided the second expedition of French explorer Jacques
              Cartier to explore bays, islands, and the St. Lawrence River,
              Canada.

1541   The Turk (Pawnee?)
              The Turk guided explorer Francisco Vásquez de Coronado's expedi-
              tion through the Texas Panhandle, Oklahoma, and the Arkansas River
              into Kansas.

1619   Tisquantum/Squanto (Wampanoag)
              Tisquantum served as a pilot for Captain Thomas Dermer, guid-
              ing him along the coast north of Cape Cod. Skilled in the English
              language, in 1621 he also served as an interpreter for the Wampanoag
              sachem Massasoit in his dealings with the Pilgrims of Plymouth
              colony.

1749–50   Nemacolin (Lenape/Delaware)
              Nemacolin guided frontiersman Thomas Cresap in clearing a trail
              between the Potomac and Monongahela Rivers. The trail, which came
              to be called Nemacolin's Path, ran through mountains from present-
              day Virginia through Maryland into Pennsylvania.

ca. 1770–71   Matonabbee (Chipewyan)
              Matonabbee, a well-known trade leader, traveled aboard Hudson
              Bay Company ships on expeditions along the west coast of Hudson Bay.
              He guided explorer Samuel Hearne along the length of the Coppermine
              River, in present-day Northwest Territories and Nunavut.

1804   Sacagawea/Sakakawea, "bird woman" (Shoshone)
              During the winter of 1803–4, the Corps of Discovery, as the Lewis
              and Clark expedition was known, hired Toussaint Charbonneau as
              an interpreter. His wife, Sacagawea, joined the expedition, serving as a
              guide, interpreter, and diplomat to dozens of Indian tribes located along
              the route from Mandan villages in present-day North Dakota to the
              Pacific Coast at the mouth of the Columbia River.

1811   Marie Aioe Dorion (Ioway)
         Marie Dorion helped guide Jacob Astor's overland expedition from the Dakota region to the Oregon coast, where the American Fur Company's outpost at Astoria was located.

1834   Black Beaver (Lenape/Delaware)
         Black Beaver, an interpreter, guided General Henry Leavenworth and Colonel Henry Dodge's expedition, known as the Dragoon Expedition, from Fort Gibson, present-day eastern Oklahoma, to southwestern Oklahoma and northern Texas. The next year he guided several other expeditions out of Fort Leavenworth, Kansas, to the southern Plains. He explored the country between the Arkansas and Colorado Rivers and the eastern Rockies of present-day Colorado.

         Jesse Chisholm (Cherokee)
         Because of his contacts with tribes and his language skills (he reportedly knew fourteen different Native languages), he found work as a guide and interpreter for numerous military expeditions. Along with Black Beaver (Lenape/Delaware), he helped guide Leavenworth and Dodge's expedition.

1845–46 Chief James Sagundai (Lenape/Delaware)
         Chief James Sagundai guided John Charles Frémont on his third western expedition into California.

         Truckee (Northern Paiute)
         Truckee guided the third western expedition of John Charles Frémont into California. Speaking his native language, English, and Spanish, he regularly interpreted between Paiute bands and non-Indians.

1850s   Irateba (Mohave)
         Irateba guided a series of U.S. Army expeditions through present-day western Arizona and southeastern California.

1853–54 Jacob Ennis, Solomon Everett, James Harrison, John Johnnycake, John Moses, John Smith, Wahone, George Washington, Weluchas, and Captain James Wolff (Lenape/Delaware)
         These guides, many of whom spoke or understood English, guided explorer John Charles Frémont's fifth expedition from Westport, present-day Kansas City, Missouri, to the Rocky Mountains.

Nine Books about Christopher Columbus

1. *1491: New Revelations of the Americas before Columbus*, by Charles Mann (2005).
2. *Columbian Consequences*, Volume 1: *Archaeological and Historical Perspectives on the Spanish Borderlands West* (1989); Volume 2: *Archaeological and*

Estimates of the North American Native Population, circa 1492

James Mooney	1910	1.153 million
Karl Sapper	1924	2.5–3.5 million
William C. MacLeod	1928	1.0 million
James Mooney	1928	1.148 million
Walter F. Wilcox	1931	1.02 million
Alfred Kroeber	1939	900,000
Angel Rosenblatt	1954	1.0 million
Homer Aschmann	1959	2.24 million
Henry F. Dobyns	1966	9.8 million
Harold E. Driver	1969	3.5 million
Douglas H. Ubelaker	1976	2.2 million
William M. Denevan	1976	4.4 million
Russell Thornton and		
Joan Marsh-Thornton	1981	1.8–5.13 million
Henry F. Dobyns	1984	18 million

Source: Paul Stuart, *Nations within a Nation: Historical Statistics of American Indians*, 1987.

Native American Population in the United States, 1850–2010

Year	Total (Includes Alaska Natives, beginning in 1960)
1850	400,764
1860	339,421
1870	313,712
1880	306,543
1890	248,253
1900	237,196
1910	265,683
1920	244,437
1930	332,397
1940	333,969
1950	343,410
1960	551,669
1970	827,268
1980	1,420,400
1990	1,959,234
2000	4,100,000
2010*	5,220,579

Source: U.S. Census Bureau
*In 2010, 2,932,248 reported being "American Indian and Alaska Native alone."

Historical Perspectives on the Spanish Borderlands East (1990); Volume 3: *The Spanish Borderlands in Pan-American Perspective* (1991), by David Hurst Thomas et al.

3. *The Columbian Exchange: Biological and Cultural Consequences of 1492*, by Alfred W. Crosby Jr. (1972).
4. *Columbus: The Four Voyages*, by Lawrence Bergreen (2011).
5. *Columbus and Other Cannibals*, by Jack D. Forbes (1992).
6. *Columbus: His Enterprise: Exploding the Myth*, by Hans Konig (1992).
7. *The Conquest of Paradise: Christopher Columbus and the Columbian Legacy*, by Kirkpatrick Sale (1991).
8. *Rethinking Columbus: The Next 500 Years*, edited by Bill Bigelow and Bob Peterson (1998).
9. *Without Discovery: A Native Response to Columbus*, edited by Ray Gonzalez (1992).

Ten Books about Colonization

1. *Aloha Betrayed: Native Hawaiian Resistance to American Colonialism*, by Noenoe K. Silva (2004).
2. *The American Discovery of Europe*, by Jack D. Forbes (2007).
3. *Beyond 1492: Encounters in Colonial North America*, by James Axtell (1992).
4. *Ceremonies of Possession in Europe's Conquest of the New World, 1492–1640*, by Patricia Seed (1995).
5. *Decolonizing Methodologies: Research and Indigenous Peoples*, by Linda Tuhiwai Smith (1999).
6. *Hawaiian Blood: Colonialism and the Politics of Sovereignty and Indigeneity*, by J. Kēhaulani Kauanui (2008).
7. *The Legacy of Conquest: The Unbroken Past of the American West*, by Patricia Nelson Limerick (1987).
8. *The Myth of the Savage and the Beginnings of French Colonialism in the Americas*, by Olive Patricia Dickason (1984).
9. *Nation Within: The History of the American Occupation of Hawai'i*, by Tom Coffman (2009).
10. *Shaking the Rattle: Healing the Trauma of Colonization*, by Barbara-Helen Hill (1995).

Fourteen Books about Explorers and Expeditions

1. *Across Arctic America: Narrative of the Fifth Thule Expedition (1927)*, by Knud Rasmussen (1999).
2. *The Atlas of North American Exploration: From the Norse Voyages to the Race to the Pole*, by William H. Goetzmann and Glyndwr Williams (1992).
3. *Captain Cook: Master of the Seas*, by Frank McLynn (2011).

4. "A Chronology of Non-Indian Explorers of North America and Their Contacts with Indians," by Carl Waldman. In *Atlas of the North American Indian*, third edition (2009).

5. *The European Challenge* (Time-Life Books: The American Indians), series edited by Henry Woodhead (1992).

6. *Explorers and Settlers: Historic Places Commemorating the Early Exploration and Settlement of the United States*, by Robert G. Ferris (1968).

7. *Explorers of the New World*, by Jake Mattox (2004).

8. *First Encounters: Spanish Explorations in the Caribbean and the United States, 1492–1570*, edited by Jerald T. Melanich and Susan Milbrath (1989).

9. *Historical Dictionary of the Discovery and Exploration of the Northwest Coast of America*, by Robin Inglis (2008).

10. *Indian Life on the Northwest Coast of North America, As Seen by the Early Explorers and Fur Traders During the Last Decades of the Eighteenth Century*, by Erna Gunther (1972).

11. *Lewis and Clark Through Indian Eyes: Nine Indian Writers on the Legacy of the Expedition*, edited by Alvin Josephy Jr. (2007).

12. *A Life Wild and Perilous: Mountain Men and the Paths to the Pacific*, by Robert M. Utley (1997).

13. *Native America, Discovered and Conquered: Thomas Jefferson, Lewis and Clark, and Manifest Destiny*, by Robert J. Miller (2008).

14. *Russians in Alaska, 1732–1867*, by Lydia Black (2004).

Seventeen Books about North American Indian Wars

1. *Andrew Jackson and His Indian Wars*, by Robert V. Remini (2001).

2. *Anóoshi Lingit Aani Ká: Russians in Tlingit America, The Battles of Sitka 1802 and 1804*, edited by Richard and Nora Dauenhauer (2008).

3. *Chronicle of the Indian Wars: From Colonial Times to Wounded Knee*, by Alan Axelrod (1992).

4. *Crucible of War: The Seven Years' War and the Fate of Empire in British North America*, by Fred Anderson (2000).

5. *Encyclopedia of Indian Wars: Western Battles and Skirmishes, 1850–1890*, by Gregory Michno (2004).

6. *European and Native American Warfare, 1675–1815*, by Armstrong Starkey (1998).

7. *A Good Year to Die: The Story of the Great Sioux War*, by Charles M. Robinson III (1995).

8. *Indian Wars*, by Robert M. Utley and Wilcomb E. Washburn (1977).

9. *Lakota and Cheyenne: Indian Views of the Great Sioux War*, edited by Jerome A. Greene (1994).

10. *The Last Indian War: The Nez Perce Story*, by Elliott West (2009).

11. *Little Bighorn Remembered: The Untold Indian Story of Custer's Last Stand*, by Herman Viola (1999).
12. *The Name of War: King Philip's War and the Origins of American Identity*, by Jill Lepore (1999).
13. *North American Indian Wars*, by Richard H. Dillon (1983).
14. *Once They Moved Like the Wind: Cochise, Geronimo, and the Apache Wars*, by David Roberts (1993).
15. *President Washington's Indian War: The Struggle for the Old Northwest, 1790–95*, by Wiley Sword (1995).
16. *The Seminole Wars: America's Longest Indian Conflict*, by John Missall and Mary Lou Missall (2004).
17. *The Shawnees and the War for America*, by Colin G. Calloway (2007).

MISSIONS AND MISSIONARIES

Fourteen Seventeenth-Century Indian Praying Towns in Massachusetts Bay Colony

Beginning with Natick in 1650, John Eliot, the English missionary known as the "Apostle to the Indians," established fourteen "praying towns" in the Massachusetts Bay Colony; others were created in Connecticut, Martha's Vineyard, and Nantucket. Eliot sought to further the colonial mission of Christianizing and Anglicizing Indians by separating them from the influences of their non-converted peers and by teaching them to live and worship like the English. After King Philip's War (1675–1676), the praying towns were largely abandoned.

Historical and contemporary sources offer conflicting information about the exact locations of the fourteen towns. The spellings of the praying towns have also varied over the centuries.

Indian Praying Town	*Possible Current Location of the Praying Town*
1. Chabanakongkomun	Webster, Massachusetts
2. Hassanamesit	Grafton, Massachusetts
3. Magunkaquog	Hopkinton, Massachusetts
4. Manchaug	Sutton, Massachusetts
5. Manexit	Fabyan, Connecticut
6. Nashobah	Littleton, Massachusetts
7. Natick	Natick, Massachusetts
8. Okommakamesit	Marlborough, Massachusetts
9. Pakachoog	Worcester, Massachusetts
10. Punkapoag	Canton, Massachusetts
11. Quantisset	Thompson, Connecticut
12. Wabaquasset	Woodstock, Connecticut
13. Wacuntug	Uxbridge, Massachusetts
14. Wamesit	Lowell, Massachusetts

> ## Quinnipiac Reservation
>
> English colonizers established what would later be called a "reservation" for the Quinnipiac people at Mioonhktuck (present-day East Haven, Connecticut) in 1638. The result of a Quinnipiac-English treaty, the terms reduced the original Quinnipiac land base to 1,200 acres, which were subject to the jurisdiction of an English magistrate or agent. The English also imposed rules forbidding the Quinnipiac from selling or leaving their lands or from receiving "foreign" Indians. The Quinnipiac were further prohibited from buying firearms or whiskey. They were required to reject their own religious practices, viewed by Puritans as the teachings of the devil, and to adopt Christian beliefs.

Nine Books about Missions and Missionaries

1. *American Indians and Christian Missions: Studies in Cultural Conflict*, by Henry W. Bowden (1981).
2. *American Protestantism and United States Indian Policy, 1869–82*, by Robert H. Keller (1983).
3. *Indians, Franciscans, and Spanish Colonization*, by Robert H. Jackson and Edward Castillo (1995).
4. *Indians, Missionaries, and Merchants: The Legacy of Colonial Encounters on the California Frontiers*, by Kent G. Lightfoot (2006).
5. *The Jesuit Relations: Natives and Missionaries in Seventeenth-Century North America*, by Allan Greer (2000).
6. *Laboring in the Fields of the Lord: Spanish Missions and Southeastern Indians*, by Jerald T. Milanich (2006).
7. *Missionary Conquest: The Gospel and Native American Cultural Genocide*, by George E. Tinker (1993).
8. *The Poor Indians: British Missionaries, Native Americans, and Colonial Sensibility*, by Laura M. Stevens (2006).
9. *Presbyterian Missionary Attitudes toward American Indians, 1837–1893*, by Michael C. Coleman (1985).

HISTORY THROUGH VISUAL AND LITERARY ARTS

Thirty Eighteenth- and Nineteenth-Century Artist-Historians of Native Peoples

During the eighteenth and nineteenth centuries, numerous artists drew and painted Native peoples who lived in present-day contiguous United States, Alaska, or Hawaii. Self-taught or trained by teachers, these artists were among those who recorded firsthand images and observations of Native life in diverse communities. According to John C. Ewers, a foremost ethnohistorian of Plains Indians and the history of the West, "the best of such painters were both fine artists and reliable historians."

1. William Bartram
2. Albert Bierstadt
3. Karl Bodmer
4. Jose Cardero
5. Jonathan Carver
6. George Catlin
7. Ludovic Choris
8. Jervis Cutler
9. Theodore R. Davis
10. Seth Eastman
11. Myron Eells
12. Charles Bird King
13. Rudolph Friederich Kurz
14. Alfred Jacob Miller
15. Thomas Moran
16. Lewis Henry Morgan
17. John Neagle
18. Charles Willson Peale
19. Titian Ramsay Peale
20. Father Nicolas Point
21. Frederic Remington
22. Peter Rindisbacher
23. Charles M. Russell
24. Charles B. J. F. de Saint-Mémin
25. Samuel Seymour
26. William Simpson
27. Gustavus Sohon
28. Tomas de Suria
29. Philip Georg Friedrich von Reck
30. John Webber

Nine Poems about History by Native Poets

1. "A Brief Guide to American History Teachers," by Carter Revard (Osage). In *Returning the Gift: Poetry and Prose from the First North American Native Writers' Festival*, edited by Joseph Bruchac (1994).
2. "Colonization," by Haunani-Kay Trask (Native Hawaiian). In *Light in the Crevice Never Seen* (1994).
3. "For History on Behalf of My Children," by Gloria Bird (Spokane). In *Full Moon on the Reservation* (1993).

4. "Histories, Places, Indians, Just Like Always," by Simon J. Ortiz (Acoma Pueblo). In *Out There Somewhere* (2002).
5. "In 1864," by Luci Tapahonso (Navajo). In *Sáanii Dahataał, The Women Are Singing: Poems and Stories* (1993).
6. "notes from central california," by Carol Lee Sanchez (Laguna Pueblo). In *Returning the Gift*, edited by Joseph Bruchac (1994).
7. "Petroglyphs," by Barney Bush (Shawnee/Cayuga). In *American Indian Writings. The Greenfield Review*, vol. 9, nos. 3 and 4 (1981).
8. "The Road Where the People Cried," by Geary Hobson (Cherokee/Chickasaw). In *The Clouds Threw This Light: Contemporary Native American Poetry*, edited by Phillip Foss (1983).
9. "Without History," by Deborah Miranda (Esselen/Chumash). In *Indian Cartography* (1999).

Twelve Biographies and Biographical Accounts

1. *100 Native Americans Who Shaped American History*, by Bonnie Juettner (2003).
2. *A to Z of American Indian Women*, second edition, by Liz Sonneborn (2007).
3. *American Indian Intellectuals of the Nineteenth and Early Twentieth Centuries*, edited by Margot Liberty (2002).
4. *As Long As the Rivers Flow: The Stories of Nine Native Americans*, by Paula Gunn Allen and Patricia Clark Smith (1996).
5. *Biographical Dictionary of American Indian History to 1900*, by Carl Waldman (2001).
6. *The Book of Elders: The Life Stories and Wisdom of Great American Indians*, by Sandy Johnson and Dan Budnik (1994).
7. *Brave Are My People: Indian Heroes Not Forgotten*, by Frank Waters (1993).
8. *The Encyclopedia of Native American Biography: Six Hundred Life Stories of Important People from Powhatan to Wilma Mankiller*, by Bruce E. Johansen and Donald A. Grinde Jr. (1998).
9. *Extraordinary American Indians*, by Susan Avery and Linda Skinner (1992).
10. *Indian Lives: Essays on Nineteenth- and Twentieth-Century Native American Leaders*, edited by L. G. Moses and Raymond Wilson (1993).
11. *The New Warriors: Native American Leaders Since 1900*, edited by R. David Edmunds (2001).
12. *The Patriot Chiefs: A Chronicle of American Indian Resistance*, by Alvin M. Josephy (1961).

Eighteen Books of Photographs

1. *Beyond the Reach of Time and Change: Native American Reflections on the Frank A. Rinehart Photograph Collection*, edited by Simon J. Ortiz (2004).
2. *Enduring Culture: A Century of Photography of the Southwest Indians*, by M. K. Keegan (1991).

3. *Hopi Photographers/Hopi Images,* compiled by Victor Masayesva Jr. and Erin Younger (1983).

4. *Native American Photography at the Smithsonian: The Shindler Catalogue,* by Paula Richardson Fleming (2003).

5. *Native Nations: Journeys in American Photography,* edited by Jane Alison (1998).

6. *Navajo and Photography: A Critical History of the Representation of an American People,* by James C. Faris (2003).

7. *The North American Indians in Early Photographs,* by Paula Richardson Fleming and Judith Lynn Luskey (1988).

8. *Partial Recall: With Essays on Photographs of Native North Americans,* edited by Lucy R. Lippard (1992).

9. *Peoples of the Plateau: The Indian Photographs of Lee Moorhouse, 1898–1915,* by Steven L. Grafe (2005).

10. *The Photograph and the American Indian,* by Alfred I. Bush and Lee Clark Mitchell (1994).

11. *Picturing Indians: Photographic Encounters and Tourist Fantasies in H. H. Bennett's Wisconsin Dells,* by Steven D. Hoelscher (2008).

12. *Pueblo Imagination: Landscape and Memory in the Photography of Lee Marmon,* with writings by Leslie Marmon Silko, Joy Harjo, and Simon Ortiz (2003).

13. *Sacred Legacy: Edward S. Curtis and the North American Indian,* edited by Christopher Cardozo (2005).

14. *Shadows on Glass: The Indian World of Ben Wittick,* by Patricia Janis Broder (1991).

15. *Spirit Capture: Photographs from the National Museum of the American Indian,* edited by Tim Johnson (1998).

16. *Trading Gazes: Euro-American Women Photographers and Native North Americans, 1880–1940,* by Susan Bernardin et al. (2003).

17. *Visual Currencies: The Native American Photograph Museums and Galleries,* edited by Henrietta Lidchi and Hulleah J. Tsinhnahjinnie (2009).

18. *Women and Warriors of the Plains: The Pioneer Photography of Julia E. Tuell,* by Dan Aadland (2000).

LEGISLATION

Five Federal Historic Preservation Laws

1906   Antiquities Act

The Antiquities Act fines or imprisons people who harm any historic or prehistoric ruin or monument, or any object of antiquity, situated on lands owned or controlled by the United States government. It authorizes the president to publicly proclaim historic landmarks, historic and prehistoric structures, and other objects of historic or scientific interest located on lands owned or controlled by the United States government to be national monuments.

1935   Historic Sites Act

The Historic Sites Act declared it national policy "to preserve for public use historic sites, buildings, and objects of national significance." This was the first assertion of historic preservation as a government duty, which was only hinted at in the 1906 act.

1966   National Historic Preservation Act

The National Historic Preservation Act established a National Register of Historic Places to include districts, sites, structures, buildings, and objects of local, state, and national significance. The same act also created State Historic Preservation Offices. Since then, states have created state registries of historic parks, tribal villages, houses, and other cultural properties significant to Native peoples. Some of the sites appear on both the national and state historic site lists.

1970   National Park Service Organic Act

The National Park Service Organic Act, which amended the 1916 law that established the National Park Service (NPS), specifies that parks, monuments, historic sites, battlefields, cemeteries, trails, and other lands belonging to the NPS system must be conserved "for the enjoyment of future generations." Since everyday NPS decisions impact Native Americans, Alaska Natives, and Native Hawaiians, the American Indian Liaison Office was created in 1995 to work with tribes on a government-to-government basis.

1992   National Historic Preservation Act Amendments

The National Historic Preservation Act Amendments allow federally recognized Indian tribes to take on more formal responsibility for preserving significant historic properties on tribal lands. Tribes may assume any or all functions of a state historic preservation officer.

Four Historic American Indian Agencies

Johnston Farm and Indian Agency, Piqua, Ohio
http://www.johnstonfarmohio.com/
An Ohio Historical Society site, Johnston Farm and Indian Agency preserves the home and farm of John Johnston, who served as U.S. Indian Agent for western Ohio from 1812 to 1829. The area includes a modern museum with exhibits that trace the story of Eastern Woodland Indians of Ohio and the Pickawillany (Miami) village site.
Lower Sioux Agency Historic Site, Redwood Falls, Minnesota
http://www.mnhs.org/places/sites/lsa/

The Lower Sioux Agency was a federal government agency established in 1853 as the administrative center of the newly created reservation. A history center exhibit explores Dakota life before and after the reservation era. The site is managed by the Lower Sioux Indian Community.

Pottawatomie (Potawatomi) Indian Pay Station Museum, St. Mary's, Kansas

The Indian Pay Station, the oldest building in Pottawatomie County, was built in 1857 by the United States government as an Indian Agency. It was used by government agents to pay treaty annuities (annual payments) due to the Potawatomi. The tribe had been removed in the 1830s from the Great Lakes region to Kansas, where they established a reservation, first in Miami County and later in Pottawatomie County.

Upper Sioux Agency State Park, Granite Falls, Minnesota

Upper Sioux Agency State Park was established to preserve the historic Yellow Medicine Agency site, where provisions of the Treaty of Traverse des Sioux of 1851 were administered.

National American Indian Heritage Month

National American Indian Heritage Month is celebrated to recognize Native cultures and to educate the public about the heritage and traditions of American Indians. It resulted from the efforts of individuals and organizations to establish a day of recognition to honor Native peoples for their contributions to the country.

In 1914, Red Fox James, a member of the Blackfeet Tribe of Montana, traveled on horseback some four thousand miles seeking national support for a day to honor American Indians. He obtained backing from twenty-four state governors, taking their letters of endorsement to Washington, DC, to present to the president of the United States. The Society of American Indians (SAI), in which Red Fox James served as a representative, issued a proclamation at its annual conference held in Lawrence, Kansas, in 1915 declaring that the second Saturday in the month of May each year would "henceforth be known as 'American Indian Day.'" SAI president Sherman Coolidge (Arapaho) called upon every person of American Indian ancestry to specially observe the day as one set aside "as a memorial to the red race of America and to a wise consideration of its future." Arthur C. Parker, SAI's national secretary, who had earlier persuaded the Boy Scouts of America to designate a day for the "First Americans," which was held from 1912 to 1915, was also involved in this measure.

The governor of New York declared the first state American Indian Day on the second Saturday in May, 1916. Illinois designated a similar day by legislative enactment in 1919, but scheduled the observance for the fourth Friday in September. In 1935, Massachusetts passed a law providing for the governor to annually issue a proclamation setting apart the third week of May as American Indian Heritage week, with exercises commemorating the tribes of the commonwealth. In more recent times, several states have designated Columbus Day in October as Native American Day, but it is not recognized as a separate national legal holiday.

Congressional resolutions and presidential proclamations also designated various American Indian weeks in the 1970s and 1980s. These were followed by longer observances, with Congress passing Public Law 101–343 in 1990, designating National American Indian Heritage Month in November. That month, according to the legislation, "concludes the traditional harvest season of American Indians and was generally a time of celebration and giving thanks." Two years later, President Bush issued a proclamation declaring 1992, the five hundredth anniversary of Columbus's landfall, as the "Year of the American Indian," consistent with Public Law 102–188, legislated by Congress.

Similar proclamations to that issued by President Bush in 1990 have continued each year since 1994. They encourage all Americans and their elected representatives to observe the designated National American Indian Heritage Month with appropriate programs, ceremonies, and activities.

http://www.loc.gov/law/help/commemorative-observations/american-indian.php

HONORING NATIONS PROJECT, HARVARD UNIVERSITY

Honoring Nations Honorees, 2002 and 2005

Honoring Nations, a national awards program initiated in 1998, highlights outstanding programs in self-governance by Native nations. At the heart of the program is the belief that tribes themselves hold the key to positive social, political, cultural, and economic prosperity. Based at the John F. Kennedy School of Government at Harvard University, Honoring Nations is administered by the Harvard Project on American Indian Economic Development. The criteria for selection of honorees include program effectiveness, significance to sovereignty, cultural relevance, transferability, and sustainability. The programs include those that foster the development and presentation of accurate history and preservation of cultural heritage sites and resources.

Southwest Oregon Research Project (SWORP), 2002
Coquille Indian Tribe (North Bend, Oregon)
    Believing that historical documents and archival collections are vital for cultural self-determination, the Coquille Indian Tribe partnered with the

University of Oregon and the Smithsonian Institution to begin the Southwest Oregon Research Project (SWORP) in 1995. Over 110,000 pages of cultural, historical, and linguistic documents collected through SWORP were placed in a central archive. The documents, copies of which were given to forty-four tribes, help tribal scholars develop and present accurate history.

Cherokee Nation History Course, 2002
Department of Human Resources
Cherokee Nation, Tahlequah, Oklahoma
Offered to tribal employees and members of Cherokee communities, the award-winning Cherokee Nation History Course began in 2000. The forty-hour, college level course provides instruction in Cherokee history, culture, and government to both Indians and non-Indians. Its benefits include building social and professional cohesion and enhancing understanding about Cherokee sovereignty.

Tribal Monitors Program, 2005
Tribal Historic Preservation Office
Standing Rock Sioux Tribe
The Standing Rock Sioux Tribe, which is located on 2.3 million acres of land in North and South Dakota, established a Tribal Monitors Program through its Historic Preservation Office in 2000. The program utilizes archeologically trained personnel, who work with tribal elders to identify and monitor significant sites. The tribe manages and protects its lands, preserving cultural and spiritual heritage and resources for present as well as future generations.

FILMS

Columbus Day Legacy (USA, 2011, 27 min.), directed by Bennie Klain (Navajo).
The film explores issues of free speech and ethnic pride associated with the Columbus Day Parade celebrated by the Italian-American community in Denver, Colorado. The documentary examines the controversy over the annual event, which sparks protests by Native Americans, raising questions about history and identity in America.

Coming to Light: Edward S. Curtis and the North American Indians (USA, 2000, 84 min.), directed by Anne Makepeace.
This film tells the story of photographer Edward S. Curtis (1868–1952), the creation of his monumental work documenting American Indians, and his changing views of the people whose images he captured. *Coming to Light* also incorporates Native voices, including descendants of individuals portrayed by Curtis, to discuss the work and its legacy today.

The Ghost Riders (USA, 2003, 58 min.), directed by Vincent Blackhawk Aamodt (Blackfoot/Lakota/Mexican).

This film features the Big Foot Memorial Ride, a three-hundred-mile journey on horseback, taken to "wipe the tears" stemming from the massacre of Lakota men, women, and children at Wounded Knee in 1890. The ride is characterized by a spirit of sacrifice and remembrance, as well as determination and hope for the future.

History of the Iñupiat: 1961, The Duck-In (USA, 2005, 30 min.), directed by Rachel Naninaaq Edwardson (Inupiaq). In Inupiaq and English with English subtitles.

In this film, Edwardson documents the successful protest of Iñupiat of Barrow, Alaska, against federal regulations interfering with subsistence hunting brought by Alaska statehood in 1959.

History of the Iñupiat: Nipaa Ilitqusipta/The Voice of Our Spirit (USA, 2008, 49 min.), directed by Rachel Naninaaq Edwardson (Inupiaq). In Inupiaq and English with English subtitles.

In this film, Iñupiat community members in Barrow, Alaska, speak of the impact of colonization, which included the arrival of devastating diseases and an educational system that undermined indigenous culture and language. This film and "The Duck-In" are part of an Inupiaq history series developed for use in classes across the North Slope.

House of Peace (USA, 1999, 29 min.), produced by G. Peter Jemison (Seneca).

This video tells the story of Ganondagan, a seventeenth-century Seneca village, now a New York State Historic Site, and documents the construction of a bark longhouse there.

The Last Conquistador (USA, 2007, 52 min.), directed by John J. Valadez and Cristina Ibarra.

This documentary examines the controversy ignited by artist John Houser's project of sculpting a massive bronze equestrian statue of Juan de Oñate, colonial explorer and governor of the New Spain province of New Mexico, for the city of El Paso, Texas. Designed to memorialize the first European explorations of a region named El Paso del Rio del Norte by the Spanish, the monument depicts Oñate astride a rearing horse as he claimed land for Spain. Acoma Pueblo and other Native Americans objected to the work, reiterating Oñate's genocidal brutality against their people.

Numbe Whageh (Our Center Place) (USA, 2005, 10 min.), directed by Nora Noranjo-Morse (Tewa, Santa Clara Pueblo).

This video explores artist Nora Naranjo-Morse's earth sculpture, commissioned by the City of Albuquerque as a response to a controversial public sculpture commemorating the four hundredth anniversary of New Mexico's "discovery" by the Spanish.

Summer Sun Winter Moon (USA, 2009, 57 min.), directed by Hugo Perez.

Summer Sun Winter Moon, which premiered on PBS in 2009, presents American Indian perspectives about Lewis and Clark's "Corps of Discovery" expedition. The film features the collaboration between classical music conductor and composer Rob Kapilow and Blackfeet poet and educator Darrell Robes Kipp to create a symphony for the Lewis and Clark Bicentennial.

Surviving Columbus (USA, 1992, 120 min.), directed by Diane Reyna (Taos Pueblo). This PBS film, which won a Peabody Award in 1993, centers on Pueblo peoples of the Southwest and their perspectives on "surviving Columbus." The documentary focuses on Pueblo-Spanish interactions from first encounters to the Pueblo Revolt of 1680, but also includes other aspects of the European invasion of indigenous homelands.

The Trail of Tears: Cherokee Legacy (USA, 2006, 115 min.), directed by Chip Richie. Named Best Documentary Feature at the American Indian Film Festival in 2006, this film explores President Andrew Jackson's Indian Removal Act of 1830 and the forced removal of Cherokees from their southeastern United States homeland to Indian Territory (present-day Oklahoma). The film is presented in the Cherokee language with English subtitles by actor Wes Studi (Cherokee). It features narration by actor James Earl Jones and the voices of actor James Garner and singer/songwriter Crystal Gayle.

RESOURCES

Brooks, Drex. *Sweet Medicine: Sites of Indian Massacres, Battlefields, and Treaties.* Albuquerque: University of New Mexico Press, 1995.

Calloway, Colin G. *First Peoples: A Documentary Survey of American Indian History.* Boston: Bedford/St. Martin's, 1999.

———, ed. *The World Turned Upside Down: Indian Voices from Early America.* Boston: Bedford Books, 1994.

Daws, Gavan. *Shoal of Time: A History of the Hawaiian Islands.* Honolulu: University of Hawaii Press, 1989 (originally published in 1968).

Deloria, Philip J. and Neal Salisbury, eds. *A Companion to American Indian History.* Malden, MA: Blackwell Publishing, 2002, 2004.

Dowd, Gregory Evans. *A Spirited Resistance: The North American Struggle for Unity, 1745–1815.* Baltimore: Johns Hopkins University Press, 1993.

Fixico, Donald L., ed. *Rethinking American Indian History.* Albuquerque: University of New Mexico Press, 1997.

Greene, Candace S., and Russell Thornton, eds. *The Year the Stars Fell: Lakota Winter Counts at the Smithsonian.* Lincoln: University of Nebraska Press, 2007.

Grumet, Robert S. *First Manhattans: A History of the Indians of Greater New York.* Norman: University of Oklahoma Press, 2011.

Hoxie, Frederick E., ed. *Indians in American History: An Introduction.* Arlington Heights, IL: Harlan Davidson, 1988.

Johansen, Bruce E. *Forgotten Founders: How the American Indian Helped Shape Democracy.* Boston: Harvard Common Press, 1982.

Josephy, Alvin M., Jr., ed. *Lewis and Clark through Indian Eyes.* New York: Alfred A. Knopf, 2006.

Kennedy, Frances H. *American Indian Places: A Historical Guidebook.* Boston: Houghton Mifflin Co., 2008.

Littlefield, Daniel F., Jr., and James W. Parins, eds. *Encyclopedia of American Indian Removal.* Santa Barbara, CA: ABC-CLIO/Greenwood Press, 2011.

Martin, Calvin, ed. *The American Indian and the Problem of History.* New York: Oxford University Press, 1987.

Miles, Tiya, and Sharon P. Holland, eds. *Crossing Waters, Crossing Worlds: The African Diaspora in Indian Country.* Durham, NC: Duke University Press, 2006.

Miller, Lee, ed. *From the Heart: Voices of the American Indian (From Montezuma and Pontiac to Crazy Horse and Chief Joseph—Eloquent Speeches from America's Indian Nations).* New York: Vintage Books, 1996.

———. *Roanoke: Solving the Mystery of the Lost Colony.* New York: Arcade Publishing, 2000.

Nabokov, Peter, ed. *Native American Testimony: A Chronicle of Indian-White Relations from Prophecy to the Present.* New York: Penguin Books, 1992.

Osorio, Jonathan Kay Kamakawiwo'ole. *Dismembering Lāhui: A History of the Hawaiian Nation to 1887.* Honolulu: University of Hawaii Press, 2002.

Richter, Daniel K. *Facing East from Indian Country: A Native History of Early America.* Cambridge, MA: Harvard University Press, 2001.

Sando, Joe S., and Herman Agoyo, eds. *Po'pay: Leader of the First American Revolution.* Santa Fe, NM: Clear Light Publishers, 2005.

Steele, Ian K. *Warpaths: Invasions of North America.* New York: Oxford University Press, 1994.

Stubben, Jerry D. *Native Americans and Political Participation: A Reference Handbook.* Santa Barbara, CA: ABC-CLIO, 2006.

Taft, Robert. *Artists and Illustrators of the Old West 1850–1900.* New York: Charles Scribner's Sons, 1953.

Thornton, Russell. *American Indian Holocaust and Survival: A Population History Since 1492.* Norman: University of Oklahoma Press, 1987.

Trafzer, Clifford E., ed. *American Indians/American Presidents: A History.* New York: HarperCollins/National Museum of the American Indian, Smithsonian Institution, 2009.

Vowell, Sarah. *Unfamiliar Fishes.* New York: Riverhead Books, 2011.

Web Sites

American Indian History, Library of Congress: http://www.loc.gov/topics/content.php?subcat=2.

Edward S. Curtis's The North American Indian, Northwestern University: http://curtis.library.northwestern.edu/.

Harvard Project's Honoring Nations Directory of Honored Programs, 1999–2006: http://hpaied.org/images/resources/general/Dir_web.pdf.

Hidden Landscapes (three-part series on New England's ancient past revealed in stone monuments, ceremonial structures, and earthworks): http://www.hiddenlandscape.com.

Indians of the Midwest, Past and Present: http://publications.newberry.org/indiansofthemidwest/.

National Association of Tribal Historic Preservation Officers (NATHPO): http://www.nathpo.org/.

National Register of Historic Places—Teaching with Historic Places: American Indian History: http://www.nps.gov/nr/twhp/topic.htm#indian.

National Register of Historic Places—Teaching with Historic Places: The Trail of Tears and the Forced Relocation of the Cherokee Nation: http://www.nps.gov/history/nr/twhp/wwwlps/lessons/118trail/118trail.htm.

Native American Bibliography Series (thirty titles to date): http://www.scarecrowpress.com/series/SeriesDesc.shtml?command=Search&db=^DB/series.db&eqCO_DEPT datarq=SCP&eqTITLEdatarq=Native%20American%20Bibliography%20Series.

The Newberry Library D'Arcy McNickle Center for American Indian and Indigenous Studies: http://www.newberry.org/mcnickle/darcyhome.html.

Potawatomi Trail of Death: http://www.kansasheritage.org/PBP/people/trail_map.html.

Wanamaker Collection of Photographs of American Indians, Mathers Museum of World Cultures: http://www.indiana.edu/~mathers/collections/photos/wanamake.html.

Oral History

The Duke Collection of American Indian Oral History online: http://digital.libraries.ou.edu/whc/duke/

Oral History Center, Department of Native Studies, University of South Dakota http://www.usd.edu/arts-and-sciences/native-studies/oral-history-center.cfm

University of Oklahoma, Western History Collections

2

Stereotypes and Myths

NATIVE AMERICAN REPRESENTATIONS

Indian Violence in Selected American Art

Countless American artworks portray American Indians as bloodthirsty aggressors attacking United States soldiers, cowboys, wagon trains, forts, and women. Captivity tales, some of which were bestsellers of their time, also delivered inflammatory accounts of Indians, likening them to devils who delivered "barbarities terrible and shocking to human nature" (Williamson 1757). Likewise, American artists painted captivity scenes that generally portrayed whites as innocent victims and Indians as aggressive villains. Works such as those listed appear in many public places, among them federal buildings and city museums.

The Attack on an Emigrant Train, painting by Carl Wimar, 1856; University of Michigan Museum of Art, Ann Arbor

Captured by Indians, painting by George Caleb Bingham, 1848; Saint Louis Art Museum, Missouri

Dangers of the Mail, painting by Frank A. Mechau, 1936; Environmental Protection Agency, Ariel Rios Federal Building, Washington, DC

Dash for the Timber, painting by Frederic Remington, 1889; Amon Carter Museum, Fort Worth, Texas

The Death of Jane McCrea, painting by John Vanderlyn, 1804; Wadsworth Atheneum Museum of Art, Hartford, Connecticut

Death Whoop, painting by Seth Eastman, 1847; in federal facility storage

Defending the Stockade, painting by Charles Schreyvogel, ca. 1905; Gaylord Broadcasting Co., Oklahoma City

Fight on the Plains, painting by N. C. Wyeth, 1916; Collection of Mr. and Mrs. Andrew Wyeth

The Murder of David Tully and Family by the Sissetoons Sioux, 1823, painting by Peter Rindisbacher, 1830; United States Military Academy, West Point Museum, West Point, New York

The Prairie Hunter, "One Rubbed Out!," painting by Arthur Tait, 1852; Gene Autry Western Heritage Museum, Los Angeles

The Prisoner, colored engraving by Henry Farny, 1886; private collection

Twenty Poems about Native Representations by Native Poets

1. "Answers to Tourists," by Karen Coody Cooper. In *Eagle Wing Press* (April 1983).
2. "Being Indian Is . . . ," by Reuben Snake. In *Akwesasne Notes* (Early Autumn 1971).
3. "Butter Maiden and Maize Girl Survive Death Leap," by Heid E. Erdrich (Ojibwe). In *Sister Nations: Native American Women Writers on Community*, edited by Heid E. Erdrich and Laura Tohe (2002).
4. "Changing Is Not Vanishing" (1916), by Carlos Montezuma (Yavapai). In *Changing Is Not Vanishing: A Collection of American Indian Poetry to 1930*, edited by Robert Dale Parker (2011).
5. "Dear John Wayne," by Louise Erdrich (Ojibwe). In *Original Fire: Selected and New Poems* (2003).
6. "Her Pocahontas," by Susan Deer Cloud. In *Sister Nations: Native American Women Writers on Community*, edited by Heid E. Erdrich and Laura Tohe (2002).
7. "The Indian List," by Alex Jacobs, Karoniaktahke (Akwesasne Mohawk). In *Sovereign Bones: New Native American Writing*, edited by Eric Gansworth (2007).
8. "Minstrel Show (1993)," by Dennis Tibbetts (Ojibwe/Shoshone). In *Team Spirits: The Native American Mascots Controversy*, edited by C. Richard King and Charles Fruehling Springwood (2001).
9. "My Heroes Have Never Been Cowboys," by Sherman Alexie (Spokane/Coeur d'Alene). In *First Indian on the Moon* (1993).
10. "My Standard Response," by Karenne Wood (Monacan). In *Markings on Earth* (2001).
11. "New Age," by Lydia Whirlwind Soldier (Sicangu Lakota). In *Memory Songs* (1999).
12. "On a Nickel," by Leta V. Meyers Smart (Omaha). In *Changing Is Not Vanishing*, edited by Robert Dale Parker (2011).
13. "Pocahontas to Her English Husband, John Rolfe," by Paula Gunn Allen (Laguna/Sioux). In *Songs from This Earth on Turtle's Back*, edited by Joseph Bruchac (1983).
14. "The Real Thing," by Marilou Awiakta. In *Through Indian Eyes: The Native Experience in Books for Children*, edited by Beverly Slapin and Doris Seale (1992).
15. "Savage Romance," by Sara Littlecrow-Russell (Anishinaabe/Han-Naxi Metís). In *The Secret Powers of Naming* (2006).
16. "Sure You Can Ask Me a Personal Question," by Diane Burns (Anishinaabe/Chemehuevi). In *The Clouds Threw This Light: Contemporary Native American Poetry*, edited by Phillip Foss (1983).
17. "Survival This Way," by Simon J. Ortiz. In *Songs from This Earth on Turtle's Back: Contemporary American Indian Poetry*, edited by Joseph Bruchac (1983).

8. *Selling the Indian: Commercializing and Appropriating American Indian Cultures*, edited by Carter Jones Meyer and Diane Royer (2001).
9. *Shoot the Indian: Media, Misperception and Native Truth*, edited by Kara Briggs, Ronald D. Smith, and Jose Barreiro (2007).
10. *Walking a Tightrope: Aboriginal People and Their Representations*, edited by Ute Lischke and David T. McNab (2005).

Stereotypes and Myths

Stereotypes and myths about American Indians can be traced back to the earliest years of European exploration and colonization. Initially, portrayals found expression in early drawings, engravings, portraits, political prints, maps and cartouches, tobacconist figures and shop signs, weather vanes, coins and medals, books, and policy measures. Then, over hundreds of years, inaccurate cultural images and invented stories about American Indians became commonplace. Today, they are expressed in a range of media, including art and film, commercial products and advertisements, national holiday cycles, sports mascots, children's games and toys, school curricula, and museum displays. These stereotypes and myths, which saturate the nation's popular culture, work to erase or distort the historical and contemporary realities of hundreds of richly diverse tribal nations and cultures. They also mask the ongoing impact of European colonization on Native peoples, minimizing or denying the facts of actual dispossession and conquest of aboriginal homelands.

Eliminating the "S" Word

The English language contains a set of words and phrases used to define or portray Native peoples.

Among them is the word "squaw," which has been removed from its cultural linguistic origins and turned into a negative label applied to all American Indian women. The offensive "s-word" has extensive use in North America, especially as a name for geographic features.

In 1995, Minnesota became the first state to require counties to rename geographic features with the word "squaw" in them. Since that time at least eight other states, including Montana, Maine, and Oregon, have passed laws to change the names of public places. Minnesota's law required that:

"On or before July 31, 1996, the commissioner of natural resources shall change each name of a geographic feature in the state that contains the word 'squaw' to another name that does not contain this word. The commissioner shall select the new names in cooperation with the county boards of the counties in which the feature is located and with their approval."

Laws of Minnesota for 1995, Chapter 53—S.F. 574

Dime Novels

In the late nineteenth and early twentieth centuries, dime novels, a popular form of literary entertainment, were published in paper-covered booklets, issued at regular intervals, and priced at five to ten cents. By the mid-1890s, massive editions of sensationalistic tales were distributed at newsstands and dry goods stores. Covering a wide variety of subjects, dime novels promoted American values of patriotism, rugged individualism, and moral behavior. Many early stories fictionalized bloody conflicts between Native peoples and heroic frontiersmen who hunted down and fought Indians, saving the Euro-American settlers from the violent danger that Indians represented. Dime novel stories, which led working-class readers to believe that Indians were plotting to kill them, helped bolster support for government policies that forced Indians off their lands.

In June of 1860, *Malaeska: The Indian Wife of the White Hunter*, considered the first dime novel, was written by Mrs. Ann S. Stephens and published by Beadle & Adams in New York City. The sensationalized tale of an Indian maiden who marries a white settler proved enormously popular, and more than 65,000 copies sold within the first few months. Although *Malaeska* and other early dime novels were published without cover illustrations, later ones were emblazoned with exciting images of damsels abducted by Indians and bloody conflicts between "savages" and courageous rugged heroes.

PLAYING INDIAN

Ten Groups That Play Indian

Playing Indian, a complex set of behaviors centered on the appropriation of Native American identity, customs, and dress, is one of the most deeply rooted practices in the nation. It cuts across race and class, gender and age, and group affiliations. The behaviors associated with playing Indian find expression in dramatic performances, ritual reenactments, as well as in songs and texts. Some people engage in the practice for life (individuals who reinvent themselves as Indian), others for a brief, one-time purpose (costume party), or on an intermittent basis over time (annual reenactments). Being Indian is treated as a role or occupation that others can appropriate, rather than recognized and respected as the complex human identity it is. Groups associated with playing Indian, a phenomenon that can be found across the country as well as internationally, include the ten listed here.

1. Athletic teams
2. Cheerleaders
3. Fraternal orders

4. Halloween costumes
5. Hobbyists
6. Mascots
7. Pageant performers
8. Secret societies
9. Scout troops
10. Thanksgiving reenactors

The Boston Tea Party

Sounding war whoops and masquerading as Mohawk Indians, a group of colonists known as the Sons of Liberty boarded ships to dump chests of tea into Boston Harbor. The incident, which occurred on December 16, 1773, was a direct protest against new taxes imposed by the British government in the American colonies. The Boston Tea Party is nationally renowned for helping to spark the American War of Independence. The protesting colonists chose to disguise themselves as Indians, the most American of identities, to hide who they really were and to signal their independence from the mother country. Although the Boston Tea Party is iconic in American history, less attention has been paid to the Indian disguise, or playing Indian, aspect of the event.

INDIAN MASCOTS AND NAMES

Twelve Educational Institutions with Indian Name or Mascot Changes

A more modern version of "Indian" performance arose in the early part of the twentieth century through the use of American Indian names in organized sports. Some of these names are general ("Indians," "Redmen"), others are tribal-specific ("Apache," "Chippewa," and "Sioux"), and still others are aligned with status or rank ("Chiefs," "Braves," and "Warriors"). Such team names, which often link American Indians with aggressive or warlike behavior, proliferate in K–12 schools, colleges and universities, and in both amateur and professional athletics.

Since the late 1960s, American Indians have agitated for changes, eventually filing lawsuits against the Cleveland Indians (especially its Chief Wahoo logo), the Atlanta Braves (known for "Chief Noc-a-Homa and the tomahawk chop"), and the Washington Redskins (especially the name "Redskins"). A number of schools, particularly at the K–12 and college levels, have changed their team names. Other teams have made cosmetic changes, such as substituting logos adorned with comic caricatures with more dignified imagery. Professional teams have been the most resistant to change.

1. Dartmouth College, New Hampshire, 1970
   Changed its "Indians" team name to "Big Green."
2. University of Oklahoma, 1970
   Retired its "Little Red" mascot.
3. Marquette University, Wisconsin, 1971
   Retired its "Willie Wampum" mascot.
4. Stanford University, California, 1972
   Changed its team name from "Indians" to "Cardinals" and eliminated its Chief Lightfoot mascot.
5. Syracuse University, New York, 1978
   Eliminated its Saltine Warrior mascot, "Big Chief Bill Orange."
6. St. Mary's College, Minnesota, 1988
   Changed its team name from "Red Men" to "Cardinals."
7. Miami University, Ohio, 1996
   Changed its team name from "Redskins" to "Redhawks."
8. Los Angeles Unified School District, California, 1997
   The district, the second largest in the nation, required three high schools and one junior high school to eliminate American Indian–themed names and mascots.
9. Dallas Public Schools, Texas, 1999
   The Dallas Public Schools retired Indian mascots from ten of its schools.
10. Southeastern Community College, Iowa, 2002
    Changed its American Indian–themed "Blackhawks" name to "Black Hawks," reflecting a bird of prey.
11. Chowan University, North Carolina, 2006
    Changed its team name from the "Braves" to the "Hawks."
12. University of Illinois at Urbana-Champaign, 2007
    Retired its Chief Illiniwek mascot to comply with the National Collegiate Athletic Association (NCAA) ruling concerning mascots, nicknames, or imagery.

Ten Organizations Opposed to Indian Names and Mascots

1. The Michigan Civil Rights Commission called for eliminating American Indian symbols from the state's athletic teams, 1988.
2. The Minnesota State Board of Education found the use of mascots depicting American Indian culture or race unacceptable, 1988.
3. The National Coalition on Racism in Sports and the Media was founded in Minneapolis, Minnesota, 1991.
4. The National Congress of American Indians passed a resolution denouncing "the use of any American Indian name or artifice associated with team mascots," 1993.
5. The University of Wisconsin's Athletic Board adopted a policy against scheduling games with teams having Native American mascots unless they were traditional rivals, 1993.

6. The National Association for the Advancement of Colored People (NAACP) unanimously passed a resolution expressing opposition to Native American names, logos, and mascots for sports teams, 1999.

7. The American Psychological Association passed a resolution recommending the immediate retirement of American Indian mascots, symbols, images, and personalities by schools, teams, and organizations, 2001.

8. The National Education Association reaffirmed its 1991–92 resolutions denouncing the use of ethnic-related mascots, nicknames, and symbols, 2001.

9. The United States Commission on Civil Rights called for educational institutions to avoid the use of ethnic nicknames and mascots, 2001.

10. The National Collegiate Athletic Association (NCAA) adopted a policy prohibiting NCAA colleges and universities from displaying hostile and abusive racial/ethnic/national origin mascots, nicknames, or imagery at any of the eighty-eight NCAA championships, 2005.

Chronology of Washington Redskins, 1992–2010

1992   Seven prominent American Indian leaders filed a petition with the U.S. Patent and Trademark Office, *Harjo et al. v. Pro-Football, Inc.*, to cancel seven federal trademark registrations for various offensive nicknames and logos used by the Washington Redskins football organization. The petition asserted violation of the Lanham Act of 1946, which prohibits registering names if they are disparaging, scandalous, contemptuous, or disreputable.

1994   The U.S. Patent and Trademark Office's Trademark Trial and Appeal Board ruled in favor of the American Indian petitioners (and against Pro-Football, Inc.) contesting the Washington football team's "Redskins" registration as illegal, thus allowing further litigation of the case.

1997   Dorsey & Whitney, a national law firm, filed a "trial memorandum" with the Trademark Trial and Appeal Board. The memorandum's conclusion states: "*Redskin(s)* is a racial slur. The record evidence overwhelmingly demonstrates that *redskin(s)* is today and always has been one of the most derogatory and offensive racial slurs for Native Americans."

1999   After hearing oral arguments in the Redskins case, the three-judge panel of the U.S. Patent and Trademark Office canceled seven registered Redskins trademarks for being disparaging to Native Americans in violation of federal trademark law. The decision did not take effect, pending an appeal by the Redskins, which argued that the team's name had been meant to honor Indians.

2003	A U.S. district court judge overturned the 1999 decision, concluding that the three judges relied on flawed or incomplete data. The ruling did not address the issue of whether the name "Redskins" actually was insulting to Indians.
2005	The U.S. Court of Appeals for the District of Columbia heard oral arguments in *Harjo et al. v. Pro-Football, Inc.*, and returned the case to a U.S. district judge for review. The NFL franchise argued that the seven plaintiffs had no standing to complain about the Redskins name because they had waited too long after the date of the first Redskin trademark, registered in 1967. But the court of appeals found that one plaintiff had standing, because he had been only a year old at that time.
2006	Six American Indian young people filed a petition, *Blackhorse et al. v. Pro-Football, Inc.*, with the Trademark Trial and Appeal Board of the U.S. Patent and Trademark Office for the cancellation of the Washington Redskins trademark term "Redskins."
2008	The district court ruled that the youngest of the seven Native American plaintiffs waited too long after turning eighteen to file the lawsuit that attempted to revoke the Redskins trademark. He turned eighteen in 1984 and joined the lawsuit eight years after coming of age. The judge did not address whether the Redskins name was offensive.
2009	A group of renowned researchers in the social sciences, including experts in the areas of stereotyping, prejudice, and discrimination, filed an amicus brief supporting Native plaintiffs suing to end the Redskins trademark. The experts told the court there is "extensive and pervasive" public harm caused by the continued use of Indian mascots in professional sports.
	The U.S. Supreme Court denied review of a lower court's ruling that said the plaintiffs in *Harjo et al. v. Pro-Football, Inc.*, should have made their legal argument sooner.
2010	Native American plaintiffs, represented by Drinker Biddle & Reath, filed protests with the U.S. Patent and Trademark Office against six pending trademark applications for the Redskins name, some dating as far back as 1992. The trademark applications were filed by the owner of the Redskins, and other entities including the Washington Redskins Cheerleaders, in hopes of protecting the trademark for use on clothing and other souvenirs and paraphernalia. The letters were filed after the Harjo litigation ended. The other legal action, *Blackhorse et al. v. Pro-Football, Inc.*, seeking to cancel existing Redskin trademarks, was still pending before the Trademark Trial and Appeal Board.

VANISHING

Ten Examples of Vanishing in Art

Artists, sculptors, and photographers are among those who expressed the widespread belief, voiced as early as the 1820s, that American Indians were destined to vanish. In some portrayals, Native individuals or family groups are framed on narrow or slippery precipices with nowhere left to go but to perish from the earth. The notion of disappearance, espoused by writers and policymakers, can be traced in part to Native population losses resulting from Euro-American colonization, but also to the federal removal of entire tribal nations from their ancestral homelands. In addition, cultural changes were believed to spell doom for Native continuance. Nostalgic, frozen-in-time renditions followed with artists hurrying to record a disappearing way of life. These are among the many examples of sculptures, paintings, and photographs centered on the vanishing theme.

1. *The Appeal to the Great Spirit*, sculpture by Cyrus E. Dallin (1908).
2. *The Dying Chief Contemplating the Progress of Civilization*, sculpture by Thomas Crawford (1856).
3. *The Dying Indian*, sculpture by Charles Rumsey (190[?]).
4. *The End of the Trail*, sculpture by James Earle Fraser (1915).
5. *The Last of Their Race*, painting by John Mix Stanley (1857).
6. *The Last War Whoop*, painting by Arthur F. Tait (1855).
7. *The Twilight of the Indian*, drawing by Frederic Remington (1897).
8. *A Vanishing Race*, photograph by Edward S. Curtis (1904).
9. *The Vanishing Race*, photograph titles ("The Sunset of a Dying Race," "A Glimpse Backward," "The Final Trail," "The Fading Sunset," "Vanishing into the Mists," "The Empty Saddle") in a book by Joseph K. Dixon (1913).
10. *Wi-jún-jon, Pigeon's Egg Head Going to and Returning from Washington*, painting by George Catlin (1837).

Eight Books with "Vanishing" or "Last" in the Title

These titles are among the many works of fiction and nonfiction that center on the theme of the vanishing Indian in American literature. Published in 1826, *The Last of the Mohicans* by James Fenimore Cooper is by far the best-known work, one of some forty novels published between 1824 and 1834 with the theme.

1. *Ishi: Last of His Tribe*, by Theodora Kroeber (1964).
2. *The Last Algonquin*, by Theodore L. Kazimiroff (1991).
3. *The Last of the Mohicans*, by James Fenimore Cooper (1826).
4. *The Long Death: The Last Days of the Plains Indians*, by Ralph K. Andrist (1964).
5. *Metamora; or, The Last of the Wampanoags*, by John Augustus Stone (1829).

6. *Tributes to a Vanishing Race*, by Irene Campbell Beaulieu (1916).
7. *The Vanishing American*, by Zane Grey (1925).
8. *The Vanishing Race: The Last Great Indian Council*, by Joseph K. Dixon (1913).

Ten Book Titles That Address or Counter Vanishing

These books or series are examples of works that counter the idea that American Indians were or are vanishing. Authors such as Chrystos (Menominee) and Simon J. Ortiz (Acoma Pueblo) express the determination of Indian people to endure culturally as well as physically. Other publications proclaim that "We Are Still Here," countering pervasive attitudes about Indian disappearance or invisibility. Still other examples include books that address American Indian population issues.

1. *American Indian Holocaust and Survival: A Population History since 1492*, by Russell Thornton (1987).
2. *American Indian Population Recovery in the Twentieth Century*, by Nancy Shoemaker (2000).
3. *Changing Is Not Vanishing: A Collection of American Indian Poetry to 1930*, edited by Robert Dale Parker (2011).
4. *Firsting and Lasting: Writing Indians out of Existence in New England*, by Jean M. O'Brien (2010).
5. *The Lasting of the Mohicans: History of an American Myth*, by Martin Barker and Roger Sabin (1995).

The End of the Trail

The End of the Trail, the most famous depiction of the vanishing Indian theme, was created by sculptor James Earle Fraser. Fraser first exhibited the sculpture, which is two and a half times larger than life-size, of a Plains Indian figure slumped on a worn horse at San Francisco's Panama-Pacific International Exposition in 1915. Shortly after its public appearance, small replicas of *The End of the Trail* went on sale everywhere, along with photographs, postcards, paperweights, bookends, ashtrays, postcards, and a flood of other commercial products featuring the image. "Garish prints, in sepia and color, showing the horse and rider silhouetted against a dying sunset," author Brian Dippie noted, "eventually decorated many American walls." One of the most recognized Indian depictions, the image continues to appear on a range of contemporary products, including computer mouse pads, night-lights, and belt buckles.

6. *Not Vanishing*, by Chrystos (1988).
7. *The People Shall Continue*, by Simon Ortiz (1994).
8. *Uncas: First of the Mohegans*, by Michael Leroy Oberg (2006).
9. *We Are Still Here: American Indians in the Twentieth Century*, by Peter Iverson (1998).
10. *We're Still Here: Contemporary Virginia Indians Tell Their Stories*, by Sandra F. Waugaman and Danielle Moretti-Langholtz (2000).

FILMS

Dime novels and Wild West shows inspired moviemakers whose images are seen by millions of people. Since the silent film era began in 1903, Hollywood has filmed Westerns with ferocious Indians attacking forts, settlements, troops, and wagon trains, until the cavalry rides to the rescue. When sound arrived in 1927, audiences heard screen Indians shrieking and whooping while pillaging, abducting, and scalping. Images of Indians as too bad or too good, but never real, have been repeated in thousands of films ever since. Films such as those listed below address a number of the stereotypes.

Cowtipping: The Militant Indian Waiter (USA, 1992, 17 min.), directed by Randy Redroad (Cherokee).

This short fictional film depicts a Cherokee café waiter facing customers who insist on sharing their ignorance about American Indians. His efforts to educate others generally end in enormous frustration and a paltry tip. The film, a blend of humor, anger, and information, is based on some of Redroad's own experiences of being stereotyped.

If the Name Has to Go . . . (USA, 2004, 24 min.), directed by Monica Braine (Assiniboine).

This documentary was produced during the Conference on the Use of Indians as Mascots, Nicknames, and Logos at the University of North Dakota in Grand Forks to examine racism through the experiences of Native Americans.

I'm Not the Indian You Had in Mind (Canada, 2007, 5 min.), directed by Thomas King (Cherokee).

This spoken-word short challenges the stereotypical portrayal of First Nations peoples in the media. Examining the power of images, King juxtaposes actors in business suits, jeans, and other contemporary attire against stock representations of Indians in film, language, and artifacts such as cigar store Indians.

Images of Indians: How Hollywood Stereotyped the Native American (USA, 2003, 25 min.), directed by Chris O'Brien and Jason Witner.

This film traces the depiction of Indians in Hollywood films gleaned from archival footage, ranging from early films to works by contemporary filmmakers. It also includes commentary by American Indian actors such as Elaine Miles and Russell Means.

Images of Indians [Video Series] (USA, 1979, 29 min. each), directed by Phil Lucas (Choctaw) and Robert Hagopian.

> This five-part documentary series looks at the stereotypical Hollywood treatment of Indians through the years. Each part of the series is available individually.

Imagining Indians (USA, 1992, 56 min.), directed by Victor Masayesva Jr. (Hopi).

> Masayesva explores Hollywood's depiction of American Indians, revealing the misappropriation of cultural and religious practices of America's indigenous people. Examining films, as well as the treatment of Indian actors and extras, he asks, "When did sacredness lose its sacredness?"

In Whose Honor? American Indian Mascots in Sports (USA, 1997, 47 min.), directed by Jay Rosenstein.

> This documentary, which aired nationally on the PBS series Point of View, traces the development of American Indian mascots in sports, especially through the story of Charlene Teters (Spokane) and her struggle against the Chief Illiniwek mascot at the University of Illinois. The film examines issues surrounding mascots, including racism, representation, and power relations.

Plastic Warriors (USA, 2004, 26 min.), directed by Amy TallChief (Osage).

> This documentary portrays Native New Yorkers, giving their responses to terms such as "squaw" and "redskin."

Reel Injun (Canada, 2009, 86 min.), directed by Neil Diamond (Cree).

> Filmmaker Neil Diamond explores the portrayal of North American Natives through a century of cinema, including the myth of "the Injun" and its influence. He incorporates clips from classic and recent films, as well as interviews with figures such as Clint Eastwood, Robbie Robertson, Sacheen Littlefeather, John Trudell, and Russell Means.

RESOURCES

Berkhofer, Robert F., Jr. *The White Man's Indian: Images of the American Indian from Columbus to the Present.* New York: Vintage Books, 1978.

Deloria, Philip J. *Indians in Unexpected Places.* Lawrence: University Press of Kansas, 2004.

———. *Playing Indian.* New Haven, CT: Yale University Press, 1998.

Dippie, Brian W. *The Vanishing American: White Attitudes and U.S. Indian Policy.* Lawrence: University Press of Kansas, 1982.

Doxtator, Deborah. *Fluffs and Feathers, An Exhibit on the Symbols of Indianness: A Resource Guide.* Rev. ed. Brantford, Ontario: Woodland Cultural Centre, 1992.

Fienup-Riordan, Ann. *Eskimo Essays: Yup'ik Lives and How We See Them.* New Brunswick, NJ: Rutgers University Press, 1991.

Glancy, Diane, and Mark Nowak, eds. *Visit Teepee Town: Native Writings after the Detours.* Minneapolis: Coffee House Press, 1999.

Hirschfelder, Arlene, Paulette Fairbanks Molin, and Yvonne Wakim, eds. *American Indian Stereotypes in the World of Children: A Reader and Bibliography.* 2nd ed. Lanham, MD: Scarecrow Press, 1999.

Hughte, Phil. *A Zuni Artist Looks at Frank Hamilton Cushing.* Zuni, NM: Pueblo of Zuni Arts and Crafts, A:shiwi A:wan Museum and Heritage Center, 1994.

Kaomea, Julie. "Dilemmas of an Indigenous Academic: A Native Hawaiian Story." In *Decolonizing Research in Cross-Cultural Contexts: Clinical Personal Narratives*, edited by Kagendo Mutua and Beth Blue Swadener. Albany, NY: SUNY Press, 2004.

King, C. Richard, and Charles Fruehling Springwood, eds. *Team Spirits: The Native American Mascots Controversy*. Lincoln: University of Nebraska Press, 2001.

Marubbio, M. Elise. *Killing the Indian Maiden: Images of Native American Women in Film*. Lexington: University Press of Kentucky, 2006.

Mihesuah, Devon A. *American Indians: Stereotypes and Realities*. Atlanta: Clarity Press, 1996.

Owings, Alison. *Indian Voices: Listening to Native Americans*. New Brunswick, NJ: Rutgers University Press, 2011.

Raheja, Michelle H. *Reservation Reelism: Redfacing, Visual Sovereignty, and Representations of Native Americans in Film*. Lincoln: University of Nebraska Press, 2011.

Smith, Paul Chaat. *Everything You Know about Indians Is Wrong*. Minneapolis: University of Minnesota Press, 2009.

Spindel, Carol. *Dancing at Halftime: Sports and the Controversy over American Indian Mascots*. New York: New York University Press, 2000.

Stedman, Raymond William. *Shadows of the Indians*. Norman: University of Oklahoma, 1982.

Tilton, Robert S. *Pocahontas: The Evolution of an American Narrative*. New York: Cambridge University Press, 1994.

West, W. Richard, Jr., et al. *Do All Indians Live in Tipis? Questions and Answers from the National Museum of the American Indian*. New York: Collins/National Museum of the American Indian, 2007.

Williamson, Peter. *French and Indian Cruelty Exemplified in the Life and Various Vicissitudes of Fortune of Peter Williamson*. York, PA: N. Nickson, 1757. Available at http://www.archive.org/stream/frenchindiancrue00will#page/n1/mode/2up.

Web Sites

American Indians in Children's Literature: http://americanindiansinchildrensliterature.blogspot.com/.

American Indian Perspectives on Thanksgiving: http://americanindian.si.edu/education/files/thanksgiving_poster.pdf.

Blue Corn Comics—The Basic Indian Stereotypes: http://www.bluecorncomics.com/. This site includes a Stereotype of the Month Contest.

National Museum of the American Indian. "Geronimo" Code Name Sparks Controversy: http://blog.nmai.si.edu/main/2011/05/geronimo-code-name-sparks-controversy.html.

Media Awareness Network. Common Portrayals of Aboriginal People: http://www.media-awareness.ca/english/issues/stereotyping/aboriginal_people/aboriginal_portrayals.cfm.

National Coalition on Racism in Sports and the Media: http://www.aics.org/NCRSM/index.htm.

STAR—Students and Teachers Against Racism: http://www.racismagainstindians.org/.

Part Two

3

Tribal Government

FIRSTS

1935   On October 4, the Confederated Salish and Kootenai Tribes of the Flathead Reservation in Montana adopted the first constitution prepared in connection with the Indian Reorganization Act of 1934.

1944   Comprised of member tribes from throughout the United States, the National Congress of American Indians has grown since its founding to become the oldest, largest, and most representative American Indian and Alaska Native organization in the country.

1974   The Red Lake Band of Chippewa Indians in Minnesota was the first tribal nation in the country to issue its own vehicle license plates.

1994   President William J. Clinton invited the leaders of all federally recognized tribes to meet with him at the White House, the first time since 1822 that tribal leaders had been invited to meet directly with a sitting U.S. president. In conjunction with the meeting, President Clinton issued a memorandum to all heads of executive departments and agencies outlining principles of government-to-government relations with Native American tribal governments.

1995   The Navajo Nation flag became the first Native American tribal flag taken to space when astronaut Bernard Harris carried it aboard the space shuttle *Discovery*.

2008   The Choctaw Nation of Oklahoma became the first tribal nation to be a recipient of the Secretary of Defense Employer Support Freedom Award, the highest recognition given by the U.S. government for the support of employees who serve in the National Guard and Reserve.

2009   The Confederated Tribes of the Umatilla Indian Reservation became the first tribe in the country to comply with, and implement, the

Sex Offender Registration and Notification Act (SORNA) passed by Congress in 2006.

2010   The first national symposium on tribal law was held in Albuquerque, New Mexico, to discuss the Tribal Law and Order Act, which was signed into law by President Barack Obama on July 29.

TRIBAL GOVERNMENT POWERS

Eight Selected Powers of Tribal Governments

Federally recognized American Indian tribes have a unique legal and political relationship with American society, one that is rooted in sovereignty predating the formation of the United States. Tribal governments are fundamental to this relationship, which is affirmed under the U.S. Constitution, as well as by treaties and agreements, congressional acts, executive orders, and judicial rulings. Tribal governments, which vary in size and structure among the 565 federally recognized tribal nations, have a government-to-government relationship with the United States federal government.

1. The power to determine and establish a form of government.
2. The power to determine tribal membership.
3. The power to exercise jurisdiction over the tribe's lands and resources.
4. The power to administer justice and enforce laws.
5. The power to regulate domestic relations of its tribal members.
6. The power to engage in commerce and trade.
7. The power to tax.
8. The power to regulate the conduct of nonmembers on tribal lands.

Selected Tribal Holidays

There are numerous holidays, commemorations, and other events held in tribal communities throughout the country. They vary by date and regularity, with a number of observances held annually and seasonally. At times, Native communities hold events during significant commemorative years such as centennials. They encompass a number of activities, including praying, memorializing, honoring, dancing, singing, and feasting.

Cherokee National Holiday: http://holiday.cherokee.org/
Held annually over Labor Day since 1953, the Cherokee National Holiday in Tahlequah, Oklahoma, commemorates the anniversary of the signing of the 1839 Cherokee Nation Constitution. The event has grown into one of the largest festivals in the state, attracting thousands of visitors.

Cheyenne Victory Day: http://www.cheyennenation.com/executive/holiday.html
Cheyenne Victory Day, observed on June 25 as a holiday of the Northern Cheyenne Tribe in Montana, commemorates the victory of the Cheyenne and their Lakota and Arapaho allies over Lieutenant Colonel George Armstrong Custer and the U.S. Army's Seventh Cavalry Regiment at the Battle of Little Bighorn, near what is now Crow Agency, Montana, on June 25 and 26, 1876. The victory is also commemorated by other tribal nations, especially by Lakota and other communities across the Plains.

Jamestown S'Klallam Federal Recognition Day: http://www.tribalmuseum. jamestowntribe.org/hsg/exhibits/exb_fedrec_acknowledge.php
After years of struggle, the Jamestown S'Klallam Tribe in Washington State became federally recognized in 1981. Each year on February 10, the tribal nation observes Federal Recognition Day and the formalization of government-to-government relations with the United States. An online exhibition, "Thirty Years and Time Immemorial: Commemorating the 30th Anniversary of the Official Federal Recognition of the Jamestown S'Klallam Tribe, February 10, 2011," documents the event in the tribe's rich history.

Klamath Tribes Annual Restoration Celebration, Oregon
Held annually on the fourth weekend in August, this event marks the anniversary of the restoration of federal recognition to the Klamath Tribes. The tribes, which include the Klamath, Modoc, and Yahooskin Bands of the Snake Indians, were terminated by the federal government in 1954. They regained federal recognition in 1986 by an act of Congress, P.L. 99–398, and have celebrated restoration since that time.

Nanih Waiya Day Celebration, Mississippi Band of Choctaw Indians
Nanih Waiya, which means "leaning hill" or "place of creation," is the ancestral Mother Mound of the Choctaw people. The sacred site, built over one thousand years ago and one of the best-documented mounds in the United States, was officially transferred back to Choctaw ownership by the State of Mississippi in 2008. Nanih Waiya Day, which was held to celebrate the return that year, is now an annual event.

Navajo Nation Sovereignty Day
Navajo Nation Sovereignty Day was first held in 1985 to celebrate the Supreme Court ruling in *Kerr-McGee Corp. v. Navajo Tribe*, which upheld the Navajo Nation's right to impose taxes on energy and other companies without approval by the U.S. Secretary of the Interior. An annual tribal holiday, the event is now held on the fourth Monday of April.

Nuwuvi Days, Chemehuevi Indian Tribe, Havasu Lake, California: http:// chemehuevi.net/newsnuwuvi.php

Nuwuvi Days festivities, held on the first weekend in June, celebrate the tribe's reinstatement as the Chemehuevi Indian Tribe through federal recognition on June 5, 1970. The celebration includes a pageant with youth contestants, who are crowned as Chemehuevi diplomats, and a parade. The event is held at the tribe's Nuwuvi Park.

Osage Nation Sovereignty Day, Oklahoma
The Osage Nation Sovereignty Day is held to celebrate the anniversary of the 2006 ratification of the Osage constitution, which gave the tribal nation independence and a new form of government for the first time in over a century. The change is an outgrowth of the passage of Public Law 108–431, An Act to Reaffirm the Inherent Sovereign Rights of the Osage Tribe to Determine Its Membership and Form a Government, signed by President George W. Bush in 2004.

Sovereigns Day, Hoopa Valley Tribe
Sovereigns Day of the Hoopa Valley Tribe in California celebrates the passage of the Hoopa-Yurok Settlement Act, P.L. 100–580, which was enacted on October 31, 1988. The legislation partitioned certain reservation lands between the Hoopa Valley Tribe and the Yurok Indians to clarify the use of tribal timber proceeds and for other purposes. Sovereigns Day is celebrated annually during the second week of August.

Tribal Recognition Day, Snoqualmie Indian Tribe, Washington State: http://www.snoqualmienation.com/
The Snoqualmie Indian Tribe observes Tribal Recognition Day as a holiday on October 12.

1875 Removal—1900 Return Commemoration, Yavapai-Apache Nation: http://yavapai-apache.org/events.html
A holiday of remembrance by the Yavapai-Apache Nation to commemorate the removal of the Yavapai and Apache people by military force from Arizona's Verde Valley and honors their return to their homeland. Held annually on the last Saturday of February at Veterans Memorial Park in Camp Verde, Arizona, the event includes a commemorative walk and cultural activities. The event is also referred to as Exodus Day.

Treaty Days, Tulalip Tribes, Washington: http://www.tulaliptribes-nsn.gov/
Treaty Days, which commemorates the signing of the Point Elliott Treaty of 1855, is an annual event held by the Tulalip Tribes in Washington. It usually takes place in January, with activities that include spiritual dancing and a feast. The first Tulalip Treaty Days celebration was held in 1912.

Choctaw Flag

During their alliance with the Confederate States of America during the U.S. Civil War, the Choctaws in Indian Territory (present-day Oklahoma) became the first United States tribe to adopt a flag. It was used between 1861 and 1864 and continued to inspire later Choctaw flags.

Navajo Nation Council Chamber

The Navajo Nation Council Chamber, located in Window Rock, Arizona, serves as the center of government for the Navajo Nation. Constructed from 1934 to 1935, the building was designated a National Historic Landmark (NHL) on August 18, 2004. According to the NHL's statement of significance documenting the designation, the Navajo Nation Council Chamber "stands today as a symbol of the New Deal revolution in federal Indian policy during the 1930s, advocating reconstitution of tribal organizations, restoration of tribal land base and promotion of traditional Indian culture." Featuring a red sandstone façade, the octagon-shaped chamber was designed to evoke a *hogan*, the traditional architectural or building form of the Navajo people. The landmark building also incorporates other Navajo cultural elements, including an east-facing main entrance and a windowless north wall. The interior includes a mural cycle, *The History and Progress of the Navajo Nation*, created by Navajo artist Gerald Nailor Sr.

http://tps.cr.nps.gov/nhl/detail.cfm?ResourceId=1299815777&ResourceType=Building

As one of the historic properties showcased for National American Indian Heritage Month, the National Register of Historic Places wrote that the Navajo Nation Council Chamber, in use since 1936, is "the only legislative headquarters in the United States owned by a American Indian tribe which has been continuously in use by that tribe."

http://www.nps.gov/history/nr/feature/indian/2005/navajo.htm

Embassy of Tribal Nations

The Embassy of Tribal Nations, a 17,000-square-foot office building in Washington, DC, opened on November 3, 2009. The facility was purchased by the National Congress of American Indians (NCAI), culminating years of planning and fundraising to have a permanent place that would enhance the presence of tribal sovereign nations in the nation's capital. Located in the Dupont Circle area of the city, near Embassy Row, the Embassy of Tribal Nations includes a work area for tribal leaders who visit Washington, as well as other offices.

Selected Statements about Tribal Government Powers

"The Congress shall have power to . . . regulate commerce with foreign nations, and among the several states, and with Indian tribes."

—United States Constitution, Article I, Section 8, Clause 3

"Indian Nations have always been considered as distinct, independent political communities, retaining their original natural rights, as the undisputed possessors of the soil . . . The very term 'nation,' so generally applied to them, means 'a people distinct from others.'"

—Chief Justice John Marshall, United States Supreme Court, *Worcester v. Georgia*

TRIBAL LEADERSHIP

First American Indian Women to Serve in Top Leadership Roles of Tribal Government

1959   Virginia S. Klinekole (Mescalero Apache) was the first female president of the Mescalero Apache tribe in New Mexico. She served two terms in that office, her final term ending in 1986. Honored for her contributions to Apache language preservation and education, Klinekole was inducted into the New Mexico Association of Bilingual Education's Hall of Fame in 1984.

1967   Betty Mae Tiger Jumper (Seminole Tribe of Florida) became the first woman elected to chair the Seminole Tribal Council.

1972   Anna Prieto Sandoval (Sycuan Band of Kumeyaay) served as tribal chair from 1972 to 1990. Sandoval helped to create one of the most successful gaming establishments in the country, leading efforts to bring jobs, health care, and housing to her people. Honored for her work and advocacy to preserve native traditions, she was inducted into San Diego's Hall of Fame in 2010.

1975   Vera Brown Starr (Yavapai-Apache) was the first woman elected chair of the Yavapai-Apache Tribe in Arizona.

1976   Mildred Cleghorn (Fort Sill Apache) was the first elected chairperson of the newly organized Fort Sill Apache Tribe in Oklahoma, serving in the leadership role until her retirement in 1995.

1978?   Juanita L. Learned was the first woman elected chairperson of the Cheyenne-Arapaho Tribes of Oklahoma.

1985   Wilma Mankiller (Cherokee) was the first woman to serve as principal chief of the Cherokee Nation in Oklahoma and the first woman to lead a large American Indian tribe. Mankiller, the recipient of many awards, was honored with the Presidential Medal of Freedom in 1998.

1987   Verna Williamson (Isleta Pueblo) became the first woman elected governor of Isleta Pueblo in New Mexico.

1988   Twila Martin-Kekahbah (Chippewa-Cree) was the first woman elected to serve as tribal chairwoman of the Turtle Mountain Band of Chippewa, serving three terms (1988–90, 1990–92, and 1994–96).

1993   Octaviana V. Trujillo (Pascua Yaqui) was the first woman elected as chairwoman of the Pascua Yaqui Tribal Council in Arizona.

1995   Joyce Dugan (Cherokee) was the first woman elected principal chief of the Eastern Band of Cherokee Indians in North Carolina.

2004   Cecelia Fire Thunder (Oglala Lakota) was elected first female president of the tribal council on the Pine Ridge Reservation in South Dakota.
            Erma Vizenor (Ojibwe) was the first woman to be elected tribal chair of the White Earth Band of Chippewa Indians in Minnesota.

2006   Glenna Wallace (Shawnee), who served on the Tribal Business Committee for eighteen years, was the first woman elected chief of the Eastern Shawnees in Oklahoma.

2010   Lynn Malerba (Mohegan) was appointed chief of the Mohegan Tribe in Connecticut, the first woman to hold the office since 1723.

2010   Paula Pechonick (Delaware) was elected chief of the Delaware Tribe of Oklahoma, the first woman to hold the office.

2011   Phyliss J. Anderson (Choctaw) was elected chief of the Mississippi Band of Choctaw Indians, becoming the first woman at the helm of the tribe's government.

Seven Books by and about Leaders in Tribal Government

1. *Chief, Champion of the Everglades: A Biography of Seminole Chief James Billie*, by Barbara Oeffener (1995).
2. *Chief: The Autobiography of Chief Phillip Martin, Longtime Tribal Leader, Mississippi Band of Choctaw Indians*, by Phillip Martin (2009).
3. *I'll Go and Do More: Annie Dodge Wauneka, Navajo Leader and Activist*, by Carolyn Niethammer (2004).
4. *In the Shadow of the Eagle: A Tribal Representative in Maine*, by Donna M. Loring (2008).
5. *The Last Warrior: Peter MacDonald and the Navajo Nation*, by Peter MacDonald (1993).
6. *Mankiller, a Chief and Her People: An Autobiography by the Principal Chief of the Cherokee Nation*, by Wilma Mankiller and Michael Wallis (1993).
7. *A Seminole Legend: The Life of Betty Mae Tiger Jumper*, by Betty Mae Tiger Jumper and Patsy West (2001).

Presidential Medal of Freedom

Among the nation's highest civilian honors, the Presidential Medal of Freedom is awarded to individuals who have made especially meritorious contributions to the security of national interests of the United States, world peace, or cultural or other significant public or private endeavors. The award is normally made annually, on or about July 4 of each year, but may be made at other times, as the president may deem appropriate. President Harry S. Truman established the Medal of Freedom in 1945 to recognize civilians for their efforts during World War II. In 1963 President John F. Kennedy re-established the honor as the Presidential Medal of Freedom.

Three Native American leaders have received the Presidential Medal of Freedom:
Annie Wauneka (Navajo), 1963
Wilma Mankiller (Cherokee), 1998
Joseph Medicine Crow (Crow), 2009

TRIBAL GOVERNMENT CENTERS

Selected Early Capitals or Tribal Centers

Madeline Island, Wisconsin
>Madeline Island, located in Lake Superior near Bayfield, Wisconsin, is the traditional cultural and religious center of Ojibwe in the region and one of the earliest settlements in the area.

Onondaga Nation ("The Keepers of the Central Fire"), New York
http://www.onondaganation.org/
>The Onondaga Nation serves as the "Firekeeper," or central council fire, of the Haudenosaunee, or Six Nations Iroquois Confederacy (besides Onondaga, the member nations are Mohawk, Oneida, Cayuga, Seneca, and Tuscarora).

Saukenuk, Illinois
>The capital of the Sauk Nation and one of the largest Indian centers in North America. Black Hawk State Historic Site, managed by the Illinois Historic Preservation Agency, manages the site.

Werowocomoco, Virginia
>Werowocomoco was the principal residence of Powhatan, paramount chief of approximately thirty Virginia Indian tribes at the time English colonists reached Virginia's shores in 1607. The village, located near the York River in present-day Gloucester County, served as the political and social center of the Powhatan chiefdom.

Five Early Tribal Sites with National Historic Status

Cherokee National Capitol, Tahlequah, Oklahoma
http://tps.cr.nps.gov/nhl/detail.cfm?ResourceId=460&ResourceType=Building
> The Cherokee National Capitol, a two-story brick building in Tahlequah, Indian Territory, served as the council house of the Cherokee National Council from 1869 to 1907, the year Oklahoma became a state. The Italianate structure then became the Cherokee County Courthouse. It was designated a National Historic Landmark on July 4, 1961.

Chickasaw National Capitol Building, Tishomingo, Oklahoma
> http://www.chickasaw.net/history_culture/index_3387.htm
> Built by the Chickasaw Nation in 1898, the Chickasaw National Capitol Building was the seat of Chickasaw Government from 1898 to 1906. The building, which was added to the National Registry of Historic Buildings in 1971, is now used for exhibit space.

Choctaw Capitol Building, Tuskahoma, Oklahoma
> Constructed in 1884 as a permanent seat of government at Tushka Homa ("home of the red warrior") by the Choctaw Nation, the Choctaw Capitol Building included rooms for the legislature, Supreme Court, principal chief, and other government offices. The building served as the tribal capitol until 1907, when Oklahoma became a state. It now serves as the Choctaw Nation Museum, with programs that include exhibits and shows for the annual Labor Day festival at the site. The Choctaw Capitol Building is a National Historic Site.

Creek National Capitol, Okmulgee, Oklahoma
http://tps.cr.nps.gov/nhl/detail.cfm?ResourceId=465&ResourceType=Building
> Erected in 1878 as the National Capitol of the Muscogee (Creek) Nation, the Victorian-style building served as the seat of Creek tribal government until 1907. In 1923, the structure became a museum, which chronicles the history of the Muscogee people before and after their forced removal from Georgia and Alabama to what is now Oklahoma. The building was designated a National Historic Landmark on July 4, 1961.

New Echota Historic Site, Calhoun, Georgia
http://tps.cr.nps.gov/nhl/detail.cfm?ResourceId=1043&ResourceType=District
http://www.gastateparks.org/NewEchota
> In 1825 the Cherokee Nation established a capital named New Echota at the headwaters of the Oostanaula River near present-day Calhoun, Georgia. Today, the site is a state park and museum with twelve original and reconstructed buildings, such as the Council House, Court House, Print Shop, missionary Samuel Worcester's home, and an 1805 store. New Echota was designated a National Historic Landmark on November 7, 1973.

Seneca Indian Council House

The Seneca Indian Council House, located at Letchworth State Park in Castile, New York, served as a space for leaders and other participants to gather and conduct meetings. The historic Council House antedates the American Revolution.

TRIBAL ALLIANCES AND CONFEDERACIES

Six Early Tribal Alliances and Confederacies

Illinois Confederation

Also referred to as the Illiniwek or the Illini Confederation, the Illinois Confederation refers to an alliance of Peoria, Kaskaskia, Tamaroa, Cahokia, Michigamea, and other tribes that lived in the upper Mississippi River valley, their population estimated at several thousand people at the time of European contact in the seventeenth century. The tribes shared cultural and historical roots, kinship ties, and other commonalities.

Iroquois Confederacy

The Iroquois Confederacy, "one of the oldest participatory democracies on earth," is composed of six tribal nations: the Seneca, Mohawk, Onondaga, Cayuga, Oneida, and Tuscarora (Onondaga Nation Web site: http://www.onondaganation.org/aboutus/facts.html). They call themselves the Haudenosaunee ("people who build the house" or "People of the Longhouse"), referring to their traditional homes and centers. The confederacy, or Iroquois League, initially consisted of the Five Nations, with the Tuscarora becoming the sixth member in 1722. The present-day homelands of these nations include territories and reservations in upstate New York and Wisconsin, communities in Oklahoma and North Carolina, and territories and reserves in Ontario and Quebec, Canada. The Onondaga Nation, considered the capital of the Haudenosaunee, continues to be the meeting place for the Grand Council of Chiefs, the traditional ruling body of the confederacy.

Three Fires Confederacy

Translated as Niswi-mishkodewin in the Anishinaabe language, the Three Fires Confederacy is also known as the Council of Three Fires, People of the Three Fires, and the United Nations of Chippewa, Ottawa, and Potawatomi Indians. The formation of the Three Fires Confederacy, consisting of Ojibwe (Chippewa), Ottawa (Odawa), and Potawatomi member nations, has been traced to AD 796 at Michilimackinac, the region around the Straits of Mackinac between Lake Huron and Lake Michigan. From its inception, the confederacy served diplomatic, political, military, and other purposes.

Wabanaki Confederacy

The Wabanaki Confederacy, believed to have been formed in about the 1680s, brought together a coalition of several northeastern Algonquian-speaking tribal nations, including Abenaki, Penobscot, Maliseet, Passamaquoddy, and Mi'kmaq. Member nations had their own names in their respective languages for the confederacy, but Wabanaki is generally translated in English as "People of the Dawnland" (easterners). The historic tribal alliance is noted for its crucial role in the long struggle for the aboriginal rights of its people.

Wabash Confederacy

Also called the Wabash Indians or the Wabash tribes, the Wabash Confederacy refers to eighteenth-century Native peoples who lived in the area of the Wabash River, or present-day Illinois, Indiana, and Ohio. The multi-tribal settlement alliance included Weas, Piankashaws, Kickapoos, and Mascoutens.

Western Confederacy

Also called the Western Indian Confederacy or the Miami Confederacy, this alliance was formed in the Great Lakes region during the late eighteenth century to resist expansion of the United States into the Northwest Territory. It consisted of members of the Council of Three Fires, the Iroquois Confederacy, Seven Nations of Canada, Wabash Confederacy (Weas, Piankashaws, and other tribal nations), and Illini Confederacy, as well as Wyandot, Mississauga, Menominee, Shawnee, Lenape, Miami, Kickapoo, Kaskaskia, Chickamauga (Cherokee), and Upper Muscogee (Creek).

The Great Tree of Peace and One Dollar Coin

In honor of Native American contributions to the development and history of the United States, the theme for the U.S. Mint's 2010 dollar coin was "Government—The Great Tree of Peace." It recognizes the Haudenosaunee (also known as the Iroquois Confederacy), featuring an image of the Hiawatha Belt with five arrows bound together, as well as the words "Haudenosaunee" and "Great Law of Peace." http://www.usmint.gov/mint_programs/nativeamerican/?action=2010NADesign

HONORING NATIONS PROJECT,
HARVARD UNIVERSITY

Honoring Nations Honorees, 1999–2010

Honoring Nations, a national awards program initiated in 1998, highlights outstanding programs in self-governance by Native nations. At the heart of the program is the belief that tribes themselves hold the key to positive social, political, cultural, and economic prosperity. Based at the John F. Kennedy School of Government at Harvard University, Honoring Nations is administered by the Harvard Project on American Indian Economic Development. The criteria for selection of honorees include program effectiveness, significance to sovereignty, cultural relevance, transferability, and sustainability. Tribal nations are honored for outstanding programs in diverse areas of tribal government.

New Law and Old Law Together, 1999
Judicial Branch, Navajo Nation
Window Rock, Arizona
www.navajocourts.org
>   The Judicial Branch of the Navajo Nation utilizes traditional methods of dispute resolution as the "law of preference" within its Western-based court model. The branch has also provided training about the Navajo judicial system and developed the Navajo Nation Bar Association, comprised of more than three hundred members who are licensed to practice in Navajo Nation courts.

Tribal Court of the Grand Traverse Band, 1999
Grand Traverse Band of Ottawa and Chippewa Indians
Suttons Bay, Michigan
>   The Tribal Court, which is constitutionally separate within the tribe, adjudicates cases such as child abuse, juvenile delinquency, contract and employment disputes, personal and property injuries, and constitutional issues. It utilizes peacemaking to resolve contentious issues, helping to foster the social fabric that binds the community together.

Enhancing Government-to-Government Relationships, 2000
Intergovernmental Affairs Department
The Confederated Tribes of Grand Ronde, Grand Ronde, Oregon
>   The Intergovernmental Affairs Department achieved positive intergovernmental relationships with federal, state, and local governments by pursuing a strategy of communication, education, cooperation, contributions, and presence. The tribe built coalitions and forged partnerships, forming a skilled team of tribal advocates and developing a legislative tracking system.

Government Reform, Diné Appropriate Government, Local Governance Projects, 2002
The Office of Navajo Government Development
Navajo Nation, Window Rock, Arizona
> Formed in 1989 by the Navajo Nation Council, the Office of Navajo Government Development has developed and informed legislative initiatives that expand tribal sovereignty and increase governmental accountability and efficiency.

Nation Building among the Chilkoot Tlingit, 2002
Chilkoot Indian Association, Haines, Alaska
> Excluded by the Alaska Native Claims Settlement Act of 1971, the Chilkoot Tlingit revived their tribal government, beginning in 1990 with the Chilkoot Indian Association. The association's self-determined initiatives included negotiating the acquisition of a land base and developing programs, leading to contracts in education, health, housing, economic development, as well as participation in government-to-government relationships.

Kake Circle Peacemaking, 2003
The Organized Village of Kake, Kake, Alaska
> The Organized Village of Kake restored its traditional method of dispute resolution, adopting Circle Peacemaking at its tribal court in 1999. The method provides a forum for bringing together those affected in each case, including victims, wrongdoers, families, leaders, and social service providers to restore relationships and community harmony.

Northwest Intertribal Court System, 2003
Confederated Tribes of the Chehalis Reservation
Mountlake Terrace, Washington
> The Northwest Intertribal Court System, which is owned by a consortium of tribes in Washington State, assists in developing courts that provide equitable justice for those falling within their jurisdiction. Its services include code writing and technical assistance to help Indian nations in developing the necessary legal infrastructure.

Navajo Nation Sales Tax, 2005
Office of the Navajo Tax Commission
Navajo Nation
http://www.navajotax.org/
> In 1974, the Navajo Tribal Council established a Navajo Tax Commission to study the viability of Navajo taxes. In a 1985 ruling on litigation initiated by coal companies against the tribe, the U.S. Supreme Court affirmed the Navajo Nation's ability to tax. By 2002, the Navajo Nation had instituted a tribal sales tax to help contribute to fiscal independence and local control.

Osage Nation Governmental Reform Initiative, 2008
Osage Nation
Pawhuska, Oklahoma
www.osagetribe.com

The U.S. Government abolished the 1881 Osage Nation Constitution and imposed its own policies and practices, to the detriment of tribal self-determination. Osage efforts resulted in the passage of P.L. 108–431, a federal law reaffirming the inherent sovereign rights of the Osage Tribe to determine its own membership and form of government. The Osage Nation Governmental Reform Initiative culminated in the adoption of a new constitution in 2006, one that reflects the participation and will of the people.

Citizen Potawatomi Nation Constitution Reform, 2010
Citizen Potawatomi Nation
Shawnee, Oklahoma
http://www.potawatomi.org/

In 2007, the Citizen Potawatomi Nation (CPN) adopted a new tribal constitution, incorporating executive, legislative, and judicial functions, as well as creating a sixteen-member legislature. Half the members of this body are elected at-large from Oklahoma to represent Citizen Potawatomis in the state, while each of the other eight members represents a legislative district outside Oklahoma. In part because of a long history of forced removal, only 38 percent of the nation's citizens live in the state of Oklahoma; hence the need to address out-of-state representation.

LEGISLATION

Legislation, 1898–2000

1898   Curtis Act
This legislation extended the provisions of the General Allotment Act (Dawes Act) of 1887 in Indian Territory (present-day Oklahoma), authorizing the allotment of Cherokee, Choctaw, Chickasaw, Creek, and Seminole lands, abolishing tribal courts, and prohibiting the enforcement of tribal laws in federal court. The act also abolished the constitutional governments of these tribal nations.

1934   Indian Reorganization Act (Wheeler-Howard Act)
Sometimes called the Indian New Deal, this legislation reversed the land allotment policies of the Dawes Act of 1887 to, instead, conserve and develop Indian lands and resources, to extend to Indians the right to form business and other organizations, and to

grant certain rights of home rule to Indians. A National Congress of American Indians report estimates that 60 percent of tribal governments are based on Indian Reorganization Act constitutions.

1936   Alaska Reorganization Act
This legislation, also known as the Alaska Native New Deal, extended the Indian Reorganization Act of 1934 to Alaska. Many Native village governments throughout the state organized and adopted constitutions under provisions of the act. Some Native businesses were chartered or financed as well.

1936   Oklahoma Indian Welfare Act
This legislation, also known as the Thomas-Rogers Act, extended principles of the Indian Reorganization Act of 1934 to tribal groups in Oklahoma. Its provisions included the right of any tribe or band of Indians in that state "to organize for its common welfare and to adopt a constitution and bylaws." The law also addressed land issues, a response to losses and divisions resulting from earlier allotment policies and practices.

1946   Indian Claims Commission
Congress established the Indian Claims Commission in order to settle land claims by American Indian tribal nations against the United States. Providing limited financial compensation for tribal claims and no return of land, the nation acquired title to millions of acres of illegally seized Indian land. In 1978, unresolved cases were returned to the U.S. Court of Claims.

1971   Alaska Native Claims Settlement Act
This act provided for the settlement of certain land claims of Alaska Natives. Its provisions included the enrollment of Natives, the organization of regional corporations of Natives, the conveyance of lands to the corporations, and the deposit of settlement funds in an Alaska Native Fund.

1975   Indian Self-Determination and Education Assistance Act
Signed into law on January 4, 1975, the Indian Self-Determination and Education Assistance Act authorized the secretary of the interior and other federal agencies to enter into contracts with, and make grants directly to, federally recognized tribes to operate certain programs themselves. The legislation also included provisions to upgrade Indian education.

1982   Indian Tribal Governmental Tax Status Act
Passed by Congress in 1982, this act treats tribal governments as state governments for a variety of specified tax purposes.

1994   The American Indian Trust Fund Management Reform Act
            The American Indian Trust Fund Management Reform Act
            requires the secretary of the interior to take specified actions to
            properly discharge U.S. responsibilities with regard to American
            Indian funds held in trust by the federal government, including
            providing adequate systems for accounting for and reporting
            trust fund balances. The legislation also established the Office
            of Special Trustee for American Indians within the Department
            of the Interior to oversee the implementation of management
            reforms.

1994   Federally Recognized Indian Tribe List Act
            This act charges the secretary of the interior with the responsi-
            bility of keeping a list of all federally recognized tribes, specifying
            that it be accurate, regularly updated, and regularly published. The
            information is needed because it is used by the various departments
            and agencies of the United States to determine the eligibility of
            certain groups for federal programs and services because of their
            status as Indians.

2000   Executive Order 13175, Consultation and Coordination with Tribal
            Governments
            Issued by President William J. Clinton on November 6, 2000,
            Executive Order 13175 directs federal agencies to consult and
            coordinate with American Indian tribal governments in order to
            establish regular and meaningful consultation and collaboration
            with tribal officials in the development of federal policies that have
            tribal implications, to strengthen the United States government-
            to-government relationships with Indian tribes, and to reduce the
            imposition of unfunded mandates upon Indian tribes.

FILMS

The Flickering Flame: The Life and Legacy of Chief Turkey Tayac (USA, 1999,
55 min.), directed by Janet Cavallo and Jason Corwin (Seneca Nation).
    This documentary tells the story of Chief Turkey Tayac (1895–1978) of the
    Piscataway Indian Nation in Maryland through interviews with family and
    friends.
The Great Law of the Iroquois (USA, 1998, 13 min.), directed by Pat Ferrero.
    This film examines the oral tradition and includes a number of Iroquois
    discussing wampum belts as mnemonic devices for treaty making and other
    cultural purposes.

Warrior Chiefs in a New Age (USA, 1992, 30 min.), directed by Dean Curtis Bear Claw (Crow).

This film portrays Crow Nation chiefs Plenty Coups and Medicine Crow and their visionary leadership. It intersperses historical films and photographs, interviews with contemporary tribal leaders, and images of Crow lands and people to tell the story.

ORGANIZATIONS

Americans for Indian Opportunity (AIO)
http://www.aio.org

Founded in 1970 by LaDonna Harris (Comanche) and other Native leaders, Americans for Indian Opportunity (AIO) is a national organization that works to enhance the cultural, social, political, and economic self-sufficiency of tribes. AIO, which is headquartered in Albuquerque, New Mexico, continues to provide leadership development and community-building initiatives based on indigenous Native values.

Indian Law Resource Center
http://www.indianlaw.org/

Founded in 1978, the Indian Law Resource Center is a nonprofit law and advocacy organization established and directed by American Indians. With offices in Washington, DC, and Helena, Montana, the center provides legal assistance to indigenous peoples of the Americas to combat racism and oppression, to protect their lands and environment, to achieve sustainable economic development and genuine self-government, as well as to achieve other human rights.

Intertribal Monitoring Association on Indian Trust Funds (ITMA)
http://www.itmatrustfunds.org/

Located in Albuquerque, New Mexico, the Intertribal Monitoring Association on Indian Trust Funds was organized in 1990 to actively monitor and have a voice in the activities of the federal government to ensure fair compensation to tribes for historical trust funds mismanagement. The organization grew to become a national tribal consortium consisting of sixty-six federally recognized tribes, whose efforts increased as it followed the trust reform activities of the government.

National American Indian Court Judges Association (NAICJA)
http://naicja.org/

Established in 1969, the National American Indian Court Judges Association is a national voluntary association of tribal court judges. Its mission is to strengthen and enhance American Indian and Alaska Native tribal justice systems through education, information sharing, and advocacy. NAICJA is housed at the Tribal Law and Government Center at the University of Kansas School of Law.

National American Indian Housing Council (NAIHC)
http://www.naihc.net/

Founded in 1974, the National American Indian Housing Council is the only national organization representing housing interests of Native people who reside in Indian communities, Alaska Native villages, and on Native Hawaiian homelands. NAIHC, which is headquartered in Washington, DC, numbers some 271 members representing 463 tribes and housing organizations.

National Congress of American Indians (NCAI)
http://www.ncai.org/

Founded in 1944 in response to federal termination and assimilation policies, the National Congress of American Indians (NCAI) works to protect tribal sovereignty and to preserve rights under treaties and agreements with the United States. NCAI, which serves member tribes from throughout the country, is the nation's oldest and largest tribal organization. Headquartered in Washington, DC, it works to inform the public and Congress about American Indians and Alaska Natives to foster better understanding of Native people and issues.

National Tribal Environmental Council (NTEC)
http://www.ntec.org/

Created in 1991, the National Tribal Environmental Council was formed with seven tribes and input from several intertribal organizations as a membership organization dedicated to protecting and preserving tribal environments. The NTEC, headquartered in Albuquerque, New Mexico, is open to any federally recognized tribe throughout the United States. NTEC now has some 186 member tribes.

Native American Rights Fund (NARF)
http://www.narf.org/

Founded in 1970, the Native American Rights Fund is the oldest and largest nonprofit law firm dedicated to assisting and defending the rights of Indian tribes, organizations, and individuals nationwide. NARF is headquartered in Boulder, Colorado, with branch offices in Washington, DC, and Anchorage, Alaska.

Native Nations Institute (NNI)
http://nni.arizona.edu/

The Native Nations Institute for Leadership, Management, and Policy was founded in 2001 by the Morris K. Udall and Stewart L. Udall Foundation and the University of Arizona as a self-determination, self-governance, and development resource for Native nations. An outgrowth of the research programs of the Harvard Project on American Indian Economic Development, it provides education and training programs designed to meet the needs of indigenous leadership and management.

Women Empowering Women for Indian Nations
http://www.wewin04.org/

Women Empowering Women for Indian Nations (WEWIN) was founded in 2004 to empower American Indian women working at all levels of government. Its founders include female tribal leaders from across the country who envisioned an organization that would nurture understanding of tribal responsibilities, issues confronting tribes, and political challenges experienced at various levels.

Regional Tribal Organizations

Affiliated Tribes of Northwest Indians (ATNI): http://www.atnitribes.org/
Alaska Federation of Natives (AFN): http://www.nativefederation.org/
Alaska Inter-Tribal Council (AITC)
All Indian Pueblo Council (AIPC): http://www.20pueblos.org/
California Council of Tribal Governments
Eight Northern Indian Pueblos Council: http://www.enipc.org/
Great Lakes Inter-Tribal Council (GLITC): http://www.glitc.org/
Great Plains Tribal Chairmen's Association (GPTCA)
Inter Tribal Council of Arizona (ITCA): http://www.itcaonline.com/
Inter-Tribal Council of California (ITCC): http://www.itccinc.org/
Inter-Tribal Council of Michigan (ITCM): http://www.itcmi.org/
Inter-Tribal Council of Nevada (ITCN): http://www.itcn.org/
Inter-Tribal Council of the Five Civilized Tribes: http://www.fivecivilizedtribes.org/
Midwest Alliance of Sovereign Tribes (MAST): http://www.m-a-s-t.org/
Montana-Wyoming Tribal Leaders Council: http://www.mtwytlc.com/
Oklahomans for Indian Opportunity
Southern California Tribal Chairmen's Association (SCTCA): http://www.sctca.net/
Tanana Chiefs Association: www.tananachiefs.org
United South and Eastern Tribes, Inc. (USET): http://www.usetinc.org/
United Tribes of Texas, Kansas and Oklahoma

RESOURCES

Austin, Raymond D. *Navajo Courts and Navajo Common Law: A Tradition of Tribal Self-Governance.* Minneapolis: University of Minnesota Press, 2009.
Case, David S., and David A. Voluck. *Alaska Natives and American Laws.* 2nd ed. Fairbanks: University of Alaska Press, 2002.
Cohen, Felix S. *On the Drafting of Tribal Constitutions.* Edited by David E. Wilkins. Norman: University of Oklahoma Press, 2007.
Edmunds, R. David, ed. *The New Warriors: Native American Leaders Since 1900.* Lincoln: University of Nebraska Press, 2001.

Evans, Laura E. *Power from Powerlessness: Tribal Governments, Institutional Niches, and American Federalism.* New York: Oxford University Press, 2011.

Harvard Project in American Indian Economic Development. *The State of Native Nations: Conditions under U.S. Policies of Self-Determination.* New York: Oxford University Press, 2008.

Healy, Donald T., and Peter J. Orenski. *Native American Flags.* Norman: University of Oklahoma Press, 2003.

Jorgenson, Miriam, ed. *Rebuilding Native Nations: Strategies for Governance and Development.* Tucson: University of Arizona Press, 2007.

O'Brien, Sharon. *American Indian Tribal Governments.* Norman: University of Oklahoma Press, 1993.

Pevar, Stephen L. *The Rights of Indians and Tribes.* New York: New York University Press, 2004.

Richland, Justin B. *Arguing with Tradition: The Language of Law in Hopi Tribal Court.* Chicago: University of Chicago Press, 2008.

Trafzer, Clifford E., ed. *American Indians/American Presidents: A History.* New York: HarperCollins/National Museum of the American Indian, Smithsonian Institution, 2009.

Treuer, Anton, et al. *Indian Nations of North America.* Washington, DC: National Geographic Society, 2010.

Ulrich, Roberta. *American Indian Nations from Termination to Restoration, 1953–2006.* Lincoln: University of Nebraska Press, 2010.

Wilkinson, Charles F. *Blood Struggle: The Rise of Modern Indian Nations.* New York: W.W. Norton, 2005.

Web Sites

Alaska Tribal Governments: http://www.englishoe.com/gpage2.html.

Council of Athabascan Tribal Governments: http://www.catg.org/whoweare.htm.

Fast Facts about Montana Tribal Governments. Prepared by the Montana Indian Education Association. http://www.billings.k12.mt.us/literacy/mont_indian/fastfacts.pdf.

Haudenosaunee Guide for Educators, Education Office, National Museum of the American Indian: http://www.nmai.si.edu/education/files/HaudenosauneeGuide.pdf.

Institute for Tribal Government: http://www.tribalgov.pdx.edu/.

Journey of a Nation (2010): http://www.choctawcinema.com/?p=250.

National Congress of American Indians. An Introduction to Indian Nations in the United States: http://www.ncai.org/Intro-to-Indian-Nations-in-the.567.0.html.

Native American Constitution and Law Digitization Project: http://thorpe.ou.edu/.

Native Nations Institute, Native Nation Building (CDs/DVDs): http://nni.arizona.edu/nnitvradio/index.php.

Office of Indian Tribal Governments at the Internal Revenue Service: http://www.irs.gov/govt/tribes/article/0,,id=96135,00.html.

Orders and Policies Regarding Consultation with Indian Tribes: http://www.schlosserlawfiles.com/consult/PoliciesReConsult%20w-IndianTribe.htm.

Tribal Court Clearinghouse, a project of the Tribal Law and Policy Institute: http://www.tribal-institute.org/lists/vaiw.htm.

USA.gov Tribal Governments and Native Americans: http://www.usa.gov/Government/Tribal.shtml.

Worldwide Guide to Women in Leadership, United States of America Native Tribes: http://www.guide2womenleaders.com/USA_Native.htm.

4

Federal-Tribal Relations

FIRSTS

1831   *Cherokee Nation v. Georgia* was the first U.S. Supreme Court case that discussed the issue of sovereignty of American Indian tribal nations, defining them as "domestic dependent nations with an unquestionable right to the lands which they occupy."

1869   Ely Samuel Parker (Seneca) was appointed as the first American Indian Commissioner of Indian Affairs by President Ulysses S. Grant, serving in the position until 1871.

1900   Robert William Kalanihiapo Wilcox was the first Native Hawaiian to serve in the U.S. Congress.

1914   Houston Benge Tehee (Cherokee) was the first American Indian to serve as the registrar of the U.S. Treasury.

1928   Charles Curtis (Kaw) became the first Native American to serve as vice president of the United States.

1969   Brantley Blue (Lumbee) was the first American Indian to serve as Indian commissioner on the Indian Claims Commission.

1978   Claudeen Bates Arthur (Navajo) became the first Native American woman to attain the rank of Field Solicitor for the U.S. Department of the Interior (DOI). She served with the DOI for four years.

1979   Frank H. Seay became the first American Indian to serve on the federal judiciary when he was appointed by President Jimmy Carter to the United States Eastern District Court of Oklahoma. While in his 50s, Judge Seay learned that his heritage included Native ancestry, likely Cherokee.

1983   Arlinda Faye Locklear (Lumbee) was the first American Indian woman to successfully argue a case before the U.S. Supreme Court.

1990   Daniel Kahikina Akaka became America's first U.S. Senator of Native Hawaiian ancestry and the only Chinese American member of the Senate. He was first elected to the U.S. House of Representatives in 1976.

1991   Barbara Booher (Uintah-Ouray Ute) became the first American Indian woman to be appointed superintendent in the National Park Service, supervising the Custer Battlefield National Monument.

1993   Ada Deer (Menominee) became the first female assistant secretary for the Bureau of Indian Affairs in the history of the U.S. Department of the Interior. Following her nomination to the office by President Bill Clinton, she was confirmed by the U.S. Senate on July 16, 1993.

1994   Robert D. Ecoffey (Oglala Lakota) was the first American Indian to serve as U.S. Marshal in the Department of Justice.

1994   President Bill Clinton became the first U.S. President to invite the leaders of all federally recognized tribes to the White House. The president pledged that his administration would work with tribal leaders to establish a true government-to-government partnership.

1996   Ben Nighthorse Campbell (Northern Cheyenne) was the first American Indian to serve as chairman of the Senate Committee on Indian Affairs.

2003   Harvard Law School announced the establishment of the Oneida Indian Nation Professorship of Law, the first endowed chair in American Indian studies at Harvard University and the only professorship of its kind east of the Mississippi River. It was made possible by the Oneida Indian Nation in New York "to help create a better understanding of the complex legal issues faced by all American Indians today and in the future."

2007   Diane Humetewa (Hopi), who was nominated by President George W. Bush and confirmed by the U.S. Senate, was the first American Indian woman to become a United States attorney, serving for the District of Arizona until August 2009.

2009   Appointed by President Barack Obama, Kimberly Teehee (Cherokee Nation) was named the first White House Senior Policy Adviser for Native American Affairs. As a member of the Domestic Policy Council, her role includes advising the president on issues impacting Indian country.

   President Obama also appointed Jodi Archambault Gillette (Standing Rock Sioux) as a deputy associate director of the Office of Intergovernmental Affairs, the administration's primary liaison to federally recognized tribes; she is the first Native American to hold the position.

2011   Stacy L. Leeds (Cherokee Nation) became the first American Indian woman to serve as dean of a law school. She had been serving as interim associate dean for academic affairs, professor of law, and director of the Tribal Law and Government Center at the University of Kansas School of Law when she was named dean of the University of Arkansas School of Law.

EXECUTIVE BRANCH

Selected Statements by U.S. Presidents

"[T]he basis of our proceedings with the Indian Nations has been, and shall be, justice during the period in which I may have anything to do in the administration of this government."
     President George Washington, 1790

"To promote this disposition to exchange lands, which they have to spare and we want . . . we shall push our trading houses, and be glad to see the good and influential individuals among them run in debt, because we observe that when these debts get beyond what the individuals can pay, they become willing to lop them off by a cession of lands."
     Thomas Jefferson to William Henry Harrison, February 27, 1803

"The great objective to be accomplished is the removal of these tribes . . . to the territory designated on conditions which shall be satisfactory to themselves and honorable to the United States."
     President James Monroe on Indian Removal, January 25, 1825

"At the establishment of the Federal Government . . . the principle was adopted of considering them as foreign and independent powers and also as proprietors of lands. . . . We have been far more successful in the acquisition of their lands than in imparting to them the principles or inspiring them with the spirit of civilization."
     President John Quincy Adams, December 2, 1828

"Professing a desire to civilize and settle them, we have at the same time lost no opportunity to purchase their lands and thrust them farther into the wilderness. By this means they have not only been kept in a wandering state, but been led to look upon us as unjust and indifferent to their fate."
     President Andrew Jackson, First Annual Message to Congress, December 8, 1829

"It is the object of this Government to be on terms of peace with you, and with all our red brethren. We constantly endeavor to be so. We make treaties with you, and will try to observe them; and if our children should sometimes behave badly, and violate these treaties, it is against our wish."
     President Abraham Lincoln, March 27, 1863, Speech to a southern Plains tribal delegation

"I determined to give all the agencies to such religious denominations as had heretofore established missionaries among the Indians.... The societies selected ... are expected to watch over them and aid them as missionaries, to Christianize and civilize the Indians . . ."

President Ulysses S. Grant, Second Annual Message to Congress, December 5, 1870

"In my judgment the time has arrived when we should definitely make up our minds to recognize the Indian as an individual and not as a member of a tribe. The General Allotment Act is a mighty pulverizing engine to break up the tribal mass."

President Theodore Roosevelt, First Annual Message, December 3, 1901

"The continued application of the allotment laws, under which Indian wards have lost more than two-thirds of their reservation lands, while the costs of Federal administration of these lands have steadily mounted, must be terminated."

President Franklin D. Roosevelt, Statement on the Wheeler-Howard Bill, April 28, 1934

"I propose a new goal for our Indian programs: A goal that ends the old debate about 'termination' of Indian programs and stresses self-determination; a goal that erases old attitudes of paternalism and promotes partnership self-help."

President Lyndon B. Johnson, Special Message to Congress on the Problems of the American Indian: "The Forgotten American," March 6, 1968

"History has shown that failure to include the voices of tribal officials in formulating policy affecting their communities has all too often led to undesirable and, at times, devastating and tragic results. By contrast, meaningful dialogue between Federal officials and tribal officials has greatly improved Federal policy toward Indian tribes. Consultation is a critical ingredient of a sound and productive Federal-tribal relationship."

President Barack Obama, Presidential Memorandum, November 5, 2009

Twelve Roles of U.S. Presidents in Federal-Tribal Relations

From President George Washington's message on government trading houses to President Barack Obama's second White House Tribal Nations Conference with leaders of tribal nations in 2010, U.S. presidents have always served critically important roles in federal-tribal relations.

1. Conducts diplomacy with tribal leaders, such as meeting with delegations.
2. Presents diplomatic gifts, such as peace medals, to American Indian leaders.
3. Negotiates and/or implements treaties and agreements.
4. Formulates federal Indian policy.

5. Appoints key figures to critical roles in Indian affairs and beyond.
6. Issues executive orders and directives.
7. Delivers addresses and messages on Indian affairs.
8. Initiates, signs, and/or vetoes legislation affecting American Indians.
9. Issues proclamations.
10. Invites American Indian delegations to participate in inaugural parades and other events.
11. Grants pardons.
12. Fosters government-to-government relations with tribal governments.

Presidential Visits to Indian Country

1883	En route to Yellowstone National Park, President Chester A. Arthur visited the Wind River Reservation in Wyoming Territory, where he was welcomed by Shoshone to their homeland. Arthur favored allotment, or the breaking up of Indian reservations into individual parcels.
1936	President Franklin D. Roosevelt made a brief stop at the Eastern Band of Cherokee in North Carolina. It would be another six decades before a U.S. president would visit an Indian reservation.
1999	President Bill Clinton visited the Pine Ridge Reservation in South Dakota, part of his New Markets Tour to encourage private investment in Indian country. He became the first sitting president to visit a reservation since Franklin D. Roosevelt in 1936.
2000	President Bill Clinton visited the Navajo Nation at Shiprock, New Mexico. His purpose was to bridge the digital divide between the Navajo Nation and the rest of the country.

Rupert Costo Statement

"The Presidents of the United States have always played a far more important role in Indian affairs than is generally recognized. Their role in determining policy, initiating actions, signing or vetoing legislative acts, and in fact deciding the fate of the Indian tribes, has always been significant and crucial."

—Rupert Costo, "Presidents of the United States in American History," *Indian Historian*, Fall 1968

Tribal Delegations

A major component of federal Indian policy centered on the practice of inviting important tribal leaders to Washington, DC, to pave the way for American expansion via diplomatic means. Tribal delegations, part of a pattern of Indian-white diplomacy in North America, can be traced to the early years of European colonization. European leaders met with Native delegates in tribal homelands, Euro-American capitals, and other locations to establish alliances, negotiate treaties, and foster friendship and loyalty. By the time the United States government was formed, tribal delegations were already firmly established as a major component of Indian-white relations.

Tribal delegations often met with the American president, a practice that continued at least through Ulysses S. Grant's administration in 1877. After meeting the president, delegates were often presented with peace medals and flags, given gifts, and taken on tours of military installations and other eastern cities to impress upon the visitors the nation's power and wealth. They also sat for drawings or photographs. Charles Milton Bell (1848–93), one of the leading portrait photographers in Washington, DC, began to photograph Native Americans in 1873. From 1879 until the 1890s, he took photographs of Indians for the Department of the Interior and the Bureau of American Ethnology.

As the nation and the government grew and demands on the president's time multiplied, the secretary of the interior gradually assumed more of the official duties associated with diplomatic relations with American Indians.

Peace Medals

Prior to the establishment of the United States, the practice of distributing peace medals to American Indian leaders already had a long history in diplomacy. Thomas Jefferson described the practice as "an ancient custom from time immemorial" that began with the European issuance of medals to negotiators of treaties, other diplomatic figures, or visitors of distinction.

Beginning with George Washington, American presidents and their agents bestowed Indian peace medals upon American Indian leaders and other tribal representatives to advance Indian-white diplomatic relations in the United States. The medals, generally silver, were intended to symbolize friendship and alliance between the American government and tribal nations. They also symbolized the power invested in the recipient of the medal. Common scenes on the medals include a crossed tomahawk and peace pipe, clasped hands, a likeness of the president issuing the medal, and scenes intended to show the advantages of Euro-American civilization over Indian customs.

The last of the medals designed specifically for American Indians was the round Benjamin Harrison medal, designed in 1890. During the nineteenth century, with changing relations between the United States government and tribal nations, the practice of presenting medals declined. Rather than signifying national allegiance, as earlier, the medals increasingly shifted to serving as rewards for good behavior or services rendered. The growing production and distribution of unofficial medals also contributed to the decline.

American Indian leaders valued peace medals as symbols of power, essential to diplomatic relations. In 1829 Thomas L. McKenney, United States commissioner of Indian affairs, wrote that "without medals, any plan of operations among the Indians, be it what it may, is essentially enfeebled." He explained that Indians viewed the practice as an "ancient right" (Prucha 1994, xiii). As cherished possessions, the medals were sometimes buried with the owners or passed to descendants. Over time, large numbers of official medals also passed into the hands of private collectors and museums.

Treaties

"All treaties made, or which shall be made, under the authority of the United States shall be the supreme law of the land; and the judges in every state shall be bound thereby, anything in the constitution or laws of any state to the contrary notwithstanding."

—U.S. Constitution, Article VI, Section 2

LEGISLATIVE BRANCH

Historical Overview of Treaties and Agreements

The legislative branch has a significant role in the federal-tribal relations, including the U.S. Senate's ratification, or approval, of American Indian treaties.

Treaties are vitally important to tribal nations, as the legal basis for the establishment of land bases and claims, distinct political status, and rights to resources such as hunting, fishing, and water. Specific treaties continue to be litigated and interpreted in courts of law, including the U.S. Supreme Court.

Treaties can be roughly divided into seven overlapping periods.
Colonial Treaties (1600–1776)
American Indian nations concluded treaties with European colonizers, including Great Britain, France, Spain, and Holland. Besides peace, friendship, and alliance,

the subjects of these agreements could also include territorial rights, trade relations, jurisdiction, boundary delineations, and use and conveyance of land.

Treaties of Alliance and Peace (1776–1816)

This period saw the start of treaties between tribal nations and the newly formed United States, beginning with the Treaty with the Delawares in 1778. The fledgling U.S. sought alliance and peace from tribal nations, who negotiated from a position of strength and could align themselves with competing colonial European powers.

The Beginning of Land Cessions (1784–1817)

Land cession treaties began in the New England and the Middle Atlantic states in exchange for goods or other payments. During this period, treaties began to be used to extinguish Indian title to land. The United States used methods that included drawing boundaries between Indian country and U.S. territory, and securing of rights of way and land for military forts and trading posts.

Treaties of Removal (1817–46)

The departure of France, England, and Spain from North America resulted in diminished bargaining power for tribal nations. During this period, the federal government sought to remove Indians from lands to accommodate the burgeoning Euro-American population. With removal treaties, tribal nations in the Southeast and Great Lakes regions exchanged their homelands for lands west of the Mississippi River in present-day Arkansas, Kansas, and Oklahoma.

Early Western Treaties (1846–64)

The gold rush in California and the addition of new territory in the U.S. contributed to a new federal policy to clarify relations between tribal nations and the United States in the West. Treaties during the period included provisions that constricted Indians to smaller, well-defined reservations.

Civil War Treaties (1861–65)

The U.S. Civil War divided tribal nations such as the Five Civilized Tribes and others, who fought on both sides of the conflict. The Confederate States signed treaties with them in exchange for their assistance to the Confederacy. During the period, the federal government also continued to negotiate treaties, including some with provisions for the allotment, or breakup into individual parcels, of tribal lands.

Peace Commissions and Treaties (1865–68)

From 1865 to 1868, various treaty-making "peace commissions" traveled to the Southern and Northern Plains to negotiate treaties, promising the benefits of Euro-American civilization in exchange for large land cessions and other provisions. A short time later, in 1871, the United States ended treaty making with tribal nations. The law did not repeal or modify treaties ratified prior to that date, and federal-tribal relations continued with government measures such as congressional acts, executive orders, and agreements.

Ten Important Facts about Treaties

Treaty making between American Indian and European nations began in the 1600s and continued with the establishment of the United States government in 1776. Between 1778 and 1871, some 370 U.S.-Indian treaties were ratified, or approved, comprising a major component of federal Indian law. Recognized as "the supreme law of the land" in the U.S. Constitution, these legal agreements continue to be a fundamental component of government-to-government relations. Treaties were negotiated in a range of locations, many of which—such as forts and the nation's capital—were strategically selected by U.S. officials in an effort to convince Indian representatives to agree to their provisions. Besides treaty documents, historical records associated with the proceedings include speeches and testimony, as well as paintings and sketches of participants and settings.

1. A treaty is a contract between two or more sovereigns that is as binding today as when it was signed.
2. According to the U.S. Constitution, "all Treaties made, or which shall be made, under the Authority of the United States, shall be the supreme Law of the Land" (Article VI, Section 2).
3. American Indian treaties have as much force as those the government made with any other nation.
4. Treaties are living documents, not outdated relics of the past. The U.S. Constitution is not invalidated by age and neither are treaties.
5. As the "supreme Law of the Land," treaties are superior to the law of any state. The U.S. Constitution states that "the Judges in every State shall be bound thereby, any Thing in the Constitution or Laws of any State to the Contrary notwithstanding" (Article VI, Section 2).
6. Although treaties have been challenged in court by states and other parties, United States courts have repeatedly upheld their validity.
7. Violations of treaties do not nullify them, any more than committing a crime nullifies the law that forbids the crime.
8. Although the U.S. government has broken Indian treaties without tribal consent, the courts have said that Congress has a moral duty to uphold treaty obligations.
9. In a number of treaties, tribes retain property rights (known as usufructuary rights) with respect to lands that were ceded; that is, surrendered or relinquished. Such rights may include traditional subsistence activities such as hunting, fishing, and gathering.
10. Congress ended treaty making with Indian nations in 1871, but provided that treaties "heretofore lawfully made and ratified" remained valid. The measure, a rider to an appropriations bill, provided that nothing "shall be construed to invalidate or impair the obligation of any treaty heretofore lawfully made and ratified with any such nation or tribe."

Selected Treaty Firsts

1778   The Treaty with the Delawares, which was signed on September 17, 1778 at Fort Pitt in Pennsylvania, was the first formal treaty between the new United States of America and a Native American nation. In this treaty of alliance, the U.S. sought free passage for its troops through Delaware territory as well as other military aid during the American War of Independence against the British.

1784   The Treaty with the Six Nations (Cayuga, Seneca, Mohawk, Oneida, Tuscarora, and Onondaga), concluded at Fort Stanwix in New York, was the first land cession treaty between American Indian nations and the United States. It provided that the Six Nations relinquish claims to specified lands, but that they "be secured in the peaceful possession of the lands they inhabit east and north" of boundary lines delineated in the treaty.

1789   The Treaty of Fort Harmar, an agreement signed at Fort Harmar, near present-day Marietta, Ohio, was the first U.S.-Indian treaty to use the word "cede." Wyandot, Delaware, Ottawa, and other tribal nations represented, agreed "to release, quit claim, relinquish and cede to the said United States" specified lands."

1794   A treaty between the United States and the Oneida, Tuscarora, and Stockbridge Indians became the first U.S.-Indian treaty to include a provision for education, stipulating: "The United States will provide, during three years after the mills shall be completed, for the expense of employing one or two suitable persons to manage the mills, to keep them in repair, to instruct some young men of the three nations in the arts of the miller and sawyer, and to provide teams and utensils for carrying on the work of the mills."

1830   Negotiated at Dancing Rabbit Creek in Mississippi, the Treaty with the Choctaw Indians, September 27, 1830, was the first of the removal treaties that the United States government signed with southeastern Indians after the passage of the Indian Removal Act of 1830.

1832   The Treaty with the Winnebago, September 15, 1832, was the first to include a provision for health care. In Article V of the treaty, the United States agreed to provide "the said nation of Winnebago Indians . . . for the services and attendance of a physician at Prairie du Chien, and of one at Fort Winnebago, each, two hundred dollars, per annum."

1851   The Fort Laramie Treaty, attended by approximately ten thousand Sioux, Crow, Cheyenne, Arapaho, Assiniboine, Gros Ventre, and Arikara, was the first great treaty conference held on the Northern Plains.

1861   The Confederate States of America created the first of nine treaties with
              tribes in Indian Territory (present-day Oklahoma) on July 10, 1861.

Six Treaty Commemorations

Treaty commemorations are held in Native communities across the country, marking historic events and binding agreements that are deeply significant to tribal nations. Depending on the occasion and time of year, these observances include a host of activities, among them community gatherings, parades, educational exhibits, athletic contests, giveaways, powwows, rodeos, and tree plantings.

Annual Tribute Day, Virginia
http://www.washingtonpost.com/wp-dyn/content/article/2010/11/24/
AR2010112406926.html
> Pamunkey and Mattaponi present gifts such as deer and turkey to the governor of the Commonwealth of Virginia each November, fulfilling tribute provisions of 1646 and 1677 colonial treaties with the English.

Canandaigua Treaty Day Celebration, Canandaigua, New York
http://www.ganondagan.org/TreatyCelebration.html
> Observed annually on November 11, this celebration commemorates the Canandaigua Treaty of 1794, a treaty between the United States and the Six Nations of the Iroquois Confederacy: Seneca, Cayuga, Onondaga, Oneida, Mohawk, and Tuscarora. It was signed in Canandaigua, New York, by representatives of the Six Nations and by Colonel Timothy Pickering, the official agent of President George Washington. The treaty established peace and friendship between the parties, with provisions that included affirming Six Nations land rights.

1855 Treaty Sesquicentennial, 150th anniversary, Walla Walla, Washington
http://www.umatilla.nsn.us/Treaty150.html
> In 2005, the Confederated Tribes of the Umatilla Indian Reservation, joined by Walla Walla (Walla Walla Treaty Commemoration Committee and Walla Walla Historic Memorials Committee), the Nez Perce Tribe, and the Yakama Nation, commemorated the Treaty of 1855 made with the United States. Several events were held in late May and early June in Walla Walla, where the historical treaty council was held.

"Return to Muckl-te-oh"—A Point Elliott Treaty Remembrance Gathering, Mukilteo, Washington
> Held in August 2010, this gathering marked the 155th anniversary of the signing of the Point Elliott Treaty by representatives of the Duwamish, Suquamish, Snoqualmie, Snohomish, Lummi, Skagit, Swinomish, and other Northwest Coast tribes, bands, and clans, as well as Territorial Governor Isaac Stevens and other government officials. The historic treaty included provisions for the

establishment of reservations, and secured "the right of taking fish at usual and accustomed grounds and stations."

Treaty Days, Tulalip Tribes, Washington
http://www.tulaliptribes-nsn.gov/
Treaty Days, which commemorates the signing of the Point Elliott Treaty of 1855, is an annual event held by the Tulalip Tribes in Washington. It usually takes place in January, with activities that include spiritual dancing and a feast. The first Tulalip Treaty Days celebration was held in 1912.

Treaty Days Celebration, Navajo Nation, Window Rock, Arizona
http://www.navajonationfair.com/TD10/info.html
The provisions of the U.S.-Navajo Treaty of 1868 included arrangements for Navajo to return to their homeland after the Long Walk of 1864, their forcible removal to internment at Bosque Redondo in New Mexico. The first annual Treaty Days Celebration in 2010 included a reading of the treaty in Navajo, a reenactment, special guest speakers, an exhibit of the Long Walk, and video presentations documenting the historic events.

Congress and Commerce

"The Congress shall have Power . . . to regulate Commerce with foreign Nations, and among the several States, and with the Indian Tribes."

—U.S. Constitution, Article I, Section 8, Clause 3

Selected Federal Policies and Legislation, 1790–2010

Indian Trade and Intercourse Act of 1790
The first of a series of laws passed by Congress "to regulate trade and intercourse with the Indians." The legislation also sought to restrain frontier whites from invading tribal lands and violating United States treaties with Indian nations.

Indian Removal Act of 1830
Successfully pushed through Congress by President Andrew Jackson, the Indian Removal Act authorized the removal of American Indian tribes from their ancestral homelands to areas west of the Mississippi River. The act enabled President Jackson to negotiate removal treaties with tribes and implement government policies centered on Euro-American land acquisition and the expulsion and relocation of Indians.

Grant's Indian Peace Policy of 1870

In an effort to reform the Indian service, President Ulysses S. Grant authorized the assignment of Indian agencies to Christian denominations, allowing them to name and oversee their own agents. The religious groups were expected to "Christianize and civilize the Indian, and to train him in the arts of peace."

Indian Appropriations Act of 1871

In a rider to an Indian appropriations bill, Congress ended further treaty making with American Indian tribes, but provided that any treaty, "lawfully made and ratified," would not be invalidated or impaired by the statute. The final treaty, with the Nez Perce, was completed in 1868. By then, the United States had ratified some 370 treaties with tribal nations. After treaty making officially ended in 1871, Congress continued to negotiate agreements with tribal nations, enacting congressional acts, statutes, and other laws.

Major Crimes Act of 1885

Congress placed seven major crimes committed by Indians on federal reservations under the jurisdiction of United States courts. This measure was a reaction to the ruling of the U.S. Supreme Court in *Ex Parte Crow Dog*, which found that the federal courts had no jurisdiction over crimes committed in the Indian country by one Indian against another.

General Allotment Act (Dawes Severalty Act) of 1887

Named for Massachusetts senator Henry L. Dawes, the sponsor of the General Allotment Act of 1887, the Dawes Act provided for the breakup of collectively held landholdings of tribes by partitioning reservation lands into individually owned parcels, or allotments, and selling the "surplus." By the time the allotment policy officially ended in 1934, over 90 million acres of land (about two-thirds of the total tribal land base) had passed from Indian to non-Indian ownership.

Indian Citizenship Act of 1924

Congress declared all non-citizen Indians born within the territorial limits of the United States to be citizens of the United States through this act. The legislation stemmed in part from the nation's recognition of services provided by American Indians during World War I.

Indian Reorganization Act (Wheeler-Howard Act) of 1934

Sometimes called the Indian New Deal, this legislation reversed the land allotment policies of the Dawes Severalty Act of 1887 to, instead, conserve and develop Indian lands and resources, to extend to Indians the right to form business and other organizations, and to grant certain rights of home rule to Indians. A National Congress of American Indians report estimates that 60 percent of tribal governments are based on Indian Reorganization Act constitutions.

Indian Claims Commission Act of 1946

Congress established the Indian Claims Commission (ICC), a special tribunal to hear and determine longstanding claims by American Indian tribes against the federal government that stemmed from land dealings that President Harry S. Truman called the "largest real estate transaction in history" (Presidential Signing Statement, August 13, 1946). The ICC provided monetary compensation through the awards it granted, much of it diminished by attorneys' fees, but no return of lands. Expected to be in effect for ten years, the Indian Claims Commission operated until 1978, when the U.S. Court of Claims reassumed jurisdiction over unresolved cases.

Indian Relocation Policy of the 1950s

As part of an effort to terminate federal obligations to American Indian tribes, the government began a relocation policy that aimed to relocate American Indian families from reservation communities to urban areas such as Chicago, Denver, Los Angeles, Oakland, and San Francisco. In 1952, the Bureau of Indian Affairs began the Voluntary Relocation Program (also known as the Employment Assistance Program), providing short-term assistance to those who relocated.

House Concurrent Resolution 108 of 1953

With House Concurrent Resolution 108, Congress initiated the policy that became known as "termination," a plan to end federal obligations to American Indian tribes, abrogating treaty and other legal responsibilities. From 1954 to 1962, Congress passed laws that terminated over one hundred tribes, bands, and communities, severing them from trust relations with the United States government. The National Congress of American Indians and other opponents of the policy, which was devastating to tribal nations, finally succeeded in ending it. The Menominee Tribe of Wisconsin and a number of other terminated tribes were eventually restored to federal status over time.

Public Law 280 of 1953

With this legislation, which altered tribal self-determination and federal-tribal relations, Congress empowered six states to take over criminal and civil jurisdiction on Indian reservations within their respective borders. The states included Alaska, California, Minnesota, Nebraska, Oregon, and Wisconsin.

Civil Rights Act of 1968

Titles II–VII of the Civil Rights Act of 1968 applied the provisions of the Bill of Rights to individual tribal members in relation to their tribal governments, authorized a model code for courts of Indian offenses, and addressed jurisdiction over criminal and civil actions.

Indian Education Act of 1972

Congress passed the Indian Education Act of 1972 to address the special educational needs of American Indian students. Its measures included providing financial assistance to local educational agencies to develop and carry out specially designed school programs, and establishing new administrative structures through the creation of an Office of Indian Education, as well as a National Advisory Council on Indian Education.

Indian Self-Determination and Education Assistance Act of 1975

The Indian Self-Determination and Education Assistance Act permitted federal authorities such as the secretary of the interior to enter into contracts with Indian tribes to plan, conduct, and administer programs and services. Congress recognized that the prolonged federal domination of Indian service programs had "served to retard" rather than enhance the progress of Indian people.

Indian Health Care Improvement Act of 1976

The Indian Health Care Improvement Act was enacted with the goal of raising the health status of Indians to the highest possible level. It provided incremental funding for health services and facilities over a seven-year period. The legislation also authorized programs to address the inadequate number of health professionals serving Indians, support for urban Indian health centers, and a feasibility study for an Indian medical school.

American Indian Religious Freedom Act (AIRFA) of 1978

This act protects and preserves the inherent right of American Indians, Eskimos, Aleuts, and Native Hawaiians to believe, express, and exercise their traditional religions, "including but not limited to access to sites, use and possession of sacred objects, and the freedom to worship through ceremonials and traditional rites." AIRFA has been viewed as a policy statement rather than a mandate granting Native people legally enforceable rights.

Indian Child Welfare Act of 1978

Aimed at ending child welfare practices that resulted in Indian parent-child separation, this legislation was enacted to establish standards for the placement of Indian children in foster or adoptive homes and to prevent the breakup of Indian families. The law included provisions specifying tribal court jurisdiction over applicable child custody proceedings.

Tribally Controlled Community College Assistance Act of 1978

The Tribally Controlled Community College Assistance Act provided grants for the operation and improvement of tribally controlled community colleges to ensure continued and expanded educational opportunities for Indian students.

Indian Gaming Regulatory Act (IGRA) of 1988
http://www.nigc.gov/
> The purpose of this legislation is to provide a statutory basis for the operation and regulation of gaming by federally recognized Indian tribes as a means of promoting tribal economic development, self-sufficiency, and strong tribal governments. IGRA also included requirements for negotiating with states with respect to specified classifications of gaming and established the National Indian Gaming Commission.

National Museum of the American Indian Act of 1989
http://anthropology.si.edu/repatriation/pdf/nmai_act.pdf
> This legislation was enacted to establish the National Museum of the American Indian (NMAI) within the Smithsonian Institution as a living memorial to Native Americans and their traditions. The act also included provisions for the identification and repatriation of Indian human remains and Indian funerary objects in the Smithsonian's possession or control. The legislation was amended in 1996, extending the repatriation requirements to applicable sacred objects and objects of cultural patrimony.

Native American Graves Protection and Repatriation Act (NAGPRA) of 1990
> NAGPRA provides a process for federally assisted museums and institutions and federal agencies to return certain Native American cultural items such as human remains, funerary objects, sacred objects, and objects of cultural patrimony to lineal descendants, culturally affiliated Indian tribes, Native Alaskan villages and corporations, and Native Hawaiian organizations.

Native American Languages Act of 1990
> Acknowledging that acts of suppression and extermination directed against Native American languages and cultures are in conflict with the United States policy of self-determination for Native Americans, Congress enacted the Native American Languages Act to preserve, protect, and promote the rights and freedom of Native Americans to use, practice, and develop Native American languages.

American Indian Trust Fund Management Reform Act of 1994
> The American Indian Trust Fund Management Reform Act requires the secretary of the interior to take specified actions to properly discharge U.S. responsibilities with regard to American Indian funds held in trust by the federal government, including providing adequate systems for accounting for and reporting trust fund balances. The legislation also established the Office of Special Trustee for American Indians within the Department of the Interior to oversee the implementation of management reforms.

Tribal Law and Order Act of 2010

The major provisions of this legislation, which addresses the criminal justice needs of American Indians, include establishing an option for tribes to increase sentencing authority for up to three years, deputizing tribal police to enforce federal law, providing tribal police with greater access to criminal history records, requiring tribal and federal officers serving Indian country to receive specialized training to interview victims of sexual assault and collect crime scene evidence, and providing programs to improve justice systems and prevent crime.

American Indian U.S. Congressmen and Senators

Since the late nineteenth century, American Indians have been elected to both houses of Congress. Indians have also been elected to state legislatures, state judiciary systems, county and city governments, and school boards.

U.S. Senate

Hiram R. Revels (Lumbee), Mississippi, 1870–71 (filled vacancy)
Matthew Stanley Quay (Abenaki), Pennsylvania, 1887–99 and 1901–4
Charles Curtis (Kaw), Kansas, 1907–13 and 1915–29
Robert L. Owen (Cherokee), Oklahoma, 1907–25
Ben Nighthorse Campbell (Northern Cheyenne), Colorado, 1993–2005

U.S. House of Representatives

Charles Curtis (Kaw), Kansas, 1893–1907
Charles D. Carter (Choctaw), Oklahoma, 1907–27
W. W. Hastings (Cherokee), Oklahoma, 1915–21 and 1923–35
Will Rogers Jr. (Cherokee), California, 1943–44
William G. Stigler (Choctaw), Oklahoma, 1943–52
Benjamin Reifel (Rosebud Sioux), South Dakota, 1961–71
Clem Rogers McSpadden (Choctaw), Oklahoma, 1973–75
Ben Nighthorse Campbell (Northern Cheyenne), Colorado, 1987–93
Brad Carson (Cherokee), Oklahoma, 2001–5
Tom Cole (Chickasaw), Oklahoma, 2003–present

United States Senate Committee on Indian Affairs Chairmen

http://indian.senate.gov/

Established in the early nineteenth century, disbanded for a period, and then existing on a temporary basis, the United States Senate Select Committee on

Indian Affairs became a permanent committee in 1984 and was re-designated as the Committee on Indian Affairs in 1993. It has jurisdiction to study the unique problems of American Indian, Native Hawaiian, and Alaska Native peoples and to propose legislation to address issues that include, but are not limited to, Indian education, economic development, land management, trust responsibilities, health care, and claims against the United States. The number of committee members has varied over time, increasing from five in 1977 to a high of eighteen at the beginning of the 103rd Congress in 1993. In subsequent terms, the committee has had either fourteen or fifteen members.

Current and Former Chairmen of the Committee

Senator Daniel K. Akaka	D-Hawaii	2011–
Senator Byron L. Dorgan	D-North Dakota	2007–11
Senator John McCain	R-Arizona	2005–7
Senator Ben Nighthorse Campbell	R-Colorado	2003–5
Senator Daniel K. Inouye	D-Hawaii	2001–3
Senator Ben Nighthorse Campbell	R-Colorado	1997–2001
Senator John McCain	R-Arizona	1995–97
Senator Daniel K. Inouye	D-Hawaii	1987–95
Senator Mark Andrews	R-North Dakota	1983–87
Senator William S. Cohen	R-Maine	1981–83
Senator John Melcher	D-Montana	1979–81
Senator James Abourezk	D-South Dakota	1977–79

Treaty with the Delawares, 1778

Negotiated by commissioners of the United States and leaders of the Delaware Nation, the first formal treaty between a Native American nation and the newly established United States government was signed at Fort Pitt in Pennsylvania on September 17, 1778. Considered a treaty of "peace and friendship" between sovereign nations, it set forth six articles of agreement. The Americans, who were engaged in the War of Independence against the British, sought free passage for U.S. troops through Delaware territory and other military aid such as "corn, meat, horses, or whatever may be in their power" and "expert warriors." In exchange, they promised goods, trade, the possibility of Delaware statehood, and other provisions.

Text of treaty: http://avalon.law.yale.edu/18th_century/del1778.asp

The Treaty of Dancing Rabbit Creek, 1830

Negotiated at Dancing Rabbit Creek in Mississippi, September 27, 1830, the treaty with the Choctaw Indians was the first of the removal treaties that the United States government signed with southeastern Indians after the passage of the Indian Removal Act of 1830. The treaty resulted in the extinguishment of Choctaw title to their lands east of the Mississippi River and the removal of a large part of the tribe from their traditional homeland to Indian Territory (present-day Oklahoma). It also served as a model for treaties of removal with other southeastern tribes. Dancing Rabbit Creek Treaty Site, which served as a traditional gathering place of the Choctaw people, was designated a National Historic Landmark in 1996.

http://tps.cr.nps.gov/nhl/detail.cfm?ResourceId=1346&ResourceType=Site

Congress Acknowledges the Contribution of the Iroquois Confederacy and Other Indian Nations to the Formation and Development of the United States

The U.S. Congress, on the occasion of the two hundredth anniversary of the signing of the U.S. Constitution, passed a resolution introduced in 1987 acknowledging the contributions made by the Iroquois Confederacy and other Indian Nations to the formation and development of the United States. The Congress also reaffirmed the constitutionally recognized government-to-government relationship with Indian tribes, which has been the cornerstone of the nation's official Indian policy. H.Con.Res.331 was passed by both the Senate and House in 1988.

http://www.senate.gov/reference/resources/pdf/hconres331.pdf

JUDICIAL BRANCH

Twenty Supreme Court Cases

1823   *Johnson v. M'Intosh*
        The Court announced the "discovery doctrine," which held that a discovering sovereign (European/United States) has "an exclusive right to extinguish the Indian title of occupancy, either by purchase or conquest."

1831   *Cherokee Nation v. Georgia*
        The Court addressed the "condition of the Indians in relation to the United States," describing tribes as "domestic dependent nations."

1832   *Worcester v. Georgia*
Describing the Cherokee Nation as "a distinct community, occupying its own territory," the Court ruled that the state of Georgia has no jurisdiction to impose its laws there.

1883   *Ex Parte Crow Dog*
The Court held that the United States had no jurisdiction over crimes committed in the Indian Country by one Indian against the person or property of another Indian.

1886   *U.S. v. Kagama*
The Court upheld the constitutionality of the Major Crimes Act in Indian Country under powers derived from Congress and its "duty of protection" to tribes.

1903   *Lone Wolf v. Hitchcock*
The Court held that Congress has plenary or absolute authority over Indian relations and that it has the power to abrogate treaty obligations.

1908   *Winters v. U.S.*
Often referred to as the Winters Doctrine, this case provides the foundation of American Indian water rights, assuring implied reserve rights to sufficient water to fulfill the purposes of the reservation.

1955   *Tee-Hit-Ton Indians v. United States*
The Court ruled that Indian occupancy, not specifically recognized as ownership by action authorized by Congress, may be extinguished by the government without compensation.

1959   *Williams v. Lee*
The Court held that the exercise of state jurisdiction, absent federal authority, in the Navajo Reservation–based civil suit would undermine tribal courts, infringing on the right of the Indians to govern themselves.

1968   *Menominee Tribe v. United States*
The Court ruled that the tribe's treaty hunting and fishing rights were not ended by the Menominee Indian Termination Act of 1954.

1974   *Morton v. Mancari*
The Court held that the Indian hiring preference system within the Bureau of Indian Affairs does not constitute racial discrimination, but is "an employment criterion reasonably designed to further the cause of Indian self-government and to make the BIA more responsive to its constituent groups."

1978   *Oliphant v. Suquamish Indian Tribe*

The Court ruled that American Indian tribal courts lack inherent sovereign power to try and to punish non-Indians for crimes committed on Indian reservations and may not assume such jurisdiction unless specifically authorized to do so by Congress.

1987   *California v. Cabazon Band of Mission Indians*
The Supreme Court upheld the right of tribal governments to regulate reservation gaming activities free from state interference or regulation.

1988   *Lyng v. Northwest Cemetery Protective Association*
The Court concluded that American Indian tribes have no First Amendment religious freedom right to prohibit the federal government from permitting timber harvesting in, or constructing a road through, a portion of a National Forest traditionally used for tribal religious purposes.

1990   *Employment Division, Department of Human Resources of Oregon et al. v. Smith et al.*
The Court ruled that the Free Exercise Clause permits the state to prohibit sacramental peyote use, and thus to deny unemployment benefits to tribal members fired for such use.

1998   *Alaska v. Native Village of Venetie Tribal Government*
The Court concluded that land owned in fee simple by the Native Village of Venetie Tribal Government pursuant to the Alaska Native Claims Settlement Act is not "Indian country."

2001   *Chickasaw Nation v. United States*
The Court ruled that a particular subsection in the Indian Gaming Regulatory Act does not exempt tribes from paying gambling related taxes that chapter 35 of the Internal Revenue Code imposes, taxes that states need not pay.

2004   *United States v. Lara*
Congress has the power to relax the restrictions imposed by the political branches on tribes' inherent prosecutorial authority.

2005   *City of Sherrill v. Oneida Indian Nation*
The Court held that repurchase of traditional tribal lands did not revive the tribal nation's ancient sovereignty over the parcels at issue.

2009   *Carcieri v. Salazar*
The Court ruled that the federal government could not place land into trust for a tribe that was not federally recognized when the Indian Reorganization Act of 1934 was enacted.

Eighteen Books about American Indians and the Law

1. *American Indian Sovereignty and the U.S. Supreme Court: The Masking of Justice*, by David E. Wilkins (1997).
2. *American Indian Tribal Law*, by Matthew L. M. Fletcher (2011).
3. *American Indians and the Law*, by N. Bruce Duthu (2008).
4. *Architect of Justice: Felix S. Cohen and the Founding of American Legal Pluralism*, by Dalia Tsuk Mitchell (2007).
5. *Arguing with Tradition: The Language of Law in Hopi Tribal Court*, by Justin B. Richland (2008).
6. *Broken Landscape: Indians, Indian Tribes, and the Constitution*, by Frank Pommersheim (2009).
7. *Conquest by Law: How the Discovery of America Dispossessed Indigenous Peoples of Their Lands*, by Lindsay G. Robertson (2005).
8. *Coyote Warrior: One Man, Three Tribes, and the Trial that Forged a Nation*, by Paul VanDevelder (2004).
9. *Crow Dog's Case: American Indian Sovereignty, Tribal Law, and United States Law in the Nineteenth Century*, by Sidney L. Harring (1994).
10. *Indian Law Stories*, edited by Carole E. Goldberg, Kevin K. Washburn, and Philip P. Frickey (2010).
11. *In the Courts of the Conqueror: The 10 Worst Indian Law Cases Ever Decided*, by Walter R. Echo-Hawk (2010).
12. *Landmark Indian Law Cases*, by National Indian Law Library, Native American Rights Fund (2002).
13. *A Lawyer in Indian Country: A Memoir*, by Alvin J. Ziontz (2009).
14. *Like a Loaded Weapon: The Rehnquist Court, Indian Rights, and the Legal History of Racism in America*, by Robert A. Williams Jr. (2005).
15. *Lone Wolf v. Hitchcock: Treaty Rights and Indian Law at the End of the Nineteenth Century*, by Blue Clark (1994).
16. *Navajo Courts and Navajo Common Law: A Tradition of Tribal Self-Governance*, by Raymond D. Austin (2009).
17. *Standing Bear Is a Person: The True Story of a Native American's Quest for Justice*, by Stephen Dando-Collins (2004).
18. *The Supreme Court and Tribal Gaming: California v. Cabazon Band of Mission Indians*, by Ralph A. Rossum (2011).

NATIONAL AGENCIES AND OFFICES

Administration for Native Americans (ANA)
http://www.acf.hhs.gov/programs/ana/

Established in 1974 through the Native American Programs Act, the Administration for Native Americans is a federal agency within the U.S. Department of Health and Human Services (DHHS), Administration for

Children and Families (ACF). ANA promotes the goals of self-sufficiency and cultural preservation for Native Americans by providing social and economic development opportunities through financial assistance, training, and technical assistance to eligible tribes and Native American communities and organizations. It is the only federal agency serving all Native Americans, including federally recognized tribes, American Indian and Alaska Native organizations, Native Hawaiian organizations, and Native populations throughout the Pacific basin (including American Samoa, Guam, and the Commonwealth of the Northern Mariana Islands).

Bureau of Indian Affairs (BIA)
http://www.bia.gov/

Secretary of War John C. Calhoun created the Bureau of Indian Affairs (also known as BIA, Indian Bureau, Indian Office, Indian Service, and Indian Affairs) within the U.S. Department of War in 1824. The bureau's duties included overseeing treaty negotiations and managing Indian schools and trade relations. In 1832, the office was formally recognized by a law of Congress, which approved the appointment of a Commissioner of Indian Affairs to oversee the work. In 1849, the BIA was transferred to the newly created Department of the Interior, where it remains to this day.

The oldest bureau of the United States Department of the Interior, the BIA provides services (directly or through contracts, grants, or compacts) to approximately 1.9 million American Indians and Alaska Natives. It is responsible for the administration and management of 55 million surface acres and 57 million acres of subsurface minerals estates held in trust by the United States for American Indians and Alaska Natives. Headquartered in Washington, DC, the BIA maintains regional offices across the country and provides services at the local tribal level.

Indian Arts and Crafts Board (IACB)
http://www.doi.gov/iacb/

The Indian Arts and Crafts Board, an agency of the U.S. Department of the Interior, was created by Congress in 1935 to promote the economic development of American Indians and Alaska Natives of federally recognized tribes through the expansion of the Indian arts and crafts market. The IACB operates three regional museums, conducts a promotional museum exhibition program, produces a "Source Directory of American Indian and Alaska Native Owned and Operated Arts and Crafts Businesses," and oversees the implementation of the Indian Arts and Crafts Act.

Indian Health Service (IHS)
http://www.ihs.gov/

The Indian Health Service (IHS) began on July 1, 1955, following the transfer of Native American health services from the Bureau of Indian Affairs to the

Public Health Service (now Health and Human Services). The IHS provides health services to approximately 1.9 million American Indians and Alaska Natives belonging to 564 federally recognized tribes in thirty-five states. The agency is divided into twelve geographic regions called "Area Offices," which provide administrative support to the facilities and personnel within their respective jurisdictions.

National Indian Gaming Commission (NIGC)
http://www.nigc.gov/
The National Indian Gaming Commission (NIGC) is an independent federal regulatory agency that was established pursuant to the Indian Gaming Regulatory Act of 1988. The commission's primary mission is to regulate gaming activities on Indian lands to ensure that they are conducted fairly and honestly by both operators and players. It includes a chairman, who is appointed by the president and must be confirmed by the Senate, and two commissioners, appointed by the secretary of the interior, each of whom serves on a full-time basis for a three-year term. The Indian Gaming Regulatory Act requires that at least two of the three commissioners be enrolled members of a federally recognized tribe and that no more than two members may be of the same political party. Headquartered in Washington, DC, the NIGC also has regional offices in Oregon, California, Arizona, Minnesota, and Oklahoma.

Office of Native American Programs (ONAP)
http://portal.hud.gov/hudportal/HUD?src=/program_offices/
public_indian_housing/ih/codetalk/onap
The Office of Native American Programs (ONAP) within the U.S. Department of Housing and Urban Development works to ensure that safe, decent, and affordable housing is available to Native American families; to create economic opportunities for tribes and Indian housing residents; to assist tribes in the formulation of plans and strategies for community development; and to assure fiscal integrity in the operation of programs. Headquartered in Washington, DC, ONAP has six area offices, located in Chicago, Oklahoma City, Phoenix, Denver, Seattle, and Anchorage.

Office of the Special Trustee for American Indians, U.S. Department of the Interior
http://www.ost.doi.gov/
The Office of the Special Trustee for American Indians (OST) was established by the American Indian Trust Fund Management Reform Act of 1994 to improve the accountability and management of Indian funds held in trust by the federal government. As trustee, the Department of the Interior (DOI) has the primary fiduciary responsibility to manage tribal trust funds as well as Individual Indian Money (IIM) accounts. The DOI manages the largest land trust in the United States.

Office of Tribal Justice (OTJ)
http://www.justice.gov/otj/about.htm
> The Office of Tribal Justice (OTJ) was originally established in 1995 as a unit within the Office of the Deputy Attorney General of the U.S. Department of Justice in response to tribal concerns. As required by the Tribal Law and Order Act of 2010 and announced by Attorney General Eric Holder on November 17, 2010, OTJ became a separate, permanent component within the organizational structure of the Justice Department. It serves as the primary point of contact for the Department of Justice with federally recognized tribes and advises the department on legal and policy matters pertaining to Native Americans.

U.S. Department of Agriculture, Office of Tribal Relations (OTR)
http://www.usda.gov/wps/portal/usda/usdahome?navid=OTR
> The Office of Tribal Relations (OTR) is the primary point of contact for tribal matters within the U.S. Department of Agriculture. OTR is responsible for government-to-government relations between the USDA and tribal governments, advising the secretary of agriculture on tribal issues, and working to build an integrated approach to issues, programs, and services that address the needs of American Indians and Alaska Natives. It is located within the Office of the Secretary.

U.S. Forest Service, Office of Tribal Relations (OTR)
http://www.fs.fed.us/spf/tribalrelations/
> The Office of Tribal Relations (OTR) was formed in 2004 to facilitate Forest Service program delivery to tribes and to institutionalize long-term relationships with tribal governments. OTR provides oversight of Forest Service programs and policy that may affect tribes, prepares and implements new and existing policy and direction, develops and supports education and training for the Forest Service and other agencies, and explores innovative ways to enhance the Forest Service's service to American Indian and Alaska Native communities. It is directed by a number of policies, executive orders, and statutes.

Statement about U.S. Government Policies

"Indians are the only race in the United States that has experienced the deliberate, official governmental effort over decades to wipe out its way of life, language, and culture. They were conquered, colonized, and subjected to social engineering, culture shock, relocation, and forced negative education."
—Elizabeth Ebbott for the League of Women Voters in Minnesota, 1985 (*Indians in Minnesota*, 4th edition. Edited by Judith Rosenblatt. Minneapolis: University of Minnesota Press, 1985).

HONORING NATIONS PROJECT, HARVARD UNIVERSITY

Honoring Nations Honorees, 1999–2002

Honoring Nations, a national awards program initiated in 1998, highlights outstanding programs in self-governance by Native nations. At the heart of the program is the belief that tribes themselves hold the key to positive social, political, cultural, and economic prosperity. Based at the John F. Kennedy School of Government at Harvard University, Honoring Nations is administered by the Harvard Project on American Indian Economic Development. The criteria for selection of honorees include program effectiveness, significance to sovereignty, cultural relevance, transferability, and sustainability. The programs include those centered on the exercise and protection of treaty rights.

Minnesota 1837 Ceded Territory Conservation Code, 1999
Department of Natural Resources, Mille Lacs Band of Ojibwe
Onamia, Minnesota
> In 1997 the Mille Lacs Band of Ojibwe successfully developed a conservation code, enabling the tribe to exercise its treaty rights to hunt, fish, and gather. The code establishes hunting and fishing regulations for tribal members, protecting natural resources while sustaining the continuation of traditional practices. The Conservation Code has withstood challenges in district courts, appeals courts, and the Supreme Court, helping to demonstrate that tribes can successfully manage natural resources programs.

Treaty Rights/National Forest Memorandum of Understanding, 2000
Member Tribes of the Great Lakes Indian Fish and Wildlife Commission
Odanah, Wisconsin
http://www.glifwc.org/
> The Great Lakes Indian Fish and Wildlife Commission (GLIFWC), a tribally chartered intertribal agency of eleven Ojibwe nations in Minnesota, Wisconsin, and Michigan, negotiated a memorandum of understanding (MOU) with the U.S. Forest Service that recognizes and implements treaty-guaranteed hunting, fishing, and gathering rights under tribal regulations. The MOU establishes standards and processes by which the federal agency and the tribes will act consistently across the National Forests located within treaty-applicable areas.

Columbia River Inter-Tribal Fish Commission, 2002
Yakama, Umatilla, Nez Perce, and Warm Springs Tribes
Portland, Oregon
http://www.critfc.org/
> Working to manage its member tribes' fisheries resources and to protect treaty rights, the Columbia River Inter-Tribal Fish Commission (CRITFC) provides

programs that include fisheries enforcement, policy development and litigation support, fish marketing, and watershed restoration. In 2000, CRITFC created the Spirit of the Salmon Fund, a charitable restricted fund that helps support the commission's mission and activities.

FILMS

Broken Treaty at Battle Mountain (USA, 1974, 60 min.) and its sequel, *To Protect Mother Earth* (USA, 1989, 60 min.), produced and directed by Joel L. Freedman.
> *Broken Treaty at Battle Mountain* portrays the Western Shoshone efforts to protect their lands and treaty rights, documenting their initial attempt to stop the government from tearing down pinon trees. *To Protect Mother Earth* documents the Dann sisters, Carrie and Mary, and other Western Shoshone as they fight to keep the government from seizing their ancestral land and conducting nuclear tests there.

Lighting the 7th Fire (USA, 1995, 48. min.), directed by Sandra Sunrising Osawa (Makah).
> This film documents the fight for treaty fishing rights and the struggle against anti-Indian racism among the Ojibwe in Wisconsin.

Standing Bear's Footsteps (USA, 2011, 56 min.), directed by Christine Lesiak
> The film documents the story of Chief Standing Bear and his people, Ponca Indians who were forcibly removed from their Nebraska homeland to Indian Territory (present-day Oklahoma) by the federal government. Their quest for justice culminated in a landmark court case establishing that Indians are "persons" under U.S. law.

The Trail of Tears: Cherokee Legacy (USA, 2006, 115 min.), directed by Chip Richie.
> This film, which is presented in both English and Cherokee, documents the events leading up to the forced removal of the Cherokee Nation from their ancestral homelands in the Southeast to Indian Territory (present-day Oklahoma) in 1838.

Tribal Nations—The Story of Federal Indian Law (USA, 2006, 60 min.), directed by Lisa Jaeger and Igor Sopronenko.
> This film documents the history of how federal Indian law has developed in the United States and examines the impact federal policies have had on Native peoples. It culminates with the self-determination era of today, ending with a look to the future for American Indian and Alaska Native people.

Usual and Accustomed Places (USA, 2000, 48 min.) directed by Sandra Sunrising Osawa (Makah).
> This film, which focuses on the Makah Nation of Washington State, documents the struggle of tribal nations in the Pacific Northwest to have their treaty fishing rights honored.

We Shall Remain: Trail of Tears (USA, 2008, 74 min.), directed by Chris Eyre (Cheyenne/Arapaho) (part of five-film series).

This episode of the five-part television film series *We Shall Remain* examines the history of the Trail of Tears, the federal removal of the Cherokee Nation from their southeastern homeland to Indian Territory (present-day Oklahoma). It features Cherokee actors such as Wes Studi, as well as Cherokee language use.

ORGANIZATIONS

American Indian Policy Center (AIPC)
http://www.airpi.org/

Founded in 1992, the American Indian Policy Center is a nonprofit organization located in St. Paul, Minnesota. The center focuses on research, policy development, and education on critical issues.

Columbia River Inter-Tribal Fish Commission (CRITFC)
http://www.critfc.org/

The Columbia River Inter-Tribal Fish Commission (CRITFC) consists of the Warm Springs, Yakama, Umatilla, and Nez Perce tribes, who joined together in 1977 to protect their treaty-reserved property and to renew their authority in fisheries management on the Columbia River. Headquartered in Portland, Oregon, CRITFC is a coordinating and technical organization to support the individual and joint exercise of sovereign authority of the member tribes.

Great Lakes Indian Fish and Wildlife Commission (GLIFWC)
http://www.glifwc.org/

Formed in 1984, the Great Lakes Indian Fish and Wildlife Commission is an agency of eleven Ojibwe nations in Minnesota, Wisconsin, and Michigan, with off-reservation treaty rights to hunt, fish, and gather in treaty-ceded lands. GLIFWC, which has its main office on the Bad River Reservation in Wisconsin, assists member nations in the implementation of off-reservation treaty seasons and in the protection of treaty rights and natural resources.

International Indian Treaty Council (IITC)
http://www.treatycouncil.org/

Founded in 1974 at a gathering of the American Indian Movement in Standing Rock, South Dakota, the International Indian Treaty Council supports indigenous peoples with treaty, land, and other rights. In 1977, the IITC became the first organization of indigenous peoples to be recognized as a nongovernmental organization (NGO) with consultative status to the United Nations Economic and Social Council. The IITC has an office at United Nations Plaza in New York, but also maintains an administrative office in Palmer, Alaska, and an information office in San Francisco, California.

Intertribal Monitoring Association on Indian Trust Funds (ITMA)
http://www.itmatrustfunds.org/
Located in Albuquerque, New Mexico, the Intertribal Monitoring Association on Indian Trust Funds was organized in 1990 to actively monitor and have a voice in the activities of the federal government to ensure fair compensation to tribes for historical trust funds mismanagement. The organization grew to become a national tribal consortium consisting of sixty-six federally recognized tribes, whose efforts increased as it followed the trust reform activities of the government.

Midwest Treaty Network (MTN)
http://treaty.indigenousnative.org/
Located in Oneida, Wisconsin, and founded in 1989, the Midwest Treaty Network was formed as an alliance of Indian and non-Indian groups supporting Native American sovereignty in the western Great Lakes region. MTN coordinated the Witness for Nonviolence to help protect Ojibwe families who were under attack by anti-treaty groups during the fishing rights crisis of the late 1980s in Wisconsin. The organization has also worked against metallic sulfide mining projects and other threats to natural resources for both Indians and non-Indians.

Northwest Indian Fisheries Commission (NWIFC)
http://www.nwifc.org/
The Northwest Indian Fisheries Commission is a support service organization for twenty Indian tribes in western Washington. Headquartered in Olympia, the NWIFC was created following the 1974 *U.S. v. Washington* ruling (Boldt Decision) that reaffirmed the tribes' treaty-reserved fishing rights and established them as natural resource co-managers with the State of Washington.

Society of American Indian Government Employees (SAIGE)
http://www.saige.org/
Established in 2001, the Society of American Indian Government Employees is a national nonprofit organization that works to promote the recruitment, development, retention, and advancement of American Indian (AI) and Alaska Native (AN) government employees. Its mission also includes assisting federal agencies in honoring and implementing the unique federal-tribal relationship and providing a national forum for issues and topics affecting AI/AN employees.

Tribal Law and Policy Institute
http://www.tribal-institute.org/
> The Tribal Law and Policy Institute is a nonprofit corporation organized to design and develop education, research, and technical assistance programs that promote the enhancement of justice in Indian country. It maintains the Tribal Court Clearinghouse, a Web site established in 1997 as a resource for American Indian and Alaska Native peoples, tribal justice systems, service providers, and others.

RESOURCES

Bighorse, Tiana. *Bighorse the Warrior.* Edited by Noel Bennett. Tucson: University of Arizona Press, 1990.

Case, David S., and David A. Voluck. *Alaska Natives and American Laws.* 2nd ed. Fairbanks: University of Alaska Press, 2002.

Castile, George Pierre. *Taking Charge: Native American Self-Determination and Federal Indian Policy, 1975–1993.* Tucson: University of Arizona Press, 2006.

Cohen, Felix, ed. *Handbook of Federal Indian Law.* Washington, DC: U.S. Government Printing Office, 1942.

Fixico, Donald Lee. *Termination and Relocation: Federal Indian Policy, 1945–1960.* Albuquerque: University of New Mexico Press, 1990.

Gibson, Ronald, ed. *Jefferson Davis and the Confederacy and Treaties Concluded by the Confederate States with Indian Tribes.* Dobbs Ferry, NY: Oceana Publications, 1977.

Hoxie, Frederick. *A Final Promise: The Campaign to Assimilate the Indians, 1880–1920.* Lincoln: University of Nebraska Press, 1984.

———, ed. *Talking Back to Civilization: Indian Voices from the Progressive Era.* Boston: Bedford/St. Martin's, 2001.

Littlefield, Daniel F., Jr., and James W. Parins, eds. *Encyclopedia of American Indian Removal.* Santa Barbara, CA: Greenwood, 2011.

Peterson, Herman A. *The Trail of Tears: An Annotated Bibliography of Southeastern Indian Removal.* Lanham, MD: Scarecrow Press, 2011.

Philp, Kenneth R., ed. *Indian Self-Rule: First-Hand Accounts of Indian-White Relations from Roosevelt to Reagan.* Logan: Utah State University Press, 1995.

Prucha, Francis Paul. *American Indian Treaties: The History of a Political Anomaly.* Berkeley and Los Angeles: University of California Press, 1994.

———. *Documents of United States Indian Policy.* 2nd ed. Lincoln: University of Nebraska Press, 1990.

———. *Indian Peace Medals in American History.* Bluffton, SC: Rivilo Books, 1994.

Trafzer, Clifford E., ed. *American Indians/American Presidents: A History.* New York: HarperCollins/National Museum of the American Indian, Smithsonian Institution, 2009.

Viola, Herman J. *Ben Nighthorse Campbell: An American Warrior.* New York: Orion Books, 1993.

———. *Diplomats in Buckskins: A History of Indian Delegations in Washington City.* Bluffton, SC: Rivilo Books, 1995.

Wilkins, David E., and K. Tsianina Lomawaima. *Uneven Ground: American Indian Sovereignty and Federal Law.* Norman: University of Oklahoma Press, 2001.

Web Sites

FEMA Indian Tribal Government Fact Sheet: http://www.fema.gov/government/grant/pdm/pdm_tribal_fact_sheet.shtm.

Forest Service National Resource Guide to American Indian and Alaska Native Relations, 1997: http://www.schlosserlawfiles.com/consult/USFSGUIDE.pdf .

Harvard Project's Honoring Nations Directory of Honored Programs, 1999–2006: http://hpaied.org./images/resources/general/Dir_web.pdf.

Indian Land Cessions in the United States, 1784–1894. U.S. Congressional Documents: http://memory.loc.gov/ammem/amlaw/lwss-ilc.html.

National Congress of American Indians. *An Introduction to Indian Nations in the United States*: http://www.ncai.org/fileadmin/initiatives/NCAI_Indian_Nations_In_The_US.pdf.

National Congress of American Indians: Federally Recognized Indian Tribes: http://www.ncai.org/Tribal-Directory.3.0.html.

Presidential Signing Statement: Bill Creating the Indian Claims Commission, August 13, 1946: http://www.presidency.ucsb.edu/ws/index.php?pid=12495#axzz1WvZM1LgG.

USA.gov Tribal Governments and Native Americans: http://www.usa.gov/Government/Tribal.shtml.

U.S. Department of Agriculture. American Indians and Alaska Natives: A Guide to USDA Programs, 2007: http://www.usda.gov/documents/AmerIndianNativeAlaskGuide-07%2011%2007.pdf.

U.S. Department of Agriculture. Natural Resources Conservation Service: http://www.nrcs.usda.gov/programs/tribalgov/.

Online Resources about U.S.-Indian Treaties

Digital Librarian: American Indian Studies:
    http://www.digital-librarian.com/american_indian_studies.html
    (Scroll down to the section on treaties.)

Indian Affairs: Laws and Treaties (Compiled and edited by Charles J. Kappler):
    http://digital.library.okstate.edu/kappler/index.htm

Native American Indian Agreements and Treaties (First People Web site):
    http://www.firstpeople.us/FP-Html-Treaties/Treaties.html

Penn Treaty Museum (online):
    http://www.penntreatymuseum.org/treaty.php

Seneca Nation's Honor Indian Treaties site:
    http://www.honorindiantreaties.com

Treaties between the United States and Native Americans (The Avalon Project from Yale Law School): http://avalon.law.yale.edu/subject_menus/ntreaty.asp

Treaty of 1868, a Web page from a National Archives and Records Administration (NARA) Online Exhibit: http://www.archives.gov/exhibits/american_originals/industry.html

The Treaty Trail: U.S.–Indian Treaty Councils in the Northwest (Washington State Historical Society): http://stories.washingtonhistory.org/treatytrail/intro.htm

Why Treaties Matter: Self-Government in the Dakota and Ojibwe Nations:
    http://www.minnesotahumanities.org/treaties

5

State-Tribal Relations

FIRSTS

1926   Jessie Elizabeth Randolph Moore (Chickasaw) became the first American Indian woman, and the second woman in Oklahoma history, elected to a state office. She was elected clerk of the Oklahoma Supreme Court. During the Great Depression, her statewide emergency relief program was adopted by the federal government in 1933 and implemented on a national scale.

1932   Dolly Smith Akers (Assiniboine) was the first American Indian woman elected to the Montana state legislature (1933–34). She became the first woman ever elected to the Assiniboine-Sioux tribal council at Fort Peck, and in 1960 became the first woman elected to chair the Fort Peck Tribal Council.

1957   Joseph R. Garry (Coeur d'Alene) was the first American Indian elected to the Idaho state legislature, serving in 1957 and 1959. He served as chair of his tribe and six terms as president of the National Congress of American Indians (NCAI), from 1953 to 1959. After Congress endorsed House Concurrent Resolution 108, which declared that Indian tribes and individuals should rapidly be "freed" from federal supervision, Garry convened an NCAI emergency conference to declare united resistance to the termination policy. Dozens of community service and Indian organizations honored his work.

1964   James D. Atcitty (Navajo) from Shiprock, New Mexico, and Monroe Jymm (Navajo) from Tohatchi, New Mexico, were the first two American Indians elected to the New Mexico House of Representatives. Atcitty served from 1964 to 1966 and Jymm from 1965 to 1967. Mr. Jymm's grandfather, nearly one hundred years old, exercised his rights of citizenship for the first time by voting for his thirty-year-old grandson.

1966   Lloyd Lynn House (Navajo/Oneida) was the first American Indian elected to the Arizona House of Representatives, serving from 1966 to 1968. He worked toward ensuring social security benefits for self-employed Navajos, including recognizing medicine men as self-employed doctors. House was proficient in Navajo, Apache, English, and Spanish.

     Tom Lee (Navajo) became the first American Indian to be elected a state senator in New Mexico, serving from 1967 to 1978. He built and owned a trading post in Twin Lakes, New Mexico, and learned how to make silver jewelry to supplement his income when the trading post business was slow.

1970s   Vivien Hailstone (Yurok/Karuk) became the first Indian to serve on the State of California's Department of Parks and Recreation Commission. She promoted Indian names for two parks, a reburial policy for Indian remains and associated grave goods, a traditional gathering policy for Indians, and the elimination of Indian stereotypes from park displays.

1971   Arthur Raymond (Lakota Sioux) was the first Sioux Indian elected to the North Dakota state legislature. A journalist, Raymond wrote an article that won first prize from the Associated Press and was also chosen by the Pulitzer awards committee for award consideration.

     "Les" Ann Hendrick (Nez Perce) was the first Nez Perce to serve as page in the Idaho House of Representatives (1971–72).

1982   Benjamin Nighthorse Campbell (Northern Cheyenne) became the first American Indian to be elected to the Colorado House of Representatives. He ran as a Democrat and won a surprise victory against an incumbent for a seat in the Colorado General Assembly, where he served for four years (two terms). Later he was elected to the U.S. House of Representatives, where he served three terms, and then to the U.S. Senate as a Republican.

1984   Jeanne Givens (Coeur d'Alene) was the first Native American woman elected to the Idaho House of Representatives (1984 and 1986).

1986   Enoch Kelly Haney (Seminole/Muscogee) was the first full-blood American Indian to serve in the Oklahoma legislature. He served in the House from 1980 to 1986 and was a state senator from 1986 to 2002. In 1988 he became the first chairman of Oklahoma's Joint Committee on State-Tribal Relations. Haney is considered the founding father of the National Caucus of Native American State Legislators, created in the early 1990s.

John David Waihe'e III became the first Native Hawaiian elected to the office of governor of Hawaii and the first indigenous person to be elected governor.

1990   Larry EchoHawk (Pawnee Nation) became the first Native American elected as a state attorney general (of Idaho) in the United States; he served from 1991 to 1995. In 1992, he was the first American Indian to head a state delegation to the Democratic National Convention, where he participated as a speaker. On April 20, 2009, President Barack Obama nominated EchoHawk to become the assistant secretary for Indian affairs within the Department of the Interior. The Senate unanimously confirmed EchoHawk to the position.

1993   Georgianna Lincoln (Athabascan) became the first Alaska Native woman to serve in the Alaska State Senate.

1996   Lynda Morgan Lovejoy (Navajo) was the first American Indian woman elected to the New Mexico House of Representatives. In 1991 she received the New Mexico Governor's Award for Outstanding New Mexico Women. In 2007, she was appointed a Democratic member of the New Mexico Senate.

1997   Sally Ann Gonzales (Yaqui) and Debora Norris (Navajo/Blackfeet) were the first Native American women to be elected to the Arizona House of Representatives. Gonzales also served on the Yaqui Tribal Council. In 2000, Norris, who at twenty-eight years of age was one of the youngest members of the state legislature, was elected first vice chairwoman of the Arizona Democratic Party and a member of the Democratic National Committee. She became the second Native American to become a state's vice chair of the Democratic Party.

Thomas Stillday Jr. (Red Lake Band of Chippewa) became the first person outside the Judeo-Christian tradition to serve as chaplain in the Minnesota State Senate. He was elected unanimously by the Minnesota Senate for a two-year term. Sixty-seven senators stood at attention for ten minutes as Chaplain Stillday prayed in Ojibwe asking that the senators be guided by the Creator as they made decisions that would affect all people.

1998   Carol Vigil (Tesuque Pueblo) became the first woman ever elected as state district judge in the United States and the first Indian to win a state judgeship in New Mexico. At her swearing-in ceremony, Vigil wore a black robe with beaded Pueblo Indian symbols of mountains, lightning, clouds, and rain. She also received the governor's award for Outstanding New Mexico Women.

2008   Denise Juneau (Mandan-Hidatsa/Blackfeet) became the first American Indian woman elected to statewide office in Montana when she won election as Superintendent of Public Instruction. Juneau, a Democrat who was named Educator of the Year in 2009 by the National Indian Education Association, supports Farm to School programs, which have popped up all over Montana.

2010   Ponka-We Victors (Ponca Tribe/Tohono O'odham Nation) became the first Native American woman to serve in the Kansas House of Representatives.

First State of the Tribes Addresses

Maine

Leaders of the Passamaquoddy Tribe, Governor Richard Doyle and Governor Richard Stevens, along with Penobscot Nation Chief Barry Dana addressed a joint session of the State of Maine's legislature in 2002. This was the first State of the Tribes address in Maine's 182-year history.

North Dakota

Tex Hall, chairman of the Mandan, Hidatsa, and Arikara Nation gave the first state address in 2003 about the relationship between tribal governments and North Dakota's state government. He was the first tribal chairman to deliver the address to a joint session of the North Dakota legislature. Before, the designated tribal chairman gave separate addresses to the House and Senate.

Wisconsin

Ray DePerry, chair of the Red Cliff Chippewa tribe, delivered the first-ever State of the Tribes address in 2005 to the Wisconsin state legislature. He labeled the event the most significant day in dealings between Wisconsin and its tribal nations.

STATE GOVERNMENTS AND AMERICAN INDIAN TRIBES

State Legislative Committees and State Executive Commissions
Dedicated to Indian Affairs

The need for state forums on Indian affairs has increased in conjunction with the need for improved state-tribal relations. Traditionally, these forums have been under the direction of the state executive branches. More legislatures, however, are recognizing the benefits of having dedicated committees on Indian affairs or state-tribal relations. This list includes both legislative and executive branch committees and commissions. http://www.ncsl.org/?tabid=13279.

Alabama

The Alabama Indian Affairs Commission (AIAC) is located in the executive branch. It has a liaison/advocacy role between the various departments of government and the Indian people of the state's nine tribal communities.

Arizona

Arizona has an annual meeting with legislators and tribal leaders. The Arizona Commission on Indian Affairs (executive branch) submits an annual report to the legislature and makes recommendations to the governor and legislators on Indian issues.

California

California has an inactive Assembly Select Committee on California Indian Nations. A Native American Heritage Committee provides protection to Native American burial sites from vandalism and inadvertent destruction; provides a procedure for the notification of most likely descendants regarding the discovery of Native American human remains and associated grave goods; brings legal action to prevent severe and irreparable damage to sacred shrines, ceremonial sites, sanctified cemeteries, and places of worship on public property; and maintains an inventory of sacred places.

Colorado

Colorado created the Colorado Commission of Indian Affairs (CCIA) (executive branch) in 1976 to be the official liaison between the two Ute tribes and the State of Colorado. The commission has also worked with off-reservation American Indian people who live in Colorado.

Connecticut

Connecticut has had an Indian Affairs Council within the state's Department of Environmental Protection (executive branch) since 1973. The council consists of three members appointed by the governor and one representative from each of the state's five tribes.

Delaware

Delaware has a state-recognized Nanticoke Indian Association (executive branch). The tribe's Nanticoke Indian Center and Nanticoke Indian Museum run programs for the public.

Florida

Florida has a Governor's Council on Indian Affairs, Inc. (executive branch) that advises the governor of Florida on matters affecting the rights and interests of the Indian people in the state. The council represents the interests of the Indian people of Florida before various state agencies and assists Florida in carrying out responsibilities to the state's Indian people.

Georgia

Georgia has a Council on American Indian Concerns (executive branch), which was created by the Georgia legislature in 1992 to help protect Indian graves and burial objects from accidental and intentional desecration. The council is the only state entity specifically authorized to address the concerns of Georgia's American Indians.

Hawaii

Hawaii has an Office of Hawaiian Affairs (executive branch) and two legislative committees (House Committee on Judiciary and Hawaiian Affairs, and Senate Committee on Water, Land and Hawaiian Affairs) that deal with Native Hawaiian issues.

Idaho

Idaho has an Idaho Council on Indian Affairs that monitors and reviews legislation and state policies that impact state-tribal relations and advises the governor, legislature, and state departments. The Idaho Commission on Human Rights (ICHR) (executive branch) helps protect persons within the state from illegal discrimination.

Indiana

Indiana has a Native American Indian Affairs Commission (executive branch). It studies problems of Native residents in the areas of employment, education, civil rights, health, and housing and makes recommendations to appropriate government agencies.

Kansas

Kansas has a legislative Joint Committee on State-Tribal Relations and an Office of Native American Affairs in the Department of Human Resources (executive branch).

Kentucky

Kentucky has a Native American Heritage Commission (executive branch), established in 1996, to recognize and promote Native American contributions and influence in Kentucky's history and culture.

Louisiana

Louisiana has a Governor's Office of Indian Affairs (executive branch), the sole purpose of which is to address Indian issues and develop a mutual relationship between the state and tribes.

Maine

Maine has a legislature with two tribal representatives, from the Penobscot Nation and the Passamaquoddy Tribe, who have seats on the floor of the House, sponsorship privilege, and membership in the State Government and Judiciary Committee. They have no voting privileges. The state also has an Indian Tribal-State Commission (executive branch).

Maryland

Maryland has a Governor's Commission on Indian Affairs (executive branch), which was created in 1976 to represent and serve the state's American Indian groups and communities.

Massachusetts

Massachusetts has a Commission on Indian Affairs (executive branch), created in 1974, that assists Native American individuals, tribes, and organizations in their relationships with state and local government agencies.

Michigan

Michigan has a Department of Human Services (executive branch) that partners with the state's twelve federally recognized American Indian tribes, state tribes, Indian organizations, the federal government, and other community and state organizations to develop a coordinated service delivery system that focuses on preserving and strengthening Indian families both on and off tribal lands.

Minnesota

Minnesota has an Indian Affairs Council (executive branch), established in 1963, that serves as the official liaison between the state and its eleven tribal governments. The council also advises state government on issues of concern to urban Indian communities. The council, which plays a central role in the development of state legislation, monitors programs that affect the state's American Indian population and tribal governments.

Montana

Montana has a State-Tribal Relations Interim Committee (legislative branch) and an Office of Indian Affairs (executive branch), established in 1951, to facilitate effective tribal-state communications. The office serves as a liaison between the state and the tribes, as well as Indian people on and off their reservations, and promotes economic development, environmental protection, education, and support for social services.

Nebraska

Nebraska has a State-Tribal Relations Committee (legislative branch) and a Commission on Indian Affairs (executive branch), established in 1971, that consists of fourteen Indian commissioners appointed by the governor and one ex officio member representing the Pawnee tribe. It is the state liaison between the state's four tribes and serves off-reservation Indian communities as well.

Nevada

Nevada has an Indian Commission (executive branch), created in 1965, that serves as a liaison between the state and the nineteen federally recognized tribes, which in turn comprise twenty-eight separate tribes, bands, and community councils. The commission has five commissioners appointed by the governor, three of whom are Native American.

New Jersey

New Jersey has a Commission on Native American Affairs (executive branch), which was created in 1995 and is located in the New Jersey Department of State. The commission ensures that the state's American Indian tribal members and communities have full opportunities for cultural, educational, social, economic, physical health, mental health, and welfare development. The commission serves as a liaison among the tribal members and the state and federal governments.

New Mexico

New Mexico has several legislative committees that meet when the legislature is in session, not in session, or when required. The Indian Affairs Department (IAD) (executive branch) has implemented groundbreaking state-tribal policies intended to improve the quality of life for the state's Indian citizens and policies designed to strengthen tribal and state relations. Its Web site notes that the IAD is the first and only cabinet-level state Indian affairs department in the nation that sets "the standard for what is possible when state and tribal governments work together to address mutual concerns in respectful and positive dialogue between sovereign governments."

New York

New York has three state agencies (executive branch) charged with specific obligations to the state's Native population: the Office of Children and Family Services (OCFS), Department of Education, and Department of Health. The OCFS has the bulk of the state's responsibilities with regard to Native Americans, serving as liaison between state agencies and tribal groups.

North Carolina

North Carolina has a House Federal Relations and Indian Affairs Committee (legislative branch) and the North Carolina Commission on Indian Affairs (executive branch), created in 1971. The commission was established to bring local, state, and federal resources into focus for implementing or continuing meaningful programs for the state's Indian citizens. There is also a State Advisory Council on Indian Education (executive branch) that identifies issues and concerns affecting academic achievement of American Indian students.

North Dakota

North Dakota has a Tribal and State Relations Committee (legislative branch) that studies tribal-state issues, including government-to-government relations, and an Indian Affairs Commission (executive branch), which was created in 1949 and is committed to creating a better North Dakota through improved tribal and state relations between Indian and non-Indian people.

Oklahoma

In 2011 Oklahoma passed an act (HB 2172) that transferred all powers, duties, and functions of the Oklahoma Indian Affairs Commission, composed of members from nine Indian Nations, to the position of Oklahoma Native American Liaison. Appointed by the governor, the liaison, who must be American Indian, represents the tribes, especially with regard to state-tribal relations.

Oregon

Oregon has a thirteen-member Legislative Commission on Indian Services (legislative and executive branches), created in 1975, that includes representation from all nine federally recognized tribes. The commission serves as the main forum in which Indian concerns are considered. It serves as a point of access for finding out about state government programs and Indian communities.

South Carolina

South Carolina has a Commission on Minority Affairs (executive branch) with a Native American Affairs section. Since 2003, the commission has served as the liaison between South Carolina's Native American population and governments and the South Carolina state government.

South Dakota

South Dakota has a State-Tribal Relations Interim Committee (legislative branch), which drafts legislation and makes policy recommendations. There is also a Department of Tribal Relations (executive branch), created in 1949, which over the years has played a vital role in resolving differences between tribal governments and the state. It recommends qualified Native Americans to boards, commissions, and positions within state government.

Tennessee

Tennessee has a Commission of Indian Affairs (executive branch) that researches and finds local, state, and federal sources of funding and other assistance for implementing or continuing programs for Indian citizens of the state.

Texas

Texas has an Office of the Attorney General (executive branch), which serves and protects the rights of all citizens of Texas through the activities of the various agencies.

Utah

Utah has an inactive Native American Legislative Liaison Committee (legislative branch) and a Division of Indian Affairs (executive branch), which serves as liaison and promotes positive intergovernmental relations with and between Utah's eight Indian tribes, the Office of the Governor, federal and state agencies, and local entities.

Vermont

Vermont has a Commission on Native American Affairs (executive branch), which assists Native American tribal councils, organizations, and individuals to secure social services, education, employment opportunities, health care, housing, and census information.

Virginia

Virginia has a Council on Indians (executive branch) composed of chiefs of all states—recognized tribes—plus two gubernatorial-appointed Indian-at-large members and an ex-officio non-voting member appointed by the governor.

Washington

Washington has a House State Government and Tribal Affairs Committee (legislative branch) that considers issues involving the government-to-government relationship of the state and Indian tribes. The Governor's Office of Indian Affairs (executive branch), created in 1969, serves as liaison between state and tribal governments in advisory, resource, consultative, and educational capacities.

Wisconsin

Wisconsin has a Special Committee on State-Tribal Relations (legislative branch) that studies issues related to American Indians and American Indian tribes and bands, and develops specific recommendations and legislative proposals relating to these issues. It includes six to twelve legislative and six to eleven tribal members. The State-Tribal Relations Initiative (executive branch) is a comprehensive program aimed at increasing the ties between state agencies and tribal governments to streamline and improve the services that governments provide to both tribal and nontribal members.

Wyoming

Wyoming has a Select Committee on Tribal Relations (legislative branch) and an Indian Affairs Council (executive branch). The committee has studied all areas in which the state is contracting with or currently providing services or funding to the tribal entities.

The Cherokee Nation, the State of Georgia, and the U.S. Supreme Court, 1831–32

Efforts by Georgia in 1828 and 1829 "to extend the laws of this State" to Cherokee lands led to important rulings in federal Indian law. In 1828 and 1829, Wilson Lumpkin, governor of Georgia, signed acts to "to annul all laws and ordinances made by the Cherokee Nation of Indians." The Cherokee Nation declared the state laws "null and void" owing to its status as "a foreign state, not owing allegiance to the United States, nor to any State of this Union." The Cherokees, who considered themselves to be sovereign, independent, and self-governing, said that Georgia, in its efforts to seize Cherokee country and force the Cherokees from their homeland, violated at least a dozen treaties the nation had made with the U.S. government. The tribe also charged that Georgia violated acts of Congress that recognized the Cherokee Nation's boundaries. The Cherokees filed suit in the Supreme Court against enforcement of Georgia's laws on their territory under Article III of the Constitution. In his opinion in *Cherokee Nation v. Georgia* (1831), Chief Justice John Marshall held that Indian tribes were "domestic, dependent nations," not "foreign states."

In 1831, Samuel Worcester, a missionary to the Cherokee Nation, was indicted in a county court for residing in the Cherokee Nation without a license or permit from the governor. Despite Worcester's argument that he was authorized by the U.S. president and the Cherokee Nation to preach the gospel, the state prosecuted him. He was convicted and sentenced to hard labor in prison for four years.

Worcester took his case to the Supreme Court, which first decided it had jurisdiction to decide the controversy. Speaking for the Court in one of its most celebrated and oft-cited opinions, *Worcester v. Georgia* (1832), Chief Justice John Marshall held that Georgia's statutes were unlawful because they were "repugnant to the Constitution, treaties, and laws of the United States." In reaching the decision, the Court held that the federal government, not individual states, possessed the exclusive right to exercise control over Indian affairs. "The Cherokee Nation . . . is a distinct community, occupying its own territory, with boundaries accurately described, in which the laws of Georgia can have no force."

State-Tribal Agreements

Working together, many state and tribal governments have found ways to cooperate in areas of mutual interest rather than engage in jurisdictional rivalries. In and around tribal lands, some states and local governments have agreed to share responsibilities for government services in the following subject areas.

1. Cultural resources agreements involving the discovery, during construction of buildings, roads, and bridges, of Native American human remains or burials.
2. Environmental agreements that give tribes increasing authority to administer programs under federal environmental protection statutes.

3. Human services agreements, including foster care programs, licensing and monitoring child care centers, and temporary assistance for needy families.
4. Law enforcement and cross-deputization agreements between tribes; state, county, and municipal police officers; and the Bureau of Indian Affairs.
5. Mutual respect and equal status agreements by state legislatures and local city and county governments acknowledging Indian tribes as separate and equal governments within state and local boundaries.
6. Tax agreements involving tribal government authority to collect taxes on transactions that occur on tribal lands, and tribal revenues, which are not taxable by state governments, including sales of motor fuel, tobacco, and cigarettes.
7. Transportation agreements involving planning, development, and maintenance projects.

Source: Susan Johnson, et al. *Government to Government: Models of Cooperation between States and Tribes*, pp. 59–79.

State Seals with American Indian Imagery

Official seals, a symbol of identity, exist for every state in the United States. They are used for a variety of purposes, such as signifying state-level offices and documents. Each seal has a unique history, incorporating designs that reflect aspects of the state's character. Several state seals include representations of American Indians.

Florida

Mandated by the state legislature in 1868, Florida's seal featured the image of a Western Plains Indian woman wearing a headdress. In 1985, the seal was revised and the figure was replaced with a representation of a Seminole woman, a Florida Native.

Hawaii

Officially adopted by the Territorial Legislature in 1959, the year Hawaii was admitted as the fiftieth state of the U.S., the seal includes Kamehameha I, who unified the Hawaiian islands, and goddess Liberty. She holds *Ka Hae Hawaii* (Hawaiian flag) in her hand.

Kansas

The Kansas seal, adopted in 1861, incorporates an image of two Indians on horseback pursuing a retreating herd of buffalo juxtaposed with Euro-American symbols of settlement.

Massachusetts

The Massachusetts state seal, adopted by the Provincial Congress in 1780, has featured an Indian figure holding an arrow pointed downward to signify peace.

The Indian image, which traces back to the Massachusetts Bay Colony seal, has been redesigned over time.

Minnesota

Minnesota's state seal, which became official in 1861, incorporates a male Indian figure riding on horseback into the distance. The image is juxtaposed with that of a Euro-American farmer plowing a field in the foreground, his weapons nearby.

North Dakota

The North Dakota seal features a full-feathered Indian on horseback riding away in pursuit of a buffalo. The scene, which incorporates North Dakota's 1889 statehood date, also includes a bow and arrows and other symbols, such as wheat and a plow.

Oklahoma

Oklahoma's seal, dated 1907 with statehood, features a large star with radiating arms that represent the Chickasaw, Choctaw, Seminole, Creek, and Cherokee nations, along with symbols from each of their respective official tribal seals. The star's center depicts two men, one Indian and one white, shaking hands in front of a liberty figure.

Before statehood, Alaska had an official seal that featured images such as Eskimo ice fishing and igloos, but replaced it in 1910 to focus on Alaska's industrial and other wealth.

Kamehameha Day in Hawaii

Kamehameha Day is an official holiday of the State of Hawaii, held on June 11 of each year. The holiday honors Kamehameha the Great (also known as Kamehameha I and Kamehameha the First), the ruler of Hawaii from 1762 until his death in 1819. He is respected for unifying and establishing the Kingdom of Hawaii in 1810.

Honoring Nations Honoree, 2010

Honoring Nations, a national awards program initiated in 1998, highlights outstanding programs in self-governance by Native nations. At the heart of the program is the belief that tribes themselves hold the key to positive social, political, cultural, and economic prosperity. Based at the John F. Kennedy School of Government at Harvard University, Honoring Nations is administered by the Harvard Project on American Indian Economic Development. The criteria for selection of honorees include program effectiveness, significance to sovereignty, cultural relevance, transferability, and sustainability. One tribal-state jurisdiction program was honored.

Joint Tribal-State Jurisdiction, 2010
Leech Lake Band of Ojibwe
Cass Lake, Minnesota

> Because Minnesota is subject to Public Law 280, criminal jurisdiction fell to county and state agencies. Statistics for tribal citizens suggested that problems were beyond the counties' and state's ability to address. The tribe wanted to intercede to better serve citizens caught up in the judicial system for substance abuse–related offenses, but lacked resources to do so. In 2006, the Leech Lake Tribal Court and Minnesota's Ninth Judicial District's Cass County District Court formed a DWI Wellness Court to adjudicate and rehabilitate substance abusers. A year later, Leech Lake established a second Wellness Court in collaboration with Itasca County District Court. The Wellness Courts operate under a joint powers agreement and serve both Native and non-Native people. A Leech Lake Tribal flag has been installed in both the Itasca and Cass County courts to symbolize the Nation's arrangement with the district courts.

Tribal Flag Plaza, Oklahoma State Capitol

Dedicated in 1996, the Oklahoma Tribal Flag Plaza on the North Mall of the Oklahoma State Capitol in Oklahoma City recognizes and honors the thirty-six tribal governments in the state. The tribes are each represented by their respective tribal flag, except for the Kickapoo, who are signified by a bare flagpole because their tribal traditions prohibit such display. The design was inspired by indigenous Spiro Mound Builders and includes a monument, whose perimeter features the name of each tribe carved in a granite edge at the base of the flagpoles. The project was a collaborative effort that included the thirty-six tribal governments of Oklahoma. http://davidmeyer.info/images/full/c010KMonument.html

STATE RECOGNITION OF AMERICAN INDIAN TRIBES

Fifteen States That Have State-Recognized American Indian Tribes

1. Alabama
2. California
3. Connecticut
4. Delaware
5. Georgia
6. Louisiana
7. Massachusetts

8. Montana
9. New Jersey
10. New York
11. North Carolina
12. Ohio
13. South Carolina
14. Vermont
15. Virginia

State-Recognized Tribes with Reservations

In 2011, there are ten small Indian reservations located in six states east of the Mississippi River.

Alabama	MOWA Choctaw Reservation north of Mobile	MOWA Band of Choctaw Indians
Connecticut	Golden Hill Reservation in Colchester and Trumbull	Paugussett Tribe
	Schaghticoke Reservation in Kent	Schagticoke Tribe
	Paucatuck Eastern Pequot Reservation in North Stonington	Paucatuck Eastern Pequot Tribe
Georgia	Tama Tribal Town (reservation) in Whigham `	Lower Muskogee Creek Tribe
Massachusetts	Nipmuc-Hassanamisco Reservation in Grafton	Nipmuc Nation
New York	Poospatuck Indian Reservation in Mastic	Unkechaug Indian Nation
Virginia	Pamunkey Reservation in King William	Pamunkey Tribe
	Mattaponi Reservation in West Point	Mattaponi Tribe

State Recognition of Tribes

Some states have recognized certain tribes within their borders. State recognition is not the same as federal recognition, which is the federal government's acknowledgment of a tribe as a sovereign nation with which it has a government-to-government relationship. Recognition leads to a tribe's eligibility to receive federal services. State recognition means a tribe has been officially recognized by its respective state, but not by the federal government. State recognition does not permit gaming or other significant non-gaming benefits. One right conferred on members of state-recognized tribes is the right to exhibit as Native American artists under the U.S. federal law, the Indian Arts and Crafts Law of 1990. Benefits and rights vary from state to state.

State recognition regulatory processes include: (1) state law recognition, passed by both houses and approved by a governor; (2) "administrative" recognition, bestowed by executive agencies empowered by statutes; (3) "legislative" recognition, which lacks a governor's signature, or joint resolutions by state legislatures; and (4) executive recognition (gubernatorial proclamation, executive orders, or historically by a treaty established between tribes and the original colonies).

Federal Recognition of Tribes

Federal recognition is the U.S. government's acknowledgment of a tribe as a sovereign nation. Such acknowledgment leads to a tribe's eligibility to receive federal services provided to federally recognized Indian tribes.

Before 1978, requests from Indian groups for federal acknowledgment as tribes were determined on an ad hoc basis. Some tribes were acknowledged by Congressional action, others by executive branch decisions, and some through cases brought in the courts. After 1978, regulations governing the administrative process for federal acknowledgment required a review of tribal petitions for federal acknowledgment conducted by the Office of Federal Acknowledgment (OFA) in the Bureau of Indian Affairs (BIA). This demanding and time-consuming process has become the dominant means of securing federal recognition, rather than by legislative or judicial means.

OFA's process requires the petitioning tribe to satisfy seven mandatory criteria, including historical and continuous American Indian identity in a distinct community. The vast majority of petitioners do not meet these strict standards; far more petitions have been denied than accepted. At the end of 2008, over three hundred groups in forty-three states had petitioned the OFA for federal recognition.

LEGISLATION

Congressional Laws Impacting State-Tribal Jurisdiction

Tribal governments have come under state jurisdiction by a variety of methods. Over the years, state officials have succeeded in pressuring Congress to increase state jurisdiction over Indians. Supreme Court rulings also have greatly increased state jurisdiction on reservations. At the same time, however, some federal laws enacted after 1953 have reduced the amount of jurisdiction available to states and increased tribal sovereignty and/or federal power.

1. The General Allotment Act of 1887 (GAA) did not give states any power over Indians themselves, but increased state authority over activities on privately owned land (individual allotments held by Indians, removed from trust status, and subsequently sold to non-Indians) within reservations. The law vastly increased state jurisdiction over portions of Indian reservations owned by non-Indians.

2. Public Law 83-280 (often referred to as P.L. 280), enacted on August 15, 1953, took away shared jurisdiction between the federal government and tribal courts in Indian country. The law authorized six *mandatory* states "to assume jurisdiction over offenses committed by or against Indians" in Indian country without consulting tribes. P.L. 280 authorized the other forty-four states, at their option, to acquire the same jurisdiction the six states had received. The states could acquire criminal jurisdiction at any time by passing a law.

    In the affected states, the federal government gave up control over crimes in Indian country (those involving Indian perpetrators and/or victims). Indian nations impacted by P.L. 280 had to deal with greatly increased state control over a broad range of reservation activities. Many Indian tribes opposed P.L. 280, objecting to the imposition of state jurisdiction in Indian country. The law did not require prior consent or consultation with affected tribes.

3. Termination Laws passed by Congress between 1953 and 1966 terminated 109 tribes. Each law ended the trust relationship between the United States and the tribes and required the tribes to distribute all of their property to their members, thus eliminating the reservation. Tribal members and their lands became fully subject to state law.

4. The Civil Rights Act of 1968 gave any state that had assumed jurisdiction under P.L. 280 the option to return all or some of its criminal/civil jurisdiction to the federal government. The federal government had the final say over whether to accept the return. Indians had no say in the matter. Over the years, a number of states returned to the federal government jurisdiction over civil and criminal matters involving Indians on their lands. The law required tribal consent for any future state jurisdiction under the law. Tribes could not undo state jurisdiction established between 1953 and 1968.

5. Congress passed several laws (authorizations of state jurisdiction) conferring some amount of state jurisdiction over certain reservations in Colorado, Maine, New York, Oklahoma, and Rhode Island. Congress gave states jurisdiction over specific subject matters, such as selling liquor in Indian country. Congress has authorized the secretary of the interior to allow state officials to inspect reservation health conditions; authorized states to seize by eminent domain any federal land allotted to an Indian, provided there is

fair compensation; and required employers in Indian country to comply with state workers' compensation laws.

6. Some federal laws enacted after Public Law 280 have reduced the amount of jurisdiction available to states, and at the same time have increased tribal sovereignty and/or federal power. The 1978 Indian Child Welfare Act gave Indian nations exclusive jurisdiction over certain custody proceedings involving Indian children. The 1988 Indian Gaming Regulatory Act has made enforcement of state gaming laws a federal, not a state, responsibility.

Six States under Public Law 280 State Jurisdiction

The following states were required to assume "jurisdiction over offenses committed by or against Indians" in Indian country without consulting with tribes. The federal government relinquished its special criminal jurisdiction involving Indian criminals or victims. A handful of tribes that strongly opposed state jurisdiction successfully proved they had satisfactory law enforcement. Most tribes failed to prove their case.

1. Alaska: All Indian Country within the state, except for Annette Islands.
2. California: All Indian Country within the state.
3. Minnesota: All Indian Country within the state, except the Red Lake Reservation.
4. Nebraska: All Indian Country within the state.
5. Oregon: All Indian Country within the state, except the Warm Springs Reservation.
6. Wisconsin: All Indian Country within the state, except the Menominee Reservation.

BOOKS

Ten Books about Indians and States

1. *Formulating American Indian Policy in New York State, 1970–1986,* by Laurence Hauptman (1988).
2. *Indian Tribes of Oklahoma: A Guide,* by Blue Clark (2009).
3. *Indians and Indian Agents: The Origins of the Reservation System in California, 1849–1852,* by George Harwood Phillips (1997).
4. *Indians in Minnesota,* by Kathy Davis Graves and Elizabeth Ebbott (2007).
5. *Indian Nations of Wisconsin: Histories of Endurance and Renewal,* by Patty Loew (2002).
6. *In the Shadow of the Eagle: A Tribal Representative in Maine,* by Donna M. Loring (2008).

7. *Oregon Indians: Voices from Two Centuries*, by Stephen Dow Beckham (2006).
8. *Pocahontas' People: The Powhatan Indians of Virginia through Four Centuries*, by Helen C. Rountree (1990).
9. *The Sioux in South Dakota History*, by Richmond L. Clow (2007).
10. *The Worlds between Two Rivers: Perspectives on American Indians in Iowa*, edited by Gretchen M. Bataille, David Mayer Gradwohl, and Charles L. P. Silet (2000).

Minnesota Tribal Nations Plaza

A plaza honoring Minnesota's eleven Indian tribes, located outside the Gopher football stadium in Minneapolis, was dedicated in 2009. The plaza was built with a $10 million grant from the Shakopee Mdewakanton Sioux Community (SMSC). It includes eleven sky markers, each eighteen feet high and each incorporating information about one of Minnesota's eleven Tribal Nations with tribal flags, images, and facts.

ORGANIZATIONS

National Caucus of Native American State Legislators
http://www.nativeamericanlegislators.org/default.aspx

The National Caucus of Native American State Legislators (formerly the National Council of Native American Legislators), headquartered in Denver, Colorado, was initially formed in 1992 and met during National Conference of State Legislatures (NCSL) meetings whenever possible. The caucus, which receives support from NCSL, works to promote a better understanding of state-tribal issues among policymakers and the public at large. Membership is open to all Native American, Alaska Native, and Native Hawaiian state legislators. The caucus holds an annual meeting once a year and also meets during the NCSL Legislative Summit. Additionally, seven policy committees meet throughout the year. The caucus also collaborates with the National Black Caucus of State Legislators, the National Hispanic Caucus of State Legislators, and the National Asian Pacific American Caucus of State Legislators on issues of common interest.

National Congress of American Indians and National Conference of State Legislators: State-Tribal Relations Project
http://www.ncai.org/Tribal-State-Relations.28.0.html

The National Congress of American Indians (NCAI) and National Conference of State Legislators (NCSL) established a twelve-member advisory council of state legislators and tribal leaders from across the country. The council meets twice a year to provide direction for all project activities and to discuss steps and models that might facilitate more collaborative relationships. NCAI's Web site has many examples of cooperative agreements between tribal governments and state governments, as well as other documents and articles related to tribal-state relations.

RESOURCES

Ashley, Jeffrey S., and Hubbard, Secody J. *Negotiated Sovereignty: Working to Improve Tribal-State Relations.* Westport, CT: Praeger, 2004.

Bays, Brad A., and Fouberg, Erin Hogan, eds. *The Tribes and the States: Geographies of Intergovernmental Interaction.* Lanham, MD: Rowman and Littlefield, 2002.

Castille, George Pierre. *State and Reservation: New Perspectives on Federal Indian Policy.* Tucson: University of Arizona Press, 1992.

Davis, Sia. *Sustainable Development: State and Tribal Initiatives.* Denver: National Conference of State Legislatures, 2007.

Davis, Sia, and Kanegis, Aura. *Improving State-Tribal Relations: An Introduction.* Denver: National Conference of State Legislatures, 2004.

Goldberg-Ambrose, Carole. *Planting Tail Feathers: Tribal Survival and Public Law 280.* Los Angeles: American Indian Studies Center, 1997.

Johnson, Susan, et al. *Government to Government Models of Cooperation between States and Tribes.* Denver: National Conference of State Legislatures, 2009.

Miller, Mark Edwin. *Forgotten Tribes: Unrecognized Indians and the Federal Acknowledgment Process.* Lincoln: University of Nebraska Press, 2006.

Rosen, Deborah A. *American Indians and State Law: Sovereignty, Race, and Citizenship, 1790–1880.* Lincoln: University of Nebraska Press, 2009.

Wilkins, Andrea. *Criminal Jurisdiction and Law Enforcement: Areas for State-Tribal Cooperation.* Denver: National Conference of State Legislatures, 2006.

———. *Economic Development in Tribal Reservations and Rural Communities.* Denver: National Conference of State Legislatures, 2004.

———. *Welfare Reform on Tribal Lands: Examples of State-Tribal Collaboration.* Denver: National Conference of State Legislatures, 2004.

Zelio, Judy. *Piecing Together the State-Tribal Tax Puzzle.* Denver: National Conference of State Legislatures, 2005.

Web Sites

Association on American Indian Affairs, FAQs about Federal Acknowledgment: http://www.indian-affairs.org/resources/aaia_faqs.htm

"Federalism and the State Recognition of Native American Tribes: A Survey of State-Recognized Tribes and State Recognition Processes across the United States," by Alexa Koenig and Jonathan Stein: http://www.gabrielinotribe.org/legal_articles/KoenigSteinFederalism_formatted_for_publication_113007.pdf

Harvard Project's Honoring Nations Directory of Honored Programs, 1999–2006: http://hpaied.org/images/resources/general/Dir_web.pdf

Office of Federal Acknowledgment: http://www.bia.gov/WhoWeAre/AS-IA/OFA/index.htm

"Piecing Together the State-Tribal Tax Puzzle," by Judy Zelio: http://www.ncsl.org/default.aspx?tabid=12662

The Process of Gaining Federal Recognition, by the Jamestown S'Klallam Tribe: http://www.tribalmuseum.jamestowntribe.org/hsg/exhibits/exb_fedrec_process.php

"Public Law 280: Issues and Concerns for Victims of Crime in Indian Country," by Jerry Gardner and Ada Pecos Melton. Tribal Court Clearinghouse, Tribal Law & Policy Institute: http://www.tribal-institute.org/articles/gardner1.htm

"Questions and Answers about Public Law 280," by Carole Goldberg. Tribal Court Clearinghouse, Tribal Law & Policy Institute: http://www.tribal-institute.org/articles/goldberg.htm

State-Recognized Indian Tribes: http://www.ncai.org/State-Recognized-Indian-Tribes.285.0.html

Part Three

6

Native Lands and Environmental Issues

FIRSTS

1990   The Draft Comprehensive Land Use Plan by the Swinomish Indian Tribal Community and Skagit County in Washington was the first comprehensive planning effort attempted by a tribe and a county to coordinate land use goals.

1997   The InterTribal Sinkyone Wilderness Council, a nonprofit land conservation consortium composed of ten federally recognized Northern California tribes, purchased a 3,845-acre parcel of redwood forestland to establish the first intertribal wilderness area in the country. The area is a small portion of the original indigenous Sinkyone territory.

1999   The Pueblo of Zuni in New Mexico opened the first eagle sanctuary owned and operated by Native Americans.

2005   Fiscal years 2005 through 2007 marked the first time the U.S. Environmental Protection Agency (EPA) selected tribal environmental issues as a national priority. Working with tribes to build capacity and increase direct implementation in Indian country and beyond, the priorities included drinking water, schools, and solid waste as initial focus areas.

2006   With the completion of its eagle aviary in January 2006, the Iowa Tribe of Oklahoma became the first tribe in the country federally permitted through the U.S. Fish and Wildlife Services to rehabilitate injured eagles.

2007   San Esteban del Rey Mission, Acoma Pueblo, was the first Native site to be named a National Trust for Historic Preservation site.

2010   The Comanche Nation Ethno-Ornithological Initiative (SIA) based in Cyril, Oklahoma, became the first permitted and tribally managed non-eagle feather repository in the country.

2011   Arizona's Kayenta Township, a political subdivision of the Navajo Nation, became the first tribal community in the United States to adopt the International Green Construction Code (IGCC). The IGCC is a building code designed to reduce the environmental impact of construction projects.

INDIAN COUNTRY

Five Indian Country Facts

1. According to 2010 figures, there are 565 federally recognized tribes in the United States, 229 of which are located in Alaska.
2. The 2010 census indicates that 5,220,579 people reported being American Indian or Alaska Native, either alone or in combination with other races (approximately 1.7 percent of the U.S. population). Of these, 2,932,248 reported being American Indian and Alaska Native alone (0.9 percent of the U.S. population). A total of 540,013 Americans reported being Native Hawaiian and Other Pacific Islander alone (0.2 percent of the U.S. population).
3. The General Allotment Act (Dawes Severalty Act) and related federal policies led to the loss of over 90 million acres of land for tribal nations between 1887 and 1934. It also resulted in fractionation—divided parcels of land with many owners (often hundreds)—of a large percentage of remaining lands.
4. The Department of the Interior (DOI) holds approximately 56 million acres of American Indian lands in trust, "perhaps the largest land trust in the world" (EDS 2003). The agency's trust responsibility includes protecting treaty rights and obligations of federally recognized tribes.
5. Indian lands comprise approximately 5 percent of the total land area of the United States, but contain an estimated 10 percent of the nation's energy reserves.

Seven Facts about American Indian Reservations

1. Reservations were created by a number of actions and agreements, including treaties, executive orders, and legislative acts.
2. The Navajo Nation (Diné Bikeyah, or Navajoland) has the largest reservation in the United States, with over 27,000 square miles extending into the states of Utah, Arizona, and New Mexico. The Navajo land base is larger than ten of the fifty states in the United States.
3. There are over one hundred federally recognized tribes in California, with nearly one hundred federal reservations, the highest number in the lower forty-eight states. A large number of them are *rancherias*, a Spanish term for small, rural settlements, and generally range in size from less than an acre to several hundred acres.
4. According to the Bureau of Indian Affairs, the Metlakatla Indian Community of the Annette Island Reserve in southeastern Alaska is the only federal Indian reservation in that state. The Alaska Native Claims Settlement Act of 1971

changed Native land title for many indigenous groups in the state through a shift to Alaska Native corporations.

5. The Seminole Tribe of Florida has six non-contiguous reservations, more than any tribe in North America. They are Big Cypress, Tampa, Hollywood, Brighton, Immokalee, and Fort Pierce.
6. There are state-recognized tribes with ten small reservations located in six states east of the Mississippi (Alabama, Connecticut, Georgia, Massachusetts, New York, and Virginia).
7. The state-recognized Golden Hill Reservation of the Paugussett Indian Nation in Connecticut, with one-quarter acre of land, is among the smallest Indian reservations in the United States. There are also tribal nations that are landless.

Ten Names for Tribal Homelands

Federal Indian reservations are areas that have been set aside for the use of American Indian tribes, the legal status and boundaries of which are defined in treaties, agreements, executive orders, federal statutes, secretarial orders, or judicial decisions. The U.S. Census Bureau recognizes federal reservations as territory over which American Indian tribes have primary governmental authority. The agency identifies ten names by which these lands and communities are known.

1. Colonies
2. Communities
3. Indian Communities
4. Indian Villages
5. Pueblos
6. Rancherias
7. Ranches
8. Reservations
9. Reserves
10. Villages

The Largest Federal Indian Reservations

After the Navajo Nation, which has the largest reservation in the United States, twelve other reservations each have more than one million acres of land, according to data drawn from *Tiller's Guide to Indian Country* (2005). The figures below are rounded off to the nearest thousand acres. Depending upon the source, four of the reservations also indicate higher figures (Cheyenne River, 2,796,000; Pine Ridge, 2,800,000; Uintah Ouray, 4,500,000; and Yakama, 1,400,000).

7. "Theory of Light," by Hershman R. John (Navajo). In *I Swallow Turquoise for Courage* (2007).
8. "To a Child Running with Outstretched Arms in Canyon de Chelly," by N. Scott Momaday (Kiowa). In *Harper's Anthology of 20th Century Native American Poetry*, edited by Duane Niatum (1988).
9. "When Earth Becomes an 'It,'" by Marilou Awiakta (Cherokee). In *Through Indian Eyes: The Native Experience in Books for Children*, edited by Beverly Slapin and Doris Seale (1992).

Natural Resources in Indian Country (Excluding Alaska)

Acres of grazing range	44,298,390
Number of natural lakes and ponds	5,770
Acres of developed oil, gas, and mineral resources	765,706
Percentage of U.S. coal reserves	30
Percentage of U.S. uranium deposits	40
Percentage of U.S. oil and natural gas deposits	4

Source: Patrick Durham, "Snapshot of Indian Country," Native American Fish and Wildlife Society, June 18, 1999

LEGISLATION

Selected Federal Legislation Affecting Native Lands, 1887–2004

General Allotment Act (Dawes Severalty Act) of 1887

Named for Massachusetts senator Henry L. Dawes, the sponsor of the General Allotment Act of 1887, the Dawes Act provided for the breakup of collectively held landholdings of tribes by partitioning reservation lands into individually owned parcels, or allotments, and selling the "surplus." By the time the allotment policy officially ended in 1934, over 90 million acres of land (about two-thirds of the total tribal land base) had passed from Indian to non-Indian ownership.

Curtis Act of 1898

Passed by Congress in 1898, this legislation extended the provisions of the General Allotment Act in Indian Territory (present-day Oklahoma), authorizing the allotment of Cherokee, Chickasaw, Choctaw, Creek, and Seminole lands, abolishing tribal courts, and prohibiting the enforcement of tribal laws in federal court. The act also abolished the constitutional governments of these tribal nations.

Indian Reorganization Act (Wheeler-Howard Act) of 1934

Sometimes called the Indian New Deal, this legislation reversed the land allotment policies of the Dawes Act of 1887 to, instead, conserve and develop Indian lands and resources, to extend to Indians the right to form business and other organizations, and to restore or grant certain rights of home rule to Indians. A National Congress of American Indians report estimates that 60 percent of tribal governments are based on Indian Reorganization Act constitutions.

Oklahoma Indian Welfare Act of 1936

This legislation, also known as the Thomas-Rogers Act, extended principles of the Indian Reorganization Act of 1934 to tribal groups in Oklahoma. Its provisions included the right of any tribe or band of Indians in that state "to organize for its common welfare and to adopt a constitution and bylaws." The law also addressed land issues, a response to losses and divisions resulting from earlier allotment policies and practices.

Indian Claims Commission Act of 1946

Congress established the Indian Claims Commission (ICC), a special tribunal to hear and determine longstanding claims by American Indian tribes against the federal government that stemmed from land dealings that President Harry S. Truman called the "largest real estate transaction in history" (Presidential Signing Statement, August 13, 1946). The ICC provided monetary compensation through the awards it granted, much of it diminished by attorneys' fees, but no return of lands. Expected to be in effect for ten years, the Indian Claims Commission operated until 1978, when the U.S. Court of Claims reassumed jurisdiction over unresolved cases.

California Rancheria Termination Act of 1958

Congress enacted the California Rancheria Termination Act in 1958, terminating the federal recognition and trust status of forty-one reservations, or rancherias. In 1964, the act was amended, terminating additional tribal lands. In 1983, a class action lawsuit resulted in the restoration of federal recognition to seventeen rancherias, but others are still awaiting reversal of termination.

Indian Land Consolidation Act of 1983, amended in 1991 and 2000

This legislation authorized any tribe, with the approval of the secretary of the interior, to adopt a land consolidation plan providing for the sale or exchange of any tribal lands or interest in lands for the purpose of eliminating undivided fractional interests in Indian trust or restricted lands or consolidating its land holdings. It also included a pilot program for the acquisition of fractional interests in trust or restricted lands.

American Indian Probate Reform Act of 2004
    The American Indian Probate Reform Act (AIPRA), which amends the Indian
    Land Consolidation Act, was enacted to improve provisions relating to probate
    of trust and restricted land, and for other purposes. Its provisions include
    replacing state law with federal probate code, a change intended to address
    fractionated land ownership (lands divided among multiple heirs), a result of
    federal allotment policies.

Selected Native Land Settlement or Recovery Actions

In some instances tribal nations have been successful in having a portion of lost or
stolen lands returned, but generally only after long years of struggle. The majority
of claims have not resulted in land return or restoration. These are examples of
federal actions that resulted in land settlement or recovery.

1970   P.L. 91-489, Makah Indian Tribe, Washington
        After nearly 150 years, the Makah Tribe recovered lands that belonged
        to it. On October 22, 1970, Congress enacted Public Law 91-489, declar-
        ing Ozette reservation to be part of the Makah's trust lands. Other lands
        belonging to the tribal nation were returned in 1984, when Congress
        passed Public Law 98-282, restoring the islands of Tatoosh and Waadah
        to Makah ownership.

1972   McQuinn Strip Act, P.L. 92-427, Warm Springs Reservation, Oregon
        Congress resolved a dispute that began in the nineteenth century about
        the boundaries of the Warm Springs Reservation, placing some 61,000
        acres of public land from the Mount Hood and Willamette national
        forests back into tribal ownership.

1972   Executive Order 11670—Providing for the Return of Certain Lands to
        the Yakima Indian Reservation
        Signed by President Richard Nixon on May 20, 1972, this Execu-
        tive Order restored some 21,000 acres of land to the Yakima (now
        Yakama) Nation in Washington State. In 1966, the Indian Claims
        Commission found that the area in question had originally been
        intended for inclusion in the Yakima Reservation. Since the commis-
        sion did not have the authority to return land, the tribe sought, and
        obtained, executive remedy.

1975   The Grand Canyon National Park Enlargement Act (P.L. 93-620),
        which was signed into law by President Gerald Ford on January 3,
        1975, included provisions for Arizona's Havasupai Tribe, indigenous
        to the area. The act enlarged the Havasupai Reservation by 185,000
        acres and designated a contiguous 95,300 acres of the enlarged park

as a permanent traditional use area of the Havasupai Indians of Havasu Canyon, Arizona.

1978   Rhode Island Claims Settlement Act
In 1975, the Narragansett Tribe filed a lawsuit against the State of Rhode Island and several landowners for the return of approximately 3,200 acres of land. An out-of-court agreement was reached for some 1,800 acres, requiring congressional approval and the appropriation of $3.5 million to purchase privately owned land. Congress passed the Rhode Island Claims Settlement Act on September 30, 1978, extinguishing aboriginal title in Rhode Island as part of the legislation.

1980   Maine Indian Claims Settlement Act
The Maine Indian Claims Settlement Act of 1980 provided for the settlement of land claims of the Passamaquoddy Tribe, the Penobscot Nation, and the Houlton Band of Maliseet Indians in the State of Maine. These indigenous lands had been originally transferred in violation of U.S. laws, including the Trade and Intercourse Act of 1790. To relinquish the claims, Congress recognized the federal status of the tribes, provided for a land acquisition fund, and made other provisions.

2000   Timbisha Shoshone Homeland Act
The Timbisha Shoshone Homeland Act, passed by Congress in 2000, provided the Timbisha Shoshone Tribe a permanent land base within its aboriginal territory, which included the area that now comprises Death Valley National Park and other areas of California and Nevada. The act restored 7,753.99 acres of land, consisting of separate parcels in those states and including the purchase of two privately owned properties.
http://www.timbisha.org/

Selected Environmental Legislation

Indian Mineral Development Act of 1982
This legislation was enacted to provide American Indian tribes with flexibility in the development and sale of their mineral resources. The IMDA made it possible for tribes to enter into joint venture or other agreements with mineral developers. IMDA's objectives included furthering the policy of Indian self-determination and maximizing the financial return for tribes from valuable resources.

Indian Dams Safety Act of 1994
This legislation provided for the establishment of a dam safety maintenance and repair program within the Bureau of Indian Affairs to ensure maintenance

The Return of Blue Lake to Taos Pueblo

In 2010, Taos Pueblo in New Mexico commemorated the fortieth anniversary of the return of its sacred Blue Lake and surrounding lands. President Richard M. Nixon signed Public Law 91-550 into law on December 15, 1970, to return 48,000 acres of land that had been unjustly taken from the Pueblo in 1906. The return marked one of the most significant occasions in the history of Taos Pueblo, the culmination of a sixty-four-year struggle with the U.S. government to reclaim religious freedom and protect sacred land. During the struggle, the Taos Pueblo issued a statement that asserted: "The story of my people and the story of this place are one single story. No man can think of us without also thinking of this place. We are always joined together."

Alaska Native Claims Settlement Act of 1971

The Alaska Native Claims Settlement Act of 1971 provided for the settlement of native land claims in Alaska by extinguishing Native title to approximately nine-tenths of the state and by allocating Alaska's Native peoples 44 million acres of their homelands. The act also provided for the enrollment of Natives, the organization of regional corporations of Natives, the conveyance of lands to the corporations, and the deposit of the legislation's monetary compensation into an Alaska Native Fund.

and monitoring of the condition of identified dams to keep them in a satisfactory condition on a long-term basis.

Tribal Forest Protection Act of 2004
    This legislation was enacted to authorize the secretary of agriculture and the secretary of the interior to enter into an agreement or contract with Indian tribes meeting certain criteria to carry out projects to protect Indian forestland.

Indian Tribal Energy Development and Self-Determination Act of 2005
    This legislation, Title V of the Energy Policy Act of 2005, was enacted to assist Indian tribes in the development of energy resources and to further the goal of Indian self-determination. Its provisions included the establishment and implementation of an Indian energy resource development program to assist consenting Indian tribes and tribal energy resource development organizations.

American Indian Trust Fund Management Reform Act of 1994

The American Indian Trust Fund Management Reform Act of 1994 requires the secretary of the interior to take specified actions to properly discharge United States responsibilities with regard to American Indian funds held in trust by the federal government, including providing adequate systems for accounting for and reporting trust fund balances. The legislation also established the Office of Special Trustee for American Indians within the Department of the Interior to oversee the implementation of management reforms.

The Office of the Special Trustee for American Indians (OST) was established to improve the accountability and management of Indian funds held in trust by the federal government. As trustee, the Department of the Interior (DOI) has the primary fiduciary responsibility to manage tribal trust funds as well as Individual Indian Money (IIM) accounts. The DOI manages the largest land trust in the United States.

http://www.ost.doi.gov/

The Cobell Settlement of the Claims Resolution Act of 2010

As trustee, the U.S. government approves leases and sales of natural resources on American Indian trust lands and is responsible for collecting payments on behalf of Indian owners. Over time, the federal government has collected billions of dollars from farming and grazing leases, oil and gas production, timber sales, and other assets on tribal lands.

In a lawsuit that became known as *Cobell v. Salazar*, the Native American Rights Fund (NARF) and other attorneys filed a lawsuit on behalf of Indian trust beneficiaries in 1996, charging that the federal government had breached its legally mandated trust responsibility for over one hundred years. The lawsuit was named for lead plaintiff Elouise Cobell, a widely recognized banker and leader from the Blackfeet Nation in Montana.

In 2010, President Barack Obama signed into law the Claims Resolution Act of 2010, which included the Cobell Settlement. The settlement resolved class action litigation over the U.S. government's oversight and accounting failures with respect to Indian trust funds.

Under the Cobell Settlement, the U.S. Department of the Interior is to distribute a fund of $1.4 billion to more than three hundred thousand Individual Indian Money (IIM) and other qualifying account holders or heirs. It also establishes a $2 billion fund for a land consolidation program, which includes college and vocational school scholarship funds for American Indian students. "This is truly an historic day in Indian Country as well as in America's history," Cobell said of the agreement. "By Congress placing a seal of approval on this settlement, a monumental step has been taken to remove a stain on our national honor" (McAllister 2010).

http://www.indiantrust.com

Settlement of Native American Farmers' Lawsuit against the U.S. Department of Agriculture

On April 30, 2011, Attorney General Eric Holder and Department of Agriculture (USDA) Secretary Tom Vilsack announced the U.S. District Court–approved settlement of *Keepseagle v. Vilsack*, a class action lawsuit filed against the USDA by Native American farmers on November 24, 1999.

Native farmers and ranchers claimed in the lawsuit that they had been denied USDA loans, resulting in the loss of hundreds of millions of dollars. Through the settlement, eligible members of the class would qualify for monetary compensation. The agreement also provides $80 million for forgiveness of farm debt for the Indian plaintiffs, as well as USDA initiatives aimed at the alleviation of racism against American Indians and other minorities in rural farm loan offices.

AWARDS

Eight Award-Winning Native Environmental Leaders

1. Matthew Coon Come (Cree)
   Matthew Coon Come, Grand Chief of the Grand Council of the Crees in Quebec, received a Goldman Environmental Prize in 1994. The prize recognized Coon Come's leadership in marshaling "local, national and international environmental, human rights and tribal communities to create a strong coalition" to stop a massive hydroelectric project on his people's land. The project, James Bay II, which would have caused irreversible damage to an immense watershed area, was slated to sell power to the states of New York, New Hampshire, Maine, and Vermont.
2. Billy Frank Jr. (Nisqually)
   Environmental leader and treaty rights activist Billy Frank Jr. has received numerous awards to honor him for his leadership and service, among

them the Common Cause Award (1985), Washington State Environmental Excellence Award (1987), American Indian Distinguished Service Award (1989), Martin Luther King Jr. Distinguished Service Award (1990), Albert Schweitzer Prize (1992), and the American Indian Visionary Award (2004) from *Indian Country Today.*

3, 4, and 5. Sarah James, Norma Kassi, and Jonathon Solomon (Gwich'in), lifetime members of the Gwich'in Steering Committee in Alaska, were recipients of the Goldman Prize in 2002 for their work to protect the Arctic National Wildlife Refuge from oil exploration, drilling, and other environmental threats.

6. Winona LaDuke (Anishinaabe)

The founding director of the White Earth Land Recovery Project (WELRP) on the White Earth Reservation in Minnesota, Winona LaDuke is the recipient of numerous awards for her work to recover land and protect the environment. In 1988, she received a Reebok Human Rights Award, with which she began the WELRP. In 1994, LaDuke was nominated by *Time* magazine as one of America's fifty most promising leaders under forty years of age. She has also been honored with the Thomas Merton Award (1996) and the Global Green USA Millennium Award (1998). LaDuke was inducted into the National Women's Hall of Fame in 2007. Her writings include the nonfiction book *All Our Relations: Native Struggles for Land and Life* (1999).

7. JoAnn Tall (Oglala Lakota)

JoAnn Tall was a recipient of the fourth annual Goldman Environmental Prize, the world's largest prize for grassroots environmentalists, in 1993. The mother of eight spent years working from her home on the Pine Ridge Reservation in South Dakota to raise awareness and take action against environmental abuses on tribal lands. Tall co-founded the Native Resource Coalition, which is dedicated to research and education on issues of land, health, and the environment. Tall's efforts included halting nuclear weapons testing in the Black Hills and preventing a proposed 5,000-acre landfill and incinerator site from being located on the Pine Ridge and Rosebud reservations.

8. Sheila Watt-Cloutier (Inuit)

Canadian activist Sheila Watt-Cloutier has received many honors for her tireless efforts on a range of environmental issues, including global warming and pollution threats, affecting Inuit regionally, nationally, and internationally. She has served as chair of the Inuit Circumpolar Council (ICC), an international nongovernmental organization representing some 150,000 Inuit of Alaska, Canada, Greenland, and Russia that holds consultative status II at the United Nations. Watt-Cloutier's awards include the Global Environmental Award, National Aboriginal Achievement Award, the Sophie Prize, Champion of the Earth Award, and International Environmental Leadership Award. In 2007 *The Globe and Mail* reported that Watt-Cloutier had been nominated for the 2007 Nobel Peace Prize.

Ecotrust Indigenous Leadership Award Honorees 2001–10

The Ecotrust Indigenous Leadership Award was founded by the families of Peter and Howard Buffett to honor outstanding individual leaders in the indigenous communities of Oregon, Washington, California, Western Montana, Nevada, Idaho, Alaska, and the Canadian provinces of British Columbia and the Yukon Territory. The honor is bestowed on those who work on issues that serve to improve the community's resource base, cultural base, economic security, or health and wellness. The award is a recognition program with endowed cash awards of $25,000 or $5,000.

http://www.ecotrust.org/indigenousleaders/honorees.html

2001	Susan Burdick
	Phillip Cash Cash
	David Hatch
	Dennis Martinez
2002	Kelly Brown
	Carol Craig
2003	Jeannette Armstrong
	Billy Frank Jr.
	Susan Masten
	Chief Nathan Matthew
2004	Clarence Alexander
	Ivan Jackson Sr.
	Sarah James
2005	Chairman W. Ron Allen
	Robi Michelle Craig
	Leaf Hillman
2006	Harold Gatensby
	Guujaaw
	Ilarion (Larry) Merculieff
2007	Roberta (Bobbie) Conner
	Carol Craig
	Alfred (Bud) Lane III
2009	Janeen Comenote
	James Manion
2010	Terry L. Cross
	Jessie Housty
	Kim Recalma-Clutesi
	Sandra Sunrising Osawa

Nuclear-Free Future Award, 1999–2010

http://www.nuclear-free.com/eng/recipients.htm#lark

The Nuclear-Free Future Award is an international prize given by the Franz Moll Foundation for the Coming Generations, based in Munich, Germany. Since 1998, it has honored and helped facilitate the ongoing work of individuals and groups to achieve a safe, sustainable future. American Indians from various tribal nations are among the laureates, honored for their work on behalf of Native lands and environments. Final selections for the prize, called "the most important anti-nuke award in the world," are determined by an international jury (Democracynow.org 2010).

1999	Dorothy Purley (Laguna Pueblo) "For her enduring struggle to make people aware of the toxic consequences of uranium mining and milling."
1999	Grace Thorpe (Sac and Fox Nation) "For her energetic anti-nuclear round-up of Indian Country to resist the creeping invasion of the nuclear industry."
2003	Corbin Harney (Western Shoshone) "For his enduring spiritual leadership and dogged perseverance in defending the sacred lands of the *Newe* from the aggressors of the Atomic Age."
2005	Joe Shirley Jr. and George Arthur (Navajo Nation) "For their passage of the Diné Resources Protection Act of 2005, a historic step assuring the preservation of their sovereign land for the generations to come." This legislation prohibits uranium mining and processing on any sites within Navajo Country.
2006	Phil Harrison (Navajo Nation) "For his many years of struggle as a visionary activist calling the uranium industry to account for its blind and poisonous greed."
2007	Charmaine White Face and Defenders of the Black Hills (Lakota) "For defending their sacred lands from further uranium mining debasement on behalf of the coming generations and all living creatures."
2008	Manuel Pino (Acoma Pueblo) "For his marathon endurance as an educator and activist fighting to preserve the sacred earth from the ravages of the uranium monster."
2010	Henry Red Cloud (Lakota Nation) "For his outstanding success in harvesting the energy of the prairie sun, helping to preserve the sacred *He Sapa* from the renewed threat of uranium mining."

HONORING NATIONS PROJECT, HARVARD UNIVERSITY

Honoring Nations Honorees, 1999–2006

Honoring Nations, a national awards program initiated in 1998, highlights outstanding programs in self-governance by Native nations. At the heart of the program is the belief that tribes themselves hold the key to positive social, political, cultural, and economic prosperity. Based at the John F. Kennedy School of Government at Harvard University, Honoring Nations is administered by the Harvard Project on American Indian Economic Development. The criteria for selection of honorees include program effectiveness, significance to sovereignty, cultural relevance, transferability, and sustainability. Honored programs are centered on land and environmental issues, including recovery and protection of vital resources.

Idaho Wolf Recovery Program, 1999
Wildlife Management Program, Nez Perce Tribe
Lapwai, ID
http://www.nezperce.org
> The Nez Perce Tribe developed the Idaho Wolf Recovery Program, initiating a plan that featured monitoring, outreach, species management and control, and research. The program, which met guidelines developed by the U.S. Fish and Wildlife Services, has resulted in an increased wolf population.

Water Quality Standards, 1999
Environment Department, Pueblo of Sandia
Bernalillo, New Mexico
> Addressing the severe contamination of the Rio Grande, the Pueblo of Sandia developed and implemented U.S. EPA–approved water quality standards, giving it control over local and regional water issues, as well as management of water quality improvement efforts. In 1997, the Pueblo received EPA's "Partnership in Environmental Excellence Award" for its success in developing an environmental management program to protect and manage tribal resources.

Cherokee Tribal Sanitation Program, 1999
Tribal Utilities, Eastern Band of Cherokee Indians
Cherokee, North Carolina
> The Eastern Band of Cherokee Indians developed a waste management system that included a tribally owned transfer station, waste collection and recycling, and bio-solids and food composting. This system, which also includes an education component, has enabled the tribe to shut down open dumps, coordinate efforts with neighboring counties, reduce levels of illegal dumping, and avoid the need for a tribal landfill.

Swinomish Cooperative Land Use Program, 2000
Office of Planning and Community Development, Swinomish Indian Tribal Community
LaConner, Washington

> The Swinomish Cooperative Land Use Program was an outcome of the first comprehensive planning effort attempted by a tribe and a county to address land use issues affecting both jurisdictions. The plan, created in 1990, articulated land use goals, established policies to guide land and resource stewardship, and outlined an implementation strategy. The program fosters a mutually beneficial government-to-government relationship, leading to other cooperative agreements with other jurisdictions.

White Mountain Apache Wildlife and Recreation Program, 2000
Wildlife and Outdoor Recreation Division, White Mountain Apache Tribe
Whiteriver, Arizona

> The White Mountain Apache Wildlife and Recreation Program has successfully fulfilled the dual role of performing wildlife conservation and management and serving as a business enterprise in connection with the tribe's recreation and tourism industry.

Safe Clean Waters, 2002
Lummi Tribal Sewer and Water District, Lummi Indian Nation
Bellingham, Washington

> The Lummi Tribal Sewer and Water District, governed by an elected board that includes two seats open to nontribal fee landowners, provides water, sanitary and sewer infrastructure, and service to some five thousand Indian and non-Indian residents living within the boundaries of the Lummi Indian Reservation. Adhering to strict health and environmental standards, the district reduced dependence on river withdrawals.

Umatilla Basin Salmon Recovery Project, 2002
Confederated Tribes of the Umatilla Indian Reservation
Pendleton, Oregon

> The Umatilla Basin Salmon Recovery Project has restored salmon to the Umatilla River while also protecting the local agriculture economy. Tribal efforts included partnering with local irrigators and community leaders, fish passage improvements, stream habitat enhancement, hatchery stations, and research.

Yakama Nation Land Enterprise, 2002
Confederated Tribes and Bands of the Yakama Nation
Toppenish, Washington

> A land purchase program of lands that were previously "checker-boarded," with alternating ownership patterns, made it possible for the Yakama Nation

to consolidate tribal fee-land areas for better management and use. The nation was then able to expand industrial, business, and agricultural activities.

Zuni Eagle Sanctuary, 2002
Zuni Fish and Wildlife Department, Pueblo of Zuni
Zuni, New Mexico
In 1999, the Pueblo of Zuni opened the first eagle sanctuary owned and operated by Native Americans. The facility provides a source of molted eagle feathers for ceremonial use while also reviving Zunis' ancient practices with respect to eagles.

Honoring Our Ancestors: The Chippewa Flowage Joint Agency Management Plan, 2003
Lac Courte Oreilles Band of Lake Superior Chippewa Indians
Hayward, Wisconsin
The Lac Courte Oreilles Band, the State of Wisconsin, and the U.S. Department of Agriculture Forest Service co-manage the Chippewa Flowage, a 15,300-acre reservoir that inundated a tribal community when it was created in 1923. The management plan provides a framework for the three governmental entities to coordinate management activities.

The Hopi Land Team, 2005
Office of the Chairman, The Hopi Tribe
Kykotsmovi, Arizona
The Hopi Tribe created the Hopi Land Team, a committee of the tribal council, as part of the effort to reclaim traditional lands. The team's work includes identifying potential purchases, evaluating their cultural and economic significance and potential, and recommending purchasing actions. The work contributes to new development initiatives, as well as helping to return critical resources and sites back to the Hopi.

Miccosukee Tribe Section 404 Permitting Program, 2005
Real Estate Services, Miccosukee Tribe of Indians of Florida
Miami, Florida
The Miccosukee Tribe of Indians of Florida contracted with the U.S. Environmental Protection Agency to issue land permits, enforce environmental codes, and manage permit violations on reservation lands, which are located primarily within Everglades National Park. The permitting program streamlined the regulatory process for tribal citizens, reducing the maze of regulations by a host of federal agencies pertaining to requirements for home improvement projects and other activities.

Yukon River Inter-Tribal Watershed Council, 2005
Koyukon and Gwich'in Athabascan, Yupik, and Tlingit

Fairbanks, Alaska

http://www.yritwc.org/

> Representing sixty Native nations in Alaska and Canada, the Yukon River Inter-Tribal Watershed Council monitors thousands of miles of the Yukon River and millions of acres of land in an effort to increase water quality and environmental standards within an enormous ecosystem. The council provides a model of partnership among diverse peoples determined to preserve their lands and life-ways.

Red Lake Walleye Recovery Program, 2006

Red Lake Band of Chippewa Indians

Red Lake, Minnesota

> The Red Lake Walleye Recovery Program has brought the walleye population back from near extinction to recovered levels in less than a decade.

FILMS

American Outrage (USA, 2007, 56 min.), directed by Beth Gage and George Gage.
> This film tells the story of sisters Carrie and Mary Dann and their fight for Western Shoshone land rights and tribal sovereignty against unlawful federal and corporate violations of the 1863 Treaty of Ruby Valley.

Backbone of the World: The Blackfeet (USA, 1997, 57 min.), directed by George Burdeau (Blackfeet).
> This documentary explores the significance of their history and land for today's Blackfeet tribal members through the lens of a filmmaker returning home to his tribe and organizing a community filmmaking workshop.

The Border Crossed Us (USA, 2005, 26 min.), directed by Rachael J. Nez (Navajo).
> The Tohono O'odham have always freely crossed borders between their communities in the United States and Mexico, but current immigration and naturalization policy are jeopardizing their ancient way of life.

Hidden Medicine (USA, 2000, 23 min.), directed by Robby Romero.
> Set in Onondaga Nation Territory in New York, with appearances by Chief Oren Lyons and Clan Mother Audrey Shenandoah, *Hidden Medicine* explores the relationship between Native peoples and the environment. Romero, the founder of Native rock group Red Thunder and nonprofit organization Native Children's Survival, also produced *America's Last Frontier*, a 2002 film/music project in support of the Gwich'in people of Alaska's North Slope and their opposition to oil drilling in the Arctic National Wildlife Refuge.

Home (USA, 2005, 7 min.), directed by Dustinn Craig (White Mountain Apache/Navajo).
> In this film, Apache, Tohono O'odham, Navajo, and members of other southwestern tribal nations discuss their connections to their homelands and what the concept of home means to them. The film was created for *HOME: Native People of the Southwest*, an exhibition at the Heard Museum in Phoenix, Arizona.

Homeland: Four Portraits of Native Action (USA, 2005, 90 min.), directed by Roberta Grossman.

> This film tells the story of Native activists and their battle to protect Native lands, preserve tribal sovereignty, and ensure cultural survival. The individuals and their respective tribal nations include Mitchell and Rita Capitan (Navajo), Barry Dana (Penobscot), Evon Peter (Gwich'in), and Gail Small (Northern Cheyenne).

In the Light of Reverence (USA, 2000, 72 min.), produced and directed by Christopher McLeod and Malinda M. Maynor (Lumbee).

> This film depicts the struggle of three Native groups to protect lands of religious significance, among them the Lakota at Devils Tower in Wyoming, the Hopi in the Four Corners of the Southwest, and the Wintu at Mount Shasta in California, from environmental threats and outside intrusion. The use of these sites for resource extraction as well as recreation and tourism poses a threat to Native religious practices.

Kaho'olawe (USA, 1997, 57 min.), directed by David H. Kalama Jr. (Native Hawaiian).

> This documentary chronicles the efforts of Native Hawaiians to recover their sacred island Kaho'olawe, an area that had been used as a military bombing range. The struggle often incorporated traditional Native Hawaiian ceremony, dance, and oratory.

The Last Days of Shishmaref (Netherlands/USA, 2008, 95 min.), directed by Jan Louter.

> This award-winning documentary chronicles the impact of global warming on the lives of several families in the village of Shishmaref, located on the barrier island of Sarichef, off Alaska's Seward Peninsula. Filmed in English and Inupiaq with English subtitles, the filmmaker reveals how rising temperatures lead to the destruction of the villagers' homes and sea-based way of life, culminating in relocation.

March Point (USA, 2008, 57 min.), directed by Annie Silverstein.

> This film follows the journey of three teenagers from the Swinomish Reservation in Washington State and their response to being asked to make a film about the threat their people face from two oil refineries that were built in an area of land that once belonged to the tribe by treaty.

Paatuwaqatsi: Water, Land and Life (USA, 2007, 60 min.), directed by Victor Masayesva Jr. (Hopi).

> This documentary follows a 78-year-old man and a 14-year-old girl as they participate in a run on the two-thousand-mile-route to the Fourth World Water Forum in Mexico City in 2006. The work highlights the message "Water Is Life," conveyed through the ancient tradition of running.

Qapirangajuq: Inuit Knowledge and Climate Change (Canada, 2010, 54 min.), directed by Zacharias Kunuk (Inuit) and Ian Mauro.

The filmmakers document the knowledge and experience of Inuit communities regarding climate change, creating the world's first Inuktitut language film on the topic. They take viewers on a journey with elders and hunters to explore the social and ecological impact of a warming Arctic. The film centers on Inuit expertise concerning environmental change and indigenous ways of adapting to it.

Return of the Red Lake Walleye (USA, 2010, 28 min.), directed by Ian W. Record.
A Native Nations Institute film, *Return of the Red Lake Walleye* documents the efforts of the Red Lake Band of Chippewa Indians, working with the State of Minnesota and the federal government, to restore culturally vital walleye to health in Red Lake. It examines how government cooperation helped forge innovative public policy solutions to make a significant difference for the people.

River of Renewal (USA, 2009, 57 min.), directed by Carlos Bolado.
Eight years in the making, this film examines the water and wildlife crisis in the Klamath basin in northern California and Oregon. It chronicles the impact on communities that harvest food from the Klamath River and offshore, including the collapse of wild salmon populations and the lack of enough water to serve irrigation and fishery needs.

The Salt Song Trail: A Living Documentary (USA, 2009, 25 min.), directed by Cara McCoy and Bridget Sandate.
This film documents Salt Songs, the sacred songs of the Nuwuvi (Southern Paiute) peoples of California, Utah, Arizona, and Nevada, which describe ancient landscapes of the people, such as early villages, hunting grounds, gathering places, and sacred sites. Reflecting a cultural and spiritual bond between the Nuwuvi and the land, the Salt Songs represent renewal and healing.

Trespassing (USA, 2005, 116 min.), directed by Carlos DeMenezes.
This film examines issues surrounding land rights, uranium mining, nuclear testing, and the disposal of nuclear waste in the Four Corners area, Nevada's Yucca Mountain, and California's Mojave Desert. It documents the perilous struggle of indigenous activists and others to protect Native lands, the air, and the water from further desecration.

Waterbuster (USA, 2006, 8 min.), directed by J. Carlos Peinado (Mandan/Hidatsa).
The filmmaker investigates the impact of the Garrison Dam project of the 1950s on the upper Missouri River basin in North Dakota, the indigenous homeland of his people. The massive project laid waste to a self-sufficient tribal community, submerged 156,000 acres of fertile land, and displaced members of North Dakota's Fort Berthold Indian Reservation.

We Live by the River (USA and Canada, 2009, 52 min.), directed by Karin Williams.
This film depicts the work of First Nations communities in the Yukon River basin in Canada to restore the watershed and wildlife damaged by years of

mining and other activities. The winner of the Denali Award at the 2010 Alaska International Film Festival, *We Live by the River* demonstrates the power of grassroots environmental movements to make a global impact.

Yukon Circles (USA, 2006, 30 min.) directed by Karin Williams.

This film documents how the 2,300-mile Yukon River, which flows through Canada and Alaska, is threatened by pollution from a variety of sources, including mining and manufacturing. To help address the problem, tribes and First Nations develop a historic agreement to work together to protect the river.

ORGANIZATIONS

Columbia River Inter-Tribal Fish Commission (CRITFC)

http://www.critfc.org/

The Columbia River Inter-Tribal Fish Commission (CRITFC) consists of the Warm Springs, Yakama, Umatilla, and Nez Perce tribes, who joined together in 1977 to renew their authority in fisheries management on the Columbia River. Headquartered in Portland, Oregon, CRITFC is a coordinating and technical organization to support the individual and joint exercise of sovereign authority of the member tribes.

Council of Energy Resource Tribes (CERT)

http://74.63.154.129/aboutus-philosophyHistory.html

Headquartered in Denver, Colorado, the Council of Energy Resource Tribes (CERT) was founded in 1975 by tribal leaders to support member tribes in managing, developing, and sustaining long-term energy goals. CERT's goal is to help build strong self-governed economies according to each member tribe's vision and priority.

Council of Large Land Based Tribes (CLLBT)

http://mtwytlc.org/tlc-programs/large-land-based-tribes.html

Co-founded by Montana state senator Jonathan Windy Boy (Chippewa-Cree) in 2001, the Council of Large Land Based Tribes (CLLBT) was established to advocate for the needs of tribal nations with large land bases (over 100,000 acres) and populations.

Great Lakes Indian Fish and Wildlife Commission (GLIFWC)

http://www.glifwc.org/

Formed in 1984, the Great Lakes Indian Fish and Wildlife Commission is an agency of eleven Ojibwe nations in Minnesota, Wisconsin, and Michigan, with off-reservation treaty rights to hunt, fish, and gather in treaty-ceded lands. GLIFWC, which has its main office on the Bad River Reservation in Wisconsin, assists member nations in the implementation of off-reservation treaty seasons and in the protection of treaty rights and natural resources.

Indian Land Tenure Foundation (ILTF)
http://www.iltf.org/

The work of the Indian Land Tenure Foundation (ILTF) began in the 1990s, when a group of Native landowners, land rights advocates, and tribal leaders met to address serious issues affecting American Indian land tenure. Created in 2002, the ILTF is headquartered in Little Canada, Minnesota, where it works toward the goals of land recovery and increased Indian ownership and control of land and assets.

Indigenous Environmental Network (IEN)
http://www.ienearth.org/

Established in 1990, the Indigenous Environmental Network (IEN) works to foster the capacity of Native communities and tribal governments to protect sacred sites, land, water, air, natural resources, and health of all living things. Headquartered in Bemidji, Minnesota, with field offices in Alaska and other states, IEN provides support, resources, and referrals to communities in North America and, in recent years, around the world.

International Institute for Indigenous Resource Management (IIIRM)
http://www.iiirm.org/

Established in Denver, Colorado, in 1997, the International Institute for Indigenous Resource Management is a law and policy research institute. Working with a small cadre of attorneys, the IIIRM's efforts include projects designed to empower Native peoples by examining the role the law can play in establishing and enhancing indigenous control over and management of lands and resources.

InterTribal Buffalo Cooperative (ITBC)
http://www.itbcbison.com/

Officially established in 1992, the InterTribal Buffalo (Bison formerly) Cooperative (ITBC) is a nonprofit tribal organization dedicated to reestablishing buffalo herds on American Indian lands in a manner that fosters cultural and spiritual revitalization, ecological restoration, and economic development. ITBC is headquartered in Rapid City, South Dakota, and its activities include coordinating education and training programs, developing marketing strategies, coordinating the transfer of surplus buffalo from national parks to tribal lands, and providing technical assistance to member tribes.

Intertribal Timber Council (ITC)
http://www.itcnet.org/

Established in 1976, the Intertribal Timber Council (ITC) is a nonprofit nationwide consortium of Indian tribes, Alaska Native corporations, and individuals dedicated to improving the management of natural resources of importance to Native American communities. Located in Portland, Oregon, the ITC has grown to over sixty tribes and Alaska Native corporations.

Inuit Circumpolar Council (ICC)

http://inuitcircumpolar.com

http://www.iccalaska.org/servlet/content/home.html

The Inuit Circumpolar Council, which was founded in 1977 by Eben Hopson of Barrow, Alaska, has grown into a major international nongovernmental organization representing approximately 155,000 Inuit of Alaska, Canada, Greenland, and Russia. The ICC holds consultative status II at the United Nations. ICC's goals include developing and encouraging long-term policies that safeguard the Arctic environment. Inuit Circumpolar Council-Alaska (ICC-AK), headquartered in Anchorage, represents Inuit from Alaska at this international forum.

National Tribal Air Association (NTAA)

http://www.ntaatribalair.org/

Founded in 2002, the National Tribal Air Association works to advance air quality issues, consistent with the needs, interests, and unique legal status of American Indian tribes and Alaska Natives. The NTAA is headquartered in Albuquerque, New Mexico, and has a membership of more than fifty principal member tribes.

National Tribal Environmental Council (NTEC)

http://www.ntec.org

The National Tribal Environmental Council (NTEC) was formed in 1991 with seven tribes and input from tribal organizations such as the Council of Energy Resource Tribes and the Native American Rights Fund as a membership organization to address environmental issues. NTEC's mission is to support American Indian tribes and Alaska Native villages in protecting, regulating, and managing their environmental resources according to their own priorities and values. The NTEC, located in Albuquerque, New Mexico, is open to any federally recognized tribe and its membership has grown to over 185 tribes.

Native American Fish and Wildlife Society (NAFWS)

http://www.nafws.org/

Incorporated in 1983, the Native American Fish and Wildlife Society is a national nonprofit organization that works to assist Native American and Alaska Native tribes with the conservation, protection, and enhancement of their fish and wildlife resources. Headquartered in Denver, Colorado, the society has both individual and tribal memberships.

Native American Land Conservancy
http://nalc4all.org/
> Founded in 1998 and located in California, the Native American Land Conservancy is an intertribal organization dedicated to the protective management of endangered Native American sacred sites and areas. NALC's work has included acquiring threatened cultural landscapes, forming cooperative agreements with tribes, public agencies, and conservation groups, and organizing conferences to promote the preservation of Native America's sacred lands.

Native American Rights Fund (NARF)
http://www.narf.org/
> Founded in 1970, the Native American Rights Fund is the oldest and largest nonprofit law firm dedicated to assisting and defending the rights of Indian tribes, organizations, and individuals nationwide. NARF is headquartered in Boulder, Colorado, with branch offices in Washington, DC, and Anchorage, Alaska. Its key areas of practice include the protection of tribal natural resources.

Northwest Indian Fisheries Commission (NWIFC)
http://www.nwifc.org/
> The Northwest Indian Fisheries Commission is a support service organization for twenty Indian tribes in western Washington. Headquartered in Olympia, the NWIFC was created following the 1974 *U.S. v. Washington* ruling (Boldt Decision) that reaffirmed the tribes' treaty-reserved fishing rights and established them as natural resource co managers with the State of Washington.

RESOURCES

Banner, Stuart. *How the Indians Lost Their Land: Law and Power on the Frontier.* Cambridge, MA: Belknap Press of Harvard University Press, 2005.

Blackhawk, Ned. *Violence over the Land: Indians and Empires in the Early American West.* Cambridge, MA: Harvard University Press, 2006.

Blue Spruce, Duane, and Tanya Thrasher, eds. *The Land Has Memory: Indigenous Knowledge, Native Landscapes, and the National Museum of the American Indian.* Chapel Hill: University of North Carolina Press/National Museum of the American Indian, Smithsonian Institution, 2008.

Democracynow.org. "Henry Red Cloud of Oglala Lakota Tribe on Native American Anti-Nuclear Activism, Uranium Mining, and the Recession's Toll on Reservations." 2010. Available at http://www.democracynow.org/2010/9/30/henry_red_cloud_of_oglala_lakota

EDS. *DOI Trust Reform As-Is Trust Business Model Report.* March 21, 2003. Available at http://www.doi.gov/ost/trust_reform/ASIS/03%20Chapter%202.pdf

Gonzalez, Mario, and Elizabeth Cook-Lynn. *The Politics of Hallowed Ground: Wounded Knee and the Struggle for Indian Sovereignty.* Urbana and Chicago: University of Illinois Press, 1998.

Grinde, Donald A., and Bruce E. Johansen. *Ecocide of Native America: Environmental Destruction of Indian Lands and Peoples.* Santa Fe, NM: Clear Light Books, 1994.

Hirst, Stephen. *I Am the Grand Canyon: The Story of the Havasupai People.* Grand Canyon, AZ: Grand Canyon Association, 2007.

Kaha'ulelio, Daniel. *Ka 'Oihana Lawai'a: Hawaiian Fishing Traditions.* Edited by Puakea Nogelmeier. Translated by Mary Kawena Pukui. Honolulu: Bishop Museum Press, 2006.

Kame'eleihiwa, Lilikala. *Native Land and Foreign Desires: Pehea La E Pono Ai? How Shall We Live in Harmony?* Honolulu: Bishop Museum Press, 1992.

Kennedy, Frances H. *American Indian Places: A Historical Guidebook.* New York: Houghton Mifflin, 2008.

LaDuke, Winona. *All Our Relations: Native Struggles for Land and Life.* Boston: South End Press, 1999.

McAllister, Bill. "Elouise Cobell Hails Historic Vote to Resolve Trust Case." *Native American Times,* November 30, 2010.

Most, Stephen. *River of Renewal: Myth and History in the Klamath Basin.* Portland: Oregon Historical Society Press, 2006.

O'Brien, Jean M. *Dispossession by Degrees: Indian Land and Identity in Natick, Massachusetts, 1650–1790.* New York: Cambridge University Press, 1997.

Pratt, Kenneth L., ed. *Chasing the Dark: Perspectives on Place, History and Alaska Native Land Claims.* Anchorage: U.S. Department of the Interior, Bureau of Indian Affairs, Alaska Region, Division of Environmental and Cultural Resources Management, ANCSA Office, 2009.

Ruppel, Kristin T. *Unearthing Indian Land: Living with the Legacies of Allotment.* Tucson: University of Arizona Press, 2008.

Smith, Bruce L. *Wildlife on the Wind: A Field Biologist's Journey and an Indian Reservation's Renewal.* Logan: Utah State University Press, 2010.

Spence, Mark David. *Dispossessing the Wilderness: Indian Removal and the Making of the National Parks.* New York: Oxford University Press, 1999.

Sutton, Imre, ed. *Irredeemable America: The Indians' Estate and Land Claims.* Albuquerque: Native American Studies, University of New Mexico, 1985.

Tiller, Veronica E. Velarde. *Tiller's Guide to Indian Country: Economic Profiles of American Indian Reservations.* Albuquerque, NM: Bow Arrow Publishing Company, 2005.

Ulrich, Roberta. *Indians, Dams, and the Columbus River,* 2nd edition. Corvallis: Oregon State University Press, 2007.

Warhus, Mark. *Another America: Native American Maps and the History of Our Land.* New York: St. Martin's Press, 1997.

Wildcat, Daniel R. *Red Alert! Saving the Planet with Indigenous Knowledge.* Golden, CO: Fulcrum Publishing, 2009.

Wilkinson, Charles F. *Messages from Frank's Landing: A Story of Salmon, Treaties, and the Indian Way.* Seattle: University of Washington Press, 2000.

Willis, John. *Views from the Reservation.* Chicago: Center for American Places/Columbia College Chicago, 2010.

Web Sites

American Indian Environmental Office Tribal Portal—U.S. Environmental Protection Agency: http://www.epa.gov/indian/index.htm

American Indians and Alaska Natives: A Guide to USDA Programs: http://www.usda.gov/documents/AmerIndianNativeAlaskGuide-07%2011%2007.pdf

Buffalo Field Campaign: http://www.buffalofieldcampaign.org/

Bureau of Indian Affairs, Division of Natural Resources: http://www.bia.gov/WhatWeDo/ServiceOverview/LandWater-Resources/index.htm

The Cultural Conservancy: http://www.nativeland.org/

Ecotrust: http://www.ecotrust.org/

Forest Service National Resource Guide to American Indian and Alaska Native Relations: http://www.fs.fed.us/people/tribal/

Harvard Project's Honoring Nations Directory of Honored Programs, 1999–2006: http://hpaied.org./images/resources/general/Dir_web.pdf

Indian Country Renewable Energy Consortium (ICREC): http://www.tribesandclimatechange.org/documents/nccc/nccc20110105_0109.pdf

Indian Land Cessions in the United States, 1784–1894. U.S. Congressional Documents: http://memory.loc.gov/ammem/amlaw/lwss-ilc.html

Indian Trust Settlement: http://indiantrust.com/

Intertribal Agriculture Council: http://www.indianaglink.com

Inter-Tribal Environmental Council: http://www.itecmembers.org/

Native Americans and the Environment: http://www.cnie.org/NAE/index.html

Native Geographies and Counter-mapping Links: http://academic.evergreen.edu/g/grossmaz/Countermapping.html

Office of the Special Trustee for American Indians: http://www.doi.gov/ost/

Our Natural Resources (ONR): http://www.ournaturalresources.org/

Presidential Signing Statement: Bill Creating the Indian Claims Commission, August 13, 1946: http://www.presidency.ucsb.edu/ws/index.php?pid=12495#axzz1WvZM1LgG

Tribal Energy and Environmental Information Clearinghouse: http://teeic.anl.gov/

U.S. Department of Agriculture Natural Resources Conservation Service: http://www.nrcs.usda.gov/wps/portal/nrcs/main/national/people/outreach/tribal

U.S. Department of the Interior Bureau of Land Management: http://www.blm.gov/wo/st/en/prog/more/CRM/tribal_consultation.html

U.S. Geological Survey Office of Tribal Relations: http://www.usgs.gov/indian/

White Earth Land Recovery Project, Callaway, Minnesota: http://nativeharvest.com/

7

Health

FIRSTS

1832   The U.S. Congress enacted the Indian Vaccination Act, the first piece of federal legislation designed to address an American Indian health problem, epidemic smallpox. The legislation enabled the government to vaccinate approximately forty to fifty thousand American Indians.

1889   The first two American Indians to become physicians graduated from medical school:
    Carlos Montezuma (Yavapai) graduated from Northwestern University's Chicago Medical College in Illinois. Following his work as a physician for the Office of Indian Affairs (1889 to 1896) and in private practice (1896 to 1922), he created the newspaper, *Wassaja.*
    Susan LaFlesche Picotte (Omaha), the first Native American woman to become a medical doctor, graduated from the Women's Medical College of Pennsylvania at the top of her class. In August 1889, she returned home to the Omaha Reservation in Nebraska, where she served as a physician.

1890   Charles Alexander Eastman (Santee Sioux), who graduated from Boston University School of Medicine in 1890, became the first American Indian agency physician on the Pine Ridge Reservation in Dakota Territory (present-day South Dakota). He tended to the wounded in the aftermath of the U.S. Army's attack on Big Foot's peaceful band at Wounded Knee.

1898   The first four American Indian women documented to be U.S. Army nurses arrived in Cuba to provide nursing services to soldiers during the Spanish-American War. Lakota nuns from reservations in Dakota Territory, they included Susan Bordeaux (the Reverend Mother M. Anthony), Ella Clark (the Reverend Sister M. Gertrude), Anna B. Pleets (the Reverend Mother M. Bridget), and Josephine Two Bears (the Reverend Sister M. Joseph).

1912   A hospital on the Omaha Indian Reservation in Nebraska, which was constructed as a facility for Dr. Susan LaFlesche Picotte (Omaha) and completed in 1913, was the first hospital built on an Indian reservation with funding from private sources.

1913   The first national study of American Indian health was conducted by the Public Health Service, and its report, *Contagious and Infectious Diseases among the Indians*, was issued to Congress.

1921   The Bureau of Indian Affairs Health Division, the forerunner to the Indian Health Service, was created.

1930   Sage Memorial Hospital School of Nursing on the Navajo Reservation in Arizona was founded, becoming the first and only accredited nursing program for Native American women in the United States. Closed in 1951, the facility was designated a U.S. National Historic Landmark in 2008.

1935   The Kiowa School of Practical Nursing in Lawton, Oklahoma, marked the first organized effort by the Indian Service to train American Indian women as nurses or nursing aides.

1956   James W. Hampton (Chickasaw/Choctaw), who graduated from the University of Oklahoma Medical School, became the first oncologist in the nation. In 2008, he and Dr. Judith Salmon Kaur (Choctaw/Cherokee) were identified as the only two oncologists in the country who are members of an Indian tribe.
         George Blue Spruce Jr. (Laguna/Ohkay Owingeh Pueblo) became the first American Indian dentist upon his graduation from dental school.

1963   Annie Dodge Wauneka (Navajo), who worked tirelessly to improve the health of her people, was the first Native American to receive a Presidential Medal of Freedom. It was awarded during the John F. Kennedy administration and presented by President Lyndon B. Johnson.

1966   Arthur McDonald (Oglala Lakota), who graduated from the University of South Dakota, was the first American Indian man to earn a PhD in psychology. In 2000, he was awarded the American Psychological Association's Presidential Citation in recognition of his "tireless efforts to gain increased psychological services to American Indians and Alaska Natives and other underserved populations in rural areas."

1969   The Indian Health Board of Minneapolis, the first urban health care program in the U.S. for Native people, was established.

1971   Bill F. Pearson (Choctaw) became the first Native American to serve as director of an Indian Health Service Sanitation Facilities Construction Program (for the Navajo Area).

1976   The Puyallup Tribal Health Authority in Washington was the first ambulatory health clinic to enter into a contract with the Indian Health Service through the Indian Self-Determination and Education Assistance Act of 1975.

Ted Mala (Inupiaq), who received his Doctor of Medicine and Surgery (MD) degree from the Autonomous University of Guadalajara in 1976, was the first Alaska Native to become a medical doctor. Dr. Mala also earned a Master of Public Health degree from Harvard University in 1980 and became the first Alaska Native Commissioner of Health and Social Services in 1990.

1978   Established by the Ramah Navajo School Board, Inc., Pine Hill Health Center in Pine Hill, New Mexico, became the first community-controlled health care system in the United States under the Indian Self-Determination and Education Assistance Act of 1975.

1979   The first formal Indian Health Service (IHS) policy affirming the importance of traditional Native healing was issued by the IHS director.

Connie Redbird Pinkerman-Uri (Choctaw/Cherokee) became the first Native American woman to hold degrees in both medicine (MD, University of Arkansas, 1955) and law (JD, Whittier College, 1979).

Jessica A. Rickert (Prairie Band Potawatomi) was the first American Indian woman to become a dentist.

1982   Everett R. Rhoades, MD (Kiowa), became the first American Indian director of the Indian Health Service (IHS). He served as the last director of the Bureau of Indian Health Service under the Health Resources and Services Administration and later, in 1988, as the first agency director when the IHS became an agency of the Public Health Service.

1992   The Porcupine Clinic, the first community-owned and operated clinic on a reservation, achieved state certification as a rural health facility. Located on the Pine Ridge Reservation in South Dakota, it was cofounded by Lorelei DeCora (Winnebago).

1993   Anna Albert, director of the Phoenix Indian Medical Center in Arizona, became the first Native American female and the first non-physician to direct any of the three Indian medical centers in the nation.

1994   Michael H. Trujillo, MD (Laguna Pueblo), became the first president-appointed and Senate-confirmed director of the Indian Health Service of the Department of Health and Human Services.

1995   The American Indian Program at Northern Arizona University School of Nursing became the first reservation-based baccalaureate program in nursing in the United States.

1997   Dr. Linda Burhansstipanov (Western Cherokee) became the first Native American to receive the American Public Health Association's Award for Excellence, which recognizes exceptionally meritorious contributions to the improvement of the health of the people.

2000   Michael E. Bird (Santo Domingo and San Juan Pueblo) became the first American Indian and the first social worker to serve as president of the American Public Health Association.

2002   Susie Walking Bear Yellowtail (Crow) became the first American Indian nurse named to the American Nursing Association's Hall of Fame.

2009   Yvette Roubideaux, MD (Rosebud Sioux), became the first woman to lead the Indian Health Service (IHS). Dr. Roubideaux was confirmed by the U.S. Senate as IHS director on May 6 and sworn in on May 12, 2009.

First Treaty Health Provision, Treaty with the Winnebago, September 15, 1832

Concluded at Rock Island, Illinois, the Treaty with the Winnebago was the first treaty to include a provision for health care.

Article V of the Treaty:
"And the United States further agree to make to the said nation of Winnebago Indians the following allowances, for the period of twenty-seven years, in addition to the considerations herein before stipulated; that is to say: for the support of six agriculturalists, and the purchase of twelve yokes of oxen, ploughs, and other agricultural implements, a sum not exceeding two thousand five hundred dollars per annum; to the Rock River band of Winnebagoes, one thousand five hundred pounds of tobacco, per annum; for the services and attendance of a physician at Prairie du Chien, and of one at Fort Winnebago, each, two hundred dollars, per annum."

U.S. INDIAN HEALTH SERVICE

Indian Health Service Area Offices

The Indian Health Service (IHS) began on July 1, 1955, following the transfer of Native American health services from the Bureau of Indian Affairs to the Public Health Service (now Health and Human Services). The IHS provides health services to approximately 1.9 million American Indians and

Alaska Natives belonging to 564 federally recognized tribes in thirty-five states. The agency is divided into twelve geographic regions called "Area Offices," which provide administrative support to the facilities and personnel within their respective jurisdictions.

Area	Service Area
1. Aberdeen	North Dakota, South Dakota, Iowa, and Nebraska
2. Alaska	State of Alaska
3. Albuquerque	New Mexico, Colorado, and Texas
4. Bemidji	Indiana, Minnesota, Michigan, and Wisconsin
5. Billings	Montana and Wyoming
6. California	California and Hawaii
7. Nashville	Eastern United States
8. Navajo	Arizona, New Mexico, and Utah
9. Oklahoma	Oklahoma, Kansas, and Texas
10. Phoenix	Arizona, California, Nevada, and Utah
11. Portland	Idaho, Oregon, and Washington
12. Tucson	Southern Arizona

Indian Health Service Urban Indian Health Programs

Urban Indian Health Programs (UIHP), which number thirty-four nonprofit programs nationwide, are funded through Indian Health Service (IHS) grants and contracts under Title V of the Indian Health Care Improvement Act, P.L. 94-437, as amended. The funding level is estimated at 22 percent of the projected need for primary care services. Eighteen additional cities have been identified as having urban Indian populations large enough to support an UIHP. http://www.ihs.gov/nonmedicalprograms/urban/Urban_index.asp

Aberdeen Area

South Dakota Urban Indian Health, Inc.	Pierre, SD
Nebraska Urban Indian Health Coalition, Inc.	Omaha, NE

Albuquerque Area

Denver Indian Health and Family Services	Denver, CO
First Nations Community Healthsource	Albuquerque, NM

Bemidji Area

Indian Health Board of Minneapolis, Inc.	Minneapolis, MN
American Indian Health and Family Services of Southeastern Michigan	Detroit, MI
Green Bay, WI*	Green Bay, WI
Gerald L. Ignace Indian Health Center, Inc.	Milwaukee, WI
American Indian Health Service of Chicago, Inc.	Chicago, IL

Billings Area

Indian Health Board of Billings	Billings, MT
North American Indian Alliance	Butte, MT

Helena Indian Alliance   Helena, MT
Indian Family Health Clinic   Great Falls, MT
Missoula Indian Center   Missoula, MT

California Area
American Indian Health Project Bakersfield   Bakersfield, CA
Native American Health Center, Inc.   Oakland, CA
Sacramento Native American Health Center   Sacramento, CA
Indian Health Center of Santa Clara Valley   San Jose, CA
American Indian Health and Services Corporation   Santa Barbara, CA
San Diego American Indian Health Center   San Diego, CA
United American Indian Involvement, Inc.   Los Angeles, CA
United American Indian Involvement, Inc.   Fresno, CA

Nashville Area
American Indian Community House, Inc.   New York, NY
North American Indian Center of Boston, Inc.   Jamaica Plain, MA

Navajo Area
Native Americans for Community Action   Flagstaff, AZ

Oklahoma City Area
Urban Inter-Tribal Center of Texas   Dallas, TX
Hunter Health Clinic   Wichita, KS

Phoenix Area
Nevada Urban Indians, Inc.   Reno, NV
Native American Community Health Center, Inc.   Phoenix, AZ
Indian Walk-In Center   Salt Lake City, UT

Portland Area
Seattle Indian Health Board   Seattle, WA
Native American Rehabilitation Association of   Portland, OR
the Northwest, Inc.
NATIVE Project   Spokane, WA

Tucson Area
Tucson Indian Center   Tucson, AZ

*IHS is currently seeking a contractor for this site.

2010 "IHS Per Capita Expenditures and Other Federal Health Care Per Capita Expenditures"

Medicare spending per beneficiary	$11,018	2009
Veterans medical spending per user	$7,154	2010
National health expenditures per capita	$6,909	2010

Medicaid spending per enrollee	$5,841	2008
Federal employee health benefits per enrollee	$4,817	2009
Indian Health Service spending per user—all	$3,348	2010
Indian Health Service spending per user—medical care	$2,741	2010

Source: U.S. Department of Health and Human Services, National Tribal Budget Recommendations for the Indian Health Service, Fiscal Year 2013 Budget: http://www.nihb.org/docs/03282011/FY%202013%20National%20Tribal%20Budget%20Recommendations_Final.pdf

National Congress of American Indians Resolution

"The National Congress of American Indians does hereby declare a State of Emergency for Indian health programs; and . . . urge(s) Congress to provide emergency funding to deal with the Indian Health Care Crisis. . ."

NCAI Resolution PHX-08-030, October 2008

DEATH AND ILLNESS AMONG NATIVE AMERICANS

Ten Leading Causes of Death among American Indians and Alaska Natives

According to the Office of Minority Health and Health Disparities (OMHD), an office of the Centers for Disease Control and Prevention (CDC), the ten leading causes of death among American Indians and Alaska Natives in the United States ranged from heart disease to influenza and pneumonia in 2007. http://www.cdc.gov/omhd/Populations/AIAN/AIAN.htm#Ten

1. Heart disease
2. Cancer
3. Unintentional injuries
4. Diabetes
5. Chronic liver disease and cirrhosis
6. Chronic lower respiratory disease
7. Stroke
8. Suicide
9. Nephritis, nephrotic syndrome, and nephrosis
10. Influenza and pneumonia

The Impact of Epidemics

American Indian populations, susceptible to European diseases for which they had no immunity, were decimated following colonization. Large-scale epidemics and wartime fatalities resulted in immense demographic losses over time. By the end of the nineteenth century, declining Native population figures seemed to support the notion of a vanishing race. The U.S. Census counted only 248,253 Indians in 1890 and 237,196 in 1900, precipitous drops from earlier periods, such as a count of 400,764 in 1850. After 1900, the population began to recover, and by 1938, Commissioner of Indian Affairs John Collier reported that Indians were "no longer a dying race."

Health Disparities

According to Indian Health Service figures (based on 2004–6 rates), American Indians and Alaska Natives die at higher rates than other Americans from tuberculosis (500 percent higher), alcoholism (514 percent higher), diabetes (177 percent higher), unintentional injuries (140 percent higher), homicide (92 percent higher), and suicide (82 percent higher). http://info.ihs.gov/Disparities.asp

The American Psychiatric Association (APA) Office of Minority and National Affairs, in a 2010 fact sheet on mental health disparities, indicates that American Indians and Alaska Natives (AI/AN) experience serious psychological distress 1.5 times more than the general population, with a high prevalence of depression, substance abuse disorders, suicide, and anxiety (including post traumatic stress disorder). The APA Office of Minority and National Affairs reports that historical traumas, including forced relocations and cultural assimilation, and other injustices continue to affect Native populations in significant ways. It concludes that AI/AN mental health disparities "are inherently tied to the historical and current sociopolitical experiences" of these communities. http://www.psych.org/Share/OMNA/Mental-Health-Disparities-Fact-Sheet--American-Indians.aspx

Statement by President Barack Obama, December 16, 2010

"We know that Native Americans die of illnesses like diabetes, pneumonia, flu—even tuberculosis—at far higher rates than the rest of the population . . . and closing these gaps is not just a question of policy, it's a question of our values—it's a test of who we are as a Nation."

Source: Remarks by the President at the White House Tribal Nations Conference, December 16, 2010: http://www.whitehouse.gov/the-press-office/2010/12/16/remarks-president-white-house-tribal-nations-conference

NATIVE AMERICAN PHYSICIANS

Association of American Indian Physicians Physician of the Year Award

Founded in 1971 and headquartered in Oklahoma City, the Association of American Indian Physicians (AAIP) is a nonprofit corporation dedicated to improving the health of American Indians and Alaska Natives. Recipients of AAIP's Physician of the Year Award are American Indian physicians honored for distinguished service and significant contributions to American Indian health. http://www.aaip.org/. AAIP identifies the following honorees by the years indicated on its website.

1996	Edwin Chappabitty Jr., MD (Comanche)
1998	Gerald Ignace, MD (Coeur d'Alene)
1999	Melvina McCabe, MD (Navajo)
2002	Joseph Bell, MD (Lumbee)
2003	Melvina McCabe, MD (Navajo)
2004	Yvette Roubideaux, MD (Rosebud Sioux)
2005	Phillip L. Smith, MD (Navajo)
2006	Kelly Moore, MD (Creek Nation)
2007	Judith Kaur, MD (Choctaw/Cherokee)
2008	Ted Mala, MD (Iñupiaq)
2009	R. Dale Walker, MD (Cherokee)
2010	Kathleen R. Annette, MD (White Earth Band of Chippewa Indians)
2011	Everett Rhoades, MD (Kiowa)

Picotte Memorial Hospital

Listed on the National Register of Historic Places in 1989 and declared a National Historic Landmark in 1993, the Dr. Susan LaFlesche Picotte Memorial Hospital was built on the Omaha Indian Reservation in 1912–13. The one-and-a-half story frame building was constructed as a facility for Dr. Picotte (Omaha), the first American Indian woman to become a medical doctor, to provide health care to her people. Susan was the daughter of Chief Joseph LaFlesche (Iron Eye), who encouraged his children to pursue education. Susan LaFlesche, who married Henry Picotte (Yankton Sioux), graduated from the Women's Medical College of Pennsylvania in 1889, returning home a year later to provide health care on the Omaha Reservation.

Dr. Picotte died two years after the hospital opened, but the building continued as a health care facility until the 1940s. It presently serves as a museum and includes exhibits devoted to Dr. Picotte's pioneering life and work.

http://www.nps.gov/history/nr/feature/indian/2001/picotte.htm

LEGISLATION

Federal Health Legislation

The provision of health care services to federally recognized tribes is a component of the federal trust responsibility of the United States, a legal relationship that has historical roots in sources such as the U.S. Constitution, treaties, agreements, laws, statutes, executive orders, and court decisions. The following legislative acts are among those that provide the legal basis for U.S. government services to American Indians and Alaska Natives.

Civilization Fund Act of 1819
Passed by Congress on March 3, 1819, the Civilization Fund Act was enacted to provide against "the further decline and final extinction of Indian tribes," authorizing annual sums for education and "such other duties as may be enjoined" to carry out the legislation's provisions. Some missionary societies, which received funds to introduce "the habits and arts of civilization," provided some rudimentary health care.

The Snyder Act of 1921
The Snyder Act, passed by Congress on November 2, 1921, formulated the basic legislative authority for Indian health care, providing "for relief of distress and conservation of health" among American Indians.

The Transfer Act of 1954
This legislation transferred the maintenance and operation of hospital and health facilities for American Indians from the Bureau of Indian Affairs to the Public Health Service (PHS) of the Department of Health, Education, and Welfare. The following year, the new PHS Division of Indian Health released "The Most Pressing Needs Study," assessing facilities and other services.

Indian Sanitation Facilities Act of 1959
This legislation authorizes the Indian Health Service to provide essential sanitation facilities, such as safe drinking water and adequate sewer and solid waste systems, to American Indian homes and communities.

Indian Self-Determination and Education Assistance Act of 1975
The Indian Self-Determination and Education Assistance Act provided that tribal governments could contract with the Bureau of Indian Affairs and the Indian Health Service to operate their own programs and services.

Indian Health Care Improvement Act of 1976
The Indian Health Care Improvement Act was enacted with the goal of raising the health status of Indians to the highest possible level. It provided incremental funding for health services and facilities over a seven-year period. The legislation also authorized programs to address the inadequate number of health professionals serving Indians, support for urban Indian health centers, and a feasibility study for an Indian medical school.

Indian Alcohol and Substance Abuse Prevention and Treatment Act of 1986
The Indian Alcohol and Substance Abuse Prevention and Treatment Act was enacted to authorize and develop a comprehensive, coordinated attack upon illegal narcotics traffic in Indian country and the deleterious impact of alcohol and substance abuse upon Indian tribes and their members.

Indian Child Protection and Family Violence Prevention Act of 1990
This legislation's goals included identifying the scope of incidents of child abuse and family violence in Indian Country and to reduce such incidents.

The Indian Health Care Improvement Act of 2010
In 2010, President Barack Obama signed into law the Patient Protection and Affordable Care Act, which permanently reauthorizes the Indian Health Care Improvement Act (IHCA). The IHCA was first made law in 1976, but it required reauthorization by Congress. IHCA of 2010 provisions include programs and services such as training and recruitment for health care professionals, construction of health care facilities, preventive health care, suicide prevention, cancer screening, injury prevention activities, and new long-term care assistance.

HONORING NATIONS PROJECT, HARVARD UNIVERSITY

Honoring Nations Honorees, 1999–2008

Honoring Nations, a national awards program initiated in 1998, highlights outstanding programs in self-governance by Native nations. At the heart of the program is the belief that tribes themselves hold the key to positive social, political, cultural, and economic prosperity. Based at the John F. Kennedy School of Government at Harvard University, Honoring Nations is administered by the Harvard Project on American Indian Economic Development. The criteria for selection of honorees include program effectiveness, significance to sovereignty, cultural relevance, transferability, and sustainability. Those honored include facilities and programs addressing a range of health issues.

Choctaw Health Center, 1999
Mississippi Band of Choctaw Indians
> Following the transfer of health care decisions from the Indian Health Service to tribal control over a ten-year period, the Mississippi Band of Choctaw Indians significantly improved its health care delivery system. The facility provides health and dental care, behavioral health care and community health promotion, education and prevention programs, and the first on-reservation disability clinic.

Institutionalized Quality Improvement Program, 1999
Puyallup Tribal Health Authority (PTHA), Puyallup Tribe of Indians
> After tribally initiated restructuring in the early 1980s, the Puyallup Tribal Health Authority became a model for other Indian nations seeking to create and sustain health systems that meet the highest standards of excellence. Among the changes, the PTHA increased patient access for urgent care visits, reduced "no show" rates, increased dental treatments, and incorporated the use of traditional healers into health care delivery.

Coeur d'Alene Tribal Wellness Center, 2000
Coeur d'Alene Tribe, Plummer, Idaho
http://www.bmcwc.com/
> Created in 1998, the Coeur d'Alene Wellness Center promotes healthy lifestyles by offering programs in fitness, aquatics, physical rehabilitation, childcare, and community health to over 2,500 Indian and non-Indian clients.

Navajo Treatment Center for Children and Their Families (formerly Navajo Child Special Advocacy Project), 2000
Division of Social Services, Navajo Nation
> Created in 1990, the Navajo Child Special Advocacy Project was initiated to provide therapy to child victims of sexual abuse, addressing the need for services and support. The program, which has five offices on the Navajo Reservation, fosters the emotional, mental, physical, and spiritual well-being of children and their families through an array of Western and Navajo therapeutic approaches.

Pharmacy On-Line Billing Initiative, 2000
Human Services Division, Fond du Lac Band of Lake Superior Chippewa
> Faced with rising pharmaceutical costs, limited Indian Health Service funds, and an inability to bill and collect from third-party insurers, the Human

Services Division contracted with a private sector firm to design and implement a computerized pharmacy billing system in 1995. The initiative, the first of its kind for Indian country, increases the Human Services Division's revenue, updates prices automatically, interfaces with the Indian Health Service's Resource Patient Management System for health record keeping, and warns of drug interactions.

White Earth Suicide Intervention Team, 2000
White Earth Chippewa Tribe, White Earth, Minnesota

Created in 1990, the White Earth Suicide Intervention Team organized to address a high rate of suicide attempts and completions among tribal members at White Earth. The program, consisting of a group of volunteers, was designed to provide support and assistance to clients and to ensure that appropriate intervention and treatment occur as needed.

The Healing Lodge of the Seven Nations, 2002
Colville, Spokane, Kalispel, Kootenai, Coeur d'Alene, Nez Perce, and Umatilla
http://www.healinglodge.org/

The Healing Lodge, a nonprofit treatment center owned by a consortium of seven tribes, was created in 1989 to help Native youth and their families heal from alcohol and drug abuse. Its services include certified and accredited inpatient chemical dependency programs, mental health counseling, family counseling, a juvenile justice improvement project, and educational and cultural activities.

Whirling Thunder Wellness Program, 2002
Winnebago Tribal Health Department, Winnebago Tribe of Nebraska

The Winnebago Tribe of Nebraska created the Whirling Thunder Wellness Program in 1995 to address the devastating effects of diabetes and substance abuse. The program's innovations include the "Team Up" diabetes patient retreat; "Kidz Cafe," which provides healthy summertime meals and snacks to children; and after-school programs that provide cultural and physical activities for participants.

Choctaw Community Injury Prevention Program, 2003
Choctaw Health Center
Mississippi Band of Choctaw Indians

In response to alarming rates of preventable accidents on its reservation, the Mississippi Band of Choctaw created a community injury prevention program in 2001. The program has saved lives, reduced injuries and disabilities, and lowered health care costs through measures such as seat belt and child safety seat campaigns, strict enforcement of motor vehicle laws, and community-wide education initiatives.

Family Violence and Victim's Services Program, 2003
Department of Family and Community Services
Mississippi Band of Choctaw Indians
http://www.refusetoabuse.org/
> The Family Violence and Victim's Services Program (FVVS) serves as a "one-stop" hub for all domestic violence and sexual assault issues on the Mississippi Choctaw Reservation. Besides providing and coordinating legal, therapeutic, and other services, FVVS has drafted a strict tribal domestic criminal code and developed community awareness activities.

Na'Nizhoozhi Center, Inc., 2003
Navajo Nation in collaboration with Zuni Pueblo, City of Gallup, McKinley County, Indian Health Services, and the State of New Mexico
> Na'Nizhoozhi Center, a collaborative effort by the Navajo Nation with Zuni Pueblo, the City of Gallup, McKinley County, Indian Health Services, and the State of New Mexico, was established in 1992 to address alcohol-related accidents and other problems in Gallup, New Mexico. The center provides services such as protective custody and culturally based inpatient and outpatient substance abuse treatment to address the needs of Native clients.

Northwest Portland Area Indian Health Board (NPAIHB), 2003
The Forty-three Federally Recognized Tribes of Oregon, Washington, and Idaho
http://www.npaihb.org/
> The Northwest Portland Area Indian Health Board, a nonprofit tribal organization that serves forty-three federally recognized tribes in Oregon, Washington, and Idaho, was created in 1972 to increase the tribes' ability to exercise control over the design and development of tribal health care delivery systems. Besides facilitating intertribal coordination and providing leadership in Indian health, the NPAIHB administers the first and largest tribal epidemiology center.

Navajo Nation Methamphetamine Task Forces, 2006
Navajo Nation Department of Behavioral Health Services, Navajo Nation
> The Navajo Nation Methamphetamine Task Forces were developed to address the crisis of methamphetamine use. The task forces utilize collaborative efforts, educational programs, community involvement, cultural teachings, and other means to combat the crisis.

Archie Hendricks Sr. Skilled Nursing Facility and Tohono O'odham Hospice, 2008
Tohono O'odham Nation
http://www.toltc.org/
> Archie Hendricks Sr. is a Medicare-certified sixty-bed skilled nursing facility directed by the Tohono O'odham Nursing Care Authority in Arizona. The facility, which combines the latest technologies and clinical care with

traditional values, provides respite care and long-term services to elders who would otherwise have to leave the community.

Pine Hill Health Center, 2008
Navajo Nation, Ramah Chapter
Pine Hill Health Center, which was established in 1978 and primarily serves the Ramah Band of Navajos, received high honors for its cancer awareness and prevention program. Recognizing that breast cancer is the second leading cause of death for American Indian women, the center initiated "Mammo Days" to provide culturally relevant breast and cervical cancer screenings.

BOOKS

Five Books about American Indian Doctors

1. *Carlos Montezuma, M.D., A Yavapai American Hero: The Life and Times of an American Indian, 1866–1923,* by Leon Speroff (2003).
2. *The Essential Charles Eastman (Ohiyesa): Light on the Indian World,* edited by Michael Oren Fitzgerald (2007).
3. *The Scalpel and the Silver Bear: The First Navajo Woman Surgeon Combines Western Medicine and Traditional Healing,* by Lori Arviso Alvord and Elizabeth Cohen Van Pelt (1999).
4. *Searching for My Destiny,* by George Blue Spruce Jr. as told to Deanne Durrett (2009).
5. *Susan La Flesche Picotte, M.D.: Omaha Indian Leader and Reformer,* by Benson Tong (1999).

FILMS

The Doe Boy (USA, 2001, 83 min.), directed by Randy Redroad (Cherokee).
Set in the Cherokee Nation of Oklahoma, *The Doe Boy* tells the story of a young man who lives with the illness of hemophilia, intensifying the complicated circumstances of his life.
Don't Get Sick after June: American Indian Healthcare (USA, 2010, 60 min.), directed by Chip Richie.
A documentary by Rich-Heape Films, this film addresses Indian health care and the Indian Health Service from Native American perspectives.
The Gift of Diabetes (Canada, 2005, 58 min.), directed by Brion Whitford and John Paskievich.

The Gift of Diabetes documents Ojibway filmmaker Brion Whitford's struggle with advanced diabetes and his efforts to regain health and well-being. On his journey, he sought to understand the source of the disease as well as possible healing for Native families and communities.

Goodnight Irene (USA, 2004, 14 min.), directed by Sterlin Harjo (Creek/Seminole).
Two young men have a life-changing encounter with an elder in an Indian Health Service clinic.

Hózhó of Native Women (USA, 1997, 29 min.), directed by Beverly R. Singer (Santa Clara Pueblo/Diné).
Native American women from diverse tribal backgrounds tell stories from their lives and cultural memory that concern wellness.

Letter from an Apache (USA, 1983, 12 min.), directed by Barbara Wilk.
An animated film that tells the story of Carlos Montezuma, or Wassaja, who became one of the first American Indian medical doctors.

Lijj' Biyiin/Horse Song (USA, 2000, 56 min.), directed by Norman Patrick Brown (Navajo).
A drama that portrays the impact of diabetes on a Navajo man and his family and their struggle to deal with it through traditional and Western health practices.

The Lisa Tiger Story: If It Can Happen to Me It Can Happen to You (USA, 1994, 27 min.), directed by Harlan McKosato (Sac and Fox).
This documentary profiles AIDS lecturer and artist Lisa Tiger (Creek/Seminole/Cherokee), who learned in 1992, at age 29, that she had tested HIV-positive. She committed herself to speaking to Native American high school students and other audiences about the risks and consequences of unprotected sex.

My Big Fat Diet (Canada, 2008, 42 min.), directed by Mary Bissell.
This film portrays the people of 'Namgis First Nation in Alert Bay, British Columbia, who agree to give up junk food and return to a more traditional way of eating for one year in order to fight obesity and diabetes.

The Necessities of Life (Canada, 2008, 102 min.), directed by Benoît Pilon.
Tivii, an Inuit hunter and family man from Baffin Island, is taken from his village and placed in a tuberculosis sanatorium in Quebec City, where he meets an Inuit orphan who helps him navigate the strange new setting. In French and Inuktitut with English subtitles.

Walking into the Unknown (USA, 2010, 60 min.), directed by Nate Maydole.
This film chronicles the journey of Dr. Arne Vainio (Mille Lacs Ojibwe), a family practice physician, as he undergoes health screenings. His experiences serve as a tool to help others, encouraging medical testing and follow-up actions for healthier lives. The Emmy-nominated film was funded by the Fond du Lac Band of Lake Superior Chippewa, with support from the Indian Health Service Special Diabetes Program.

ORGANIZATIONS

Alaska Native Health Board (ANHB)
http://www.anhb.org/

> Established in 1968 and located in Anchorage, the Alaska Native Health Board is recognized as the statewide voice on Alaska Native health issues. ANHB's work includes serving as advisor to the director of the Alaska Area Native Health Service, the U.S. Senate Committee on Indian Affairs, and the House Interior and Insular Affairs Committee on federal legislation and appropriations affecting Alaska Native health programs.

Alaska Native Tribal Health Consortium (ANTHC)
http://www.anthc.org/

> Established in 1997 and based in Anchorage, the Alaska Native Tribal Health Consortium is a nonprofit health organization that manages statewide health services for Alaska Native people. ANTHC is owned and managed by Alaska Native tribal governments and their regional health organizations.

Association of American Indian Physicians (AAIP)
http://www.aaip.org/

> Founded in 1971 as an educational, scientific, and charitable nonprofit corporation, the Association of American Indian Physicians is dedicated to improving the health of American Indians and Alaska Natives. The association is headquartered in Oklahoma City, providing leadership, support, and services on a nationwide basis.

National Alaska Native American Indian Nurses Association (NANAINA)
http://www.nanainanurses.org/

> The National Alaska Native American Indian Nurses Association was founded upon its predecessor organization, the American Indian Nurses Association, and later, the American Indian Alaska Native Nurses Association, which disbanded in 1984. The organization was established to advocate for improved health care services for American Indians and Alaska Natives (AI/AN) throughout the United States and to foster the development of AI/AN nurses.

National Council of Urban Indian Health (NCUIH)
http://www.ncuih.org/index

> Founded in 1998 and based in Washington, DC, the National Council of Urban Indian Health is a membership-based organization devoted to the development of quality, accessible, and culturally sensitive health care programs for American Indians and Alaska Natives living in urban areas. It serves as a resource center providing advocacy, education, training, and leadership for urban Indian health care providers.

National Indian Council on Aging (NICOA)
http://www.nicoa.org/

>   Established in 1976 and headquartered in Albuquerque, New Mexico, the
>   National Indian Council on Aging was founded by members of the National
>   Indian Tribal Chairmen's Association to advocate for improved health and
>   social services to American Indian and Alaska Native elders. NICOA provides
>   advocacy and services at the national level, representing a voting membership
>   consisting of AI/AN elders across Indian Country.

National Indian Health Board (NIHB)
http://www.nihb.org/

>   Established in 1972 and headquartered in Washington, DC, the National Indian
>   Health Board is a nonprofit organization that serves all federally recognized
>   American Indian and Alaska Native (AI/AN) tribal governments by advocating
>   for the improvement of health care delivery to AI/AN people. Besides
>   advising Congress, the Indian Health Service, and other agencies about health
>   disparities and service issues in Indian country, the NIHB conducts research
>   and provides policy analysis, program development, technical assistance, and
>   a variety of other services.

National Indian Women's Health Resource Center (NIWHRC)
http://www.niwhrc.org/

>   Formed in 1998 in Albuquerque, New Mexico, the National Indian Women's
>   Health Resource Center is a national nonprofit organization whose mission is
>   to assist American Indian and Alaska Native women achieve optimal health
>   and well being throughout their lives. The members include health providers,
>   health planners, health administrators, and elected tribal leaders concerned
>   about the health status of Native women.

National Native American AIDS Prevention Center (NNAAPC)
http://www.nnaapc.org/

>   Founded in 1987 and based in Denver, Colorado, the National Native American
>   AIDS Prevention Center addresses the impact of HIV/AIDS on American
>   Indians, Alaska Natives, and Native Hawaiians through culturally appropriate
>   advocacy, research and education, and policy development. NNAAPC helps
>   organizations that serve Native communities to plan, develop, and manage HIV/
>   AIDS prevention, intervention, care, and treatment programs.

National Native American EMS Association (NNAEMSA)
http://www.healthfinder.gov/orgs/HR3401.htm

>   The National Native American EMS Association was established to provide
>   support to EMS, rescue, and public safety organizations that provide services
>   on Native American and Alaska Native lands. NNAEMSA seeks significant

improvements in the quality of patient care available to all people within each EMS service district.

Native Vision

http://www.nativevision.org/

Founded in 1997, Native Vision is a partnership of the Johns Hopkins Center for American Indian Health and the National Football League Players Association that mobilizes NFL players and other professional athletes as mentors for Native youth. Native Vision promotes three major areas of well-being for individuals and families: healthy minds, healthy bodies, and healthy families.

Native Wellness Institute

http://www.nativewellness.com/

Founded in 2000 and based in Gresham, Oregon, the Native Wellness Institute is a nonprofit organization that provides Native-specific and wellness-related training and technical assistance to Native people, communities, tribes, and organizations throughout North America.

Society of American Indian Dentists (SAID)

http://www.aaip.org/?page=SAID

Founded in 1990 and incorporated as a nonprofit organization in Arizona, the Society of American Indian Dentists was organized to meet the needs of Native dentists, dental students, and dental auxiliaries. SAID's mission includes promoting dental health in American Indian communities, encouraging Native youth to pursue dentistry careers, and providing role model leadership, support, and assistance.

Urban Indian Health Institute (UIHI)

http://www.uihi.org/

Established as a division within the Seattle Indian Health Board in 2000, the mission of the Urban Indian Health Institute is to support the health and well-being of urban Indian communities through information, scientific inquiry, and technology. It is one of eleven tribal epidemiology centers; UIHI focuses on the nationwide urban American Indian/Alaska Native population, while the other ten centers serve tribes regionally.

RESOURCES

Davies, Wade. *Healing Ways: Navajo Health Care in the Twentieth Century.* Albuquerque: University of New Mexico Press, reprint edition, 2009.

DeJong, David H. *"If You Knew the Conditions": A Chronicle of the Indian Medical Service and American Indian Health Care, 1908–1955.* Lanham, MD: Lexington Books, 2008.

————. *Plagues, Politics, and Policy: A Chronicle of the Indian Health Service, 1955–2008.* Lanham, MD: Lexington Books, 2011.

Dixon, Mim, and Yvette Roubideaux, eds. *Promises to Keep: Public Health Policy for American Indians and Alaska Natives in the 21st Century.* Washington, DC: American Public Health Association, 2001.

Iverson, Peter. *Carlos Montezuma and the Changing World of American Indians.* Albuquerque: University of New Mexico Press, 1982.

Keller, Jean A. *Empty Beds: Indian Student Health at Sherman Institute, 1902–1922.* East Lansing: Michigan State University Press, 2002.

Moerman, Daniel E. *Native American Medicinal Plants: An Ethnobotanical Dictionary.* Portland, OR: Timber Press, 2009.

Nebelkopf, Ethan, and Mary Phillips, eds. *Healing and Mental Health for Native Americans: Speaking in Red.* Lanham, MD: AltaMira Press, 2004.

Rhoades, Everett R., ed. *American Indian Health: Innovations in Health Care, Promotion, and Policy.* Baltimore: The Johns Hopkins University Press, 2000.

Ruby, Robert H. *A Doctor among the Oglala Sioux Tribe: The Letters of Robert H. Ruby, 1953–1954.* Edited by Cary C. Collins and Charles V. Mutschler. Lincoln: University of Nebraska Press, 2010.

Sandefur, Gary D., Ronald R. Rindfuss, and Barney Cohen, eds. *Changing Numbers, Changing Needs: American Indian Demography and Public Health.* Washington, DC: National Academy Press, 1996.

Sarche, Michelle C. et al., eds. *American Indian and Alaska Native Children and Mental Health: Development, Context, Prevention, and Treatment.* Santa Barbara, CA: Praeger, 2011.

Smith-Morris, Carolyn. *Diabetes among the Pima: Stories of Survival.* Tucson: University of Arizona Press, 2006.

St. Pierre, Mark. *Madonna Swan: A Lakota Woman's Story.* Norman: University of Oklahoma Press, 1991.

Witko, Tawa M., ed. *Mental Health Care for Urban Indians: Clinical Insights from Native Practitioners.* Washington, DC: American Psychological Association, 2006.

Web Sites

A Chronological History of IHS: http://academic.udayton.edu/health/02organ/Indian02.htm

American Indian Health (United States National Library of Medicine): http://americanindianhealth.nlm.nih.gov/

American Indians and Alaska Natives in Health Careers: http://aianhealthcareers.org/index.html

Broken Promises: Evaluating the Native American Health Care System (U.S. Commission on Civil Rights, 2004): http://www.usccr.gov/pubs/nahealth/nabroken.pdf

Center for American Indian Health, Johns Hopkins Bloomberg School of Public Health: http://www.jhsph.edu/caih

Harvard Project's Honoring Nations Directory of Honored Programs, 1999–2006: http://hpaied.org./images/resources/general/Dir_web.pdf

Health of Native People of North America: An Annotated Mediagraphy: http://wings.buffalo.edu/publications/mcjrnl/v1n2/gray.html

Healthy Indian Country Initiative Promising Prevention Practices Resource Guide (National Indian Health Board, 2009): http://nihb.org/docs/04072010/2398_NIHB%20HICI% 20Book_web.pdf

"If you knew the conditions . . .": Health Care to Native Americans (online version of an exhibit held at the National Library of Medicine): http://www.nlm.nih.gov/exhibition/if_you_knew/if_you_knew_01.html

Index of Native American Health Resources on the Internet/WWW Virtual Library—American Indians: http://www.hanksville.org/NAresources/indices/NAhealth.html

Mayo Clinic Native Circle: The American Indian/Alaska Native Cancer Information Resource Center and Learning Exchange: http://mayoresearch.mayo.edu/mayo/research/cancercenter/native_circle.cfm

Mental Health Disparities: American Indians and Alaska Natives (American Psychiatric Association Fact Sheet): http://www.psych.org/Share/OMNA/Mental-Health-Disparities-Fact-Sheet--American-Indians.aspx

Native American Cancer Research: http://natamcancer.org/

Native American Programs, American Diabetes Association: http://www.diabetes.org/in-my-community/programs/native-american-programs/

One Sky Center, The American Indian/Alaska Native National Resource Center for Substance Abuse and Mental Health Services: http://www.oneskycenter.org/

Strong Heart Study (Center for American Indian Health Research): http://strongheart.ouhsc.edu/

Elders

National Resource Center for American Indian, Alaska Native and Native Hawaiian Elders at the University of Alaska, Anchorage: http://elders.uaa.alaska.edu/

National Resource Center on Native American Aging (NRCNAA) at the University of North Dakota: http://ruralhealth.und.edu/projects/nrcnaa/

Native Web Resource Database, Health and Elder Resources: http://www.nativeweb.org/resources/health_elder_resources

Wisdom of the Elders: http://www.wisdomoftheelders.org/

Women

Minority Women's Health: American Indians/Alaska Natives (U.S. Department of Health and Human Services Office on Women's Health): http://womenshealth.gov/minority-health/american-indians/

8

Native American Religions

FIRSTS

1615   Roman Catholic Recollet missionaries arrived in New France (Canada) and were accepted as emissaries from the French traders with whom the Indians traded. This was the first time a community of American Indians provided Europeans access to their society. This began the long history of Catholic missionization among Native peoples.

1651   John Eliot, seventeenth-century missionary, established in Natick, Massachusetts, the first of fourteen "praying towns," in which American Indians of various tribes were moved from their former Native communities and converted to Christianity. After the town was established, Waban (Nipmuc) became the first Massachusetts chief to embrace Christianity.

1657   Skanudharova (Huron) is believed to have been the first Native American woman to enter Catholic religious life.

1660   The first Indian church in New England was established by John Eliot. It was built in Natick, Massachusetts, for newly converted Christian Indians.

1670   Hiacoomes (Wampanoag) preached his first sermon as a consecrated minister to the Wampanoag people on Martha's Vineyard, Massachusetts. He was the first Indian preacher ordained through the missionary program of John Eliot.

1680   Po'pay (Ohkay Owingeh/formerly known as San Juan Pueblo) was one of the first North American Indians to successfully lead a revolt against the Spanish occupiers of the Southwest who denied Pueblo villagers the right to practice their ancient religious traditions and forced them to accept Christianity.

1765   Christian clergyman Samson Occum (Mohegan) was the first Native American to preach to a white audience in Europe. He was instrumental in raising funds to establish Eleazar Wheelock's Indian Charity School (renamed Dartmouth College in New Hampshire).

1769   Junipero Serra, Franciscan missionary from Spain, founded San
            Diego de Alcala, the first in a series of twenty-one missions built along
            the coastal trail of California. Indians from many California tribes
            and bands were confined in the missions to be Christianized and
            "civilized."

1855   James Bouchard (Delaware) was the first American Indian to be
            ordained a Roman Catholic priest. Converted to Catholicism in 1846,
            he was assigned to work with miners in California, although his
            preference was to minister to his own people.
                Allen Wright (Choctaw) was the first American Indian from Indian
            Territory (present-day Oklahoma) to receive a Master of Arts from
            the Union Theological Seminary in New York City. He was ordained
            to the Presbyterian ministry and became an honorary member of the
            American Board of Commissioners of Foreign Missions.

1881   David Pendleton Oakerhater (Cheyenne) was the first American Indian
            ordained an Episcopal deacon. He served for fifty years at a mission
            in Indian Territory (present-day Oklahoma). In 1985, the Episcopal
            Church included his name on its calendar of saints.
                For the first time, American Indians were explicitly forbidden to
            practice their religions by order of President Chester A. Arthur. He
            authorized the secretary of the interior to ban the practice of dances,
            rites, and customs that were "contrary to civilization." The ban resulted
            in imprisonment and punishment for many Indians living on reserva-
            tions as well as those away at boarding school.

1884   Kateri Tekakwitha (Mohawk), also known as the "Lily of the Mohawks,"
            was the first Native American to be venerated by the Roman Catholic
            Church. In 1884 the Jesuits submitted her name for canonization; in
            1932 her name was formally presented to the Vatican; in 1943, she was
            venerated; and in 1980 Kateri was beatified (declared blessed).

ca. 1891   Josephine Crowfeather (Lakota Sioux), also known as Sacred White
            Buffalo and Mother Mary Catherine, and the Reverend Francis M. Craft
            (Iroquois) founded the first Indian Christian sisterhood, the Congrega-
            tion of American Sisters. Crowfeather was also the first Lakota Sioux
            woman to become a nun.

1903   Albert Negahnquet (Potawatomi) was one of the first full-blood
            American Indians to be ordained a Roman Catholic priest. Ordained in
            Rome, he returned to the United States to work among Indian people
            in Oklahoma and then in Minnesota.

1906   President Theodore Roosevelt proclaimed Devils Tower in Wyoming
            the first national monument under the Antiquities Act. A sacred site to

over twenty American Indian tribes, it is called Mato Tipi (Bear's Lodge or Bear's Tipi) by Lakota people.

1912   Edward Ahenakew (Plains Cree) became the first American Indian to be ordained an Anglican minister.

1914   Jonathan Koshiway (Sac/Fox) founded the second peyote church and the first one to be legally incorporated.

1918   The Native American Church (NAC), the first church of the Peyote Religion was organized and incorporated in Reno, Oklahoma. The NAC has since spread to many states and to Indian tribes outside of the Plains people.

1938   The first successful efforts to repatriate Native American sacred objects to their rightful caretakers occurred when the sacred Midipadi (or Waterbuster Clan Bundle) was returned to the Hidatsa People of North Dakota by the Museum of the American Indian.

ca. 1941   James C. Ottipoby (Comanche) was the first American Indian priest to be commissioned in the American Chaplain Corps. He served during World War II.

1943   Philip B. Gordon (Ojibwa) was the first ordained American Indian priest to offer the invocation at the convening of the U.S. House of Representatives. It took place on July 11.

ca. 1947   Roe B. Lewis (Pima/Tohono O'odham) was the first American Indian to be ordained a minister in the United Presbyterian Church.

1952   Gloria Ann Davis (Navajo/Choctaw) was the first American Indian to enter the Order of the Blessed Sacrament in the Roman Catholic Church.

1954   Vine Deloria Sr. (Yankton Dakota/Sioux) was the first American Indian appointed to a national executive post in the Episcopal Church. His appointment put him in charge of all Indian missions.

1956   Frank Takes Gun (Crow) was elected as the first president of the newly named and organized Native American Church of North America (formerly known as the Native American Church). He worked with tribal governments to legitimize the church on their respective reservations.

1961   Charles Kekumano (Native Hawaiian) was named by Pope John XXIII as an honorary chaplain of the papal household, with the title of monsignor, the first Native Hawaiian to hold such an honor.

1972   Harold Stephen Jones (Santee Dakota Sioux) became the first American Indian to be consecrated as suffragan bishop of the Episcopal Diocese of South Dakota.

1973   P. Annette Anderson (Mono) became the first woman to direct an Indian Ministries program for a major church group. She served as national director of Indian ministries for the American Baptist Churches.

1975   Frank Fools Crow (Oglala Lakota) was the first leader of a Native religion to offer the invocation at the convening of the U.S. Senate. Fools Crow said the prayer in Lakota, and it was translated into English.

1976   George P. Lee (Navajo) was the first Native American to be appointed to the highest office of the Church of Jesus Christ of Latter-Day Saints. In 1989, he was removed from office, the first excommunication imposed on a high-ranking official in over forty-six years.

1986   Donald E. Pelotte (Abenaki) was the first Native American to be ordained bishop in the Roman Catholic Church. The elevation to bishop made him the highest-ranking Indian in the Catholic Church. Pelotte, who served the Gallup, New Mexico, diocese for twenty-two years, is also the only known Roman Catholic to have ordained his own twin brother, Father Dana F. Pelotte, to the priesthood, in 1999.

1997   Charles J. Chaput (Prairie Band Potawatomi) became the first American Indian archbishop, when Pope John Paul II appointed him archbishop of Denver, Colorado. In 1988 Pope John Paul II had named him bishop of Rapid City, South Dakota.

2003   The first National Day of Prayer to Protect Native American Sacred Places took place across the country. Native and non-Native people gathered at sacred sites to hold solstice events and ceremonies emphasizing the need to protect sacred lands.

2007   Jacqueline Left Hand Bull-Delahunt (Rosebud Sioux) was elected chair of the Baha'i National Spiritual Assembly of America. She is the first American Indian leader and third woman to hold that position in the religion.

        Bishop Francis A. Quinn apologized to the Miwok Indians for cruelties the Catholic Church committed against them two centuries before. The historic apology took place during a Mass at the Church of St. Raphael in San Rafael, California.

2010   Father Maurice Henry Sands (Ojibway/Ottawa/Potawatomi) became the first Native American priest chosen as a consultant to the U.S. Conference of Catholic Bishops' Secretariat of Cultural Diversity. In 2005, he became Detroit, Michigan's first Native American priest.

NATIVE AMERICAN RELIGIONS IN AMERICAN CULTURE

Eleven Native American Views about Native and Non-Native Religions, 1805–1999

Since contact with Europeans, Native people have expressed their preference for their own religious practices; they have also put forth their reasons for rejecting Christianity.

1. "Brother, you say there is but one way to worship and serve the Great Spirit; if there is but one religion, why do you white people differ so much about it? Why not all agree, as you can all read the book? . . . Brother, we do not wish to destroy your religion, or take it from you. We only want to enjoy our own."
   Red Jacket (Seneca), 1805
2. "Cast your eyes abroad over the world, and see how many different systems of religion there are in it, almost as many as there are nations—and is not this the work of the Lord? . . . Your declaiming so violently against our modes of worshiping the [Creator], in my opinion, is not calculated to benefit us as a nation. We are willing to receive good advice from you; but we are not willing to have the customs and institutions which have been kept sacred by our fathers, and handed down to us, thus assailed and abused."
   John Hicks (Wyandot), 1812
3. "You speak of the 'good book' that you have in your hand; we have many of these in our village; we are told that all your words about the Son of the [Creator] are printed in that book, and if we learn to read it, it will make good people of us. I would now ask why it don't make good people of the pale faces living all around us?"
   Neumonya (Ioway), 1844
4. "They will teach us to quarrel about God, as Catholics and Protestants do on the Nez Perce Reservation and other places. We do not want to learn that. We may quarrel with men sometimes about things on earth, but we never quarrel about the Great Spirit. We do not want to learn that."
   Chief Joseph (Nez Perce), 1870s
5. "Our religion seems foolish to you, but so does yours to me. The Baptists and Methodists and Presbyterians and the Catholics all have a different God. Why cannot we have one of our own?"
   Sitting Bull (Lakota), 1889
6. "We want to keep our religion as any other white people would like to keep his . . . The religious beliefs and ceremonies and forms of prayer of each of our Pueblos are as old as the world and they are holy."
   Pueblo leaders, 1923
7. "My People, the Indians, worship the same Being as that worshiped by our white brothers, but only in our own way and in our beliefs, which I know is very strange to the white people. But this is the only form of worship the red man, my people, have known for generations past. . ."
   Chief Dick Washakie (Shoshone), ca. 1930

8. "The reason for the survival of the Hopis has been our dedication to and faithfulness to our one God of the universe, and our adherence to our traditions and learnings. As long as we do this same thing, we will survive as a people and be of service to the rest of humanity."
   Daisy Albert (Hopi), 1954

9. "I challenge anyone concerned about the problem of drug abuse to find examples of dope peddlers selling the holy medicine [Peyote] in America's school yards and play grounds. The idea is preposterous. We don't have a peyote abuse problem in this nation."
   Reuben A. Snake Jr. (Winnebago), 1990

10. "While missionaries did indeed manage to 'save some souls,' most Indians preferred their own religions and were determined to practice them no matter the cost."
    Devon A. Mihesuah (Choctaw), 1996

11. "The religious traditions of the indigenous tribes that have survived are based on centuries, or millennia, of close observations of the natural world . . . Our ties to the land have evolved a very unique set of diverse forms of worship among the tribes, and they are vastly different from Judeo-Christian religions."
    Walter Echo-Hawk (Pawnee), 1999

Federal Suppression of Native Religions

By the nineteenth century, the hostility of missionaries and others to Native religious leaders and cultural practices characterized as "heathenish," "injurious," and "evil" had resulted in restrictive government policy measures. In 1883, Interior Secretary Henry M. Teller established Courts of Indian Offenses on federal Indian reservations to "compel these imposters to . . . discontinue their practices, which are not only without benefit to the Indians but positively injurious to them" (http://rclinton.files.wordpress.com/2007/11/code-of-indian-offenses.pdf).

Nevertheless religious leaders continued to conduct ceremonies, or dances, rites, and prayers, and preside over life-cycle events, despite the insistence of the Bureau of Indian Affairs (BIA) in the early 1920s that religious ceremonies be restricted to "one each month in the daylight hours of one day in the midweek" and that "none take part in the dances or be present who are under fifty years of age." The courts punished Indians who participated in religious ceremonies by imprisoning them or withholding rations, which they depended on for food after buffalo and other means of sustenance were nearly eradicated. At their height, the courts were imposed on approximately two-thirds of the nation's Indian reservations.

The rules for the courts were amended when John Collier became Commissioner of Indian Affairs during the administration of President Franklin D. Roosevelt in

1933. He eliminated references to the bans on dances, such as the sacred Lakota Sun Dance, and other Native customs, including giveaways, the ceremonial presentation of gifts to honor an individual or group. The modern version of rules for the Court of Indian Offenses can be found at 25 C.F.R. (Code of Federal Regulations), Part 11, Indian Law and Order on Indian Reservations.

Appropriation and Commercialization of Native American Religions

Some individuals and groups appropriate and exploit cultural and intellectual property by acting in the name of American Indians without the proper credentials or authority to do so. Such practices, rooted in colonization, include bogus shamans who offer pseudo-religious workshops or sweat lodges and pipe ceremonies, as well as offering vision quests to non-Indians for a fee. Other practices involve initiating members and performing "borrowed" rituals; the tribally unauthorized use of American Indian sacred music to sell CDs; the tribally unauthorized production, use, or sale of tribal religious images and/or ritual objects (pipes, turtle shell rattles, medicine pouches, tobacco ties, and prayer feathers); and the appropriation of American Indian identities, names, and credentials by outsiders who then pose as legitimate tribal spokespeople or religious practitioners.

Tribal nations condemn these practices as cultural exploitation, detrimental to the survival and well-being of their people. Abusing private Native religious practices desecrates their sacredness, disrespects tribal sovereignty, and endangers the people.

SACRED SITES

Five Sacred Places Protected

1. Blue Lake, New Mexico

    The sacred Taos Pueblo site located in the Sangre de Cristo Mountains was seized unjustly by the federal government in 1906 and made part of Carson National Forest. In December 1970, President Richard M. Nixon returned Blue Lake and the surrounding 40,000 acres of land to the Taos people, a culmination of a sixty-four year struggle of the pueblo to reclaim and protect sacred land.
2. Cave Rock, Nevada

    Cave Rock, a large rock formation sacred to the Washoe Tribe of California and Nevada, is located on national forest land near Lake Tahoe, Nevada. The heart of the Cave Rock site was dynamited by two highway road tunnels in 1931 and 1957, as well as desecrated by vulgar graffiti, the installation of over forty-six different bolted climbing routes, and the cementing over of cave openings. In 2003 the U.S. Forest Service banned rock climbing at the site to protect cultural, historical, and archaeological features of the site. The ruling protects Cave Rock from climbing, but not on the basis of sacred lands protection.

3. Kootenai Falls, Montana

A major waterfall on the Kootenai River near Libby, Montana, is sacred to Kootenai Indians of Montana, Idaho, and British Columbia. After an administrative law judge from the Federal Energy Regulatory Commission (FERC) visited the falls, in June 1987 FERC denied a license to seven Montana-Idaho electric cooperatives that tried to win approval for a dam and hydroelectric plant at Kootenai Falls.

4. Medicine Wheel/Medicine Mountain National Historic Landmark, Wyoming

The Medicine Wheel/Medicine Mountain (MWMM) in the Big Horn Mountains of Wyoming is sacred to tribal nations including Arapaho, Blackfeet, Crow, Cheyenne, Lakota, and Shoshone. In 1991, the U.S. Forest Service proposed measures to develop the Medicine Wheel area as a tourist attraction, as well as proposing future logging activities in the vicinity. A Medicine Wheel Coalition negotiated and signed a 1996 landmark Historic Preservation Plan with the U.S. Forest Service, as well as state and local government agencies, designed to ensure that the entire area around the MWMM is managed in a manner that protects it as a sacred site.

5. Mount Adams, Washington

A mountain sacred to Yakama people was taken by the federal government around the turn of the twentieth century and included in the Clifford Pinchot National Forest. It was returned to the Yakamas in May of 1972.

Five Desecrated and Endangered Sacred Sites

1. Celilo Falls, Oregon

Celilo Falls, an ancient place of worship and fishery on the Columbia River, was sacred to the Umatilla, Nez Perce, Yakama, and Warm Springs Indians. The site was flooded by the Dalles Dam, which was completed in 1957.

2. Glen Cove, California

A sacred Ohlone burial site in Vallejo, California, where local Indians lived and buried their dead at the Glen Cove Shellmound, is endangered. The Greater Vallejo Recreation District wants to "improve" the site by adding a park, paved parking lot, picnic tables, paved trails, and restrooms.

3. Mount Taylor, New Mexico

The National Trust for Historic Preservation named Mount Taylor, near Grants, New Mexico, to its 2009 list of America's 11 Most Endangered Historic Places. The sacred mountain, named for President Zachary Taylor, is known to the Acoma Pueblo people as Kaweshtima, or "place of snow," and to the

Navajos as *Tsoodzil,* their Sacred Mountain to the South. A pilgrimage site for as many as thirty Native American tribes, Mount Taylor has been threatened by proposals for uranium mining and recreational development projects.

4. Rainbow Natural Bridge, Utah

    Rainbow Natural Bridge, a huge sandstone arch sacred to the Navajo, Paiute, and Pueblo peoples, was desecrated by the completion of Glen Canyon Dam on the Colorado River in 1963 and the rising of Lake Powell.

5. San Francisco Peaks, Arizona

    San Francisco Peaks, a site in the Coconino National Forest, is sacred to Apache, Havasupai, Hopi, Hualapai, Navajo, and Zuni. The peaks were desecrated by the development of the Snow Bowl, a portion of the peaks used for downhill skiing, approved by the U.S. Forest Service. Litigation has failed to prevent the possibility of operators of the ski area using treated sewage effluent for snowmaking.

Thirteen Books about Sacred Sites

1. *Cave Rock: Climbers, Courts, and a Washoe Indian Sacred Place,* by Matthew S. Makley and Michael J. Makley (2010).
2. *For This Land: Writings on Religion in America,* by Vine Deloria Jr. (Dakota) (1999).
3. *Navajo Sacred Places,* by Klara Bonsack Kelley and Harris Francis (1994).
4. *Places of Power: Ancient American Sacred Sites,* by Corson Hirschfeld (1989).
5. *Sacred Lands of Indian America,* by Jake Page (2001).
6. *Sacred Objects and Sacred Places: Preserving Tribal Traditions,* by Andrew Guilford (2000).
7. *Sacred Places in North America: A Journey into the Medicine Wheel,* by Courtney Milne (1995).
8. *Sacred Sites and Repatriation,* by Joe Edward Watkins (2005)
9. *Sacred Sites: The Secret History of Southern California,* by Susan Suntree (2010).
10. *Spirit of the Land: Sacred Places in Native North America,* by Courtney Milne (1994).
11. *The Taos Indians and the Battle for Blue Lake,* by R. Gordon C. McCutchan (1991).
12. *Vision Quest: Men, Women and Sacred Sites of the Sioux Nation,* by Don Doll (1994).
13. *Where the Lightning Strikes: The Lives of American Indian Sacred Places,* by Peter Nabokov (2006).

Five Films about Sacred Sites

1. *In the Light of Reverence* (USA, 2000, 72 min.), directed by Christopher McLeod.

    The film is a documentary about three Native communities and the sacred lands they struggle to protect: the Hopis of Arizona and the Colorado

Plateau in the Southwest, the Wintu and Mt. Shasta in California, and the Lakota and Devils Tower in Wyoming.

2. *Mato Paha* (USA, 2008, 38 min.), directed by Mitchell Zephier (Lakota).

    Mato Paha, the Lakota name for Bear Butte, located in South Dakota, dramatically illuminates the struggle between Native traditionalists from thirty tribes who regard Mato Paha as a place of quiet sanctity, fasting, and prayer, and the convenience stores, other non-Indian businesses, campgrounds, and biker bars that are encroaching on the sacred mountain.

3. *Our Sacred Land* (USA, 1985, 28 min.), directed by Chris Spotted Eagle (Houma).

    The film looks at American Indian religious freedom and treaty rights, especially focusing on Bear Butte and the Black Hills in South Dakota, two of the most sacred areas to the Sioux Nation.

4. *Paha Sapa: The Struggle for the Black Hills* (USA, 1998, 60 min.), directed by Mel Lawrence.

    The film depicts the struggle of the Sioux Nation to regain the Black Hills of South Dakota, land sacred to many Native peoples. In 1980, the U.S. Supreme Court awarded the Sioux Nation a monetary settlement for the loss of the Black Hills. The Sioux want their sacred land back, not the monetary award.

5. *The Snowbowl Effect* (USA, 2005, 56 min.), directed by Klee Benally (Diné/Navajo).

    This documentary explores the controversy surrounding the San Francisco Peaks, a sacred site revered by more than a dozen tribes, that is part of public lands managed by the U.S. Forest Service. Tribal officials, spiritual leaders, Forest Service officials, ski resort representatives, and environmentalists weigh in on the impact on the peaks of the expansion of a ski resort and snowmaking with wastewater.

Sacred Sites

Traditional practices of Native Americans are inseparably bound to land and natural formations including mountains, lakes, piles of rocks, unusually shaped mounds, middens, caves, burial grounds, ceremonial grounds, doctoring sites, and medicine or training sites. Sacred sites are often the centerpiece of a tribe's creation stories and oral histories. Ceremonies, vision quests, prayers, fasts, or pilgrimages must take place at certain lakes, hot springs, places where ancestors left petroglyphs, and other isolated sanctuaries. They may be areas where plants, herbs, minerals, and waters may be taken.

Because Indian tribes lost much of their land through treaties with the U.S. government, many traditional tribal prayer sites are located on lands controlled by the U.S. Forest Service, U.S. Park Service, U.S. Bureau of Land

Management, and states. These land managers take into account the needs of developers and recreational users, but do not readily take into account the profound effect these decisions have on sacred places critical to Native populations.

Federal and state laws exist to protect Native sacred sites, but at times they are ignored. Many sacred sites are threatened or desecrated by logging and mining operations, hydroelectric plants and other public works projects, Forest Service regulations, urban housing, highways, tourism, looting, pollution, and vandalism. Many sacred grounds have been fenced off, cutting off Native access to these places, which are not interchangeable for religious purposes. Rock climbers and hikers who have access to sacred areas often disrupt the grounds. New Agers, intruders, and others who flock to sacred areas disturb Native people in prayer there.

Mato Tipi (Devils Tower)

For centuries, over twenty Plains Indian tribes have made pilgrimages to a volcanic stump-shaped monolith rising 1,280 feet over the Belle Fourche River in northeastern Wyoming. The tribes use this sacred landmark for funerals, prayer offerings, sweat lodge ceremonies, Sun Dance rituals, and vision seeking. The site gained global fame in 1977 thanks to the blockbuster film *Close Encounters of the Third Kind*.

Lakotas call it Mato Tipi (Bear's Lodge), but it is known as Devils Tower to non-Indians. The name Devils Tower originated in 1875 during an expedition led by Col. Richard Irving Dodge. His interpreter misinterpreted the name to mean Bad God's Tower, later shortened to the Devils Tower. The first site to become a national monument, it received that designation from President Teddy Roosevelt in 1906 to protect the wildlife there. In 1956, the U.S. Post Office issued a three-cent stamp in honor of the tower's fiftieth anniversary as a national monument.

In the 1990s, the National Park Service tried to balance the competing interests of Indians and recreational rock climbers. Since 2006, the NPS Climbing Management Plan advocates for a June Voluntary Climbing Closure to encourage respect for American Indian tribes who view the tower as a sacred site. June is a culturally significant time to many Plains Indian Nations, when many ceremonies traditionally occur. Although voluntary, this closure has been very successful, resulting in an 80 percent reduction in the number of climbers during June.

PEYOTE RELIGION AND REVITALIZATION MOVEMENTS

Eight Facts about Peyote Religion

1. Peyote, a small spineless cactus, is used ceremonially to heal, pray, prophesy, and seek spiritual aid. Its origins trace back at least ten thousand years in the Rio Grande valley in present-day Mexico and Texas.
2. The ceremonial eating of peyote as a sacrament in the Peyote Religion is analogous to the centrality of bread and wine within churches.
3. Since the early twentieth century, accounts of the use of peyote in the Peyote Religion have represented it either as a sacrament, the holy medicine of Native American worship, or "the greatest and most insidious evil" (Lindquist 1923, 69).
4. Peyote plays a central and vital role in the Native American Church, which was established in Oklahoma in 1918 by adherents to the Peyote Religion.
5. Opposition to the Peyote Religion can be traced back to the early Spaniards in the Southwest. Christian missionaries and U.S. government agents also opposed the religious practice at the end of the nineteenth century. Peyotists were subject to raids, arrests, and imprisonment.
6. In 1990, in *Employment Division, Department of Human Resources of Oregon, et al. v. Smith et al.*, the Supreme Court ruled that the "free exercise of religion" clause in the First Amendment of the U.S. Constitution did not extend to the Native American Church because of its sacramental use of peyote.
7. Reuben A. Snake (Winnebago), Peyote Road Man or leader, became the prime mover in securing passage by Congress of a 1994 law, signed by President Bill Clinton, that exempted the religious use of peyote from federal and state controlled substance laws and prohibited discrimination against those who use peyote for religious purposes.
8. Laws regulating peyote use vary by state, although most follow the stipulations of the 1994 law. Use of peyote (religious or non-religious) outside of the ceremonies of the Native American Church is far more likely to be viewed as illegal by state authorities.

Seventeen Religious Revitalization Movements

As Native American groups began to experience dispossession, removal, and other assaults on their way of life, religious movements developed. These movements offered hope that lands would be restored, buffalo and game return, and oppressors disappear. Spiritual leaders emphasized a return to Native traditions, introduced new ceremonies and songs, and preached against alcohol and other destructive ways introduced by the Euro-American newcomers. Dreamers and prophets were often leaders of these religions.

1. Big Head Religion: 1874–77 among northern California tribal groups
2. Bole-Maru Religion: 1800s among north-central California tribal groups
3. Cherokee Religious Revival: 1811–13 in North Carolina area
4. Dream Dance: 1872 among Modoc and Klamath in southern Oregon
5. Drum Religion: around 1880 among tribes of the Midwest and western Great Lakes area
6. Earth Lodge Religion: around 1872 among tribes of northern California and southern Oregon
7. Feather Dance, Kiowa: 1894–1916 among the Kiowa of Western Oklahoma
8. Feather Religion: 1904 among tribal groups in the middle Columbia Plateau region
9. Ghost Dance of 1870: among the Northern Paiute in Nevada
10. Ghost Dance of 1889–90: among Great Basin and Plains Indian tribes
11. Handsome Lake Religion: 1799 to present day among Iroquois nations of New York and Canada
12. Holy Ground Religion: 1920s to present day among Apaches in Arizona
13. Indian Shaker Religion: 1881 to present day among Salish tribes in Puget Sound area of Washington and spread to California groups
14. Prophet Dance: around 1770 among tribes in the Columbia Plateau region of the Northwest Coast
15. Shawnee Prophet Religious Movement: 1806–22 among tribes in present-day Ohio area
16. Washani Religion: around 1850 into the twentieth century among tribes of the Columbia Plateau of the Pacific Northwest and Great Basin region
17. Washat Dance (Religion): late 1850 to present day among Yakama and other Native groups in present-day Washington State and Oregon

Seven Books about Revitalization Movements

1. *American Indian Prophets: Religious Leaders and Revitalization Movements*, edited by Clifford Trafzer (1986).
2. *Coming Down from Above: Prophecy, Resistance, and Renewal in Native American Religions*, by Lee Irwin (2008).
3. *Ghost Dances and Identity: Prophetic Religion and American Indian Ethnogenesis in the Nineteenth Century*, by Gregory Ellis Smoak (2006).
4. *Kenekuk, the Kickapoo Prophet*, by Joseph B. Herring (1988).
5. *The Lakota Ghost Dance of 1890*, by Rani-Henrik Andersson (2008).
6. *Prophets of the Great Spirit: Native American Revitalization Movements in Eastern North America*, by Alfred A. Cave (2006).
7. *The Shawnee Prophet*, by R. David Edmunds (1985).

LEGISLATION

Eleven Laws and Native American Religions

Antiquities Act of 1906

This act, which resulted from concerns about protecting ancient Indian ruins and artifacts ("antiquities"), allowed the president to set aside valuable public natural areas as park and conservation lands. Devils Tower in Wyoming became the first U.S. national monument under the act.

Migratory Bird Treaty Act of 1918

The Migratory Bird Treaty Act, originally passed in 1918, is the federal law that protects over eight hundred migratory birds under four international treaties between the U.S. and Canada, Japan, Mexico, and Russia. Under the act, no one may pursue, hunt, capture, kill, possess, sell, buy, barter, import, export, or transport any migratory bird, its parts (including feathers), nests, or eggs, except with a valid federal permit. The act permits Alaska Natives to take migratory birds for nutritional and other essential needs.

Bald and Golden Eagles Protection Act of 1940 and 1962

These federal acts are designed to protect endangered eagle populations by generally prohibiting their sale and possession. The laws provide for certain exceptions, including one for traditional religious and cultural uses by Native Americans. The scope of the exceptions has not been clearly defined in the law, leading to conflicts between practitioners and the U.S. Fish and Wildlife Service.

National Historic Preservation Act of 1966, amended in 1992

Amendments to the National Historic Preservation Act, originally passed in 1966, required federal agencies to consult with tribes about the effects their actions may have on religious places. The 1992 amendments made such sites eligible for the National Register of Historic Places if they met certain criteria. In 1996, President William Clinton issued an executive order that required extra precaution for any federal construction project that might interfere with a Native American sacred site.

American Indian Religious Freedom Act (AIRFA) of 1978

The act protects and preserves the inherent right of "American Indians, Eskimos, Aleuts, and Native Hawaiian" people to believe, express, and exercise their traditional religions, including "access to sites, use and possession of sacred objects, and freedom to worship through ceremonials and traditional rites." AIRFA has been viewed as more of a policy statement than a mandate giving Native people legally enforceable rights.

Archaeological Resources Protection Act of 1979

The act was designed to protect archaeological sites and objects located on public and American Indian lands from "uncontrolled excavation and pillage." The act requires that applicants seeking permits to work on Indian lands or public lands with religious sites must obtain the consent of Indian landowners or tribes having jurisdiction. Penalties for violating the act include fines and imprisonment.

National Museum of the American Indian Act of 1989

This law provides for identifying and repatriating to Native Americans any Indian human remains and funerary objects collected or controlled by the Smithsonian Institution. A 1996 amendment to the law extended repatriation requirements to sacred objects and objects of cultural patrimony. The number of American Indian human remains in the Smithsonian collection at the time was estimated at eighteen thousand.

Native American Graves Protection and Repatriation Act of 1990

This landmark act helps to protect Native American gravesites from looting and requires the repatriation to tribes of culturally identifiable remains, funerary objects, and objects of cultural patrimony taken from federal or tribal lands if certain legal criteria are met. The law does not apply to burial remains found on state or private lands. The act gives tribes legal means to reclaim artifacts of religious or ceremonial significance from federally supported museums.

Religious Freedom Restoration Act (RFRA) of 1993

The act addressed the U.S. Supreme Court's 1990 ruling (*Employment Division, Department of Human Resources of Oregon, et al. v. Smith et al.*) that the "free exercise of religion" clause in the First Amendment of the U.S. Constitution did not extend to the Native American Church because of its sacramental use of peyote. RFRA restored the "compelling interest" requirement in which governments would have to show an overriding public interest was being served by interfering with a religious practice. In 1997, the U.S. Supreme Court declared RFRA unconstitutional in *City of Boerne v. P. F. Flores.*

American Indian Religious Freedom Act Amendments of 1994

This landmark legislation guaranteed American Indians the right to use peyote, a small spineless cactus, in religious ceremonies. A coalition of Native American Church leaders, tribal leaders, and attorneys developed the strategy for enacting separate peyote legislation after Congress failed to pass a bill that would have protected sacramental peyote. Technically this law amends the American Indian Religious Freedom Act of 1978.

Religious Land Use and Institutionalized Persons Act of 2000

The Religious Land Use and Institutionalized Persons Act of 2000 provided stronger protection for religious freedom in prison. The law gave prisoners a powerful tool for challenging prison regulations that burden their religious freedom. Federal and state prisons had prohibited incarcerated Native people from conducting ceremonies central to their spiritual beliefs. Many prisons also banned the possession of tobacco ties and prayer pipes; long hair; and participation in sweat lodges.

NATIVE RELIGIOUS LEADERS

Fourteen Autobiographies and Biographies of Native Religious Leaders

1. *Black Elk Speaks: Being the Life Story of a Holy Man of the Oglala Sioux,* by Black Elk (Oglala Lakota) as told through John G. Neihardt (1932).
2. *Crow Dog: Four Generations of Sioux Medicine Men,* by Leonard Crow Dog (Sicangu Lakota) with Richard Erdoes (1996).
3. *Dakota Cross-Bearer: The Life and World of a Native American Bishop* [Harold Stephen Jones (Santee Dakota)], by Mary E. Cochran (2004).
4. *Fools Crow* [Frank Fools Crow (Lakota)], by Thomas E. Mails (1979).
5. *Hosteen Klah: Navaho Medicine Man and Sand Painter,* by Franc Johnson Newcomb (1964).
6. *The Indian Priest: Philip B. Gordon, 1885–1948* [Philip B. Gordon (Ojibway)], by Paula Delfeld (1977).
7. *Lame Deer: Seeker of Visions* [John Lame Deer (Lakota)], with Richard Erdoes (1972).
8. *Not for Innocent Ears: The Spiritual Traditions of a Desert Cahuilla Medicine Woman* [Ruby Modesto (Cahuilla)], as told to Guy Mount (1980).
9. *Pretty Shield: Medicine Woman of the Crows,* as told to Frank Linderman (1931).
10. *Render unto Caesar: Serving the Nation by Living Our Catholic Beliefs in Political Life,* by Charles J. Chaput (Prairie Band Potawatomi) (2008).
11. *Reuben Snake, Your Humble Serpent: Indian Visionary and Activist* [Reuben Snake (Winnebago)], as told to Jay C. Fikes (2006).
12. *Sanapia: Comanche Medicine Woman,* by David E. Jones (1984).
13. *Silent Courage: An Indian Story: The Autobiography of George P. Lee,* by George P. Lee (Navajo) (1987).
14. *Yellowtail, Crow Medicine Man and Sun Dance Chief: An Autobiography* [Yellowtail (Crow)], as told to Michael Oren Fitzgerald (1991).

Black Elk's World

http://www.firstpeople.us/articles/Black-Elk-Speaks/Black-Elk-Speaks-Index.html The full text of *Black Elk Speaks,* the story of the Lakota visionary and healer Nicholas Black Elk (1863–1950) as told to John G. Neihardt. The electronic version includes twenty-five chapters.

FILMS

Kinaalda: Navajo Rite of Passage (USA, 1999, 56 min.), directed by Lena Carr (Navajo).

> In this documentary, the story of a young Navajo girl's coming-of-age ceremony parallels the story of a Navajo woman who did not have the ceremony.

Life Spirit (USA, 1993, 24 min.), directed by Fidel Moreno (Yaqui/Huichol).

> *Life Spirit* features interviews with nine U.S. Native leaders who express the importance of repatriation of ceremonial materials and their value to living cultures.

Native Spirit and *The Sun Dance Way* (USA, 2007, 54 min., 57 min.), directed by Jennifer Casey.

> Two documentaries draw heavily on the words of the late Sun Dance Chief, Thomas Yellowtail, and provide an account of the Sun Dance ceremony and the spiritual context of which it is the central expression. There are ninety minutes of special features including a sweat lodge, vision quest, pipe prayer, and biography of Thomas Yellowtail.

The Peyote Road (USA, 1992, 59 min.), directed by Fidel Moreno (Yaqui/Huichol), Gary Rhine, and Phil Cousineau.

> *The Peyote Road* documents the centuries-old sacramental use of peyote and addresses the 1991 *Employment Division v. Smith* Supreme Court decision, which denied First Amendment religious liberty protection to Native peyote ceremonies, which are part of one of the oldest tribal religions in the Western hemisphere.

A Seat at the Table: Struggling for American Indian Religious Freedom (USA, 2004, 90 min.), directed by Gary Rhine.

> This documentary features eight American Indian leaders who discuss the myriad problems faced by contemporary Native Americans in practicing their religious ceremonies and beliefs. The film interweaves the commentaries with sequences shot in threatened American Indian sacred sites and scenes from the third Parliament of the World's Religions in Cape Town, South Africa.

We Pray with Tobacco (USA, 1998, 60 min.), directed by John and Ismana Carney.

> The sacred significance of tobacco is explained through interviews, storytelling, traditional singing, drumming, and reenactments.

White Shamans and Plastic Medicine Men (USA, 1995, 26 min.), directed by Terry Macy and Daniel Hart.

> The documentary presents the opinions regarding the issues of the marketing of Native American spiritual and religious practices by non-Indians.

Your Humble Serpent: The Wisdom of Reuben Snake (USA, 1996, 70 min.), directed by Gary Rhine.

> The portrait of Reuben Snake (Winnebago), which includes interviews with relatives and friends, provides a look at an American Indian leader who created the

Native American Religious Freedom Project. The project led to the passage of the 1994 legislation providing First Amendment protection of sacramental peyote.

ORGANIZATIONS

Association on American Indian Affairs (AAIA)
http://www.indian-affairs.org/programs/aaia_programs.htm
> The Association on American Indian Affairs, a nonprofit membership organization headquartered in Rockville, Maryland, was launched in 1922. It conducts programs in sacred site protection and repatriation.

Friends Committee on National Legislation (A Quaker Lobby in the Public Interest) http://fcnl.org/issues/nativeam
> The site contains information about issues of importance to Native Americans. The Friends Committee on National Legislation, a public lobby organization founded in 1943 and based in Washington, DC, encourages "respectful relations with Native peoples" and advocates that the federal government "should relate directly to tribal governments, respecting their sovereignty" (http://fcnl .org/about/govern/policy/equity_and_justice).

National Congress of American Indians (NCAI)
http://www.ncai.org/Cultural-Protection.71.0.html
> The National Congress of American Indians, founded in 1944 and based in Washington, DC, created a Sacred Lands Protection Coalition (SLPC) to collaborate with the Seventh Generation Fund, the Native American Rights Fund, and the Association on American Indian Affairs. The SLPC plays a key role in efforts to strengthen legal protections for sacred sites and to secure administrative accommodations for their use by Indian religious practitioners.

Seventh Generation Fund For Indian Development
http://www.7genfund.org
> The Seventh Generation Fund, founded in 1977 and headquartered in Arcata, California, has programs in environmental health and justice aimed at preserving, protecting, and restoring the traditional, cultural, and spiritual values of sacred places.

Tekakwitha Conference
http://groups.creighton.edu/tekconf
> The Tekakwitha Conference, incorporated in 1979 and headquartered in Great Falls, Montana, sponsors local Native Catholic groups, known as "Kateri Circles." The conference hosts a national convention each year that attracts hundreds of Native American Catholics.

RESOURCES

Beck, Peggy V., Anna Lee Walters, and Nia Francisco. *The Sacred: Ways of Knowledge, Sources of Life.* Tsaile, AZ: Navajo Community College Press, 1977.

Bowden, Henry Warner. *American Indians and Christian Missions: Studies in Cultural Conflict.* Chicago: University of Chicago Press, 1985.

Cousineau, Phil, ed. *A Seat at the Table: Huston Smith in Conversation with Native Americans on Religious Freedom.* Berkeley: University of California Press, 2006.

Deloria, Vine, Jr. *God is Red: A Native View of Religion.* 30th anniversary edition. Golden, CO: Fulcrum, 1993.

Echo-Hawk, Roger C., and Walter Echo-Hawk. *Battlefields and Burial Grounds: The Indian Struggle to Protect Ancestral Graves in the United States.* Minneapolis: Lerner Publications, 1994.

Jenkins, Philip. *Dreamcatchers: How Mainstream America Discovered Native Spirituality.* New York: Oxford University Press, 2004.

Lindquist, G. E. E. *The Red Man in the United States.* New York: G. H. Duran, 1923.

Long, Carolyn N. *Religious Freedom and Indian Rights: The Case of Oregon v. Smith.* Lawrence: University Press of Kansas, 2000.

Maroukis, Thomas Constantine. *The Peyote Road: Religious Freedom and the Native American Church.* Norman: University of Oklahoma Press, 2010.

Mihesuah, Devon, ed. *A Repatriation Reader: Who Owns American Indian Remains?* Lincoln: University of Nebraska Press, 2000.

O'Brien, Suzanne J. Crawford, and Dennis Francis Kelley, eds. *American Indian Religious Traditions: An Encyclopedia* (3 vols.). Santa Barbara, CA: ABC-CLIO, 2005.

Smith, Huston, and Reuben Snake, eds. *One Nation Under God: The Triumph of the Native American Church.* Santa Fe, NM: Clear Light Publishers, 1996.

Stewart, Omer C. *Peyote Religion: A History.* Norman: University of Oklahoma Press, 1987.

Thomas, R. Murray. *Manitou and God: North-American Indian Religions and Christian Culture.* Santa Barbara, CA: Praeger, 2007.

Tinker, George E. (Osage/Cherokee). *Missionary Conquest: The Gospel and Native American Cultural Genocide.* Minneapolis: Fortress Press, 1993.

Treat, James, ed. *Native and Christian: Indigenous Voices on Religious Identity in the United States and Canada.* New York: Routledge, 1996.

Vecsey, Christopher, ed. *Handbook of American Indian Religious Freedom.* New York: Crossroad, 1991.

Wenger, Tisa. *We Have a Religion: The 1920s Pueblo Indian Dance Controversy and American Religious Freedom.* Chapel Hill: University of North Carolina Press, 2009.

Web Sites

Canyon Records: Native American Church/Peyote/Healing: http://www.canyonrecords.com/store

Devils Tower: http://www.nps.gov/deto/historyculture/sacredsite.htm

Is Nothing Sacred: Corporate Responsibility for the Protection of Native American Sacred Sites: http://www.sacredland.org/PDFs/csr_dl.pdf

Kifaru Productions: http://www.kifaru.com/index.html

help Indians as stockholders, borrowers, and depositors" (*Time* 1974). The bank folded in the late 1980s.

1979   The Seminole Tribe of Florida opened the first high-stakes bingo hall and casino in the United States. The facility was the forerunner of the Indian gaming movement throughout North America.

1985   The Jicarilla Apache Tribe of New Mexico became the first Indian tribe to issue a tax-free bond using the provisions of the Indian Tribal Governmental Tax Status Act of 1982 to issue bonds paying tax-free interest to the purchasers. The bond was worth more than $30 million.

1987   The Blackfeet Tribe of Montana opened the Blackfeet National Bank (BNB) in Browning, Montana, the first national bank on an Indian reservation owned by an Indian tribe. Elouise Cobell (Blackfeet) was instrumental in its founding. In 2001, it was acquired by Native American Bancorporation, a bank holding company founded in 1998, which acquired the BNB as a wholly owned subsidiary and changed the name to Native American Bank, N.A. The Browning branch provides financial services to consumers, small businesses, and agricultural enterprises.

1988   Richard Mike (Navajo) opened the first Burger King restaurant on the Navajo Reservation at Kayenta, Arizona. Mike, whose father was a code talker, designed part of the restaurant as a code talker museum.

1994   Dave Anderson (Chippewa/Choctaw) opened his first Famous Dave's BBQ Shack in Hayward, Wisconsin. In November 1995, Famous Dave's was named first-place winner for its Rich & Sassy BBQ sauce at the American Royal Barbecue Sauce Contest in Kansas City, Missouri—the largest and most prestigious barbeque contest in the world—and other awards followed. Over 170 Famous Dave's restaurants are located in thirty-seven states.

1996   The leaders of the City of Greater Marysville, Washington, Chamber of Commerce expanded the name of its chamber to the Greater Marysville Tulalip Chamber of Commerce. While the Tulalip Tribes were already members, the chamber recognized the tribes' growing role in the region's economy and acknowledged the strength that comes from partnering after decades of mistrust and stereotypical thinking. To date, it is the first and only U.S. Chamber of Commerce to partner with a tribal nation. A new regional facility at the crossroads of the two communities opened in 2002.

Rebecca L. Adamson (Cherokee), founder and president of First Nations Development Institute, received the Robert W. Scrivner Award for Creative Grantmaking by the Council of Foundations, the first award to acknowledge Ms. Adamson's framework for Native economic development, which incorporates traditional knowledge and values. The same year, she received the Jay Silverheels Achievement Award from the National Center for American Indian Enterprise Development for her contributions to the Native community. In 2001, Independent Sector awarded her the John W. Gardner Leadership Award.

1999   The Morongo Band of Mission Indians opened the first Coco's Restaurant owned by an American Indian Tribe. It is located in Cabazon, California.

2000   Oweesta was the first national Native institution to be certified as a Community Development Financial Institutions (CDFI) Fund intermediary through the U.S. Department of the Treasury, dedicated to providing technical assistance, training, research, and lending for local Native CDFIs in all fifty states.

2005   The Indigenous Internet Chamber of Commerce (IICC) became the first cross-continent Chamber of Commerce. It unites indigenous peoples of the Western Hemisphere, from Greenland to Argentina, through communication, technology, education, and commerce. IICC provides a connecting place for Native people to market their products and services to a world market.

2007   The Seminole Tribe of Florida purchased the Hard Rock International, Inc., business family for approximately $965 million. It was the first American Indian tribe to acquire an international corporation. The Seminole acquired 124 Hard Rock Cafes, five hotels, and several Hard Rock Live concert venues, as well as the world's largest collection of rock and roll memorabilia, some seventy thousand pieces.

Pojoaque Pueblo of New Mexico teamed up with Hilton Hotels to create the Buffalo Thunder Resort, the first time the renowned hotel chain became involved in a joint project with a tribal government.

2008   The Tanka Bar, made by Native American Natural Foods on South Dakota's Pine Ridge Reservation, became the first national brand product to originate from an Indian reservation.

The Coushatta Tribe of Louisiana recognized and honored official representatives of the State of Israel, the first Indian tribe to extend a welcome. The tribe has become an exclusive importer of Aya Natural, an Israeli company that markets an all-natural, olive oil–based line of skin care products.

2009   The National Center for American Indian Enterprise Development, which celebrated its fortieth anniversary, compiled a "40 Under 40" list of Native Americans aged 18–39 who were selected for their leadership, initiative, and dedication to propelling Native businesses and communities forward.

2010   Margo Gray-Proctor (Osage Nation) became the first woman to chair the National Center for American Indian Enterprise Development, which represents thousands of business owners.

The Mashantucket Pequot Gaming Enterprise of Mashantucket, Connecticut, and 2,500 dealers represented by UAW Local 2121 reached the first labor contract negotiated under tribal law. The landmark agreement left in place a federal appeals court ruling that sovereign Indian nations are subject to the National Labor Relations Act.

2011   NativeOne Institutional Trading LLC, a California financial firm, became the first Native-owned business to become a member of the New York Stock Exchange. It offers services and products to all tribes and Canadian First Nations, as well as institutional investors, state treasurers, pension funds, and endowments.

2011   Turkey became the first foreign nation officially represented at the annual Reservation Economic Summit of the National Center for American Indian Enterprise Development. The Turkish delegation proposed developing business-to-business relations.

The Yocha Dehe Wintun Nation of California launched a state-of-the-art sustainable olive oil enterprise, the first of its kind in the United States.

BUSINESSES OWNED BY AMERICAN INDIANS AND ALASKA NATIVES

Ten Facts about Businesses Owned by American Indians and Alaska Natives in 2007

The U.S. Census Bureau's 2007 Survey of Business Owners defines American Indian– and Alaska Native–owned businesses as firms in which American Indians and Alaska Natives own 51 percent or more of the stock or equity of the business. Alaska Native regional corporations and villages and tribally owned businesses are outside the scope of survey. These business ventures range from retail food and arts and crafts stores (including some that are Internet based), gas stations, and restaurants, to construction companies, radio stations, and commercial fishing companies.

1. There were $34.4 billion in receipts for Native-owned businesses, up 28 percent from 2002.
2. American Indian/Alaska Native–owned firms represented 0.9 percent of all U.S. non-farm firms.
3. There were 236,967 Native-owned non-farm businesses, up 17.7 percent from 2002.

4. A total of 30.5 percent of Native-owned businesses were in the construction industry, repair, maintenance, or personal and laundry services.
5. Of the 236,967 Native-owned businesses, 23,704 had paid employees, a decrease of 3.2 percent from 2002. Their payrolls totaled $5.9 billion, an increase of 15.4 percent. Receipts from these employer businesses totaled $27.5 billion, up 25.1 percent.
6. There were 213,263 Native-owned businesses with no paid employees, an increase of 20.6 percent from 2002. These non-employer businesses generated $6.9 billion in receipts, an increase of 40.7 percent from 2002.
7. The number of Native-owned businesses with receipts of $1 million or more increased 26.7 percent, from 3,631 in 2002 to 4,599 in 2007.
8. The number of Native-owned businesses with one hundred employees or more decreased by 9.0 percent, from 178 to 162.
9. California had the most Native-owned firms, with 45,629; Oklahoma had 21,194, and Texas 19,057.
10. American Indian– and Alaska Native–owned businesses accounted for 10.0 percent of businesses in Alaska, 6.3 percent in Oklahoma, and 5.3 percent in New Mexico.

Twelve Businesses Owned by Tribes, American Indians, Individuals,
and Native Hawaiians in 2010

The following list of businesses owned and operated by tribes, American Indians, individuals, and Native Hawaiians reflects a diversity of firms.

1. Ad-Pro
   http://www.adproweb.com
   > Founded in 1988, the award-winning company Ad-Pro, headquartered in Huntington Beach, California, specializes in advertising and graphic design services, convention exhibits, promotional items, printing, silkscreen imprinting, public relations, signage, marketing, and Web and multimedia services.
2. Arrow Strategies
   http://www.arrowstrategies.com
   > Founded in 2002, the award-winning Arrow Strategies is a leading provider of full-service staffing solutions, including contract, contract-to-hire, and permanent placements of high-end professionals in information technology, engineering, accounting/finance, and professional services. Arrow Strategies is headquartered in Bingham Farms, Michigan.
3. Cherokee Nation Industries
   http://www.cherokee-corp.com/
   > Established in 1969, Cherokee Nation Industries, located in Stilwell, Oklahoma, utilizes a portfolio of 8(a), HUBZone, Small Disadvantaged

and Minority Business Enterprise companies to leverage business opportunities and enhance financial opportunities in aerospace and defense, telecommunications, technology solutions, staffing, office products, and construction management.

4. Choctaw Office Supply
   http://wb019.britlink.com/BL5/choctawofficesupply
   Founded in the late 1980s on the Choctaw Reservation in Choctaw, Mississippi, the company sells office supplies, furniture, and cleaning and janitorial supplies.

5. Dancing Rabbit Golf Club
   http://www.dancingrabbitgolf.com
   Built on the ancestral lands of the Mississippi Choctaw in Choctaw, Mississippi, the award-winning Dancing Rabbit Golf Club, designed by Tom Fazio and Jerry Pate, features two championship golf courses that opened in 1997 and 1999.

6. Dawson
   http://www.dawson8a.com
   Founded in 1994, Dawson, a for-profit firm owned by the Hawaiian Native Corporation, a nonprofit organization, originally provided environmental remediation services throughout the Hawaiian Islands. It has evolved into a provider of energy conservation, construction, and military munitions response program services to commercial and federal clients throughout the United States.

7. Kah-Nee-Ta High Desert Resort and Casino
   http://www.kahneeta.com
   Kah-Nee-Ta Resort, located on the Confederated Tribes of Warm Springs Reservation in Oregon, includes a lodge, which opened in 1972, championship golf course, a double Olympic-sized pool, spa, riding stables, hiking trails, and casino, opened in 1995, as well as an award-winning museum.

8. Native American Natural Foods
   http://www.tankabars.com
   Founded in 2005 and based on South Dakota's Pine Ridge Reservation, Native American Natural Foods makes the award-winning Tanka products, created from real buffalo meat and cranberries and based on a centuries-old recipe for using fruit to preserve dried meat.

9. Native Threads
   http://www.nativethreads.com
   Founded in 1990, Native Threads (NT), a clothing company headquartered in Valley Center, California, creates contemporary designs with messages that are traditional, cultural, and conscious of the social, political, and economic current trends that affect Native peoples.

10. Navajo Arts and Crafts Enterprise
    http://www.gonavajo.com
       Alarmed at the volume of counterfeit products flooding into the Four
       Corners region, Navajo Arts and Crafts Guild was conceived by tribal
       leaders in 1941 to protect craft traditions and the livelihood of Nava-
       jo craftspeople and artisans. Today, Navajo Arts and Crafts Enterprises
       (NACE), headquartered in Window Rock, Arizona, remains the official
       marketing channel of the Navajo Nation for arts and crafts.

11. Sister Sky Bath and Beauty Products
    http://sistersky.com/aboutus.htm
       Founded in 1999 and headquartered in Spokane, Washington, two sis-
       ters launched Sister Sky, an award-winning company that manufactures
       herbal bath and body care products including lotions, shampoos, condi-
       tioners, and body wash.

12. Sole Nation Health
    http://solenationhealth.com/
       Founded in the early 1990s and headquartered in Mesa, Arizona, the
       footwear company is dedicated to the prevention of diabetic-related foot
       problems.

Six Key Findings Regarding Native American Unemployment 2010

From the first half of 2007 to the first half of 2010, the national American Indian
   unemployment rate increased 7.7 percentage points to 15.2 percent. This
   increase was 1.6 times the size of the increase among white Americans.
By the first half of 2010, the unemployment rate for Alaska Natives jumped
   6.3 percentage points to 21.3 percent—the highest regional unemployment
   rate for American Indians.
Since the start of the recession, American Indians in the Midwest experienced
   the greatest increase in unemployment, growing by 10.3 percentage points to
   19.3 percent.
By the first half of 2010, slightly more than half—51.5 percent—of American Indians
   nationally were working, down from 58.3 percent in the first half of 2007.
In the first half of 2010, only 44 percent of American Indians in the Northern Plains
   were working, the worst employment rate for Native Americans regionally.
The employment situation is the worst for American Indians in some of the same
   regions where it is best for whites: Alaska and the Northern Plains.

Source: Algernon Austin, "Different Race, Different Recession: American Indian Unemployment in 2010." *Economic Policy Institute*, Issue Brief #289, November 18, 2010.

American Indian Chambers of Commerce

American Indian Chambers of Commerce are advocacy organizations for American Indian businesses. They provide networking opportunities, mentoring, training and development, legislative updates, collaboration with other businesses, and social events. The following states and regions have American Indian chambers of commerce:

Arizona
California
Colorado: Rocky Mountain area
Colorado: Western American Indian Chamber, Denver
Hawaii
Kansas
Minnesota
Nevada
New Mexico
North Carolina
Oklahoma
Oregon
South Carolina
South Dakota: Pine Ridge area
Texas
Washington, DC
Wisconsin

Native Hawaiian–Owned Businesses, 2007

The U.S. Census Bureau reported that people of Native Hawaiian origin owned 55.6 percent of all Native Hawaiian and Other Pacific Islander–owned businesses in 2007. The number of businesses increased 31.1 percent between 2002 and 2007, to 37,957. They earned $6.5 billion in receipts in 2007, a 51.6 percent increase from 2002.

Source: Survey of Business Owners: Native Hawaiian—and Other Pacific Islanders—Owned Businesses: 2007. U.S. Census Bureau, 2011.

HONORING NATIONS PROJECT, HARVARD UNIVERSITY

Honoring Nations Honorees, 1999–2010

Honoring Nations, a national award program launched in 1998, highlights outstanding programs in self-governance by Native nations. At the heart of the program is the belief that tribes themselves hold the key to positive, social, political, cultural, and economic prosperity. Based at the John F. Kennedy School of Government at Harvard University, Honoring Nations is administered by the Harvard Project on American Indian Economic Development. The criteria for selection of honorees include program effectiveness, significance to sovereignty, cultural relevance, transferability, and sustainability. The programs honored include outstanding tribal businesses and corporations.

Pte Hca Ka, Inc., 1999
Cheyenne River Tribe
Gettysburg, South Dakota

> The tribally owned and chartered corporation, founded in 1991, manages and develops a biologically sound tribal buffalo herd and financially sound enterprise. It helped restore the centrality of buffalo to Lakota life by making animals available to tribal members for ceremonial use, traditional feasts, tribal schools, elder programs, and national Indian events.

Tax Initiative Economic Development, Kayenta Township Commission, 1999
Navajo Nation
Kayenta, Arizona

> The Navajo Nation Council created Kayenta Township as a municipal style government. In 1997, the first Kayenta Township Commission levied a retail sales tax, which became a significant revenue stream for the self-sufficient township, located near Monument Valley, a popular tourist destination.

Economic Development Corporation: Ho-Chunk, Inc., 2000
Winnebago Tribe of Nebraska
Winnebago, Nebraska

> Launched in 1994, Ho-Chunk, Inc. (HCI) has diversified the tribe's business interests while maintaining a separation between itself and tribal government. According to its Web site, in 2010 HCI operated eighteen subsidiaries in eight states, Washington, DC, and three countries. HCI industries include information technology, construction, government contracting, wholesale distribution, marketing, media, and retail.

Small Business Development Program (SBDP) Corporate Commission, 2000
Milles Lacs Band of Ojibwe Indians
Onamia, Minnesota

> Created in 1996 and organized under a tribal corporation, SBDP provides technical assistance, management and business skills training, education, and

low-interest loans to the band's entrepreneurial members. The program's micro and macro loans have helped people start up agricultural, construction, service, retail, and home-based enterprises.

Yukaana Development Corporation, 2000
Louden Tribal Council
Galena, Alaska

Created by the Louden Tribal Council (Athabascan Indians), in 1997 as a for-profit corporate environmental remediation business, the Yukaana Development Corporation (YDC) led a successful effort to clean up contamination caused by a local U.S. Air Force base. YDC provides workforce training and jobs. Community members have become qualified for asbestos abatement and lead-based paint removal.

Bringing Financial and Business Expertise to Tribes, Borrego Springs Bank, 2002
Viejas Band of Kumeyaay Indians
Mesa, California

The Borrego Springs Bank (the Viejas Band has been a majority owner since 1996) offers services to tribal and Native-owned businesses to foster economic self-sufficiency and improve their access to capital, credit counseling and loans, trust assistance, housing programs, fund management assistance, infrastructure loans, tax deferral programs, and federal lending programs. This became the first tribally owned bank in California.

Quil Ceda Village, 2003
Tulalip Tribes
Tulalip, Washington

In 1998, Tulalip Tribes created Quil Ceda Village (QCV) as a tribal city located within the tribes' reservation. QCV boasts a business park, nationwide retailers, an open-air outlets mall, casino, and infrastructure (roads, water, and sewage). The anchor stores, businesses, and casino employ thousands of people, many of them Tulalip citizens.

Migizi Business Camp, Education Department, 2005
Little River Band of Ottawa Indians
Manistee, Michigan

In early 2000, the tribal planning and education departments of the Little River Band created a business camp for tribal youth in seventh through twelfth grades, living on or off the reservation. Students learned small business development concepts and entrepreneurial skills. At the end of the camp, they made business plan presentations to a panel, which awarded cash prizes.

ONABEN: Native American Business Network, 2005
Confederated Tribes of Grand Ronde, Confederated Tribes of the Warm Springs Reservation, Confederated Tribes of Siletz Indians, Confederated Tribes of the

Umatilla Indian Reservation, Cowlitz Indian Tribe, and Confederated Tribes of the Colville Reservation Tigard, Oregon

> Founded in 1991 by a consortium of Pacific Northwest nations, ONABEN encourages the development of the private sector on reservations by providing business mentoring, referrals to start-up financing, and access to teachers and business people. ONABEN is regarded as the "go-to" organization when tribes or individuals need assistance in developing micro-enterprise.

Siyeh Development Corporation, 2005
Blackfeet Nation
Browning, Montana

> In 1999 the Blackfeet Nation established Siyeh Corporation, a for-profit business, to generate and manage businesses on behalf of, but separate from, the tribal government. Siyeh's successful business ventures include StarLink Cable, which provides over forty television channels, and the Blackfeet Heritage Center and Art Gallery. Siyeh is named for a revered Blackfeet leader.

Citizen Potawatomi Community Development Corporation, 2006
Citizen Potawatomi Nation
Shawnee, Oklahoma

> Founded in 2003, the Citizen Potawatomi Community Development Corporation (CPCDC) was created to stimulate small businesses and entrepreneurs that provide products and services for Citizen Potawatomi Nation members nationwide and to all Oklahoma American Indians. Its award-winning pro-

---

Community Development Financial Institution (CDFI) Fund

Created in 1994, the CDFI Fund, a program of the U.S. Treasury Department, works to expand the capacity of financial institutions to provide credit, capital, and financial services to underserved populations and communities throughout the United States by providing direct monetary awards and training.

The CDFI Fund has a longstanding commitment to Native American, Alaska Native, and Native Hawaiian communities. The fund's 2001 publication, the congressionally mandated Native American Lending Study, identified seventeen barriers to credit and capital, including the lack of financial institutions on or near Native communities. Between 2002 and 2011, the CDFI Fund awarded more than 175 grants totaling $31 million to Native CDFIs serving almost one hundred Native communities. These institutions enable locally based organizations to create jobs, develop businesses, and provide housing, home ownership, and community development financial services.

grams include business development, financial education, credit counseling, and commercial and emergency employee loans.

Project Pueblo: Economic Development Revitalization Project, 2010
Ysleta del Sur Pueblo
El Paso, Texas

Between 2006 and 2010, the Ysleta del Sur Pueblo developed a Comprehensive Economic Development Strategy, a new set of economic and business policies, new business and commercial laws and regulations, and a new mindset geared toward long-term planning.

CASINOS AND GOLF COURSES

Fourteen Facts about American Indian Casinos

1. In 1987, the U.S. Supreme Court in *California v. Cabazon Band of Mission Indians* confirmed the authority of tribal governments to establish gaming operations independent of state regulation.
2. In 1988, Congress passed the Indian Gaming Regulatory Act (IGRA), which provided a regulatory framework for Indian gaming.
3. Indian tribes are the primary regulators of Class I (traditional games) and Class II gaming (bingo, pull tabs, lotto, punch boards, and certain card games not prohibited by the state in which the casino is located).
4. Regulation of Class III gaming (baccarat, blackjack, chemin de fer, slot machines, and electronic facsimiles of any game of chance) is addressed in tribal-state compacts and varies by state.
5. Tribal-state compacts are agreements that establish rules to govern the conduct of Class III gaming activities. The secretary of the interior must approve the contracts.
6. Congress vested the federal National Indian Gaming Commission (NIGC) (http://www.nigc.gov) with broad authority to issue regulations regarding Class II and Class III gaming.
7. According to the NIGC, in 2009, there were 456 casinos with Class II and Class III facilities in twenty-nine states.
8. The NIGC announced that gross gaming revenues in 2010 totaled about $26.5 billion, matching revenues from 2009.
9. According to the NIGC, gaming revenues are not distributed equally among the gaming tribes. Facilities with annual revenues of less than $100 million constitute over 80 percent of the more than four hundred operations, while fewer than 20 percent of the operations generate about 70 percent of the $26.5 billion in revenues.
10. Federal law mandates that tribal gaming income be spent on five general purposes.

11. Tribal gaming is subject to stringent regulation, overseen by the federal National Indian Gaming Commission, the U.S. Treasury, and tribal and state authorities.

12. Tribes spend hundreds of millions of dollars annually on purchasing goods and services from non-Native firms.

13. Indian gaming brings tangible economic benefits to Indian nations and non-Indian communities around them. It employs thousands of tribal members and non-Indian workers nationwide.

14. Indian casinos extend beyond gaming and may include shops, restaurants, golf courses, swimming pools, spas, big name entertainment, and convention facilities.

Eleven Books about American Indian Casinos

1. *Casino and Museum: Representing the Mashantucket Pequot Identity*, by John J. Bodinger de Uriarte (2007).
2. *Gambling and Survival in Native North America*, by Paul Pasquaretta (2003).
3. *High Stakes: Florida Seminole Gaming and Sovereignty*, by Jessica R. Cattelino (2008).
4. *Indian Gaming*, by Stuart A. Kallen, editor (2006).
5. *Indian Gaming and Tribal Sovereignty: The Casino Compromise*, by Steven Andrew Light and Kathryn R. L. Land (2005).
6. *Indian Gaming and the Law*, by William R. Eadington and Judy Cornelius (1998).
7. *Indian Gaming: Tribal Sovereignty and American Politics*, by W. Dale Mason (2000).
8. *Indian Gaming: Who Wins?* by Angela Mullis (2000).
9. *New Capitalists: Law, Politics, and Identity Surrounding Casino Gaming on Native American Land*, by Eve Darian-Smith (2003).
10. *New Politics of Indian Gaming: The Rise of Reservation Interest Groups*, by Kenneth Hanson and Tracy Skopek (2011).
11. *Tourism and Gaming on American Indian Lands*, edited by Alan A. Lew and George A. Van Otten (1998).

Sixteen Native American Golf Courses

Tourism development in Indian country has led to many tribal governments building and managing golf courses. Dozens of Native-owned golf courses stretching from Florida to California attract visitors to reservations. Tribes have hired many of the best course designers in the nation to create physically beautiful and challenging courses. Some Native courses have been named as among the best public courses in America.

Arizona
Fort McDowell Yavapai Nation: We-Ko-Pa Golf Club

California
Pechanga Band of Luiseño Indians: The Journey at Pechanga

Florida
Miccosukee Tribe: Miccosukee Golf and Country Club

Idaho
Coeur d'Alene Tribe: Circling Raven Golf Club

Kansas
Prairie Band Potawatomi Nation: Firekeeper Golf Course

Louisiana
Tunica-Biloxi Tribe: Tamahka Trails Golf Club

Michigan
Hannahville Indian Community of the Potawatomi Nation: Sweetgrass Golf Club

Minnesota
Bois Forte Band of Chippewa: The Wilderness at Fortune Bay Casino

Mississippi
Mississippi Band of Choctaw Indians: Dancing Rabbit Golf Club (two courses)

Nebraska
Santee Sioux Tribe: Santee Sioux Golf Club

Nevada
Paiute Nation: Paiute Golf Resort

New Mexico
Santa Clara Pueblo: Black Mesa Golf Club

New York
Oneida Indian Nation: Turning Stone Resort (three courses)

North Carolina
Eastern Band of Cherokees: Sequoyah National Golf Club

Oregon
Cayuse, Umatilla, and Walla Walla Tribes: Wildhorse Golf Club

Washington
Squaxin Island Tribe: Salish Cliffs Golf Club

LEGISLATION

*Thirteen Selected Federal Laws Promoting Business and Economic
Development in Indian Country*

Congress has enacted many laws designed to promote business and economic
development in Indian country.

Buy Indian Act of 1910

The Buy Indian Act "grants a purchasing priority to the products of Indian
industry" and also promotes the employment of American Indians. In 1976, the
Bureau of Indian Affairs adopted the policy to contract with qualified Indian
contractors to the maximum practicable extent. In more recent times, some tribal
governments began adopting Buy Indian resolutions in their business codes.

Small Business Act of 1953 and Amendments

The Small Business Act of 1953, amended a number of times, created the
Small Business Administration (SBA). SBA grew to include specialized outreach to socially and economically disadvantaged individuals of certain racial
or ethnic heritage, Indian tribes, Alaska Native corporations, Native Hawaiian
organizations, and community development corporations. The 7(a) loan program helps start-up and existing small businesses obtain financing through
bank and non-bank institutions. The 8(a) program provides federal procurement assistance to economically disadvantaged businesses.

Indian Self-Determination and Education Assistance Act of 1975

The Indian Self-Determination and Education Assistance Act recognized
American Indian tribes' desires to control their own destinies. Through the
use of "638 contracts," tribal governments have carried out on their reservations economic development programs formerly provided by the Bureau of
Indian Affairs.

Indian Tribal Government Tax Status Act of 1982

The Indian Tribal Government Tax Status Act treats Indian tribes like
states so that they can issue tax-free bonds for projects "customarily" financed
by states and local governments, such as schools, roads, and government
buildings. The law also treats subdivisions of an Indian tribal government as
a political subdivision of a state as long as the subdivision has been delegated
the right to exercise one or more of the substantial governmental functions of
the Indian tribal government.

Indian Gaming Regulatory Act of 1988
 The Indian Gaming Regulatory Act established the jurisdictional framework that governs Indian gaming. The law also established the National Indian Gaming Commission, an independent regulatory authority to regulate gaming on Indian lands.

Indian Employment, Training, and Related Services Demonstration Act of 1992
 The Indian Employment, Training, and Related Services Demonstration Act, amended by the Omnibus Indian Advancement Act of 2000, has allowed federally recognized tribal governments and Alaska Native entities to combine federal funds, which they receive under grant programs related to employment and training, into a single plan with a single budget and one reporting system. A single comprehensive program reduces administrative costs. The 2000 law authorized tribes to devote up to 25 percent (depending on their local unemployment rate) to economic development efforts.

Omnibus Budget Reconciliation Act of 1993
 The Omnibus Budget Reconciliation Act included two federal income tax incentives designed to stimulate economic development on Indian reservations throughout the United States.

Riegle Community Development and Regulatory Improvement Act of 1994
 The Riegle Community Development and Regulatory Improvement Act established the Community Development Financial Institutions Fund (CDFI Fund). Since 2001, the CDFI Fund has worked to overcome barriers preventing access to credit, capital, and financial services in Native American, Alaska Native, and Native Hawaiian communities.

Taxpayer Relief Act of 1997
 The Taxpayer Relief Act enabled tribes to apply to the Empowerment Zone and Enterprise Community (EZ/EC) program established by a 1993 law, which at the time made Indian reservation lands ineligible for tax incentives and federal government grants. The law also included portions of Oklahoma that were previously reservations.

Small Business Reauthorization Act of 1997
 The Small Business Reauthorization Act provides federal contract preferences to qualified small businesses owned and controlled by Indian tribes located in "Historically Underutilized Business Zones" (HUBZone). HUBZones include all lands on federally recognized Native American reservations.

Native American Business Development, Trade Promotion, and Tourism Act of 2000
 The Native American Business Development, Trade Promotion, and Tourism Act provides financial, legal, and technical assistance and adminis-

trative services to develop tribal and Indian-owned businesses, expand trade, and encourage economic development on Indian lands. The law required tourism demonstration projects to be conducted by Indian tribes in five U.S. regions.

Indian Tribal Energy Development and Self-Determination Act (Title V in Energy Policy Act of 2005) of 2005

The Indian Tribal Energy Development and Self-Determination Act reformed the way Indian lands are leased for energy purposes by replacing federal decision making with tribal decision making. A major stumbling block to tribal energy development plans was the inefficiency of the federal review and approval process for land leases and business agreements.

American Recovery and Reinvestment Act of 2009

The American Recovery and Reinvestment Act infused millions of dollars into Indian country to spur long-term economic development and near-term economic recovery in Indian communities. Monies were allocated to intensive training programs in construction trades to equip unemployed and underemployed Indian trainees with the job skills needed to participate in infrastructure activities and maintenance on federal government facilities.

Five General Purposes of the 1988 Indian Gaming Regulatory Act

The Indian Gaming Regulatory Act required Indian tribes to use net revenue from gaming for five general purposes:
1. To fund tribal government operations or programs
2. To promote general welfare of tribes and their members
3. To promote tribal economic development
4. To donate to charitable organizations
5. To help fund operations of local government agencies

BOOKS

Twelve Cultural Tourism Books

Non-Native people have been visiting American Indian reservations, especially in the Southwest, since the 1800s. Since the 1960s, American Indian tribes and individual entrepreneurs have taken control of the tourist industry to fuel economic development. Among the enterprises drawing tourist revenues are tours of reservations, pueblos, ancient and historic sites; Native museums and cultural centers; luxury spa resorts, hotels, bed-and-breakfast operations, restaurants, golf courses, campsites, festivals, powwows, rodeos, casinos, and arts and crafts stores.

1. *A Hiker's Guide to California Native Places: Interpretive Trails, Reconstructed Villages, Rock-Art Sites, and the Indigenous Cultures They Evoke*, by Nancy Salcedo (1999).
2. *Alaska's Totem Poles*, by Pat Kramer (2008).
3. *Indian America: A Traveler's Companion*, by Eagle Walking Turtle (1995).
4. *Insight Guide: American Southwest*, by Scott Rutherford (2002).
5. *Insight Guide: Native America*, edited by John Gattuso (2002).
6. *Native Peoples of Alaska: A Traveler's Guide to Land, Art, and Culture*, by Jan Halliday, Patricia J. Petrivelli, and Alaska Native Heritage Center (1998).
7. *Native Peoples of the Northwest: A Traveler's Guide to Land, Art, and Culture*, by Jan Halliday and Gail Chehak (2002).
8. *North American Indian Landmarks: A Traveler's Guide*, by George Cantor (1993).
9. *Trading Post Guidebook: Where to Find the Trading Posts, Galleries, Auctions, Artists, and Museums of the Four Corners Region*, by Patrick Eddington and Susan Makov (1995).
10. *The Traveler's Guide to Native America: The Great Lakes Region*, by Allen Hayward (1992).
11. *A Traveler's Guide to Native America: The Southwest Region*, by Allen Hayward (1993).
12. *Traveling Indian Arizona*, by Anne O'Brien (2005).

FILMS

Christmas in the Clouds (USA, 2005, 97 min.), directed by Kate Montgomery.
   Christmas in the Clouds, shot at Robert Redford's Sundance Resort, is a romantic comedy set in a Native American–run Utah ski resort that is having a snowless year. It's a tale of love, tribal enterprise, and mistaken identity. The director, who cast predominantly Native actors, portrays modern Native people free of stereotypes.
Naturally Native (USA, 1998, 108 min.), directed by Jennifer Wynne Farmer and Valerie Red-Horse (Cherokee).
   This feature film follows the lives and struggles of three Indian sisters trying to start their own cosmetic business based on traditional native herbs and plants. The film deals with obstacles the sisters encounter in

finding financing for their business. *Naturally Native* is the first mainstream dramatic feature film to be funded by an American Indian tribal nation, the Mashantucket (Western) Pequot Tribal Nation of Connecticut. It is also one of the first features to explore Indians' relationship with corporate America.

ORGANIZATIONS

American Indian Alaska Native Tourism Association
http://www.aianta.org

American Indian Alaska Native Tourism Association (AIANTA) is a nonprofit association of Native American tribes and tribal businesses, organized in 1999, to promote Indian country tourism. Headquartered in Albuquerque, New Mexico, the association is made up of member tribes from the Eastern, Plains, Midwest, Southwest, Pacific Northwest, and Alaska regions. AIANTA serves as the voice and resource for its constituents in marketing and expanding tourism, especially internationally, plus providing training and networking with tourism professionals. It works with the Bureau of Indian Affairs and private entities for the development, growth, and sustenance of Indian country tourism.

American Indian Business Leaders (AIBL)
http://www.aibl.org

The American Indian Business Leaders (AIBL), organized in 1994, supports and promotes the education and development of future American Indian business leaders. Headquartered on the University of Montana campus in Missoula, AIBL encourages all students to participate in its activities, regardless of race, academic major, or career objectives.

American Indian Business Network (AIBN)
http://www.americanindianbusiness.net

The American Indian Business Network, established in 2003 by the National Indian Gaming Association, is a forum for Indian businesses to showcase products and network with other business owners, customers, and tribal leaders. Headquartered in Washington, DC, AIBN has focused on "buy Indian" tribal initiatives, tribally owned casinos, and other enterprises.

First Nations Development Institute
http://www.firstnations.org

The First Nations Development Institute, founded in 1980, works with rural and reservation-based Native communities throughout the United States to build sustainable reservation economies. Headquartered in Longmont, Colorado, the award-winning nonprofit First Nations has been working to restore Native American control and culturally compatible stewardship of the assets they own—be they land, human potential, cultural heritage, or natural resources—and to establish new assets for ensuring the long-term vitality of Native communities.

National Center for American Indian Enterprise Development
http://www.ncaied.org/default.php

The National Center for American Indian Enterprise Development (NCAIED), launched in 1969, was initially a grassroots organization focused on California's urban populations. In 1988, the organization renamed itself to reflect the expanding scope of its work in urban and reservation-based business development. Headquartered in Mesa, Arizona, NCAIED has been dedicated to developing relations between Indian enterprises and private industry. NCAIED, which awards the prestigious Jay Silverheels Achievement Award, hosts a large annual gathering of Indian businesses, federal government agencies, and corporate parties.

National Indian Gaming Association
http://www.indiangaming.org

The National Indian Gaming Association (NIGA), established in 1985, is a nonprofit organization of 184 Indian nations, with other non-voting associate members representing organizations, tribes, and businesses engaged in tribal gaming enterprises from around the country. Headquartered in Washington, DC, NIGA works with the federal government and Congress to develop policies and practices and to provide technical assistance and advocacy on gaming-related issues.

National Tribal Development Association
http://www.ntda.info

The National Tribal Development Association (NTDA), founded in 1995, is a nonprofit American Indian organization that provides a wide range of economic development services to American Indians and Alaska Natives nationwide. Headquartered on the Rocky Boy's Indian Reservation in Box Elder, Montana, NTDA offers services including economic analysis, commercial code development, marketing and promotions, graphic design, loan preparation, entrepreneurship development, small business technical assistance, financial records management, and IT and technical support.

Native American Bank
http://www.nabna.com

The Native American Bank (NAB), established in 2001 and now owned by a collection of over twenty-five tribal nations, tribal enterprises, and Alaska Native corporations, assists Native American and Alaska Native individuals,

enterprises, and governments in reaching their goals by providing affordable and flexible banking and financial services. Headquartered in Denver,
Colorado, NAB concentrates on pooling Indian economic resources to increase
Indian economic independence by fostering a climate of self-determination in
investment, job creation, and sustainable economic growth.

Native American Business Alliance
http://n-a-b-a.org/default.htm

The Native American Business Alliance (NABA), formed in 1995, facilitates
relationships between private and public businesses and Native American–
owned companies. Headquartered in Detroit, Michigan, NABA puts Native
businesses in front of diversity managers of corporate America, especially at its
annual procurement conference.

Native American Community Development Corporation
http://www.nacdc.org

The Native American Community Development Corporation (NACDC), the nonprofit affiliate of Native American Bancorporation that has been in operation since
2001, aims to remove barriers that exist in Indian country that prohibit the flow of
capital and credit. Headquartered in Browning, Montana, NACDC addresses critical needs in Native communities related to growth of family assets and sustainable
economic development. NACDC, an affiliate of Native American Bank (NAB),
collaborates with NAB and its owner tribes and Alaska Native corporations.

Native American Finance Officers Association
http://www.nafoa.org

Native American Finance Officers Association (NAFOA) created a network
of financial and business management professionals serving tribes and their
enterprises. Headquartered in Phoenix, Arizona, NAFOA provides the latest in
financial and accounting information, training, technical assistance, and business management information.

Lakota Funds

Lakota Funds was established in 1986 in Kyle, South Dakota, on the Pine Ridge
(Oglala Lakota) Reservation by Oglala Lakota College, the First Nations Development Institute team, and Lakota community leaders. It became the best-known example (regarded by many as the first) of a Native community development financial
institution (CDFI) in the United States.

When Lakota Funds started, there were two Native-owned businesses on the
reservation. In 2009 there were over 328 licensed businesses. Besides creating an

> entrepreneurial environment, Lakota Funds has co-founded the Pine Ridge Area Chamber of Commerce, developed the first Native American–owned, tax credit–financed housing project in America, lent out $4.7 million to over 350 borrowers, and created nearly a thousand jobs.

Oweesta

http://www.oweesta.org

Oweesta (from the Mohawk word for money), a subsidiary of the First Nations Development Institute, was founded in 1986. Headquartered in Rapid City, South Dakota, since 1999, Oweesta provides training, technical assistance, investments research, and advocacy for the development of Native CDFIs and other support organizations in Native communities.

RESOURCES

Braun, Sebastian Felix. *Buffalo, Inc.: American Indians and Economic Development.* Norman: University of Oklahoma Press, 2008.

Harmon, Alexandra. *Rich Indians: Native People and the Problem of Wealth in American History.* Chapel Hill: University of North Carolina Press, 2010.

Harvard Project on American Indian Economic Development. *The State of the Native Nations: Conditions under U.S. Policies of Self-Determination.* New York: Oxford University Press, 2008.

Hosmer, Brian, and Colleen O'Neill, eds. *Native Pathways: American Indian Culture and Economic Development in the 20th Century.* Boulder: University of Colorado Press, 2004.

Johansen, Bruce, ed. *Encyclopedia of Native American Economic History.* Westport, CT: Greenwood Press, 1999.

Jorgensen, Miriam, ed. *Rebuilding Native Nations: Strategies for Governance and Development.* Tucson: University of Arizona Press, 2007.

O'Neill, Solleen M. *Working the Navajo Way: Labor and Culture in the Twentieth Century.* Lawrence: University Press of Kansas, 2005.

Smith, Dean Howard. *Modern Tribal Development: Paths to Self-Sufficiency and Cultural Integrity in Indian Country.* Lanham, MD: AltaMira Press, 2000.

Tiller, Veronica E. Velarde, ed. *Tiller's Guide to Indian Country: Economic Profiles of American Indian Reservations.* Albuquerque: BowArrow Publishing, 2005.

Time. "Banking: Minority Report." January 7, 1974. Available at http://www.time.com/time/magazine/article/0,9171,910981,00.html

Web Sites

American Indian Chambers of Commerce: http://www.nativeworkplace.com/RNCC.html

American Indian Report: Falmouth Institute's Online Magazine: www.americanindianreport. com

Business Development in Indian Country (by Kate Spilde Contreras, 2007): http://www .ncai.org/ncai/econpolicy/BusinessDevelopmentPaper.pdf

Harvard Project on American Indian Economic Development: http://hpaied.org

Harvard Project's Honoring Nations Directory of Honored Programs, 1999–2006: http:// hpaied.org/images/resources/general/Dir_web.pdf

Joint Occasional Papers on Native Affairs (JOPNA) (includes publications in PDF format regarding tribal economic development): http://www.jopna.net

National Indian Gaming Association: http://www.indiangaming.org

National Indian Gaming Commission: http://www.nigc.gov

National Indian Law Library, Native American Business and Economic Development Law Resources: http://www.narf.org/nill/resources/ecobib.htm

Native Hawaiian Organizations Association Directory: http://www.nhoassociation.org/ nhos/directory.htm

Native Tourism: http://www.nativetourism.org

The Nature and Components of Economic Development in Indian Country (by Stephen Cornell and Miriam Jorgensen, 2007): http://udallcenter.arizona.edu/publications/ sites/default/files/104_en.pdf

Oregon Native American Business and Entrepreneurial Network: http://www.onaben.org

U.S. Census Bureau, American Indian and Alaska Native Heritage Month (November 2010): http://www.census.gov/newsroom/releases/archives/facts_for_features_special _editions/cb10ff22.html

U.S. Census Bureau, Facts on the American Indian and Alaskan Native Population: http:// www.census.gov/newsroom/minority_links/aian.html

10

Military Service and War

FIRSTS

1777–78   The six individual member nations of the Iroquois Confederacy determined their own stance during the American Revolution. The Mohawk, Onondaga, Cayuga, and Seneca sided with the British, while the Oneida and Tuscarora supported the American rebels. This decision created the first division within the Iroquois in over two hundred years.

1822   David Moniac (Creek) was the first American Indian admitted into the United States Military Academy and the first to graduate from it. He became a major in the U.S. Army.

1864   Stand Watie (Cherokee) was the only Native American on either side of the Civil War to rise to the rank of brigadier general. Jefferson Davis, president of the Confederate States, appointed him brigadier general in the Confederate army. He was the last Confederate general to concede to the Union army, at Doaksville, Choctaw Nation, in 1865, over two months after General Robert E. Lee's surrender.

1865   Ely Samuel Parker (Seneca) was promoted to brigadier general at the end of the Civil War, the highest rank held by an Indian in the U.S. Army. Military secretary to General Ulysses S. Grant, he penned the final copy of the Confederate army's surrender at the Appomattox Courthouse, Virginia, in 1865.

1913   Joseph J. Clark (Cherokee) was the first midshipman of American Indian ancestry to attend the United States Naval Academy; he graduated in 1917. In 1953, he retired as a full admiral in the U.S. Navy, the first person of Native ancestry to attain such a high rank in that service.

1918   During World War I, the Choctaw language became the first American Indian language used to transmit messages by radio and telephone in World War I. Fourteen Choctaw soldiers sent messages in their language that were never deciphered, even when intercepted, by the German army.

1921   The Haskell unit of the Kansas National Guard was the first and only all–American Indian National Guard organized by the Indian Service. It inspired in 1924 the formation of the all-Indian Troop C of the 114th Cavalry, a unit of the Kansas National Guard.

1940   For the first time in history, American Indians registered for the draft.

1941   James C. Ottipoby (Comanche) was the first American Indian commissioned in the American Chaplain Corps.

1942   Clarence L. Tinker (Osage) was the first Native American to attain the rank of major general in the U.S. Air Force. In that year he became the first American general lost in action during World War II. Tinker Air Force Base in Oklahoma City was named in his honor.

        The original twenty-nine Navajo code talkers in the U.S. Marines were the first Native group to develop a special Type One Code based on their language. The code was never deciphered.

1945   Louis Charlo (Salish/Kootenai) was among the U.S. Marines who helped hoist the first American flag at Iwo Jima. That event was overshadowed by the second flag raising, which occurred on the same day (February 23) and became iconic.

1948   Allan Houser (Chiricahua Apache) created *Comrade in Mourning*, the first public monument in the United States done by a Native American. The work was a memorial to Indian servicemen who died during World War II.

1952   Herbert Kaili Pililaau (Native Hawaiian) was the first Hawaiian to receive the Medal of Honor.

1960s   Loretta S. Jendritza (Navajo) was the first Navajo woman to earn the rank of major during her service in the U.S. Air Force.

1970s   Marcia Ann Biddleman (Seneca) was the highest-ranking woman Marine and the only woman Marine officer to serve as a weather forecaster. A first lieutenant with the U.S. Marine Corps, she was the first recipient of the Women Officer Basic Course Leadership Award.

1981   Sandra L. Hinds (tribal affiliation unknown) became the first Native woman to graduate from the United States Naval Academy.

1982   Dolores K. Smith (Cherokee) was the first American Indian woman to graduate from the United States Air Force Academy.

1984   Brigitte T. Wahwassuck (Potawatomi) was the first American Indian woman to graduate from the United States Military Academy.

1986   Chief Hollis E. Roberts presented posthumous Choctaw Nation Medals of Valor to the families of the nation's code talkers. This was the first official recognition the Oklahoma Choctaw code talkers had been given.

A plaque was dedicated at Arlington National Cemetery in Virginia, the first national memorial honoring Native American veterans. It reads: "Dedicated to Our Indian Warriors and Their Brothers Who Have Served Us Well—The Vietnam Era Vets—We Are Honored To Remember You—The Indigenous People of America."

2003   Lori Piestewa (Hopi) became the first woman in the U.S. Armed Forces to be killed in action in Operation Iraqi Freedom. She is believed to be the first Native American woman killed in combat in a foreign war. She was posthumously decorated with the Purple Heart and the National Defense Service Medal.

2005   James D. Fairbanks (White Earth Chippewa) became the first American Indian to serve as Force Master Chief Petty Officer of the Seabees, the construction battalions of the U.S. Navy. A recipient of the Bronze Star, his military career included service in Operations Enduring and Iraqi Freedom.

2009   Maine became the first state in the union to commemorate its Native American veterans. It established June 21 of each year as Native American Veterans Day in the state. Penobscot tribal elder and decorated World War II veteran, Charles Norman Shay, said the annual commemoration will "remind the general public, as well as our own Native communities, about Native American contributions and sacrifices to the spirit of freedom, and to honor those who have served or are now serving our country."

2010   Pedro "Pete" Molina (Yaqui) became the nation's first assistant secretary for Native American Veterans Affairs. The position was created by the State of California to oversee providing services to Native veterans in California, which has the largest population of American Indian veterans in the country.

NATIVE PARTICIPATION IN U.S. WARS

Native Participation in U.S. Wars: 1917 to 1991

Participation in World War I (1917–18): Nearly 12,000 served in the military.

Participation in World War II (1941–45): More than 25,000 American Indians served between 1941 and 1945 (plus 40,000 in war-related industries in U.S. cities).

Participation in Korean War (1950–53): An estimated 29,700 served.

Participation in Vietnam (1965–75): An estimated 42,500 served, of whom 90 percent were volunteers. Many women served; however, the exact number has not been documented.

Participation in Persian Gulf War (1991): An estimated 3,000 Native American men and women served in the Persian Gulf in Operation Desert Storm.

Six Books about American Indian Participation in the Civil War

1. *The American Indian in the Civil War, 1862–1865*, by Annie Heloise Abel (1992; reprint of 1919 edition).
2. *Between Two Fires: American Indians and the Civil War*, by Laurence Hauptman (1995).
3. *The Blue, the Gray, by and the Red: Indian Campaigns of the Civil War*, by Thom Hatch (2003).
4. *The Iroquois in the Civil War: From Battlefield to Reservation*, by Laurence Hauptman (1993).
5. *Lincoln and the Indians: Civil War Policy and Politics*, by David A. Nichols (1978).
6. *Red Fox: Stand Watie and the Confederate Indian Nations during the Civil War Years in Indian Territory*, by Wilfred Knight (1987).

Sixteen Books about American Indian Participation in World War I and World War II

1. *American Indians and World War II: Toward a New Era in Indian Affairs*, by Alison R. Bernstein (1991).
2. *Code Talker*, by Chester Nez, with Judith Schiess Avila (2011).
3. *The Comanche Code Talkers of World War II*, by William C. Meadows (2003).
4. *Crossing the Pond: The Native American Effort in World War II*, by Jere Bishop Franco (1999).
5. *Indians in World War I: At Home and At War*, by Thomas A. Britten (1997).
6. *The Navajo Code Talkers*, by Doris A. Paul (1973).
7. *Navajo Weapon: The Navajo Code Talkers*, by Sally McClain (2002).
8. *No One Ever Asked Me: The World War II Memoirs of an Omaha Indian Soldier*, edited by Hollis D. Stabler and Victoria Smith (2008).
9. *North American Indians in the Great War*, by Susan Krouse (2007).
10. *Power of a Navajo: Carl Gorman: The Man and His Life*, by Henry Greenberg (1996).
11. *The Red Man's on the Warpath: The Image of the "Indian" and the Second World War*, by R. Scott Sheffield (2004).
12. *Unsung Heroes of World War II: The Story of the Navajo Code Talkers*, by Deanne Durrett (1998).
13. *Warriors: Navajo Code Talkers*, by Kenji Kawano (1990).
14. *When the Wind Was a River: Aleut Evacuation in World War II*, by Dean Kohlhoff (1995).

15. *Winds of Freedom: The Story of the Navajo Code Talkers of World War II,* by Margaret T. Bixler (1992).
16. *World War II and the Indian,* by Kenneth William Townsend (2000).

Six Books about American Indian Participation in Vietnam and Iraq

1. *America's First Warriors: Native Americans and Iraq,* by Steven Clevenger (2010).
2. *A Hundred Miles of Bad Road: An Armored Cavalryman in Vietnam,* by Dwight W. Birdwell and Keith William Nolan (2000).
3. *Of Uncommon Birth: Dakota Sons in Vietnam,* by Mark St. Pierre (2003).
4. *Red Earth: A Vietnam Warrior's Journey* (novel), by Philip H. Red Eagle (1997).
5. *Strong Hearts and Wounded Souls: Native American Veterans of the Vietnam War,* by Tom Holm (1996).
6. *Year in Nam: A Native American Soldier's Story,* by Leroy TeCube (Apache) (1999).

Honoring Native Veterans

Many Native families send their soldiers to war armed with eagle feathers, prayers of protection, and ceremonial sweats to prepare them. They welcome them back with honoring or mourning ceremonies and purification rites to cleanse away the pressures of war. Vietnam veteran and counselor Harold Barse explains: "Our families were there to greet us when we got home; they provided a soldier dance, prayer meetings, peyote meetings, stuff to make us feel good . . . to recognize us for our experiences and to honor us for the sacrifices that we made" (Brende and Parson 1985, 155–56). According to historian and Vietnam veteran, Tom Holm, "the dances and honoring songs helped the veterans purge their grief and vent their emotions" (King 1989, 29).

Tribal communities decorate towns and highways with patriotic banners and ribbons. At nearly every powwow, intertribal ceremony, graduation, and other gatherings, American Indian veterans are honored. All year round, tribal newspapers run advertisements for powwows to honor tribal veterans. Photographs of outgoing and returning soldiers regularly appear in Native newspapers. Many tribal communities have honored war veterans with permanent memorials.

The tradition of honoring veterans at powwows, which are held throughout the year in nearly every state, on reservations, in small towns and metropolitan areas, in school gyms, universities, museums, and parks, means that Indian soldiers are honored frequently. Families especially gather to remember and recognize their veterans on Memorial Day and Veterans Day with parades and powwows. During powwows, honor songs are sung for veterans. Soldiers may speak publicly about their war deeds, and families provide giveaways or meals for the gathering.

Native Women in the Military

Accounts tell about Native women joining their husbands in battle or taking the place of husbands or brothers who were wounded or killed. In 1777, Tyonjanegen, an Oneida woman, fought beside her husband, an American army officer, against the British. She reloaded his gun for him after he was shot in the wrist during battle. Buffalo Calf Road Women (Cheyenne), a strong fighter, was renowned for saving her wounded brother at the Battle of the Rosebud in 1876. She rode onto the battlefield, grabbed her brother, and carried him to safety. The Cheyenne called the battle "The Fight Where the Girl Saved Her Brother." At one time, Minnie Hollow Wood (Lakota) was the only woman in her tribe who earned the right to wear a war bonnet, for her actions against the U.S. Cavalry in the 1876 Battle of the Little Bighorn. During the 1870s and 1880s, legendary Apache warrior Lozen, sister of chief Victorio, fought in campaigns against Mexicans and Americans and stole army horses with ease, one of her favorite pastimes. Besides Lozen, historians have identified at least four other Apache women who were as courageous and skillful as men. During the Spanish-American War (1898), four Roman Catholic nuns from South Dakota worked as military nurses in Cuba. Native women also joined the Army nurse corps during World War I.

During World War II, nearly eight hundred Native women served in all military branches as officers and enlisted personnel. As nurses, they cared for survivors of the Bataan death camps in the Pacific theater and served in MASH units in the Korean and Vietnam wars. Some saw active duty in Pearl Harbor, Hawaii, in Women Accepted for Volunteer Emergency Service (WAVES). Today, many Native women from all four service academies have served in active duty in both of the Iraq wars.

MEDALS OF HONOR

Medals of Honor, 1869–2011

American Indians have played prominent roles in the military history of this country since its very beginning. The number of Indians receiving Medals of Honor attests to this. Created in 1861, the Medal of Honor is given to candidates whose acts "far exceeded any just demand of duty."

Name	Date Earned	Awarded Medal
Indian War Campaigns		
Alchesay (Apache)	1872–73	April 12, 1875
Blanquet (Apache)	1872–73	April 12, 1875

Chiquito (Apache)	1872–73	April 12, 1875
Co-Rux-Te-Chod-Ish (Pawnee)	July 8, 1869	August 24, 1869
Elsatsoosu (Apache)	1872–73	April 12, 1875
Factor, Pompey (Seminole)	April 25, 1875	May 28, 1875
Jim (Apache)	1872–73	April 12, 1875
Kelsay (Apache)	1872–73	April 12, 1875
Kosoha (Apache)	1872–73	April 12, 1875
Machol (Apache)	1872–73	April 12, 1875
Nannasaddie (Apache)	1872–73	April 12, 1875
Nantaje (Apache)	1872–73	April 12, 1875
Paine, Adam (Seminole)	September 26–27, 1874	October 13, 1875
Payne, Isaac (Seminole)	April 25, 1875	May 28, 1875
Rowdy (Apache)	March 7, 1890	May 15, 1890
Ward, John (Seminole)	April 25, 1875	May 28, 1875

World War II

Barfoot, Van T. (Choctaw)	May 23, 1944	October 4, 1944
Boyington, Gregory "Pappy" (Sioux)	September 12, 1943– January 3, 1944	October 5, 1945
Childers, Ernest (Oklahoma Creek)	September 22, 1943	April 12, 1944
Evans, Ernest E. (Cherokee/ Creek)	October 25, 1944	November 24, 1945
Harmon, Roy W. (Cherokee)	July 12, 1944	October 2, 1945
Montgomery, Jack (Oklahoma Cherokee)	February 22, 1944	January 10, 1945
Reese, John N., Jr. (Oklahoma Creek)	February 9, 1945	October 19, 1945

Korea

George, Charles (Eastern Band Cherokee)	November 30, 1952	March 10, 1954
Harvey, Raymond (Chickasaw)	March 9, 1951	July 5, 1951
Kaho'ohanohano, Anthony T. (Native Hawaiian)	September 1, 1951	May 2, 2011
Keeble, Woodrow W. (Dakota)	October 20, 1951	March 3, 2008

| Pililaau, Herbert Kaili (Native Hawaiian) | September 17, 1951 | June 18, 1952 |
| Red Cloud, Mitchell, Jr. (Winnebago) | November 5, 1950 | April 3, 1951 |

Vietnam

| Thornton, Michael Edwin (Cherokee) | October 31, 1972 | October 15, 1973 |
| Williams, James E. (Cherokee) | October 31, 1966 | May 14, 1968 |

American Indian Scouts

In 1866, during the Indian wars, the U.S. Army established the Indian Scouting Service. Apache, Crow, Delaware, Pawnee, Shoshone, and Tonkawa Indian men signed up as scouts, motivated by their intimate knowledge of the terrain, their skill at following trails left by enemies, plus the willingness of some tribal groups to settle scores against their rivals. They pursued traditional enemies for steady pay, prestige, and material wealth—the promise of horses or other loot. Some were pragmatists, believing that scouting for the army might benefit their group with favorable government treatment. After Indians were confined to reservations, scouting gave some men a chance to escape the tedium of reservation life, distinguish themselves as warriors, gain status, or enjoy adventure and travel. Some scouts saw action in Cuba during the Spanish-American War (1898), and some accompanied Gen. John J. Pershing's expedition to Mexico in pursuit of Pancho Villa in 1916. Between 1872 and 1890, sixteen Native members of the Scouting Service were awarded Congressional Medals of Honor. The Scouting Service was disbanded in 1943.

Selected Military Awards

1946   Hawila Kaleohano (Native Hawaiian) was awarded a Medal of Freedom for valor in capturing alive a Japanese pilot who attacked the islands of Oahu and Nihau in 1941.

1999   Charles Chibitty, the last surviving member of the original Comanche code talkers, received the Knowlton Award, which recognizes individuals for outstanding intelligence work, during a ceremony at the Pentagon's Hall of Heroes.

2008   Joseph Medicine Crow (Crow) was awarded the Bronze Star by the U.S. Army for his service during World War II. At the same time, the French government made him a knight of the French Legion of Honor.

Master Sgt. Woodrow Keeble (Sisseton-Wahpeton Oyate), a veteran of World War II and the Korean War, received the Medal of Honor more than twenty-five years after he died. President George Bush apologized that the country waited decades to honor him for his valor.

2009   Joseph Medicine Crow (Crow) received the Presidential Medal of Freedom, the highest civilian honor awarded to individuals by the United States. During World War II, Medicine Crow became legendary after stealing some fifty horses from a Nazi war camp.

CODE TALKERS

Choctaw Nation Code Talkers, World War I and World War II

Choctaw soldiers from Oklahoma served as code talkers during World War I. October of 1918 was the first time in modern warfare that messages were transmitted in a Native American language to communicate military information. The Germans never broke the code. In appreciation for their work, on November 3, 1989, the French government honored Choctaw code talkers with the "Chevalier de l'Ordre National du Mérite" (Knight of the National Order of Merit), the second-highest level of civilian award France bestows.

During World War II, Choctaw code talkers also contributed to the war effort. The following eighteen servicemen using their Native language over field radios to coordinate military positions.

1. Albert Billy
2. Mitchell Bobb
3. Victor Brown
4. Ben Carterby
5. George Davenport
6. Joe Davenport
7. James Edwards
8. Tobias Frazier
9. Ben Hampton
10. Noel Johnson
11. Otis Leader
12. Solomon Louis
13. Pete Maytubby

14. Jeff Nelson
15. Joseph Oklahombi
16. Robert Taylor
17. Walter Veach
18. Calvin Wilson

In 2008, the U.S. government passed the Code Talkers Recognition Act, which will grant Congressional Gold Medals to Choctaw Code Talkers, or next of kin, for service to the nation.

Seventeen Comanche Nation Code Talkers, World War II

The Comanche code talkers from Oklahoma developed one of the most successful military codes of World War II, saving countless lives and hastening the end of the war in Europe. In appreciation for their work, on November 3, 1989, the French government honored seventeen Comanche code talkers with the "Chevalier de l'Ordre National du Mérite" (Knight of the National Order of Merit), the second-highest level of civilian award France bestows. In 2008, the U.S. government passed the Code Talkers Recognition Act, which will grant Congressional Gold Medals to Comanche Code Talkers, or next of kin, for service to the nation.

1. Charles Chibitty
2. Haddon Codynah
3. Robert Holder
4. Forrest Kassanovoid
5. Wellington Mihecoby
6. Edward Nahquaddy
7. Perry Noyabad
8. Clifford Otitivo
9. Simmons Parker
10. Melvin Permansu
11. Dick (Roderick) Red Elk
12. Elgin Red Elk
13. Larry Saupitty
14. Morris Tabbyetchy (Sunrise)
15. Anthony Tabbytite
16. Ralph Wahnee
17. Willie Yacheschi

Eight Meskwaki Code Talkers, World War II

The Meskwaki of Iowa were among some eighteen tribes who supplied code talkers. Eight soldiers were trained to use their language as a secret code to encrypt orders relayed over walkie-talkies. Neither the Germans nor the Japanese ever cracked this code. The soldiers who were stationed in Northern Africa died before receiving recognition.

1. Edward Benson
2. Dewey Roberts
3. Frank Sanache
4. Willard Sanache
5. Melvin Twin
6. Mike Wayne Wabaunsee
7. Judy Wayne Wabaunsee
8. Dewey Youngbear

Navajo Code Talkers, World War II

Twenty-nine Navajos fluent in Navajo and English, some only fifteen years old, constructed and mastered the Navajo Code while serving in the U.S. Marine Corps. Eventually four hundred Navajo marines from Arizona and New Mexico served in the code talker program, taking part in many campaigns in the Pacific theater, usually in two-men teams conversing by field telephones. The entire military operation at Iwo Jima was directed by orders of Navajo code talkers. They sent more than eight hundred messages without error. When the marines raised the flag at Mount Suribachi, the code talkers relayed the message in the code: "sheep-uncle-ram-ice-bear-ant-cat-horse-itch," which spelled "Suribachi." The Navajo code talking program remained top secret until 1968 when the United States government declassified it.

The code talkers devised an alphabet to spell words or represent objects, many taken from nature, that had logical association with military terms and names of places. Thus, the Navajo code word for observation plane was *Ne-ahs-jah,* or "owl" in Navajo. "Saipan" was spelled *Dibeh* ("sheep,"), *Wol-la-chee* ("ant"), *Tkin* ("ice"), *Bo-so-dih* ("pig"), *Wol-la-chee* ("ant"), and *Nesh-chee* ("nut"). Code talkers chose alternative words for *e, t, a, o, i,* and *n,* the six most frequently used letters in the English language. Instead of using "ant" for *a* to spell out a code word, they also used Navajo words for "apple" and "axe."

A	Wol-la-chee	Ant
B	Shush	Bear
C	Moasi	Cat
D	Be	Deer
E	Dzeh	Elk
F	Ma-e	Fox
G	Klizzie	Goat
H	Lin	Horse
I	Tkin	Ice

J	Tkele-cho-gi	Jackass
K	Klizzie-yazzie	Kid
L	Dibeh-yazzie	Lamb
M	Na-as-tso-si	Mouse
N	Nesh-chee	Nut
O	Ne-ahs-jah	Owl
P	Bi-so-dih	Pig
Q	Ca-yeilth	Quiver
R	Gah	Rabbit
S	Dibeh	Sheep
T	Than-zie	Turkey
U	No-da-ih	Ute
V	A-keh-di-glini	Victor
W	Gloe-ih	Weasel
X	Al-na-as-dzoh	Cross
Y	Tsah-as-zih	Yucca
Z	Besh-do-tliz	Zinc

Navajo Code Talkers Honors

For decades after the end of the war, the Navajo code talkers were sworn to secrecy about the existence of a code, until 1968 when the U.S. government declassified it. The Navajo code talkers have now attained visibility in American popular culture and mainstream American history, overshadowing code talkers from the Choctaw, Comanche, Hopi, Meskwaki, Sioux, and over a dozen other tribes.

1971   President Richard Nixon presented Certificates of Appreciation to the Navajo code talkers.

1982   President Ronald Reagan's presidential proclamation revealed to the world the contribution of the Navajo code talkers. President Reagan proclaimed August 14, 1982, as National Navajo Code Talker Day.

1989   Code talkers reunited in Phoenix, Arizona, at the unveiling of a *Tribute to Navajo Code Talkers*, a sculpture by Doug Hyde (Nez Perce), the nation's first permanent tribute to the code talkers.

       The Navajo Code Talker Association set up a museum in Gallup, New Mexico, where historic photographs, posters, and other items were displayed.

1992   The Pentagon honored the Navajo code talkers with a permanent exhibit that documented the history of the code. Keith Little, one of the code talkers in attendance, translated a prayer for peace phoned in by another code talker in Arizona.

2000 President Bill Clinton signed legislation granting Congressional Gold Medals, the highest civilian honor the U.S. Congress can bestow, to the original twenty-nine code talkers and Silver Medals to about three hundred Navajo soldiers who followed them to the Pacific theater.

2001 President George Bush presented Congressional Gold Medals to five code talkers who attended the ceremony (of the original twenty-nine) and medals to families of four men who were unable to attend.

2002 Hollywood released *Windtalkers,* an action/adventure film starring Adam Beach (Saulteaux) as a code talker. Directed by John Woo, the film dwells on protecting the Navajo code "at all costs."

2007 The Navajo Council established Navajo Code Talker Day, a tribal holiday held every year on August 14.

Eleven Sioux Code Talkers, World War II

Sioux Indians from North and South Dakota used dialects of their Siouan language, Dakota, Lakota, and Nakota, in a top-secret code in both Europe and the Pacific during World War II. They manned radio communications networks to advise of enemy actions. In 2008, the U.S. government passed the Code Talker Recognition Act, which will grant Congressional Gold Medals posthumously to Sioux Code Talkers for their service to the nation.

1. John Bear King
2. Simon Brokenleg
3. Iver Crow Eagle Sr.
4. Eddie Eagle Boy
5. Walter C. John
6. Phillip "Stoney" LaBlanc
7. Baptiste Pumpkinseed
8. Guy Rondell
9. Edmund St. John
10. Charles Whitepipe
11. Clarence Wolfguts

REPRESENTATION OF NATIVE AMERICANS IN THE MILITARY

Eleven Poems about Twentieth and Twenty-First-Century Combat by Native Poets

1. "American Flag Dress," by Ray A. Young Bear (Meskwaki). In *The Rock Island Hiking Club* (2001).

2. "El Alamein" [World War II], by Steve Crow (Cherokee). In *Harper's Anthology of 20th Century Native American Poetry,* edited by Duane Niatum (1988).
3. "Father Scarmark—World War I Hero—and Democracy," by Ray A. Young Bear (Meskwaki). In *The Rock Island Hiking Club* (2001).
4. "From Which War," by Phillip Yellowhawk Minthorn (Nez Perce). In *Songs from This Earth on Turtle's Back: Contemporary American Indian Poetry,* edited by Joseph Bruchac (1983).
5. "In 1969 XXXX Coloradoans Were Killed in Vietnam," by Simon Ortiz (Acoma Pueblo). In *From Sand Creek* (1981).
6. "ogichidag," by Jim Northrup (Chippewa). In *Walking the Rez Road* (1993).
7. "Red Blues in a White Town the Day We Bomb Iraqi Women and Children," by Adrian C. Louis (Paiute). In *Among the Dog Eaters* (1992).
8. "time wounds all heels," by Jim Northrup (Chippewa). In *Walking the Rez Road* (1993).
9. "Universal Soldier," by Buffy Sainte-Marie (Cree). In *The Buffy Sainte-Marie Songbook* (1971).
10. "The Warrior, for Ira Hayes," by Paula Gunn Allen (Laguna Pueblo/Sioux). In *Life Is a Fatal Disease: Collected Poems 1962–1995* (1996).
11. "Wokiksuye Olowan: Memory Songs, dedicated to Vietnam Vets," by Lydia Whirlwind Soldier (Lakota). In *Memory Songs* (1999).

Thirteen Selected Native Names of U.S. Helicopters

Army Regulation AR 70-28 (1969) set the naming policy for the army's aircraft. Some helicopters were named for Indian tribes and terms because they "appeal to the imagination and reflect mobility, agility, flexibility, firepower and endurance of the equipment" (Griffin 1989, 18). Although the 1969 policy was rescinded in 1988, AR 70-28 specifies that names will not be changed (http://www.globalsecurity.org/military/systems/aircraft/mds.htm). Native names for tribal nations and distinguished leaders, as well as geographic features, plants, and objects, have provided names for missiles, gunboats, sloops-of-war, mine layers, patrol boats, battleships, attack cargo ships, Coast Guard cutters, aircraft carriers, submarines, and many other kinds of naval vessels.

1. Apache attack helicopter (1975)
2. Black Hawk combat assault helicopter (1974)
3. Cayuse light observation helicopter (1963)
4. Cheyenne attack helicopter (prototype) (1967)
5. Chickasaw utility helicopter (1949)
6. Chinook cargo helicopter (1961)
7. Choctaw cargo helicopter (1954)
8. Kiowa light observation helicopter (1979)
9. Kiowa Warrior (1991)

10. Mojave cargo helicopter (1953)
11. Osage helicopter trainer (1964)
12. Sioux light observation helicopter (1946–73)
13. Sioux scout (1963)

Seven Comic Book Representations of Natives in the Military

1. Red Hawk, Native American; freelance fighter pilot (no tribal affiliation)
   First appearance: *Blazing Comics*, No. 1, June 1944
   One of the earliest, if not the earliest Native military character
2. Johnny Cloud (also known as "Flying Cloud"), Navajo
   First Appearance: *DC All-American Men of War*, No. 82, November/December 1960
   Lieutenant, U.S. Army Air Corps, World War II; European theater; led air patrol called "Happy Braves"
3. Little Sure Shot (also known as "Louis Kiyahani"), Apache
   First Appearance: *DC Our Army at War*, No. 127, February 1963
   U.S. Army scout, European theater of war, World War II
4. Private Jay Little Bear (alias "Chief," with no tribal affiliation)
   First Appearance: *DC Captain Savage & His Leatherneck Raiders*, No. 1, January 1968
   Marine, World War II era, Pacific theater
5. Red Wolf (also known as "Johnny Wakely"), Cheyenne
   First Appearance: *Marvel Spotlight I*, No. 1, November 1971
   U.S. Army scout in "Old West," United States during the late nineteenth century
6. Franklin E. Talltree (also known as "Airborne"), Navajo
   First Appearance: *Marvel G.I. Joe, a Real American Hero*, No. 11, 1982
   Paratrooper; character's "Indianness" concealed
7. Charlie Iron-Knife (also known as "Spirit Tracker," with no tribal affiliation)
   First Appearance: *Marvel G.I. Joe, a Real American Hero*, No. 31, January 1985
   Member of G.I. Joe, paramilitary group; shaman or healer

Indian Scout Stereotype

Since the first military encounters with American Indians hundreds of years ago, non-Indians have subscribed to the myth that Indians have inherent superhuman abilities in war, traits acquired genetically rather than learned. In the mythology, Indians could "detect the presence of an enemy from a bent blade of grass or could conceal themselves in an open field" (Holm 1992, 9). The stereotype followed Native soldiers into the twentieth and twenty-first centuries. During both World Wars, Vietnam, and the Gulf Wars, Native soldiers disproportionately performed the most dangerous assignments in the U.S. military, perhaps because of the mistaken belief that Indians were innately better at war, racially endowed, could "read their environments," and had "enthusiasm for fighting." They heard phrases such as "Chief, walk point," and "You Indians have that sixth sense." They were sent out on night ambushes and other dangerous missions because they were "supposed to see through the dark." None of these mistaken beliefs account for the fact that keen senses were part of the traditional training of Native hunters and warriors learned in childhood and adolescence. Harold Barse (Kiowa/Wichita/Sioux), a Vietnam veteran and counselor, notes that many Native American soldiers volunteered for dangerous service because they "believed in their fighting skills . . . They believed in their own stereotype."

Ira Hayes

Ira Hamilton Hayes, a Pima Indian born on the Gila River Indian Reservation in Arizona in 1923, was one of six United States marines who raised the American flag atop Mount Suribachi on the Japanese island of Iwo Jima on February 23, 1945. Joe Rosenthal's Pulitzer Prize–winning photograph immortalized the act and made national heroes of Hayes and two others who survived Iwo Jima. Hayes never reconciled himself to the constant adulation, believing the soldiers who died were the heroes and wishing "that guy had never made that picture."

Despite his reticence about being a hero, Hayes traveled to California to take a bit part in the 1949 film, *Sands of Iwo Jima*, starring John Wayne. While in California, Hayes posed for sculptor Felix de Weldon, who created the nation's first Iwo Jima monument, a bronze cast replica of Rosenthal's photograph. The Marine Corps War Memorial was dedicated in 1954 at the entrance to Arlington National Cemetery near Washington, DC.

Hayes returned to his Arizona reservation, where according to James Bradley, author of *Flags of Our Fathers* (2000), "Ira's home life became hell. Day and night, his phone rang off the hook, and people pounded on the door." In 1955, he died of exposure to the cold. Buried in Arlington National Cemetery with full military honors, Hayes has been characterized as "a hero to everyone but himself." Bradley notes that "today a battle-scarred Ira Hayes would be diagnosed with post-traumatic stress syndrome, and there would be understanding and treatment available to him. But in the late forties and early fifties, Ira had to suffer alone."

Hayes' life has been recounted in films, several books, and in the song "Ballad of Ira Hayes," written by Peter LaFarge and recorded by Johnny Cash in 1964. The recording by Cash, who was concerned about Native Americans, became a top ten country hit. Since then, the ballad has been recorded by Pete Seeger (1963), Bob Dylan (1973), and numerous other musicians. In 1985, the Ira Hayes Memorial Library opened at Sacaton, capital of the Gila River Indian Community.

Taylor, Alan. *Divided Ground: Indians, Settlers, and the Northern Borderland of the American Revolution.* New York: Knopf, 2006.

Viola, Herman J. *Warriors in Uniform.* Washington, DC: National Geographic, 2007.

Web Sites

The American Indian as Participant in the Civil War (by Annie Heloise Abel, 1910): http://www.gutenberg.org/ebooks/12541

American and Canadian Indians in the Military: http://www.thepeoplespaths.net/military.htm

Congressional Medal of Honor Society: www.cmohs.org/recipient-archive.php

Indians and the American Revolution: http://www.americanrevolution.org/ind1.html

Native Americans and the U.S. Military, Naval History and Heritage Command: http://www.history.navy.mil/faqs/faq61-1.htm

American Indian Code Talkers: http://www.nmai.si.edu/education/codetalkers

Native Americans in the U.S. Navy: http://www.history.navy.mil/special%20Highlights/NativeAmerican/NativeAmericansInUSN.pdf

Part Four

11

Education

FIRSTS

1568   Society of Jesus (Jesuit) missionaries organized a school in Havana, Cuba, for Indian boys brought from Florida, the first of many mission schools established to extend Christian teachings and other Euro-American customs among Native groups in North America.

1665   Caleb Cheeshahteaumuck (Wampanoag) became the first American Indian to graduate from Harvard's Indian College.

1784   Western schooling was first introduced in Alaska at Three Saints Bay, Kodiak Island, the site of the first Russian settlement.

1831   Lahainaluna Seminary was founded by Protestant missionaries in Lahaina, Maui, the first mission school founded in Hawaii. It became known as Lahainaluna school and now serves as a public secondary school (Lahainaluna High School).

1860   The first federal boarding school was opened at the Yakima (Yakama) Indian Agency in Washington State, the result of an 1855 treaty agreement between the United States and the Yakima.

1915   Henry Rowe Cloud (Winnebago) established the first college preparatory school for American Indians, later serving as the first American Indian superintendent of Haskell Institute in Lawrence, Kansas.

1920   John Joseph Mathews (Osage) became the first American Indian to be offered a Rhodes Scholarship.

1966   Rough Rock Demonstration School was established by the Navajo Nation, the first Native community in the United States to assume control of a Bureau of Indian Affairs (BIA) school. Rough Rock, located in Arizona, paved the way for other American Indian schools to become tribally controlled.

1968   Navajo Community College (renamed Diné College in 1997) in Arizona became the first community college chartered and controlled by an American Indian tribe.

1969   The National Indian Education Association (NIEA) was first formed in Minneapolis, Minnesota, becoming the oldest and largest national education organization devoted exclusively to educational issues of American Indians, Alaska Natives, and Native Hawaiians.

1970   Organized by Jeannette Henry Costo (Cherokee) and Rupert Costo (Cahuilla), the first Convocation of American Indian Scholars was held at Princeton University in New Jersey. It brought together Native teachers and administrators actively involved in Indian education.

1982   The University of California at Los Angeles (UCLA) established the first interdisciplinary Master of Arts program in American Indian Studies in the nation.

1983   Oglala Lakota College and Sinte Gleska College, both in South Dakota, became the first two tribal colleges accredited to offer bachelor's degrees. In 1989 Sinte Gleska became the first tribal college to offer a master's degree.

    Henrietta Mann Morton (Southern Cheyenne), also known as Henrietta Whiteman, became the first American Indian woman appointed as director of the Office of Indian Education in the Bureau of Indian Affairs.

1986   Rupert Costo (Cahuilla) and his wife Jeannette Henry Costo (Cherokee), who helped to establish the University of California, Riverside (UCR), endowed the first academic chair in the field of American Indian history in the nation at UCR.

1992   The first White House Conference on Indian Education was held in Washington, DC, federally mandated in part to develop recommendations for the improvement of educational programs for American Indians.

1994   Christine Zuni Cruz (Isleta Pueblo/Ohkay Owingeh) became the first tenured Native law professor at the University of New Mexico. In 2000, she assisted law students in establishing the first electronic public-access journal dedicated solely to the law of indigenous peoples (UNM School of Law *Tribal Law Journal*, tlj.unm.edu).

1996   Regis Pecos (Cochiti Pueblo) became the first American Indian to be appointed as a member of the Princeton University Board of Trustees.

1997   Dorothy Sunrise Lorentino (Comanche) became the first American Indian to be named to the National Teachers Hall of Fame.

1998   Carrie Billie (Navajo) served as the first executive director of the White House Initiative on Tribal Colleges and Universities.

2002   Richard W. West (Southern Cheyenne) became the first Native American named to the Stanford University Board of Trustees.

2005   Southern Ute Indian Academy in Colorado became the first tribal school to earn certification as a National Wildlife Schoolyard Habitat site.

2006   Loriene Roy (White Earth Chippewa Indians), professor at the University of Texas at Austin's School of Information, was elected president of the American Library Association (ALA) for the 2007–8 term, becoming the first American Indian elected to the position.

2007   Cassandra Manuelito-Kerkvliet (Navajo) was chosen as president of Antioch University Seattle, becoming the first Native American woman to ascend to the presidency of an accredited university outside the tribal college system.

2008   LuAnn Leonard (Hopi) became the first Native American to be appointed to the Arizona Board of Regents.

2009   The Native American Contemplative Garden, an outdoor reflective space, was dedicated at the University of California, Davis (UCD) to honor the original Patwin inhabitants of lands now encompassed by UCD's campus. The garden is believed to be the first of its kind at any public university in the nation.

2010   Edmund Manydeeds (Standing Rock Sioux) became the first Native American to be appointed to the University of Wisconsin system's Board of Regents.
        The Payne Family Native American Center at the University of Montana, which opened in May 2010, became the first facility in the nation built especially to accommodate a Department of Native American Studies and an American Student Services office.

2011   Tiffany Smalley became the first Wampanoag to graduate from Harvard College since 1665, when Caleb Cheeshahteaumuck received his degree. Harvard University also granted a posthumous degree to Cheeshahteaumuck's classmate Joel Iacommes (Wapanoag), who died in a shipwreck before graduating.

First Treaty Educational Provision, Treaty with the Oneida, Tuscarora, and Stockbridge, 1794

A 1794 United States Treaty with the Oneida, Tuscarora, and Stockbridge Indians became the first treaty to include a provision for education, stipulating: "The United States will provide, during three years after the mills shall be completed, for the expense of employing one or two suitable persons to manage the mills, to keep them in repair, to instruct some young men of the three nations in the arts of the miller and sawyer, and to provide teams and utensils for carrying on the work of the mills."

Following this treaty, numerous others included educational provisions. It is estimated that over eighty treaties promised teachers, schoolhouses, and books to American Indian tribes. The United States also guaranteed the services of blacksmiths, farmers, millers, or carpenters in the majority of the treaties.

EDUCATIONAL INSTITUTIONS AND NATIVE AMERICAN EDUCATION

Twenty-Five Off-Reservation Boarding Schools, 1879–1902

Beginning in the late nineteenth century, the federal government established a system of boarding schools that removed American Indian youngsters from their homes and communities to undergo a strict regimen of English-only instruction, Christian religious teachings, manual labor, summer work placements, and industrial training. Boarding school officials regulated every aspect of student life in an effort to achieve Euro-American goals of eradicating tribal cultural and religious practices.

1.	Carlisle, Pennsylvania	1879
2.	Chemawa, Oregon (Salem)	1880
3.	Albuquerque, New Mexico	1884
4.	Chilocco, Oklahoma	1884
5.	Genoa, Nebraska	1884
6.	Lawrence, Kansas (Haskell)	1884
7.	Grand Junction, Colorado	1886
8.	Carson City, Nevada	1890
9.	Fort Mojave, Arizona	1890
10.	Santa Fe, New Mexico	1890
11.	Phoenix, Arizona	1891
12.	Pierre, South Dakota	1891
13.	Fort Lewis, Colorado	1892
14.	Fort Shaw, Montana	1892

15.	Flandreau, South Dakota	1893
16.	Mount Pleasant, Michigan	1893
17.	Pipestone, Minnesota	1893
18.	Tomah, Wisconsin	1893
19.	Greenville, California	1895
20.	Wittenberg, Wisconsin	1895
21.	Morris, Minnesota	1897
22.	Chamberlain, South Dakota	1898
23.	Fort Bidwell, California	1898
24.	Rapid City, South Dakota	1898
25.	Riverside, California	1902

Source: Annual Report of the Commissioner of Indian Affairs, 1905, 41

Twelve Early American Indian Schools on the National Register of Historic Places and Landmark Districts

1. Armstrong Academy Site, in present-day Bryan County, Oklahoma
   Founded as a mission school for Choctaw boys in 1844, Armstrong Academy was closed in 1861 at the outbreak of the U.S. Civil War. It reopened as a school in 1883, but was destroyed by fire in 1921.
2. Bear Mountain Indian Mission School, Amherst, Virginia
   http://www.monacannation.com/museum.shtml
   Bear Mountain Indian Mission School was a historic school for Monacan Indians in Virginia, a state-recognized tribal group now centered around Bear Mountain in Amherst County. In the late 1870s a log cabin was built and used as a church for the Monacan people, later becoming a school. Today, the structure is listed on the U.S. National Register of Historic Places.
3. Bloomfield Academy Site, near present-day Achille, Oklahoma
   Founded in 1852 by the Reverend J. H. Carr, the Bloomfield Academy was a Chickasaw school for girls that operated until 1949. Control of the school passed to the U.S. Government following the passage of the Curtis Act in 1898.
4. Carlisle Indian Industrial School, Carlisle, Pennsylvania
   http://tps.cr.nps.gov/nhl/detail.cfm?ResourceId=486&ResourceType=District
   Founded in 1879 by Richard H. Pratt, the Carlisle Indian School was the forerunner of the federal boarding school system. After the school's closing in 1918, the U.S. Army used the facility to treat soldiers wounded in World War I and later established a War College on the campus.
5. Cherokee Female Seminary
   http://www.nsuok.edu/GettingStarted/NSUsHeritage.aspx
   First Cherokee Female Seminary (1851–87)
   The Cherokee Nation opened the first Cherokee Female Seminary in 1851 in Indian Territory (present-day Oklahoma), a boarding school that was destroyed by fire in 1887.

Cherokee Female Seminary (1889–1909)

In 1889, the Cherokee Nation rebuilt the Cherokee Female Seminary on a 40-acre site and maintained the school until 1909, when the State of Oklahoma purchased it for the newly created Northeastern State Normal School in Tahlequah. Seminary Hall is the oldest building on present-day Northeastern State University's campus.

6. Chilocco Indian Agricultural School, Newkirk, Oklahoma

    http://www.nps.gov/history/nr/feature/indian/2006/chilocco.htm

    The Chilocco Indian Agricultural School, an off-reservation school established by the federal government in Indian Territory (present-day Oklahoma), operated from 1884 to 1980.

7. Hampton Institute (present-day Hampton University), Hampton, Virginia

    http://www.hamptonu.edu/

    Founded in 1868 to educate newly freed African Americans, Hampton Normal and Agricultural Institute also operated an off-reservation boarding school program for American Indian students from 1878 to 1923. The campus includes a National Historic Landmark District with buildings such as Wigwam, which was constructed to house Indian male students.

8. Haskell Institute (present-day Haskell Indian Nations University), Lawrence, Kansas

    http://www.haskell.edu/

    Founded in 1884 as the United States Indian Industrial Training School, the off-reservation Indian boarding school was renamed Haskell Institute in 1887. The school was accredited as a junior college in 1970 and became Haskell Indian Nations University in 1993. The campus comprises a National Historic Landmark District.

9. Shawnee Indian Mission State Historic Site, Fairway, Kansas

    http://www.kshs.org/portal_shawnee_indian_mission

    Built by Methodist missionaries in 1839, the Shawnee Indian Mission served as a boarding school for children from Shawnee and other tribes until 1862. The 12-acre site, which includes three historic buildings, period rooms, and exhibits, is administered by the Kansas Historical Society.

10. Sherman Indian Museum, Riverside, California

    http://www.shermanindianmuseum.org

    Sherman Institute, a federal Indian boarding school that opened in Riverside, California, in 1902, is documented in the Sherman Indian Museum, which is housed in the current school's only original architecture. The institute is now known as Sherman Indian High School, an off-reservation boarding high school for Native students in grades nine through twelve.

11. Stewart Indian School, Carson City, Nevada

    http://www.nps.gov/nr/travel/nevada/ste.htm

    The Stewart Institute, which was founded in 1890, was the only federal Indian school created by an act of a state legislature. Located three miles

North Dakota

Cankdeska Cikana Community College, Fort Totten, North Dakota	1974
Fort Berthold Community College, New Town, North Dakota	1973
Sitting Bull College, Fort Yates, North Dakota	1973
Turtle Mountain Community College, Belcourt, North Dakota	1972
United Tribes Technical College, Bismarck, North Dakota	1969

Oklahoma

College of the Muscogee Nation, Okmulgee, Oklahoma	2004
Comanche Nation College, Lawton, Oklahoma	2002

South Dakota

Oglala Lakota College, Kyle, South Dakota	1971
Sinte Gleska University, Mission, South Dakota	1971
Sisseton Wahpeton College, Sisseton, South Dakota	1979

Washington

Northwest Indian College, Bellingham, Washington	1973

Wisconsin

College of Menominee Nation, Keshena, Wisconsin	1993
Lac Courte Oreilles Ojibwa Community College, Hayward, Wisconsin	1982

Wyoming

Wind River Tribal College, Ethete, Wyoming	1997

Six Tribal Colleges Named in Honor of Tribal Leaders

Cankdeska Cikana (Little Hoop) Community College, Fort Totten, North Dakota
http://www.littlehoop.edu/

> Established as Little Hoop Community College by the Spirit Lake Tribe in 1974, the Board of Regents officially changed the name of the Dakota institution to Cankdeska Cikana Community College in 1995. It is named in honor of military veteran Paul Yankton Sr., who was named Cankdeska Cikana (Little Hoop) in the Dakota language. An honored warrior, he was the recipient of two Purple Hearts; he died on November 29, 1944, while serving with the United States Army in Lorraine, France.

Chief Dull Knife College, Lame Deer, Montana
http://www.cdkc.edu/

> Located on the Northern Cheyenne Reservation in Lame Deer, Montana, Chief Dull Knife College was originally chartered in 1975 by tribal ordinance as the Northern Cheyenne Indian Action Program. The institution later became

---

southeast of Carson City, the Stewart Indian School remained open until 1980.

12. Wheelock Academy, present-day Millerton, Oklahoma
    http://tps.cr.nps.gov/nhl/detail.cfm?ResourceId=719&ResourceType=District
    http://www.youtube.com/watch?v=N3VmacnCfng
    Built in about 1832 in the Choctaw Nation, Indian Territory (present-day Oklahoma), Wheelock Academy began as a mission school for girls. In 1842, it became the first Choctaw National Academy, serving as a model for the school system established by the Five Civilized Tribes.

Three Colonial Colleges with Charters
Establishing American Indian Education

1. Harvard College, Cambridge, Massachusetts (1650)
   http://hul.harvard.edu/huarc/charter.html
   Harvard's charter avowed "education of the English and Indian youth of this country, in knowledge and godliness."
2. The College of William and Mary, Williamsburg, Virginia (1693)
   http://scrc.swem.wm.edu/wiki/index.php/Charter
   Its royal charter specified "that the Christian faith may be propagated amongst the Western Indians."
3. Dartmouth College, Hanover, New Hampshire (1769)
   http://www.dartmo.com/charter/charter.html
   Dartmouth College was chartered for "the education and instruction of Youth of the Indian Tribes in this Land . . . which shall appear necessary and expedient for civilizing and christianizing; and also of English Youth and any others."

Early Indian Education at the College of William and Mary in Virginia

The College of William and Mary was chartered in 1693, including in its mission a plan to provide schooling to American Indian children, agreeing to keep them "in Sicknesse and health, in Meat, drink, Washing, Lodgeing, Cloathes, Medicines, bookes and Education from the first beginning of Letters till they are ready to receive Orders and be thought Sufficient to be sent abroad to preach and Convert the Indians." Estimates of the Indian enrollment vary, but generally indicate small numbers of students (young males), among them hostages taken in frontier wars. The Brafferton School was constructed at the College of William and Mary for Native scholars in 1723, but the building was soon turned to other educational uses.

Thirty-Six Tribal Colleges and Universities

Starting with the establishment of the Navajo Community College (now Diné College) by the Navajo Nation in 1968, American Indian nations began to establish tribal colleges and universities (TCUs) to address the higher education needs of their communities. In 2010, there were thirty-six such institutions in the United States, (thirty-three of them fully accredited and three in Associate Status), serving some thirty thousand full- and part-time students. TCUs also offer a range of vocational certificate programs.

Alaska

Ilisagvik College, Barrow, Alaska	1995

Arizona

Diné College (Formerly Navajo Community College), Tsaile, Arizona	1968
Tohono O'odham Community College, Sells, Arizona	1998

Kansas

Haskell Indian Nations University, Lawrence, Kansas	1970

Michigan

Bay Mills Community College, Brimley, Michigan	1981
Keweenaw Bay Ojibwa Community College, Baraga, Michigan	1975
Saginaw Chippewa Tribal College, Mount Pleasant, Michigan	1998

Minnesota

Fond du Lac Tribal and Community College, Cloquet, Minnesota	1987
Leech Lake Tribal College, Cass Lake, Minnesota	1990
White Earth Tribal and Community College, Mahnomen, Minnesota	1997

Montana

Blackfeet Community College, Browning, Montana	1974
Chief Dull Knife College, Lame Deer, Montana	1975
Aaniiih Nakoda College, Harlem, Montana	1984
Fort Peck Community College, Poplar, Montana	1978
Little Big Horn College, Crow Agency, Montana	1980
Salish Kootenai College, Pablo, Montana	1977
Stone Child College, Box Elder, Montana	1984

Nebraska

Nebraska Indian Community College, Macy, Nebraska	1972
Little Priest Tribal College, Winnebago, Nebraska	1996

New Mexico

Navajo Technical College, Crownpoint, New Mexico	1979
Institute of American Indian Arts, Santa Fe, New Mexico	1962
Southwestern Indian Polytechnic Institute, New Mexico	1971

known as Dull Knife Memorial College, but was officially renamed Chief Dull Knife College in 2001. It is named in honor of one of the Northern Cheyenne's most respected nineteenth century leaders, Chief Dull Knife (also known as Morning Star), who fought on behalf of his people to maintain their sovereignty and homelands.

Little Priest Tribal College, Winnebago, Nebraska
http://www.littlepriest.edu/
Located in Winnebago, Nebraska, Little Priest Tribal College was chartered by the Winnebago Tribe of Nebraska in 1996. It is named in honor of Chief Little Priest, known as the last war chief of the Winnebago people. The institution strives to fulfill its educational mission, keeping in mind Little Priest's dying words, which were to "be strong, and educate my children."

Sinte Gleska University, Mission, South Dakota
http://www.sintegleska.edu/
Since its founding on the Rosebud Reservation in 1971, Sinte Gleska University has transitioned from Rosebud College Center, to Sinte Gleska Community College, to Sinte Gleska College during its development. One of the first two-year tribal colleges accredited to offer four-year bachelor's degrees, the university is named in honor of Sinte Gleska (Spotted Tail), a famous chief of the Sicangu band of Lakota.

Sitting Bull College, Fort Yates, North Dakota
http://www.sittingbull.edu/
Sitting Bull College began as Standing Rock Community College at Fort Yates, North Dakota, in 1973. The institution, which was accredited by the North Central Accreditation Association in 1987, was renamed in honor of renowned Hunkpapa Lakota leader Sitting Bull (Tatanka Iyotake) in 1996. Sitting Bull's visionary leadership and words, "Let us put our minds together to see what we can build for our children," are fundamental to education.

Stone Child College, Box Elder, Montana
http://www.stonechild.edu/
Chartered by the Chippewa-Cree Tribe on the Rocky Boy's Reservation in 1984, Stone Child College (SCC) is named for the nineteenth-century Chippewa leader Ah-se-ne-win, or Stone Man, often translated as Rocky Boy. Stone Child is another translation of the leader's name. SCC, which is accredited by the Northwest Commission on Colleges and Universities, offers associate degrees and certificate programs in various fields.

Commissioner of Indian Affairs Directive
Aimed at Indian Schools in 1889

In 1889, Commissioner of Indian Affairs Thomas J. Morgan directed Indian agents and school superintendents to inculcate patriotism in all Indian schools by instructing tribal youth "in the elements of American history, acquainting them with the leading acts in the lives of the most notable and worthy historical characters." To that end, Morgan called for regular instruction "in the form of familiar talks," the use of civics textbooks, the organization of debating societies, the distribution of rules of order to advanced students, the erection of flagstaffs to fly the American flag, the performance of patriotic songs and readings, and the observance of national holidays with appropriate exercises "to awaken reverence for the nation's power, gratitude for its beneficence, pride in its history, and a laudable ambition to contribute to its prosperity." Commissioner Morgan also directed that Indian school teachers "should carefully avoid any unnecessary reference to the fact that [their students] are Indians" ("Instructions to Indian Agents in Regard to Inculcation of Patriotism in Indian Schools," issued by Commissioner of Indian Affairs Thomas J. Morgan in December 1889, in Prucha 1996, 180–81).

Statements from American Indian Education Reports and Studies

"Our Nation's policies and programs for educating American Indians are a national tragedy. They present us with a national challenge of no small proportions."
—*Indian Education: A National Tragedy—A National Challenge*, Senate Report, 1969

"More than three hundred books were examined in the course of this study. Not one could be approved as a dependable source of knowledge about the history and culture of the Indian people in America. Most of the books were, in one way or another, derogatory to the Native Americans. Most contained misinformation, distortions, or omissions of important history."
—The American Indian Historical Society (Rupert Costo, editor, and Jeannette Henry, author), *Textbooks and the American Indian*, 1970

"What we have found out about Indian education in the course of this study is not new, especially to Indians. The history of education for American Indians is a history of reports, studies, task forces, and more studies. They all make the same sharp criticism and similar recommendations. Somehow the rhetoric never translates into action."
—NAACP Legal Defense and Educational Fund, with the cooperation of the Center for Law and Education, Harvard University, *An Even Chance: A Report on Federal Funds for Indian Children in Public School Districts*, 1971

"The children are a gift to us all, to their families, to their Indian nations, to the United States and to the world . . . (W)hat is lacking in us that we cannot nurture the richness of these children?"

—Leonard Haskie (Navajo), *Indian Nations At Risk*, 1991

White House Initiative on Tribal Colleges and Universities (TCUs)

The White House Initiative on Tribal Colleges and Universities (WHITCU) was established by Executive Order No. 13021, which was signed by President Bill Clinton on October 19, 1996. Located within the U.S. Department of Education in Washington, DC, the WHITCU works to ensure that the nation's tribal colleges and universities (TCUs) are more fully recognized and have full access to federal programs benefiting other higher educational institutions. Since its creation, it has led the implementation of Executive Order 13270, Tribal Colleges and Universities, signed by President George W. Bush on July 3, 2002.

Source: http://www2.ed.gov/about/inits/list/whtc/edlite-index.html

EDUCATORS

National Indian Education Association (NIEA) Educator of the Year Recipients

Founded in 1969 and incorporated in 1970, the National Indian Education Association (NIEA) is the largest and oldest Indian education organization in the country. NIEA, headquartered in Washington, DC, is a membership-based organization committed to increasing educational opportunities and resources for American Indian, Alaska Native, and Native Hawaiian students while protecting cultural and linguistic traditions. The organization bestows Educator of the Year and other honors at its annual convention, which draws large numbers of teachers, administrators, students, parents, and other participants from across the country (www.niea.org/data/files/convention/nieaconvprogram2006.pdf).

1977	Dr. William G. Demmert Jr. (Tlingit/Sioux)
1978	Dr. Robert J. Swan (Chippewa-Cree)
1979	Evaulu Russell (Kiowa)
1980	Stuart Tonemah (Kiowa-Comanche)
1981	Dr. Murton McCluskey (Blackfeet)

1982	Agnes Chavis (Lumbee)
1983	Dr. Michael Doss (Crow)
1984	Dr. Gerald Gipp (Hunkpapa Lakota)
1985	Tom Thompson (Blackfeet)
1986	Dr. Larry LaCounte (Chippewa)
1987	Dr. Lloyd Elm (Onondaga)
1988	Lionel Bordeaux (Sicangu Lakota)
1989	Dr. Joseph McDonald (Salish-Kootenai)
1990	Dr. Janine Pease Pretty-on-Top (Crow)
1991	Dr. Cornell Pewewardy (Comanche-Kiowa)
1992	Dr. Joseph Mann (Navajo)
1993	Edward Parisian (Chippewa-Cree)
1994	Dorothy Kiyukan (Prairie Band of Potawatomi)
1995	Dr. David M. Gipp (Hunkpapa Lakota)
1996	Dr. John W. Tippeconnic III (Comanche)
1997	Dr. Karen Gayton Swisher (Hunkpapa Lakota)
1998	Dr. Sandra K. Fox (Oglala Lakota)
1999	Carmen Taylor (Salish/Oneida)
2000	Dr. Barry Harding (Lumbee)
2001	Dr. Sue Ann Warner (Comanche)
2002	Danielle Walking Eagle (Sicangu Lakota)
2003	William Mehojah (Kaw)
2004	Joyce Silverthorne (Salish-Kootenai)
2005	Richard B. Williams (Oglala Lakota)
2006	Vida Stabler (Omaha)
2007	Dr. Larry Kimura (Native Hawaiian)
2008	Dr. David Kekaulike Sing (Native Hawaiian)
2009	Denise M. Juneau (Mandan/Hidatsa)
2010	Michelle M. Parada (Luiseño)
2011	Keiki Kawai'ae'a (Native Hawaiian)

HONORING NATIONS PROJECT, HARVARD UNIVERSITY

Honoring Nations Honorees, 1999–2010

Honoring Nations, a national awards program initiated in 1998, highlights outstanding programs in self-governance by Native nations. At the heart of the program is the belief that tribes themselves hold the key to positive social, political, cultural, and economic prosperity. Based at the John F. Kennedy School of Government at Harvard University, Honoring Nations is administered by the Harvard Project on American Indian Economic Development. The criteria for selection of honorees include program effectiveness, significance to sovereignty, cultural relevance, transferability, and sustainability. Honoring Nations has recognized a range of American Indian education programs.

Navajo Studies Department, 1999
Rough Rock Community School, Navajo Nation
> The Navajo Tribal Council named the Navajo Studies Department of Rough Rock Community School, which became the first tribal contract school in the country in 1966, as the only Navajo studies program on the reservation. Students from any of the Nation's 110 chapters are eligible to attend to study Navajo culture, history, and language.

Rosebud Sioux Tribal Education Department and Code, 1999
Education Department, Rosebud Sioux Tribe
> To address negative academic conditions among reservation youth, the Rosebud Sioux Tribe created a tribal education department (TED) and developed a code to regulate and coordinate aspects of tribal and public schools as well as myriad programs. The measures enabled the Rosebud Sioux Tribe to play a greater role in educating its youth, contributing to reduced dropout rates and increased graduation rates.

Two Plus Two Plus Two Program, 2000
Hopi Junior/Senior High School, Hopi Nation
> The Two Plus Two Plus Two college transition program was developed as a partnership between Hopi Junior/Senior High School, Northland Pioneer College, and Northern Arizona University in 1997. The program has contributed to increased Hopi enrollment in institutions of higher education, helping students acquire skills they can bring back to the reservation.

Ya Ne Dah Ah (Ancient Teachings) School, 2002
Education Department, Chickaloon Village Tribal Council, Chickaloon, Alaska
http://www.chickaloon.org
> Ya Ne Dah Ah School, which began full-time operation in 1993, is an independent school of the Chickaloon Village. It became Alaska's only tribally owned

and operated full-time primary school and day care facility, operating in a one-room school without federal and state funding. It received high honors for its cultural and academic achievements.

Akwesasne Freedom School, 2005
Friends of the Akwesasne Freedom School
Akwesasne Mohawk Nation
http://freedom-school.org

> Founded in 1979, the Akwesasne Freedom School (AKS) is an independent elementary/middle school that conducts year-round, full-day classes for grades pre-kindergarten through grade eight. The school combines solid academics with a strong foundation in Mohawk culture.

Hopi Education Endowment Fund, 2006
The Hopi Tribe
http://www.hopieducationfund.org

> Created by the Hopi Tribe in 2000, the Hopi Education Endowment Fund (HEEF) was established as a charitable, nonprofit public benefit program to meet the present and future educational needs of the Hopi people. The fund's purposes include providing financial assistance to Hopi students of all ages as well as support for other educational initiatives.

Morongo Tutoring Program, 2006
Morongo Band of Mission Indians (Banning, CA)
http://www.morongonation.org

> Created in 1991, the Morongo Tutoring Program is a comprehensive program that includes in-school and after-school tutoring, extended education, summer school, and an annual college/career day. The program's measures have helped to increase graduation rates to approximately 90 percent, the highest in tribal history.

Intercultural Leadership Initiative, 2008
Lac du Flambeau Band of Lake Superior Chippewa Indians

> The Intercultural Leadership Initiative (ILI) works to reduce racial tensions and promote cultural understanding between students from the Lac du Flambeau Reservation and the non-Indian population in school settings. The ILI seeks to ease the transition of reservation students transferring to an off-reservation high school, improve academic success, and reduce dropout rates.

Leadership Institute at the Santa Fe Indian School, 2010
All Indian Pueblo Council

> Founded in 1997, the Leadership Institute at the Santa Fe Indian School works to create a learning environment in which community members learn and teach as well as actively contribute to the success of their tribal nations. The

institute is guided by the themes of leadership, community service, public policy, and critical thinking. It has four programs: Community Institutes, Summer Policy Academy, high school symposia, and enrichment opportunities.

LEGISLATION

Education Legislation, 1819–1994

Civilization Fund Act of 1819

Passed by Congress on March 3, 1819, the Civilization Fund Act authorized an annual "civilization fund" to introduce "the habits and arts of civilization" to American Indians through educational instruction.

Snyder Act of 1921

The Snyder Act, passed by Congress on November 2, 1921, provided authorization for the expenditure of federal funds appropriated for education, health, and other expenses in connection with the administration of American Indian affairs.

Johnson-O'Malley Act of 1934

Passed by Congress on April 16, 1934, the Johnson-O'Malley Act authorized federal contracts with states or territories to receive support for providing educational, medical, and other services to American Indians.

Navajo Community College Act of 1971

The Navajo Community College Act authorized Congress to fund the construction and operation of a tribal college on the Navajo Reservation. Established in 1968 and renamed Diné College in 1997, it was the first college established by American Indians for American Indians. The college set a precedent for later tribally controlled community colleges on or near reservations.

Indian Education Act of 1972

Congress passed the Indian Education Act of 1972, an act to amend the Higher Education Act of 1965 and related acts, to address the special educational needs of American Indian students. Its measures included providing financial assistance to local educational agencies to develop and carry out specially designed school programs, and establishing new administrative structures through the establishment of an Office of Indian Education (OIE) as well as a National Advisory Council on Indian Education (NACIE).

Indian Self-Determination and Education Assistance Act of 1975

The Indian Self-Determination and Education Assistance Act of 1975 authorized federal authorities such as the secretary of the interior to enter into contracts with Indian tribes to plan, conduct, and administer programs and services. Congress recognized that the prolonged federal domination of Indian service programs had "served to retard" rather than enhance the progress of Indian people.

Tribally Controlled Community College Assistance Act of 1978
(renamed in 1998 the Tribally Controlled College or University Assistance Act)
    This legislation was enacted to provide grants for the operation and improvement of tribally controlled community colleges to ensure continued and expanded opportunities for American Indian students.

Bureau of Indian Education, U.S. Department of the Interior

The Bureau of Indian Education (BIE), an educational bureau overseen by the assistant secretary for Indian affairs in the U.S. Department of the Interior, provides services to federally recognized American Indian and Alaska Native tribes. It implements federal education laws and provides funding to 183 elementary and secondary day and boarding schools and peripheral dormitories, located on sixty-four reservations in twenty-three states and serving approximately forty-two thousand students. Of these schools, 124 are tribally controlled under P.L. 93-638 Indian Self-Determination and Education Assistance Act contracts or P.L. 100-297, the Tribally Controlled Schools Act. The Bureau of Indian Education directly operates 59 schools. The BIE also serves post-secondary students through higher education scholarships and support funding to twenty-six tribal colleges and universities. In addition, it oversees two post-secondary institutions: Haskell Indian Nations University in Lawrence, Kansas, and Southwestern Indian Polytechnic Institute in Albuquerque, New Mexico.

Source: http://www.bie.edu/

Office of Indian Education, U.S. Department of Education

The Office of Indian Education (OIE) was established through provisions of the Indian Education Act of 1972 (legislation to amend the Higher Education Act of 1965), which Congress enacted as a response to "Indian Education: A National Tragedy—A National Challenge," the final report of a Special Senate Subcommittee on Indian Education in 1969. Besides creating the OIE and providing financial assistance to local educational agencies to develop and implement school programs designed to meet the special needs of Indian students, the legislation also established the National Advisory Council on Indian Education (NACIE) among its provisions. OIE's

primary functions include grants management, evaluation, interagency coordination, and communication. It is located within the Office of Elementary and Secondary Education of the U.S. Department of Education in Washington, DC.

Source: http://www2.ed.gov/about/offices/list/oese/oie/index.html

Tribally Controlled Schools Act of 1988
This legislation was enacted to further the goals of the Indian Self-Determination and Education Assistance Act for increased tribal control over programs
and services. The Tribally Controlled Schools Act of 1988 provides for grants to
Indian tribes and organizations that operate tribally controlled schools eligible
for assistance.

Native American Languages Act of 1990
This law encourages and supports the use of Native American languages as a
medium of instruction to foster Native American language survival, equal educational opportunity, and increased student knowledge of culture and history.
It also stipulates evaluations by federal departments and agencies to bring their
policies and procedures into compliance with the measure.

Alaska Native Educational Equity, Support, and Assistance Act of 1994
The purposes of this legislation are to recognize the unique educational needs
of Alaska Natives, to authorize the development of supplemental educational
programs to benefit Alaska Natives, to supplement existing programs and
authorities in the area of education, and to provide direction and guidance to
appropriate federal, state, and local agencies to focus resources on meeting the
educational needs of Alaska Natives. This law was reauthorized as Title VII,
Part C of the No Child Left Behind Act of 2001.

Equity in Educational Land-Grant Status Act of 1994
The Equity in Educational Land-Grant Status Act authorized land-grant status to
twenty-nine tribal colleges and universities, thus entitling them to funding and
benefits for the improvement of agriculture and sciences programs and facilities.

POEMS AND BOOKS

Ten Poems about Schooling by Native Poets

1. "At the Door of the Native Studies Director," by Robert H. Davis (Tlingit). In
   Harper's Anthology of 20th Century Native American Poetry, edited by Duane
   Niatum (1988).

2. "The Cornwall Seminary," by Adin C. Gibbs (Delaware). In *Changing Is Not Vanishing: A Collection of American Indian Poetry to 1930*, edited by Robert Dale Parker (2011).
3. "For Heather, Entering Kindergarten," by Roberta Hill Whiteman (Oneida). In *Harper's Anthology of 20th Century Native American Poetry*, edited by Duane Niatum (1988).
4. "For Misty Starting School," by Luci Tapahonso (Navajo). In *A Breeze Swept Through* (1987).
5. "Indian Blood," by Mary Tall Mountain (Koyukon). In *The Clouds Threw This Light: Contemporary Native American Poetry*, edited by Phillip Foss (1983).
6. "Indian Boarding School: The Runaways," by Louise Erdrich (Ojibwe). In *Original Fire: Selected and New Poems* (2003).
7. "Indian Education Blues," by Ed Edmo (Shoshone/Bannock). In *Returning the Gift: Poetry and Prose from the First North American Native Writers' Festival*, edited by Joseph Bruchac (1994).
8. "Margaret/Haskell Indian School," by Carolyn Marie Dunn (Muscogee/Seminole/Cherokee). In *Reinventing the Enemy's Language*, edited by Joy Harjo and Gloria Bird (1997).
9. "Moccasins to School Again," by Heather Harris (Cree/Métis). In *A Broken Flute: The Native Experience in Books for Children*, edited by Doris Seale and Beverly Slapin (2005).
10. "Tribal Identity Grade Three," by Silvia Ross (Chukchansi). In *The Dirt Is Red Here: Art and Poetry from Native California*, edited by Margaret Dubin (2002).

Nine Memoirs and Other Books about School Life and More

1. *As Long as the Rivers Flow*, by Larry Loyie (Cree), with Constance Brissenden (2003).
2. *Children Left Behind: The Dark Legacy of Indian Mission Boarding Schools*, by Tim Giago (Lakota) (2006).
3. *First Person, First Peoples: Native American College Graduates Tell Their Life Stories*, edited by Andrew Garrod and Colleen Larimore (1997).
4. *Indian School Days*, by Basil H. Johnston (Ojibway) (1989).
5. *The Middle Five: Indian Schoolboys of the Omaha Tribe*, by Francis La Flesche (Omaha). Originally published in 1900, with many reprints of this classic account.
6. *My People the Sioux*, by Luther Standing Bear (Lakota) (1928).
7. *No Parole Today* (prose memoir and poetry), by Laura Tohe (Navajo) (1999).
8. *No Turning Back: A Hopi Indian Woman's Struggle to Live in Two Worlds*, by Polingaysi Qöyawayma (Elizabeth Q. White) (1964).
9. *Pipestone: My Life in an Indian Boarding School*, by Adam Fortunate Eagle (Ojibwe) (2010).

FILMS

Indian Boarding Schools: Keeping Culture Alive (USA, 2007, each 27 min.), directed by Allan Holzman.

>This two-part series examines federal Indian boarding school history with the films *Beyond the Mesas* (part one) and *Beautiful Resistance* (part two). Produced with the involvement of the Hopi Cultural Preservation Office, *Beyond the Mesas* documents the removal of Hopi youngsters to institutions such as Sherman Institute, Phoenix Indian School, and Ganado Mission School. *Beautiful Resistance* tells the story of contemporary Native artists and their creativity as they express family and tribal experiences and stories through their art.

In the White Man's Image (USA, 1992, 60 min.) directed by Christine Lesiak.

>Part of the series *The American Experience*, the PBS documentary *In the White Man's Image* tells the story of Richard Pratt and the founding of the Carlisle Indian boarding school in Carlisle, Pennsylvania.

Ma Ka Malu Ali'i: The Legacy of Hawaii's Ali'i (USA, 2007, 57 min.), directed by Lisa Altieri (Native Hawaiian) and Steve Okino.

>This documentary explores the visionary efforts made by five members of the *ali'i*, Hawaiian royalty, to provide for the education of children, as well as other services. The charitable institutions they created have endured to the present.

Older Than America (USA, 2007, 102 min.), directed by Georgina Lightning (Cree).

>This film explores Indian boarding school life, experiences that have shaped generations of Native American and First Nations lives.

The Only Good Indian (USA, 2009, 114 min.), directed by Kevin Willmott.

>Set in Kansas during the early 1900s, a Native American teenager in this drama is taken from his family and forced to attend a distant Indian boarding school. When he runs away, he is tracked by a former U.S. Army scout.

Only the Devil Speaks Cree (Canada, 2002, 32 min.), directed by Pamela Matthews (Cree).

>This film about boarding school experiences was inspired by the filmmaker's mother.

Our Spirits Don't Speak English: Indian Boarding School (USA, 2008, 80 min.), directed by Chip Richie.

>This documentary examines Indian boarding schools, providing Native American perspectives on the federally supported educational system designed to eradicate tribal cultures.

Spirit of the Dawn (USA, 1994, 29 min.), directed by Heidi Schmidt Emberling.

>*Spirit of the Dawn* explores the changes in American Indian education from boarding school institutions of the past to classrooms of today. The documentary incorporates the story of two sixth graders from the Crow Reservation in Montana.

Where the Spirit Lives (Canada, 1989, 96 min.), directed by Bruce Pittman.

Set in 1937 in Western Canada, *Where the Spirit Lives* tells the story of a Black-foot girl taken from her home on a reserve and sent to a residential school to undergo cultural transformation.

A Windigo Tale (Canada, 2009, 90 min.), directed by Armand Garnet Ruffo (Ojibway).

Filmed on the Six Nations Reserve in Ontario and in the Ottawa Valley, *A Windigo Tale* is a drama based on the history of the residential school system, which removed generations of children from their families for schooling in Euro-Canadian society.

ORGANIZATIONS

American Indian College Fund (AICF)

http://www.collegefund.org/

Founded in 1989, the American Indian College Fund was established to raise private-sector funds for tribal colleges and to complement the efforts of its sister organization, the American Indian Higher Education Consortium (AIHEC). Originally located in New York City, the fund has been headquartered in Denver, Colorado, since 2002. Besides providing scholarships to American Indian students, the organization also supports cultural preservation projects, capital construction, and other programs at tribal colleges.

American Indian Graduate Center (AIGC)

http://www.aigc.com/

Headquartered in Albuquerque, New Mexico, the American Indian Graduate Center is a national nonprofit organization that provides educational assistance to American Indian and Alaska Native graduate students throughout the country. It was founded in 1969 as American Indian Scholarships, but changed its name to AIGC in 1989.

American Indian Higher Education Consortium (AIHEC)

http://www.aihec.org

The American Indian Higher Education Consortium, located in Alexandria, Virginia, was founded in 1972 by the presidents of the first six tribal colleges in the country. Today, the organization has grown to represent thirty-six tribal colleges in the United States and one Canadian institution. AIHEC's mission is to support the work of these institutions as well as the national movement for Indian self-determination.

American Indian Library Association (AILA)

http://www.ailanet.org/

Founded in 1979, the American Indian Library Association, an affiliate of the American Library Association, is a membership action group that addresses library-related needs of American Indians and Alaska Natives. AILA works to improve Indian library, cultural, and informational services in school, public, and research libraries on reservations and beyond.

Futures for Children
http://www.futuresforchildren.org/
Futures for Children provides mentoring, training, and programs to American Indian students and their families. Located in Albuquerque, New Mexico, the organization serves Hopi, Navajo, and Pueblo tribal communities.

National Aboriginal Achievement Foundation (NAAF)
http://www.naaf.ca/
The National Aboriginal Achievement Foundation is an organization dedicated to raising funds to deliver programs that provide the tools necessary for Aboriginal peoples, especially youth, to achieve their potential. It is the largest supporter of aboriginal education outside of the federal government in Canada. NAAF also sponsors the National Aboriginal Achievement Awards, Canada's largest and most influential annual showcase of aboriginal achievement. NAAF is headquartered in Ohsweken, Ontario.

National Advisory Council on Indian Education (NACIE)
http://www2.ed.gov/about/offices/list/oese/oie/nacie.html
The National Advisory Council on Indian Education (NACIE) was authorized by section 7141 of the Elementary and Secondary Education Act of 1965 and is governed by the provisions of the Federal Advisory Committee Act. NACIE's fifteen members are appointed by the president of the United States and serve as special government employees. The council's functions include advising the secretary of education concerning the funding and administration of applicable programs with American Indians as participants.

National Indian Education Association (NIEA)
http://www.niea.org/
Founded in 1969 and incorporated in 1970, the National Indian Education Association is the largest and oldest Indian education organization in the country. NIEA is a membership-based organization committed to increasing educational opportunities and resources for American Indian, Alaska Native, and Native Hawaiian students while protecting cultural and linguistic traditions. It is headquartered in Washington, DC.

National Indian Head Start Directors Association (NIHSDA)
http://www.nihsda.org/
Formed in 1979, the National Indian Head Start Directors Association became the recognized voice for American Indian programs within the federal Head

Start Bureau, National Head Start Association, and other early childhood development associations. NIHSDA promotes and supports high quality comprehensive early childhood development and education services, advocating on behalf of American Indian and Alaska Native preschoolers.

Native American and Indigenous Studies Association (NAISA)
http://www.naisa.org/
Founded in 2008, the Native American and Indigenous Studies Association is a professional organization dedicated to supporting scholars and others who work in the academic field of Native American and indigenous studies. The association, which hosts a scholarly meeting in Native studies, has more than seven hundred members from diverse nations and peoples.

Nihewan Foundation
http://www.nihewan.org/
Founded by Academy Award–winning singer/songwriter Buffy Sainte-Marie (Cree) in 1969, the Nihewan Foundation is a nonprofit educational organization dedicated to improving the education of and about Native American people and cultures. Nihewan's programs include scholarships and the Cradleboard Teaching Project, which partners indigenous and non-indigenous school classes across a range of settings.

Tribal Education Departments National Assembly (TEDNA)
http://www.tedna.org/
The Tribal Education Departments National Assembly was established in 2003 as a membership organization to represent the education departments of American Indian and Alaska Native tribes. TEDNA fosters effective relationships with governmental and educational agencies, facilitates communication, and supports the rights of member nations with respect to their educational goals.

RESOURCES

Adams, David Wallace. *Education for Extinction: American Indians and the Boarding School Experience, 1875–1928*. Lawrence: University Press of Kansas, 1995.

Archuleta, Margaret L., Brenda J. Child, and K. Tsianina Lomawaima, eds. *Away from Home: American Indian Boarding School Experiences, 1879–2000*. Phoenix: Heard Museum, 2000.

Benham, Maenette K. P. A., and Ronald H. Heck. *Culture and Educational Policy in Hawai'i: The Silencing of Native Voices*. Mahwah, NJ: Lawrence Erlbaum Associates, 1998.

Benham, Maenette K. P. A., and Wayne J. Stein, eds. *The Renaissance of American Indian Higher Education: Capturing the Dream*. Mahwah, NJ: Lawrence Erlbaum Associates, 2003.

Child, Brenda J. *Boarding School Seasons: American Indian Families, 1900–1940*. Lincoln: University of Nebraska Press, 1998.

Cobb, Amanda J. *Listening to Our Grandmothers' Stories: Bloomfield Academy for Chickasaw Females, 1852–1949.* Lincoln: University of Nebraska Press, 2000.

Faircloth, Susan C., and John W. Tippeconnic III. *The Dropout/Graduation Rate Crisis among American Indian and Alaska Native Students: Failure to Respond Places the Future of Native Peoples at Risk.* Los Angeles: The Civil Rights Project/Proyecto Derechos Civiles at UCLA, 2010. Available from www.civilrightsproject.ucla.edu.

Jones, Guy W., and Sally Moomaw. *Lessons from Turtle Island: Native Curriculum in Early Childhood Classrooms.* St. Paul, MN: Redleaf Press, 2002.

Katanski, Amelia V. *Learning to Write "Indian": The Boarding-School Experience and American Indian Literature.* Norman: University of Oklahoma Press, 2005.

Khachadoorian, Angelle A. *Inside the Eagle's Head: An American Indian College.* Tuscaloosa: University of Alabama Press, 2010.

Lincoln, Kenneth, ed. *Gathering Native Scholars: UCLA's 40 Years of American Indian Culture and Research.* Los Angeles: UCLA American Indian Studies Center, 2009.

Lomawaima, K. Tsianina. *They Called It Prairie Light: The Story of the Chilocco Indian School.* Lincoln: University of Nebraska Press, 1994.

———, and Teresa L. McCarty. *To Remain an Indian: Lessons in Democracy from a Century of Native American Education.* New York: Teachers College Press, 2006.

Mihesuah, Devon A. *Cultivating the Rosebuds: The Education of Women at the Cherokee Female Seminary, 1851–1909.* Urbana: University of Illinois Press, 1993.

Modica, Andrea, and Rebecca Carroll. *Real Indians: Portraits of Contemporary Native Americans and America's Tribal Colleges.* New York: Melcher Media, 2003.

Oppelt, Norman T. *The Tribally Controlled Indian College: The Beginnings of Self-Determination in American Indian Education.* Tsaile, AZ: Navajo Community College Press, 1990.

Owings, Alison. *Indian Voices: Listening to Native Americans.* New Brunswick, NJ: Rutgers University Press, 2011.

Prucha, Francis Paul. *The Churches and the Indian Schools, 1888–1912.* Lincoln: University of Nebraska Press, 1979.

———, ed. *Documents of United States Indian Policy.* 2nd ed., expanded. Lincoln: University of Nebraska Press, 1996.

Reyhner, Jon Allan, and Jeanne M. Oyawin. *American Indian Education: A History.* Norman: University of Oklahoma Press, 2006.

Szasz, Margaret Connell. *Indian Education in the American Colonies, 1607–1783.* Albuquerque: University of New Mexico Press, 1988.

Warner, Linda Sue, and Gerald E. Gipp, eds. *Tradition and Culture in the Millennium: Tribal Colleges and Universities.* Charlotte, NC: Information Age Publishing, 2009

Journals

American Indian Culture and Research Journal: http://www.books.aisc.ucla.edu/cat-aicrj.asp

American Indian Quarterly: http://www.nebraskapress.unl.edu/product/American-Indian -Quarterly,673174.aspx

Journal of American Indian Education: http://jaie.asu.edu/

Ōiwi: A Native Hawaiian Journal: http://www.hawaii.edu/oiwi

Tribal College Journal of American Indian Higher Education: http://www.tribalcollegejournal .org/

Wicazo Sa Review: http://www.upress.umn.edu/journal-division/Journals/wicazo-sa-review
Winds of Change (AISES): http://www.aises.org/what/woc

Web Sites

Aboriginal Healing Foundation: http://www.ahf.ca/

A Guide to Native American Studies Programs in the United States and Canada (by Robert M. Nelson, 2011): https://facultystaff.richmond.edu/~rnelson/asail/guide/guide.html

Alaska Native Knowledge Network: http://www.ankn.uaf.edu/

Alaskool Central: http://www.alaskool.org

American Indian College Fund: http://www.collegefund.org/

American Indian Education Knowledgebase, Mid-Continent Comprehensive Center: http://www.mc3edsupport.org/community/knowledgebases/Project-7.html

American Indian Library Association: http://www.ailanet.org/

American Indian Science and Engineering Society: http://www.aises.org/

Carlisle Indian Industrial School Research Pages: http://home.epix.net/~landis/

Chilocco Indian Agricultural School: http://www.nps.gov/history/nr/feature/indian/2006/chilocco.htm

Harvard Project's Honoring Nations Directory of Honored Programs, 1999–2006: http://hpaied.org./images/resources/general/Dir_web.pdf

Indian Residential Schools Settlement, Canada: http://www.residentialschoolsettlement.ca/

Indians of the Midwest, Past and Present: http://publications.newberry.org/indiansofthemidwest/

Truth and Reconciliation Commission of Canada: http://www.trc.ca/

Website Resources for Hawaiian Agencies: http://www.k12.hi.us/~kaiapuni/HLIP/resources/resAgencies.htm

White House Conference on Indian Education. Final Report. Executive Summary. May 22, 1922. http://www.tedna.org/pubs/1990whitisconf.pdf

12

Native Languages

FIRSTS

1663	Published in the Massachuset language in 1663, *Mamusse Wunneetupa-natamwe Up-Biblum God*, developed by missionary John Eliot, was the first Bible printed in any language in North America.
ca. 1815	Jane Johnston Schoolcraft, Bamewawagezhikaquay, Woman of the Sound the Stars Make Rushing Through the Sky (Ojibwe), the first known Native American literary writer, began writing poetry and other works in Ojibwe and English in about 1815.
1978	Hawaii became the first state to declare a native language (Hawaiian) as its official language (along with English).
2001	*Atanarjuat: The Fast Runner* (2001), directed by Zacharias Kunuk (Inuit), was Canada's first Native-language feature film to be written, produced, directed, and acted by Inuit.
2006	The University of Hawaii at Hilo established a PhD program in the Hawaiian language. In addition to being the first doctoral program for the study of Hawaiian, it was the first doctoral program established for the study of any Native language in the United States. Both the master's (established in 2002) and doctoral programs are considered by global scholars as pioneering in the revival of Native languages.
2007	The first endangered-language software developed through Rosetta Stone was created for the Mohawk language (Kanien'kehaka). The work was sponsored by Kanien'kehaka Onkwawén:na Raotitiohkwa, the Mohawk language and cultural center of Kahnawake, Quebec, Canada.
2008	A showing of *Stories of the Cherokees* marked the first time a Cherokee language film premiered at the famed Cannes Film Festival in France. The fifteen-minute film was shown at the festival's Short Film Corner.
2009	Nkwusm, a Salish language immersion school on the Salish-Kootenai Reservation in Arlee, Montana, had its first graduation, June 12, 2009.

2010   The Cherokee Nation in Oklahoma worked with Apple, Inc., to develop Cherokee-language software for the iPhone, iPod, and iPad. Cherokee became the first American Indian language supported by Apple devices.

University of Hawaii at Hilo's Ka Haka 'Ula O Ke'elikōlani College of Hawaiian Language presented the first doctorate in Hawaiian and Indigenous Language and Culture Revitalization to a Native Hawaiian student, Kauanoe Kamanâ.

Qapirangajuq: Inuit Knowledge and Climate Change, directed by Zacharias Kunuk (Inuit) and Ian Mauro, became the world's first Inuktitut-language film on climate change.

NATIVE LANGUAGES

Seven Name Changes of Tribal Nations or Reservations

Changed From	Changed To	Date	Location
Papago Tribe	Tohono O'odham Nation (Desert People)	1986	Arizona
Devils Lake Sioux	Spirit Lake Tribe (Mni Wakan Oyate)	1996	North Dakota
Wisconsin Winnebago Tribe	Ho-Chunk Nation (People of the Big Voice)	1994	Wisconsin
Canoncito Reservation	Tohajiilee Indian Reservation	1999	New Mexico
Sisseton Wahpeton Sioux Tribe	Sisseton Wahpeton Oyate	2002	South Dakota
San Juan Pueblo	Ohkay Owingeh Pueblo	2006	New Mexico
Santo Domingo Pueblo	Kewa Pueblo	2009	New Mexico

Twenty-Six States with Native Language Names

Beginning with Massachusetts and Connecticut during the colonial period, twenty-six states have names that have been traced or attributed to diverse Native languages.*

Alabama
Alabama (*Alibamu*), the Muskogean name of a tribal nation of the Creek Confederacy.

Alaska
Aleut, *Alaxsxaq*, "the mainland, the land facing the sea."

Arizona
Possibly of O'odham (Pima) origin, translated as "having a little spring."

Arkansas
Illinois and French variations of the name for the *Ugakhpa* (*Quapaw*), "downstream people"; also *Akansas*, or "wind people."

Connecticut
Mohegan, *Quinnitukqut*, "beside the long river."

Idaho
An English corruption of the Kiowa-Apache word *Idaahe*, "enemy." The name has also been traced to the Coeur d'Alene language, meaning "greetings by surprise."

Illinois
The name has been traced to a French adaptation of a Miami word, *Ilenweewa*, "s/he speaks normally." It is also associated with *Illiniwek*, a historic confederation of Algonquian tribes.

Iowa
Ioway, the name of a tribal nation indigenous to the area.

Kansas
Kaw (also Kansa), the name of a tribal nation in the central Midwest.

Kentucky
Wyandot, *Kentahteh*, "tomorrow, the coming day"; Iroquois, "meadow" or "prairie"; Shawnee, referring to the head of a river; or an Algonquian word for a river bottom.

Massachusetts
The name can be traced to the Massachuset, an Algonquian group indigenous to the area, and is generally interpreted as a reference to the area's Great Blue Hills.

Michigan
A French adaptation of the Anishinaabe (Ojibwe) term *Mishigami*, "large water" or "large lake."

Minnesota
The Dakota (Sioux) name for the Minnesota River, from *mni* (water) and *sota*, "cloudy, muddy."

Mississippi
From *misi-ziibi* ("great river"), the Anishinaabe (Ojibwe) name for the Mississippi River.

Missouri
The name is said to come from the Algonquian language, variously translated as "town of the large canoes" or "muddy water." It is associated with the

Missouria, a tribal group that lived along what became known as the Missouri River.

Nebraska
Otoe-Missouri name for the Platte River, meaning "flat water."

North Dakota
The word *Dakota*, which refers to the Dakota/Lakota indigenous to the area, is generally translated as "friend" or "ally."

Ohio
A Wyandot name referring to the Ohio and Allegheny rivers, translated as "large, great." A French mistranslation is "beautiful river."

Oklahoma
Choctaw, *Okla* and *Humma*, "red person" or "red people."

Oregon
The origin of the name "Oregon," a matter of speculation, has been traced to the Algonquian terms *wauregan* and *olighin*, translated as "good and beautiful." Alternatively, the name is said to derive from an engraver's error in naming the *Ouisiconsink* (Wisconsin River) on a French map. A recent theory is that "Oregon" comes from *ooligan*, an indigenous term for the grease from smelt (fish), a trade item.

South Dakota
The word *Dakota*, which refers to the Dakota/Lakota indigenous to the area, is generally translated as "friend" or "ally."

Tennessee
Of Cherokee or Yuchi origin, the name of a Native village or town (*Tanasqui*; a Cherokee town named *Tanasi*); also "meeting place," "winding river," or "river of the great bend."

Texas
Taysha, a word in the Caddoan language of the Hasinai, translated "Hello, Friend," adopted in Spanish as *Tejas* and in English as *Texas*.

Utah
Navajo, *Yuttahih*, "higher-ups, people who are higher."

Wisconsin
The name has been traced to the Mascouten (Miami, Kickapoo) words *Mescous-ing Miskous*, translated as "red stone" by Jacques Marquette in 1673, but these

terms were later disputed. *Mescousing* became *Ouisconsin* by 1682 and *Wisconsin* in the early nineteenth century.

Wyoming

The name of this state comes from the Lenape (Delaware) word *Mecheweami-ing*, "at/on the big plains" or "mountains and valleys alternating" and was first used to name the Wyoming Valley in Pennsylvania.

*Although it is not derived from a Native language, the name "Indiana" is interpreted as "land of Indians."

Bible Translations

Beginning in the seventeenth century, the Bible has been translated in its entirety into several Native languages in North America. Portions of the Bible, as well as prayer books, hymnals, stories, and other religious works, have also been translated into countless indigenous languages. Native translators, including Cockenoe and John Printer, and their work on the first complete Bible to be published in America, contributed to these linguistic achievements.

Language	Title or Translation and Date
Massachuset	*Mamusse Wunneetupanatamwe Up-Biblum God.* Cambridge, Massachusetts, 1663
Western Cree	*Kunache kehche musenuhekun.* London, 1861.
Eastern Arctic Inuit	Using the Latin alphabet, Moravian missionaries in Labrador completed a translation of the Bible, 1871.
Dakota	*Dakota Wowapi Wakan* (The Holy Bible). New York, 1880.
Gwich'in	*Ettunetle Rsotitinyoo.* London, 1898.
Navajo	*Diyin God Bizaad.* New York, 1985.
Inuktitut (Inuit)	Translated in Inuktitut syllabics under one cover, *Gudib UKausingit* (God's Word) was dedicated on January 20, 2009. (A translation of the New Testament was completed in 1992.)

Translation of the Bible into Navajo

The Navajo translation of the Bible, *Diyin God Bizaad* (Holy God, His Word, 1985), which took over forty years to complete, involved the work of separate teams of Protestant missionaries and Navajo interpreters through the Wycliffe Bible Translators and later the American Bible Society. The New Testament was translated in

1956, with efforts to produce a revised version initiated in 1968, simultaneous with work on the Old Testament. The 1,583-page Bible was dedicated in January 1986 on the Navajo reservation. Linguist Turner Blount, who headed the Wycliffe translating team, noted: "No Navajo translation can be done without the help of native speakers to convey proper meanings," in the complex, tonal language.

Thirty-Six English Loanwords from Native Languages

Abalone	Moccasin	Skunk
Adirondack	Moose	Squash
Anorak	Mukluk	Succotash
Appalachian	Opossum	Tamarack
Bayou	Pecan	Terrapin
Caribou	Pemmican	Tipi
Catalpa	Persimmon	Toboggan
Chipmunk	Podunk	Totem
Hickory	Quahog	Ulu
Honk	Quonset	Wampum
Igloo	Raccoon	Wigwam
Kayak	Sequoia	Woodchuck

Four Native Language Immersion and Reclamation Programs

American Indian language instruction can be found in a variety of settings throughout North America, including immersion programs and course offerings. Native peoples are working to preserve and maintain tribal languages, which were eradicated or endangered through policies and practices associated with European colonization, among them population loss, boarding schools, and English-only mandates.

1. Akwesasne Freedom School (NY)
   http://freedom-school.org/
   Concerned about the lack of cultural and linguistic offerings in local public schools, Mohawk parents founded the Akwesasne Freedom School (AFS) in 1979. Six years later, in 1985, the parents administering the school made the decision to adopt a total Mohawk immersion curriculum, doing so without approval or funding from state or federal governments. AFS, an independent elementary school, immerses its students in levels Pre-K to 6 in the Kanienkeha (Mohawk) language and culture. Levels 7, 8, and 9 are transition classes with both Mohawk and English instruction.

2. Nkwusm Salish Language Revitalization Institute (MT)
   http://salishworld.com/
   Chartered in the state of Montana in 2003, the Nkwusm Salish Language Revitalization Institute works to research, promote, and preserve the Salish language. The institute is based on the Flathead Reservation, the home of the Confederated Salish and Kootenai Tribes, in Arlee, Montana. Nkwusm operates an immersion preschool and primary school, with twenty-five students from age two to thirteen enrolled for the 2011–2012 school year. It also operates three other programs centered on curriculum development, fluent speaker training, and an adult immersion program for school staff. Nkwusm's mission is to recreate a process whereby language is passed along as it once was, from parent to child.

3. The Piegan Institute (MT)
   http://www.pieganinstitute.org/
   Founded in 1987, the Piegan Institute is headquartered on the Blackfeet Indian Reservation in Montana. The institute's objectives are to increase the number of Blackfeet language speakers, to increase the cultural knowledge base of community members, and to actively influence community-based change. Projects include operating an immersion program for grades K–8, conducting research, and producing print and non-print materials on Blackfeet language and history.

4. Wôpanâak Language Reclamation Project (MA)
   http://www.wlrp.org/
   The Wôpanâak Language Reclamation Project (WLRP) was formed in 1993 under the direction of Jessie Little Doe Baird (Mashpee Wampanoag), who earned a master's degree in Algonquian linguistics from MIT in 2000. The project represents the joint collaborative efforts of members of the Assonet Band of Wampanoag, the Mashpee Wampanoag Tribe, the Wampanoag Tribe of Aquinnah, and the Herring Pond Band of Wampanoag to restore Wôpanâak (Wampanoag language) as a principal means of expression of their people. According to the WLRP, this is the first effort to reclaim an American Indian language with no living speakers.

Native Languages Used in Code Talking during
World War I and World War II

World War I	World War II
Cherokee	Assiniboine
Cheyenne	Cherokee
Choctaw	Chippewa
Comanche	Choctaw
Osage	Comanche
Yankton Sioux	Creek

Hopi
Kiowa
Menominee
Navajo
Oneida
Pawnee
Sac and Fox/Meskwaki
Seminole
Sioux
   (Lakota, Dakota,
   Nakota)
Winnebago

Estimate of the Number of Native Languages

By some estimates, more than three hundred native languages once existed in what is now the continental United States, as different from each other as English and Chinese. But that number is now greatly diminished. Loss of Native speakers and Native population losses caused by European diseases, English-only requirements in schools, and other factors have had a negative impact on the survival of these languages. Today, many tribal nations and tribal members are working to reclaim or revitalize them.

Sequoyah and the Cherokee Syllabary

Born in the Cherokee Nation in the southern Appalachian region in a year estimated to be between 1760 and 1765, Sequoyah (also known as George Guess) became renowned as the inventor of the Cherokee syllabary, an eighty-five-character writing system he completed in 1821. He was raised by his Cherokee mother, later working as a trader, blacksmith, and silversmith. Sequoyah completed the syllabary, composed of characters to represent syllables of the Cherokee language, after twelve years of work.

In 1825 the Cherokee Nation's General Council voted to make Sequoyah's alphabet official, appointing a committee to raise funds to establish a printing office. The syllabary contributed to rapid literacy, helping to inform tribal citizens about issues of the day as well as contributing to the preservation of history, culture, and religious practices.

Historic sites devoted to Sequoyah's life and work include the Sequoyah Birthplace Museum in Tennessee and Sequoyah's Cabin in Oklahoma.

The Sequoyah Birthplace Museum
http://www.sequoyahmuseum.org/
> Located in Vonore, Tennessee, the Sequoyah Birthplace Museum is a property of the Eastern Band of Cherokee Indians. Its mission is to promote understanding and appreciation of the history and culture of the Cherokee Indians, particularly the life and contributions of Sequoyah.

Sequoyah's Cabin, U.S. National Historic Landmark, Sallisaw, Oklahoma http://www.okhistory.org/outreach/homes/sequoyahcabin.html
> Sequoyah, the inventor of the Cherokee syllabary, or writing system, built a one-room log cabin shortly after moving from the southeastern homeland of his people to Oklahoma in 1829. The cabin became the property of the Oklahoma Historical Society in 1936 and was designated as a National Historic Landmark in 1966.

New Words Council

The New Words Council works to ensure that the Alutiiq language of the Kodiak Archipelago in Alaska continues to grow, with knowledgeable elders meeting monthly to discuss the development of new words. The *Nuta'at Niugnelistat* (New Word Makers) use methods that include literal translations (such as Kicarwik, "place to anchor," the Alutiiq word for the city of Anchorage) to accomplish their work. They also translate the function or characteristics of words in English. In this way, the council developed words for computer, *umiartusqaq* ("thing that always thinks"), and e-mail, *cukasqaq kaliqaq* ("fast paper").
http://alutiiqmuseum.org/alutiiq-language/new-words.html

HONORING NATIONS PROJECT, HARVARD UNIVERSITY

Honoring Nations Honorees, 1999–2005

Honoring Nations, a national awards program initiated in 1998, highlights outstanding programs in self-governance by Native nations. At the heart of the program is the belief that tribes themselves hold the key to positive social, political, cultural, and economic prosperity. Based at the John F. Kennedy School of Government at Harvard University, Honoring Nations is administered by the Harvard Project on American Indian Economic Development. The criteria for selection of honorees include program effectiveness, significance to sovereignty, cultural relevance, transferability, and sustainability. Exemplary Native language preservation projects and revitalization initiatives are among the outstanding programs.

Ojibwe Language Program, 1999
Department of Education, Mille Lacs Band of Ojibwe
Onamia, Minnesota
http://www.millelacsband.com
> This tribally funded program was created in 1995 to teach the Ojibwe language to students ranging from toddlers to young adults. The program utilizes elder-youth interaction, instructional materials such as songbooks and comic books, and other resources to teach the language. The program has also provided instruction in Ojibwe language, history, and culture to local public schools.

Cherokee National Youth Choir, 2003
Cherokee Nation
Tahlequah, Oklahoma
http://youthchoir.cherokee.org/
> Founded in 2000, the Cherokee National Youth Choir consists of forty Cherokee young people from northeastern Oklahoma who perform traditional songs in the Cherokee language. The Cherokee Nation's principal chief, Chad Smith, envisioned the choir as a way to engage children in the Cherokee language and culture. The award-winning choir has performed nationally and produced CDs, available at sources such as http://cdbaby.com.

The Cherokee Language Revitalization Project, 2005
Cherokee Nation Language Department
The Cherokee Nation, Tahlequah, Oklahoma
http://www.cherokee.org/culture/language/default.aspx
> After surveying the Cherokee population and finding no fluent tribal language speakers under the age of forty, the Cherokee principal chief declared a state of emergency that launched revitalization initiatives. The project's multifaceted efforts include a language immersion program for preschoolers, a university partnership degree program for certifying Cherokee language teachers, and community language activities.

AWARDS

Awards for Native Language Work

Jessie Little Doe Baird (Mashpee Wampanoag)
> Jessie Little Doe Baird received a MacArthur Fellows award in 2010 for "reviving a long-silent language and restoring to her Native American community a vital sense of its cultural heritage and to the nation a link to our complex past." The MacArthur program awards five-year, unrestricted fellowships to individuals across all ages and fields who show exceptional merit and promise of continued creative work.

Virginia Beavert (Yakama)
Virginia Beavert, linguist and teacher, has been honored for her lifetime of work to preserve and revitalize the Sahaptin language, a Plateau Penutian language spoken in south central Washington and northern Oregon. She received the Washington Governor's Heritage Award in 2006, the Ken Hale Prize from the Society for the Study of the Indigenous Languages of the Americas (SSILA) in 2008, and an honorary Doctor of Humane Letters degree from the University of Washington in 2009. Beavert co-authored *Ichishkíin Sinwit Yakama/Yakima Sahaptin Dictionary* (University of Washington Press, 2010), the first modern published dictionary of any Sahaptin dialect.

Sharon Burch (Diné)
Sharon Burch received the National Association for Independent Record Labels and Distributors INDIE Award, Best North American Native Music, for her album *Touch the Sweet Earth* in 1995. Burch sings many of her songs in the Navajo language.

Vi Hilbert (Upper Skagit)
Named a Washington State Living Treasure in 1989, Vi Hilbert also received other honors for her work to preserve the Lushootseed (Puget Salish) language and culture, including a National Heritage Fellowship from the National Endowment for the Arts in 1994. In 2008, she was the recipient of the Ken Hale Prize from the Society for the Study of the Indigenous Languages of the Americas (SSILA). Hilbert's life and work are featured in *Huchoosedah: Traditions of the Heart*, a 1995 television documentary by KCTS/BBC Wales.

Keith Secola (Bois Forte Ojibwe) and Karen Drift (Bois Forte Ojibwe)
Keith Secola and Karen Drift received a Native American Music Award for Best Linguistic Recording for *Anishinabemoin*, 2007.

Emory Sekaquaptewa (Hopi)
Honored with the Heard Museum's national Spirit of the Heard Award in 1997, University of Arizona professor Emory Sekaquaptewa has been referred to as the "Noah Webster of the Hopi Nation" for his work to preserve the language and culture of his people. He co-edited *Hopi Dictionary: Hopiikwa Lavaytutuveni: A Hopi-English Dictionary of the Third Mesa Dialect* (published in 1998), which includes some thirty thousand entries and is the first Hopi language dictionary. Sekaquaptewa, who, among his many accomplishments, also founded and was chief judge of the Hopi appellate court, received the 1989 Arizona Indian Living Treasure award and the first Ken Hale Award from the Society for the Study of the Indigenous Languages of the Americas (SSILA) in 2003.

Ofelia Zepeda (Tohono O'odham)
>   Linguist and cultural preservationist Ofelia Zepeda, who received a MacArthur
>   Fellows award in 1999, was honored for her "singular work in advancing the
>   field of native language scholarship," work that positions her "as a unique force
>   on behalf of the continued life of endangered languages." She wrote the first
>   Tohono O'odham grammar book and has authored and edited many other
>   publications as well. Zepeda is also a renowned poet, whose books include
>   *Ocean Power: Poems from the Desert* and *Where Clouds Are Formed.*

LEGISLATION

Native American Languages Legislation

Native American Languages Act of 1990
>   This law encourages and supports the use of Native American languages as
>   a medium of instruction to foster Native American language survival, equal
>   educational opportunity, and increased student knowledge of culture and his-
>   tory. It also stipulates evaluations by federal departments and agencies to bring
>   their policies and procedures into compliance with the measure.

Native American Languages Act of 1992
>   This legislation amended the Native American Programs Act of 1974 to pro-
>   vide a grant program for the purpose of assisting Native Americans to ensure
>   the survival and continuing vitality of their languages.

Statements Concerning the Use of American Indian Languages

"Your attention is called to the regulation of this office which forbids instruction
in schools in any Indian language. This rule applies to all schools on an Indian
reservation, whether Government or mission schools. The education of Indians in
the vernacular is not only of no use to them, but is detrimental to their education
and civilization."

—J. D. C. Atkins, Commissioner of Indian Affairs, July 16, 1887

"The Congress finds that the status of the cultures and languages of Native
Americans is unique and the United States has the responsibility to act together with Native Americans to ensure the survival of these unique cultures
and languages."

—Native American Languages Act of 1990

"Indigenous people have the right to revitalize, use, develop and transmit to future generations their histories, languages, oral traditions, philosophies, writing systems and literatures, and to designate and retain their own names for communities, places, and persons."
—United Nations Draft Declaration of the Rights of Indigenous Peoples, 1993

"It is hard to comprehend the variety of American Indian languages that once existed, with more than fifty language families. The languages of Western Europe, by comparison, fall into just three families—Indo-European, Finno-Ugric, and Basque."

—Elizabeth Seay, *Searching for Lost City*, 2003

Esther Martinez Native American Languages Preservation Act of 2006
This legislation amended the Native American Programs Act of 1974 to provide for the revitalization of Native American languages through Native American language immersion programs and other instructional measures.

POEMS AND CDS

Seven Poems about Language by Native Poets

1. "Acoma Poems," by Simon J. Ortiz (Acoma Pueblo). In *Out There Somewhere* (2002).
2. "English Only," by Sara Littlecrow-Russell (Anishinaabe/Han-Naxi Metís). In *The Secret Powers of Naming* (2006).
3. "Nam Shim," by Lance Henson (Southern Cheyenne). In *Harper's Anthology of 20th Century Native American Poetry*, edited by Duane Niatum (1988).
4. "Grandfather," by Lance Henson (Southern Cheyenne). Henson's translation of "Nam Shim." In *Harper's Anthology of 20th Century Native American Poetry*, edited by Duane Niatum (1988).
5. "An Onondaga Trades with a Woman Who Sings with a Mayan Tongue," by Gail Tremblay (Onondaga/Micmac). In *Returning the Gift: Poetry and Prose from the First North American Native Writers' Festival*, edited by Joseph Bruchac (1994).
6. "Our Tongues Slapped into Silence," by Laura Tohe (Navajo). In *No Parole Today* (1999).
7. "There Is No Word for Goodbye," by Mary Tall Mountain (Athabascan). In *Harper's Anthology of 20th Century Native American Poetry*, edited by Duane Niatum (1988).

Ten Recordings with Songs in Native Languages

1. *American Indian Christmas*, by Jana Mashonee (2005). Ten songs in various Native American languages.
2. *Anishinabemoin*, by Keith Secola and Karen Drift (2007). Bois Forte Band of Ojibwe. Native American Music Award (NAMMY) for Best Linguistic Recording.
3. *Baswewe "Echo,"* by Mille Lacs Band of Ojibwe (1998). Songbook/cassette featuring twenty-five songs in Ojibwe.
4. *Beautiful Beyond: Christian Songs in Native Languages*, by various artists (2004). Smithsonian Folkways.
5. *Children's Songs in the Cherokee Language*, by Cherokee Nation. http://www .cherokee.org/PressRoom/Downloads/1/Default.aspx
6. *Colors of My Heart*, by Sharon Burch (Diné) (1999). Also other CDs in the Navajo language.
7. *Innu*, by Kashtin (1994). Also other CDs performed in the Innu-aimun or Montagnais language of Labrador and Quebec.
8. *Rarenneháwi* ("He Carries a Song"), by Teddy Peters and Eddy Lawrence in the Kanien' Kĕha (Mohawk) language. NAMMY (Native American Music Award) nominee for Best Linguistic Recording in 2007.
9. *Songscapes of Native America*, the Cultural Conservancy Compilation Music CD, 2005. This CD includes songs in five Native languages.
10. *Voices of the Creator's Children*, by Cherokee National Youth Choir, featuring Rita Coolidge (2002).

FILMS

Twelve Films with Native Languages

Atanarjuat/The Fast Runner (Canada, 2001, 172 min.), directed by Zacharias Kunuk (Inuit).

> *Atanarjuat* is Canada's first Native-language feature film to be written, produced, directed, and acted by Inuit. It is an action thriller set in ancient Igloolik, a community with four thousand years of continuous habitation in what is now Arctic Canada. The film unfolds as a life-threatening struggle between natural and supernatural characters. Part of a trilogy, the other two films are *The Journals of Knud Rasmussen* (2006) and *Before Tomorrow* (2009). http://www.isuma.tv/atanarjuat

Cane Music (USA, 2005, 6 min.), directed by Nathan Young (Pawnee/Delaware/Kiowa). In Cherokee with English subtitles.

> Produced by the Fort Gibson Public Schools in Oklahoma, this film by Cherokee high school students tells the story of how Owl taught Deer the music of the cane flute.

Finding My Talk: A Journey into Aboriginal Languages (Canada, 1999, 48 min.), directed by Paul M. Rickard (Cree).

> This documentary follows Cree filmmaker Paul M. Rickard as he discovers the efforts of many individuals working to revitalize indigenous languages in their communities. During his travels, Rickard visits diverse programs and settings, including those centered on Tlingit, Mohawk, and Inuktitut languages. He returns home with a renewed appreciation for his own Native language. His film served as a pilot for *Finding Our Talk*, a thirteen-part series of documentaries on indigenous languages. http://www.mushkeg.ca/

First Speakers: Restoring the Ojibwe Language (USA, 2010, 56 min.), directed by Dianne Steinbach and John Whitehead.

> This film, a production of Twin Cities Public Television (TCPT), documents efforts to restore the Ojibwe language, which is endangered because of historical forces and policies such as English-only mandates. Narrated by writer Louise Erdrich, Ojibwe elders, scholars, teachers, and students reveal some of the work underway, including that of two immersion schools. In 2011, TCPT was awarded an Upper Midwest Emmy for the documentary. The film is available online at: http://www.mnvideovault.org/index.php?id=21088&select_index=0&popup=yes

Horse You See (USA, 2007, 8 min.), directed by Melissa Henry (Navajo). In Navajo with English subtitles.

> A Navajo horse explains the essence of being himself.

Kanien'Keha:Ka/Living the Language (Canada, 2008, 62 min.), directed by Tracey Deer (Mohawk) and Paul M. Rickard (Cree). In Mohawk and English with English subtitles.

> This two-part film examines the Mohawk Nation of Akwesasne, located on both sides of the international border between the United States and Canada, and its efforts to save the indigenous language. The documentary portrays the Akwesasne Mohawk language revitalization movement, which began in 1979, and included the creation of the Akwesasne Freedom School.

Language of America: An Indian Story (USA, 2009, 81 min.), directed by Ben Levine.

> *Language of America* follows members of three New England tribes, the Passamaquoddy, Wampanoag, and Narragansett, as they work to address Native language loss. Filmed over a period of six years, the documentary demonstrates how language provides a window into the beauty and richness of distinctive cultures and what is at stake when cultural and linguistic traditions are lost.

Qapirangajuq: Inuit Knowledge and Climate Change (Canada, 2010, 54 min.), directed by Zacharias Kunuk (Inuit) and Ian Mauro.

> This film, the world's first Inuktitut-language film on climate change, explores the social and ecological impacts of a warming Arctic. Drawing from a long history of experience and knowledge, Inuit speak firsthand of the changes to the land and ecosystem. Their perspectives both support and challenge mainstream ideas about this critical issue.

Stories of the Cherokees (USA, 2007, 15 min.), directed by Andrew Sikora. In Cherokee and English.

> Filmed within the Cherokee Nation of Oklahoma, *Stories of the Cherokees* was inspired by the tribal nation's oral history traditions. The film, which promotes Cherokee culture and language through the perspectives of indigenous storytellers and actors, features native speakers as well as language immersion students. *Stories of the Cherokee* made its European debut at the Cannes Film Festival in 2008.

Transitions: Destruction of a Mother Tongue (USA, 1991, 30 min.), directed by Darrell Kipp (Blackfeet) and Joe Fisher (Blackfeet).

> Produced by Native Voices Public TV Workshop, this film documents the impact of language loss on the Blackfeet people and explores the relationship between language and culture.

We Still Live Here: Âs Nutayuneân (USA, 2011, 56 min.), directed by Anne Makepeace.

> This film documents cultural and linguistic revival among the Wampanoag of southeastern Massachusetts, including the work of linguist Jessie Little Doe Baird (Mashpee Wampanoag) and other tribal members to revitalize their Native language. Their efforts in the Wôpanâak Language Reclamation Project resulted in the first Wôpanâak speaker to be born in over a century and a MacArthur Foundation "Genius Grant" for Baird to continue the endeavor.

Why Save a Language? (USA, 2006, 27 min.), directed by Sally Thompson.

> Produced by the Regional Learning Project at the University of Montana, this film features tribal members explaining why Native languages are important and discussing their language revitalization efforts.

ORGANIZATIONS

Advocates for Indigenous California Language Survival
http://www.aicls.org/

> Founded in 1992, Advocates for Indigenous California Language Survival is a nonprofit organization established to foster the restoration and revival of indigenous California languages so they may be retained as a permanent part of the living cultures of Native California. It is located in Vallejo, California.

Alaska Native Language Center (ANLC)
http://www.uaf.edu/anlc/

> The Alaska Native Language Center (ANLC), located at the University of Alaska, Fairbanks, was established by state legislation in 1972 as a center for the study of the twenty Native languages of Alaska. Internationally known for its work, the ANLC publishes research, maintains an archival collection of more than ten thousand language items, provides materials for teachers and other language

workers throughout Alaska, and offers consulting and training services to school districts, as well as other services. The ANLC staff also teach through the Alaska Native Language Program, which offers degrees in Central Yup'ik and Inupiaq Eskimo at the University of Alaska Fairbanks.

American Indian Language Development Institute (AILDI)
http://www.u.arizona.edu/~aildi/index.html

Founded in 1978 with support from the National Endowment for the Humanities, the American Indian Language Development Institute (AILDI) held its first training institute in San Diego, California, focusing on the Yuman language family. Since that time, AILDI has trained Native American language educators, practitioners, and researchers from across the United States and other parts of the world. Located at the University of Arizona in Tucson, AILDI's mission includes mobilizing efforts to document, revitalize, and promote indigenous languages.

Center for American Indian Languages (CAIL)
http://www.cail.utah.edu/

The Center for American Indian languages at the University of Utah, Salt Lake City, is a research center devoted to assisting scholars and communities to preserve their linguistic resources. CAIL's objectives include working with communities where languages and cultures are endangered, assisting with revitalization efforts, training students to address scholarly and practical needs, and providing community outreach.

Indigenous Language Institute (formerly known as the Institute for Preservation of Original Languages of the Americas)
http://www.ilinative.org/

Founded as the Institute for the Preservation of the Original Languages of the Americas (IPOLA) in 1992, the organization became a national center working to revitalize indigenous languages in the Americas. IPOLA was changed to the Indigenous Language Institute (ILI) in 2000 to reflect changes in leadership, services, and scope of working relations. ILI is located in Santa Fe, New Mexico.

Intertribal Wordpath Society (IWS)
http://www.ahalenia.com/iws/

Located in Norman, Oklahoma, the Intertribal Wordpath Society is a nonprofit organization whose purpose is to promote the teaching, awareness, use, and status of Oklahoma Indian languages. Its activities include providing exhibits and educational programs for the general public, producing language-related materials, engaging in teacher training, and providing information about the status of Native languages in Oklahoma. IWS also hosts the Celebration of Oklahoma Indian Language and Culture, an annual event held in Norman in October.

National Alliance to Save Native Languages
http://www.savenativelanguages.org/
> The National Alliance to Save Native Languages was founded in 2006 to promote the revitalization of Native languages. The alliance, which is located in Washington, DC, is a coalition of tribes, schools, organizations, and individuals.

Native Languages of the Americas
http://www.native-languages.org
> Native Languages of the Americas is a Minnesota-based nonprofit corporation dedicated to the survival of Native American languages, particularly through the use of Internet technology. Created in 1998, the organization's Web site provides links to information about Native language sources, including a list of thirteen ways to support American Indian languages from home.

Society for the Study of the Indigenous Languages of the Americas (SSILA)
http://linguistlist.org/ssila/
> Founded in 1981 and incorporated in 1997, the Society for the Study of the Indigenous Languages of the Americas is an international scholarly organization focusing on American Indian linguistics. Membership is open to all those interested in the scientific study of the languages of Native peoples of North, Central, and South America.

RESOURCES

Boyden, Linda. *Giveaways: An ABC Book of Loanwords from the Americas.* Albuquerque: University of New Mexico Press, 2010.

Bright, William. *Native American Placenames of the United States.* Norman: University of Oklahoma Press, 2004.

Clark, John R. K. *Hawai'i Place Names: Shores, Beaches, and Surf Sites.* Honolulu: University of Hawaii Press, 2002.

Cutler, Charles L. *O Brave New Words! Native American Loanwords in Current English.* Norman: University of Oklahoma Press, 1994.

Davis, Jeffrey E. *Hand Talk: Sign Language among American Indian Nations.* New York: Cambridge University Press, 2010.

Farnell, Brenda. *Do You See What I Mean?: Plains Indian Sign Talk and the Embodiment of Action.* Austin: University of Texas Press, 1995.

Galla, Candace K., Stacey Oberly, G. L. Romero, Maxine Sam, and Ofelia Zepeda, eds. *American Indian Language Development Institute: Thirty Year Tradition of Speaking from Our Heart.* Tucson: American Indian Language Development Institute, University of Arizona, 2010.

Golla, Victor. *California Indian Languages.* Berkeley and Los Angeles: University of California Press, 2011.

Hinton, Leanne. *Flutes of Fire: The Indian Languages of California.* Berkeley, CA: Heyday Books, 1993.

———, with Matt Vera and Nancy Steele. *How to Keep Your Language Alive: A Common-sense Approach to One-on-One Language Learning.* Berkeley, CA: Heyday Books, 2002.

Kroskrity, Paul V., and Margaret C. Fields, eds. *Native American Language Ideologies: Beliefs, Practices, and Struggles in Indian Country.* Tucson: University of Arizona Press, 2009.

Ortiz, Simon J. *The Good Rainbow Road/Rawa 'Kashtyaa' Tsi Hiyaani: A Native American Tale in Keres and English,* followed by a translation into Spanish. Tucson: University of Arizona Press, 2004.

Reyhner, Jon, ed. *Teaching Indigenous Languages.* Flagstaff: Northern Arizona University, 1997.

Seay, Elizabeth. *Searching for Lost City: On the Trail of America's Native Languages.* Guilford, CT: The Lyons Press, 2003.

Spack, Ruth. *America's Second Tongue: American Indian Education and the Ownership of English, 1860–1900.* Lincoln: University of Nebraska Press, 2002.

White Hat, Albert, Sr. *Reading and Writing the Lakota Language.* Salt Lake City: University of Utah Press, 1999.

Web Sites

AAIA Language Program YouTube Videos (Dakota Language): http://www.youtube.com/user/AAIALanguageProgram

Advocates for Indigenous California Language Survival: http://www.aicls.org/

Aha Pūnana Leo: http://www.ahapunanaleo.org

Alaska Native Language Center (ANLC): http://www.uaf.edu/anlc/

Center for Advanced Research on Language Acquisition (CARLA): Less Commonly Taught Languages: http://www.carla.umn.edu/lctl/

Endangered Language Fund: Native Voices Endowment: http://www.endangeredlanguagefund.org/native_voices.php

Eyak Language Project/*q'aayaa tl'hix* (A New Beginning): http://sites.google.com/site/eyaklanguageproject/home

First Voices (a group of Web-based tools and services designed to support Aboriginal people engaged in language archiving, language teaching, and culture revitalization): http://www.firstvoices.com/

Hand Talk: American Indian Sign Language: http://sunsite.utk.edu/pisl/index.html

Hans Rausing Endangered Language Project, Online Resources for Endangered Languages (OREL): http://www.hrelp.org/languages/resources/orel/

Harvard Project's Honoring Nations Directory of Honored Programs, 1999–2006: http://hpaied.org/images/resources/general/Dir_web.pdf

Heritage Languages in America, Center for Applied Linguistics: http://www.cal.org/heritage/

Ka Haka 'Ula O Ke'elikōlani College of Hawaiian Language: http://www.olelo.hawaii.edu.

Lakota Berenstain Bears Project: http://lakotabears.com

MLA Statement on Native American Languages in the College and University Curriculum: https://facultystaff.richmond.edu/~rnelson/asail/MLA.pdf

Native Words, Native Warriors (companion Web site to the traveling Smithsonian Institution exhibition): http://www.nmai.si.edu/education/codetalkers/html/

Sacred Earth Network Endangered Languages Program: http://sacredearthnetwork.org/elp/default.cfm

Song: *Awesiiyag* (Animals), Ziibiwing Center, Saginaw Chippewa Indian Tribe: http://www.sagchip.org/ziibiwing/ZiibiwingCenter/audioplayer/OjibweSong.htm

SpokenFirst, A Resource for News about American Indian Languages: http://falmouthinstitute.com/language/

Teaching Indigenous Languages: http://jan.ucc.nau.edu/~jar/TIL.html

Website Resources for Hawaiian Language: http://www.k12.hi.us/~kaiapuni/HLIP/resources/resHawnLang.htm

13

Science and Technology

FIRSTS

1935   Arthur C. Parker (Seneca Nation) became the first president of the Society of American Archaeology (SAA), serving in that leadership position until 1936. His career contributions included research in archaeology, cultural anthropology, history, education, and the development of museum anthropology.

1948   Mary G. Ross (Cherokee) was the first Native American woman engineer and first female engineer at Lockheed. She was a pioneer in aerospace engineering. The Council of Energy Resource Tribes (CERT) named an award in her honor, the Mary G. Ross Award, which is presented at CERT's annual American Spirit Award Dinner, held in conjunction with the Indian Energy Solutions conference.

1950   Isabella Aiona Abbott, who graduated from the University of California at Berkeley, was the first Native Hawaiian woman to receive a PhD in science. She became an internationally known botanist, the leading expert on Pacific algae.

    Bernard Anthony Hoehner (Standing Rock Sioux) became the first American Indian veterinarian, ca. 1950.

1966   William R. Pogue, of Choctaw descent, was the first Native American to become an astronaut. His assignment was as command module pilot for *Skylab 4*, and he was launched into space in 1973, spending what was then a record eighty-four days on the mission.

1972   Fred Begay (Navajo) was the first member of his tribal nation to earn a PhD in physics in the United States, earning his degree in nuclear physics from the University of New Mexico. Dr. Begay went on to work at Los Alamos National Laboratory, where he created and coordinated math and science education programs. In 1994, he received the National Science Foundation Lifetime Achievement Award for making stellar efforts in nuclear fusion and substantive contributions to minority students.

1973   Frank Dukepoo (Hopi) was the first Native American geneticist and also the founder of the National Native American Honor Society, which he established in 1982.

1976   Edna Lee Paisano (Nez Perce/Laguna Pueblo) was the first American Indian to be hired as a full-time employee for the U.S. Census Bureau. A statistician, she was featured in a 1981 publication titled *Women, Numbers and Dreams.*

1980   Clarkson University in Potsdam, New York, established the first collegiate chapter of the American Indian Science and Engineering Society in the country.

1992   Suzanne Van Cooten (Chickasaw) is believed to have become the first Native female meteorologist in the country. Dr. Van Cooten has worked in a variety of weather-related roles, including serving as research scientist with the National Oceanic and Atmospheric Administration's (NOAA) National Weather Service.

1995   The Navajo Nation flag became the first Native American tribal flag taken to space when astronaut Bernard Harris carried it aboard the space shuttle *Discovery.*

1996   John Herrington, a member of the Chickasaw Nation, was the first tribally enrolled Native American to become an astronaut. In 2002, he became the first tribal member to fly in outer space and the first to walk in outer space.

2003   Intertribal Information Technology Company (IITC), which specializes in data conversion and data management, became the first business owned by a consortium of tribes and Native groups to be certified in the Small Business Administration 8(a) business development program.

2004   Marigold Linton (Cahuilla/Cupeno), cognitive psychologist, was the first Native American woman to become president of the Society for the Advancement of Chicanos and Native Americans in Science (SACNAS), serving until 2007. Recognized for her lifetime work to increase the representation of Native Americans in scientific endeavors, Dr. Linton was honored with a Presidential Award for Excellence in Science, Mathematics, and Engineering Mentoring (PAESMEM) at the White House in 2011.

2010   The inaugural First Nations Launch: Tribal College High-Powered Rocket Competition was initiated through the College of Menominee Nation (CMM) and the Wisconsin Space Grant Consortium (WSGC). This first-ever national tribal college competition, centered on rocket building and launching, was held near Burlington, Wisconsin.

Alaska Native, or Native Hawaiian cultural preservation programs. The scholarship is named in honor of archaeologist and historian Arthur C. Parker (1881–1955), from the Cattaraugus Reservation of the Seneca Nation of New York, who served as the first president of SAA.

1998	Angela J. Neller
1999	Iwalani Ching
2000	Randy Thompson
2001	Cynthia Williams
2002	Nola Markey
2003	Kalewa Sye Arie Correa
2004	Sean P. Naleimaile
2005	Larae Buckskin
2006	Maria Kapuanalani Evans-Mason
2007	Ora V. Marek

Choctaw Solar Car Race

In 2010, an eleven-student team from Choctaw Central High School in Choctaw, Mississippi, won the Hunt-Winston Solar Car race with *Tushka Hashi III* ("sun warrior"), coming in first overall and first in the advanced division in the eight-day, 853.5-mile cross-country drive from Fort Worth, Texas, to Boulder, Colorado. The team won the overall championship as well as the Hunt Award for Engineering Excellence, an Appreciation Award for Excellent Team Spirit, and day trophies for being the first car to reach each daily destination. The race was part of the Hunt-Winston School Solar Car Challenge, an annual solar-powered car competition for high school students that began in 1995. Its objectives center on encouraging student learning in science, engineering, and technological skills, specifically solar power. Student teams design, build, and drive a vehicle meeting the required specifications and standards for the competition.

Besides learning technical skills such as building a battery box in the solar car, wiring and rewiring lithium ion batteries, and adding a battery-monitoring system, the students shared varied responsibilities and tasks to create a cohesive team. *Tushka Hashi III* garnered attention during the challenge for its aerodynamic design and its frontrunner status, highlighting its impressive team. The Choctaw drivers completed the race in a total of 24.5 hours, with an average speed of 35 miles per hour.

2008   Marie Sina Faatuala

2009   Travis Maki

2010   Paulette Faith Steeves

2011   Kamakana Christian Ferreira

SACNAS Distinguished Scientist Award

1999   Fred Begay, PhD (Navajo), Los Alamos National Laboratory
2006   Donna Nelson, PhD (Cherokee/Chickasaw/Choctaw)

SCIENCE AND TECHNOLOGY BUSINESSES, ENTERPRISES, AND PROGRAMS

Eight Science and Technology Businesses and Enterprises

1. Ao'ao O Na Loko I a O Maui (Association of the Fishponds of Maui)
   http://www.mauifishpond.com
   > Ao'ao O Na Loko I a O Maui is a nonprofit organization, created in 1998 by residents of Maui, Hawaii, to become the leader on Maui of fishpond restoration. The organization's board includes Native Hawaiians and non-Native educators, fishermen, scientists, and others who have concerns about the deterioration of South Maui's most visible Hawaiian fishpond.

2. HEBCO, Inc.
   http://www.hebco.com
   > HEBCO, located in Oklahoma City, Oklahoma, is a business providing solutions in engineering, technical publications, data management, training, and advisory services. It has been a Native American, woman-owned business since 1983.

3. Horizon Engineering Services Company
   http://www.horizoneng.com
   > Horizon Engineering Company is a civil engineering firm, founded in 1998 by Margaret Gray-Proctor (Osage Nation) and Carl Cannizarro. Located in Tulsa, Oklahoma, Horizon Engineering has worked with tribes providing coordination and project management between the tribe and the design team during the scheduling, master planning, bidding, negotiations, and construction phases of projects.

4. Lakota Solar Enterprises
   http://lakotasolarenterprises.com
   > Lakota Solar Enterprises (LSE), one of the first Native-owned and operated renewable energy businesses, is located on the Pine Ridge

Reservation, South Dakota. Established in 2006, LSE manufactures solar air collectors and solar heating systems, and offers training workshops. The New York–based Interstate Renewable Energy Council selected LSE for one of five 2010 Innovation Awards.

5. Red Willow Production Company
   http://www.rwpc.us

   An operation of the Southern Ute Tribe in Ignacio, Colorado, Red Willow Production Company finds and develops economic oil and gas reserves using best available technology and best industry practices to maximize the benefits to the Southern Ute Tribe and its members. At the same time, RWPC carefully manages the environmental impacts of its successful oil and gas production operation. http://www.sugf.com/

6. Sacred Power Corporation
   http://sacredpowercorp.com/home.htm

   Since 2001, Sacred Power, a Native American–owned and operated small business, has provided government, commercial, and residential customers with photovoltaic (PV), renewable, and distributive energy systems. These include both PV polycrystalline and thin-film, wind turbines, solar hot water systems, solar hot air systems, and other distributive energy systems. Sacred Power, located in Albuquerque, New Mexico, launched a 2011 Super Bowl XVL campaign to raise awareness about the solar industry.

7. Spirit Electronics Inc.
   http://www.spiritelectronics.com

   Spirit Electronics, located in Phoenix, Arizona, provides supply-chain solutions and electronic component distribution for global technology leaders in aerospace, defense, and communications industries. It has been a Native American, woman-owned business since 1979.

Chickasaw Nation Science-Technology-Math Academy

In 2011, the Chickasaw Nation officially opened the Chickasaw Nation Science-Technology-Math Academy, in Ada, Oklahoma. This innovative building houses the tribal robotics program and the Chickasaw Nation Aviation and Space Academy (CNASA). CNASA is a summer learning program designed to engage Chickasaw students in aviation, space, science, or math. The academy building provides participating students a place to meet, conduct research, build robots, simulate tournament play, and utilize the flight simulator for science programs such as LEGO and Metal Mayhew robotics.

It also provides a classroom with SmartBoard technology, as well as a large shop area and other facilities.
http://www.chickasaw.net/

8. Tall Bear Solar
   http://tallbeargroup.com
   > Tall Bear Group Solar was launched in 2008 by Richard Tall Bear (Sisseton Wahpeton Dakota) in response to client requests for assistance in procuring solar energy systems for projects ranging from small residential and business clients to tribally owned utilities. Tall Bear won the "Native American 40 Under 40" award presented by the National Center for American Indian Enterprise Development in 2009 for his groundbreaking business.

Alaska Native Science and Engineering Program (ANSEP)

ANSEP, headquartered in Anchorage, works with students from the time they are in middle school all the way through to doctoral programs. ANSEP increases university recruitment and retention rates through hands-on middle and high school outreach initiatives, rigorous summer bridging programs, focused academic learning communities, organized student cohorts, networks of peer and professional mentors, community-based learning, professional internships, and undergraduate and graduate research projects.

ANSEP was founded by Dr. Herb (Ilisaurri) Schroeder, who serves as its executive director. Dr. Schroeder is the recipient of numerous awards for his work, among them the 2004 Presidential Award for Excellence in Science, Mathematics, and Engineering, which is administered by the National Science Foundation on behalf of the White House. The following year he received the Denali Award, the top honor bestowed on non-Natives by the Alaska Federation of Natives.

Source: http://www.ansep.net/

POEMS

Nine Poems Dealing with Science and Technology by Native Poets

1. "Ancient Wisdom Advancing Modern Science and Technology," by Michael Avritt (San Felipe Pueblo). In *Winds of Change* (Winter 2002).
2. "Grandmother, Salish Mathematician," by Teresa Iyall-Santos (Coeur d'Alene/Yakama). In *Sister Nations: Native American Women Writers on Community*, edited by Heid E. Erdrich and Laura Tohe (2002).
3. "Gravity," by Sherman Alexie (Spokane/Coeur d'Alene). In *First Indian on the Moon* (1993).
4. "Liquid Crystal Thoughts," by Carter Revard (Osage). In *How the Songs Come Down: New and Selected Poems* (2005).

5. "Lunar Eclipse," by Diane Glancy (Cherokee). In *Songs from This Earth on Turtle's Back*, edited by Joseph Bruchac (1983).
6. "Meditating on Star Light While Traveling Highway 2," by Anita Endrezze (Yaqui). In *Harper's Anthology of 20th Century Native American Poetry*, edited by Duane Niatum (1988).
7. "My Grandfather Was a Quantum Physicist," by Duane Big Eagle (Osage). In *Songs from This Earth on Turtle's Back*, edited by Joseph Bruchac (1983).
8. "Outer Space, Inner Space," by Gladys Cardiff (Eastern Cherokee). In *That's What She Said: Contemporary Poetry and Fiction by Native American Women*, edited by Rayna Green (1994).
9. "Star Vision," by Marilou Awiakta (Cherokee). In *Abiding Appalachia: Where Mountain and Atom Meet* (1994).

FILMS

Dancing with Photons (USA, 1997, 30 min.), directed by Beverly Morris (Aleut).
This film tells the story of Dr. Fred Begay, nuclear physicist, and describes how his Navajo teachings assist him in his work.
The Mystery of Chaco Canyon: Unveiling the Ancient Astronomy of Southwestern Pueblo Indians (USA, 1999, 56 min.), directed by Anna Sofaer.
The Mystery of Chaco Canyon, a sequel to Sofaer's film *The Sun Dagger*, examines Chaco Canyon in northwestern New Mexico, one of the most impressive archaeological sites in North America. As the film documents, between AD 850 and AD 1150, the Chacoan people designed and constructed massive ceremonial buildings in a complex celestial pattern throughout their desert homeland. Pueblo leaders also speak of the ancestral significance of Chaco to their world today.
Pearl (USA, 2010, 107 min.), directed by King Hollis.
The first feature-length film produced by the Chickasaw Nation, *Pearl* is the story of Eula "Pearl" Carter Scott, a Chickasaw aviator who became the youngest licensed pilot in American history. Pearl, who was mentored by aviator Wiley Post, first piloted a plane at age twelve and earned her license at age thirteen in 1928. By age fourteen, she was performing as a barnstormer and commercial pilot. Filmed at various locations in Oklahoma, *Pearl* features several Chickasaw cast members.
Qayaqs and Canoes: Native Ways of Knowing (USA, 2001, 56 min.), directed by Bob Jenkins and Jerry Lavine.
Produced by the Alaska Native Heritage Center in Anchorage and narrated by Vernon Chimegalrea (Yup'ik), *Qayaqs and Canoes* documents Alaska Native master craftsmen as they build eight traditional watercraft. Linking cultural history, stories, and experiences, the builders revitalize time-honored knowledge and technical skills of their ancestors.

ORGANIZATIONS

Alaska Native Science Commission (ANSC)
http://www.nativescience.org/

> The Alaska Native Science Commission (ANSC), located in Anchorage, was established in 1994 to bring together research and science in partnership with the Native community. It serves as a clearinghouse for proposed research, as well as an information and archive base for research involving the Native community.

American Indian Council of Architects and Engineers (AICAE)
http://www.aicae.org/

> Established in 1976, the American Indian Council of Architects and Engineers is a nonprofit corporation whose members are American Indian architecture, engineering, and design professionals throughout the United States.

American Indian Institute for Innovation (AIII)
http://theaiii.com/

> The American Indian Institute for Innovation (AIII) was founded by Stacy Phelps (Sisseton Wahpeton Oyate) as an outgrowth of his work with American Indian students, which began in 1992. Headquartered in Rapid City, South Dakota, AIII is focused on efforts that include increasing the number of Native students in the fields of science, technology, engineering, and math. Phelps, a mechanical engineering and educational technology graduate, received a Presidential Award for Excellence in Science, Mathematics, and Engineering Mentoring at the White House in 2010.

American Indian Science and Engineering Society (AISES)
http://www.aises.org/

> Founded in 1977, the American Indian Science and Engineering Society is a national nonprofit organization that provides academic, financial, and cultural support to American Indians and Alaska Natives from middle school through graduate school. AISES works to address the severe underrepresentation of American Indians in the science and engineering fields.

Indigenous Education Institute (IEI)
http://www.indigenouseducation.org/

> The Indigenous Education Institute (IEI) is a nonprofit organization created in 1995 with a mission to preserve, protect, and apply traditional indigenous knowledge in a contemporary setting. IEI, located in Santa Fe, New Mexico, has developed numerous projects as well as educational materials in science disciplines such as astronomy.

American Indian Science and Engineering Society (AISES)

Founded in 1977, the American Indian Science and Engineering Society (AISES) is a national nonprofit organization that works to substantially increase the representation of American Indians and Alaska Natives in science, technology, engineering, and math disciplines. The organization's founders included hydrologist Al Qöyawayma (Hopi), engineer George Thomas (Cherokee), geologist Carol Metcalf Gardipe (Penobscot/Passamaquoddy), chemical engineer A. T. Anderson (Mohawk), geologist Jim Shorty (Navajo), and NASA technology manager Jerry Elliot (Osage/Cherokee). They knew there was a great need to address the vast underrepresentation of American Indians in science and technology fields. Since 1977, AISES has worked to enhance Native participation at every level in these disciplines, creating programs and networks involving students, professionals, mentors, and leaders.

AISES, which is headquartered in Albuquerque, New Mexico, has grown to include over 170 chartered college and university chapters throughout the United States and Canada, ten professional chapters, some 150 affiliated schools that enroll more than thirty thousand K–12 Native American students, and nearly three thousand active members, with over a thousand Sequoyah Fellows (lifetime members). The organization also provides support services through internship and scholarship programs; hosts an annual conference that attracts thousands of students, professionals, agencies, and sponsors; and sponsors other educational events. AISES publishes a quarterly magazine, *Winds of Change*, an annual college guide, and other publications. It also maintains a Web site with links to other resources.

Source: http://www.aises.org/

Indigenous Peoples Council on Biocolonialism (IPCB)
http://www.ipcb.org/

The mission of the Indigenous Peoples Council on Biocolonialism is to assist indigenous peoples in the protection of their genetic resources, indigenous knowledge, and cultural and human rights from the negative effects of biotechnology. Based in Nixon, Nevada, the organization provides educational and technical support in the protection of indigenous resources, knowledge, and rights.

Indigenous Women in Science Network (IWSN)
http://iwsnetwork.org/

The Indigenous Women in Science Network was established in 2008 to create a community of mutual support for Native women in the sciences. IWSN, which held its first conference the following year in Portland, Oregon, is also committed to empowering emerging scientists and working to counteract the underrepresentation of Native women in the fields of science and engineering.

National EPA–Tribal Science Council (TSC)
http://www.epa.gov/osp/tribes/who.htm

> The National EPA–Tribal Science Council (TSC) was created to help integrate Environmental Protection Agency (EPA) and tribal interests concerning environmental science issues. The TSC includes a tribal representative from each of the nine EPA regions with federally recognized tribes, with an additional tribal representative designated in Region 10 to represent Alaska Native communities.

Native American Intellectual Property Enterprise Council (NAIPEC)
http://nativeamericaninventors.org/

> The Native American Intellectual Property Enterprise Council was founded by inventor T. David Petite (Chippewa) to support invention and innovation in Native American communities by providing quantitative patenting, copyright, and trademark assistance. The nonprofit organization, which is supported by a network of partners and experts, works to facilitate opportunities and to help create new knowledge-based enterprises.

Society for Advancement of Chicanos and Native Americans in Science (SACNAS)
http://www.sacnas.org

> The Society for Advancement of Chicanos and Native Americans in Science is a national society of scientists that works to foster the success of Hispanic/Chicano and Native American scientists, from college students to professionals, in attaining advanced degrees, careers, and positions of leadership. Founded in 1973, SACNAS is headquartered in Santa Cruz, California.

Society for American Archaeology (SAA)
http://www.saa.org/

> Founded in 1934 and headquartered in Washington, DC, the Society for American Archaeology is an international organization dedicated to the research, interpretation, and protection of the archaeological heritage of the Americas. In 1997, the SAA board established a Native American Scholarship program named in honor of Arthur C. Parker (Seneca), SAA's first president. In addition, the organization provides scholarships from a National Science Foundation grant awarded to the SAA for Parker scholarship applicants. In 2009, SAA added two new awards in support of Native American undergraduate and graduate archaeology education.

RESOURCES

Abbott, Isabella Aiona. *Marine Red Algae of the Hawaiian Islands.* Honolulu: Bishop Museum Press, 1999.

Adney, Edwin, and Howard Chapelle. *The Bark Canoes and Skin Boats of North America.* 2nd ed. Washington, DC: Smithsonian Institution Press, 1983.

Boyer, Paul. *Tribal College and University Profiles: New Directions in Math and Science.* Pablo, MT: Salish Kootenai College Press, 2008.

Cajete, Gregory. *Native Science: Natural Laws of Interdependence.* Santa Fe, NM: Clear Light Publishers, 1999.

Deutsch, Stacia, and Rhody Cohon. *John B. Herrington.* Broomall, PA: Mason Crest Publishers, 2009.

Fienup-Riordan, Ann. *Yuungnaqpiallerput/The Way We Genuinely Live: Masterworks of Yup'ik Science and Survival.* Oakland: Oakland Museum of California, 2007.

James, Keith, ed. *Science and Native American Communities: Legacies of Pain, Visions of Promise.* Lincoln: University of Nebraska Press, 2001.

Kawagley, A. Oscar. *A Yupiaq Worldview: A Pathway to Ecology and Spirit.* Prospect Heights, IL: Waveland Press, 1995.

Keoke, Emory Dean, and Kay Marie Porterfield. *American Indian Contributions to the World: 15,000 Years of Inventions and Innovations.* New York: Checkmark Books, 2002.

Kimmerer, Robin Wall. *Gathering Moss: A Natural and Cultural History of Mosses.* Corvallis: Oregon State University Press, 2003.

MacDonald, John. *The Arctic Sky: Inuit Astronomy, Star Lore, and Legend.* Toronto: Royal Ontario Museum, 1998.

Maryboy, Nancy C., and David Begay. *Sharing the Skies: Navajo Astronomy.* 4th ed. Tucson: Rio Nuevo Publishers, 2010.

Miller, Dorcas S. *Stars of the First People: Native American Star Myths and Constellations.* Boulder, CO: Pruett Publishing Co., 1997.

Moerman, Daniel E. *Native American Ethnobotany.* Portland, OR: Timber Press, 1998.

Nabhan, Gary Paul. *Enduring Seeds: Native American Agriculture and Wild Plant Conservation.* Tucson: University of Arizona Press, 2002.

Pogue, William R. *But for the Grace of God: An Autobiography of an Aviator and Astronaut.* Rogers, AR: Soar with Eagles, 2011.

Steinbright, Jan. *Qayaqs and Canoes: Native Ways of Knowing.* Anchorage: Alaska Native Heritage Center, 2002.

St. John, Jetty. *Native American Scientists.* Mankato, MN: Capstone Press, 1996.

Verheyden-Hilliard, Mary Ellen. *Engineer from the Comanche Nation, Nancy Wallace.* Bethesda, MD: Equity Institute, 1985.

———. *Scientist from the Santa Clara Pueblo, Agnes Naranjo Stroud-Lee.* Bethesda, MD: Equity Institute, 1985.

Watkins, Joe E. *Indigenous Archaeology: American Indian Values and Scientific Practice.* Walnut Creek, CA: AltaMira, 2000.

Wildcat, Daniel R. *Red Alert! Saving the Planet with Indigenous Knowledge.* Golden, CO: Fulcrum Publishing, 2009.

Williamson, Ray A. *Living the Sky: The Cosmos of the American Indian.* Norman: University of Oklahoma Press, 1987.

Journals

The SACNAS News (Society for Advancement of Chicanos and Native Americans in Science): http://sacnas.org/about/stories/sacnas-news

Tribal College Journal of American Indian Higher Education (TCJ): http://www.tribal collegejournal.org/

Winds of Change (AISES): http://www.aises.org/what/woc

Web Sites

16 Indian Innovations: From Popcorn to Parkas: http://news.nationalgeographic.com/news/2004/09/0914_040913_information_about_indians.html

All Nations Louis Stokes Alliance for Minority Participation (ANLSAMP): http://www.pathwaystoscience.org/programhub.asp?sort=LSA-AllNations&subsort=partners

American Indians and Alaska Natives in Health Careers: http://aianhealthcareers.org/index.html

Ancient Observatories—Chaco Canyon: http://www.exploratorium.edu/chaco/

Ancient Observatories—Timeless Knowledge: http://solar-center.stanford.edu/AO/

Biographies of Native American, Chicano/Latino Scientists, Mathematicians, and Engineers: http://bio.sacnas.org/biography/default.asp

First Nations Launch: Tribal College High-Powered Rocket Competition: http://www.uwgb.edu/wsgc/fnl/

JustGarciaHill, A Virtual Community for Minorities in Sciences: http://JustGarciaHill.org/

Native Americans and the Environment: http://www.cnie.org/NAE/

Native American Ethnobotany Database: Food, Drugs, Dyes, and Fibers of Native North American Peoples (Daniel E. Moerman, Summer 2003): http://herb.umd.umich.edu/

Native Hawaiian Science and Engineering Mentorship Program: http://nhsemp.eng.hawaii.edu/

Native Seeds/Search: http://www.nativeseeds.org/

Native Tech: http://www.nativetech.org/

Science in Indian Country, U.S. Environmental Protection Agency: http://www.epa.gov/osp/tribes/contacts.htm

Society of Indian Psychologists: http://www.aiansip.org/

Native Science Field Programs: http://www.nativesciencefieldcenters.org/

U.S. Geological Survey Native American Tribal Liaison Team: http://www.usgs.gov/indian/

14

Food

FIRSTS

1998   Loretta Barrett Oden (Citizen Potawatomi Nation) and her son, the late chef Clayton Oden, opened the Corn Dance Café in Hotel Santa Fe, New Mexico, the first restaurant to showcase the bounty of food indigenous to the Americas. The restaurant closed in 2001.

     Native Vines Winery became the first winery owned and operated by American Indians in the United States. Located in Lexington, North Carolina, Native Vines was started by Darlene Gabbard (Lumbee).

2004   Yakama Juice, owned by the Yakama Nation of Washington State, became America's first Native-owned juice plant, producing organic juices as well as purified water and sports drinks. The Yakama Nation sold the company in 2010.

2008   The Tanka Bar, produced by a Native-owned and operated company, is the first high-protein energy bar made primarily of buffalo meat. Produced on the Pine Ridge Reservation in South Dakota by Native American Natural Foods, the company uses a recipe based on *wasna*, a traditional Lakota recipe similar to pemmican, to make a bar of smoke-dried buffalo meat blended with cranberries, salt, garlic, onion, and other natural ingredients.

2009   The first design in the new Native American dollar coin series of the U.S. Mint pays tribute to Three Sisters gardening, the joint planting of corn, beans, and squash. Although these three vegetables were grown in many Native cultures, the term "Three Sisters" originated with the Iroquois.

     Nuui Cunni Farmers' Market of the Kern River Paiute Council became the first farmers' market approved to be held on U.S. Forest Service land. It is in Isabella, California.

2010   Karlene Hunter (Oglala Lakota), CEO of Native American Natural Foods, the parent company of Tanka Bar, was named the 2010 recipient of the Cliff Adler "Heart in Business" Award, one of the natural foods industry's top honors. Hunter became the first Native American natural foods industry leader to receive the award in its twenty-one-year history. *Backpacker Magazine* awarded the Tanka Bar Spicy Pepper Blend with a 2010 Editors' Choice Award. In 2011, Native American Natural Foods received an Innovation Award from Social Venture Network, a national network of socially responsible entrepreneurs.

2011   At a White House ceremony, the Three Sisters—squash, corn, and beans—were planted together for the first time in the White House Kitchen Garden.

The Yocha Dehe Wintun Nation of California started a state-of-the-art sustainable olive oil enterprise, the first of its kind in the United States.

Three Sisters Coin

The first Native American series coin, released in January 2009, depicts on the reverse side of the Sacagawea "Golden Dollar" a Native American woman sowing seeds of the Three Sisters: corn, squash, and beans. Throughout history, these three vegetables have nourished Native peoples living across the continental United States. Corn, squash, and beans were traditionally planted together.

By leading with agriculture, the first coin in the series highlights one of the greatest of American Indian accomplishments, introducing dozens of foods to the world diet, as well as honoring indigenous skill in domesticating and growing these crops.

FOODS THAT CHANGED THE WORLD'S DIET

Native American Cultivated and Wild Plant Foods That Changed the World's Diet

Many traditional foods of Native people have made their way into the diet of mainstream America and supermarkets around the world.

Acorns of oak trees
Beans of all shapes and sizes
Berries: blackberries, black currants, blueberries, cassioberries, chokeberries, cranberries, juneberries, elderberries, huckleberries, raspberries, strawberries
Corn/maize
Jerusalem artichokes
Maple syrup
Nuts of beech, chestnut, hickory, and walnut trees

Peppers
Persimmon fruit
Pinon pine seed (also called a nut)
Potatoes
Prickly pear fruit
Squashes (pumpkins, summer, winter)
Sunflower seeds
Sweet potatoes/yams
Tomatoes
Wild rice
Wild turnips

Potato Chips

Potatoes have been cultivated by American Indians for thousands of years. The potato chip, however, is a modern invention, created by George Crum, believed to be from the Mohawk Nation. He was a cook who worked at Moon Lake Lodge in Saratoga Springs, New York. In 1853, a customer sent a plate of French fries back to the kitchen because they were too thick and soggy. Crum cut the potatoes into paper-thin slices and fried them. These crisp "saratoga" chips delighted Crum's customer. Crum never tried to widely distribute his potato chips. But other potato chip makers did, and now the snack is eaten by people all over the world.

Sixteen Native American Ceremonies That Honor the Gifts of Food

1. Acorn Feast (Hupa) in California
2. Bean Ceremony (Iroquois) in New York and Canada
3. Bread Dance (Shawnee) in Oklahoma
4. Busk, also called Green Corn Ceremony (Creek, Seminole, Yuchi, and other tribes) in the Southeast
5. Corn Dance (Keresan, Tewa, and Towa Pueblos) in New Mexico
6. Cranberry Day (Wampanaog) in Massachusetts
7. First Catch (Iñupiat) Alaska
8. First Salmon Rites of tribes in North Pacific Coast (Northern California, Oregon, and Washington, Northern Great Basin, and Plateau areas)
9. Green Corn Ceremony (Seminole and Creek) in Oklahoma
10. Green Corn Festival (Iroquois) in New York and Canada
11. Harvest (Thanksgiving) Festival for Crops (Zuni) in New Mexico
12. Peach Dance (Havasupai) in Arizona
13. Powamu/Bean Dance (Hopi) in Arizona
14. Raspberry Ceremony (Iroquois) in New York and Canada

15. Root Feast (Confederated Tribes of the Warm Springs Reservation) in Oregon
16. Strawberry Festival (Iroquois) in New York and Canada

Table of Foods with the Highest Antioxidant Properties (USDA)

In 2004, the United States Department of Agriculture released the largest study to date of food antioxidant sources. Many of the top twenty foods are traditional Native American foods. Antioxidants, such as vitamins A, C, and E and selenium, help reduce the risk of chronic diseases.

Rank	Food	Serving Size
1.	Small red bean	½ cup
2.	Wild blueberry	1 cup
3.	Red kidney bean	½ cup
4.	Pinto bean	½ cup
5.	Blueberry, cultivated	1 cup
6.	Cranberry	1 cup
7.	Artichoke heart	1 cup
8.	Blackberry	1 cup
9.	Prune	½ cup
10.	Raspberry	1 cup
11.	Strawberry	1 cup
12.	Red Delicious apple	One
13.	Granny Smith apple	One
14.	Pecan	1 oz.
15.	Sweet cherry	1 cup
16.	Black plum	One
17.	Russet potato	One
18.	Black bean	½ cup
19.	Plum	One
20.	Gala apple	One

TRIBAL AND NATIVE-OWNED FOOD BUSINESSES AND GARDENS

Seventeen Tribal and Native-Owned Food Businesses

1. Bedré Fine Chocolate: http://www.bedrechocolates.com
   This Chickasaw Nation–owned company's products include dark and milk chocolate, white fudge crisps, peanut clusters, and pecan-caramel sensations.

Bedré Fine Chocolate
2001 West Airline Road
Pauls Valley, OK 73075

2. Cooking Post: http://www.cookingpost.com/comersus7f/store/comersus _index.asp

A tribal enterprise of Santa Ana Pueblo, the Cooking Post offers a selection of foods, coffee, and teas from companies owned by Native people.
The Cooking Post
Pueblo of Santa Ana
2 Dove Road
Bernalillo, NM 87004

3. Coquille Cranberries: http://www.coquillecranberries.com

This Coquille Indian Tribe business offers freshly harvested, quick-frozen, bulk frozen, sweet and dried cranberries; cranberry juice, juice concentrate, and other preserves.
Coquille Cranberries
3201 Tremont Avenue
North Bend, OR 97459

4. First American Natural Foods: http://firstamericannaturalfoods.com/home

An Alaska Native privately owned company, First American Natural Foods is a wholesale and retail food broker specializing in the following markets: seafood, beef, bison, fruits, vegetables, and juice.
First American Natural Foods
Anchorage, AK 99504

5. Ho'oli Estate: http://www.hooliestate.com

Ho'oli Estate is a twenty-five-year-old Native Hawaiian company that sells organic Kona coffee and organic macadamia nuts.
Ho'oli Estate
Honomalino Acres
Captain Cook, HI 96704

6. Lakota Foods: http://lakotafoods.com/t-contact.aspx

This Lower Brule Sioux Tribe of South Dakota business sells popcorn products.
Lakota Foods
PO Box 132
Industrial Park Lot #2
Lower Brule, SD 57548

7. Lickity Split Chocolate: http://www.lickitysplitchocolate.com

A for-profit business owned and operated by Native American youth (ages eight to eighteen) from the Southwest makes and sells chocolate lollipops with Native designs, candy bars, and truffles.
Lickity Split Chocolate Studio, LLC
87 South Main Street
Blanding, UT 84511

8. Little River Smokehouse

    This Native American–owned and operated supplier specializes in a wide range of jerky, including buffalo jerky, snack sticks, spicy sausage, and summer sausage dried and smoked in the company's smokehouse.

    Little River Smokehouse

    445 Main Street

    Harlem, MT 59526

9. McGreevy's Mid West Meat Co., Inc.: http://www.mcgreevys.com

    This Native American–owned and operated certified 8(A) company supplies restaurants, hotels, and institutions with quality beef, pork, lamb, poultry, and brand-name related provisions, including cheese, hams, bacon, and more.

    McGreevy's Mid West Meat Co., Inc.

    230 N. West Street

    Wichita, KS 67203

10. Native American Natural Foods: http://www.tankabars.com

    A Native American–owned company produces Tanka Bars (buffalo meat and cranberries), Tanka Bites (buffalo and cranberry bites), Tanka Dogs (buffalo hotdogs), Tanka Wild Sticks (buffalo, cranberry, and wild rice), and Tanka Wild Gourmet Summer Sausage, products that are gluten-free, nitrates-free, msg-free, and hormone-free.

    Native American Natural Foods

    Pine Ridge Reservation

    287 Water Tower Road

    Kyle, SD 57762

11. Native Harvest: http://nativeharvest.com/catalog/1/wild_rice

    Native Harvest is the primary outlet for products of the White Earth Land Recovery Project, a nonprofit organization seeking to recover lost homelands of the White Earth Indian Reservation, Minnesota. The online catalog includes wild rice products, dried corn, fruit spreads, honey, buffalo sausage, maple syrup, candy, butter, coffee, tea, jelly, and granola.

    Native Harvest

    White Earth Land Recovery Project

    607 Main Avenue

    Callaway, MN 56521

12. Native Vines Winery

    A Native American–owned and operated company sells a line of vinifera wines, as well as specialty and fruit wines.

    Native Vines Winery

    1336 North Highway 150

    Lexington, NC 27295

13. Red Lake Nation Foods Incorporated: http://www.redlakenationfoods.com/index.html

    The Red Lake Nation business offers wild rice (and blends), wild berry jellies, jams, and syrups.

Red Lake Nation Foods Incorporated
PO Box 547
Hwy. #1 North
Red Lake, MN 56671

14. Sugpiaq: http://www.sugpiaq.com

An Alaska Native–owned company sells wild Alaskan seafood salmon, halibut, black cod, pacific cod, weathervane scallops, both fresh and flash frozen.
Sugpiaq, Inc.
645 G. Street, #744
Anchorage, AK 99501

15. Umpqua Indian Foods: http://www.umpquaindianfoods.com/xcart/home.php

This business, owned by the Cow Creek Band of Umpqua Tribe of Indians, sells steak jerky in six flavors, meat snacks, snack foods, honey, jams and jellies, candy, and saltwater taffy.
Umpqua Indian Foods
315 Main Street
Canyonville, OR 97417

16. Wilderness Delights: http://www.wildernessdelights.com

A Native American–owned business sells huckleberries, fresh and frozen, as well as mushrooms.
Wilderness Delights
PO Box 173
White Swan, WA 98952

17. Yakama Nation Land Enterprise: www.ynle.com

This Yakama Nation–owned business sells asparagus, apples, pears, peaches, nectarines, and plums.
Yakama Nation Land Enterprise
PO Box 151
Toppenish, WA 98948

Ten Native American Gardens and Farmers' Markets

1. Amah Mutsun Relearning Garden at the University of California Santa Cruz Arboretum

2. Amos Owen Garden of American Indian Horticulture, in honor of Dakota elder Amos Owen, Mankato, Minnesota: http://www.hmdb.org/marker.asp?marker=21588

3. Dream of Wild Health Farm, Native-owned organic farm, Hugo, Minnesota: http://dreamofwildhealth.org

4. Fort Belknap College Demonstration Farm, two-year college serving Gros Ventre and Assiniboine Tribes, Harlem, Montana: http://www.fbcc.edu/?page=sponsored_programs/extension

5. Maximizing Family Resources through Gardening project, Turtle Mountain Community College, Belcourt, North Dakota: http://www.turtle-mountain .cc.nd.us/community/anishinabe/garden.asp

6. Mazopiya: http://www.mazopiya.com
Mazopiya ("store" in Dakota) in Prior Lake, Minnesota, on the Shakopee Mdewakanton Dakota Reservation, is a natural food market that sells products that are in season, locally produced using sustainable practices, organic, minimally packaged, free of growth hormones and antibiotics, and fair trade.

7. Northwest Indian Treatment Center Healing Gardens, Elma, Washington: http://www.squaxinisland.org/government/northwest-indian-treatment -center

8. Nuui Cunni Farmers' Market, owned by the Kern River Paiute Council, Isabella, California: http://www.nuuicunni.com/page/Farmer

9. Oneida Farmers Market, Oneida Nation of Wisconsin, Oneida, Wisconsin: http://www.oneidanation.org/ocifs/page.aspx?id=532

10. United Tribes Technical College, Dragon Fly Garden, Bismarck, North Dakota

HONORING NATIONS PROJECT, HARVARD UNIVERSITY

Honoring Nations Honorees

Honoring Nations, a national awards program initiated in 1998, highlights outstanding programs in self-governance by Native nations. At the heart of the program is the belief that tribes themselves hold the key to positive social, political, cultural, and economic prosperity. Based at the John F. Kennedy School of Government at Harvard University, Honoring Nations is administered by the Harvard Project on American Indian Economic Development. The criteria for selection of honorees include program effectiveness, significance to sovereignty, cultural relevance, transferability, and sustainability. The honored programs center on foods central to tribal cultures.

Umatilla Basin Salmon Recovery Project, 2002
Confederated Tribes of the Umatilla Reservation
The project successfully restored a thriving salmon population to the Umatilla River after a seventy-year absence, while also protecting the local irrigated agriculture economy. Salmon have been central to the culture, economy, religion, and diet of the Cayuse, Umatilla, and Walla Walla tribes.

Oneida Nation Farms, 2005
Oneida Nation of Wisconsin
http://www.oneidanation.org/farm
In 1978, the Oneida Nation established the Oneida Nation Farms, beginning with 150 acres of land and twenty-five head of cattle. In 2005, the operation

included over 8,000 acres of agricultural and conservation lands; four hundred cattle and one hundred buffalo; major crops such as soybeans and corn; and diverse produce such as apples, several kinds of berries, snap beans, squash, and pumpkins. The farm is based on sustainable development and respect for the value of whole foods and a healthy diet.

POEMS AND BOOKS

Twelve Poems about Food by Native Poets

1. "Chili," by Eugene Holgate (Taos Pueblo). In *Rising Voices*, edited by Arlene Hirschfelder and Beverly Singer (1993).
2. "Communing before Supermarkets," by Carter Revard (Osage). In *Winning the Dust Bowl* (2001).
3. "Fish Fry at Panhandle Bar," by Adrian C. Louis (Paiute). In *Blood Thirsty Savages* (1994).
4. "Green Chile," by Jimmy Santiago Baca (Apache/Chicano). In *Black Mesa Poems* (1986).
5. "How to Make Good Baked Salmon from the River," by Nora Marks Dauenhauer (Tlingit). In *The Droning Shaman.*
6. "In September: Ode to Tomatoes," by Denise Sweet (Anishinaabe). In *Wisconsin Poetry, Academy of Sciences, Arts, and Letters* (1991).
7. "I Still Eat All of My Meals with a Mussel Shell," by Shaunna Oteka McCovey (Yurok/Karuk). In *The Smokehouse Boys* (2005).
8. "The Planting of the Blue Corn," by Edgar Gabriel Silex (Tigua Pueblo). In *Through All the Displacements* (1995).
9. "The Sweet and Vinegary Taste," by Cheryl Savageau (Abenaki). In *Dirt Road Home* (1995).
10. "Sweeten the Mango," by Haunani-Kay Trask (Native Hawaiian). In *Light in the Crevice Never Seen* (1999).
11. "White Corn Sister," by Peter Blue Cloud (Mohawk). In *Clans of Many Nations* (1995).
12. "Wine and Cheese," by Eric Gansworth (Onondaga). Available online: http://www.hanksville.org/storytellers/ericg/writing/Wine.Cheese.html (1998).

Sixteen Native American Cookbooks

1. *American Indian Cooking: Recipes from the Southwest,* by Carolyn Niethammer (1999).
2. *The Art of American Indian Cooking,* by Yeffe Kimball and Jean Anderson (1960, reprinted in 2000).
3. *Body, Mind and Spirit: Native Cooking of the Americas,* by Beverly Cox and Martin Jacobs (2004).

4. *Cape Cod Wampanoag Cookbook: Wampanoag Indian Recipes*, by Earl Mills (Wampanoag) (2001).
5. *Enduring Harvests: Native American Foods and Festivals for Every Season*, by E. Barrie Kavasch (1995).
6. *Foods of the Americas: Native Recipes and Traditions*, by Fernando Divina and Marlene Divina (Chippewa/Cree) (2004). Winner of a 2005 James Beard Award.
7. *Foods of the Southwest Indian Nations*, by Lois Ellen Frank (Kiowa) (2002). Winner of a 2003 James Beard Award.
8. *Hopi Cookery*, by Juanita Tiger Kavena (Creek/Hopi) (1980).
9. *The Mitsitam Cafe Cookbook: Recipes from the Smithsonian National Museum of the American Indian*, by Richard Hetzler (2010). The book won second place in the "Best Local" category at the Gourmand World Cookbook Awards, 2011.
10. *Native Harvests: American Indian Wild Foods and Recipes*, by E. Barrie Kavasch (2005).
11. *Native Indian Wild Game, Fish, and Wild Foods Cookbook*, by Lovesick Lake Native Women's Association (1996).
12. *New Native American Cooking: More Than 125 Traditional Foods and Contemporary Dishes Made from America's Indigenous Ingredients*, by Dale Carson (Abenaki) (1996).
13. *The New Native American Cuisine: Five-Star Recipes from the Chefs of Arizona's Kai Restaurant*, by Marion Betancourt, Michael O'Dowd, and Jack Strong (Confederated Tribes of Siletz Indians of Oregon) (2009).
14. *Pueblo Indian Cookbook: Recipes from the Pueblos of the American Southwest*, by Phyllis Hughes (1977).
15. *Seaweed, Salmon, and Manzanita Cider: A California Feast*, by Margaret Dubin and Sara-Larus Tolley (2009).
16. *Spirit of the Harvest: North American Indian Cooking*, by Beverly Cox and Martin Jacobs (1991).

Contemporary Native American Chefs

Native chefs create dishes with regional foods that have been used by Native peoples in the Americas for hundreds of years. The chefs aim to preserve Native American culinary traditions while taking a forward-thinking approach to modern Native American cookery and cuisine.

Fred Bitsoie (Navajo)
Nephi Craig (White Mountain Apache/Navajo)
Loretta Barrett Oden (Citizen Band Potawatomi)
Jack Strong (Confederated Tribes of Siletz Indians in Oregon)
Walter Whitewater (Navajo)
Walter Wolfman (Salish)

FILMS

Corn Is Life (USA, 1983, 16 min.), directed by Patricia Barey.

The film explores the central roles that corn has played in the life of every Hopi for centuries. It continues to be an essential food, a holy substance, used in every ritual of Hopi religious life.

Diabetes and Desert Foods: Examples from O'odham Traditions (USA, 1991, 20 min.), produced by Native Seeds/SEARCH Native American Research and Training Center.

The video gives an overview of changes in the Native American diet from traditional times to the present, especially the health effects of those changes on O'odham people. The film argues that the nutritional value of wild and domesticated desert plants can control diabetes, and also tells how people can choose healthier food in grocery stores.

The Gift (Canada, 1998, 49 min.), directed by Gary Farmer (Cayuga).

The film explores the traditional, spiritual, economic, and political importance of corn, a sacred plant, to Native peoples in North and South America.

Grab (USA, 2011, 60 min.), directed by Billy Luther (Navajo/Hopi/Laguna Pueblo).

Each year residents of the Laguna Pueblo in New Mexico honor individual family members by throwing food and gifts from the rooftops of their homes to the community that gathers below. Luther's film follows three families as they prepare for this ancient tradition.

Manoomin: A Minnesota Way of Living (USA, 2005, 22 min.), directed by Theresa Konechne.

The documentary informs people about the complex issues surrounding genetic engineering, patenting, and other issues surrounding wild rice, the state grain of Minnesota. Wild rice cleans lakes and provides important habitat for migrating waterfowl. Its continuation is the key to the survival of the Minnesota way of life, culture, community health, and future generations of Ojibwe people. Ricers, activists, tribal elders, and members of the scientific and academic community discuss the dangers that genetically modified wild rice poses to the natural environment and to Ojibwe cultural and spiritual life.

Mino-Bimadiziwin: The Good Life (USA, 1998, 59 min.), directed by Deb Wallwork.

The documentary is about the tradition of wild rice harvesting among the Ojibwe of Minnesota. Interviews illuminate the economic and spiritual aspects of the ancient tradition.

More Than Frybread (USA, 2011, feature length), produced by Travis Holt Hamilton.

This mockumentary and comedy is about frybread, or bannock, a Native American staple. Frybread is a flat wheat bread made by North American Indians, cooked by frying the dough in deep fat until light brown and puffed on both sides. The indie film tells the fictional story of the First Annual Arizona State Frybread Championship competition held among Arizona's twenty-two tribes.

Seasoned with Spirit: A Native Cook's Journey (USA, 2006, five episodes, 27 min. each), produced by Matt and Renard Cohen, Native American Public Telecommunications, and Connecticut Public Television.

A five-part cooking series offers viewers a culinary celebration of America's bounty, combining Native American history and culture with recipes inspired by indigenous foods. Loretta Barrett Oden (Citizen Potawatomi Nation), a renowned chef, ethnobotanist, and food historian, hosts the Emmy award–winning series, which was filmed in Native locations.

Search for the World's Best Indian Taco (USA, 2010, 15 min.), directed by Steven Judd (Kiowa/Choctaw).

A Choctaw grandfather regales his grandson with tall tales about his lifelong quest for the world's best Indian taco.

ORGANIZATIONS

American Indian Foods
http://www.americanindianfoods.com
A program of the Intertribal Agriculture Council since 1998, American Indian Foods (AIF) is an important economic program that promotes the efforts of thousands of American Indian farmers and ranchers, some of whom grow foods the same way their ancestors did hundreds of years ago. The AIF showcases products of American Indian food businesses at food and beverage events.

Indigenous Seed Sovereignty Network
http://nativeharvest.com/node/244
The Indigenous Seed Sovereignty Network is a network of organizations working to restore traditional food knowledge and oppose efforts to patent, modify, or control Native food resources. The network organizes legislatively against genetic engineering of wild rice and other traditional crops. It also opposes biopiracy of medicinal and other plants.

Intertribal Agriculture Council
http://www.indianaglink.com
The Intertribal Agriculture Council (IAC), founded in 1987 and based in Billings, Montana, pursues and promotes the conservation, development, and use of Native agricultural resources that are vital to the economic and social welfare of many Native American and Alaska Native people. Its American Indian Foods (AIF) program showcases the efforts of tribal businesses and American Indian–owned food businesses through food show events. IAC has grown to

become the respected voice within the Indian community and among federal government agencies on agricultural policies and programs in Indian country.

Native Seeds/SEARCH
http://www.nativeseeds.org/
A Tucson-based nonprofit conservation organization and seed bank, founded by ethnobotanist and author Gary Nabhan, Native Seeds/SEARCH (NS/S) preserves native plants in the Southwest and northwestern Mexico. NS/S established the Native American Outreach Program in 2005 to help increase network initiatives with farmers, gardeners, nations/tribes, and organizations. Outreach programs include information about traditional agricultures and seed saving, workshops, and free seeds to Native peoples in the Greater Southwest region.

Native Women in Agriculture
Founded in 2004, Native Women in Agriculture (NWIA) addresses agricultural issues relating to education, food systems, viability, and preservation of cultural identification. NWIA especially focuses on better agricultural education and assistance for youth, which has led NWIA to conduct an annual youth writing competition.

Renewing America's Food Traditions
http://www.slowfoodusa.org/index.php/programs/details/ark_of_taste
Managed by Slow Food USA, Renewing America's Food Traditions (RAFT) is an alliance of farmers, chefs, fishers, agricultural historians, ranchers, nurserymen, retail grocers, consumers, and conservationists who have joined together to restore and celebrate America's biologically and culturally diverse food traditions through conservation, education, promotion, and regional networking. One of RAFT's programs, the US Ark of Taste, is a catalog of over two hundred rare regional foods that includes many Native food products.

RESOURCES

Caduto, Michael J., and Bruchac, Joseph. *Keepers of Life: Discovering Plants through Native American Stories and Earth Activities for Children*. Golden, CO: Fulcrum Publishing, 1994.

——. *Native American Gardening: Stories, Projects, and Recipes for Families*. Golden, CO: Fulcrum Publishing, 1996.

Fussell, Betty. *The Story of Corn*. Albuquerque: University of New Mexico Press, 2004.

Hutchens, Alma R. *Handbook of Native American Herbs*. Boston: Shambhala Publications, 1992.

LaDuke, Winona (White Earth Chippewa), and Sarah Alexander. *Food is Medicine: Recovering Traditional Foods to Heal the People*. Minneapolis: Honor the Earth/White Earth Land Recovery Project, 2004.

Mihesuah, Devon. *Recovering our Ancestors' Gardens: Indigenous Recipes and Guide to Diet and Fitness.* Lincoln: University of Nebraska Press, 2005.

Moerman, Daniel E. *Native American Food Plants.* Portland, OR: Timber Press, 2010.

Nabhan, Gary Paul, ed. *Saving and Savoring the Continent's Most Endangered Foods.* White River Junction, VT: Chelsea Green Publishing, 2008.

Price, V. B., and Baker H. Morrow. *Canyon Gardens: The Ancient Pueblo Landscapes of the American Southwest.* Albuquerque: University of New Mexico Press, 2007.

Vennum, Thomas. *Wild Rice and the Ojibway People.* St. Paul: Minnesota Historical Society, 1988.

Viola, Herman J., and Carolyn Margolis, eds. *Seeds of Change: A Quincentennial Commemoration.* Washington, DC: Smithsonian Institution Press, 1991.

Weatherford, Jack. *Indian Givers: How the Indians of the Americas Transformed the World.* New York: Fawcett Columbine, 1988.

Weiner, Michael A. *Earth Medicine, Earth Food: The Classic Guide to the Herbal Remedies and Wild Plants of the North American Indians.* New York: Ballantine, 1990.

Wilson, Gilbert. *Buffalo Bird Woman's Garden: Agriculture of the Hidatsa Indians.* Minneapolis: Minnesota Historical Society Press, 1917 (reprinted 1987).

Web Sites

16 Indian Innovations From Popcorn to Parkas: http://news.nationalgeographic.com/news/2004/09/0914_040913_information_about_indians.html

American Native Food: http://www.tahtonka.com/food.html

Guide to USDA Programs for American Indians and Alaska Natives: http://www.usda.gov/news/pubs/indians/open.htm

Harvard Project's Honoring Nations Directory of Honored Programs, 1999–2006: http://hpaied.org/images/resources /general/Dir_web.pdf

Indian Health Service, Division of Diabetes Treatment and Prevention: http://www.diabetes.ihs.gov/index.cfm?module=resourcesfstorysp

Intertribal Buffalo Cooperative: http://www.itbcbison.com

Keepseagle et al. v. Vilsack, Fact Sheet about Native American Farmers and Ranchers Class Action Lawsuit Against the U.S. Department of Agriculture for Decades of Discrimination in Farm Loans: http://www.cmht.com/media/pnc/7/media.787.pdf

Native American Cuisine: http://nativerecipes.com/

Native American Culinary Association: http://nativeculinary.com/forum/index.php

Pemmican: http://w4.lns.cornell.edu/~seb/pemmican.html

Part Five

15

Visual Arts

FIRSTS

1906   Angel DeCora Dietz (Winnebago) became the first director of a newly established art department at the Carlisle Indian School in Carlisle, Pennsylvania.

1934   Maria Martinez (San Ildefonso Pueblo), regarded as one of the greatest modern Pueblo potters, was the first Native American woman to receive a bronze medal for Indian achievement from the Indian Council Fire.

1948   Allan Houser (Chiricahua Apache) created *Comrade in Mourning*, the first public monument in the United States done by a Native American. The work, a memorial to Indian servicemen who died during World War II, was commissioned by Haskell Institute in Lawrence, Kansas, and dedicated in 1949.

1951   Lloyd Kiva New (Cherokee), who participated in the Atlantic City International Fashion Show, was the first Native American to show designs at an international fashion show. In 1962, New co-founded the Institute of American Indian Arts in Santa Fe and served as its first art director and longtime president.

1963   George Morrison (Grand Portage Band of Chippewa) became the first Native artist to be appointed to the faculty of a major art school, the Rhode Island School of Design.

1964   Helen Cordero (Cochiti Pueblo) created the first pottery storyteller doll, revitalizing early Pueblo figural art into a new form.

1965   Located on the Morongo Reservation, the Malki Museum was the first tribal museum founded by Native Americans on a reservation in California. Its facilities include the Temalpakh Ethnobotanical Garden, which contains botanical species used in the daily life of the Cahuilla.

1971   Dennis C. Numkena (Hopi), architect, artist, and designer, formed Numkena Architects, the first Native American–owned architectural firm. The recipient of the Arizona Indian Living Treasure Award in 2002, among other honors, Numkena designed buildings that included the Anasazi Resort Condominiums in Phoenix and the Pyramid Lake Paiute Tribe Museum in Nevada.

1985   Artists Jaune Quick-To-See Smith and Harmony Hammond organized *Women of Sweetgrass, Cedar, and Sage*, the first exhibition of contemporary Indian women's art.

The nation's first extensive art exhibition on the topic of Native HIV/AIDS was held in New York City's only Indian-owned and operated gallery, American Indian Community House Gallery.

1989   Established by an act of Congress in 1989, the National Museum of the American Indian is the first national museum dedicated to the preservation, study, and exhibition of the life, languages, literature, history, and arts of Native Americans.

1992   Allan Houser (Chiricahua Apache), sculptor, became the first American Indian artist to receive the National Medal of Arts.

2005   Cliff Fragua (Jemez Pueblo) became the first American Indian artist to have a sculpture placed in the U.S. Capitol's Statuary Hall. It is a marble statue of Po'pay, the leader of the Pueblo Revolt of 1680.

Zig Jackson (Mandan/Hidatsa/Arikara) became the first contemporary Native American photographer to be represented in the Library of Congress's collections when he contributed a gift of twelve large silver gelatin prints.

2007   Nora Naranjo-Morse (Santa Clara Pueblo) became the first Native American woman to create an outdoor sculpture in Washington, DC. Titled *Always Becoming*, it was built on site at the National Museum of the American Indian.

Marvin Oliver (Quinault/Isleta Pueblo) became the first non-Italian artist to be commissioned for a public art piece in Perugia, Italy, Seattle's sister city. Perugia named one of its parks in Seattle's honor, Orca Park, which features Oliver's monumental bronze sculpture, *Sister Orca*.

2009   The Native Arts and Cultures Foundation was launched as the first permanently endowed national foundation dedicated to promoting the revitalization, appreciation, and perpetuation of Native arts and cultures. Based in Portland, Oregon, the foundation fosters indigenous arts in American Indian, Alaska Native, and Native Hawaiian communities.

Fashion designers Dorothy Grant (Haida), Patricia Michaels (Taos Pueblo), and Virgil Ortiz (Cochiti, Pueblo) showed during New York Fashion Week, a historic first for Native American designers.

Fritz Scholder (Luiseño) became the first American Indian and the first painter to be inducted into the California Hall of Fame.

NATIVE ARTISTS

Twelve Native Architects

1. Richard K. Begay Jr. (Navajo): http://www.members.tripod.com/rkbegay/
2. Duane Blue Spruce (Laguna/Ohkay Owingeh Pueblo)
3. Douglas Cardinal (Blackfoot/Métis): http://www.djcarchitect.com/
4. Michael Fredericks (Yu'pik): http://www.rimfirstpeople.com/
5. Daniel J. Glenn (Crow): http://www.glennandglennarchitects.com
6. Johnpaul Jones (Cherokee/Choctaw): http://www.jonesandjones.com/
7. Michael Laverdure (Turtle Mountain Band of Chippewa): http://www.dsgw .com/firstamericans.html
8. Anthony Monroe (Yakama): http://www.northwestnativearchitecture.com/
9. Dyron Murphy (Navajo): http://www.dm-architects.com
10. Dennis Numkena (Hopi): http://www.numkena.com (online museum)
11. Dennis Sun Rhodes (Northern Arapaho): http://greathorsegroup.com/
12. Rina Swentzell (Santa Clara Pueblo)

Thirteen Native Fashion Designers

1. Marcus Amerman (Choctaw): http://www.marcusamerman.com/
2. Tammy Beauvais (Mohawk): http://www.tammybeauvais.com/
3. Betty David (Spokane)
4. Dorothy Grant (Haida): http://www.dorothygrant.com/
5. Louie Gong (Nooksack/Squamish/Chinese/French/Scottish): http://www.eighthgeneration.com/
6. Victorialyn McCarthy (Navajo)
7. Patricia Michaels (Taos Pueblo)
8. Lloyd Kiva New (Cherokee)
9. Virgil Ortiz (Cochiti Pueblo): http://www.virgilortiz.com/
10. Wendy Ponca (Osage)
11. Penny Singer (Diné): http://www.pennysinger.com/
12. Margaret Roach Wheeler (Chickasaw/Choctaw): http://www.margaretroach-wheeler.com/
13. Margaret Wood (Navajo/Seminole): http://www.margaretwood.net/

Fifteen Native Photographers

1. Dorothy Chocolate (Diné)
2. Thomas Eaton (Tsimshian)

3. Jean Fredericks (Hopi)
4. Benjamin A. Haldane (Tsimshian)
5. Zig Jackson (Mandan/Hidatsa/Arikara)
6. Carm Little Turtle (Apache/Tarahumara)
7. Lee Marmon (Laguna Pueblo)
8. Larry McNeil (Tlingit/Nisga'a)
9. Paul Natonabah (Navajo)
10. Shelley Niro (Mohawk)
11. Peter Pitseolak (Inuit)
12. Horace Poolaw (Kiowa)
13. Owen Seumptewa (Hopi)
14. Richard Throssel (Cree)
15. Hulleah J. Tsinhnahjinnie (Navajo/Creek/Seminole)

Twenty-Seven Native Sculptors

1. Manasie Akpaliapik (Inuit)
2. Lawrence Jerry Beck(Yup'ik)
3. Blackbear Bosin (Comanche/Kiowa)
4. Joe Cajero (Jemez Pueblo)
5. Amanda Crowe (Cherokee)
6. Cliff Fragua (Jemez Pueblo)
7. Retha Walden Gambaro (Creek)
8. Bill Glass (Cherokee)
9. Bob Haozous (Chiricahua Apache)
10. Edgar Heap of Birds (Cheyenne/Arapaho)
11. Allan Houser (Chiricahua Apache)
12. Doug Hyde (Nez Perce)
13. Oreland C. Joe (Ute/Navajo)
14. Bruce LaFountain (Turtle Mountain Chippewa)
15. Edmonia Lewis (Mississauga Ojibwe)
16. David Montour (Potawatomi/Ottawa/Mohawk/Cayuga)
17. George Morrison (Ojibwe)
18. Michael Naranjo (Santa Clara Pueblo)
19. Nora Naranjo-Morse (Santa Clara Pueblo)
20. Marvin Oliver (Quinault/Isleta Pueblo)
21. Bill Prokopiof (Aleut)
22. Mark Swazo (Tesuque Pueblo)
23. Roxanne Swentzell (Santa Clara Pueblo)
24. Frederick Peso (Mescalero Apache)
25. Nelson Tsosie (Navajo)
26. Kathy Whitman-Elk Woman (Mandan/Hidatsa)
27. Larry Yazzie (Navajo)

The Kiowa Five (sometimes called the Kiowa Six)

The Kiowa Five, a group of Kiowa artists prominent in the development of contemporary American Indian painting, were part of the early "Oklahoma school" of art work, generally characterized by paintings of tribal ceremonial and social scenes in colorful, flat, two-dimensional styles. These artists actually numbered six, when Lois Smoky (Bougetah, "of the dawn"), who also participated, is counted. Their artistic talent was first recognized and began to be nurtured as students at Saint Patrick's Indian Mission School in Anadarko, Oklahoma. During the late 1920s, the Kiowa Five studied at the University of Oklahoma, where they were mentored by school art director Oscar B. Jacobson, who promoted their work through international exhibition and other venues. The Jacobson House Native Art Center, his former residence in Norman, Oklahoma, honors this artistic legacy. See www.jacobsonhouse.com.

1. Spencer Asah (ca. 1905–54)
2. James Auchiah (1906–74)
3. Jack Hokeah (ca. 1902–69)
4. Stephen Mopope (1898–1974) (See Anadarko Post Office Murals)
5. Monroe Tsatoke (1904–37)
6. Lois Smoky (1907–81)

MUSEUMS, FAIRS, FESTIVALS, MARKETS, AND ASSOCIATIONS

Fourteen Tribal Museums and Centers

1. Ah-Tah-Thi-Ki Museum, Big Cypress Seminole Indian Reservation, Clewiston, Florida
   http://www.ahtahthiki.com
2. Ak-Chin Him Dak Eco-Museum, Maricopa, Arizona
   http://www.ak-chin.nsn.us/about.html
3. Aquinnah Cultural Center, Aquinnah, Massachusetts
   http://www.wampanoagtribe.net/Pages/Wampanoag_ACC/index
4. Chickasaw Cultural Center, Sulphur, Oklahoma
   http://www.chickasawculturalcenter.com/
5. Makah Cultural and Research Center, Neah Bay, Washington
   http://www.makah.com/mcrchome.html
6. Malki Museum, Banning, California
   http://www.malkimuseum.org/
7. Mashantucket Pequot Museum and Research Center, Mashantucket, Connecticut
   http://www.pequotmuseum.org/
8. The Museum at Warm Springs, Warm Springs, Oregon
   http://www.museumatwarmsprings.org/

9. Museum of the Cherokee Indian, Cherokee, North Carolina
   http://www.cherokeemuseum.org/
10. Navajo Nation Museum, Window Rock, Arizona
    http://www.navajonationmuseum.org/
11. Oneida Nation Museum, Oneida, Wisconsin
    http://museum.oneidanation.org/
12. Poeh Center, Santa Fe, New Mexico
    http://www.poehcenter.com/
13. Southern Ute Cultural Center and Museum, Ignacio, Colorado
    http://www.succm.org/
14. Ziibiwing Center of Anishinabe Culture and Lifeways, Mt. Pleasant, Michigan
    http://www.sagchip.org/ziibiwing/

National Museum of the American Indian

Established by an act of Congress in 1989 (amended in 1996), the National Museum of the American Indian (NMAI) is the sixteenth museum of the Smithsonian Institution in Washington, DC. It is the first national museum dedicated to the preservation, study, and exhibition of the life, languages, literature, history, and arts of Native Americans. NMAI opened on the National Mall in Washington, DC, on September 21, 2004.

The museum's collections, assembled largely by George Gustav Heye (1874–1957), are extensive. They span all major culture areas of the Americas, most of those of Canada, and a significant number of cultures from Central and South America as well as the Caribbean. The collections range from Paleo-Indian objects to contemporary works. The holdings also include film and audiovisual collections, paper archives, and a photography archive depicting historic as well as contemporary Native life.

Besides the museum in Washington, DC, NMAI has two other facilities. The George Gustav Heye Center, which opened in 1994 in Manhattan, serves as NMAI's exhibition and education facility in New York City. The Cultural Resources Center, which opened in 1999 in Suitland, Maryland, houses the collections and research programs of the museum.

Source: http://www.nmai.si.edu/

Seven American Indian Art Fairs, Festivals, and Markets

1. American Indian Arts Marketplace at the Autry, Los Angeles, California (November): http://theautry.org/
2. Eiteljorg Museum Indian Market, Indianapolis, Indiana (June): www.eiteljorg.org/

3. Gallup Inter-Tribal Indian Ceremonial, Gallup, New Mexico (August): http://www.theceremonial.com/
4. Heard Museum Guild Indian Fair and Market, Phoenix, Arizona (March): http://heardguild.org/events/indianfairandmarket.php
5. Northern Plains Indian Art Market, Sioux Falls, South Dakota (September): http://www.npiam.org/
6. Red Earth Native American Cultural Festival, Oklahoma City, Oklahoma (June): www.redearth.org/
7. Santa Fe Indian Market, Santa Fe, New Mexico (August): http://swaia.org/

Osage Tribal Museum

Osage Tribal Museum, Pawhuska, Oklahoma
http://www.osagetribalmuseum.com

When it opened in 1938, the Osage Tribal Museum became the only museum in the nation owned by an American Indian tribe. The building, originally constructed in 1872 as a chapel, schoolhouse, and dormitory, was adapted for use as a museum as a Public Works Administration (WPA) project. The Osage Tribal Museum was placed on the National Register of Historic Places in 1987. Today, the facility continues to collect, preserve, interpret, and celebrate Osage Native history, culture, and traditions.

Five American Indian Basketweaver Associations

1. California Indian Basketweavers Association: http://www.ciba.org/
2. Maine Indian Basketmakers Alliance: http://www.maineindianbaskets.org/
3. Northwest Native American Basketweavers Association: http://www.nnaba.org/
4. Oklahoma Native American Basketweavers Association: http://onaba.org/
5. Tohono O'odham Basketweavers Organization: http://www.tocaonline.org/

U.S. FEDERAL GOVERNMENT AND NATIVE AMERICAN ART

Seven American Indian Sculptures in the U.S. Capitol
and U.S. House of Representatives

An 1864 law authorized the U.S. president to invite each state to furnish two statues, in marble or bronze, of deceased persons who were "illustrious for their historic renown or for distinguished civic or military services." Seven sculptural figures, located throughout the U.S. Capitol building, honor two Native women and five Native men, each notable in his or her state's history.

Hawaii
King Kamehameha, bronze statue by Thomas R. Gould, 1969. Located in the National Statuary Hall, the United States Capitol.

Nevada
Sarah Winnemucca (Paiute), bronze by Benjamin Victor, 2005. Located in the Capitol Crypt (first floor).

New Mexico
Po'pay (Ohkay Owingeh, formerly known as San Juan Pueblo), marble by Cliff Fragua from Jemez Pueblo, 2005. Located in the Capitol Rotunda.

North Dakota
Sakakawea [Sacagawea] (Shoshone), bronze by Leonard Crunelle, 1909 (copied by Arizona Atelier in 2003). Located in the Capitol Crypt (first floor).

Oklahoma
Will Penn Adair Rogers (Cherokee), bronze by Jo Davidson, 1939. Located in the House of Representatives, second floor.

Sequoyah (Cherokee), bronze by Vinnie Ream Hoxie, 1917. Located in the National Statuary Hall, the United States Capitol.

Wyoming
Chief Washakie (Shoshone), bronze by Dave McGary, 2000. Located in the House of Representatives, first floor.

American Indian Art on U.S. Postage Stamps

Following the first depiction of an American Indian on a United States postage stamp in 1898, other stamps have featured Native themes, including tribal arts such as those listed here. An online exhibit, *The American Indian in Stamps: Profiles in Leadership, Accomplishment and Cultural Celebration*, highlights this aspect of U.S. postage. http://postalmuseum.si.edu/ARAGOAmericanIndian

American Folk Art, Pueblo Art	Denomination	Date Issued
Pueblo Art: Zia	13 cent	April 13, 1977
Pueblo Art: San Ildefonso	13 cent	April 13, 1977
Pueblo Art: Hopi	13 cent	April 13, 1977
Pueblo Art: Acoma	13 cent	April 13, 1977
American Folk Art, Indian Art	**Denomination**	**Date Issued**
Heiltsuk, Bella Bella	15 cent	September 25, 1980
Chilkat Tlingit	15 cent	September 25, 1980

Tlingit	15 cent	September 25, 1980
Bella Coola	15 cent	September 25, 1980
Navajo Art (four different designs)	22 cent	September 4, 1986
Wood Carving: Cigar-Store Figure	22 cent	October 1, 1986

Art of the American Indian

The Art of the American Indian commemorative stamps, with ten designs illustrating objects from diverse tribal cultures, were issued at the Santa Fe Indian Market on August 21, 2004. The issue, each in 37-cent denominations, also celebrated the 2004 opening of the National Museum of the American Indian in Washington, DC.

1. Acoma pot
2. Ho-Chunk bag
3. Kutenai parfleche
4. Luiseño basket
5. Mimbres bowl
6. Mississippian effigy
7. Navajo weaving
8. Seminole doll
9. Seneca carving
10. Tlingit sculptures

Indian Arts and Crafts Board (IACB)

The Indian Arts and Crafts Board, an agency of the U.S. Department of the Interior, was created by Congress in 1935 to promote the economic development of American Indians and Alaska Natives of federally recognized tribes through the expansion of the Indian arts and crafts market. The IACB operates three regional museums, conducts a promotional museum exhibition program, produces a "Source Directory of American Indian and Alaska Native Owned and Operated Arts and Crafts Businesses," and oversees the implementation of the Indian Arts and Crafts Act.
The three Indian Arts and Crafts Board Museums are:

1. Sioux Indian Museum, Rapid City, South Dakota, founded in 1939
2. Museum of the Plains Indian, Browning, Montana, founded in 1941
3. Southern Plains Indian Museum, Anadarko, Oklahoma, founded in 1947–48

Source: http://www.doi.gov/iacb/

HONORING NATIONS PROJECT, HARVARD UNIVERSITY

Honoring Nations, 2000–2008

Honoring Nations, a national awards program initiated in 1998, highlights outstanding programs in self-governance by Native nations. At the heart of the program is the belief that tribes themselves hold the key to positive social, political, cultural, and economic prosperity. Based at the John F. Kennedy School of Government at Harvard University, Honoring Nations is administered by the Harvard Project on American Indian Economic Development. The criteria for selection of honorees, among them cultural centers and museum programs, include program effectiveness, significance to sovereignty, cultural relevance, transferability, and sustainability.

Poeh Center: Sustaining and Constructing Legacies, 2000
Poeh Cultural Center, Pueblo of Pojoaque
Santa Fe, New Mexico
http://www.poehcenter.com/

> The Pueblo of Pojoaque established the Pojoaque Pueblo Construction Services Corporation (PPCSC) in 1993 to generate new revenues for, and to oversee the construction and maintenance of, the Poeh Center and Museum. Having completed the Poeh Center and other work, the PPCSC bids profitably on commercial projects throughout New Mexico, thus providing a sustainable funding stream for cultural and educational activities. The Poeh Center is able to provide programs and internships in arts and museum professions to young tribal members.

Cultural Education and Revitalization Program, 2006
Makah Cultural and Research Center, Makah Nation
Neah Bay, Washington
http://www.makah.com/

> The Cultural Education and Revitalization Program was honored for its work in the Makah Cultural and Research Center, including serving as the hub of the community and stewards of a world-class museum collection. Programs are guided by the needs of the tribal nation and its citizens, with language taught by certified teachers, collection labels categorized in the Makah language, and other work done in accordance with cultural traditions and standards. "By claiming and caring for the treasures of their ancestors," Honoring Nations indicated, "the Makah Nation ensures the cultural viability of its people."

Ziibiwing Center of Anishinabe Culture and Lifeways, 2008
Saginaw Chippewa Indian Tribe of Michigan
Mt. Pleasant, Michigan
www.sagchip.org/ziibiwing

Opened in 2004, the Ziibiwing Center of Anishinabe Culture and Lifeways serves as the cultural hub of the Saginaw Chippewa community, educating tribal citizens and the general public through a rich array of exhibits and programs. One of the features of the facility is the Nindakenjigewinoong Research Center ("the place where you find things out at"), where students and other researchers can search historical and contemporary collections for information about the tribe. Other activities include repatriation efforts, Anishinabe language programs, oral history endeavors, and an art market.

AWARDS AND HONORS

Indian Arts and Crafts Association (IACA) Artist of the Year

The Indian Arts and Crafts Association is an international nonprofit trade association established in 1974 to promote, preserve, and protect authentic American Indian arts and crafts. Based in Albuquerque, New Mexico, IACA sponsors retail and wholesale markets that bring together artists, retailers, wholesalers, museums, and collectors. During the spring market, artist members compete for the IACA Artist of the Year awards. The honor, which acknowledges creativity and craftmanship, includes financial benefits as well as one year of extensive promotion by the association (http://swaia.org/Awards/Lifetime_Achievements/index.html).

Artist of the Year, Indian Arts and Crafts Association

1982	Virginia Stroud (Cherokee/Creek)
1983	Carolyn Bobelu (Zuni)
1984	Jean Bales (Iowa)
1985	Charles Pratt (Cheyenne/Arapaho)
1986	Mark Silversmith (Navajo)
1987	Clifford Brycelea (Navajo)
1988	Jake Livingston (Navajo)
1989	Bill Rabbit (Cherokee)
1990	Angelina Frances Medina (Acoma/Zia)
1991	Denny Haskew (Potawatomi)
1992	John Balloue (Cherokee)
1993	Naveek (Navajo)
1994	Carol Snow (Seneca)
1995	Andy Lee Kirk (Isleta Pueblo)

1996	Jesse T. Hummingbird (Cherokee)
1997	Michael Kirk (Isleta Pueblo)
1998	Bruce Contway (Sioux/Chippewa-Cree)
1999	Pahponee (Kansas/Kickapoo)
2000	George Shukata Willis (Choctaw)
2001	Alfred Joe (Navajo)
2002	Mary Small (Jemez Pueblo)
2003	Lorraine Caté (Santo Domingo Pueblo)
2004	Charles Pratt (Cheyenne/Arapaho)
2005	Cliff Fragua (Jemez Pueblo)
2006	Amelia Joe Chandler (Navajo)
2007	Shane R. Hendren (Navajo)
2008	Mary Lou Big Day (Crow)
2009	Alfred Joe (Navajo)
2010	Mary Small (Jemez Pueblo)
2011	Earl Plummer (Navajo)

National Endowment for the Arts (NEA) National Heritage Fellows

The National Endowment for the Arts annually awards one-time-only National Heritage Fellowships for master folk and traditional artists. The fellowships, which began in 1982, are intended to recognize the recipients' artistic excellence and support their continuing contributions to our nation's traditional arts heritage. American Indian, Alaska Native, and Native Hawaiian artists are among the recipients of the lifetime honors.

1982	Georgeann Robinson (Osage), Bartlesville, Oklahoma: Ribbon worker
1983	Ada Thomas (Chitimacha), Charenton, Louisiana: Basketmaker
1984	Margaret Tafoya (Santa Clara Pueblo), Espanola, New Mexico: Potter Paul Tiulana (Iñupiat), Anchorage, Alaska: Mask maker, dancer, singer Emily Kau'i Zuttermeister, Kaneohe, Hawaii: Hula master
1985	Meali'i Kalama, Honolulu, Hawaii: Hawaiian quilter Alice New Holy Blue Legs (Lakota Sioux), Oglala, South Dakota: Quill artist

1986   Helen Cordero (Cochiti Pueblo), Cochiti, New Mexico: Potter
        Joyce Doc Tate Nevaquaya (Comanche), Apache, Oklahoma: Flutist
        Jenny Thlunaut (Tlingit), Haines, Alaska: Chilkat blanket weaver

1989   Vanessa Paukeigope Morgan (Kiowa), Anadarko, Oklahoma: Regalia
        maker
        Chesley Goseyun Wilson (Apache), Tucson, Arizona: Fiddle maker

1990   Maude Kegg (Ojibwe), Onamia, Minnesota: Storyteller, craftsman
        Kevin Locke (Lakota), Mobridge, South Dakota: Flute player, singer,
        dancer

1991   George Blake (Hupa/Yurok), Hoopa, California: Native American
        craftsman
        Rose Frank (Nez Perce), Lapwai, Idaho: Native American cornhusk
        weaver
        Esther Littlefield (Tlingit), Sitka, Alaska: Regalia maker

1992   Walker Calhoun (Cherokee), Cherokee, North Carolina: Cherokee
        musician, dancer, teacher
        Belle Deacon (Athabascan), Grayling, Alaska: Basketmaker
        Gerald R. Hawpetoss (Menominee/Potawatomi), Milwaukee, Wisconsin:
        Regalia maker

1993   Nicholas and Elena Charles (Yup'ik), Bethel, Alaska: Woodcarvers, mask
        makers, skin sewers
        Nalani Kanaka'ole and Pualani Kanaka'ole Kanahel, Hilo, Hawaii: Hula
        masters
        Everett Kapayou (Mesquakie), Tama, Iowa: Native American singer

1994   Mary Mitchell Gabriel (Passamaquoddy), Princeton, Maine: Basket-
        maker
        Violet Hilbert (Skagit), Seattle, Washington: Storyteller

1995   Mary Holiday Black (Navajo), Mexican Hat, Utah: Basketweaver
        Nathan Jackson (Tlingit), Ketchikan, Alaska: Woodcarver, metalsmith,
        dancer
        Nellie Star Boy Menard (Lakota Sioux), Rosebud, South Dakota: Quilt
        maker

1996   Solomon and Richard Ho'opi'I, Pukalani and Wailuku, Hawaii: Hawaiian
        singers
        Eva McAdams (Shoshone), Fort Washakie, Wyoming: Regalia maker
        Dolly Spencer (Iñupiat), Homer, Alaska: Doll maker

1997   Georgia Harris (Catawba), Atlanta, Georgia: Potter

1998   Bruce Caesar (Sac and Fox/Pawnee/German), Anadarko, Oklahoma: Silversmith

Sophia George (Yakama/Colville), Gresham, Oregon: Beadworker

1999   Lila Greengrass Blackdeer (Ho-Chunk), Black River Falls, Wisconsin: Black ash basketmaker, needleworker

Ulysses Goode (Western Mono), North Fork, California: Basketmaker

Mary Louise Defender Wilson (Dakotah/Hidatsa), Shields, North Dakota: Traditionalist, storyteller

2000   Nettie Jackson (Klickitat), White Swan, Washington: Basketmaker

Genoa Keawe, Honolulu, Hawaii: Native Hawaiian singer, ukelele player

2001   Evalena Henry (Apache), Peridot, Arizona: Basketweaver

Fred Tsoodle (Kiowa), Mountain View, Oklahoma: Sacred song leader

2002   Loren Bommelyn (Tolowa), Crescent City, California: Tradition bearer

Rose Cree and Francis Cree (Ojibwe, Turtle Mountain), Dunseith, North Dakota: Basketmakers, storytellers

Clara Neptune Keezer (Passamaquoddy), Perry, Maine: Basketmaker

2003   Agnes "Oshanee" Kenmille (Salish), Ronan, Montana: Beadworker, regalia maker

2004   Gerald "Subiyay" Miller (Skokomish), Shelton, Washington: Tradition bearer, carver, basketmaker

2005   Grace Henderson Nez (Navajo), Ganado, Arizona: Weaver

James Ka'upena Wong, Waianae, Hawaii: Hawaiian chanter

2006   Delores Elizabeth Churchill (Haida), Ketchikan, Alaska: Cedar bark weaver

Esther Martinez (Tewa), Ohkay Owingeh, New Mexico: Tewa linguist, storyteller, teacher

George Na'ope, Hilo, Hawaii: Kumu Hula (hula master)

2007   Pat Courtney Gold (Wasco), Scappoose, Oregon: Wasco Sally bag weaver

Julia Parker (Kashia Pomo), Lee Vining, California: Basketmaker

2008   Horace P. Axtell (Nez Perce), Lewiston, Idaho: Drum maker, singer, tradition bearer

Oneida Hymn Singers of Wisconsin, Oneida, Wisconsin: Oneida hymn singers

2009   Teri Rofkar (Tlingit), Sitka, Alaska: Weaver and basketmaker

2010   Gladys Kukana Grace, Honolulu, Hawaii: Lauhala (palm leaf) weaver

2011   Ledward Kaapana, Kaneohe, Hawaii: Ukelele and slack key guitarist

Southwestern Association for Indian Arts (SWAIA) Lifetime Achievement Awards

Located in Santa Fe, New Mexico, the Southwestern Association for Indian Arts (SWAIA) established the Lifetime Achievement Award in 1995 to recognize artists whose body of work reflects a lifetime of integrity and excellence, artists who have made significant contributions to the work of American Indian art. The awards, some given posthumously, are presented at SWAIA's honoring reception, the event that officially opens Santa Fe Indian Market. In 2009, SWAIA joined with the Allan Houser Estate to present the "SWAIA Lifetime Achievement Allan Houser Legacy Award." (http://www.swaia.org/)

1995	Allan Houser (Chiricahua Apache) Maria Martinez (San Ildefonso Pueblo)
1996	Charles Loloma (Hopi) Margaret Tafoya (Santa Clara Pueblo)
1997	Pablita Velarde (Santa Clara Pueblo)
1998	Marie Zieu Chino (Acoma Pueblo) Helen Cordero (Cochiti Pueblo) Woody Crumbo (Potawatomi) Carl Gorman (Navajo)
1999	Kenneth Begay (Navajo) Fred Kabotie (Hopi) Julia Jumbo (Navajo) Nampeyo (Hopi) Patrick Swazo-Hinds (Tesuque Pueblo)
2001	Pop Chalee (Taos Pueblo) Lloyd Kiva New (Cherokee) Geronima Montoya (San Juan Pueblo) Rose Naranjo (Santa Clara Pueblo)
2002	Bob Chavez (Cochiti Pueblo) Julian Lovato (Santo Domingo Pueblo) Alex Seotewa (Zuni Pueblo) Lucy Whitehorse (Navajo)
2003	Harrison Begay (Navajo) Lucy Lewis (Acoma Pueblo) Matilda Thomas (Tohono O'Odham) Jose Rey Toledo (Jemez Pueblo)
2004	Ignacia Duran (Tesuque Pueblo) Dextra Quotskuyva (Hopi) Ramoncita Sandoval (San Juan Pueblo) Clara Sherman (Navajo)

2005   Lucy Lowden (Jemez Pueblo)
            Josephine Nahohai (Zuni Pueblo)
            Joe Sando (Jemez Pueblo)
            Fritz Scholder (Luiseño)
            Ruth Schultz (no affiliation listed)

2006   R. C. Gorman (Navajo)
            Lee Marmon (Laguna Pueblo)
            Grace Medicine Flower (Santa Clara/Pojoaque Pueblos)
            Joyce Growing Thunder Fogarty (Assiniboine Sioux)

2007   Michael Naranjo (Santa Clara Pueblo)
            Pearl Sunrise (Navajo)
            Harry Fonseca (Maidu/Hawaiian/Portuguese)
            Peter Garcia (Ohkay Owingeh)
            Lydia Pesata (Jicarilla Apache)

2008   Mary Cain (Santa Clara)
            Blue Corn (San Ildefonso)
            Mary Holiday Black (Navajo)
            Lawrence and Griselda Saufkie (Hopi)

2009   Lifetime Achievement Allan Houser Legacy Awards
            Sam English (Turtle Mountain Chippewa)
            Sofia Medina (Zia Pueblo)
            Oscar Howe (Yanktonai Dakota) (1915–83)

2010   Lifetime Achievement Allan Houser Legacy Awards
            Zuni Olla Maidens
            Family of Tonita and Juan Cruz Roybal (San Ildefonso Pueblo)
            Otellie Loloma (Hopi) (1922–93)
            N. Scott Momaday (Kiowa)

2011   Lifetime Achievement Allan Houser Legacy Awards
            Tonita Peña (San Ildefonso Pueblo)
            Popovi Da (San Ildefonso Pueblo)
            Joseph Lonewolf (Santa Clara Pueblo)

Five Places Named in Honor of Native American Artists

Blue Eagle Hall, Haskell Indian Nations University (HINU) Lawrence, Kansas
    Blue Eagle Hall, a business administration building on HINU'S campus in
    Lawrence, Kansas, is named for Acee Blue Eagle (1907–59), Creek/Pawnee artist.
    In 1934, he joined the Work Projects Administration (WPA) Public Works of Art
    Project, later accepting a teaching appointment at Bacone College in Oklahoma.
    Blue Eagle established the school's art department and became known for shaping
    what came to be called the Bacone style of painting. He was a prolific painter whose
    works included public murals and garnered widespread acclaim.

Angel DeCora Memorial Museum/Research Center, Little Priest Tribal College (LPTC), Winnebago, Nebraska

http://www.winnebagotribe.com/cultural_center.html

> Opened in 2002, the Angel DeCora Memorial Museum/Research Center, located at LPTC in Winnebago, Nebraska, is named in honor of illustrator, painter, and teacher Angel DeCora. DeCora (1869–1919), a member of the Winnebago Tribe of Nebraska, was one of the first Native American artists to gain acceptance in the mainstream art world. A graduate of Smith College in Massachusetts, she also studied with famed illustrator Howard Pyle. DeCora (also known by her married name, Dietz) served as the first teacher of American Indian art at the Carlisle Indian School in Pennsylvania.

C. N. Gorman Museum, University of California, Davis

http://gormanmuseum.ucdavis.edu/

> The C.N. Gorman Museum at the University of California, Davis (UCD) was founded in 1973 and later named in honor of Navajo artist Carl Nelson Gorman (1907–98). Gorman served in the U.S. Marines as a member of the Navajo code talkers, who transmitted military intelligence via code in their tribal language during World War II. His work at UCD included serving as a founding faculty member of Native American Studies and becoming the first faculty member to teach Native American art on that campus. Gorman was known as an innovator, using varied styles and media.

Allan Houser Art Park, Institute of American Indian Arts (IAIA), Santa Fe, New Mexico

http://www.iaia.edu/museum/about/galleries/

> Allan Houser Art Park at IAIA's Museum of Contemporary Native Arts in Santa Fe, New Mexico, was dedicated in 1993 to honor Allan Houser (1914–94), one of the most renowned artists of the twentieth century. Houser (Chiricahua Apache), part of the inaugural faculty at the newly established IAIA in 1962, created the school's sculpture department while continuing to produce artworks. He retired from teaching in 1975 to devote full time to his own work. During his career, he had nearly fifty solo exhibitions in museums and galleries in the United States, Europe, and Asia, and received numerous honors and awards. The Allan Houser Art Park provides a special place for participating artists to exhibit large-scale works.

Oscar Howe Gallery, University of South Dakota

http://www.oscarhowe.org/

> The Oscar Howe Gallery at the University of South Dakota (USD) is named in honor of Yanktonais Sioux artist, Oscar Howe (1915–83), who became internationally famous as an artist. His achievements include helping to define the Native American fine arts movement between the 1940s and 1960s. Howe had a twenty-six-year association with USD, the institution that now owns the largest single collection of his work. The Oscar Howe Memorial Association at USD, Vermillion, maintains a Web site devoted to the artist's life and work.

National Medal of Arts

Established by Congress in 1984, the National Medal of Arts is the highest award given to artists and arts patrons by the federal government. It is awarded by the president of the United States, who is authorized to award no more than twelve medals each year. This lifetime achievement award is given to individuals or groups who "are deserving of special recognition by reason of their outstanding contributions to the excellence, growth, support and availability of the arts in the United States." Since 1984, over 250 recipients in the fields of visual, performing, and literary arts have been honored, including these extraordinary Native American artists.

1992   Allan Houser (Chiricahua Apache), sculptor
1999   Maria Tallchief (Osage), ballerina
2007   N. Scott Momaday (Kiowa), author, essayist, poet, professor, painter

http://www.nea.gov/honors/medals/

LEGISLATION

Indian Arts and Crafts Legislation, 1935–2000

Indian Arts and Crafts Act of 1935
> This legislation created the Indian Arts and Crafts Board within the Department of the Interior to promote the economic welfare of Indian tribes through the development of Indian arts and crafts, as well as the expansion of the market for such products.

National Museum of the American Indian Act of 1989
> This legislation was enacted to establish the National Museum of the American Indian (NMAI) within the Smithsonian Institution as a living memorial to Native Americans and their traditions. The act also included provisions for the identification and repatriation of Indian human remains and Indian funerary objects in the Smithsonian's possession or control. The legislation was amended in 1996, extending the repatriation requirements to applicable sacred objects and objects of cultural patrimony.

Indian Arts and Crafts Act of 1990
> This legislation makes it unlawful to offer or display for sale or sell any good in a manner that falsely suggests it is American Indian–produced, an Indian product, or the product of a particular Indian or Indian tribe or Indian arts and crafts organization within the United States.

Indian Arts and Crafts Enforcement Act of 2000

Through this act, which amends the Indian Arts and Crafts Act of 1990, Congress sought to strengthen the cause of action for misrepresentation of Indian arts and crafts. It clarifies the definition of "Indian product" and provides specific examples of items that may be marketed as Indian products and those that may not.

BOOKS

Eight Books about Ledger Art

Ledger art, named for accounting ledger books that were a source of paper, is the term for Plains Indian narrative drawing or painting dating from the late nineteenth century. The genre represents a transition from hide painting, reflecting the loss of land and destruction of buffalo herds, as well as the establishment of reservations. With new art tools provided by government agents, traders, and military figures, ledger artists created art works that portrayed the rich cultural ways of their people and documented social and cultural changes underway. Today, artists such as Arthur Amiotte (Oglala Lakota) and Michael Horse (Yaqui/Mescalero Apache/Zuni) create contemporary works that incorporate and continue ledger art traditions in today's world.

1. *Art from Fort Marion*, by Joyce M. Szabo (2008).
2. *Cheyenne Dog Soldiers: A Ledgerbook History of Coups and Combat*, by Jean Afton, Richard N. Ellis, David Fridtjof Halaas, and Andrew E. Masich (2000).
3. *The Five Crows Ledger: Biographic Warrior Art of the Flathead Indians*, by James D. Keyser (2000).
4. *Howling Wolf and the History of Ledger Art*, by Joyce M. Szabo (1994).
5. *A Kiowa's Odyssey: A Sketchbook from Fort Marion*, edited by Phillip Earenfight (2007).
6. *Plains Indian Drawings, 1865–1935*, by Janet Catherine Berlo (1996).
7. *Silver Horn: Master Illustrator of the Kiowas*, by Candace S. Greene (2001).
8. *Warrior Artists: Historic Cheyenne and Kiowa Indian Ledger Art Drawn by Making Medicine and Zotom*, by Herman Viola (1998).

Sixteen Books about Native Artists

1. *Allan Houser: An American Master (Chiricahua Apache, 1914–1994)*, by W. Jackson Rushing III (2004).
2. *Arthur Amiotte Collages 1988–2006*, by Janet Catherine Berlo (2006).
3. *The Art of Dan Namingha*, by Thomas Hoving (2000).
4. *Born of Fire: The Life and Pottery of Margaret Tafoya*, by Charles S. King (2008).

5. *Child of the Fire: Edmonia Lewis and the Problem of Art History's Black and Indian Subject*, by Kirsten Pai Buick (2010).
6. *Fire Light: The Life of Angel De Cora, Winnebago Artist*, by Linda M. Waggoner (2008).
7. *Fritz Scholder: Indian/Not Indian*, edited by Lowery Stokes Sims (2008).
8. *Helen Cordero and the Storytellers of the Cochiti Pueblo*, by Nancy Howard (1995).
9. *The Legacy of a Master Potter: Nampeyo and Her Descendants*, by Mary Ellen Blair and Laurence R. Blair (1999).
10. *The Legacy of Maria Poveka Martinez*, by Richard L. Spivey (2003).
11. *Lucy M. Lewis: American Indian Potter*, by Susan Peterson (second edition, 2004).
12. *Lumhee Holot-Tee: The Art and Life of Acee Blue Eagle*, by Tamara Liegerot Elder (2006).
13. *Nampeyo and Her Pottery*, by Barbara Kramer (1996).
14. *Oscar Howe: Artist*, by Oscar Howe, John R. Milton, and John A. Day (second edition, 2004).
15. *T. C. Cannon: He Stood in the Sun*, by Joan Frederick (1995).
16. *Turning the Feather Around: My Life in Art*, by George Morrison, as told to Margot Fortunato Galt (1998).

FILMS

Aboriginal Architecture: Living Architecture (Canada, 2005, 65 min.), directed by Paul M. Rickard (Cree).

> This film explores the diversity of North American Native architecture, focusing on seven tribal communities to reveal how Native architects are reinterpreting traditional forms for contemporary purposes. The filmmaker focuses on Pueblo, Mohawk, Inuit, Crow, Navajo, Coast Salish, and Haida forms to discuss the renaissance of Native design.

Always Becoming Sculpture Project (USA, 2007, 17 min.), directed by Dax Thomas (Laguna/Acoma).

> This film centers on the work of Nora Naranjo-Morse (Santa Clara Pueblo), the first Native American woman to create an outdoor sculpture in Washington, DC. Named *Always Becoming*, it is located on the grounds of the National Museum of the American Indian. Naranjo-Morse discusses the artistic process involved with creating the sculpture.

Darren Vigil Gray: Counterclockwise (USA, 2002, 30 min.), directed by Vanessa Vassar.

> This film profiles Jicarilla Apache artist Darren Vigil Gray and his work.

Earl's Canoe (USA, 1999, 27 min.), directed by Thomas Vennum.

> Produced by the Smithsonian Institution, Office of Folklife Programs, this film portrays Ojibwe craftsman Earl Nyholm as he makes a birchbark canoe from start to finish on Madeline Island in Wisconsin.

Faithful to Continuance: Legacy of the Plateau People (USA, 2002, 58 min.), directed by David Schneiderman and Penny Phillips.

> This film explores Plateau culture through the eyes of contemporary artists Elaine Timentwa Emerson (Colville/Methow/Okanagan), Joe Fedderson (Colville/Okanagan), Pat Courtney Gold (Warm Springs/Wasco), Maynard White Owl-Lavadour (Umatilla/Cayuse/Nez Perce), Lillian Pitt (Warm Springs/Yakama/Wasco), and Elizabeth Woody (Warm Springs/Wasco/Navajo) and their work in various traditional and nontraditional media.

Fritz Scholder: Indian/Not Indian Exhibition Video (USA, 2008, 10 min.) directed by Daniel Davis.

> This film profiles artist Fritz Scholder (Luiseño) and serves as an introduction to a National Museum of the American Indian exhibition of the same name. Scholder (1937–2005) is known for his pathbreaking art, which helped to debunk popular clichés about American Indians.

From the Roots: California Indian Basketweavers (USA, 1996, 28 min.), directed by Sara Greensfelder.

> Produced for the California Indian Basketweavers Association, Native California weavers speak of the history and contemporary status of their art. They also address the challenges they face, including restricted access to plant gathering and environmental hazards in areas where plants are gathered.

James Luna: A Performance Rehearsal at the National Museum of the American Indian (USA, 2005, 10 min.).

> Produced by the National Museum of the American Indian, this film explores the work of performance artist James Luna (Luiseño), who shares perspectives about his approach and material as well as their relationship to audiences.

Mi'kmaq Baskets: The Tradition (Canada, 2003, 24 min.), directed by Brian J. Francis (Mi'kmaq) and Sam Grana. In English and Mi'kmaq with English subtitles.

> This film documents the art of Mi'kmaq basketry at the Waycobah First Nation in Nova Scotia. Basketmakers speak about their work in their native language and create baskets of split ash, quill, and birch bark.

A Return Home (2008, 31 min.), directed by Ramona D. Emerson (Navajo).

> The filmmaker explores the experience of her mother, B. Emerson Kitsman, a contemporary painter who has returned to her childhood home in the Navajo Nation. She addresses the meaning of home as well as what it means to be a Native artist.

Roxanne Swentzell (USA, 2005, 24 min.), directed by Alex Traube.

> This film, part of the *Living Portraits of New Mexico Artists and Writers* film series, profiles renowned sculptor Roxanne Swentzell (Santa Clara Pueblo). One of Swentzell's works, *For Life in All Directions*, appears at the National Museum of the American Indian in Washington, DC.

Unconquered: Allan Houser and the Legacy of One Apache Family (USA, 2009, 32 min.), directed by Bryan Beasley.

Narrated by actor Val Kilmer, this multi-award-winning documentary tells the story of painter and sculptor Allan Houser (Chiricahua Apache) and his family, addressing the unjust incarceration of their people, as well as the multigenerational creation of world-renowned art. The film is one part of an exhibition by the same name at the Oklahoma History Center.

Weaving Worlds (USA, 2008, 57 min.), directed by Bennie Klain (Navajo). In Navajo and English with English subtitles.

This film portrays Navajo rug weavers and explores their intricate relationships with reservation traders, presenting a portrait of economic and cultural survival through the art of weaving.

Welcome Home (USA, 2005, 13 min.), produced by the National Museum of the American Indian.

This film depicts the Native Nations procession and other events at the September 2004 grand opening of the National Museum of the American Indian in Washington, DC.

When the Season Is Good: Artists of Arctic Alaska (USA, 2005, 65 min.), directed by Andrew Okpeaha Maclean (Iñupiaq).

In this film, four contemporary Alaska Native artists from the Bering Sea and Arctic regions—an ivory carver, a skin sewer, a sculptor, and a painter—share their stories. They express the relationship of their art to culture, economics, and survival in some of the most remote areas of the world.

ORGANIZATIONS

Alaska Native Arts Foundation (ANAF)
http://alaskanativearts.org/

Founded in late 2002, the Alaska Native Arts Foundation (ANAF) is a nonprofit corporation that works to increase awareness about Alaska's Native people, cultures, and art forms. Headquartered in Anchorage, ANAF's objectives include improving the economic well-being of Alaska Native artists, invigorating training of the next generation of indigenous artists, and enhancing the success of Alaska Native artists.

American Indian Council of Architects and Engineers (AICAE)
http://www.aicae.org/

Established in 1976, the American Indian Council of Architects and Engineers is a nonprofit corporation whose members are American Indian architecture, engineering, and design professionals throughout the United States.

Council for Indigenous Arts and Culture (CIAC)
http://www.ciaccouncil.org

Incorporated in 1998, the Council for Indigenous Arts and Culture is a nonprofit organization established to foster, develop, and contribute to the support and understanding of authentic Native American Arts. CIAC has two offices, a midwestern office located in Hobart, Indiana, and a western office in Zuni, New Mexico.

Crow's Shadow Institute of the Arts (CSIA)
http://www.crowsshadow.org

Incorporated as a nonprofit organization in 1992, Crow's Shadow Institute of the Arts provides opportunities for Native Americans through artistic development, emphasizes fine art printmaking, and offers other professional and educational services. The facility is located in St. Andrew's Mission School on the Umatilla Reservation near Pendleton, Oregon.

ECHO: Education through Cultural and Historical Organizations
http://www.echospace.org/

ECHO was launched in 2001 as a joint project of Peabody Essex Museum in Salem, Massachusetts; the Alaska Native Heritage Center in Anchorage, Alaska; the Iñupiat Heritage Center in Barrow, Alaska; the Bishop Museum in Honolulu, Hawaii; the New Bedford Oceanarium and New Bedford Whaling Museum in New Bedford, Massachusetts; and the Mississippi Band of Choctaw Indians. The nonprofit organization provides educational programs and resources, technology training, and student internships; shares museum collections; and organizes a performing arts festival.

First Peoples Fund
http://www.firstpeoplesfund.org/

Founded in 1995, the mission of First Peoples Fund is to honor and support creative community-centered Native artists and to nurture the collective spirit that allows them to sustain their people. Based in Rapid City, South Dakota, the fund works to provide support and voice to artists nationwide who share their inspiration, wisdom, knowledge, and gifts with their communities.

Indian Arts and Crafts Association (IACA)
www.iaca.com

Established in 1974 and based in Albuquerque, New Mexico, the mission of the Indian Arts and Crafts Association is to promote, preserve, and protect authentic American Indian arts and Crafts. The association has grown to become an international organization representing American Indian arts, including Native artists, consumers, retailers, wholesalers, museums, government agencies, suppliers, and supporting members.

Inuit Art Foundation (IAF)
http://www.inuitart.org/

Located in Ottawa, Ontario, Canada, the Inuit Art Foundation began with the launch of *Inuit Art Quarterly* (AIQ) magazine in 1986, "the only magazine in the world dedicated to Inuit art," promoting the work of Inuit artists worldwide. The IAF, which is owned and governed by Inuit artists and northern cultural workers, was formally incorporated in 1989 as the first aboriginal arts service organization in Canada.

National Association of Tribal Historic Preservation Officers (NATHPO)
http://www.nathpo.org/
Founded in 1998, the National Association of Tribal Historic Preservation Officers is a nonprofit membership organization of tribal government officials who implement federal and tribal preservation laws. NATHPO's main office is in Washington, DC, where its activities include monitoring the U.S. Congress, administration, and state activities on issues that affect all tribes.

Native Arts and Cultures Foundation (NACF)
http://www.nativeartsandcultures.org
Launched in 2009 and based in Portland, Oregon, the Native Arts and Cultures Foundation is the first permanently endowed national foundation dedicated to promoting the revitalization, appreciation, and perpetuation of Native arts and cultures. The foundation's mission includes supporting the diversity of artistic expression in American Indian, Alaska Native, and Native Hawaiian communities.

Native Women in the Arts (NWIA)
http://www.nativewomeninthearts.com/
Established in 1993, Native Women in the Arts is a nonprofit organization for First Nations, Inuit, and Métis women from diverse artistic disciplines who share a common interest in culture, art, community, and the advancement of indigenous peoples. The Toronto-based organization produces artistic programming while developing, supporting, and cultivating Aboriginal women in the performing arts, literary arts and publishing, visual arts, and community development projects.

Southwestern Association for Indian Arts (SWAIA)
http://swaia.org/
The mission of the Southwestern Association for Indian Arts is to be an advocate for Native American arts and cultures, especially those in the Southwest, and to create economic and cultural opportunities for artists. Its activities include producing and promoting the annual Santa Fe Indian Market, bestowing a Lifetime Achievement Award each year, sponsoring business training seminars, and developing other programs and events that support, promote, and honor Native artists.

UNRESERVED American Indian Fashion and Art Alliance
http://www.unreservedalliance.org/
Founded in 2009 by American Indian entrepreneurs and leaders from the international worlds of fashion and art, UNRESERVED was established to

foster educational, economic, and sustainable opportunities while creating global awareness about Native talent. The organization, which is headquartered in New York City, works to advance the visions and voices of Native American apparel designers and artists.

RESOURCES

Abbott, Lawrence, ed. *I Stand in the Center of the Good: Interviews with Contemporary Native American Artists.* Lincoln: University of Nebraska Press, 1994.

Archuleta, Margaret, and Rennard Strickland, eds. *Shared Visions: Native American Painters and Sculptors in the Twentieth Century.* New York: The New Press, 1993.

Broder, Patricia Janis. *Earth Songs, Moon Dreams: Paintings by American Indian Women.* New York: St. Martin's Press, 1999.

Cazimero, Momi, et al. *Na Maka Hou: New Visions, Contemporary Native Hawaiian Art.* Honolulu Academy of Arts, 2001.

Chalker, Kari. *Totems to Turquoise: Native North American Jewelry Arts of the Northwest and Southwest.* New York: Harry N. Abrams, 2004.

Congdon-Martin, Douglas. *Storytellers and Other Figurative Pottery.* Atglen, PA: Schiffer Publishing, 1990.

Cummings, Denise K., ed. *Visualities: Perspectives on Contemporary American Indian Film and Art.* East Lansing: Michigan State University Press, 2011.

Dubin, Lois Sherr. *Grand Procession: Contemporary Artistic Visions of American Indians.* Denver: Denver Art Museum, 2011.

Everett, Deborah, and Elayne L. Zorn. *Encyclopedia of Native American Artists.* Westport, CT: Greenwood Press, 2008.

Hill, Rick, ed. *Creativity Is Our Tradition: Three Decades of Contemporary Indian Art at the Institute of American Indian Arts.* Santa Fe: Institute of American Indian and Alaska Native Culture and Arts Development, 1992.

Hutchinson, Elizabeth. *The Indian Craze: Primitivism, Modernism, and Transculturation in American Art, 1890–1915.* Durham, NC: Duke University Press, 2009.

Kalahele, Imaikalani. *Kalahele: Poetry and Art.* Honolulu: Kalamaku Press, 2002.

Kamehiro, Stacy L. *The Arts of Kingship: Hawaiian Art and National Culture of the Kalakaua Era.* Honolulu: University of Hawaii Press, 2009.

Krinsky, Carol Herselle. *Contemporary Native American Architecture: Cultural Regeneration and Creativity.* New York: Oxford University Press, 1996.

Lester, Patrick D. *Biographical Directory of Native American Painters.* Norman: University of Oklahoma Press, 1995.

Lippard, Lucy R., ed. *Partial Recall, with Essays on Photographs of Native North Americans.* New York: The New Press, 1992.

McFadden, David, and Ellen N. Taubman. *Changing Hands: Art Without Reservation.* Vol. 1, *Contemporary Native American Art from the Southwest.* Vol. 2, *Contemporary Native Art from the West, Northwest and Pacific.* New York: Museum of Arts and Design, 2002, 2005.

McLerran, Jennifer. *A New Deal for Native Art: Indian Arts and Federal Policy, 1933–1943.* Tucson: University of Arizona Press, 2009.

McMaster, Gerald, and Clifford E. Trafzer, eds. *Native Universe: Voices of Indian America.* Washington, DC: National Museum of the American Indian, Smithsonian Institution/ National Geographic, 2004.

Rader, Dean. *Engaged Resistance: American Indian Art, Literature, and Film from Alcatraz to the NMAI.* Austin: University of Texas Press, 2011.

Roalf, Peggy, ed. *Strong Hearts: Native American Visions and Voices.* New York: Aperture Foundation, 1995.

Rushing, W. Jackson III. *Native American Art in the Twentieth Century: Makers, Meanings, Histories.* New York: Routledge, 1999.

Wood, Margaret. *Native American Fashion: Modern Adaptations of Traditional Designs.* 2nd ed. Phoenix, AZ: Native American Fashions, 1997 (originally published in 1981).

Magazines and Journals

American Indian Art magazine: http://www.aiamagazine.com/

American Indian magazine, National Museum of the American Indian: http://www.nmai .si.edu/subpage.cfm?subpage=support&second=membership&third=magazine

Inuit Art Quarterly: http://www.inuitart.org/magazine/

Native Peoples magazine: http://www.nativepeoples.com/

'Ōiwi: A Native Hawaiian Journal: http://www.hawaii.edu/oiwi

SNAG (Seventh Native American Generation) magazine: http://www.snagmagazine.com

Web Sites

American Indian Art Dealers Directory: http://www.american-indian-art-dealers-directory .com/

Antique Tribal Art Dealers Association: http://www.atada.org/

Arctic Studies Center: http://www.mnh.si.edu/arctic/

Harvard Project's Honoring Nations Directory of Honored Programs, 1999–2006: http:// hpaied.org/images/resources /general/Dir_web.pdf

The Indian Craft Shop, Department of the Interior: http://www.indiancraftshop.com/

Jessica R. Metcalfe (Turtle Mountain Chippewa). Beyond Buckskin: About Native American Fashion: http://beyondbuckskin.blogspot.com/

National Association of Tribal Historic Preservation Officers (NATHPO). Tribal Museums and Cultural Centers: http://tribalmuseums.org/museum.html

The Native American Artists Resource Collection at the Billie Jane Baguley Library and Archives of the Heard Museum in Phoenix, Arizona: http://www.heard.org/library/ artistsresources.html

Native Art Network: http://www.nativeart.net/

Native Treasures Indian Arts Festival: http://www.nativetreasuressantafe.org/

Native Web Resources: http://www.nativeweb.org/resources/art_artisans_galleries/clothing_ textiles/

Plains Indian Ledger Art: https://plainsledgerart.org/

Pow Wow Network: http://www.powwownetwork.com/

16

Literary and Spoken Arts

FIRSTS

1663	Caleb Cheeshahteaumuck (Wampanoag) wrote one of the first known pieces of writing by a Native North American. He wrote *Honoratissimi Benefactores* in Latin while attending Harvard's Indian College.
1772	Samson Occom (Mohegan) probably wrote the first book published in English by an American Indian. He wrote *A Sermon Preached at the Execution of Moses Paul, an Indian*. It was so popular that it was reprinted at least nineteen times and translated into Welsh in 1827.
1794	Hendrick Aupaumut (Mahican) wrote *A Short Narration of My Last Journey to the Western Country* about his work as government liaison to American Indian tribes of the frontier West. His work, published in 1827, was the first official report by a Native American person reporting on other Native peoples.
ca. 1815	Jane Johnston Schoolcraft (Ojibwe) has been recognized as the first Native American literary writer, the first known Indian woman writer, the first known Indian poet, the first known poet to write poems in a Native American language, and the first known American Indian to write out traditional Indian stories.
ca. 1827	David Cusick (Tuscarora) was the first person of his tribe to record ancient tribal stories and one of the first Native people to preserve information about tribal social and cultural customs. He also was the first Native to use Western pictorial art to interpret Iroquoian spirituality.
1829	William Apess (Pequot) wrote the first full-length Native American autobiography, *A Son of the Forest*. He was one of the most prolific nineteenth-century Native American writers.

1847	George Copway (Ojibway) published the first full-length travelogue by a Native person, *The Life, History, and Travels of Kah-ge-ga-gah-bowh*. By 1848, it was reprinted seven times. Copway has been credited with becoming Canada's first Native literary celebrity to become prominent in the United States.
1854	John Rollin Ridge/Yellow Bird (Cherokee) published the first novel by a Native person, *The Life and Adventures of Joaquin Murieta*. In 1868, his poetry was published posthumously in what is believed to be the first book-length collection of poetry by a Native.
1881	Susette LaFlesche (Omaha), writing under the name "Bright Eyes," published "Nedawi" in *St. Nicholas*, a children's magazine. It is believed to be the first non-legend short story written by a Native person.
1883	Sarah Winnemucca Hopkins (Paiute) published *Life Among the Piutes: Their Wrongs and Claims*, the first autobiography written by a Native American woman. In 1884, she established the first all-Indian school, the Peabody School for Indian Children, in Lovelock, Nevada, which lasted four years.
1891	Sophia Alice Callahan (Creek) wrote the first novel by a Native woman. *Wynema: A Child of the Forest*, a fictional account of the murder of Sitting Bull and the Wounded Knee massacre.
1899	Simon Pokagon (Potawatomi) wrote *Queen of the Woods*, believed to be the first novel about Indian life by an American Indian. The plot deals with a man's return to his tribal culture after years of living among non-Indians.
1927	Mourning Dove/Christine Quintasket (Colville) wrote *Cogewea: The Half-Blood*, considered the first novel published by a Native American woman in the twentieth century. She depicted the Montana cattle range.
1969	N. Scott Momaday (Kiowa) became the first (and only, to date) Native American to win the Pulitzer Prize for Fiction for his novel, *House Made of Dawn*. In 1989, he was the first literary artist to receive the Jay Silverheels Achievement Award from the National Center for American Indian Enterprise.
1981	Leslie Marmon Silko (Laguna Pueblo) received a MacArthur "Genius" Foundation Award, the first Native American to receive the award. In 2000, she received a Lannan Literary Award for Fiction. Silko has authored notable works including *Ceremony* and *Almanac of the Dead*.

1992	The first North American Native writers festivals, "Returning the Gift," took place in Norman, Oklahoma, in 1992.
1994	*Light in the Crevice Never Seen*, by Haunani-Kay Trask, was the first book of poetry by an indigenous Hawaiian to be published in North America.
1998	*'Ōiwi: A Native Hawaiian Journal* became the first journal dedicated to the literary and artistic expressions of Native Hawaiians. Founded by D. Mahealani Dudoit, *'Ōiwi* is located in Honolulu, Hawaii.
2006	For the first time in its 131-year history, the prestigious American Library Association (ALA) elected a Native woman as its president: Loriene Roy (White Earth Chippewa). Passionate about literacy for Native American children long before she became ALA president, she founded "If I Can Read, I Can Do Anything," a national reading club for Native children, in 2000.
2010	Linda Hogan (Chickasaw) was nominated for the position of U.S. Poet Laureate, believed to be the first Native American to receive this honor.

Returning the Gift Writers' Festival

"Returning the Gift," the first North American Native Writers' Festival, took place in Norman, Oklahoma, in 1992. An unprecedented gathering of over three hundred Native writers from the United States (including Hawaii), Canada, Mexico, and Central America, the four-day festival brought more Native writers together in one place than at any other time in history. "Returning the Gift" co-organizer Joseph Bruchac (Abenaki) observed that the festival "both demonstrated and validated our literature and our devotion to it, not just to the public, but to ourselves" (Bruchac 1994, xxi). An observation by Chief Tom Porter (Mohawk Nation) led to the name for the 1992 gathering, and the ones that followed. He said that Native writers were "actually returning the gift—the gift of storytelling, culture, and continuance—to the people, the source from whence it had come" (Bruchac 1994, xxv). Returning the Gift festivals, sponsored by Wordcraft Circle and Native Writers' Circle of the Americas, have taken place in many locations from coast to coast since the first gathering in 1992.

In 1994, the University of Arizona published *Returning the Gift: Poetry and Prose from the First North American Native Writers' Festival*. The anthology, which includes works from around the continent, represented a wide range of tribal affiliations, languages, and cultures.

NATIVE AMERICAN WRITERS
AND STORYTELLERS

Fifteen American Indian Novelists, 1854–1974

1. Denton R. Bedford (Minsee): *Tsali*, 1972
2. Sophia Alice Callahan (Creek): *Wynema, a Child of the Forest*, 1891
3. Dallas Chief Eagle (Lakota): *Winter Count*, 1967
4. Ella Cara Deloria (Dakota): *Waterlily*, written in the 1940s, published in 1988
5. Janet Campbell Hale (Coeur d'Alene): *The Owl's Song*, 1974
6. John Joseph Mathews (Osage): *Sundown*, 1934
7. D'Arcy McNickle (Salish Kootenai): *The Surrounded*, 1936; *Runner in the Sun: A Story of Indian Maize*, 1954
8. N. Scott Momaday (Kiowa): *House Made of Dawn*, 1968
9. Mourning Dove, also known as Humishuma and Christine Quintasket (Colville): *Cogewea: The Half-Blood*, 1927
10. John Milton Oskison (Cherokee): *Black Jack Davy*, 1926; *Brothers Three*, 1935; *The Singing Bird*, written before 1947; *Wild Harvest: A Novel of Transition Days in Oklahoma*, 1925
11. Chief George Pierre (Colville): *Autumn's Bounty*, 1972
12. Chief Simon Pokagon (Potawatomi): *O-Gî-Mäw-Kwe Mit-I-Gwä-Kî (Queen of the Woods)*, 1899
13. John Rollin Ridge/Yellow Bird (Cherokee): *The Life and Adventures of Joaquin Murieta: The Celebrated California Bandit*, 1854
14. John Tebbel (Ojibwa): *The Conqueror*, 1951
15. James Welch (Blackfeet/Gros Ventre): *Winter in the Blood*, 1974

Eleven Native American Writers of Mysteries and Thrillers

1. Sherman Alexie (Spokane/Coeur d'Alene)
   http://www.fallsapart.com
2. A. A. (Aaron Albert) Carr (Navajo/Laguna Pueblo)
   http://www.nativewiki.org/Aaron_Albert_Carr
3. Robert Conley (Cherokee)
   http://www.nativewiki.org/Robert_J._Conley
4. George Todd Downing (Choctaw)
   http://digital.library.okstate.edu/encyclopedia/entries/D/DO013.html
5. Jean Hager (Cherokee)
   http://www.fantasticfiction.co.uk/h/jean-hager
6. Sara Sue Hoklotubbe (Cherokee)
   http://www.hoklotubbe.com
7. Thomas King (Cherokee)
   http://www.nativewiki.org/Thomas_King

8. Carole LaFavor (Ojibwe)
   http://en.wikipedia.org/wiki/Carole_LaFavor
9. Mardi Oakley Medawar (Cherokee)
   http://www.ipl.org/div/natam/bin/browse.pl/A498
10. Louis Owens (Mississippi Choctaw/Oklahoma Cherokee)
    http://www.ipl.org/div/natam/bin/browse.pl/A73
11. Ron Querry (Choctaw)
    http://www.ipl.org/div/natam/bin/browse.pl/A81

Seven Native American State Poet Laureates

1. Jim Weaver McKown Barnes (Choctaw): Oklahoma State Poet Laureate, 2009–11
2. Louise Erdrich (Chippewa): North Dakota Associate Poet Laureate, 2005
3. Maggie Culver Fry (Cherokee): Oklahoma State Poet Laureate, 1977–95
4. Denise Low (Delaware/Cherokee): Kansas Poet Laureate, 2007–9
5. N. Scott Momaday (Kiowa): Oklahoma Centennial State Poet Laureate, 2007–9
6. Henry Real Bird (Crow): Montana Poet Laureate, 2009–11
7. Denise Sweet (Anishinabe/Ojibwe): Wisconsin Poet Laureate, 2004–8

Twelve Native American Authors of Children's Literature

The following Native American authors write fiction, historical fiction, poetry, and stories for children about Native people, places, histories, and cultures.

1. Joseph Bruchac (Abenaki)
2. Yvonne Dennis (Cherokee)
3. Louise Erdrich (Chippewa)
4. Joy Harjo (Creek)
5. George Littlechild (Muscogee Creek)
6. N. Scott Momaday (Kiowa)
7. Joel Monture (Mohawk)
8. Simon J. Ortiz (Acoma Pueblo)
9. Cynthia Leitich Smith (Muscogee Creek)
10. Virginia Driving Hawk Sneve (Lakota)
11. Luci Tapahonso (Navajo)
12. Tim Tingle (Oklahoma Choctaw)

Eleven Native American Contemporary Storytellers

1. M. Cochise Anderson (Chickasaw/Choctaw)
   http://aboriginalpeopleschoice.com/artists/cochise

2. Rosella Archdale (Lakota/Dakota)
   http://www.pbs.org/circleofstories/storytellers/rosella_archdale.html
3. Lloyd Arneach (Eastern Band of Cherokee)
   http://www.arneach.com
4. Hoskie Benally (Diné/Navajo)
   http://www.pbs.org/circleofstories/storytellers/hoskie_benally.html
5. Joseph Bruchac (Abenaki)
   http://www.josephbruchac.com
6. Donna Couteau (Sac and Fox)
   http://leafarrow.tripod.com
7. Joe Cross (Caddo)
   http://leafarrow.tripod.com
8. Geri Keams (Navajo)
   http://gerikeams.com
9. Henry Real Bird (Crow)
   http://www.worldofpoetry.org/usop/land.htm
10. Gene Tagaband (Tlingit/Cherokee)
    http://www.genetagaban.com
11. Tchin (Narragansett/Blackfeet)
    http://www.pbs.org/circleofstories/storytellers/tchin.html

Six Anthologies of Interviews and Autobiographical Essays by Native Writers

1. *Here First: Autobiographical Essays by Native American Writers*, edited by Arnold Krupat and Brian Swann (2000).
2. *I Tell You Now: Autobiographical Essays by Native American Writers*, edited by Brian Swann and Arnold Krupat (1987).
3. *Speaking for the Generations: Native Writers on Writing*, edited by Simon Ortiz (1998).
4. *Survival This Way: Interviews with American Indian Poets*, edited by Joseph Bruchac (1987).
5. *This Is about Vision: Interviews with Southwestern Writers*, edited by John F. Crawford, William Balassi, and Annie O. Eysturoy (1990).
6. *Winged Words: American Indian Writers Speak*, edited by Laura Coltelli (1990).

Seventeen Anthologies of Contemporary Native American Poetry and Storytelling

1. *Blue Dawn, Red Earth: New Native American Storytellers*, edited by Clifford E. Trafzer (1996).
2. *Carriers of the Dream Wheel: Contemporary Native American Poetry*, edited by Duane Niatum (1975).

3. *Changing Is Not Vanishing: A Collection of American Indian Poetry to 1930*, by Robert Dale Parker (2010).
4. *A Gathering of Spirit: A Collection by North American Indian Women*, edited by Beth Brant (1988).
5. *Harper's Anthology of 20th Century Native American Poetry*, edited by Duane Niatum (1988).
6. *The Man to Send Rain Clouds: Contemporary Stories by American Indians*, edited by Kenneth Rosen (1974).
7. *Native American Writing in the Southeast: An Anthology, 1875–1935*, edited by Daniel F. Littlefield Jr. and James Parins (1995).
8. *Neon Pow-Wow: New Native American Voices of the Southwest*, edited by Anna Lee Walters (1993).
9. *New and Old Voices of Wah'Kon-Tah: Contemporary Native American Poetry*, edited by Robert K. Dodge and Joseph B. McCullough (1987).
10. *New Voices from the Longhouse: An Anthology of Contemporary Iroquois Writing*, edited by Joseph Bruchac (1989).
11. *Reinventing the Enemy's Language: Contemporary Native American Women's Writings of North America*, edited by Joy Harjo and Gloria Bird (1997).
12. *The Remembered Earth: An Anthology of Contemporary Native American Literature*, edited by Geary Hobson (1979).
13. *Returning the Gift: Poetry and Prose from the First North American Native Writers' Festival*, edited by Joseph Bruchac (1994).
14. *Stories Migrating Home: A Collection of Anishinaabe Prose*, edited by Kimberly Blaeser (1999).
15. *Talking Leaves: Contemporary Native American Short Stories: An Anthology*, edited by Craig Lesley (1991).
16. *That's What She Said: Contemporary Poetry and Fiction by Native American Women*, edited by Rayna Green (1984).
17. *Voice of the Turtle: American Indian Literature 1900–1970*, edited by Paula Gunn Allen (1994).

Books of Poems and Stories by Young Native Americans

1. *Night Is Gone, Day Is Still Coming: Stories and Poems by American Indian Teens and Young Adults*, edited by Annette Piña Ochoa, Betsy Franco, and Traci L. Gourdine (2003).
2. *A Rainbow at Night: The World in Words and Pictures by Navajo Children*, edited by Bruce Hucko (1996).
3. *Rising Voices: The Writings of Young Native Americans*, edited by Arlene Hirschfelder and Beverly Singer (1992).
4. *When the Rain Sing: Poems by Young Native Americans*, edited by the National Museum of the American Indian (1999).

Oral Tradition

The oral tradition, a rich source of knowledge in tribal cultures today, is a body of history, stories, prayers, and other works that Native people have preserved and transmitted orally for countless generations. Spoken works such as religious texts, songs, chants, speeches, ritual, oratory, laws, dramas, and ancient stories have been recited from memory in the languages of Native peoples. Some accounts may only be told under certain circumstances, such as at a specific time of the year, or by particular speakers, such as qualified religious practitioners who require rigorous, extensive, and specialized training. Some stories owned by specific families or clans can only told by those who inherit the right to tell them.

The oral tradition requires close attention to and respect for words and respect for speakers and storytellers. The tradition requires extensive memorization. Texts can range in length from short stories to lengthy accounts told over several days. Native people admire gifted individuals who can deliver a good story and value the skills necessary to communicate through spoken words.

Although European conquest either destroyed or endangered many indigenous languages, the body of oral works that survived is rich and continues to play an essential role in revitalizing and preserving Native cultures. Some of the oral knowledge survived intact in tribal languages, including stories that are retold today essentially the same way as they were hundreds of years ago. Other oral accounts continue to be transmitted, but altered through the use of English or other European languages. New knowledge may be added, reflecting changed circumstances and interactions with Euro-Americans and other groups.

AWARDS

American Book Awards for Fiction and Memoir, 1980–2010

The American Book Awards, established in 1978 by the Before Columbus Foundation, recognize outstanding literary achievement from the entire spectrum of America's diverse literary community.

1980	*Ceremony,* by Leslie Silko (Laguna Pueblo)
1981	*Back Then Tomorrow,* by Peter Blue Cloud (Mohawk)
1982	*Songs for the Harvester of Dreams,* by Duane Niatum (Klallam)
1983	No listing
1984	*The Mama Poems,* by Maurice Kenny (Mohawk)
1985	*Love Medicine,* by Louise Erdrich (Turtle Mountain Chippewa)

1986   *Seeing Through the Sun*, by Linda Hogan (Chickasaw)
   The Sun Is Not Merciful, by Anna Lee Walters (Navajo)

1987   *Fools Crow*, by James Welch (Blackfeet)

1988   *Griever: An American Monkey King in China*, by Gerald Vizenor (Chippewa)

1990   *Spider Woman's Granddaughter: Traditional Tales and Contemporary Writing by Native American Women*, by Paula Gunn Allen (Laguna Pueblo/Sioux)
   Hand into Stone, by Elizabeth A. Woody (Navajo/Wasco)

1991   *Lakota Woman*, by Mary Crow Dog (Lakota), with Richard Erdoes
   Haa Tuwunaagu Yis, for Healing Our Spirit: Tlingit Oratory, edited by Nora Marks Dauenhauer (Tlingit) and Richard Dauenhauer
   In Mad Love and War, by Joy Harjo (Muscogee Creek)

1992   *To the American Indian: Reminiscences of a Yurok Woman*, by Lucy Thompson (Che-ne-wah Weitch-ah-wah) (Yurok)

1993   *Claiming Breath*, by Diane Glancy (Cherokee)

1994   *Bloodlines: Odyssey of a Native Daughter*, by Janet Campbell Hale (Coeur d'Alene)

1995   *The Light People*, by Gordon Henry Jr. (Chippewa)

1996   *Reservation Blues*, by Sherman Alexie (Spokane/Coeur d'Alene)

1997   *Nightland*, by Louis Owen (Choctaw/Cherokee)

1998   *On Native Ground: Memoirs and Impressions*, by Jim Barnes (Choctaw)
   Dog Road Woman, by Allison Adelle Hedge Coke (Huron/Cherokee)

1999   *Survivor's Medicine*, by E. Donald Two-Rivers (Ojibwe)
   Home to Medicine Mountain (children's book), by Chiori Santiago and Judith Lowry (Mountain Maidu/Hamawi Pit-River)

2000   *Year in Nam: A Native American Soldier's Story*, by Leroy TeCube (Jicarilla Apache)

2001   *The Island of Lost Luggage*, by Janet McAdams (Creek/Irish/Scottish)

2002   *Shell Shaker*, by LeAnne Howe (Choctaw)

2003   *Perma Red*, by Debra Magpie Earling (Salish and Kootenai)
   Raising Ourselves: A Gwich'in Coming of Age Story from the Yukon River, by Velma Wallis (Athabascan)

2005	*The Red Cedar of Afognak: A Driftwood Journey* (children's book), by Alisha S. Drabek (Alutiiq) and Karen R. Adams
2007	*Blonde Indian: An Alaska Native Memoir*, by Ernestine Hayes (Tlingit)
2008	*Anóoshi Lingít Aaní Ká: Russians in Tlingit America, the Battles of Sitka 1802 and 1804*, edited by Nora Marks Dauenhauer, Richard Dauenhauer, and Lydia Black
2010	*Flood Song*, by Sherwin Bitsui (Navajo)
2011	*Shrouds of White Earth*, by Gerald Vizenor (White Earth Chippewa) *Extra Indians*, by Eric Gansworth (Onondaga Nation)

Native Writers' Circle of the Americas Lifetime Achievement Awards, 1992–2011

One of three categories of literary awards given by the Native Writers' Circle of the Americas. The awards are voted upon by Native American writers, making them among the few literary awards presented to Native Americans by Native Americans.

1992	N. Scott Momaday (Kiowa)
1993	Simon J. Ortiz (Acoma Pueblo)
1994	Leslie Marmon Silko (Laguna Pueblo)
1995	Joy Harjo (Muscogee Creek)
1996	Vine Deloria Jr. (Dakota)
1997	James Welch (Blackfeet)
1998	Linda Hogan (Chickasaw)
1999	Joseph Bruchac (Abenaki)
2000	Louise Erdrich (Turtle Mountain Chippewa)
2001	Gerald Vizenor (Chippewa) and Paula Gunn Allen (Laguna Pueblo/Sioux)
2002	Maurice Kenny (Mohawk)
2003	Geary Hobson (Cherokee/Quapaw/Chickasaw)
2004	Lee Francis III (Laguna Pueblo)
2005	Carter Revard (Osage)
2006	Luci Tapahonso (Navajo)
2007	Robert J. Conley (Cherokee)

2008   Jack D. Forbes (Powhatan/Delaware)

2009   Elizabeth Cook-Lynn (Dakota)

2010   Sherman Alexie (Spokane/Coeur d'Alene)

2011   Wilma Mankiller (Cherokee)

*Native Writers' Circle of the Americas First
Book Awards for Prose, 1992–2009*

One of three categories of literary awards given by the Native Writers' Circle of the Americas. The awards are voted upon by Native American writers, making them some of the few literary awards presented to Native Americans by Native Americans.

1992   *Stacey's Story,* by Robert L. Perea (Pine Ridge Sioux)
            The Lasting of the Mohegans, by Melissa Tantaqudeon Zobel (Melissa Jane Fawcett) (Mohegan)
            "The Star Quilter" in *Where the Pavement Ends,* by William S. Yellow Robe Jr. (Assiniboine)

1993   *Red Earth,* by Philip H. Red Eagle (Sioux/Klallam)

1994   *Calling through the Creek,* by Gus Palmer (Kiowa)

1995   *Boston Mountain Tales,* by Glenn J. Twist (Cherokee/Creek)

1997   *Life with the Little People,* by Robert J. Perry (Chickasaw)
            The Oklahoma Basic Intelligence Test, by D. L. Birchfield (Choctaw/Chickasaw)

1999   *Night Sky, Morning Star,* by Evalina Zini Lucero (Isleta/San Juan Pueblo)

2000   *Naming Ceremony,* by Chip Livingston (Florida Creek)

2001   *Naturally Native,* by Valerie Red Horse (Cherokee)

2002   *An Inquest Every Sunday,* by Edythe S. Hobson (Arkansas Quapaw)

2003   *The Power of a Name,* by Susan Supernaw (Creek/Munsee)

2004   *Back to the Blanket: Reading, Writing, and Resistance for American Indian Literary Critics,* by Kimberly G. Roppolo (Cherokee/Choctaw/Creek)

2005   *Tundra Berries,* by Mia Heavener (Central Yup'ik)

2006   *Yellowbird,* by Judy R. Smith (Quinnipiac/Mohican)
            Welcome to the City of Rainbows, by Frederick White (Haida)

2007   *Attugu Summa/Come and See What It Is*, by Mary Lockwood (Malemuit/Inupiaq)

2009   *Te Ata and Other Plays*, by JudyLee Oliva (Chickasaw)

Native Writers' Circle of the Americas First Book Awards for Poetry, 1992–2009

One of three categories of literary awards given by the Native Writers' Circle of the Americas. The awards are voted upon by Native American writers, making them some of the few literary awards presented to Native Americans by Native Americans.

1992   *Full Moon on the Reservation*, by Gloria Bird (Spokane)
        Leaving Holes, by Joe Dale Tate Nevaquaya (Yuchi/Comanche)

1993   *Trailing You*, by Kimberly Blaeser (White Earth Chippewa)

1994   *Outlaws, Renegades and Saints*, by Tiffany Midge (Standing Rock Sioux)

1995   *Songs for Discharming*, by Denise Sweet (White Earth Chippewa)

1996   *Winter Count Poems*, by Charles G. Ballard (Quapaw/Cherokee)

1997   *Indian Cartography*, by Deborah A. Miranda (Costanoan/Esselen/Ohlone)

1998   *What I Keep*, by Jennifer K. Greene (Salish/Kootenai/Chippewa/Cree)

1999   *The Island of Lost Luggage*, by Janet McAdams (Alabama Creek)

2000   *Markings on Earth*, by Karenne Wood (Monacan)

2001   *Billboard in the Clouds*, by Suzanne Rancourt (Abenaki)

2002   *Down River From Here*, by Renee Matthew (Koyukon)
        The Fork-in-the-Road Indian Poetry Store, by Phillip Carroll Morgan (Choctaw/Chickasaw)

2003   *Wild Plums*, by Marlon D. Sherman (Oglala Lakota)

2004   *Silence on the Rez*, by Christina M. Castro (Jemez Pueblo/Taos Pueblo)
        Stirring Up the Water, by Cathy Ruiz (Cree/Métis)

2005   *Smuggling Cherokee*, by Kim Shuck (Cherokee/Sac and Fox)

2006   *Picked Apart the Bones*, by Rebecca Hatcher Travis (Chickasaw)

2007   *Amazing Grace*, by Kade L. Twist (Cherokee)

2008   *Wicked Dew,* by Steve Russell (Cherokee)

2009   *Smoked Mullet Cornbread Memory,* by L. Rain Cranford-Gomez (Louisiana Choctaw/Creek/Louisiana Creole/Nakoda Métis/Celtic American)

Additional Literary Awards

1969   N. Scott Momaday (Kiowa) won the Pulitzer Prize for Fiction for his novel, *House Made of Dawn.*

1974   Maggie Culver Fry (Cherokee) published *The Umbilical Cord,* her second book of poetry. It was nominated for a Pulitzer Prize.

1984   Louise Erdrich (Turtle Mountain Chippewa) received the National Book Critics Circle Award for her novel *Love Medicine.* Erdrich has won numerous other awards, including a Pushcart Prize in Poetry, a Guggenheim Fellowship, and a Scott O'Dell Award for Historical Fiction. In 2009, *The Plague of Doves,* which won the 2009 Anisfield-Wolf Book Award, was named a finalist for a 2009 Pulitzer Prize in fiction.
    Maurice Kenny (Mohawk) received the American Book Award for *The Mama Poems.* That year, he also received the National Public Radio Award for Broadcasting.

1986   James Welch (Blackfeet/Gros Ventre) received an American Book Award, Los Angeles Times Book Prize, and the Pacific Northwest Booksellers Award for his third novel, *Fools Crow.* In 2000, the French government presented Welch with the *Chevalier de l'Ordre des Arts et des Lettres* and honored him with full knighthood.

1989   Michael Dorris (Modoc) received the National Book Critics Circle Award for nonfiction for *The Broken Cord: A Family's Ongoing Struggle with Fetal Alcohol Syndrome.*

1990   The University of Nebraska Press awarded its first annual Native American Prose Award to Diane Glancy (Cherokee) for her manuscript *Claiming Breath.* The award, given for literary merit, originality, and familiarity with Native North American Indian life, includes publication of the winning manuscript.

1992   William S. Yellow Robe Jr. (Assiniboine) was the first recipient of the First Book Award for Drama from the Native Writers' Circle of the Americas/Returning the Gift for his *The Star Quilter.* He also received a Native American Achievers award from the Smithsonian National Museum of the American Indian for his work in Native American theater. He was the first playwright to receive a Princess

Grace Foundation Theater Fellowship, a Jerome Fellowship from the Minneapolis Playwright's Center, and a New England Theater Foundation Award for Excellence.

1994   Roberta Hill Whiteman (Oneida) received the Lila Wallace–Reader's Digest annual Writers' Award for her second poetry collection, *Philadelphia Flowers.*

Linda Hogan (Chickasaw) received the Lannan Literary Award for Poetry. Her novel *Mean Spirit*, a winner of the Oklahoma Book Award and the Mountains and Plains Book Award, was nominated for a Pulitzer Prize in Fiction in 1991.

1995   Susan Power (Standing Rock Sioux) received a $7,500 Ernest Hemingway Award for first fiction for *The Grass Dancer.*

1996   Simon J. Ortiz (Acoma Pueblo) received a Lila Wallace–Reader's Digest annual Writers' Award. Among his many awards, he was an Honored Poet at the 1981 White House Salute to Poetry.

1997   Joy Harjo (Muskogee Creek) received a Lila Wallace–Reader's Digest Annual Writers' Award. As part of the award, Harjo agreed to partner with Atlatl, Inc., a nonprofit arts organization, to create programs for the public.

2000   Virginia Driving Hawk Sneve (Lakota), a writer of children's literature, won the National Humanities Medal. In 1992 she won the Native American Prose Award from the University of Nebraska Press.

2002   Vine Deloria Jr. (Standing Rock Dakota) received the Wallace Stegner Award from the Center of the American West in Boulder, Colorado. The annual award honors individuals who, through literature, art, history, or an understanding of the West, have made a significant contribution to the cultural identity of the West.

2007   Sherman Alexie (Spokane/Coeur d'Alene) received the National Book Award in Young People's Literature for his young adult novel *The Absolutely True Diary of a Part-time Indian.* He has won numerous awards and honors, including the 1993 Lila Wallace–Reader's Digest annual Writers' Award, the 1996 American Book Award, *The New Yorker: 20 Writers for the 21st Century* (1999), and the 2010 PEN/Faulkner Award for Fiction.

Paula Gunn Allen (Laguna Pueblo/Sioux) received a Lannan Literary Fellowship.

2009   Mary Louise Defender Wilson (Dakotah/Hidatsa) received the Bush Foundation's Enduring Vision Award. Defender Wilson (Wagmuhawin, "Gourd Woman"), celebrated for her gift of storytelling, also received, among her many honors, the National Heritage Fellowship from the National Endowment for the Arts, the nation's highest honor for a traditional artist.

2010   Sherman Alexie (Spokane/Coeur d'Alene) received the PEN/ Faulkner Award for Fiction for *War Dances*, a collection of short stories and poems.

N. Scott Momaday

In 1969, N. Scott Momaday (Kiowa) received the Pulitzer Prize for his novel *House Made of Dawn*. This award and the many awards and prizes that followed for both his poetry and his prose have made him one of the most widely published and read of Native American writers. As one writer put it, "Arguably, Native American literature would not be what it is today without his works" (Jusinski 2010). His writing catalyzed the flowering of Native American literature in the United States. When asked by a reporter in 2010 how he would describe himself—as a poet, a playwright, or a painter—Momaday said, "Oh, I am a poet. Yeah. I think poetry is the queen of literature. I'd rather be a poet than anything else" (Jusinski 2010).

Momaday's numerous awards and honors include a Guggenheim Fellowship, a National Institute of Arts and Letters Award, the Golden Plate Award from the American Academy of Achievement, the Premio Letterario Internazionale "Mondello," Italy's highest literary award, the Saint Louis Literary Award, the 2003 Humanities Award from the Autry Center for the American West, and the National Medal of Arts in 2007. In 2010, the Western Writers of America (WWA) presented him with the Owen Wister Award for lifetime achievement. UNESCO named him an Artist for Peace in 2003, the first American to be so honored since the United States rejoined UNESCO.

THEATER AND COMEDIANS

Eight Native Theater Companies

1. Chilkat Dancers Storytelling Theater
   The Chilkat Dancers Storytelling Theater, a troupe of Tlingit performers based in Haines, Alaska, uses elaborate costumes and masks to interpret traditional stories of Tlingit culture.
2. Native American Theater Ensemble
   Founded in 1972 by Hanay Geiogamah (Kiowa/Delaware), the troupe gave its premiere performance at La Mama in New York City, and later toured widely in North America, Europe, and elsewhere.

3. Native Voices at the Autry
   A full Equity company, established in 1999, that partners with the Autry National Center of the American West in Los Angles, California, Native Voices at the Autry (NVA) commissions one new play and mounts two Equity performances each year.
4. Perseverance Theater
   Alaska's professional theater, founded in 1979, has a strong history of work with the Alaska Native community. A Wallace Foundation award in 2003 enabled it to expand its work with Alaska Native artists and audiences.
5. Red Eagle Soaring Native American Theater Group
   Founded in 1990 in Seattle, Washington, by a group of Native theater artists, Red Eagle Soaring (RES) tours productions of plays for youth. From the beginning, RES's highest priority has been to serve the Native youth of the greater Seattle area, and in recent years has become almost exclusively a youth theater group.
6. Red Earth Performing Arts
   Established in 1974, Red Earth Performing Arts is one of the first Native American theater groups. The company disbanded in the late 1980s but was reestablished in 2003. The organization tours, giving performances in Native communities, and provides community, classroom, and teacher workshops.
7. Spiderwoman Theater
   Founded in 1976 by sisters Lisa Mayo, Gloria Miguel, and Muriel Miguel (Kuna/Rappahannock), Spiderwoman Theater has become the oldest continually running women's theater company in North America.
8. Thunderbird Theatre
   Founded in 1974, Thunderbird Theatre is the theater production organization for Haskell Indian Nations University, located in Lawrence, Kansas. It provides Native American theater to both Native and non-Native audiences to explore and expand the direction and form of Native American theater and to initiate the training of Native American theater professionals.

Fourteen Native American Comedians

1. Charlie Ballard (Sac and Fox/Ottawa/Chippewa)
   http://www.charlieballard.com
2. Don Burnstick (Cree)
   http://donburnstick.com
3. Vaughn Edward EagleBear (Colville/Lakota)
   http://www.vaughneaglebear.com
4. & 5. James and Ernie, comedy duo from the Navajo Nation (James Junes and Ernest Tsosie III)
   http://www.jamesandernie.com/index1.htm
6. Charlie Hill (Oneida/Mohawk/Cree)
   http://www.myspace.com/charliehillcomedian

7. Andrew "Drew" Lacapa (Apache/Hopi/Tewa)
   http://www.nativestars.com/comedians/lacapa
8. Tatanka Means (Oglala Lakota/Omaha/Navajo)
   http://www.tatankameans.com
9. Howie Miller (Canadian Cree)
   http://www.howiemiller.com
10. Larry Omaha (Yaqui/Zapotec)
    http://www.larryomaha.net
11. J. R. Redwater (Standing Rock Sioux)
    http://www.myspace.com/jrredwater
12. Jim Ruel (Bay Mills Band of Ojibwe)
    http://www.nativecomedian.com
13. Williams and Ree: The Indian and the White Guy (Terry Ree [Lakota] and Bruce Williams [not Lakota])
    http://www.williamsandree.com
14. Marc Yaffee (Navajo)
    http://www.marcyaffee.net/site/index.php

Native Voices at the Autry

Native Voices at the Autry, established in 1999 by co-creator Randy Reinholz (Choctaw), is a Native theater company housed at the Autry National Center of the American West in Los Angeles, California. It is the country's only Equity theater company dedicated to producing new works by Native American playwrights. Native Voices produces plays about Native experience told by Native writers for Native and non-Indian audiences.

For the past seven years, its Young Native Voices Theater Education Project has provided workshops and residencies for Native American youngsters. Young playwrights are paired with professional mentors for an intensive playwriting or theater workshop, culminating in public staged readings of their plays.

www.autrynationalcenter.org/nativevoices/index.php

NATIVE AMERICAN LITERARY PUBLISHERS

Eight Native Literary Publishers

1. Chickasaw Nation Press, located in Ada, Oklahoma
2. Greenfield Review Press, founded by Joseph Bruchac (Abenaki), located in Greenfield Center, New York

3. & 4. Malki Museum and Ballena Presses, founded by Morongo Band of Cahuilla, located in Banning, California

5. Sequoyah Research Center Digital Library, Chapbook Series, literary works of Native writers past and present, located in Little Rock, Arkansas

6. Sycuan Press, founded by the Sycuan Band of the Kumeyaay Nation of California, located in El Cajon, California

7. Theytus, founded by Randy Fred (Nuu-chah-nulth), the oldest indigenous publishing house in Canada, located on the Penticton Indian Reserve in British Columbia

8. Wigwaas Press, founded by Louise Erdrich (Chippewa), located in Minneapolis, Minnesota

Honoring Nations Honoree, 2008

The Chickasaw Press
http://www.chickasawpress.net
Division of History and Culture
Chickasaw Nation of Oklahoma
Ada, Oklahoma

In 2008, the Harvard Project on American Indian Economic Development honored the Chickasaw Nation Press, a program of the Chickasaw Nation of Oklahoma. The press, founded in 2006, publishes biographies, poetry collections, and essays written by Chickasaw citizens, works that offer readers an entry into the Chickasaw worldview. Authors touch on spirituality, federal assimilation efforts during the boarding school era, other aspects of federal policies, and the success of Chickasaw citizens in many walks of life.

The press employs Chickasaw citizens and encourages community members to participate in its activities, as authors and in other ways. In one project, young members of the tribe were hired to interview elders. The press also sponsors a series of history classes open to the entire workforce.

Besides helping a tribal nation reclaim authority over the way its history is told and the way contemporary events are interpreted, the books are a resource for non-Indian neighbors. Books written from a Chickasaw perspective help outsiders revise their misconceptions and gain a better understanding of what sovereignty means to the tribe.

FILMS

On and Off the Res' with Charlie Hill (USA, 2000, 58 min.), directed by Sandra Osawa (Makah).

A documentary about America's foremost Indian comedian, Charlie Hill (Oneida Nation of Wisconsin), reveals Hill's struggles to enter the world of stand-up comedy. Performance clips show him on influential shows such as *The Tonight Show Starring Johnny Carson* and *The Richard Pryor Show,* and television series *Moesha* and *Roseanne.*

Sun, Moon, and Feather (USA, 1989, 30 min.), directed by Jane Zipp and Bob Rosen.

This prize-winning comedy/documentary is about Native American sisters growing up in Brooklyn during the 1930s and 1940s. Lisa, Gloria, and Muriel Miguel have been performing for more than a decade as the Spiderwoman Theater. The film blends excerpts from home movies shot over a thirty-year period, scenes of family powwows (and medicine shows) for white tourists, musical theater, and personal memoirs.

Trudell (USA, 2004, 80 min.), directed by Heather Rae (Cherokee).

Poet, musician, orator, actor, and activist John Trudell (Santee Dakota) has been fearless in confronting difficult realities that exist in history and culture. Trudell, a leader of the American Indian Movement, began reciting his poetry in public appearances in the 1980s and eventually, encouraged by musician friends, began releasing cassettes of his poetry backed by traditional Indian chants and drums. The filmmaker weaves together archival footage, impressionistic scenes, a soundtrack, and interviews with Kris Kristofferson, Robert Redford, Jackson Browne, and Gary Farmer (Cayuga).

Native Literatures: Generations

Native Literatures: Generations, a quarterly online magazine founded in 2010, provides a global forum for original works of literature by writers from indigenous nations of North America and Hawaii. The poetry, fiction, creative nonfiction, drama, and mixed-genre media will be accessible online for only three months. The magazine's goal is to support writers in their endeavors by offering a venue for linking them with new audiences and potential publishers.
http://www.nativeliteratures.com

ORGANIZATIONS

Association for the Study of American Indian Literatures
https://facultystaff.richmond.edu/~rnelson/asail

The Association for the Study of American Indian Literatures (ASAIL), founded in 1972, is a professional membership organization that promotes the study, criticism, and research of American Indian written and oral literary traditions. ASAIL sponsors panels at the Modern Language Association's annual meeting and other literature conferences. ASAIL's journal, *Studies in American Indian Literatures*, publishes essays and reviews about American Indian literature.

Before Columbus Foundation
http://www.beforecolumbusfoundation.com
 The Before Columbus Foundation (BCF) was founded in 1976 as a non-profit educational and service organization dedicated to promoting and disseminating contemporary American multicultural literature. In 1978, the BCF (authors, editors, and publishers representing the multicultural diversity of American literature) created a book award program that honors excellence in American literature without restriction or bias with regard to race, sex, creed, and cultural origin. The BCF is located in Oakland, California.

The Native Writers' Circle of the Americas
http://www.hanksville.org/storytellers/awards
 Native Writers' Circle of the Americas, headquartered in Albuquerque, New Mexico, is an organization of Native American writers, most notable for its literary awards, presented annually in three categories: First Book of Poetry, First Book of Prose, and Lifetime Achievement. The awards are voted upon by Native American writers, making them among the few literary awards presented to Native Americans by Native Americans.

Project HOOP (Honoring Our Origins and Peoples through Native American Theater)
http://www.hoop.aisc.ucla.edu/nativetheaterprofiles.htm
 Project HOOP is a national American Indian theater and performing arts advocacy program located at the University of California, Los Angeles. The purpose of Project Hoop is to establish Native theater as an integrated subject of study and creative development in tribal colleges, Native communities, K–12 schools, and mainstream institutions, based on Native perspectives, traditions, views of spirituality, histories, cultures, languages, communities, and lands.

Wordcraft Circle of Native Writers and Storytellers
http://www.wordcraftcircle.org
 Wordcraft Circle of Native Writers and Storytellers was founded in 1992 by Lee Francis III. An international membership organization headquartered in Albuquerque, New Mexico, Wordcraft's unique purpose ensures that the voices of Native writers and storytellers—past, present, and future—are heard throughout the world. It urges members to "return their gift" of creativity by mentoring and volunteering both within Wordcraft Circle and in their local communities

as well. Wordcraft conducts, coordinates, and sponsors seminars, workshops, forums, meetings, and other educational activities across the country that emphasize writing and storytelling.

RESOURCES

Brooks, Joanna, ed. *The Collected Writings of Samson Occom, Mohegan: Literature and Leadership in Eighteenth-Century Native America.* New York: Oxford University Press, 2006.

Browne, Ray B. *Murder on the Reservation: American Indian Crime Fiction.* Madison: University of Wisconsin Press, 2004.

Bruchac, Joseph, ed. *Returning the Gift: Poetry and Prose from the First North American Writers' Festival.* Tucson: University of Arizona Press, 1994.

Einhorn, Lois J. *The Native American Oral Tradition: Voices of the Spirit and Soul.* New York: Praeger, 2000.

Evers, Larry, and Barry Toelken. *Native American Oral Traditions: Collaborations and Interpretations.* Logan: Utah State University Press, 2001.

Green, Richard. *Te Ata: Chickasaw Storyteller, American Treasure.* Norman: University of Oklahoma Press, 2002.

Hart, James D. *Oxford Companion to Native American Literature.* Edited by Phillip Leininger. 6th ed. New York: Oxford University Press, 1996.

Jaskoski, Helen, ed. *Early Native American Writings: New Critical Essays.* New York: Cambridge University Press, 1996.

Johnson, Rubellite Kawena. *Essays in Hawaiian Literature.* Honolulu: R. K. Johnson, 2001.

Jusinski, Charlotte. "Literary pioneer N. Scott Momaday discusses culture, history and the writing life." *Santa Fe Reporter,* January 21, 2010. Available at http://www.sfreporter.com/santafe/article-5151-writing-his-world.html

Littlefield, Daniel F., Jr. *A Biobibliography of Native American Writers 1772–1924.* Metuchen, NJ: Scarecrow Press, 1981; *A Supplement,* 1985.

Macdonald, Gina, and Andrew F. Macdonald. *Shaman or Sherlock? The Native American Detective.* Santa Barbara, CA: Praeger, 2001.

Martinez, David, ed. *The American Indian Intellectual Tradition: Anthology of Writings from 1772 to 1972.* Ithaca, NY: Cornell University Press, 2011.

Molin, Paulette F. *American Indian Themes in Young Adult Literature.* Lanham, MD: Scarecrow Press, 2005.

Owens, Louis. *Other Destinies: Understanding the American Indian Novel.* Norman: University of Oklahoma Press, 1992.

Parker, Robert Dale, ed. *The Sound the Stars Make Rushing through the Sky: The Writings of Jane Johnston Schoolcraft.* Philadelphia: University of Pennsylvania Press, 2007.

Peyer, Bernd C., ed. *The Singing Spirit: Early Short Stories by North American Indians.* Tucson: University of Arizona Press, 1989.

Porter, Joy, and Kenneth M. Roemer, eds. *The Cambridge Companion to Native American Literature.* New York: Cambridge University Press, 2005.

Purdy, John Lloyd. *Writing Indian, Native Conversations.* Lincoln: University of Nebraska Press, 2009.

Seale, Doris, and Beverly Slapin, eds. *A Broken Flute: The Native Experience in Books for Children*. Walnut Creek, CA: AltaMira Press, 2005.

Swann, Brian, and Arnold Krupat. *Recovering the Word: Essays on American Indian Literature*. Berkeley: University of California Press, 1987.

Treuer, David. *Native American Fiction: A User's Manual*. Minneapolis: Graywolf Press, 2006.

Vizenor, Gerald. *Narrative Chance: Postmodern Discourse on Native American Indian Literatures*. Norman: University of Oklahoma Press, 1993.

Warrior, Robert. *The People and the Word: Reading Native Nonfiction*. Minneapolis: University of Minnesota Press, 2005.

Weaver, Jace. *That the People Might Live: Native American Literatures and Native American Community*. New York: Oxford University Press, 1997.

Weaver, Jace, Craig S. Womack, and Robert Warrior. *American Indian Literary Nationalism*. Albuquerque: University of New Mexico Press, 2006.

Womack, Craig S. *Red on Red: Native American Literary Separatism*. Minneapolis: University of Minnesota Press, 1999.

Wright-McLeod, Brian. "Poetry Recordings," "Poetry Compilations," and "Contemporary Spoken Word Recordings." In *The Encyclopedia of Native Music: More Than a Century of Recordings from Wax Cylinder to the Internet*. Tucson: University of Arizona Press, 2005.

Audio-Video Resources

Goin' Native: The American Indian Comedy Slam—Part 2: "The Comedians"
http://www.youtube.com/watch?v=8Bp5BAJfk4Q
> Includes clips of: Charlie Hill, Howie Miller, Vaughn EagleBear, Marc Yaffee, Jim Ruel, J. R. Redwater, and Larry Omaha.

Goin' Native: The Indian Comedy Slam. Showtime, 80 minutes. http://www.sho.com/site/movies/movie.do?seriesid=0&seasonid=0&episodeid=134477
> This history-making original concert, filmed in January 2009, showcases the funniest Native American stand-up comedians performing today. Featured alongside host Charlie Hill are Larry Omaha, Howie Miller, J. R. Redwater, Marc Yaffee, Jim Ruel, and Vaughn EagleBear.

Lannan Literary Voices
http://www.lannan.org/lf/lit/video
> The Lannan Foundation produced full-length video programs featuring major poets and writers from around the world reading and discussing their work. The foundation has built an audio archive section of its Web site, where audio files from some of the titles in the video library are available for listening. Two Lannan Foundation award winners, Joy Harjo (Muscogee Creek) in 1996 and Linda Hogan (Chickasaw) in 1995, are included in the library.

Native American Novelists, produced by Films Media Group
http://ffh.films.com/id/7847/Leslie_M_Silko.htm
> Films produced in the late 1990s of novelists N. Scott Momaday (Kiowa), Leslie M. Silko (Laguna Pueblo), Gerald Vizenor (Chippewa), and James Welch (Blackfeet/Gros Ventre).

Thrasher, Tanya (Cherokee), ed. "'Pulling Down the Clouds': Contemporary Native Writers Read Their Work." CD of fifteen writers who took part in the NMAI Native Writers Series, 2004–6. NMAI Publications, 2007.

Words and Place: Native Literature from the American Southwest: Eight videos. http://parentseyes.arizona.edu/wordsandplace

> In the late 1970s, videotapes were produced at the University of Arizona with the permission of the Indian communities recorded. Each program, recorded in a Native language with English subtitles, presents one American Indian singer, storyteller, or author performing from his or her repertoire in a natural setting in the community. The five speakers also talk about the relation of their oral tradition to their native communities.

Web Sites

California Indian Storytellers Association: http://www.cistory.org

Circle of Stories Storytellers: http://www.pbs.org/circleofstories/storytellers/

Harvard Project's Honoring Nation Directory of Honored Programs, 1999–2006: http://hpaied.org/images/resources/general/Dir_web.pdf

Haskell Indian Nations University Native American Playwrights: http://www.haskell.edu/theatre/playwrights.html

Indian Reading Series: Stories and Legends of the Northwest: http://apps.educationnorthwest.org/indianreading

Native American Authors: http://www.ipl.org/div/natam

National American Indian Theater and Performing Arts Alliance/American Indian Playwrights Guild: http://www.nativetheater.org

Native American Storyteller Native American Authors: Gregg Howard: http://www.youtube.com/watch?v=SlHtzU133NI

Native Village Books, Literature, Storytelling Library: http://www.nativevillage.org/Libraries/Books,%20Lit,%20Storytelling%20Library.htm

Native Wiki: Nativewiki.org/Main_Page

Northwest Indian Storytelling Festival: http://www.worldpulse.com/pulsewire/exchange/events/29326

'Ōiwi: A Native Hawaiian Journal: http://www.hawaii.edu.oiwi

Debbie Reese (Nambe Pueblo), American Indians in Children's Literature Blog: http://americanindiansinchildrensliterature.blogspot.com/

Cynthia Leitich Smith Children's and Young Adult Literature Resources: http://www.cynthialeitichsmith.com

Tribal Writers Digital Text Project: http://www.anpa.ualr.edu/digital_library/digital_library.htm

Turtle Island Storytellers Network: http://www.turtleislandstorytellers.net/

17

Film

FIRSTS

1909–11   The Carnegie Museum Alaska-Siberian Expedition produced ten thousand feet of film, four reels longer than Robert Flaherty's *Nanook of the North*. Some consider the footage the first feature-length documentary.

1913   Lillian St. Cyr (Winnebago), who used the stage name Princess Red Wing, starred in Cecil B. DeMille's movie *Squaw Man*, the first full-length feature film made in Hollywood.

1914   *In the Land of the Head Hunters*, made by photographer Edward S. Curtis, was the first full-length feature with an all-Native American cast. The fictionalized story, written by Curtis, set the stage for other ethnographic films such as Robert Flaherty's better-known *Nanook of the North* (1922).

1922   *Nanook of the North* became the first significant nonfiction feature film. It was made by filmmaker Robert Flaherty, whose stereotypic images of Canadian Inuit influenced how Alaska Eskimo people would be presented by later filmmakers.

1926   Chief Yowlachie (Yakama), also known as Daniel Simmons, was the first Indian to play a non-Indian in film. He played a Chinese man in *Tell It to the Marines*.

1932   Ray Wise (Inupiaq), who later changed his name to Ray Mala, became the first Alaska Native lead actor in Hollywood. He starred in the silent film *Igloo* for Universal Pictures.

1934   *Eskimo*, a film produced by Irving Thalberg, won the first Oscar for Best Film Editing at the Academy Awards.

1949   Jay Silverheels, also known as Harry Smith (Six Nations Mohawk), became the first indigenous actor to play a Native American on television. He played the stoic, monosyllabic Tonto, the Lone Ranger's companion, until 1957.

1970   Chief Dan George (Salish) was the first known Native American to be nominated for an Academy Award for Best Supporting Actor, for his performance in *Little Big Man*.

1975   Sandra Sunrising Osawa (Makah) was the first Native American independent filmmaker to produce for commercial television with a groundbreaking ten-part series on Native Americans that aired on stations in New York, Dallas, Los Angeles, and Chicago.

1979   Jay Silverheels, also known as Harry Smith (Six Nations Mohawk), became the first North American Indian to have his name embedded on Hollywood's Walk of Fame. He received the 1,707th star. He was the first Native actor to play the role of Apache leader Geronimo in three major motion pictures: *Broken Arrow* (1950), *Battle at Apache Pass* (1952), and *Walk the Proud Land* (1956).

1980   With the exception of a voice-over narration, *Windwalker* became the first feature film made entirely in the Cheyenne and Crow languages with subtitles in English.

1982   Buffy Sainte-Marie (Cree) became the first known Native American to win an Oscar at the Academy Awards. She was awarded Best Original Song (along with cowriters Jack Nitzsche and Will Jennings) for composing "Up Where We Belong," the theme song from *An Officer and a Gentleman*.

1991   *Awakening* was the first film written and directed by a Navajo, Norman Patrick Brown, presented entirely in the Navajo language.

1996   *Grand Avenue* was HBO's first-ever production about Native people in a contemporary story.

1997   The Mashantucket (Western) Pequot Tribal Nation of Connecticut produced a motion picture, *Naturally Native*, the first time any tribe financially backed an entire film project. It was also the first film about Native women written, directed, produced and starring Native American women.

1998   *Smoke Signals*, an independent film, is considered the first major feature film to be written, directed, coproduced, and acted by American Indians to find a mainstream distributor. It was directed by Chris Eyre (Cheyenne/Arapaho). The movie was based on stories from Sherman Alexie's book, *The Lone Ranger and Tonto Fistfight in Heaven* (1993). It became the first feature film directed by an American Indian to receive a national theatrical release.

2000   Filmmaker, stage and screen actor Gary Farmer (Cayuga) was the first recipient of the Bernie Whitebear Community Service Award for his work in Native cinema and media. In 2001, he won the Taos Mountain Award, given annually by the Taos Talking Pictures Film Festival to an outstanding Native American film professional.

2001   *Atanarjuat/The Fast Runner* was the first Native language feature film to be produced, written, directed, and acted by Inuit. It was directed by Zacharias Kunuk (Inuit) and Norman Cohn. The film had an enormous impact on U.S. audiences.

2005   *Christmas in the Clouds*, a film showcased on the independent film circuit in 2001, winning, among other awards, Official Selection at the Sundance Film Festival, opened nationwide. It was the first Native American romantic comedy set at a tribal ski resort in Utah.

2006   Chris Eyre (Cheyenne/Arapaho) won the Directors Guild of America award for Outstanding Directorial Achievement in Children's Programs for *Edge of America*, becoming the first Native American to win the award.

2010   'Ōiwi Film Festival was the first festival to feature only Native Hawaiian filmmakers.

2011   Donavan Seschillie (Diné), Jake Hoyungowa (Diné/Hopi), and Deidra Peaches (Diné), from Flagstaff, Arizona, became for the first time the youngest Native filmmakers to premiere a film at the Sundance Institute's film festival, held in January in Park City, Utah. Their sixteen-minute film, "Rocket Boy," was picked as one of only 81 short films to be shown at Sundance, out of 6,467 entries.

EARLY FILM STARS AND FEATURE FILMS

Twenty Early Native American Film Stars, 1909–49

American Indians have acted in movies since the silent film era. The film industry used them primarily as extras and in bit parts, and rarely gave them speaking lines, much less leading roles—just enough to keep them marginally employed. A few Native actors, however, managed to attain stardom.

1. Chief John Big Tree (Seneca)
    The Primitive Lover (1922); *The Huntress* (1923); *The Iron Horse* (1924); *The Red Rider* (1925); *The Frontier Trail* (1926); *The Frontiersmen* (1927); *Winners of the Wilderness* (1927); *Spoilers of the West* (1927); *Sioux Blood* (1929); *Red Fork Range* (1931); *Custer's Last Stand* (1936); *Drums Along the Mohawk* (1939); *Stagecoach* (1939); *Western Union* (1941); *She Wore a Yellow Ribbon* (1949)

2. Monte Blue (Cherokee)
   Told in the Hills (1919); *Ride, Ranger, Ride* (1936); *The Outcasts of Poker Flat* (1937); *Hawk of the Wilderness* (1938)
3. Chief Darkcloud/Elijah Tahamont (Sioux or Abenaki)
   Song of the Wildwood Flute (1910); *The Squaw's Love* (1911); *What Am I Bid?* (1919)
4. Dove Eve Darkcloud (Algonquin)
   Desert Gold (1919)
5. Mona Darkfeather (Seminole)
   At Old Fort Dearborn (1912)
6. William Eagleshirt (Sioux)
   Last of the Line (1914); *The Conqueror* (1917)
7. Ray Mala/Ach-nach-chiak/Ray Wise (Inupiaq)
   Igloo (1932); *Eskimo* (1933); *Call of the Yukon* (1938); *The Great Adventures of Wild Bill Hickok* (1938); *North West Mounted Police* (1940); *Girl from God's Country* (1940)
8. Chief Many Treaties/William Hazlett (Blackfeet)
   The Pioneers (1941); *Overland Mail* (1942); *The Deerslayer* (1943); *The Law Rides Again* (1943); *Buffalo Bill* (1944); *Buffalo Bill Rides Again* (1947)
9. Princess Red Wing/Lillian St. Cyr (Winnebago)
   Red Wing's Gratitude (1909); *The Squaw Man* (1914); *The Thundering Herd* (1914)
10. Rodd Redwing (Chickasaw)
    Apache Chief (1949)
11. William "Will" Penn Adair Rogers (Cherokee)
    Fifty silent films, beginning with *Laughing Bill Hyde* (1918); twenty-one "talkies," beginning with *They Had to See Paris* (1929) and ending with *In Old Kentucky* (1935)
12. Jay Silverheels/Harry Smith (Six Nations Mohawk)
    The Prairie (1947); *Laramie* (1949)
13. Chief Luther Standing Bear (Lakota)
    White Oak (1921); *Santa Fe Trail* (1930); *The Conquering Horde* (1931); *Texas Pioneers* (1932); *The Miracle Rider* (1935)
14. Charles Stevens (Apache)
    Tom Sawyer (1930); *Winners of the West* (1940); *My Darling Clementine* (1946); *Buffalo Bill Rides Again* (1947); *The Cowboy and the Indians* (1949)
15. Jim Thorpe (Sac and Fox)
    Battling with Buffalo Bill (1931); *Behold My Wife* (1934); *Rustlers of Red Dog* (1935); *Treachery Rides the Range* (1936); *Prairie Schooners* (1940)
16. Chief Thunder Cloud/Victor Daniels (Cherokee)
    Laughing Boy (1934); *Rustlers of Red Dog* (1935); *Custer's Last Stand* (1936); *Ride, Ranger, Ride* (1936); *Riders of the Whistling Skull* (1937); *Flaming Frontiers* (1938); *The Great Adventures of Wild Bill Hickok* (1938); *The Lone*

Ranger (1938); *Geronimo* (1940); *Young Buffalo Bill* (1940); *Western Union* (1941); *Overland Mail* (1942); *Daredevils of the West* (1943); *Buffalo Bill* (1944); *Outlaw Trail* (1944); *The Phantom Rider* (1946); *Romance of the West* (1946); *The Prairie* (1947)

17. Chief Thunderbird (Cherokee)
    Battling with Buffalo Bill (1931); *Rustlers of Red Dog* (1935); *Wild West Days* (1937); *North West Mounted Police* (1940)
18. Chauncey Yellow Robe (Sioux)
    The Silent Enemy (1930)
19. James Young Deer (Winnebago)
    The Mended Lute (1909); *The True Heart of an Indian* (1909); *Yaqui Girl* (1910)
20. Chief Yowlachie/Daniel Simmons (Yakama)
    War Paint (1926); *The Red Raiders* (1927); *Sitting Bull at the Spirit Lake Massacre* (1927); *The Glorious Trail* (1928); *Hawk of the Hills* (1929); *Santa Fe Trail* (1930); *North West Mounted Police* (1940); *Winners of the West* (1940); *White Eagle* (1941); *Canyon Passage* (1946); *The Prairie* (1947); *The Senator Was Indiscreet* (1947); *The Dude Goes West* (1948); *The Paleface* (1948); *Red River* (1948); *The Cowboy and the Indians* (1949); *Ma and Pa Kettle* (1949); *Mrs. Mike* (1949)

Nine Early Feature Films with All–Native Casts, 1913–34

1. *Hiawatha*: silent film with all-Indian cast, 1913
2. *In the Land of the Head Hunters*: silent film with all-Native cast, 1914
3. *Before the White Man Came*: silent film with all-Indian cast, 1920
4. *The Daughter of Dawn*: silent film with Oklahoma cast of Kiowa and Comanche tribal members, 1920
5. *Nanook of the North*: silent film with all-Inuit cast, 1922
6. *Kivalina of the Ice Lands*: silent film with all-Eskimo cast, 1925
7. *Silent Enemy*: early sound film with all-Native cast, 1930
8. *Igloo*: early sound film with all-Iñupiat cast, 1932
9. *Eskimo*: early sound film with an almost all-Native cast, 1934

In the Land of the Head Hunters, 1914

In 1913, Seattle-based photographer Edward Curtis traveled to British Columbia, Canada, to make a silent movie about Indians "before the white man came" and before the Indians vanished, a belief widely held at the time. For three years, he documented the traditions and dances of the Kwakwaka'wakw (also known as the Kwakiutl). The seventy-minute film, a fictional story written by Curtis, incorporated non-professional Kwakiutl actors performing dances forbidden by the Canadian government in its attempt to force assimilation. Curtis paid Kwakiutl craftsmen to make traditional masks, war canoes, clothing, and totem poles; he even had his actors wear wigs to cover their European-style haircuts.

The film, *In the Land of the Head Hunters*, the first full-length feature to have an exclusively Native cast, debuted in New York and Seattle in 1914 to critical success but box office failure. The public wanted tipis and horses, not ceremonial Kwakiutl masks and dances. The ceremonies that Curtis documented are still performed today. In fact, Kwakiutl cultural groups have used the movie to watch the dance movements and canoe paddling.

The Curtis film, which was restored to its original form in 2008, has been credited with inspiring other ethnographic films such as Robert Flaherty's better-known *Nanook of the North* (1922).

Non-Indian Actors as Indians

Hollywood has churned out hundreds of movies about Native Americans since the turn of the twentieth century. Not so long ago, Hollywood hired Caucasian actors who were painted a brownish-red and wore wigs to portray Indian peoples. Bankable non-Indian stars, including Dame Judith Anderson, Yul Brynner, Cyd Charisse, Tony Curtis, Yvonne DeCarlo, Leonard Nimoy, Elvis Presley, and Jennifer Tilly, landed major parts playing Indians. Some American Indian actors worked as extras and bit players who were rarely given speaking lines, much less leading roles.

It took decades of protest against distorted Hollywood Indian images before some Native American actors began to break into Hollywood. Since the 1970s, a number of accomplished Native actors gained star billing, playing important roles in major films. Adam Beach (Saulteaux), Irene Bedard (Iñupiat/Cree), Tantoo Cardinal (Cree/Metis), Graham Greene (Oneida), Kimberly Norris Guerrero (Colville/Salish-Kootenai/Cherokee), Wes Studi (Cherokee), and Sheila Tousey (Menominee), among many others, have been cast in Hollywood and indie movies.

AWARDS

American Indian Film Institute's Award-Winning Feature Films, 1990–2010

The annual American Indian Film Festival, the cornerstone of the American Indian Film Institute (AIFI) since 1975, takes place in San Francisco, California. AIFI has shown hundreds of feature films, documentaries, shorts, and docu-dramas, as well as public service, industrial, and music videos, from American Indian and Canada First Nations communities. Each year the AIFI gives awards in various categories. The films listed below won Best Feature Film awards in the years 1990 to 2010.

1990   *Dances with Wolves* (USA, 180 min.), directed by Kevin Costner.
         An historical drama about the relationship between John Dunbar, a Civil War soldier, and a noble tribe of Lakota (Sioux) Indians, *Dances with Wolves* became an immensely popular and financially successful movie that prompted endless commentaries. The film is distinguished by the significant amount of dialogue in the Lakota language (with subtitles).

1991   No feature film award

1992   *Incident at Oglala* (USA, 90 min.), directed by Michael Apted.
         This documentary feature deals with events surrounding the 1975 fatal shooting of two FBI agents and one American Indian on the Pine Ridge Reservation in South Dakota.

1993   *Medicine River* (Canada, 94 min.), directed by Stuart Margolin.
         Idiosyncrasies of a small Blackfoot community draw in Will, a Toronto photographer raised by his Blackfoot mother in Medicine River. He returns after twenty years to attend his mother's funeral.

1994   *Lakota Woman: Siege at Wounded Knee* (USA, 110 min.), directed by Frank Pierson.
         This feature chronicles the life of Mary Crow Dog from her youth and boarding school years to her time (seventy-one days) spent at Wounded Knee, Pine Ridge Reservation, South Dakota.

1995   *Dance Me Outside* (Canada, 84 min.), directed by Bruce McDonald.
         This film tells the story of life on an Indian reserve in Ontario: two men are trying to get into college to train to be mechanics, but they find themselves having to deal with girls, family, . . . and murder.

1996   *Grand Avenue* (USA, 165 min.), directed by Daniel Sackheim.
         This feature chronicles the lives of three Native contemporary families in Santa Rose, California.

1997   No feature film award

1998   *Smoke Signals* (USA, 89 min.), directed by Chris Eyre (Cheyenne/Arapaho).
         The road trip of two friends from Idaho to the Southwest reveals the struggles of contemporary Native Americans and issues of identity.

1999   *UnBowed* (USA, 120 min.), directed by Nanci Rossov.

This feature deals with racism through the eyes of Native Americans forced into a "Negro" school in the American South during the 1890s.

2000   *Backroads* (USA, 83 min.), directed by Shirley Cheechoo (Cree).

Set on a fictional Canadian reservation, this dark drama explores the racism and abuse that explode into the lives of four sisters and the forces that lead to a fateful conclusion.

2001   *The Doe Boy* (USA, 83 min.), directed by Randy Redroad (Cherokee).

Set in the Cherokee Nation of Oklahoma, *The Doe Boy* tells the story of a young man of mixed parentage who is never quite at home in the complicated circumstances of his life, including his hemophilia. Eventually he must find a way to be his own man, facing love, death, and the perils of his illness.

2002   *Atanarjuat* (*The Fast Runner*) (Canada, 172 min.), directed by Zacharias Kunuk (Inuit).

An action thriller set in pre-contact Igloolik in what is now Arctic Canada, the film unfolds as a life-threatening struggle between powerful natural and supernatural characters.

2003   *Dreamkeeper* (USA, 174 min.), directed by Steve Barron.

On a road trip from South Dakota to an Albuquerque powwow, a grandfather tells traditional Native stories to his grandson, who is having trouble with local Native gang members, and brings him back to a Native place.

2004   *Edge of America* (USA, 105 min.), directed by Chris Eyre (Cheyenne/Arapaho).

Inspired by a true story that took place in New Mexico, this upbeat feature follows a girls' high school basketball team as the players learn how to win. Led by their coach, the girls discover the values of passion, dedication, and discipline as they climb from the bottom of their division to compete for the state title.

2005   *Johnny Tootall* (Canada, 90 min.), directed by Shirley Cheechoo (Cree).

Johnny, discharged from the Bosnian war, returns home with inner demons only to find equally difficult struggles within his family and community.

2006   *Expiration Date* (USA, 94 min.), directed by Rick Stevenson.

Charlie Silvercloud III, who carries around a family curse, has eight days left to live. He meets a girl who won't let him die in peace.

2007   *Imprint* (USA, 84 min.), directed by Michael Linn.

When a Native American attorney prosecutes a Lakota teen in a controversial murder trial, things spin out of control, and strange visions and ghostly voices propel her on an unexpected journey in this supernatural thriller.

2008   *Before Tomorrow* (Canada, 93 min.), directed by Marie-Hélène Cousineau and Madeline Piujuq Ivalu (Inuit).

Set in 1840, a time before many Inuit in northern Canada had met non-European people, Ningiuq, an old woman of strength and wisdom, feels dread about something she does not understand. When an unspeakable tragedy is discovered, troubling answers begin to emerge.

2009   *Barking Water* (USA, 85 min.), directed by Sterlin Harjo (Seminole/Creek).

A fifty-something once-upon-a-time couple (one of whom is dying) takes a redemptive road trip across Oklahoma. As they take to the open road for Frankie's last ride, the journey becomes one of shared memory, love, and forgiveness.

2010   *A Windigo Tale* (Canada, 91 min.), directed by Armand Garnet Ruffo (Ojibway).

Filmed on the Six Nations Reserve in Ontario and in the Ottawa Valley, *A Windigo Tale* is a drama based on the history of the residential school system, which removed generations of children from their families for schooling in Euro-Canadian society.

Award-Winning Native American and First
Nation Independent Filmmakers

1975   Independent producer Sandra Sunrising Osawa (Makah) received NBC's Outstanding Producer Award for the ten-part series about Native Americans that she produced for commercial television. Renowned as one of America's premier Native film producers, directors, and documentarians, her 1995 piece, *Lighting the 7th Fire*, inaugurated Native American programming on POV, a showcase for nonfiction on public television. In 1996, she received the Taos Mountain Award for lifetime achievement.

1984   Independent filmmaker Victor Masayesva (Hopi) won the Gold Hugo at the Chicago International Film Festival for his acclaimed work, *Itam Hakim Hopiit*, which was produced in the Hopi language and subtitled in English. The film is a poetic visualization of Hopi philosophy and prophecy. In 1995, Masayesva won the American

Film Institute's Maya Deren Award for Independent Film and Video Artists.

1991   Independent filmmakers Roy Bigcrane (Salish) and Thompson Smith directed *The Place of Falling Waters*, a film about the impact of the Kerr Dam on tribes in western Montana. They won awards from the National Educational Film Festival and the Parnu (Estonia) International Film Festival.

1991   Independent filmmaker Dean Curtis Bear Claw (Crow) directed *Warrior Chiefs in a New Age*. He won the New Visionary Award at the Two Rivers Film Festival in Minneapolis, Minnesota, for his portrait of Chief Plenty Coups and Medicine Crow. He also won the Best Native Filmmaker award at the Parnu (Estonia) International Film Festival.

1997   Independent filmmaker Beverly Singer (Santa Clara Pueblo) received a Sundance Institute award for *Hózhó of Native Women*, in which Native American women tell stories about how they merge traditional ways with contemporary life. A founding member of the Native American Producers Alliance, she authored *Wiping the War Paint off the Lens* (2001), a book on Native American independent filmmaking.

1998   Independent filmmaker Chris Eyre (Cheyenne/Arapaho) has won many fellowships, honors, and awards for his work in directing films. His first feature, *Smoke Signals*, was one of the five highest-grossing independent films in 1998. It won the Sundance Filmmakers Trophy and Audience Awards and Best Film honors at the American Indian Film Festival. In 2006 he received the Peabody Award and Parents' Choice Award for his HBO feature film, *Edge of America*. In 2008 Eyre directed the first three episodes of *We Shall Remain*, a mini-series that establishes Native history as an essential part of American history, from PBS's history series, "American Experience."

2001   Independent filmmaker Randy Redroad (Cherokee) won Perrier's Bubbling Under First-Time Filmmaker Award at the Taos Talking Pictures Film Festival for *The Doe Boy*. The film, about a mixed-blood Cherokee boy coming to terms with his identity as he hunts for deer, was also selected as the American winner of the 2000 Sundance NHK International Filmmakers Award.

2001   Zacharias Kunuk (Inuit) directed and produced *Atanarjuat/The Fast Runner*, a groundbreaking film that was the first Native language feature film to be produced, written, directed, and acted by Inuit. *Atanarjuat*, which portrays a traditional epic myth spoken entirely in Inuktitut, won the 2001 Camera d'Or for Best First Feature at the Cannes International

Film Festival. In 2004, Kunuk won the first Sun Hill Award for Excellence in Native American Filmmaking, a new annual honor from the Harvard Film Archive.

2004   Alanis Obomsawin (Abenaki) received the 2004 International Documentary Association (IDA) Pioneer Award at the IDA Distinguished Documentary Achievement Awards Gala, sponsored by Eastman Kodak and the Sundance Channel. At the 2004 imagineNATIVE Film and Media Arts Festival, Obomsawin received the Milestone Award for Lifetime Achievement.

2006   Filmmaker Sterlin Harjo (Creek/Seminole) won the Tribeca All Access Program's top Creative Promise Award for his new screenplay *Before the Beast Returns*, about a lifelong loser's quixotic journey towards self-awareness.

Native American Independent Filmmakers

In 1991, George Burdeau (Blackfeet), a Peabody Award–winning producer and founding director of the Communications Department at the Institute of American Indian Arts in Santa Fe, New Mexico, said "The image of Indians has been so erroneous for so many years that the only way it can be changed is for Native Americans to produce films themselves." Today, Native Americans are doing just that. Native producers, writers, directors, and actors have embraced film and video, today's most popular storytelling media, to create documentaries and feature films that challenge Hollywood's make-believe Indian screen images, tell Native stories, entertain audiences, and define contemporary Native American identity. Native filmmakers document people and practices meaningful to their nations, probe political issues and social problems facing Native communities, retell tribal histories from American Indian perspectives, explore treaty rights, and document religious freedom struggles. Figuratively speaking, Native films are, in the words of the title of a book written by filmmaker Beverly Singer (Santa Clara Pueblo), "wiping the war paint off the lens."

FILM FESTIVALS

Eight Major Native Film Festivals

Native American film festivals give Native independent and tribal community film, video, and audio makers the opportunity to tell their stories and histories in their own words, with their own imagery, symbols, and cultural points of view.

Without these events, many of the documentaries or feature movies would not be seen by Native and mainstream audiences. The following major film festivals take place on a regular basis.

1. American Indian Film Festival, San Francisco, California
   Founded in 1975, the festival takes place annually in November.
2. Dreamspeakers Festival, Edmonton, Alberta, Canada
   Founded in 1996, the festival takes place annually in June.
3. Indigenous World Film Festival, Anchorage, Alaska
   Founded in 2005, the festival takes place annually in February.
4. International Cherokee Film Festival, Tahlequah, Oklahoma
   Founded in 2004, the festival takes place annually in October.
5. Los Angeles Skins Fest, Los Angeles, California
   Founded in 2007, the festival takes place annually in November.
6. Native American Film and Video Festival, National Museum of the American Indian, Smithsonian Institution, New York, New York
   Founded in 1979, the festival takes place biannually in November.
7. Red Nation Film Festival, Los Angeles, California
   Founded in 2003, the festival takes place annually in November.
8. Sundance Film Festival, Park City, Utah
   From 1994 to 2004, the festival, held annually in January, presented Native films as part of a dedicated screening category. In 2005, the festival began incorporating Native and indigenous films into its official film program.

FILMS

Coming to Light (USA, 2000, 85 min.), directed by Anne Makepeace.
   Coming to Light tells the story of Edward S. Curtis, whose photographs of American Indians taken during the early 1900s have become world famous. Curtis's monumental work and the Native people whose lives he documented are balanced with responses by Native people who are descended from individuals that Curtis photographed.
Images of Indians (USA, 1980, 30 min. each), directed by Phil Lucas (Choctaw).
   A five-part documentary series explores the stereotypical Hollywood treatment of Indians through the years, especially as portrayed and perpetuated by Hollywood westerns. Each part available individually.
Images of Indians: How Hollywood Stereotyped the Native American (USA, 2003, 25 min.), directed by Chris O'Brien and Jason Witmer.
   A documentary traces Hollywood's depiction of Native Americans in Western films through interviews and archive footage, from the earliest Edison movies to the latest Indian filmmakers.

In the Land of the War Canoes (USA, 1997, 47 min.), directed by Edward S. Curtis. Originally titled *In the Land of the Head Hunters* (1914), the silent film by Curtis offers a re-creation of Kwakiutl (Kwakwaka'wakw) life on Vancouver Island before the advent of Europeans, including meticulously re-created clothing, dances, and rituals. In 1972, the only surviving print of the film was restored, along with songs recorded by Kwakiutl residents of Vancouver Island.

Jay Silverheels: The Man Behind the Mask (Canada, 2000, 44 min.), directed by David Finch and Maureen Marovitch.

Jay Silverheels is a film about the legacy of Jay Silverheels, also known as Harry Smith (Six Nations Mohawk), who played the role of Tonto, the Lone Ranger's "faithful" companion, on ABC from 1949 to 1957. Several Native actors speak about how Silverheels inspired them.

Reel Injun (Canada, 2009, 85 min.), directed by Neil Diamond (Cree).

This documentary explores the Hollywood Indian, tracing the evolution of the film image of Natives from the silent film era to today, with clips from hundreds of classic and recent movies, including Native-directed film. The filmmaker includes candid interviews with celebrated Native and non-Native actors, activists, film critics, and historians.

The Quileute Nation and the Twilight Saga (2008–10)

The Twilight Saga refers to a series of books by Stephenie Meyer and three movies (*Twilight* [2008], *New Moon* [2009], and *Eclipse* [2010]), based on the novels. The movies have drawn tourists from all over the world to the Quileute Reservation (the saga's setting) along the Pacific coast, a four-hour drive west of Seattle. The series and movies fictionalize the Quileute tribe and its origins, especially regarding the wolf, central to Quileute beliefs.

The films have also catapulted the careers of four Native actors who appeared in *New Moon* and *Eclipse*: Kiowa Gordon (Hualapai), Alex Meraz (Purepecha, Mexico), Chaske Spencer (Lakota), and Bronson Pelletier (Cree/Metis). The actors were cast as the Wolf Pack, shape shifters who change from humans to werewolves to guard the Quileute reservation from vampires.

To clarify misconceptions resulting from the Twilight novels and films, the Quileute Nation of La Push, Washington, and the Seattle Art Museum collaborated on "Behind the Scenes: The Real Story of the Quileute Wolves." The 2010 exhibit set the record straight as to the nation's history, culture, ceremonies, and artworks pertaining to the wolf.

http://www.seattleartmuseum.org/exhibit/exhibitDetail.asp?eventID=18532

ORGANIZATIONS

American Indian Film Institute

http://www.aifisf.com

A major Native American media arts center in San Francisco, California, incorporated in 1979, encourages Native and non-Native filmmakers to create works with Native voices, viewpoints, and stories that are excluded from the mainstream. Programs include an annual film festival of works by and about Native peoples, a research library, and outreach to tribes and youth.

Film and Video Center of the National Museum of the American Indian in New York City

http://www.nmai.si.edu/subpage.cfm?subpage=collections&second=film

The Film and Video Center in New York City presents screenings of Native productions and information services concerning Native films, video, radio, television, and electronic media throughout the Americas and Hawaii. The center's "Native Networks" initiative has developed professional meetings for Native Americans in media.

Native American Producers Alliance

An organization of independent producers, directors, writers, technicians, and talent, NAPA provides information on member productions and a talent director.

Native American Public Telecommunications

http://www.nativetelecom.org

Native American Public Telecommunications (NAPT), located in Lincoln, Nebraska, serves Native producers and Indian Country in partnership with public television and radio. NAPT works with Native producers to develop, produce, and distribute educational telecommunications programs for all media including public television and public radio. NAPT supports training to increase the number of American Indians and Alaska Natives producing quality public broadcasting programs, which includes advocacy efforts promoting increased control and use of information technologies by American Indians and Alaska Natives and the policies to support this control.

Sundance Institute's Native American and Indigenous Program

http://www.sundance.org/programs/native-film

Sundance Institute's Native American and Indigenous Program provides fellowships for emerging Native American, Native Hawaiian, and Alaska Native filmmakers. The Native Forum, a group of events for the international indigenous community, includes panel and filmmaker discussions and networking opportunities. The Sundance Film Festival, Native labs, and workshops in Park City, Utah, bring together writers, directors, and producers of Native and indigenous cinema.

RESOURCES

Aleiss, Angela. *Making the White Man's Indian: Native Americans and Hollywood Movies.* Westport, CT: Praeger, 2005.

Buscombe, Edward. *"Injuns!" Native Americans in the Movies.* London, UK: Reaktion Books, 2006.

Cody, Iron Eyes. *Iron Eyes, My Life as a Hollywood Indian.* New York: Everest House, 1984.

Cummings, Denise K. *Visualities: Perspectives on Contemporary American Indian Film and Art.* East Lansing: Michigan State University Press, 2011.

Evans, Michael Robert. *The Fast Runner: Filming the Legend of Atanarjuat.* Lincoln: University of Nebraska Press, 2010.

Fienup-Riordan, Ann. *Freeze Frame: Alaska Eskimos in the Movies.* Seattle: University of Washington Press, 1995.

Hertzberg, Bob. *Savages and Saints: The Changing Image of American Indians in Westerns.* Jefferson, NC: McFarland & Co., 2008.

Hilger, Michael. *The American Indian in Film.* Metuchen, NJ: Scarecrow Press, 1986.

———. *From Savage to Nobleman: Images of Native Americans in Film.* Lanham, MD: Scarecrow Press, 1995.

Kilpatrick, Jacquelyn. *Celluloid Indians: Native Americans and Film.* Lincoln: University of Nebraska Press, 1999.

King, C. Richard. *Media Images and Representations.* New York: Chelsea House Publishers, 2006.

Lewis, Randolph. *Alanis Obomsawin: The Vision of a Native Filmmaker.* Lincoln: University of Nebraska Press, 2006.

Marubbio, M. Elise. *Killing the Indian Maiden: Images of Native American Women in Film.* Lexington: University Press of Kentucky, 2009.

Morgan, Lael. *Eskimo Star: From the Tundra to Tinseltown: The Ray Mala Story.* Kenmore, WA: Epicenter Press, 2011.

Prats, Armondo José. *Invisible Natives: Myth and Identity in the American Western.* Ithaca: Cornell University Press, 2002.

Rader, Dean. *Engaged Resistance: American Indian Art, Literature, and Film from Alcatraz to the NMAI.* Austin: University of Texas, 2011.

Raheja, Michelle H. *Reservation Reelism: Redfacing, Visual Sovereignty, and Representations of North Americans in Film.* Lincoln: University of Nebraska Press, 2011.

Rollins, Peter C., and John E. O'Connor. *Hollywood's Indian: The Portrayal of Native Americans in Film.* Lexington: University Press of Kentucky, 2003.

Singer, Beverly R. *Wiping the War Paint off the Lens: Native American Film and Video.* Minneapolis: University of Minnesota Press, 2001.

Web Sites

American Indian Film Gallery Online: http://www.jfredmacdonald.com/aifg

American Indian Film Institute: http://www.aifisf.com

American Indians in Silent Films: http://www.loc.gov/rr/mopic/findaid/indian1.html

Four Directions Talent: http://fourdirectionstalent.com/

Native Americans in the Movies: A Bibliography of Materials in the UC Berkeley Library: http://www.lib.berkeley.edu/MRC/IndigenousBib.html

Native Celebs/Native Entertainment: A–Z of Native actors, news, casting notices: http://www.nativecelebs.com

Native Networks, Film and Video Center, National Museum of the American Indian: http://www.nativenetworks.si.edu

NativeVue Film and Media Connection: http://www.nativevue.org

Shenandoah Films (Indian-owned distributor of videos/DVDs produced by Native filmmakers): http://www.shenandoahfilms.com

18

Music and Dance

FIRSTS

1913   Gertrude Simmons Bonnin, or Zitkala-Sa ("red bird") (Yankton Sioux), collaborated with musician William Hanson to create *The Sun Dance*, the first opera coauthored by a Native American.

1918   *Shanewis: The Robin Woman*, composed by Charles Wakefield Cadman and based on the life of singer and entertainer Tsianina Redfeather Blackstone (Creek), was the first American opera with a modern setting to be produced in two consecutive seasons (1918 and 1919) at New York City's Metropolitan Opera.

1926   The first large, intertribal, off-reservation powwow dance organized by American Indians was held at the Haskell Institute in Lawrence, Kansas.

1949   Maria Tallchief (Osage), the New York City Ballet's first prima ballerina, starred in *Firebird*, the ballet that gained her international stardom and gave the New York City Ballet its first box office hit. Tallchief's numerous recognitions include Kennedy Center honors in 1996, Maria Tallchief Day in Chicago on March 12, 1998, and a National Medal of the Arts award in 1999.

1959   Keely Smith (Cherokee) and her musical collaborator Louis Prima won the first Grammy awarded for Best Performance by a Vocal Group or Chorus for their duet "That Old Black Magic," a Top Twenty hit.

1971   Willie Dunn (Mi'kmaq) produced Canada's first music video for his song "The Ballad of Crowfoot." The short video, which examines the situation of Native people in North America through the life of a legendary nineteenth-century Blackfoot leader, can be seen online at http://www.nfb.ca/film/ballad_of_crowfoot.

1980   Daystar, founded by Rosalie Jones (Blackfeet/Chippewa), was the first dance company in the United States created with all-native performers and specializing in the portrayal of the personal and tribal stories of Indian America.

1982   Buffy Sainte-Marie (Cree) became the first-known Native American to win an Oscar at the Academy Awards, honored for Best Original Song. She, Jack Nitzsche, and Will Jennings won for "Up Where We Belong," the theme song for the film *An Officer and a Gentleman.*

1987   Ulali, a trio with members Pura Fé (Tuscarora), Soni Moreno (Apache/Yaqui/Mayan), and Jennifer Kreisberg (Tuscarora), became the first Native American women's a cappella group to create its own sound from traditional roots and personal contemporary styles.

1988   John Kim Bell (Kahnawake Mohawk), who began his career conducting major Broadway musical productions in New York, produced, co-composed, and directed *In the Land of Spirits* in Canada, the first full-scale aboriginal ballet, among his other firsts.

1989   Louis Ballard (Quapaw/Cherokee) was the first American composer to have an entire program dedicated to his works in the new Beethoven House Chamber Music Hall, in Bonn, Germany.

Following its 1989 founding, Sound of America Records (SOAR) became the first company to release traditional Native American music on compact disc.

1990   The American Indian Dance Theatre became the first Native American dance troupe to have its own primetime national television performance special when it was featured on PBS's "Great Performances" series.

1993   Rosalie Jones (Blackfeet/Pembina Chippewa) was the first American Indian to receive a National Endowment for the Arts Choreographer's Fellowship. She used to create *No Home but the Heart,* a dance-drama that explores dimensions of her mother's family's experiences of physical displacement and spiritual return.

1994   The first convention of American Indian composers was held in Boulder, Colorado.

1997   *Canyon Trilogy,* a 1989 album by flute artist R. Carlos Nakai (Navajo/Ute), went gold in 1997, selling more than five hundred thousand copies in the United States, and becoming the first album of its genre to achieve that level of popularity.

2003   Mary Youngblood (Seminole/Aleut) became the first Native American woman to win a Grammy award, when her work *Beneath the Raven Moon* was named best Native American Music Album.

2004	Red Rhythms: Contemporary Methodologies in American Indian Dance, the first national conference illuminating the contributions of Native dancers and choreographers, was held at the University of California at Riverside.
2009	Bill Miller (Mohican) became the first Native American composer to perform an original Native American classical work in Israel. The work, *The Last Stand*, is a symphonic commemoration of the Battle of Little Big Horn (1876).
2010	Dancing Earth, a contemporary dance troupe under the direction of choreographer Rulan Tangen, became the first indigenous dance company to receive a National Dance Project production grant from the New England Foundation for the Arts.

OSHTALI: Music for String Quartet became the first album with works solely by American Indian student-composers, featuring classical music of students in the Chickasaw Nation Summer Arts Academy under the guidance of composer-in-residence Jerod Impichchaachaaha' Tate (Chickasaw). The CD, available on Thunderbird Records, features the string quartet ETHEL.

Litefoot (Cherokee) became the first Native American actor or musician to develop and produce his own branded line of sneakers. Named the "Litefoot," the shoe is a collaboration with Sole Nation Health, an American Indian–owned footwear company.

MUSICIANS

Thirteen Native Classical Musicians

1. Steven Alvarez (Yaqui/Mescalero Apache/Upper Tanana Athabascan), composer, percussionist, and film and stage producer
2. Timothy Archambault (Kichesipirini Algonquin First Nation), composer and flute artist
3. Dawn Avery (Mohawk), composer, cellist, vocalist, and educator: http://www.dawnavery.com/
4. Gabriel Ayala (Yaqui), classical guitarist and teacher: http://www.ayalaguitarist.com/
5. Louis W. Ballard (Quapaw/Cherokee), known as the father of Native American composition
6. John Kim Bell (Kahnawake Mohawk), conductor, pianist, composer: http://www.johnkimbell.com/
7. Raven Chacon (Navajo), composer and artist: http://adagio.calarts.edu/~rchacon/
8. Barbara Croall (Odawa), composer and performer

9. Brent Michael Davids (Stockbridge-Munsee), composer and flute artist: http://www.brentmichaeldavids.com/concertmusic.html
10. Timothy Long (Muskogee Creek/Choctaw), conductor and pianist
11. Barbara McAlister (Cherokee), mezzo soprano opera singer: http://barbaramcalister.com/
12. George Quincy (Choctaw), composer and conductor: http://www.georgequincy.com/
13. Jerod Impichchaachaaha' Tate (Chickasaw), composer and artistic director http://www.jerodtate.com/

Fourteen Native Jazz Musicians

1. Mildred Bailey (Coeur d'Alene/Spokane)
2. Sharel Cassity (Cherokee)
3. Joy Harjo (Muscogee Creek)
4. Illinois Jacquet (Sioux)
5. Julia Keefe (Nez Perce)
6. Andrea Menard (Metis)
7. Russell "Big Chief" Moore (Tohono O'odham)
8. Jim Pepper (Kaw/Creek)
9. Oscar Pettiford (Choctaw/Cherokee)
10. Larry Redhouse (Navajo)
11. Della Reese (Cherokee)
12. Keely Smith (Cherokee)
13. Fredrick Whiteface (Lakota)
14. Lee Wiley (Cherokee)

Mildred Bailey

Jazz musician Mildred Bailey (Coeur d'Alene/Spokane) was featured on a twenty-nine-cent U.S. postage stamp issued on September 17, 1994.

Nineteen Native Bands

1. Blackfire: http://blackfire.net/
2. Bluedog
3. Jim Boyd Band: http://www.nativestars.com/bands/jimboyd
4. Brulé and AIRO: http://www.brulerecords.com/home.html
5. Burning Sky
6. Cecil Gray and Red Dawn Blues Band: http://www.reddawnbluesband.com/
7. Clan/Destine

8. Dark Water Rising: http://www.darkwaterrising.net/
9. Digging Roots: http://www.diggingrootsmusic.com/staging/
10. Firecat of Discord: http://www.thestudigroup.com/firecat.html
11. Gary Small Band: http://garysmallband.com/
12. Graywolf Blues Band
13. Indigenous: http://www.indigenousmusic.net/
14. Pamyua: http://tribalfunk.wordpress.com/music/
15. Redbone
16. Rezawrecktion: http://www.raw-xpressions.com/rezawrecktion/
17. Robby Bee and the Boyz from the Rez
18. WithOut Rezervation
19. XIT

Cherokee National Youth Choir

The Cherokee National Youth Choir, which was launched in the Cherokee Nation in 2000, performs traditional songs in the tribal language. The choir was the brainchild of Principal Chief Chad Smith, who envisioned it as a way to keep Native youth involved with language and culture. Forty young people, drawn from grades six through twelve in northeastern Oklahoma communities, make up the choir's membership, with auditions held every year to fill available places. The choir's debut album, *Voices of the Creator's Children*, featuring musician Rita Coolidge, was completed in 2002 and won the top award for "Best Gospel Christian Recording" at the fifth annual Native American Music Awards. Named an Honoring Nations honoree in 2003, the Cherokee National Youth Choir has performed at nationwide venues such as the Smithsonian Institution and Ground Zero. In 2008, the choir became the third recipient of the Governor's Award at the Twelfth Annual Oklahoma Music Hall of Fame event. The Cherokee National Youth Choir has also produced numerous other award-winning albums, including *Learning As We Sing*, which was awarded Best Audio CD at the International Cherokee Film Festival in 2009.

http://youthchoir.cherokee.org/

DANCE

Twenty-Two Native Dance Troupes and Companies

1. Alaska Kuteeyaa Dancers, Seattle, Washington: http://www.kuteeyaadancers.com/
2. American Indian Dance Theater, Los Angeles, California: http://americanindiandancetheater.net/

 3. Black Hawk Performance Company, Chicago, Illinois: http://www.ssa
    .uchicago.edu/
 4. Chilkat Dancers, Alaska Indian Arts, Haines, Alaska
 5. Dancing Earth Indigenous Contemporary Dance Creations, San Francisco,
    California: http://www.dancingearth.org/
 6. Daystar: Contemporary Dance-Drama of Indian America, Rochester, New
    York: http://www.daystardance.com/east.htm
 7. Divi Shadende: http://divishadende.com/index.html
 8. Earth Dance Theater, San Francisco, California
 9. Earth in Motion World Indigenous Dance, North Bay, Ontario, Canada:
    http://ipaa.ca/about/membership-directory/earth-motion/
10. Hālau Kawaihoa and Noa Noa Te Tiare Polynesian Dance Company, Kaneohe,
    Hawaii: http://www.kawaihoa.org/
11. Jones Benally Family, Flagstaff, Arizona: http://www.blackfire.net/about/
12. Kaha:wi Dance Theatre, Toronto, Ontario, Canada: http://www.kahawidance
    .org
13. Lakota Sioux Indian Dance Theatre: http://www.lakotadancetheatre.org/
14. Lda Kut Naxx Sati' Yatx'i (All Nation's Children Dancers), Juneau, Alaska:
    http://members.tripod.com/COAN_Dancers/
15. Many Moccasins Dance Troupe, Winnebago, Nebraska: http://www
    .viewfinderphotographs.com/talent_management.php
16. Native Spirit Productions, Phoenix, Arizona: http://www.nativespirit.com/
17. Red Crooked Sky, Southeastern Virginia: http://www.redcrookedsky.com/
18. Red Sky Performance, Toronto, Ontario, Canada: http://www.redskyperformance
    .com/
19. Tewa Dancers from the North, Ohkay Owingeh, New Mexico
20. Thunderbird American Indian Dancers, New York, New York
21. Warriors of AniKituhwa, Cherokee, North Carolina: http://www
    .cherokeemuseum.org/education-warriors.htm
22. Wichozani Dance Theatre, Riverside, California: http://vwichozani.tripod.com/

Ten Native Choreographers

 1. Marla Bingham (Mashpee Wampanoag): http://www.marlabingham.com
 2. Michael Greyeyes (Plains Cree): http://www.imdb.com/name/nm0340729/
 3. Belinda James (Ohkay Owingeh): http://divishadende.com/index.html
 4. Emily Johnson (Yup'ik): http://catalystdance.com/
 5. Rosalie Jones (Blackfeet/Pembina Chippewa): http://www.daystardance.com/
    east2.html
 6. Sandra Laronde (Teme-Augama-Anishnaabe, Ontario): http://www
    .redskyperformance.com/
 7. Muriel Miguel (Kuna/Rappahannock): http://www.spiderwomantheater.org/
 8. Santee Smith (Mohawk): http://www.santeesmithdance.com/

9. Rulan Tangen (Métis): http://dancingearth.org/company.html
10. Raoul Trujillo (Apache/Ute): http://www.raoultrujilloinfo.com/

Five American Indian Ballerinas

Known as the "American Indian ballerinas," five Oklahoma natives rose to prominence in ballet from the 1940s through the 1960s. The dancers became internationally renowned for their contributions to the world of ballet. In 1991 the dedication of Chickasaw artist Mike Larsen's *Flight of Spirit*, a permanent mural commissioned for the Oklahoma State Capitol to honor the ballerinas, brought them there for their first public appearance together. Six years later, they were reunited at the capitol to each receive the Oklahoma Cultural Treasure Award, designated by the governor of Oklahoma and the Oklahoma Arts Council. http://arts.ok.gov/Art_at_the_Capitol/Capitol_Collection/Larsen/Flight_of_Spirit.html

1. Yvonne Chouteau (Cherokee)
2. Rosella Hightower (Choctaw)
3. Moscelyne Larkin (Peoria/Shawnee)
4. Maria Tallchief (Osage)
5. Marjorie Tallchief (Osage)

Five American Indian Dances Featured on U.S. Postage Stamps

The U.S. Postal Service issued a set of five thirty-two-cent American Indian Dances commemorative stamps on June 7, 1996, during the Red Earth Festival in Oklahoma City, Oklahoma. Illustrated by Keith Birdsong (Cherokee/Muskogee), three of the stamps feature the Hoop Dance, Fancy Dance, and Traditional Dance, which are performed by tribally diverse dancers at powwows nationwide. The other two stamps feature the Raven Dance, which is performed by Northwest Coast tribes, and the Butterfly Dance, a dance of Pueblo tribes from the Southwest.

1. Butterfly Dance
2. Fancy Dance
3. Hoop Dance
4. Raven Dance
5. Traditional Dance

Eleven Poems with Music and Dance Themes by Native Poets

1. "Dancing the Sky," by Karenne Wood (Monacan). In *Beyond Jamestown: Virginia Indians Yesterday and Today*. Teacher's Guide (2007).
2. "Glossary of a Powwow," by Sherman Alexie (Spokane/Coeur d'Alene). In *The Summer of Black Widows* (1996).

3. "Gone Dancing," by Deborah A. Miranda (Esselen/Chumash). In *Indian Cartography* (1999).
4. "The Gourd Dancer," by N. Scott Momaday (Kiowa). In *Songs from This Earth on Turtle's Back: Contemporary American Indian Poetry*, edited by Joseph Bruchac (1983).
5. "Indian Singing in 20th-Century America," by Gail Tremblay (Onondaga/Micmac). In *Reinventing the Enemy's Language*, edited by Joy Harjo and Gloria Bird (1997).
6. "Jingles You Made," by Kimberly Blaeser (Anishinaabe). In *Apprenticed to Justice* (2007).
7. "The Motion of Songs Rising," by Luci Tapahonso (Navajo). In *Sáanii Dahataal: The Women Are Singing* (1993).
8. "The Place the Musician Became a Bear," by Joy Harjo (Muskogee/Creek). In *How We Became Human: New and Selected Poems: 1975–2001* (2002).
9. "The Powwow Crowd," by Roberta Hill Whiteman (Oneida). In *Philadelphia Flowers* (1996).
10. "Two Standards," by Elise Paschen (Osage). In *Reinventing the Enemy's Language*, edited by Joy Harjo and Gloria Bird (1997).
11. "Veteran's Dance 1995," by Denise Sweet (Anishinaabe). In *Songs for Discharming* (1997).

Ten Music and Dance Festivals

1. Canadian Aboriginal Festival, Brantford, Ontario, Canada: http://www.canab.com/
2. Chickasaw Chamber Music Festival, Chickasaw Nation, Ada, Oklahoma: http://www.chickasawmusicfestivals.org/
3. Ganondagan Native American Dance and Music Festival, Ganondagan State Historic Site, Victor, New York: http://www.ganondagan.org/NADMF.html
4. Gathering of Nations Powwow, Albuquerque, New Mexico: http://www.gatheringofnations.com/
5. Indian Summer Festival, Milwaukee, Wisconsin: http://www.indiansummer.org/
6. Manito Ahbee Festival, Winnipeg, Manitoba, Canada: http://www.manitoahbee.com/
7. Nā Hōkū Hanohano Music Festival, Honolulu, Hawaii: http://www.nahokumusicfestival .com/
8. Native Roots and Rhythms Festival, Santa Fe, New Mexico: http://www.nrrfestival.com/
9. Red Earth Native American Cultural Festival, Oklahoma City, Oklahoma: http://www.redearth.org/red-earth-festival/
10. Waila Festival, Tucson, Arizona

Federal Ban on American Indian Religious Observances, including Dances

In 1883 Secretary of the Interior Henry M. Teller established Courts of Indian Offenses on federal Indian reservations, ultimately prohibiting the Sun Dance and other religious observances and making such practices subject to punishment. Encouraged to observe the Fourth of July, American Indians incorporated dance and other cultural expressions on that day, in the spirit (and under the cover) of the national day of celebration. Seizing the opportunity to perform dances and other cultural practices, a number of Plains tribes changed the time of their Sun Dance to coincide with the holiday, calling it "the Great Holy Day" or "Big Holy Day" in tribal languages such as Lakota and Blackfeet. What appeared to be secular dances and celebrations to outsiders became a vehicle to continue Native traditions.

Today, a number of tribes such as Quapaw in Oklahoma, Red Lake Chippewa in Minnesota, and Northern Cheyenne in Montana continue to hold powwows on the Fourth of July. These and other powwow celebrations provide opportunities for Native people to make the holiday their own, expressing diverse tribal traditions through music, dance, and ceremony.

Heard Museum World Championship Hoop Dance Contest

The World Championship Hoop Dance Contest, first held at the New Mexico State Fair in 1991, was co-founded by Dennis Zotigh (Kiowa/Santee Dakota/Ohkay Owingeh Pueblo) and his father Ralph Zotigh (Kiowa). The contest was moved to the Heard Museum in Phoenix, Arizona, the following year, where it continues as a popular annual event. The Hoop Dance, a dance that is symbolic of the circle of life, is generally performed by a single dancer who uses multiple hoops to create designs such as animals, butterflies, birds, and a world globe while dancing to the beat of the drum. Many tribal nations claim the dance originated with them, but the modern form is generally traced to Tony White Cloud (Jemez Pueblo), who began performing a stylized version of the dance using several hoops made of willow shaped into a circle. White Cloud invented culturally significant hoop formations and performed at a number of venues, influencing other American Indians, who adapted the dance for their own use.

The Heard Museum World Championship Hoop Dance Contest has grown over the years, now encompassing both male and female dancers competing in a range of categories. Some seventy to eighty individuals participate, drawing thousands of spectators. Championship dancers have included Eddie Swimmer (Cherokee), the first World Champion; Quentin Pipestem (Tsuu T'ina Nation in Alberta, Canada), the first adult champion at the Heard; and Lisa Odjig (Odawa/Anishinaabe from Ontario), who became the first female adult to win the competition, in 2000. Hoop dancing, a popular art form across Native North America, continues to evolve with the development of new techniques and designs.

http://heard.org/hoop/abouthoop.html

POWWOWS

Six Interesting Facts about Powwows

1. The term powwow has been traced to the Algonquian language family, specifically to the Narragansett words *pau wau,* first recorded in 1605, which refer to a shaman or a council of Indians. Over time, the word (with various spellings) came to be applied to Indian dance events held in communities throughout North America.
2. Powwows, held in communities of all sizes across the country and beyond, are celebrations of Native culture and heritage. Male and female dancers of all ages participate, dancing to the music of participating drum groups. A significant number of powwows feature dance competitions, with prize money awarded in various categories. Powwows may be held as separate events or in conjunction with other activities such as exhibits, fairs, or rodeos. They vary in size, purpose, and venue (outdoor or inside arenas).
3. Sponsored by the Confederated Salish and Kootenai Tribes and first held in 1898, the annual Arlee Powwow in Arlee, Montana, is the oldest continuous powwow held in the same location. It is held on the Fourth of July.
   http://www.cskt.org/about/publicrelations.htm
4. Crow Fair, which is held annually by the Apsáalooke (Crow) Nation in Montana, is known as the Teepee Capital of the World because of the large number of tipis (estimated at between twelve and fifteen thousand) and the huge size of the event. The one-week celebration, with thousands of participants and visitors, includes powwow dancing, daily parades, an all-Indian rodeo, and horse races.
5. Gathering of Nations bills itself as "North America's Biggest Powwow." Held in Albuquerque, New Mexico, the annual number of Native dancers and singers is estimated at over three thousand, representing more than five hundred tribes from the United States and Canada.
   http://www.gatheringofnations.com/
6. Black Lodge Singers, based in White Swan, Washington, are likely the most recorded drum group performing powwow music, with more than twenty albums on the Canyon Records label alone. Led by Kenny Scabby Robe of the

Blackfeet Nation, the northern drum group has won Native American Music Awards and received a Grammy Award nomination in 2004. Their extensive body of work includes albums of powwow songs for children.

Powwow Dances

Powwows incorporate a number of dances, most of them with origins in specific tribal nations or regions of the country, such as Northern and Southern Plains tribes. The performances include a variety of categories for both males and females. Powwows also incorporate dances in which everyone is invited to participate, especially intertribal or round dances. These dances are generally interspersed with competition dancing, where dancers in specific categories compete for prize money.

Powwows may also feature specialty dancing, including tribally specific performances, and honoring ceremonies. Following are some examples of dances.

Men's Dances

Traditional Dance

Traditional dances can be traced to early dance forms and styles, such as those rooted in tribal-specific warrior societies and Omaha/Grass Dance traditions. Through their footwork and other movements, the dancers tell a story relating to war, valor, hunting, and other feats. The regalia worn, depending on factors such as tribal origins and personal preferences, generally include a single back bustle with cloth trailers hanging from it, shirt, leggings, breastplate, roach or headdress, and feather fan.

Grass Dance

Although origin accounts vary, the Grass Dance (also called the Omaha Dance) is generally traced to the Omaha Tribe, a Great Plains tribal nation. The name refers to the dance's association with tall prairie grasses. Grass Dancers evoke swaying waves of grass, as well as representations such as "flattening the grass" through their dancing. Their outfits add to the effect, with colorful fringes, ribbons, or yarn replacing grasses originally tucked into belts and armbands. Other regalia include shirt, pants, aprons, leggings, armbands, cuffs, moccasins, and a roach.

Fancy Dance

Men's Fancy Dance, which is accompanied by very rapid drumbeats, is a free-form style of dancing that requires athleticism and endurance. The dancers, generally young, tend to wear vibrant colors in regalia such as feather bustles, decorated shirts, fringed aprons, and beaded yokes and moccasins.

Women's Dances

Women's Traditional Dance

The women's traditional dance varies, but is generally characterized by two footwork forms, one in which the dancer moves forward step by step, and the other in which she dances in one place. By tradition, the dancer's feet remain on the ground, symbolizing her close relationship to the earth. The regalia include buckskin or cloth dresses, beaded yokes, leggings, and moccasins. The dancer generally carries a fan and a folded shawl.

Jingle Dress Dance

Originating among the Ojibwe, this dance is named for the tin, cone-shaped jingles that are sewn in rows on the dresses worn by the dancers. With the dancer's movements, the cones make a distinctive sound as they jingle against one another. Before the late 1960s and early 1970s, the dance, which has religious healing origins, was performed primarily in Ojibwe communities. It has since become popular nationwide, favored by a diverse range of female dancers across the country.

Fancy Dance

Also referred to as a Fancy Shawl or Butterfly Dance, this fast-paced dance is performed by young female dancers. Their regalia include a dress (or skirt and top), leggings and moccasins, and a fringed shawl worn over their shoulders and arms. The dancer, with athleticism and grace, often evokes the beauty and movement of a butterfly.

Eleven Books about Powwows

1. *Chicago's 50 Years of Powwows*, by the American Indian Center of Chicago (2004).
2. *A Dancing People: Powwow Culture on the Southern Plains*, by Clyde Ellis (2006).
3. *Drumbeat . . . Heartbeat: A Celebration of the Powwow*, by Susan Braine (1995).
4. *Faces from the Land: Twenty Years of Powwow Tradition*, by Ben Marra and Linda Marra (2009).
5. *Heartbeat of the People: Music and Dance of the Northern Pow-Wow*, by Tara Browner (2002).
6. *Jingle Dancer*, by Cynthia Leitich Smith (2000).
7. *Long Powwow Nights*, by David Bouchard and Pam Aleekuk (2009).
8. *Powwow*, by George Ancona (1993).
9. *Powwow*, edited by Clyde Ellis, Luke Eric Lassiter, and Gary H. Dunham (2005).
10. *Powwow's Coming*, by Linda Boyden (2007).
11. *We Dance Because We Can: People of the Powwow*, by Diane M. Bernstein and Don Contreras (1996).

AWARDS

Grammy Award for Best Native American Music Album

The National Academy of Recording Arts and Sciences (NARAS), also known as the Recording Academy, established the Best Native American Music Album as a new category for its annual Grammy Awards in 2001. Headquartered in Los Angeles, the Academy, which honors outstanding achievements in the music industry, announced a restructuring of award categories in 2011. It ended the Native American category, placing it into a newly created Best Regional Roots Music Album with Native Hawaiian, Zydeco/Cajun, and other entries.

2001   *Gathering of Nations Pow Wow*, by Tom Bee (Dakota) and Douglas Spotted Eagle (also known as Douglas Wallentine)

2002   *Bless the People—Harmonized Peyote Songs*, by Giuli Doyle, Robert Doyle, Jack Miller, Johnny Mike (Navajo), and Verdell Primeaux (Dakota/Ponca)

2003   *Beneath the Raven Moon*, by Thomas A. Wasinger and Mary Youngblood (Aleut/Seminole)

2004   *Flying Free*, by Black Eagle (Jemez Pueblo)

2005   *Cedar Dream Songs*, by Bill Miller (Mohican)

2006   *Sacred Ground—A Tribute to Mother Earth*, by Jim Wilson

2007   *Dance with the Wind*, by Mary Youngblood (Aleut/Seminole)

2008   *Totemic Flute Chants*, by Robert Mirabal (Taos Pueblo)

2009   *Come to Me Great Mystery – Native American Healing Songs*, by Thomas A. Wasinger

2010   *Spirit Wind North*, by Bill Miller (Mohican)

2011   *2010 Gathering of Nations Pow Wow: A Spirit's Dance*, by various artists

Juno Award for Aboriginal Recording of the Year

Conducted by the Canadian Academy of Recording Arts and Sciences (CARAS), the annual Juno Awards are Canada's primary national honors for achievements in music. In 1994, the organization began recognizing Aboriginal music with an award category. Initially called "Best Music of Aboriginal Canada Recording" (1994–2002), it became known as the "Aboriginal Recording of the Year" (2003–present).

Best Music of Aboriginal Canada Recording

1994   *Wapistan,* by Lawrence Martin

1995   *Arctic Rose,* by Susan Aglukark

1996   *ETSI Shon, "Grandfather Song,"* by Jerry Alfred and the Medicine Beat

1997   *Up Where We Belong,* by Buffy Sainte-Marie

1998   *The Spirit Within,* by Mishi Donovan

1999   *Contact from the Underworld of Redboy,* by Robbie Robertson

2000   *Falling Down,* by Chester Knight and the Wind

2001   *Nipaiamianan,* by Florent Vollant

2002   *On and On,* by Eagle and Hawk

Aboriginal Recording of the Year

2003   *Lovesick Blues,* by Derek Miller

2004   *Big Feeling,* by Susan Aglukark

2005   *Taima,* by Taima

2006   *Hometown,* by Burnt Project 1

2007   *Sedzé,* by Leela Gilday

2008   *The Dirty Looks,* by Derek Miller

2009   *Running for the Drum,* by Buffy Sainte-Marie

2010   *We Are,* by Digging Roots

2011   *CerAmony,* by CerAmony

Native American Music Awards

The annual Native American Music Awards, or NAMMYs, began in January 1998 as "the first and only national Awards show in the world honoring Native American and aboriginal music" (http://www.nativeamericanmusicawards. com/aboutus.cfm). Founded by Ellen Bello, the annual awards event now involves over two hundred artists who submit recordings for nomination consideration in over thirty categories. People can listen to music tracks of featured artists and cast votes for their favorites at the organization's Web site: http://www.nativeamericanmusicawards.com

Native American Music Awards Hall of Fame

Date of Induction	Musician	Tribe
1998	Jimi Hendrix	Cherokee
1998	Buddy Red Bow	Lakota
1999	Hank Williams	Choctaw
2000	Jim Pepper	Creek/Kaw
2001	Crystal Gayle	Cherokee
2002	Kitty Wells	Cherokee
2006	Doc Tate Nevaquaya	Comanche
2007	Link Wray	Shawnee
2008	Ricky Medlock	Blackfoot
2008	Janice Marie Johnson	Stockbridge-Munsee
2008	Felipe Rose	Taino/Lakota
2008	Redbone	Intertribal
2009	Ritchie Valens	Yaqui
2011	Nokie Edwards	Cherokee
	Keith Secola	Ojibwa

Native American Music Awards Lifetime Achievement

1998	Robbie Robertson
1999	Tom Bee and XIT
2000	Fredrick Whiteface
2000	Rita Coolidge
2001	R. Carlos Nakai
2003	John Densmore
2006	Tiger Tiger
2007	Joanne Shenandoah
2007	Bill Miller
2009	Stevie Salas
2010	Bobby Bullet St. Germaine

Native American Music Awards Living Legend

1998	John Trudell
1999	Chief Jim Billie

2000	Navajo Code Talkers
2001	Neville Brothers
2002	Floyd Red Crow Westerman
2009	Tommy Allsup

Native American Music Awards—Best Pow Wow Recording

1998	Black Lodge Singers (Blackfeet)
1999	Various artists (intertribal), *Gathering of Nations*
2000	Various drum groups (intertribal), *Gathering of Nations '98*
2001	Northern Cree (Cree), *Rockin the Rez*
2002	Red Bull, *Traditional* (Turtle Island)
2003	Black Eagle (Taos Pueblo), *Flying Free*
2004–05	Black Lodge, Star Society, Moccasin Flats, *Blackfoot Pow Wow*
2006	Black Eagle (Taos Pueblo), *Straight Up Northern*
2007	Northern Cree and Friends, *Long Winter Nights*
2008	Blackfoot Confederacy, *Hear the Beat*
2009	Midnite Express, *Band of Brothers*
2010	The Boyz, *Boyz Will Be Boyz*
2011	Black Thunder Singers (Oglala Lakota/Inupiaq/Micmac), *Black Thunder*

Native American Music Awards—Best Rap/Hip Hop Recording

1998	Litefoot ("Best Rap Artist")
1999	Litefoot, *The Life & Times*
2000	Litefoot, *Rez Affiliated*
2001	Rollin Fox, *Strictly Native*
2002	Litefoot, *Tribal Boogie*
2003	Tribal Live, *True II Life: The 10 Letter Theory*
2004–05	Shadowyze, *Red Hawk Woman*
2006	Buggin Malone, *Spirit World*
2007	Night Shield, *The Total Package*

2008	Dago Braves, *Native American Hustle*
2009	Rezhogs, *All Day All Night*
2010	Chase Monchamp (Chase Manhattan), *Tribal Tribulations*
2011	Naka Nula Waun, *Scars and Bars*

Native American Music Awards—Songwriter of the Year

1998	Robert Mirabal (Taos Pueblo)
1999	Bill Miller (Mohican), *Ghost Dance*
2000	Robert Mirabal (Taos Pueblo), *Taos Tales*
2001	Robert Mirabal (Taos Pueblo), *Music from a Painted Cave*
2002	Gary Small (Northern Cheyenne), *Wild Indians*
2003	Joseph FireCrow (Cheyenne), *Legend of the Warrior*
2004–05	Felipe Rose (Taino/Lakota), *Red Hawk Woman*
2006	Jim Boyd (Colville), *Them Old Guitars*
2007	Arigon Starr (Kickapoo), *The Red Road*
2008	Star Nayea (tribal affiliation unknown), *Silenced My Tongue*
2009	Samantha Crain (Choctaw), *The Confiscation: A Musical Novella*
2010	Brad Clonch (Mississippi Choctaw) and Jeff Carpenter (Chickasaw), *Fight for Survival*
2011	Josh Halverson (Mdewakanton Sioux), *These Times*

FILMS

Dancing from the Heart (USA, 2007, 44 min.), directed by Marilyn Hunt.
>   This film documents Andrew Garcia (Ohkay Owingeh) and his family dance group, the Tewa Dancers from the North, as they present dance and culture traditions of Ohkay Owingeh (formerly San Juan Pueblo) in New Mexico.

Dancing on Mother Earth (USA, 2003, 57 min.), directed by Jim Virga.
>   This film presents a behind-the-scenes look at singer-songwriter Joanne Shenandoah (Oneida Nation), interweaving concert footage, interviews, and family scenes to depict her life and work.

En Pointe: The Lives and Legacies of Ballet's Native Americans (USA, 2000, 60 min.), directed by Shawnee Brittan.
>   This film depicts the lives and legacies of the internationally renowned ballerinas Maria Tallchief (Osage), Rosella Hightower (Choctaw), Marjorie Tallchief (Osage), Yvonne Chouteau (Cherokee), and Moscelyne Larkin (Peoria/Shawnee).

How the Fiddle Flows (Canada, 2002, 48 min.), directed by Gregory Coyes (Métis Cree).

Following Canada's rivers along fur-trading routes, this documentary traces the development of fiddling among Métis, Aboriginal people who intermarried with Europeans. The film is narrated by actress Tantoo Cardinal (Métis) and features well-known fiddlers and dancers associated with the rich blend of musical traditions.

John Kim Bell: The First North American Indian Conductor (Canada, 1984, 41 min.), directed by Anthony Azzopardi, CBC.

This documentary tells the story of John Kim Bell (Kahnawake Mohawk) and his path to becoming a symphonic conductor.

Kawdan's Song (USA, 2006, 16 min.), directed by Annabel Wong (Salt River Pima).

This film tells the story of a young woman from the Salt River Pima–Maricopa community in Arizona who travels to New York City for a violin audition. Besides being the lead actress, Laura Ortman (White Mountain Apache) also composed the score.

Making a Noise: A Native American Musical Journey with Robbie Robertson (USA, 1998, 57 min.), directed by Dana Heinz Perry.

This film documents the journey of Robbie Robertson (Mohawk), musician from the legendary rock group, The Band, on his return to the Six Nations Reserve in Ontario for a reunion with relatives and friends. The film also features Rita Coolidge, Buffy Sainte-Marie, John Trudell, and other Native American musicians.

Maria Tallchief (USA, 2007, 57 min.), directed by Sandra Sunrising Osawa (Makah).

Produced by Upstream Productions and broadcast on PBS in 2007, this film explores the life and artistry of Maria Tallchief (Osage), America's first prima ballerina.

Pepper's Pow Wow (USA, 1995, 57 min.), directed by Sandra Sunrising Osawa (Makah).

This documentary pays tribute to legendary jazz saxophonist and composer Jim Pepper (Kaw/Creek), tracing his life and music.

Rockin' Warriors (USA, 1997, 56 min.), directed by Andy Bausch.

This film explores Native American rock and roll, including its popularity in Europe. Filmed on reservations in Arizona, at concerts in Germany, and other locations, *Rockin' Warriors* features interviews and performance footage of Native artists including Buffy Sainte-Marie, Robert Mirabal, Joy Harjo and Poetic Justice, John Trudell, Ulali, Keith Secola, Song Catchers, and Tom Bee.

Singing Our Stories (Canada, 1998, 49 min.), directed by Annie Fraziér Henry (Blackfoot/Sioux/French).

This film depicts the lives and musical roots of Native women across North America, including performers such as Walela, Ulali, Zuni Olla Maidens, and 'Namgis Traditional Singers from the North Pacific Coast.

Song Journey (USA, 1994, 57 min.), directed by Arlene Bowman (Navajo).

The filmmaker travels the powwow dance circuit, where she learns about the role of Native American female musicians in continuing and expanding Native music traditions.

Songkeepers (USA, 1999, 48 min.), directed by Bob Hercules and Bob Jackson.

This film centers on distinguished flute artists Tom Mauchahty-Ware (Kiowa), Sonny Nevaquaya (Comanche), R. Carlos Nakai (Navajo/Ute), Kevin Locke (Lakota), and Hawk LittleJohn (Cherokee). Narrated by singer Rita Coolidge (Cherokee), *Songkeepers* reveals the meaning and role of the flute through the stories and lives of the featured musicians.

Trudell (USA, 2004, 80 min.), directed by Heather Rae (Cherokee).

Filmmaker Heather Rae documents the work of poet, musician, actor, and political activist John Trudell (Santee Sioux), a leader of the American Indian Movement who also became a creative force in rock and roll. Rae intersperses archival footage with interviews with friends and colleagues such as Kris Kristofferson, Robert Redford, Jackson Browne, and Gary Farmer (Cayuga) to tell Trudell's story.

Waila! Making the People Happy (USA, 2009, 58 min.), directed by Dan Golding (Quechan).

This documentary explores the history of Waila, the lively contemporary dance music of Akimel and Tohono O'odham communities in southern Arizona, through the experiences of the Joaquin family and their journey to performing at Carnegie Hall. Waila, which stems from *baila*, the Spanish word for dance, is a form of music that incorporates polka and Mexican *tejano*, *cumbias*, and *Norteño*.

Water Flowing Together (USA, 2007, 79 min.), directed by Gwendolen Cates. In English, Navajo, and Spanish with English subtitles.

This documentary explores the life of Jock Soto (Navajo/Puerto Rican), who left his family at the age of sixteen to pursue his dream of becoming a dancer. During his twenty-five-year career, he was one of the most recognized performers in the dance world, serving as a principal dancer in the New York City Ballet.

When Your Hands Are Tied (USA, 2006, 56 min.), directed by Mia Boccella Hartle.

A not-for-profit educational film, *When Your Hands Are Tied* explores the ways in which Native youth express themselves in the contemporary world, especially contemporary rockers, rappers, and multimedia artists from the Southwest.

The World of American Indian Dance (USA, 2003, 60 min.), directed by Randy Martin.

This film, the first American Indian–produced documentary to air on a major television network, premiered on NBC on April 19, 2003. Filmed at the Crow Fair in Montana with a cast and crew from various tribal backgrounds, *The World of American Indian Dance* explores the meaning and origin of a number of dances across diverse Native American cultures.

ORGANIZATIONS

First Americans in the Arts (FAITA)
http://www.firstamericans.org/

First Americans in the Arts (FAITA) was created to recognize, honor, and promote American Indian participation in the entertainment industry, including the areas of film, television, theater, and music. FAITA presents annual awards recognizing outstanding achievement, performances, and contributions to the Native American entertainment community.

First Nations Composer Initiative (FNCI)
http://www.fnci.org/
Launched in 2006 by the American Composers Forum, the First Nations Composer Initiative is dedicated to the encouragement and support of American Indian, First Nations, Alaska Native, and indigenous musical traditions in all its forms. FNCI, which is based in St. Paul, Minnesota, seeks to help create opportunities for American Indians in these endeavors.

Gathering of Nations
http://www.gatheringofnations.com/
Founded in 1983, the Gathering of Nations is a nonprofit organization that promotes Native cultural traditions, hosting events and programs that include the Annual Gathering of Nations Powwow, Miss Indian World Traditional Talent Presentations, and the Indian Trader's Market in Albuquerque, New Mexico. In September 2010, the American Bus Association designated the Gathering of Nations Powwow as one of the Top 100 Events in North America for 2011.

Hawai'i Academy of Recording Arts (HARA)
http://www.nahokuhanohano.org/
The origins of the Hawai'i Academy of Recording Arts (HARA) and Na Hoku Hanohano Awards can be traced to 1978 and KCCN-AM Radio, then the world's only all-Hawaiian music radio program. HARA, a nonprofit organization, was formed in 1982 to promote Hawaii's recording industry and the music of Hawaii. Headquartered in Honolulu, HARA's work includes directing programs and events, as well as awarding scholarships.

Hula Preservation Society
http://www.hulapreservation.org
Established in 2000, the Hula Preservation Society (HPS) in Kaneohe, Hawaii, is a nonprofit organization dedicated to documenting, preserving, and sharing the life stories of the eldest living hula masters and their efforts to perpetuate hula. Since that time, HPS has extended its work to include elders with firsthand accounts of hula masters and teachings. The organization is dedicated to preserving the past and sharing the future.

International Native American and World Flute Association
http://www.worldflutes.org/
> Founded in 1987, the International Native American and World Flute Association was established to foster the advancement, appreciation, preservation, and understanding of the Native American flute as well as other flute traditions in the world. The organization, based in Suffolk, Virginia, provides a listing of Native American flute events by state on its Web site.

Kawaihoa Foundation
http://www.kawaihoa.org/foundation.html
> The Kawaihoa Foundation, also known as Hālau Kawaihoa, is a nonprofit organization located in Kaneohe, Hawaii, established to promote and preserve the hula, Polynesian dances, and other ethnic arts. Dance styles are taught as passed down through generations and teachings.

RESOURCES

Bogeyaktuk, Anatole, and Charlie Steve. *Taprarmiuni Kassiyulriit: Stebbins Dance Festival,* edited by Ann Fienup-Riordan. Fairbanks: Alaska Native Language Center and University of Alaska Press, 2004.

Browner, Tara, ed. *Music of the First Nations: Tradition and Innovation in Native North American.* Champaign: University of Illinois Press, 2009.

Geiogamah, Hanay, and Jaye T. Darby. *American Indian Performing Arts: Critical Directions.* Los Angeles: UCLA American Indian Studies Center, 2010.

Heth, Charlotte, ed. *Native American Dance: Ceremonies and Social Traditions.* Washington, DC: National Museum of the American Indian/Starwood Publishing, 1992.

Kois, Dan. *Israel Kamakawiwo'ole's Facing Future.* New York: Continuum, 2010.

Murphy, Jacqueline Shea. *The People Have Never Stopped Dancing.* Minneapolis: University of Minnesota Press, 2007.

Prinzing, Scott S. *American Indian Music: More Than Just Flutes and Drums. A Guide to American Indian Music Prepared for the Office of Public Instruction.* Helena, MT: MusEco Media and Education Project, Montana Office of Public Instruction, 2009. http://opi.mt.gov/pdf/IndianEd/Resources/09MoreThanDrums.pdf

Soto, Jock. *Every Step You Take: A Memoir.* New York: HarperCollins, 2011.

Tallchief, Maria, with Larry Kaplan. *America's Prima Ballerina.* New York: Henry Holt and Co., 1997.

Troutman, John W. *Indian Blues: American Indians and the Politics of Music, 1879–1934.* Norman: University of Oklahoma Press, 2009.

Worl, Rosita, et al. *Celebration: Tlingit, Haida, Tsimshian Dancing on the Land.* Published by Sealaska Heritage Institute in association with the University of Washington Press, 2008.

Wright-McLeod, Brian. *The Encyclopedia of Native Music.* Tucson: The University of Arizona Press, 2005.

Web Sites

American Indians: Index of Native American Music Resources on the Internet (WWW Virtual Library): http://www.hanksville.org/NAresources/indices/NAmusic.html

Bill Miller's List of Ten Essential Songs for Native Musicians: http://www.americanindiannews.org/2010/12/10-essential-songs-for-native-musicians/

Canyon Records: http://canyonrecords.com/

Drumbeat Indian Arts: http://drumbeatindianarts.com

Indian House Records: http://www.indianhouse.com/

Indigenous Action Media: http://www.indigenousaction.org/

Makoché Recording Company: http://www.makoche.com/

Native American Music Association: www.nativeamericanmusicawards.com

Native Hip-Hop: http://www.nativehiphop.net/

Native Radio: www.nativeradio.com

Native Village Music and Dance Library: http://www.nativevillage.org/Libraries/Music%20and%20Dance_library.htm

PowWows.com: http://tv.powwows.com/

Red Earth Records: http://www.oocities.org/redearthrecords/

RPM (Revolutions Per Minute) Indigenous Music Culture: http://rpm.fm/

RPM's 10 Must-Hear Tracks by Native Musicians: http://indiancountrytodaymedianetwork.com/2011/07/rpms-10-must-hear-tracks-by-native-musicians/

Sound of America Records: http://www.soundofamerica.com/

Sweetgrass Records: http://www.sweetgrassrecords.com/

19

Print, Radio, and Television

PRINT

Firsts: Print

1826   *The Literary Voyager or Muzzeniegun,* a weekly magazine, was the first publication established to publish information about American Indians on a regular basis. It was published by Henry Rowe Schoolcraft, whose Ojibwe wife, Jane Johnston Schoolcraft, contributed many articles.

1828   The *Cherokee Phoenix* became the first tribal newspaper in North America and the first paper to publish news in an American Indian language. The weekly, published in the Cherokee Nation, New Echota, Georgia, was printed in English and the Cherokee syllabary.

Elias Boudinot (Cherokee) was the first editor of a tribal newspaper. He edited the *Cherokee Phoenix* from 1828 until 1832.

1834   Newspapers *Ka Lama Hawaii* and *Ke Kuma Hawaii* were the first periodicals published in the Hawaiian language.

1835   *Siwinowe Kesibwi* ("Shawnee Sun") was the first periodical published entirely in a Native American language. It was printed in a Shawnee orthography developed by Jotham Meeker at Shawnee Mission, Kansas.

1857   John Rollin Ridge, also known as Cheesquatalawny or Yellow Bird (Cherokee), was the first American Indian to edit a non-Indian newspaper. He founded the *Sacramento Daily and Weekly Bee* in 1857, which later became known as the *Sacramento Bee,* one of the nation's prominent newspapers.

1964   The American Indian Historical Society, founded by prominent national leaders Rupert Costo (Cahuilla) and his wife, Jeannette Henry Costo (Cherokee), produced the first issue of *Indian Historian* in order "to correct the record, to write history as it should be written, to interpret correctly the aboriginal past, to report honestly the immense contributions to modern society made by the Indian American." The journal lasted eighteen years.

1970   The American Indian Press Association was founded in Washington, DC. It provided news to member newspapers and a network of Indian journalists.

1973   The first issue of *Wassaja*, a national advocacy newspaper of American Indian life, was published by its founder, Rupert Costo (Cahuilla). The newspaper included articles focused on self-determination, land and water rights, housing, treaties, and other significant issues, along with poetry, book reviews, cartoons, and feature stories. The paper ceased publication in 1984.

1978   Gary Fife (Cherokee/Creek) became the first Native American Ford Fellow in Education Journalism. He went on to produce and host *National Native News*, a national radio news service for Native people.

1981   The *Lakota Times*, published by Tim Giago (Oglala Lakota), became the first independently owned Indian newspaper in the United States.

1983   The *Navajo Times Today* became the first modern daily American Indian newspaper published for an American Indian audience.

1990–91   Tim Giago (Oglala Lakota) became the first American Indian accepted into Harvard University's Nieman Fellowship program for journalists.

1991   The *Lakota Times* opened the first Native American Washington, DC, newspaper bureau. It also became the first national Native American weekly newspaper, thanks to a sizable investment from the Freedom Forum.

1994   The first gathering of UNITY took place in Atlanta, Georgia. It began as an alliance of print and broadcast journalists of color: Native American, Asian American, African American, and Hispanic American.

2000   Tom Arviso (Navajo) became "the first and only full-blood Native American to have been selected for a Knight Fellowship" in journalism (Knight Digital Media Center: http://www.knightdigitalmediacenter.org/seminars/fellow/tom_arviso_jr). He studied newspaper management at Stanford University.

2011   The premiere issue of *This Week From Indian Country Today*, a new weekly magazine, was published by Indian Country Today Media Network. It replaced *Indian Country Today* (*Lakota Times*), the award-winning weekly newspaper. The magazine and Web site blend news, entertainment, business, politics, and education.

Ten Early Native American Newspapers, 1828–78

Early Native American newspapers, published by Indian nations and individuals ("nontribal"), presented historical events from Native points of view. The American Native Press Archives in Little Rock, Arkansas, houses these titles in one of the largest collections of Native newspapers and periodicals in the world.

1828–34   The *Cherokee Phoenix and Indians' Advocate*
                 Tribal newspaper: Cherokee Nation; New Echota, Cherokee Nation

1844–1906   The *Cherokee Advocate*
                 Tribal newspaper: Cherokee Nation; Tahlequah, Cherokee Nation

1848–49   The *Choctaw Telegraph*
                 Nontribal newspaper: Doaksville, Choctaw Nation

1850–55   *The Choctaw Intelligencer*
                 Nontribal newspaper: Doaksville, Choctaw Nation

1858–?   The *Chickasaw and Choctaw Herald*
                 Nontribal newspaper: Tishomingo City, Chickasaw Nation

1875–76   *The Indian Progress*
                 Nontribal newspaper: Muskogee, Creek Nation, and Vinita, Cherokee Nation

1876–present   *The Indian Journal*
                 Intertribal newspaper: Muskogee, Creek Nation; became official city paper of Eufaula, Oklahoma, in 1903 to present day

1878   The *Choctaw News*
                 Tribal newspaper: Chahta Tamaha, Choctaw Nation

1882–1912   The *Indian Chieftain*, 1882–1902/ *Vinita Weekly Chieftain*, 1902–5/ *The Weekly Chieftain*, 1905–12; Nontribal newspaper: Vinita, Cherokee Nation, later Oklahoma

1903–26   *The Tomahawk*
                 Tribal newspaper: Minnesota Chippewa; White Earth, Minnesota

Ten Early American Indian Boarding School Newspapers

1879–81   *The Hallequah*
                 Seneca, Shawnee, and Wyandotte Industrial Boarding School
                 Quapaw Agency, Indian Territory (present-day Oklahoma)

1880–83   *School News*
                 Carlisle Indian Industrial School
                 Carlisle, Pennsylvania

1884–86	*Indian Citizen* Indian Industrial School Forest Grove, Oregon
1884–1937	*The Word Carrier of the Santee Normal Training School* Santee, Nebraska
1885–88	*The Glacier* Tlingit Training Academy Ft. Wrangell, Alaska
1885–1900	*The Indian Helper* Indian Industrial School Carlisle, Pennsylvania
1886–1907	*Talks and Thoughts of the Hampton Indian Students* Hampton Institute, Hampton, Virginia
1887–91	*The Pipe of Peace* Genoa Indian School Genoa, Nebraska
1896–1912	*Anishinabe Enamid* Ottawa Indian Boarding School Harbor Springs, Michigan
1897–1964	*The Indian Leader* Haskell Institute Lawrence, Kansas

Fifteen Native American Journalists

1. Tom Arviso Jr. (Navajo), editor and publisher of the *Navajo Times*. In 1997, he was awarded the Native American Journalists Association's Wassaja Award for "extraordinary service to Native journalism." In 1998, he was honored by the Arizona Newspapers Association with the Freedom of Information Award. In 2009 he won the Zenger Award from the University of Arizona School of Journalism for his staunch advocacy of freedom of the press.
2. Paul DeMain (Ojibwe/Oneida) received the Wassaja Award in 2002 from the Native American Journalists Association for his reporting on imprisoned activist Leonard Peltier and the murder of Anna Mae Aquash. A past president of the Native American Journalists Association, since 1987 he has been the chief executive officer and manager of Indian Country Communications, Inc., which publishes *News from Indian Country*.
3. Lori Edmo-Suppah (Shoshone/Bannock) won the Native American Journalists Association's Wassaja Award in 1995 for her contributions to Native journalism. She has also been honored with the Catherine L. Hughes Fellowship from the Maynard Institute for Journalism Education.

4. Tim Giago (Oglala Lakota) founded and edited the *Lakota Times* (later called *Indian Country Today*) in South Dakota, which became the largest independently owned American Indian newspaper. He won the *Baltimore Sun's* H. L. Mencken Writing Award for distinguished editorial writing in 1985. He returned the award in 1990 because of racist remarks Mencken made in his published diaries. In 1997, Giago won the Golden Quill Award from the International Society of Newspaper Editors for editorial writing for a non-daily newspaper.

5. Suzan Shown Harjo (Cheyenne/Hodulgee Muscogee), a columnist for *Indian Country Today*, a leading Native American newspaper, received the Native American Journalists Association's award for Best Column Writing (2004 and 2005). Founding co-chair of the Howard Simons Fund for American Indian Journalists, she was news director of the American Indian Press Association, founded in 1970.

6. Ronald D. Holt (Nez Perce), longtime news reporter in Indian country, was the first president of the Washington, DC–based National Indian Media Association (NIMA), which he founded around 1991. Holt hoped NIMA would result in better representation of Native people in mainstream media.

7. Richard V. LaCourse (Yakama), considered by many to be the dean of Native Americans in news media, led generations of Native people into journalism and founded several tribal newspapers during his thirty-three years in the field. He was a founder of the American Indian Press Association in Washington, DC, and became the first Native journalist to report on Congress from a tribal perspective.

8. Karen Lincoln Michel (Ho-Chunk) won the Wassaja Award in 1992 for her coverage of a Ho-Chunk gaming controversy, published in the *LaCrosse Tribune* in Wisconsin.

9. Jodi Rave (Mandan/Hidatsa/Arikara), a journalist with the *Lincoln Star Journal*, won the Thomas C. Sorenson Award for distinguished journalism in 2002. She also was awarded a Nieman Fellowship at Harvard.

10. Rose W. Robinson (Hopi) and other journalists founded (in 1970) the American Indian Press Association (AIPA), later renamed Native American Journalists Association, and became its executive director. She provided news to over 150 Indian newspapers until the AIPA's demise in 1976.

11. Howard Rock (Inupiaq) and Tom Snapp started a modest statewide newspaper, *Tundra Times*, in 1962, which grew to become the journalistic voice for Alaska's Native peoples. Rock served as editor of the paper until his death in 1976. In 1975, he was nominated for a Pulitzer Prize.

12. Laverne Sheppard (Shoshone/Bannock) held editorial positions with *Sho-Ban News* and the *Bengal* (Idaho State University). Executive director of the Native American Journalists Association in 1990, she aimed to revitalize tribally owned media and increase the percentage of Native journalists working in the mainstream press.

13. Amanda Takes War Bonnet (Lakota) founded (in 2004), edited, and published *Lakota Country Times*, a Lakota-owned and operated online and print independent weekly color newspaper.

14. Loren Tapahe (Navajo) published the *Navajo Times* when it became the first tribally owned U.S. Indian newspaper to go daily in the early 1980s. He founded the *Arizona Native Scene* newspaper in 1995, which serves the Native American communities in and around the Phoenix area and other parts of Arizona.

15. Charles Trimble (Oglala Lakota) received the 2009 Native American Journalists Association Award for Best Column in a Daily/Weekly Newspaper. He was one of the founders of the American Indian Press Association in 1970.

Rupert Costo and Jeannette Henry Costo

Rupert Costo (Cahuilla) and his wife, Jeannette Henry Costo (Cherokee), prominent national leaders in the fight for the economic and social rights for American Indians, turned to journalism and publishing as a way to channel their activism. In 1964 the Costos helped found the San Francisco–based American Indian Historical Society, whose mission was to "correct the historical record as to the true story of the Indians." The same year, the American Indian Historical Society began publishing *The Indian Historian*, a publication founded "to write history as it should be written"; in 1971 it launched the *Weewish Tree*, a publication for Indian children, which was published for ten years.

In 1973, the Costos started *Wassaja*, a national advocacy newspaper of Indian affairs. The paper's title came from the Yavapai name of Dr. Carlos Montezuma, "whose life was dedicated to the struggle for our people for self-determination." The first issue, published in January, presented "facts, information, carefully sifted out from rumors and gossip." Its circulation had reached over forty-two thousand copies when it ceased publication in 1984. The Costos also started the Indian Historian Press, an American Indian–controlled, for-profit publishing house that published fifty-two titles before it closed its doors.

At the end of his life, in 1986, Rupert Costo endowed the Rupert Costo Chair in American Indian History at the University of California, Riverside. He and his wife also established the Costo Library of the American Indian, one of the larger collections of research materials relating to Native life in the United States, especially strong on twentieth century California Indian cultures, tribal politics, and the rise of Indian sovereignty in the 1970s. The University of California, Riverside renamed the Student Services Building as Costo Hall in honor of the contributions of the Costos to the university.

Mark Trahant

Mark Trahant (Shoshone/Bannock) began his newspaper career at nineteen years of age when he revived the *Sho-Ban News* as a weekly, a paper that serves his home reservation in Fort Hall, Idaho, to this day. His dynamic career has since spanned both mainstream and American Indian media. For his work in remaking the *Navajo Times* weekly into a daily, he was honored by the National Press Foundation in 1985 with a special citation as Editor of the Year.

Trahant spent four years covering the West as a reporter for the *Arizona Republic* (1986 to 1990). While he was at the *Republic,* he was a finalist for the Pulitzer Prize in 1989 for coauthoring an investigative review of federal Indian policy. He became executive news editor of the *Salt Lake Tribune* for three years, where he coordinated news gathering, copy editing desks, and sports, and wrote a twice-weekly column. He followed this position by becoming editor and publisher of the *Moscow-Pullman Daily News* (Idaho) for two years. For almost five years, 1996 to 2000, he was a columnist for the *Seattle Times.*

Trahant resigned his columnist position to become chief executive of the Robert C. Maynard Institute for Journalism Education, an Oakland, California–based non-profit organization, from 2000 to 2003. His work focused on his long-time concern that the nation's news media reflect America's diversity in staffing, content, and business operations.

After a stint as editorial page director of the *Seattle Post-Intelligencer* (2003–4), he became a Kaiser Family Foundation Fellow for almost eighteen months, during which time he examined and wrote about the Indian Health Service and its relevance to the national health reform debate. Since 2010, he has been an independent journalist. He writes "Trahant Reports," a copyrighted column that can be repackaged or reprinted for free.

Trahant has received numerous honors, including the Elias Boudinot Award for Lifetime Contributions to Journalism and the Newspaper Guild's Heywood Brun award. He also received the Paul Tobenkin Memorial Award, the highest award Columbia School of Journalism bestows for the coverage of race, bigotry, and discrimination. Trahant, a past president and member of the Native American Journalists Association, is a trustee of the Freedom Forum.

RADIO

Firsts: Radio

ca.1930   Ora Eddleman Reed (Cherokee) was the first Native talk radio show host. She broadcast from Casper, Wyoming.

1934   Sadie Brower Neakok (Inupiaq) was the first radio announcer to broadcast the news in the Iñupiat language. Once a week, she broadcast from the Alaska Communication Station (ACS) in Barrow to people who had battery-operated radios.

late 1960s   Suzan Shown Harjo (Cheyenne/Hodulgee Muscogee) and Frank Ray Harjo, her husband, produced *Seeing Red*, the first regularly broadcast Native news program in the United States. *Seeing Red* was aired on WBAI-FM Radio in New York.

1970   WYRU-AM was the first commercial Native-licensed radio station, broadcasting from Red Springs, North Carolina. It was licensed to the Lumbee Tribe.

1971   Radio Tuktoyaktuk began broadcasting in English and Inuktitut, the beginning of Native-language broadcasting in Canada.

         KYUK-AM, established in Bethel, Alaska, as part of the Public Broadcasting System, became the first station to broadcast in Yup'ik.

1972   KTDB-FM became the first Indian-owned and operated non-commercial station in the United States. Established in the Ramah Navajo community, it broadcasts local, state, and national news in Navajo and English from Pine Hill, New Mexico.

1977   KMDX-FM became the first Native-owned commercial radio station, broadcasting in Parker, Arizona. It was owned by Gilbert Leivas, a member of the Colorado River Indian Tribes.

1984   CKON-FM was the first Native station that received its operating license from a sovereign Indian Nation, the Mohawk Nation Council of Chiefs. The commercial community radio station, founded by Ray Cook and Doug George Kanentiio, both Mohawks, provides twenty-four-hour live programming.

1987   *National Native News* (NNN) became the nation's first daily radio news service covering American Indian and Alaska Native issues for Native and non-Native listeners. Produced from a Native perspective, NNN's five-minute programs can be heard on public radio stations nationwide and in Canada. NNN has received many national and regional awards for providing valuable service to Native communities.

1991   KGHR-FM was the country's first Indian high school radio station, broadcasting from Tuba City, Arizona.

1993   Kenneth Maryboy (Navajo), a KTNN radio broadcaster in Window Rock, Arizona, did the first play-by-play broadcast of an NBA game (Phoenix Suns vs. San Antonio Spurs) in the Navajo language.

1995   *Native America Calling* (NCC) premiered on American Indian Radio on Satellite (AIROS), becoming the nation's first daily all-Native live radio talk show. Produced by the Koahnic Broadcast Corporation since 1996, NCC is also available at http://www.nativeamericacalling.com.

1996   KNBA signed on as the nation's first urban Native radio station, in Anchorage, Alaska. KNBA was a project of Koahnic Broadcast Corporation. "Koahnic" means "live air" in the Ahtna dialect.

Ernie Manuelito (Navajo), a KTNN radio broadcaster in Window Rock, Arizona, provided the first play-by-play of a Super Bowl football game (Dallas Cowboys vs. Pittsburgh Steelers) in Navajo, which was broadcast to radios and television screens all over the reservation.

Native American Radio Broadcasting in the "Lower 48" and Alaska, 1970–96

1970   WYRU-AM, a commercial radio station licensed to the Lumbee Tribe, began broadcasting from Red Springs, North Carolina.

1971   KYUK-AM, a public radio station, began broadcasting from Bethel, Alaska, in English and Yup'ik.

1972   KTDB-FM, a non-commercial station, began broadcasting in English and Navajo for the Ramah Navajo community from Pine Hill, New Mexico.

1975   KEYA-FM, a non-commercial station, began broadcasting to Turtle Mountain Chippewa people at Belcourt, North Dakota. It is the second-oldest Indian-owned and operated public radio station in the nation.

1976   KSUT-FM broadcast to the Southern Ute in Ignacio, Colorado, as well as to other southwestern tribes and non-Natives.

1977   KMDX, a Native-owned commercial station, broadcast from Parker, Arizona.

1978   KINI-FM broadcast to the Rosebud Sioux from St. Francis Mission on the Rosebud Sioux Reservation in South Dakota.

KNDN-AM broadcast from Farmington, New Mexico, where it became "All Navajo, All the Time."

KSHI-FM began broadcasting from Zuni Pueblo, New Mexico.

KNCC-FM began broadcasting at Tsaile, Arizona, making the Navajo reservation the first reservation with two radio stations.

1980   KIDE-FM, a non-commercial station, began broadcasting from the Hoopa Reservation in California.

1982   KNNB-FM broadcast to the White Mountain Apaches on the Fort Apache Indian Reservation in Whiteriver, Arizona.

WOJB-FM broadcast to the Lac Courte Oreilles reservation from Hayward, Wisconsin.

1983   KILI-FM broadcast to Oglala Sioux from Porcupine on the Pine Ridge Reservation in South Dakota.

KABR-AM began broadcasting in English and Navajo from the Alamo Reservation in New Mexico.

KMHA-FM signed on the air, serving the communities of the Mandan, Hidatsa, and Arikara Nations on the Fort Berthold Reservation.

1984   CKON-FM began broadcasting to the St. Regis Mohawk Reservation from Rooseveltown, New York.

1986   KTNN-AM, a commercial station, began broadcasting in Window Rock, Arizona. The radio station, owned and operated by the Navajo Nation, airs programs in Navajo, Hopi, Apache, Pueblo, and Ute languages.

1990   KCIE-FM began broadcasting to the Jicarilla Apache people in Dulce, New Mexico.

1991   K-TWINS, a combination of two commercial FM stations (KTWI and KTWS) that operated as one, began broadcasting from Kahneeta on the Confederated Tribes of Warm Springs Reservation and Bend, Oregon.

KGHR-FM began broadcasting from Greyhills High School in Tuba City, Navajo Nation in Arizona.

1994   The American Indian Radio on Satellite (AIROS) Network began service to a growing number of Indian radio stations.

1996   KNBA-FM began broadcasting in Anchorage, Alaska, with an offering of commercial-free music, news, and cultural, and local programming.

Award-Winning Native American Radio Broadcasters and Programs

1981   Peggy Berryhill (Muskogee) received the Outstanding Individual in Radio Award from the Native American Public Broadcasting Corporation and the American Indian Film Institute. She is an award-winning producer of documentaries. In 2011, Berryhill received the Bader Award for a lifetime of vital contributions to community radio.

1988   KTNN-AM of Window Rock, Arizona, received the Crystal Radio Award from the National Association of Broadcasters for outstanding public service.

1991   KYUK, a public radio/television station providing bilingual programming to Alaska's fifty-two Yup'ik villages, won the Wassaja Award from the Native American Journalists Association. It also won recognition from the Corporation for Public Broadcasting (CPB) for outstanding community service. CPB awarded the station's "Respect the River" campaign second place in its national community outreach and public service competition.

1993   *National Native News* (NNN) won an Excellence in Programming Award from the National Federation of Community Broadcasters. NNN also received a $100,000 grant from the John D. and Catherine T. MacArthur Foundation.

1998   Two American Indian Radio on Satellite (AIROS) programs received awards from the National Federation of Community Broadcasters (NFCB). The NFCB Golden Reel Award for National Music and Entertainment Series was presented to *Native Sounds—Native Voices* National Edition. *Different Drums* received a NFCB Silver Reel for the same series.

2001   Radio producers Nellie Moore (Inupiaq) and D'Anne Hamilton (Inupiaq) received the Wassaja Award from the Native American Journalists Association. The team produced *Independent Native News*, aired daily on hundreds of radio stations.

Gold and Silver Reel Awards from the National
Federation of Community Broadcasters

1989   **Gold**—*American Indian Lesbians: A Portrait in the Twin Cities*, Petra Hall, MIGIZI

1990   **Gold**—*National Native News*, Gary Fife, Alaska Public Radio Network
        Silver—*Mining in Juneau*, Claire Elizabeth Richardson, KTOO

1991   **Gold**—*Native Voices, Yokaia, Part I*, Joseph Leon, KZYX
        Gold—*Mending the Hoop*, Alex Van Oss, Dick Brooks, and Dale Looks Twice, Soundprint
        Gold—*National Native News*, Gary Fife, Alaska Public Radio Network

1993   **Gold**—*National Native News*, Gary Fife, Alaska Public Radio Network
        Gold—*The Black Hills: A Lakota Vision, Part Four*, Milt Lee, KILI

1994   **Gold**—*Radio and PSA Entries*, Martha Scott, KYUK
        Gold—*Does Mother Earth Have AIDS?* Milt and Jayme Lee, KILI
        Gold—*A Song for Wounded Knee*, Milt and Jayme Lee

1995   **Gold**—*The 20th Annual Honor the Earth Pow-Wow*, Dave Kellar, WOJB

1997 **Silver**—*Gavel to Gavel Coverage of the 1996 Alaska Federation of Natives Convention*, Stephen C. Hamlin, KBRW

1998 **Gold**—*Native Sounds—Native Voices*, John Gregg, AIROS
Silver—*Different Drums*, Tricia King, AIROS

2000 **Silver**—*Earthsongs #38*, produced by Gregg McVicar, Koahnic Broadcast Corporation
Silver—*Voices from the Circle: Native American New Year*, produced by Jim DeNomie and Barbara Jersey, WYMS-FM, Milwaukee, WI

2003 **Silver**—*Earthsongs: I Ku Maumau*, Gregg McVicar, Koahnic Broadcasting Corporation

TELEVISION

Firsts: Television

1949 Jay Silverheels/Harry Smith (Mohawk) became the first Native American to be a featured star in a television series. He appeared in over 220 episodes of *The Lone Ranger* (ABC) between 1949 and 1957. He played the stoic, monosyllabic Tonto, the Lone Ranger's companion.

1975 Sandra Sunrising Osawa (Makah) was the first Native American filmmaker to produce for commercial television: *The Native American Series*, a groundbreaking ten-part series for KNBC-TV.

1981 The Inuit Broadcasting Corporation became the first Native-language television network in North America. It was also the first indigenous media project in the world to be broadcast by satellite. It is television by, for, and about Inuit.

1987 Nancy M. Tuthill (Quapaw/Shawnee) was the first Native person to become an editor in Broadcast Standards and Practices for ABC Television.

1989 Hattie Kauffman (Nez Perce) became the first Indian reporter to report a news story on national television. She reported about an airplane crash in Honolulu, Hawaii, for ABC's *World News Tonight*. She is the national news correspondent for CBS's *The Early Show*.

1992 Jeanie Greene (Inupiaq) began *Heartbeat Alaska*, the first Native-owned, produced, and staffed news program ever offered nationwide in U.S. television history. Greene, the producer, host, and reporter, has won several media awards for her popular program.

1995   Sandra Sunrising Osawa (Makah) became the first Native American filmmaker to produce a program for *Point of View* (POV)—*Lighting the 7th Fire*—which aired nationally on public broadcasting stations.

1996   Lena Carr (Navajo) became the first Native woman to win an Emmy, for *War Code: Navajo*, a National Geographic Television Explorer episode, broadcast on TBS. She won the award for Outstanding Historical Programming.

2008   The Tulalip Tribes in Washington State became the first Indian tribe with its own cable channel. It provides programming to subscribers of Tulalip Broadband, the tribe's Internet and cable provider, a local cable station, KANU-TV 99, and worldwide by live Web-stream.

2009   'Ōiwi TV became the first Native Hawaiian TV station. Its on-demand digital media network provides news, language lessons, documentaries, and cartoons. 'Ōiwi was cofounded by filmmaker Nä'älehu Anthony (Native Hawaiian).

2011   A partnership between the San Manuel Band of Mission Indians and San Bernardino–based KVCR Television helped launch the nation's first twenty-four-hour Native American television channel, a groundbreaking media initiative emphasizing the factual history, culture, and current events of Native Americans and Alaska Natives.

Twenty-Four Native Actors with Recurring Roles
(Three or More Episodes) in United States Television and Cable Series

1. Apesanahkwat (Menominee): *Northern Exposure*, 1993–95 (CBS); *Walker: Texas Ranger*, 1994–95 (CBS)
2. Joseph Ashton (Navajo/Lakota/Cherokee): *L.A. Doctors*, 1998–99 (CBS); voice-over work on *Rocket Power*, 1999–2003 (Nickelodeon)
3. Adam Beach (Saulteaux): *Law and Order: Special Victims Unit*, 2007–8 (NBC); *Big Love*, 2010 (HBO)
4. Tantoo Cardinal (Cree/Metis): *Dr. Quinn, Medicine Woman*, 1993 (CBS)
5. Tia Carrere (Native Hawaiian): *General Hospital*, 1985–87 (ABC)
6. Gregory Cruz (Chiricahua Apache/Mexican): *Saving Grace*, 2007–10 (TNT)
7. Graham Greene (Oneida): *Northern Exposure*, 1992 (CBS); *Lonesome Dove: The Series*, 1994 (CBS)
8. Michael Horse (Yaqui/Mescalero Apache/Zuni): *Twin Peaks*, 1990–91 (ABC); *The Untouchables*, 1993 version (ABC)
9. Karina Lombard (Lakota): *The L Word*, 2004–9 (Showtime)
10. Mitch Longley (Passamaquoddy/Penobscot): *Another World*, 1991–92 (NBC); *General Hospital*, 1997–99 (ABC); *Port Charles*, 1997–2000 (ABC); *Judging Amy*, 2001–2 (CBS); *Joan of Arcadia*, 2003–4 (CBS); *Las Vegas*, 2003–8 (NBC)

11. Randolph Mantooth (Seminole): *Emergency*, 1972–79 (NBC); *Loving*, 1987–90, 1993–95 (ABC); *The City*, 1995–97 (ABC); *As the World Turns*, 2003–4 (CBS); *One Life to Live*, 2007 (ABC)

12. A Martinez (Apache/Blackfeet): *Barnaby Jones*, 1976–79 (CBS); *Centennial*, 1979 (NBC); *Quincy, M.E.*, 1979–80 (NBC); *Santa Barbara*, 1984–92 (NBC); *L.A. Law*, 1990–94 (NBC); *General Hospital*, 1999–2002 (ABC); *For the People*, 2002–3 (Lifetime); *CSI: Crime Scene Investigation*, 2005–7 (CBS); *One Life to Live*, 2008–9 (NBC)

13. Elaine Miles (Umatilla/Nez Perce/Cayuga): *Northern Exposure*, 1990–95 (CBS)

14. Joseph Jason Namakaeha Momoa (Hawaiian): *Baywatch Hawaii*, 1999–2001 (KHON-TV)

15. Nick Ramus (Blackfeet): *Dr. Quinn, Medicine Woman*, 1993–95 (CBS)

16. Buffy Sainte-Marie (Cree): *Sesame Street*, 1976–81 (PBS)

17. Frank Salsedo (Klamath): *Walker, Texas Ranger*, 1995–2000 (CBS); *Power Rangers Zeo*, 1996 (Fox Network)

18. Larry Sellers (Lakota/Osage/Cherokee): *Dr. Quinn, Medicine Woman*, 1993–99 (CBS)

19. Jay Silverheels/Harry Smith (Mohawk): *The Lone Ranger*, 1949–57 (ABC)

20. Shannyn Sossamon (Native Hawaiian descent): *Moonlight*, 2007 (CBS)

21. Wes Studi (Cherokee): *Kings*, 2009 (NBC)

22. Sheila Tousey (Menominee): *Law and Order: Special Victims Unit*, 2003–4 (NBC)

23. Kateri Walker (Saginaw Chippewa): *As the World Turns*, 1993 (CBS)

24. Floyd Red Crow Westerman (Sisseton-Wahpeton Dakota): *Walker, Texas Ranger*, 1993–94 (CBS); *Dharma and Greg*, 1997–2001 (ABC); *X-Files*, 1995–99 (Fox Network)

North American Indian Television Broadcasting, 1980–2011

1980   Inuit Tapirisat (Inuit Brotherhood) established Inukshuk, an experimental television station, and was given access to a Canadian Broadcasting Corporation (CBC) satellite channel. The station provided regionally oriented programs.

1981   The Inuit Broadcasting Corporation (IBC) in Canada, the only Native American broadcast network in North America, was established to broadcast several hours of Native-oriented programs per week in English and Inuktitut.

1988   The Salish Kootenai College of Pablo, Montana, launched KSKC-TV, a public television station that serves the Flathead Reservation through broadcast and cable systems. Local programs, documentaries, PBS programs, and classes became televised.

1992   Jeanie Greene (Inupiaq) launched *Heartbeat Alaska*, a television news program available throughout Alaska and on some thirty broadcasting stations across the country, in Canada, Greenland, and Eastern Russia.

2003   *Northwest Indian News* (NWIN), a half-hour program focusing on regional issues and events, began airing on the Dish Network, select cable systems, and www.colourstv.org. It was launched by the Tulalip Tribes Communications Department in Bellingham, Washington.

2010   *Native Heartbeat*, a television magazine program, was launched on NBC and local network TV affiliates. Programs highlight Indian culture, government, and history as told by journalists through short documentaries and news-oriented stories.

2011   KVCR Television, based in San Bernardino, California, launched the nation's first twenty-four-hour Native American television channel, thanks to a $6 million donation by the San Manuel Band of Serrano Mission Indians. The one-of-a-kind channel emphasizes history, culture, and current events of Native Americans.

Ten Native American Television Anchors, Producers, and Reporters

1. Cherokee Ballard (Cherokee)
   Television news journalist, Oklahoma. In 2002, she won the staff Peabody Award for coverage of the Oklahoma City bombing.
2. Tom Beaver (Oklahoma Creek)
   Television reporter, Minneapolis, Minnesota, during the 1970s; one of the few Indian people employed by the television industry in the Twin Cities area.
3. Conroy Chino (Acoma Pueblo)
   Investigative reporter and anchor, Albuquerque, New Mexico. In 1983, he was selected as a Nieman Fellow at Harvard University, where he studied journalism.
4. Tim Giago (Oglala Lakota)
   Television host in 1975 at KEVN, a community-owned station in Rapid City, South Dakota.
5. Jeanie Greene (Iñupiaq)
   Television producer, reporter, and host of *Heartbeat Alaska* since 1992. The award-winning program is available throughout Alaska, through public broadcasting stations across the United States, as well as in Canada, Greenland, and Eastern Russia.
6. Ronald D. Holt (Nez Perce)
   Television journalist, Billings, Montana; twenty years working in commercial and public broadcasting. A veteran television producer and journalist, in 1993 he became the first Native American to own a commercial television station: FOX-TV in Billings, Montana.

Four Online "Television" Companies

- www.americanindiantv.com: American Indian Television (AITV), which debuted in 2007, is an American Indian–centric television network featuring video and film programming delivered directly to TV sets and PCs via Internet Protocol Television (IPTV) in North America and throughout the world.
- www.IndianCountryTV.com: Launched by *News from Indian Country* in 2009, IndianCountryTV.com includes a daily "Native News Update," older news programs, and a video library of featured programs.
- www.isuma.tv/isuma-productions: Isuma TV, launched in 2008, is an Internet video portal for indigenous independent filmmakers with unique indigenous-language content available twenty-four hours a day to help films and filmmakers reach a wider audience, help audiences see themselves in their own language, and help worldwide viewers see indigenous reality from its own point of view. Isuma TV has offices in Montreal and New York.
- www.rezkast.com: RezKast is a free Native American YouTube-like social networking site, launched in 2008 by the Coeur d'Alene Tribe of Idaho, that also provides a free video and photo hosting service.

7. Hattie Kauffman (Nez Perce)
   Television reporter for ABC's *Good Morning America* (1987–90) and CBS's *Early Show* (1999 to present day). She became the first Native American journalist to file a report on a national news broadcast. She was a reporter and anchor at KING-TV Seattle (1981–87), where she earned four Emmy Awards for her work.

8. Harriet Skye (Hunkpapa Lakota)
   Weekly television talk show host, Bismarck, North Dakota. She was the first Native American to host a weekly television show.

9. Mary Kim Titla (San Carlos Apache)
   Television news reporter, Tucson and Phoenix, Arizona, 1986–2005. While reporting, Titla has racked up a few awards, which include being a finalist for a Rocky Mountain Emmy. She has won first place awards from the Associated Press, Arizona Press Club, and the Native American Journalists Association. In 2005, she launched an Internet magazine called *Native Youth Magazine*.

10. Linda White Wolf (Oklahoma Chickasaw/Maori)
    Television host and producer, television morning show segments, *Arizona Native News* (ANN), Phoenix, Arizona; ANN was launched in 2005 on KAZ-TV. White Wolf's interviews with celebrities, musical artists, sports, and political figures can be seen on YouTube.

ORGANIZATIONS

Center for Native American Public Radio

Launched in 2004, the Center for Native American Public Radio, located in Flagstaff, Arizona, is a centralized service bureau that provides technical, fundraising, and program support to nearly thirty public radio stations serving Native listeners.

Koahnic Broadcast Corporation
www.koahnicbroadcast.org

Founded in 2006, Koahnic Broadcast Corporation is a nonprofit, Alaska Native–governed and operated media center located in Anchorage, Alaska. It provides American Indian and Alaska Native news and cultural programs to public radio listeners everywhere.

Longhouse Media
http://longhousemedia.org

Launched in 2005, Longhouse Media is an indigenous media arts organization, located in Seattle, Washington, that has developed programs for indigenous communities. It partners with tribes, schools, museums, cultural centers, and health clinics to offer workshops and training in digital media. It focuses on its acclaimed youth media program, "Native Lens," established in 2003, which teaches filmmaking to Native youth.

Native American Journalists Association
http://www.naja.com

Formed in 1984, the Native American Journalists Association, located in Norman, Oklahoma, aims to improve communications among Native people and between Native Americans and the general public. Since 2002, its report "Reading Red" has dealt with Indian media representations.

Native American Public Telecommunications
www.nativetelecom.org

Native American Public Telecommunications (NAPT), founded in 1976, supports the creation, promotion, and distribution of Native public media. NAPT, located in Lincoln, Nebraska, produces and develops educational programs for all media, including public television and public radio.

Native Networks
www.nativenetworks.si.edu/nn.html

Native Networks, established in 2001 by the National Museum of the American Indians, New York, New York, provides information about media makers (film, video, radio, television, and new media) throughout the Americas.

Native Public Media

www.nativepublicmedia.org

>   Established in 2004, Native Public Media headquartered in Flagstaff, Arizona, is a nonprofit organization advocating for policies and regulations that strengthen Native voices through media, especially radio and broadband, that are community-based, local, and democratic.

Native Voice One

http://www.nv1.org

>   Native Voice One (NV1), established in 2006, educates, advocates, and celebrates Native American life and culture by providing a program service from Native points of view. NV1, located in Albuquerque, New Mexico, enables Native people, especially those without access to the many Native-owned and operated radio stations based in reservations and villages, to stay connected.

UNITY: Journalists of Color, Inc.

http://www.unityjournalists.org

>   UNITY: Journalists of Color, Inc., established in 1994, began as a nonprofit, strategic alliance of journalists of color (Asian American, Black American, Hispanic, and Native American) advocating for accurate news coverage about people of color and challenging the industry to diversity at all levels. In 2011, the National Association of Black Journalists voted to leave UNITY. UNITY is located in McLean, Virginia.

American Native Press Archives

The Sequoyah Research Center, a facility that hosts the American Native Press Archives (ANPA), was named in honor of the great Cherokee linguist who created the Cherokee syllabary. The center is dedicated to collecting and preserving the printed words of Native American individuals, nations, and organizations.

The American Native Press Archives, founded by Daniel F. Littlefield Jr. (Cherokee) and James Parins, has been collecting and archiving the products of Native press and press history since it was founded in 1983. Its newspaper and periodical collection is one of the largest in the world. Although there are older titles, the center emphasizes the period since World War II. Holdings are supplemented with microform copies of titles unavailable in hard copy.

The ANPA, located in Little Rock, Arkansas, also maintains files on an estimated 4,500 Native writers, with an emphasis on materials written in the century preceding 1925. ANPA notes that these files, which include biographical information on writers and copies of their works, make it the most comprehensive resource center for the study of Native literature during that era.

ANPA oversees a number of manuscript collections, including papers of individual writers, records of Native media organizations, records of Native nations, agency records, and papers from Native organizations. Its Web site provides access to a comprehensive bibliographic database by Native writers, sources for Indian removal research, and links to other Internet resources.

Source: www.anpa.ualr.edu

RESOURCES

Adare, Sierra S. *"Indian" Stereotypes in TV Science Fiction: First Nations' Voices Speak Out.* Austin: University of Texas Press, 2005.

Blackman, Margaret B. *Sadie Brower Neakok, an Iñupiaq Woman.* Seattle: University of Washington Press, 1989.

Briggs, Kara, Ronald D. Smith, and Jose Barreiro, eds. *Shoot the Indian: Media, Misperception and Native Truth.* Buffalo, NY: American Indian Policy and Media Initiative, 2007.

Chavez, Raul S. *Childhood Indians: Television, Film, and Sustaining the White (Sub) Conscience.* Seattle, WA: CreateSpace, 2010.

Hafsteinsson, Sigurjón Balder, and Marian Bredin, eds. *Indigenous Screen Cultures in Canada.* Winnipeg: University of Manitoba Press, 2010.

Keith, Michael, *Signals in the Air: Native Broadcasting in America.* Westport, CT: Praeger, 1995.

Littlefield, Daniel F., Jr., and James W. Parins. *American Indian and Alaska Native Newspapers and Periodicals, 1826–1924.* Westport, CT: Greenwood Press, 1984.

Morgan, Lael. *Art and Eskimo Power: The Life and Times of Alaskan Howard Rock.* Kenmore, WA: Epicenter Press, 1989.

Murphy, James E., and Sharon M. Murphy. *Let My People Know: American Indian Journalism, 1828–1978.* Norman: University of Oklahoma Press, 1981.

Parins, James W. *John Rollins Ridge: His Life and Works.* Lincoln: University of Nebraska Press, 1991.

Perdue, Theda, ed. *Cherokee Editor: The Writings of Elias Boudinot.* Athens: University of Georgia Press, 1996.

Trahant, Mark N. *Pictures of Our Nobler Selves: A History of Native American Contributions to News Media.* Nashville, TN: The Freedom Forum First Amendment Center, 1995. Available from http://www.freedomforum.org/templates/document.asp?documentID=14530.

Native Public Media and the Federal Communications Commission (FCC)

Loris Ann Taylor (Hopi), president and CEO of Native Public Media, Inc., led a team to publish the first seminal study in 2009 on "New Media, Technology, and Internet Use in Indian Country." She was instrumental in helping to establish the first FCC Tribal Priority for broadcasting and the new FCC Office of Native Affairs and Policy.

In 2010, the FCC estimated that less than 10 percent of the Native population was connected to high-speed Internet. After discussions with tribal officials, the FCC announced the establishment of an Office of Native Affairs and Policy as part of its national broadband plan. The FCC said the tribal office would serve all federally recognized tribes and other Native American organizations to improve broadband services.

The FCC's Tribal Home Page says that the FCC recognizes that the telecommunications penetration rate on many tribal lands falls far below the national average. It has taken a series of steps, through regulatory action, consumer information, and tribal outreach, to address the lack of telecommunications deployment and subscribership throughout Indian country.

Web Sites

American Indian Policy and Media Initiative: http://buffalostate.edu/communication/americanindianinitiative.xml

American Indian Radio on Satellite (AIROS): http://www.airos.org

American Native Press Archives: http://www.anpa.ualr.edu

FCC's Tribal Homepage: http://transition.fcc.gov/indians/

Indianz.com: http://64.38.12.138

National Native News (NNN): http://nativenews.net

Native American Entertainment Network: http://naenetwork.com

Native Hawaiian Radio KAHU: http://tunein.com/radio/KAHU-917-s126359/

NDN Sports: http://www.ndnsports.com

"New Media, Technology and Internet Use in Indian Country" (Traci Morris—Native Public Media, and Sascha Meinrath—New America Foundation): http://nativepublicmedia.org/images/stories/documents/npm-naf-new-media-study-2009.pdf

News from Indian Country: http://www.indiancountrynews.com

'Ōiwi TV: http://www.oiwi.tv

Pechanga.net: http://pechanga.net

RezKast: http://www.rezkast.com

This Week From Indian Country Today: http://indiancountrytodaymedianetwork.com

Part Six

20

Sports and Games

FIRSTS

1897   Frank Hudson (Laguna Pueblo) was selected for football's Walter Camp for All-American Second Team. He was the first recorded American Indian to be inducted.

1908   Ikua Purdy (Native Hawaiian) became the first Hawaiian cowboy to win a Cheyenne, Wyoming, championship with a rope and steer tying time of one minute, six seconds (some accounts say fifty-six seconds). In 1999, he was voted into the Rodeo Hall of Fame, the first Hawaiian ever to be nominated.

1913   Albert Andrew Exendine (Delaware) was head coach at Georgetown University from 1913 to 1922, believed to be the first Indian to become head coach of a college team.

1931   Pepper Martin (Osage), a St. Louis Cardinal baseball player, was named the first Associated Press Athlete of the Year.

1939   Chester L. Ellis (Seneca) won the national Golden Gloves Championship in the bantamweight division; later he won the International Golden Gloves Championship. He was the first American Indian to win boxing championships at the national and international levels.

1951   Allie P. Reynolds (Creek), a pitcher for the Cleveland Indians and the New York Yankees, became the first player in American League history to pitch two no-hit games. He was also second among his contemporaries to have thirty-seven shutouts.

1953   Charles Albert Bender (Chippewa) was the first Native American elected to the Baseball Hall of Fame.

        Fred Sasakamoose (Sandy Lake Cree) was drafted by the Chicago Black Hawks as a center, the first American Indian skater to play in the National Hockey League.

1960   Leon A. Miller (Cherokee) became the first American Indian inducted into the Lacrosse Hall of Fame in Baltimore, Maryland.

1972   The first induction ceremony of the American Indian Athletic Hall of Fame took place at Haskell Indian Junior College in Lawrence, Kansas. Fourteen athletes were named.

Takamiyama Daigorô (Native Hawaiian, born as Jesse Wailana Kuhaulua) was the first foreign-born *rikishi* ("strong man," or professional sumo wrestler) to win the top division championship.

Angelita Rosal (Sioux) became the first American Indian woman to make the United States women's national table tennis team.

1974   Golfer Rod Curl (Wintu) won the Colonial National Open, edging Jack Nicklaus by one strike. Curl was one of the first American Indians to compete at a national level in golf.

Carl Huntington (Athabascan) was the first Alaska Native to win the Iditarod Trail Sled Dog Race, the 1,150-mile Anchorage-to-Nome (Alaska) competition that began in 1973.

1975   The Mescalero Apache Tribe of New Mexico built the first tribally owned eighteen-hole championship golf course, at a seven-thousand-foot elevation.

1976   Jackson Sundown (Waaya-Tonah-Toesits-Kahn) (Nez Perce), the bronc-riding champion of the 1916 Pendleton (Oregon) Round-Up, was inducted into the Rodeo Hall of Fame at the National Cowboy and Western History Museum in Oklahoma City, Oklahoma. He was the first Native rodeo champion to be honored.

1982   Rell Kapolioka'ehukai Sunn (Native Hawaiian) won first place in the International Professional Surfing ratings.

1990   The first Olympic-style sports event exclusively for indigenous peoples of the United States and Canada took place in Edmonton, Alberta, Canada. The North American Indigenous Games incorporated at least sixteen different sporting events and a cultural component.

Jason Stevens (Navajo) captured first place in the "B" division of the Eighteenth Annual World Chess Open, held in Philadelphia, Pennsylvania. He was the first Native American to win in any section in a World Open.

1993   A National Basketball Association (NBA) game, a matchup of the Phoenix Suns and San Antonio Spurs, was broadcast in the Navajo language, the first play-by-play broadcast of an NBA game in a native language.

1995   Ryneldi Becenti (Navajo) was the first Native American woman to play professional basketball for a foreign nation—the Swiss team. In her senior year at Arizona State, she was an honorable mention All-American. In 1997, she was signed as a free agent by the Phoenix Mercury.

1996   Cheri Becerra (Omaha) was the first Native American woman to win a medal in the wheelchair track of the Olympics. She placed third in her first Olympics, finishing the 800-meter in a time of 1:55:49 at the Summer Paralympics in Atlanta, Georgia.

Dr. George Blue Spruce Jr. (Laguna/Ohkay Owingeh/Pueblo) was inducted into the American Indian Athletic Hall of Fame, the first male tennis player to be selected.

1999   Golfer Notah Begay III (Navajo/San Felipe Pueblo/Isleta Pueblo) won his first of four PGA tournaments in the Reno-Tahoe Open. He became the third player in the history of professional golf to shoot a fifty-nine on a U.S. pro tour, the Nike Dominion Open in 1998.

2000   Jay Dee "B. J." Penn (Native Hawaiian) was the first non-Brazilian winner of the World Jiu-Jitsu Championship in the black belt category.

2001   Seventh-grader Jordyn Brown (Cheyenne River Sioux) became the first American Indian female inducted into the U.S. Martial Arts Hall of Fame. She was honored as a Junior Martial Artist of the year.

Brian Ching (Native Hawaiian) was drafted by the Los Angeles Galaxy soccer team, the first Hawaiian to be drafted by Major League Soccer.

Cory Wetherill (Navajo) was the first American Indian to compete in the Indy 500 car race. He finished nineteenth. He captured a third and fourth place finish in the 1998 and 1999 PPG Dayton Indy Lights series, the stepping-stone to the Indy 500.

2002   The Oklahoma University Sooners' basketball coach Kelvin Sampson (Lumbee) became the first Native American coach to make it to the Final Four of the National Collegiate Athletic Association (NCAA) tournament. In 2003, the Sooners reached the Elite Eight.

2003   The Mohegan Tribe of Connecticut became the first Indian nation to own a professional sports team. It purchased a Women's National Basketball Association (WNBA) franchise, which it named the Connecticut Sun. From 1999 to 2002, the team was known as the Orlando Miracle, playing in Orlando, Florida.

Jordan Tootoo, a forward for the Nashville Predators, became the NHL's first Inuit player.

2005   The Yakama Nation of Washington State became the first Indian nation to purchase a professional men's basketball team. It purchased the minor league Yakima Sun Kings basketball team, which it renamed the Yakama Sun Kings.

2006   The Barrow Whalers of Barrow High School in Alaska played the first official football game in the Arctic, against Delta Junction High School (Delta Junction, Alaska). After Barrow recorded its first win two weeks later, the coaches and players jumped into the Arctic Ocean, a hundred yards from the field.

2007   The Native American Basketball Invitational (NABI), launched in 2003, became the first Native-owned basketball tournament to receive NCAA certification.

The Lady Indians, a Sequoyah High School basketball team in Tahlequah, Oklahoma, participated in the Nike Tournament of Champions in Phoenix, Arizona, the first all-Indian school to receive one of the coveted invitations. The three-time defending state champions in their classification opened the season ranked in the top ten in *Sports Illustrated*'s national poll.

2008   Sam Bradford (Cherokee) was the first American Indian to win the Heisman Trophy. He was a quarterback with the University of Oklahoma Sooners.

2011   Salt River Field at Talking Stick became the first Major League Baseball spring training stadium built on Native land. The facility is on the land of the Salt River Pima-Maricopa Indian Community in the metropolitan Phoenix, Arizona, area. The stadium will serve as spring training home for the Arizona Diamondbacks and the Colorado Rockies.

John Baker (Inupiaq Eskimo) won the Iditarod Trail Sled Dog Race, the first Eskimo to do so since the 1,150-mile Anchorage-to-Nome (Alaska) competition began in 1973. He was the fourth Alaska Native to win the race, the longest sled-dog race in the world.

Jacoby Ellsbury (Navajo) became the first American Indian to be named the American League Player of the Week. He was center fielder for the Boston Red Sox.

SPORTS AND GAMES IN TRADITIONAL AND CONTEMPORARY NATIVE AMERICAN LIFE

Twelve Sports and Games in Traditional Native Life

1. Archery
2. Dice Games
3. Double Ball
4. Footracing
5. Hand Games
6. Hidden Ball or Moccasin Game

7. Hoop and Pole
8. Lacrosse
9. Ring and Pin
10. Shinny
11. Snow Snake
12. Stick Games

Seven Popular Sports among Native Children

1. Basketball
2. Boxing
3. Golf
4. Lacrosse
5. Rodeo
6. Running
7. Skateboarding

Seven Facts about Lacrosse

Lacrosse, which derives its name from the French language, *jouer a la crosse,* has its origins in a tribal game played by Native peoples living northeast and southeast of the Mississippi River, around the Great Lakes, and into Canada. It originated long before European explorers landed in North America.

1. Modern-day lacrosse descends from and resembles games played by various Native communities. These games have been called:
   dehuntshigwa'es in the Onondaga Language("men hit a rounded object")
   da-nah-wah'uwsdi in the Cherokee Language ("little war")
   tewaarathon in the Mohawk language ("little brother of war")
   baaga'adowe in the Ojibwe language ("plays lacrosse")
   kabocha-toli in the Choctaw language ("stick-ball")
2. Native leaders used the game to resolve disputes and to prevent war between American Indian nations and communities. Lacrosse was also played to toughen young warriors for combat, for recreation, as part of festivals, and for the bets involved. Finally, lacrosse was played for religious reasons: for the pleasure of the Creator, to pray and heal the sick.
3. In the Native version of lacrosse, a contest often involved entire tribes and went on for days. Goals were miles apart, and there were no time-outs, penalties, or break periods. Players could be removed for harmful behavior or for fighting. There was also a women's version, which used much shorter sticks with larger heads.
4. The modern field game lasts an hour and is played by ten-person teams on a field 110 yards long. The object of the game is to throw a ball from a webbed stick past the goaltender. The winner is the team that scores the most goals when the match ends.

Iroquois Nationals Lacrosse

Honoring Nations Honoree, 2002
Iroquois Nationals Lacrosse
Haudenosaunee/Iroquois Confederacy
Rooseveltown, New York

Honoring Nations, a national awards program initiated in 1998, highlights outstanding programs in self-governance by Native nations. At the heart of the program is the belief that tribes themselves hold the key to positive social, political, cultural, and economic prosperity. Based at the John F. Kennedy School of Government at Harvard University, Honoring Nations is administered by the Harvard Project on American Indian Economic Development. The criteria for selection of honorees include program effectiveness, significance to sovereignty, cultural relevance, transferability, and sustainability.

The award-winning Iroquois Nationals Lacrosse team, sanctioned by the Haudenosaunee Grand Council of Chiefs, represents a sovereign nation in world competition. It has successfully engaged state departments, embassies, and consulates around the world to recognize Iroquois sovereignty. Team members travel using Haudenosaunee passports. In June 2010, however, a passport dispute with the governments of the United States and Britain was not resolved before the team's first game in the world championship tournament.

Skateboarding

Skateboarding, one of the most popular sports in Native communities, has inspired American Indian and Native Hawaiian communities to host skateboard competitions and build skate parks to encourage their youth to pursue a safe and physically demanding sport. Native entrepreneurs own skateboard companies and sponsor community-based skate teams. Native artists, musicians, and filmmakers, inspired by their skating experiences, credit the sport with teaching them a successful work ethic.

In 2010, *Ramp It Up: Skateboard Culture in Native America*, an exhibition at the National Museum of the American Indian on the National Mall, celebrated American Indian skate culture. According to the exhibition curator, skateboards were born from Hawaiian surf culture, rooted in ancient traditions of the Polynesian Islands. The exhibition featured rare archival photographs and film of Native skaters as well as skate decks, with culturally significant designs, from Native companies and contemporary artists.

5. At one time, the lacrosse stick was usually made from hickory wood because of its strength, with a small net at the end. Lacrosse sticks were so treasured that many players requested to be buried with their stick beside them. Today, while handcrafted sticks are still used and passed on through the generations, sticks are more often made from plastic, aluminum, graphite, and titanium, with pockets made of nylon mesh.

6. In the 1920s, box lacrosse was most popular on Iroquois reservations. Invented in Canada, box lacrosse took advantage of the availability of idle hockey rinks in summertime.

7. The Iroquois Nationals lacrosse team, created in 1983, represent the six nations that make up the Haudenosaunee/Iroquois Confederacy. The Nationals are recognized as full members of the Federation of International Lacrosse.

OLYMPICS

Seven Native American Olympic Firsts

1. Louis Tewanima (Hopi) was the first American to win an Olympic medal in the 10,000-meter race. He won the silver medal in the 1912 Olympics in Stockholm, Sweden.

2. Clarence "Taffy" Abel (Chippewa) became the first American to carry the United States flag in an Olympic opening ceremony at the 1924 Olympic Winter Games in Chamonix, France. He remains the only Native American to have carried the U.S. flag at an Olympic opening ceremony.

3. William Winston "Billy" Kidd (Abenaki) was the first American male, along with Jimmie Heuga, to win an Olympic alpine medal. He won the silver medal in the slalom in the 1964 Winter Olympics in Innsbruck, Austria.

4. William Mervin "Billy" Mills (Oglala Lakota) is the first and only American to date to win the gold medal in the 10,000-meter run. He won the medal at the 1964 Summer Olympics in Tokyo, Japan.

5. Kelsey Nakanelua was the first Native Hawaiian to compete in the Olympic Games in track and field. He competed in the 100-meter run in the 2000 Olympic Games in Sydney, Australia.

6. Naomi Lang (Karuk) was the first Native woman to compete in Winter Olympics. She placed eleventh in ice dancing at the 2002 Olympics in Salt Lake City, Utah.

7. Natasha Kai (Native Hawaiian) was the first player from Hawaii selected for the United States Olympic Women's soccer team, which played in Beijing, China, in 2008.

Native American Olympians 1904–2010

1904   Summer Olympics, St. Louis, Missouri
       Frank Pierce (Seneca) qualified to run in the marathon but dropped out.

1908   Summer Olympics, London, England
            Frank Mt. Pleasant (Tuscarora) placed sixth in the broad jump
            and sixth in the triple jump.
            Louis Tewanima (Hopi) placed ninth in the marathon.
            Jim Thorpe (Sac and Fox) placed ninth in the marathon.

1912   Summer Olympics, Stockholm, Sweden
            Duke Kahanamoku (Native Hawaiian) won the gold medal for
            the 100-meter freestyle, men's swimming, and silver as a member of
            a 4x200-meter freestyle relay.
            Andrew Sockalexis (Penobscot) placed fourth in the marathon.
            Louis Tewanima (Hopi) won the silver medal in the 10,000-meter
            run and placed sixteenth in the marathon.
            Jim Thorpe (Sac and Fox) won gold medals in the decathlon and
            pentathlon, placed seventh in the long jump, and fourth in the high
            jump.

1920   Summer Olympics, Antwerp, Belgium
            Duke Kahanamoku (Native Hawaiian) won the gold medal for
            the 100-meter freestyle, men's swimming, and gold for the 4x200-
            meter freestyle relay.
            Pua Kealoha (Native Hawaiian) won the silver medal for the
            100-meter freestyle, men's swimming, and the gold for the 4x200-
            meter freestyle relay.
            Warren Kealoha (Native Hawaiian) won the gold medal for the
            100-meter backstroke, men's swimming.

1924   Summer Olympics, Paris, France
            Duke Kahanamoku (Native Hawaiian) won the silver medal for
            the 100-meter freestyle, men's swimming.
            Samuel Kahanamoku (Native Hawaiian) won the bronze medal
            for the 100-meter freestyle, men's swimming.
            Warren Kealoha (Native Hawaiian) won the gold medal for the
            100-meter backstroke, men's swimming.

1924   Winter Olympics, Chamonix, France
            Clarence "Taffy" Abel (Chippewa) was captain of the silver
            medal–winning Olympic hockey team.

1932   Summer Olympics, Los Angeles, California
            Wilson "Buster" Charles (Oneida) placed fourth in the decathlon.
            Duke Kahanamoku (Native Hawaiian) was a member of the U.S.
            water polo team.

1936   Summer Olympics, Berlin, Germany
        Ellison Myers "Tarzan" Brown (Narragansett) competed in the marathon but disqualified because a bystander helped him rub out a muscle cramp.

1948   Summer Olympics, London, England
        Jesse "Cab" Renick (Choctaw) was captain of the gold medal–winning U.S. Olympic basketball team.

1964   Summer Olympics, Tokyo, Japan
        Ben Nighthorse Campbell (Northern Cheyenne), captain of the judo team, placed fourth in the competition. He carried the Olympic Flag during the closing ceremonies.
        William Mervin "Billy" Mills (Oglala Lakota) won the gold medal in the 10,000-meter run and placed fourteenth in the marathon.

1964   Winter Olympics, Innsbruck, Austria
        Billy Kidd (Abenaki) won the silver medal in slalom/Alpine skiing.

1972   Winter Olympics, Sapporo, Japan
        Henry Boucha (Chippewa) was one of three members of the silver medal–winning U.S. Olympic hockey team classified as high-schoolers.

1984   Summer Olympics, Los Angeles, California
        Alwyn Morris (Mohawk) won the gold and bronze medals in kayaking.

2000   Summer Olympics, Sydney, Australia
        Kelsey Nakanelua (Native Hawaiian) competed in the 100-meter run.
        Logan Maile Lei Tom (Native Hawaiian) placed fourth as a member of the U.S. Olympic volleyball team.

2002   Winter Olympics, Salt Lake City, Utah
        Blair Burk (Oklahoma Choctaw) won the silver medal in calf roping.
        Naomi Lang (Karuk) placed eleventh in ice dancing with partner Peter Tchernyshev.
        Bud Longbrake (Cheyenne River Sioux) competed in saddle bronc riding.
        Tom Reeves (Cheyenne River Sioux), captain of the U.S. rodeo team, was a saddle bronc silver medalist.

2004   Summer Olympics, Athens, Greece
        Kelsey Nakanelua (Native Hawaiian), competed in the 100-meter run.

Logan Maile Lei Tom (Native Hawaiian) placed fifth as a member of the U.S. Olympic volleyball team.

2008   Summer Olympics, Beijing, China
Jacob Deitchler (Chippewa) competed for the United States in Greco-Roman wrestling.

Natasha Kai (Native Hawaiian) won the gold medal as a member of the U.S. women's soccer team.

Logan Maile Lei Tom (Native Hawaiian) won the silver medal as a member of the U.S. Olympic volleyball team; she was named "Best Scorer" at the 2008 games.

2010   Winter Olympics, Vancouver, Canada
Callan Chythlook-Sifsof (Yup'ik/Inupiaq Eskimo) placed twenty-first in women's snowboard cross.

Timeline of Jim Thorpe's Accomplishments and Awards

1904–1912   Jim Thorpe (Sac and Fox) was a star athlete at the Carlisle Indian Industrial School in Pennsylvania. He led the school to the national collegiate championship in football.

1912   Jim Thorpe won gold medals in decathlon and pentathlon at the 1912 Summer Olympics in Stockholm, Sweden. Sweden's King Gustav V told Thorpe, "Sir, you are the greatest athlete in the world." Thorpe's reply was, "Thanks, King."

Thorpe won the Amateur Athletic Union (AAU) All-Around Championship decathlon.

Thorpe was named first team all-American for a second consecutive year after the Carlisle Indians finished the season 12-1-1, leading the nation in scoring.

1920   Thorpe was named the first president of the American Professional Football Association. Two years later it was renamed the National Football League (NFL).

1950   Thorpe was selected by the Associated Press as the Greatest Football Player of the Half-Century and the Greatest Male Athlete of the Half-Century.

1951   Thorpe was named to the National College Football Hall of Fame.

1953   The towns of Mauch Chunk and East Mauch Chunk, Pennsylvania, combined and were renamed Jim Thorpe, Pennsylvania.

1955   The NFL named its annual most valuable player award the Jim Thorpe Trophy.

1958	Thorpe was elected to the National Indian Hall of Fame in Anadarko, Oklahoma.
1961	Thorpe was elected to the Pennsylvania Hall of Fame.
1963	Thorpe was inducted as a charter member of the Pro Football Hall of Fame in Canton, Ohio.
1973	The Oklahoma Historical Society opened Jim Thorpe's family house (between 1917 and 1923), located in Yale, Oklahoma, as an historic site. The Amateur Athletic Union reinstated Thorpe's amateur status.
1975	Thorpe was enshrined in the National Track and Field Hall of Fame. A portion of Oklahoma Highway 51 was renamed Jim Thorpe Memorial Highway.
1977	A *Sport Magazine* national poll named Thorpe the Greatest American Football Player in History.
1983	The International Olympic Committee returned replicas of Thorpe's gold medals to the Thorpe family. They are displayed under a portrait of Thorpe that hangs in the rotunda of Oklahoma's State Capitol in Oklahoma City. (The medals were taken away from Thorpe in 1913 because he had played semi-professional baseball in 1909.) The United Indian Development Association awarded its Jay Silverheels Achievement Award to Thorpe posthumously.
1984	The U.S. government issued a commemorative twenty-cent football-themed postage stamp of Jim Thorpe. In 1998, the government also issued a thirty-two-cent stamp focusing on his achievements in track and field and baseball. The Jim Thorpe Longest Run was organized, in which teams of Indian runners left upstate New York and ran in relays across the United States, ending in Los Angeles, California, in time for the 1984 Summer Olympics. A powwow was held to honor the return of his medals.
1997	The National Congress of American Indians declared Thorpe the greatest all-around athlete and greatest football player of the century.
1999	A resolution of the U.S. House of Representatives named Thorpe America's Athlete of the Century.
2000	A majority of respondents to an ABC Wide World of Sports Internet poll voted for Thorpe as the twentieth century's greatest athlete.
2001	Wheaties, a cereal known since 1954 as the "Breakfast of Champions," chose an image of Thorpe in a football uniform for the cover of its cereal box.

Eighteen Events of the World Eskimo-Indian Olympics

Founded in 1961, the world-famous World Eskimo-Indian Olympics (www.weio.org) are held each July in Fairbanks, Alaska. The four days of games test athletic skill, strength, endurance, concentration, and agility in sports passed down from one generation to another over the centuries. In addition to the games and a Race of the Torch, there are dance, art, storytelling, and cultural displays, as well as fish-cutting, seal-skinning, sewing competitions, muktuk eating, and a Native Baby Contest. The Olympics begin with the lighting of seal-oil lamps that stay lit for the duration of the games.

1. Alaskan high kick (men and women)
2. Arm pull (men and women)
3. Blanket toss (men and women)
4. Drop the bomb (men and women)
5. Ear pull (men and women)
6. Ear weight (men and women)
7. Eskimo stick pull (men and women)
8. Four-man carry
9. Greased pole walk (men and women)
10. Indian stick pull (men and women)
11. Kneel jump (men and women)
12. Knuckle hop or seal hop (men and women)
13. One-foot high kick (men and women)
14. Two-foot high kick (men and women)
15. One-hand reach (men and women)
16. Scissor broad jump (men and women)
17. Toe kick (men and women)
18. Race of the Torch (men and women)

Cheri Becerra (Omaha), Wheelchair Olympian

Cheri Becerra, a T10 paraplegic, placed third in her first Olympics, held in Atlanta, Georgia, finishing the 800-meter in a time of 1:55.49. The woman's 800-meter is the only wheelchair track event recognized by the Olympic Games. At the 2000 Sydney, Australia, Olympic Games, she finished in fifth place with a time of 1:57.19, just 1.12 seconds behind first place. Becerra became paraplegic as a result of transverse myelitis, which she contracted when she was four years old.

Becerra participated in the 1996 Paralympics, held right after the Olympics. She brought home two silvers, in the 100-meter (16.74) and 200-meter (29.64), and two bronzes, in the 400-meter (55.29) and 800-meter (1:53.41). In the 2000 Paralympics, Cheri finished first in the 100-meter (16.59) and the 400-meter (55.29). She set a world record in the semi-finals of the 200-meter (28.78), the only person to break under 29 seconds in that event.

AMERICAN INDIAN ATHLETIC HALL OF FAME

First Fourteen Inductees into the American Indian Athletic Hall of Fame, 1972

The American Indian Athletic Hall of Fame, located on the campus of Haskell Indian Nations University in Lawrence, Kansas, selects great American Indian athletes "on the basis of an outstanding, colorful, exciting and action-punctuated record of performance." In 1972, its founding year, fourteen athletes were inducted.

1. Alexander Arcasa (Colville), Football 1909–12
2. Charles "Chief" Bender (White Earth Chippewa), Baseball 1903–17
3. Wilson "Buster" Charles (Oneida), Olympic Decathlon 1927–31
4. Albert A. Exendine (Delaware), Football 1902–7
5. Joseph N. Guyon (Chippewa), Football 1911–27
6. Jimmie Johnson (Stockbridge-Munsee), Football 1899–1905
7. John Levi (Arapaho) Football, 1921–25
8. John "Tortes" Meyers (Cahuilla), Baseball 1908–17
9. Allie P. Reynolds (Creek), Baseball 1942–54
10. Theodore "Tiny" Roebuck (Choctaw), Football 1923–27
11. Reuben Sanders (Tutuni/Rogue River), Football 1890s
12. Louis Tewanima (Hopi), Track and Field 1907–12
13. Jim Thorpe (Sac and Fox), Football/Baseball/Track 1907–19
14. Louis Weller (Caddo), Football 1929–31

NATIVE AMERICAN PROFESSIONAL BALL PLAYERS

Native American Professional Baseball Players, 1897–2011

In Chronological Order
Years Played and Team(s)
* Denotes a team on which the player is still active, as of this writing.

Louis Sockalexis (Penobscot): 1897–99 Cleveland Spiders
Bill Phyle (Lakota): 1898–1906 Chicago Orphans, New York Giants, St. Louis Cardinals
Charles "Chief" Bender (Ojibwe): 1903–25 Philadelphia Athletics, Chicago White Sox, Baltimore Terrapins, Philadelphia Phillies
Ed Pinnance (Ojibwe): 1903 Philadelphia Athletics
Louis Bruce (Mohawk): 1904 Philadelphia Athletics
Louis LeRoy (Seneca): 1905–10 New York Highlanders, Boston Red Sox
Frank Jude (Ojibwe): 1906 Cincinnati Reds
Walter Perry Johnson (Paiute): 1907–27 Washington Senators
Ed Summers (Kickapoo): 1908–12 Detroit Tigers
John Tortes Meyers (Cahuilla): 1909–17 New York Giants, Brooklyn Robins, Boston Braves

Zachariah Davis Wheat (Cherokee): 1909–27 Brooklyn Superbas, Brooklyn Dodgers, Brooklyn Robins, Philadelphia Athletics

William Cadreau (Chief Chouneau) (Ojibwe): 1910 Chicago White Sox

Paddy Mayes (Creek): 1911 Philadelphia Phillies

Mike Balenti (Cheyenne): 1911–13 Cincinnati Reds, St. Louis Browns

Frank Harter (Cherokee): 1912–14 Cincinnati Reds and Indianapolis Hoosiers

Jim Thorpe (Sac and Fox Nation): 1913–19 New York Giants, Cincinnati Reds, Boston Braves

George Howard Johnson (Winnebago): 1913–15 Cincinnati Reds, Kansas City Packers

Ben Tincup (Cherokee): 1914–18, 1928 Philadelphia Phillies, Chicago Cubs

Jim Bluejacket (Cherokee): 1914–16 Brooklyn Tip-Tops, Cincinnati Reds

McKinley Davis Wheat (Cherokee): 1915–21 Brooklyn Robins, Philadelphia Phillies

William Marriott (Cherokee): 1917–27 Chicago Cubs, Boston Braves, Brooklyn Robins

Virgil Cheeves (Cherokee): 1920–27 Chicago Cubs, Cleveland Indians, New York Giants

Jesse Petty (Cherokee): 1921–30 Cleveland Indians, Brooklyn Robins, Pittsburgh Pirates, Chicago Cubs

Moses J. Yellowhorse (Pawnee): 1921–22 Pittsburgh Pirates

Albert Clyde Youngblood (Choctaw): 1922 Washington Senators

Ike Kahdot (Potawatomie): 1922 Cleveland Indians

Homer Blankenship (Cherokee): 1922–28 Chicago White Sox, Pittsburgh Pirates

Emmett Bowles (Potawatomie): 1922 Chicago White Sox

Pryor McBee (Choctaw): 1926 Chicago White Sox

Pepper Martin (Osage): 1928–44 St. Louis Cardinals

Art Daney (Choctaw): 1928 Philadelphia Athletics

Roy Johnson (Cherokee): 1929–38 Detroit Tigers, Boston Red Sox, New York Yankees, Boston Bees

Elon Chester Hogsett (Cherokee): 1929–44 Detroit Tigers, St. Louis Browns, Washington Senators

Bob Johnson (Cherokee): 1933–45 Philadelphia Athletics, Washington Senators, Boston Red Sox

Euel Moore (Chickasaw): 1934–36 Philadelphia Phillies, New York Giants

Rudy York (Cherokee): 1934–48 Detroit Tigers, Boston Red Sox, Chicago White Sox, Philadelphia Athletics

Vallie Eaves (Cherokee): 1935–42 Philadelphia Athletics, Chicago White Sox, Chicago Cubs

Bob Neighbors (Cherokee): 1939 St. Louis Browns

Allie Reynolds (Muscogee/Creek): 1942–54 Cleveland Indians, New York Yankees

Cal McLish (Choctaw): 1944–64 Brooklyn Dodgers, Pittsburgh Pirates, Chicago Cubs, Cleveland Indians, Cincinnati Reds, Chicago White Sox, Philadelphia Phillies

Charlie Cozart (Cherokee): 1945 Boston Braves

Jess Pike (Creek): 1946 New York Giants

Pat Cooper (Choctaw): 1946–47 Philadelphia Athletics

Jack Aker (Potawatomie): 1964–74 Kansas City Athletics, Oakland Athletics, Seattle Pilots, New York Yankees, Chicago Cubs, Atlanta Braves, New York Mets

Gene Locklear (Lumbee): 1973–77 Cincinnati Reds, San Diego Padres, New York Yankees

Dwight Lowry (Lumbee): 1984–88 Detroit Tigers, Minnesota Twins

Kyle Lohse (Nomlaki/Wintun): 2001 *Minnesota Twins, Cincinnati Reds, Philadelphia Phillies, St. Louis Cardinals

Shane Victorino (Native Hawaiian): 2003 San Diego Padres, 2005 *Philadelphia Phillies

Bobby Madritsch (Lakota): 2004–5 Seattle Mariners

Jacoby Ellsbury (Navajo): 2007 *Boston Red Sox

Joba Chamberlain (Winnebago): 2007 *New York Yankees

Native American Professional Football Players, 1909–2011

Years Played and Teams(s)

* Denotes a team on which the player is still active, as of this writing.

Jim Thorpe (Sac and Fox): 1909–10 Canton Bulldogs and New York Giants

Joe Guyon (Chippewa): 1920–27 Canton Bulldogs, Washington Senators, Cleveland Indians, Oorang Indians, Rock Island Independents, Kansas City Cowboys, New York Giants

Louis "Rabbit" Weller (Caddo): 1933 Boston Redskins

Orien Crow (tribe unknown): 1933–34 Boston Redskins

Jack Jacobs (Creek): 1942–49 Green Bay Packers

Tahnee Robinson (Shoshone), Basketball Player

Tahnee Robinson (Shoshone) collected quite a few firsts in 2011. She was the first Wyoming-born player, the first University of Nevada player, and the first American Indian ever to be drafted by the Women's National Basketball Association (WNBA). Among her many honors, for the 2010–11 season she was selected as one of five finalists for the prestigious Sullivan Award, given by the Amateur Athletic Union each year to the nation's top amateur athlete. She was the only Native in the group. In April 2011, the Connecticut Sun signed Tahnee Robinson to a training camp contract.

In February 2011, at the University of Nevada, Reno's Lawlor Events Center, Robinson was celebrated with a pre-game, traditional Native American gifting ceremony, rarely seen in a college basketball game. A senior point guard on the UNR women's basketball team, she received a Pendleton blanket from the Pyramid Lake Veterans' and Warriors Association in honor of her community service to Native people in northern Nevada.

Billy Wilson (tribe unknown): 1951–60 San Francisco 49ers

Jack Bighead (tribe unknown): 1954–55 Baltimore Colts, Los Angeles Rams

Phil King (tribe unknown): 1958–66 New York Giants

Chuck Shonta (tribe unknown): 1960–67 Boston Patriots

Dale Lindsey (tribe unknown): 1965–73 Cleveland Browns

Jim Riley (tribe unknown): 1967–71 Miami Dolphins

Marv Hubbard (tribe unknown): 1969–77 Oakland Raiders

Sonny Sixkiller (Cherokee): 1974–76 Toronto Northmen, Philadelphia Bell, and Hawaiians

Joey Browner (Cherokee): 1983–92 Minnesota Vikings, Tampa Bay Buccaneers

Ed McDaniel (Choctaw/Chickasaw): 1992–2001 New York Jets

Kailee Wong (Native Hawaiian): 1998–2006 Minnesota Vikings, Houston Texans

Chester David "Tuff" Harris (Crow): 2007 Miami Dolphins; 2008 Tennessee Titans; 2009 *Pittsburgh Steelers

Sam Bradford (Cherokee): 2010 *St. Louis Rams

Levi Horn (Northern Cheyenne): 2010 *Chicago Bears

COMPETITIONS

Running Competitions

Running activities have taken place throughout North and South America since ancient times. There are stories of racing contests in almost every tribe's oral history. In addition to the physical, mental, and health benefits, people ran for trade, communication, and spiritual reasons. The tradition of running is still very much alive. In recent times, Native youth and adults have competed in national and international long-distance running competitions, breaking records and winning prestigious awards.

1876	Clocked by U.S. Army officers with stop-watches, Big Hawk Chief (Pawnee) ran a mile in three minutes, fifty-eight seconds. Other runners did not equal that record until 1954.
1901	Bill Davis (Mohawk) placed second in the Boston Marathon with a time of 2:34:45.
1907	Tom Longboat (Onondaga) won the Boston Marathon with a time of 2:24:54, a new course record.
1908	Louis Tewanima (Hopi) placed ninth in the Summer Olympic marathon in London, England.
1912	Louis Tewanima (Hopi) won the silver medal in the Summer Olympic 10,000-meter race in Stockholm, Sweden. Andrew Sockalexis (Penobscot) won second place in the Boston Marathon with a time of 2:21:52.

1928	Andy Payne (Cherokee) won the Transcontinental Footrace of 1928. Sponsored by the Route 66 Association, the race stretched from Los Angeles, California, to New York City. Payne completed the distance of 3,423.5 miles in 573 hours, 4 minutes, and 34 seconds, averaging six miles an hour. An annual Andy Payne Bunion Run held every May in Oklahoma City commemorates this long-distance runner.
1936	Ellison Brown (Narragansett) won the Boston Marathon with a time of 2:33:40. He did it again in 1939 with a time of 2:28:51.
1964	Billy Mills (Oglala Lakota) won the gold medal in the 10,000-meter race at the Summer Olympics in Tokyo, Japan, setting an Olympic record time of 28:24.4.
1979	Patti Lyons (Micmac) was the second female finisher in the Boston Marathon, with a time of 2:38:22.
1980	Patti Catalano (Micmac) set the U.S. marathon record for women in October 1980 in New York City with a time of 2:29:34, the first American woman to finish in under two and a half hours. She won the Honolulu Marathon four years in a row, 1978 to 1981. During her career, she held every American distance record from the five mile to the marathon, and the world records in the half marathon and 30K. From April 1980 to April 1981, she ran forty-eight distance races, winning forty-four of them.
1981–82	Al Waquie (Jemez Pueblo) won the Pike's Peak Marathon two years in a row, with times of 3:26:17 and 3:29:53. He also won the Empire State Building Run-Up several times.
1992	Phillip Castillo (Acoma Pueblo) was the first Native American to win a collegiate cross-country title. He became the NCAA Division II National cross-country champion.

Five Native Competitive Games

1. The Arctic Winter Games
   http://www.arcticwintergames.org
   Launched in 1970, the Arctic Winter Games were first held in Yellowknife, Northwest Territories, Canada, with contingents from Canada and Alaska. The games, held every two years, include circumpolar sport competitions such as skiing, and endurance games traditionally played by Inuit and Dene people. The games promote the benefits of sport and promote cultural values and social exchanges.
2. Lori Piestewa National Native American Games
   http://www.gcsg.org/events/nativegames/

Held in conjunction with Arizona's Grand Canyon State Games, which began in 2001, the Lori Piestewa National Native American Games attract competitors who range in age from toddlers to elders. Athletes compete for medals in seven sports. The games were renamed in honor of Lori Piestewa, the first Native woman to die while serving in the U.S. military. She was killed in Iraq in 2003.

3. Louis Tewanima Footrace
http://tewanimafootrace.org
Founded in 1974 by the Hopi Athletic Association, an annual footrace is held in honor of U.S. Olympian Louis Tewanima (Hopi), winner of the silver medal in the 10,000-meter race at the 1912 Olympics in Stockholm, Sweden. The race, primarily a 5K and 10K, takes place on Labor Day weekend and begins and ends on top of Second Mesa.

4. Native Youth Olympics
http://www.anchorage.net/764.cfm
Started in 1972, the Native Youth Olympics involves events based on the games and life skills of past generations of Alaska Natives, played as a way to test their hunting and survival skills, and to increase strength, endurance, agility, and the balance of mind and body. The three-day competition is open to students from seventh to twelfth grade, regardless of ethnicity.

5. North American Indigenous Games
Started in 1990, the North American Indigenous Games is a multisport event for youth and adults, staged intermittently, that draws thousands of First Nations, Metis, Inuit, and Native American athletes who compete and are awarded medals in sixteen summer sports events. In addition to the competitions, the games include a parade, demonstrations of traditional sports, and cultural performances.

BOOKS

Six Biographies of Native American Athletes

1. *Allie Reynolds: Super Chief,* by Bob Burke and Royse Parr (2002).
2. *Chief Bender's Burden: The Silent Struggle of a Baseball Star,* by Tom Swift (2008).
3. *Indian Summer: The Tragic Story of Louis Francis Sockalexis, the First Native American in Major League Baseball,* by Brian McDonald (2003).
4. *The Man Who Ran Faster Than Everyone: The Story of Tom Longboat,* by Jack Batten (2002).
5. *Native American Son: The Life and Sporting Legend of Jim Thorpe,* by Kate Buford (2010).
6. *60 Feet Six Inches and Other Distances from Home: The (Baseball) Life of Mose YellowHorse,* by Todd Fuller (2002).

FILMS

4wheelwarpony (USA, 2008, 8 min.), directed by Dustinn Craig (White Mountain Apache/Navajo).

> Young Apache skateboarders from Whiteriver on the White Mountain Apache Indian Reservation in Arizona link past to present. Dressed as White Mountain Apache scouts of the 1880s, they reenact their culture in motion within skateboard culture. The video is named after a White Mountain Apache skateboard Company.

Bares, Broncs and Bulls in the Navajo Nation (USA, 2010, 17 min.), produced by Levi's Workwear and VBS TV.

http://www.vbs.tv/newsroom/bares-broncs-and-bulls-part-2-of-2-49

> The online documentary is about Navajo cowboys from the Triple B (Bares, Broncs, and Bulls) Association filmed on the Navajo Nation's Monument Valley. The athletes' on-screen comments tell the story of rodeos, which originated with Spanish *vaqueros* (cowboys).

Black Cloud (USA, 2004, 95 min.), directed by Rick Schroder.

> This film is a contemporary story about a young Navajo boxer who overcomes personal challenges while struggling to make it onto the U.S. Olympic boxing team. The movie was inspired by the true story of Navajo boxer Lowell Bahe's attempts to qualify for the 2008 Olympics.

Chiefs (USA, 2003, 83 min.), directed by Daniel Junge.

> The documentary chronicles two years in the lives of the Chiefs, a boys' high school basketball team from the Wind River Reservation in Wyoming (Northern Arapaho and Eastern Shoshone).

Chiefs and Champions (Canada, 2004, 24 min. each), directed by Annie Frazier Henry (Blackfoot/Sioux) and Ken Malenstyn.

> The first season of *Chiefs and Champions* is a six-part series that looks at world-class athletes from Canada and other parts of North America: Roger Adolph, boxing; Ross Powless, lacrosse; Alwyn Morris, kayaking; Waneek Horn-Miller, water polo; Fred Sasakamoose, hockey; and Tom Longboat, distance running.

The Continuity Box Offense (USA, 2005, 65 min.), directed by Kelvin Sampson (Lumbee).

> Sampson, the University of Oklahoma's renowned head coach, describes his highly successful continuity box offense in a demonstration clinic setting. He also demonstrates four of his favorite drills to promote competition in practice.

Edge of America (USA, 2003, 105 min.), directed by Chris Eyre (Cheyenne/Arapaho).

> Inspired by a true New Mexico story, this feature follows a girls' high school basketball team as it learns how to win. Led by their coach, the girls discover the values of passion, dedication, and discipline as they climb from the bottom of their division to compete for the state title.

The End of the Race (USA, 1981, 27 min.), directed by Hector Galán.

> The documentary looks at the survival of traditional Pueblo culture through the eyes of four Pueblo Indian cross-country runners of New Mexico. Through the profiles, the film explores cultural values associated with running.

Games of the North: Playing for Survival (USA, 2011, feature length), directed by Jonathon Stanton.

> This documentary features four Inuit athletes and their ties to the Arctic Games held biennially for a week in March. The film follows the athletes as they trek across Alaska—living, competing, and training.

The Great American Footrace (USA, 2002, 57 min.), directed by Dan Bigbee (Comanche) and Lily Shangreaux (Oglala Lakota).

> The documentary depicts an extraordinary 3,422-mile cross-country trek, won by nineteen-year-old Cherokee Indian Andy Payne (Oklahoma Cherokee). Facing scorching temperatures and intermittent supplies of food and water, and competing without modern running shoes or equipment, only 55 men (out of 199 runners) finished the 84-day race from Los Angeles to New York.

Hand Game: The Native North American Game of Power and Chance (USA, 1999, 57 min.), directed by Lawrence Johnson.

> The documentary traces the historic roots of contemporary gambling by providing a close-up look at the world of traditional gaming in eight communities in the American Northwest. Although casino gaming has received major media coverage, the ancient hand game, also called bone, grass, or stick game, is the most widely played gambling game in North America.

Heart of the Sea: Kapolioka'lehukai (USA, 2002, 57 min.), directed by Lisa Denker and Charlotte Lagarde.

> The film deals with the life of championship Hawaiian surfer Rell Kapolioka'ehukai Sunn, who carved the way for women in a sport dominated by men. She became an activist cancer survivor and an inspiring hero to Hawaii's Native community and surfers everywhere.

In Whose Honor: American Indian Mascots in Sports (USA, 1997, 47 min.), directed by Jay Rosenstein.

> The documentary looks at the practice of "honoring" American Indians as mascots and nicknames in sports. It follows the story of Charlene Teters (Spokane) and her struggles with the University of Illinois as she tries to protect Indian cultural symbols and identity. At the same time, the film also looks at issues of racism, stereotypes, minority representation, and impact of mass media images in the world of sports.

Jim Thorpe: The World's Greatest Athlete (USA, 2009, 86 min.), directed by Tom Weidlinger.

> The biography traces the life of a Native athlete, Jim Thorpe (Sac and Fox), who became a sports icon in the first half of the twentieth century. The documentary uses in-depth interviews with Thorpe's surviving children, simple re-creations, and images from over seventy-five archives.

Lady Warriors (USA, 2002, 90 min.), directed by John Goheen.

Documentary tells the story of the Lady Warriors, a Tuba City, Arizona, high school girls' cross-country team on the Navajo Reservation that won four straight state championships. Milfred Tewanima (Hopi), whose great-grandfather won the silver medal in the 10,000-meter race at the 1912 Olympics, coached the team.

Off the Rez (USA, 2011, 86 min.), directed by Jonathan Hock.

Shoni Schimmel (Umatilla), a high school junior living on Oregon's Umatilla Reservation, was the star basketball player on the local team. Her mother, Ceci Moses, took a job coaching a high school team in Portland, Oregon, leaving the reservation for a couple of years to prove that her daughter (and other Native women) could become champions off the reservation. In 2010, freshman Schimmel joined the Lady Cards, the University of Louisville (Kentucky) basketball team.

Playing for the World: 1904 Fort Shaw Indian Girls' Basketball Team (USA, 57 min.), directed by John Twiggs.

The historical documentary recounts the adventures of ten girls who made up a basketball team from the Fort Shaw (Montana) Government Indian Boarding School. The team, which became renowned for defeating every team it played (including a few boys' teams), traveled to the 1904 St. Louis World's Fair, where the girls were proclaimed "Champions of the World."

Rocks with Wings (USA, 2002, 113 min), directed by Rick Derby.

This documentary, filmed over the course of thirteen years, is a portrait of the Lady Chieftains, the legendary girls' basketball team from Shiprock, New Mexico. Primarily kids from the nearby Navajo reservation, the Chieftains were coached by Jerry Richardson, an African American from Texas.

Run to the East (USA, 2011, 87 min.), directed by Henry Lu.

The documentary follows three Navajo high school seniors competing in national track meets. The runners discuss how running teaches endurance, strength, and how to deal with struggle and pain. The runners also discuss the need to combat negative images in mainstream media that associate Native people with drugs and alcohol.

Snowsnake: Game of the Haudenosaunee (USA, 2006, 11 min.), produced by NMAI Resource Center, George Gustav Heye Center.

The film, which features a master snow-snake maker and player, Fred Kennedy (Seneca), introduces the traditional game played by Iroquois men in competitions throughout Haudenosaunee lands in the Northeast and in Canada.

ORGANIZATIONS

All Indian Rodeo Cowboys Association
http://www.aircarodeo.com

The All Indian Rodeo Cowboys Association (AIRCA), located in St. Michael's, Arizona, was founded in 1957, inspired by cowboys and cowgirls who embraced the traditions of sheepherders, ranchers, and farmers of the Navajo Nation. Since its inception, AIRCA has been encouraging young Indians to get involved in rodeo sports events.

NABI Foundation
http://nabifoundation.org

Founded in 2003, the NABI (Native American Basketball Invitational) Foundation, located in Phoenix, Arizona, is committed to supporting Native American youth by implementing programs that encourage higher education, sports, health and wellness, and community building. In 2003, it established a basketball invitational, the first Native tournament to become NCAA certified. NABI has also introduced baseball and softball programs, as well as college and career fairs.

National Coalition on Racism in Sports and Media
http://www.aimovement.org/ncrsm

Founded in 1991, the National Coalition on Racism in Sports and Media (NCRSM) was organized to address the use of Indians as sports team mascots, as well as to fight the powerful influence of major media that choose to promulgate messages of oppression. NCRSM, while best known for its front-line demonstrations outside sports stadiums across America, has been responsible for an educational effort that has made the issue of racial stereotyping a household discussion topic.

Native American Olympic Team Foundation
http://www.snow-riders.org

The Native American Olympic Team Foundation (NAOTF) is a partnership of United States tribal leaders, elders, and Olympians dedicated to creating a healthy generation of Native Olympians. Founded in 1996, the NAOTF has support from sixty ski areas/communities, the snow sports industry, and tribal sponsors in the United States and Canada.

Native American Sports Council
http://www.nascsports.org

Founded in 1993 and headquartered in Denver, Colorado, the Native American Sports Council (NASC) is a nonprofit member of the U.S. Olympic Committee, which is based in Colorado Springs, Colorado. NASC is dedicated to promoting community wellness through culturally appropriate youth-oriented sports programs. The NASC conducts community-based multisport programs and athlete-development programs that enable emerging elite athletes to be identified and developed for national, international, and Olympic competition. The NASC organizes the Native American Indigenous Games every year.

Native Vision

http://www.nativevision.org

> Founded in 1997, Native Vision is a partnership between the Johns Hopkins Center for American Indian Health and the National Football League Players Association. Headquartered in Baltimore, Maryland, Native Vision mobilizes NFL players and other professional athletes to mentor reservation-based Native youth. Programs include activities focused on fitness, school completion, nutrition, and decreased substance abuse.

Nibwaakaawin

http://allnationsskatejam.com/ansjwordpress

> Nibwaakaawin (Wisdom) is an organization based in Adrian, Michigan, dedicated to promoting safe and healthy physical activity through skateboarding, a fast-growing sport on Indian reservations. Programs include the All Nations Skate Jam, the largest skateboard competition for Native youth, which began in 2007; and skate clinics, camps, and regional skate jams.

Notah Begay III Foundation (NB3 Foundation)

http://www.nb3foundation.org

> The Notah Begay III Foundation is a nonprofit organization headquartered in Santa Ana Pueblo, New Mexico, that was started by golfer Notah Begay III and his father in 2005. Since that time, Notah, his family, numerous supporters, and tribal partners have worked hard to help the foundation impact the lives and well-being of Native American youth in New Mexico and across Indian country. Since its inception, the Notah Begay III Foundation has supported Native American youth golf and soccer programs.

Running Strong for American Indian Youth

http://www.indianyouth.org

> Established in 1986 by Olympic champion Billy Mills and Eugene Krizek, Running Strong for American Indian Youth, headquartered in Alexandria, Virginia, is dedicated to helping American Indian people meet their immediate survival needs—food, water, and shelter. Programs include food distribution and nutrition, water wells, youth programs, cultural and language preservation, and housing assistance.

Wings of America American Indian Youth Development Programs

http://www.wingsofamerica.org

> Established in 1988 by the Earth Circle Foundation and headquartered in Santa Fe, New Mexico, Wings of America was created with the goal of empowering at-risk American Indian youth. Through youth development programs incorporating running, Wings helps Indian youth overcome their life challenges and maintain their heritage. Running has an integral place in the spiritual and cer-

emonial traditions of American Indian people. Wings sponsors races, Native college runners, and running camps, among other activities.

RESOURCES

Bloom, John. *To Show What An Indian Can Do: Sports at Native American Boarding Schools*. Minneapolis: University of Minnesota Press, 2005.

Colton, Larry. *Counting Coup: A True Story of Basketball and Honor on the Little Big Horn*. New York: Warner Books, 2000.

D'Orso, Michael. *Eagle Blue: A Team, a Tribe, and a High School Basketball Season in Arctic Alaska*. New York: Bloomsbury, 2006.

Howe, LeAnne. *Miko Kings: An American Indian Baseball Story*. San Francisco: Aunt Lute Books, 2006.

Jenkins, Sally. *The Real All Americans: The Team That Changed a Game, a People, a Nation*. New York: Doubleday, 2007.

King, C. Richard. *The Native American Mascot Controversy: A Handbook*. Lanham, MD: Scarecrow Press, 2010.

———, ed. *Native Americans and Sport in North America: Other People's Games*. New York: Routledge, 2007.

———, ed. *Native Americans in Sports*. Armonk, NY: Sharpe Reference, 2003.

———, ed. *Native Athletes in Sport and Society: A Reader*. Lincoln: University of Nebraska Press, 2006.

———, and Charles Fruehling Springwood. *Team Spirits: The Native American Mascots Controversy*. Lincoln: University of Nebraska Press, 2001.

Nabokov, Peter. *Indian Running: Native American History and Tradition*. Santa Barbara, CA: Capri Press, 1981.

Oxendine, Joseph B. *American Indian Sports Heritage*. Champaign, IL: Human Kinetics Books, 1988; Lincoln: University of Nebraska Press, 1995.

Peavy, Linda, and Ursula Smith. *Full-Court Quest: The Girls from Fort Shaw Indian School: Basketball Champions of the World*. Norman: University of Oklahoma Press, 2008.

Powers-Beck, Jeffrey. *The American Indian Integration of Baseball*. Lincoln: University of Nebraska Press, 2004.

Spindel, Carol. *Dancing at Halftime*. New York: New York University Press, 2003.

Vennum, Thomas. *American Indian Lacrosse: Little Brother of War*. Washington, DC: Smithsonian Press, 1994.

Web Sites

Alaska Native Sports Association: http://www.aknsa.com/

American Indian Athletic Hall of Fame: http://americanindianathletichalloffame.com

Baseball Biography Project: http://bioproj.sabr.org/bioproj.cfm?a=1

Harvard Project's Honoring Nations Directory of Honored Programs, 1999–2006: http://hpaied.org/images/resources/general/Dir_web.pdf

Native American Boxing Council: http://nativeboxing.com

North American Indian Tennis Association: http://naita.info

Peabody Museum of Archaeology and Ethnology, "Against the Winds: American Indian Running Traditions": http://140.247.102.177/mcnh_running

21

Exhibitions, Pageants, and Shows

FIRSTS

1876   The Smithsonian Institution opened the first major exhibition of American Indian art at the Centennial International Exposition in Philadelphia.

1898   The first U.S. postage stamp to feature American Indians was issued as part of a series marking the Trans-Mississippi and International Exposition in Omaha, Nebraska. The stamp, based on an engraving by artist Seth Eastman, depicted a Plains tribesman on horseback pursuing a buffalo.

1908   Ikua Purdy (Native Hawaiian) became the first Hawaiian cowboy to win the World's Steer Roping Championship in Cheyenne, Wyoming. He won the roping championship with a record time of one minute, six seconds (some accounts indicate 56 seconds). In 1999 Purdy was voted into the Rodeo Hall of Fame, the first Hawaiian to be nominated.

1916   Jackson Sundown, Waaya-Tonah-Toesits-Kahn (Nez Perce), was the first Native American to win the World Saddle Bronc Championship at the Pendleton Round-Up. In 1976, the legendary horseman (1863–1923) also became the first Native American to be inducted into the Rodeo Hall of Fame at the National Cowboy and Western History Museum in Oklahoma.

1926   Norma Smallwood (Cherokee), representing the state of Oklahoma, was the first Native American to win the Miss America title.

EXHIBITIONS

Fourteen Expositions

World's fairs and expositions are important vehicles for representing American Indians to millions of visitors. Such events, which become especially intense during commemorative years, have included anthropological displays, Indian villages, living exhibits, model Indian schools, and assemblages of "races of mankind." The array of programming and products has been extensive, with pageants and reenactments, print and nonprint advertisements, media coverage, posters, coins, decorations, replicas, school curricula, and flurries of books. From the Centennial International Exhibition of 1876, the first official world's fair in the United States, to the present-day, these events have helped shape and reinforce public perceptions of Native peoples.

Centennial International Exhibition, Philadelphia, Pennsylvania, 1876
World's Columbian Exposition, Chicago, Illinois, 1893
Cotton States and International Exposition, Atlanta, Georgia, 1895
Trans-Mississippi and International Exposition, Omaha, Nebraska, 1898
Pan-American Exposition, Buffalo, New York, 1901
Louisiana Purchase Exposition, St. Louis, Missouri, 1904
Lewis and Clark Centennial Exposition, Portland, Oregon, 1905
Jamestown Tercentenary Exposition, Virginia, 1907
Alaska-Yukon-Pacific Exposition, Seattle, Washington, 1909
Panama-Pacific International Exposition, San Francisco, California, 1915
Columbus Quincentenary, 1992
Lewis and Clark Bicentennial, 2003–6
Jamestown, America's 400th Anniversary, Virginia, 2007
Santa Fe 400th Anniversary, New Mexico, 2010

Nine Poems about Exhibitions and Other Events by Native Poets

1. "The 500-Year-Old Poem," by Denise Sweet (Anishinaabe). In *Songs for Discharming* (1997).
2. "Columbus Day," by Jimmy Durham (Cherokee). In *Through Indian Eyes: The Native Experience in Books for Children,* edited by Beverly Slapin and Doris Seale (1992).
3. "The Crow Fair of Yesteryear," by Frederick M. Howe III (Crow/Blackfeet). In *Night Is Gone, Day Is Still Coming: Stories and Poems by American Indian Teens and Young Adults,* edited by Annette Pina Ochoa, Betsy Franco, and Traci L. Gourdine (2003).
4. "A Horse Called Tradition," by William Bray (Muskogee, Creek). In *Returning the Gift: Poetry and Prose from the First North American Native Writers' Festival,* edited by Joseph Bruchac (1994).

"The Red Man's Greeting," by Simon Pokagon

An excerpt from a speech delivered by Potawatomi leader Simon Pokagon on the opening day of the 1893 World's Columbian Exposition in Chicago, an event marking the four hundredth anniversary of Christopher Columbus's first voyage to America:

"In behalf of my people, the American Indians, I hereby declare to you, the pale-faced race that has usurped our lands and homes, that we have no spirit to celebrate with you the great Columbian Fair now being held in this Chicago city, the wonder of the world.

No; sooner would we hold the high joy day over the graves of our departed than to celebrate our own funeral, the discovery of America. And while . . . your hearts in admiration rejoice over the beauty and grandeur of this young republic and you say, 'Behold the wonders wrought by our children in this foreign land,' do not forget that this success has been at the sacrifice of *our* homes and a once happy race."

Source: Frederick E. Hoxie, ed. *Talking Back to Civilization: Indian Voices from the Progressive Era.* Boston: Bedford/St. Martin's, 2001.

American Indian Exposition, Anadarko, Oklahoma

Held annually in August in Anadarko, Oklahoma, the American Indian Exposition (AIE) is one of the oldest and largest intertribal ceremonial and cultural gatherings in the nation. It is sponsored by tribal nations that include Apache, Arapaho, Caddo, Cheyenne, Comanche, Delaware, Fort Sill Apache, Kiowa, Osage, Otoe-Missouri, Pawnee, Ponca, and Wichita. It is Indian-owned and operated, with a board of directors elected annually.

The American Indian Exposition is an outgrowth of the Craterville Park Indian Fair, which was held from 1924 through 1933, near Cache, Oklahoma. The AIE, then called the Southwestern Indian Fair, presented its first event in 1932. In 1935, it was incorporated as the American Indian Exposition dedicated to "promoting and retaining Indian cultural life, handicrafts, arts, crafts, and farming and livestock skills by providing a yearly showcase." The gathering, which draws thousands of visitors to Anadarko, features dancing, parades, arts, crafts, exhibits, pageants, and sporting events.

http://www.americanindianexposition.org/

5. "Independence Day," by Linda Noel (Konkow Maidu). In *The Dirt Is Red Here: Art and Poetry from Native California*, edited by Margaret Dubin (2002).

6. "Jamestown Revisited," by Karenne Wood (Monacan). In *Markings on Earth* (2001).

7. "A New Story," by Simon J. Ortiz (Acoma Pueblo). In *Songs from This Earth on Turtle's Back*, edited by Joseph Bruchac (1983).

8. "Quincentennial Ghostdance Song," by Annette Arkeketa (Otoe-Missouria/Creek). In *Returning the Gift: Poetry and Prose from the First North American Native Writers' Festival*, edited by Joseph Bruchac (1994).

9. "Rodeo Queen," by Tiffany Midge (Hunkpapa Sioux/German). In *Outlaws, Renegades and Saints: Diary of a Mixed-Up Halfbreed* (1996).

PAGEANTS

Native American Contestants in the Miss America Pageant, 1926–2008

1926   Norma Smallwood (Cherokee), competing as Miss Oklahoma, was crowned Miss America, the first Native American to win this title.

1941   Mifaunwy Shunatona (Otoe/Pawnee/Wyandotte), competing as Miss Oklahoma, was a semifinalist at the Miss America Pageant.

1971   Susan Supernaw (Muscogee-Munsee), competing as Miss Oklahoma, won a Special Judges Award at the Miss America Pageant.

2002   Rebekah Revels (Lumbee) resigned as Miss North Carolina in connection with rule-violation allegations against her, ultimately preventing her from competing in the Miss America Pageant.

2003   Erika Harold (Cherokee/Choctaw/African American), competing as Miss Illinois, was crowned Miss America.

2008   Elyse Umemoto (Yakama), competing as Miss Washington, became the second runner-up at the Miss America Pageant.

Miss Indian America, 1953–89

The Miss Indian America competition began in 1953 and was held annually in Sheridan, Wyoming, until it moved to Bismarck, North Dakota, in 1985. Features associated with the event included a pageant parade, a fashion show of traditional tribal dress, and a ceremonial giveaway at which the contestant bestowed gifts on her sponsor. The young women were judged on factors such as demonstrating knowledge of their respective tribal cultures, as well as their performances in talent contests. (http://www.pageantopolis.com/national/indian_america.htm)

1953	Arlene Wesley (Yakima)
1954	Mary Louise Defender (Sioux)
1955	Rita McLaughlin (Hunkpapa Sioux)
1956	Sandra Gover (Pawnee)
1957	Dolores Jean Shorty (Navajo), whose title was assumed by Ruthe Larson (Gros Ventre)
1958	Not held
1959	Delores Racine (Blackfeet)
1960	Vivian Arviso (Navajo)
1961	Brenda Bearchum (Northern Cheyenne/Walla Walla/Yakima)
1962	Ramona Soto (Klamath)
1963	Williamette Youpee (Sisseton/Yankton Sioux)
1964	Michelle Portwood (Arapahoe)
1965	Marcelle Ahtone (Kiowa)
1966	Wahleah Lujan (Taos Pueblo)
1967	Sarah Ann Johnson (Navajo)
1968	Thomasine Hill (Crow/Pawnee)
1969	Margery Haury (Cheyenne/Arapahoe/Navajo/Sioux)
1970	Virginia Stroud (Western Cherokee)
1971	Nora Begay (Navajo)
1972	Louise Edmo (Shoshone-Bannock)
1973	Maxine Norris (Papago), resigned; Claire Manning (Shoshone/Paiute) took over title
1974	Pageant not held; Claire Manning became known as Miss Indian America XXI
1975	Deana Jo Harragarra (Kiowa/Otoe)
1976	Kristine Rayola Harvey (White Mountain Apache)
1977	Gracie Ann Welsh (Chemehuevi/Mohave/Yavapai)
1978	Susan Arkeketa (Otoe-Missouria/Creek)
1979	Pageant not held

1980	Melanie Tallmadge (Winnebago/Minnesota Sioux)
1981	Jerilyn Lebeau (Cheyenne River Sioux)
1982	Vivian Juan (Papago)
1983	Pageant not held
1984	Anne-Louise Willie (White Mountain Apache/Paiute)
1985	Jorja Frances Oberly (Osage/Comanche/Nez Perce)
1986	Audra Arviso (Navajo)
1987	Linda Kay Lupe (White Mountain Apache)
1988	Bobette Kay Wildcat (Shoshone)
1989	Wanda Johnson (Navajo)

Five Native American Pageants

1. Miss Indian Nations Pageant: http://min.unitedtribespowwow.com/royalty.asp
2. Miss Indian Teen World National Scholarship Pageant: http://missindianteenusa.com/
3. Miss Indian World, Gathering of Nations: http://www.gatheringofnations.com/miss_indian_world/past_winners.htm
4. Miss NCAI, National Congress of American Indians: http://www.ncai.org/Miss-NCAI.12.0.html
5. Miss World Eskimo-Indian Olympics: http://www.weio.org/PDF/Former%20Miss%20WEIO.pdf

Holidays

Pressured to observe the Fourth of July and other holidays as part of the Americanizing process, American Indians turned the celebrations to their own purposes. Holiday festivities helped to provide a cover for the continued observance of cultural and religious ceremonies that had been banned by the government in the nineteenth century. Hence, tribal groups scheduled feast days and ceremonials during the Fourth of July, Memorial Day, and Arbor Day, circumventing repressive anti-Indian measures. In a number of communities, Native people held parades, gave away American flag–embellished gifts, conducted banned tribal dances, and performed honoring ceremonies for veterans and other community members. They transformed, or Indianized, American holidays to make them their own, incorporating Native rituals, foods, and arts into national observances that continue to flourish.

American Indians have always had a rich array of tribal holidays and festivals, as diverse as the multiplicity of tribal nations across the continent. These observances include seasonal harvests to give thanks for life-sustaining plants, animals, fish, and crops; ceremonies to mark the seasons; New Year celebrations; and observances to mark important stages or events, such as naming ceremonies, puberty rites, and mourning rituals. Native people also commemorate important events in their communities, among them the signing of treaties, historic removals, and the start of new schools, clinics, legislation, and other achievements.

Boarding School Pageants: *Hiawatha*

Intent on fulfilling the goals of federal Indian policy during the nineteenth century, school officials implemented or sanctioned extracurricular activities that celebrated American patriotism, reinforced Euro-American culture and religion, and worked to erase Native cultures and languages. School-sanctioned pageants and plays featured American Indian students cast as individuals and groups exalted in American history, among them Christopher Columbus and the Pilgrims. Educators had students dramatize Euro-American perceptions of warlike or hostile Indians, as in scenarios depicting historical events, as well as noble, romanticized Indians in *Hiawatha* and other works.

Published in 1855, Henry Wadsworth Longfellow's *The Song of Hiawatha* sold some fifty thousand copies in its first six months in print. Longfellow based his work on various Indian legends, crediting ethnologist Henry Rowe Schoolcraft as his primary source. Although the name Hiawatha comes from an actual historical figure, the founder of the Iroquois Confederacy, Longfellow based his fictional lead character upon the Ojibway culture hero, Manabozho (also Nanabozho, Nanabush). Added to the mixture of cultural elements are the presence of Dakota or Sioux characters and the influence of the Finnish folk epic *Kalevala* on the poem's sing-song meter.

Longfellow's *Hiawatha* achieved worldwide fame, becoming a popular selection for pageants, staged spectacles, song and dance, and dramatic performances, especially during the early 1900s. It was a staple of boarding schools (and beyond), where authorities approved its storyline focused on Indian nobility and disappearance. Hiawatha and his female counterpart, Minnehaha, served as popular dramatic roles for young men and women. The work also spawned many spinoffs: portrayals of the lead figures appeared on countless commercial products, among them dolls, moccasins, plates, figureheads, and printed materials.

SHOWS

Twelve Indian Medicine Shows

Especially popular in America during the nineteenth century, Indian medicine shows provided a variety of entertainment acts, along with a platform for traveling showmen to pitch and sell "patent" (over-the-counter) medicinal elixirs, or cure-alls, and other products to audiences. Shows, numbering in the hundreds between 1865 and 1900, ranged from a single horse and wagon team to large tent operations with a variety of performers, including non-Indians in "red-face" costuming. The Indian medicine shows were, in effect, early versions of Wild West shows. The Oregon Indian Medicine Company and the Kickapoo Indian Medicine Company were among the best known.

Founded by Colonel Thomas Augustus Edwards in 1876, the Oregon Indian Medicine Company was initially headquartered in Pittsburgh, Pennsylvania, but later moved to Corry, Pennsylvania. Its principal cure-all was Ka-Ton-Ka, but also produced products such as Nez Perce Catarrh Snuff and War Paint Ointment. The company ended shortly after 1904.

Founded by John Healy and Charles "Texas Charlie" Bigelow in 1881, the Kickapoo Indian Medicine Company became the largest medicine show in America. It operated out of Boston (1881–84), New York City (1884–87), New Haven (1887–97), and Clintonville, Connecticut (1897–1912). The enterprise, with its traveling troupes, publications, advertisements, and elixirs, had no connection to the Kickapoo Nation, which is located in present-day Oklahoma and Mexico.

1. Blackhawk Medicine Company
2. Choctaw Indian Medicine Show
3. Indian Medicine Show Company
4. Iroquois Famous Indian Remedies Company of Harlem
5. Kickapoo Indian Medicine Company
6. Kiowa Indian Medicine and Vaudeville Company
7. Nevada Ned's Big Indian Village
8. Old-Fashioned Indian Medicine Company
9. Old Indian Medicine Company
10. Oregon Indian Medicine Company
11. Pawnee Indian Remedy Company
12. Winona Medicine Company of the Sioux Tribe

Seventeen Indian Medicine Show Potions

Propelled by a longstanding belief in Native American knowledge of herbs and plants, Indian medicine shows often engaged Indians or Indian impersonators to help sell patent (over-the-counter) medicines titled with appropriated as well as fabricated tribal names. The potions were advertised or pitched as cure-alls for all manner of ailments, with pitchmen even claiming to have been "snatched from the jaws of death" by Kickapoo Indian Sagwa (originally compounded of aloes and stale beer) and other such products.

1. Cherokee Liniment
2. Donald McKay's Indian Worm Eradicator
3. Indian Ka-Ton-Ka
4. Indian Root Pills
5. Kickapoo Indian Sagwa
6. Kickapoo Indian Worm Killer
7. Modoc Oil
8. Nez Perce Catarrh Snuff
9. Old Indian Liver and Kidney Tonic
10. Old Sachem Bitters and Wigwam Tonic
11. Red Jacket Stomach Bitters
12. Seminole Cough Balsam
13. Tippecanoe Nostrum
14. Wa-Hoo Bitters
15. Warm Springs Consumption Cure
16. Wasco Cough Drops
17. White Beaver's Laugh Cream, the Great Lung Healer

Twenty-One Wild West Shows

Wild West shows, which incorporated stage play, circus and vaudeville themes, sharpshooting demonstrations, buffalo hunting exhibitions, and other theatrical elements in performances across North America and Europe, were a popular form of entertainment from the late 1800s into the twentieth century. William Frederick "Buffalo Bill" Cody and other showmen hired a range of performers for the shows, including Lakota, Pawnee, and other Plains Indians to lend authenticity to staged portrayals of the American west.

1. Allen Bros. Wild West (1929–34)—Charles and Mert H. Allen
2. Arlington & Beckman's Oklahoma Ranch Wild West (1913)—Edward Arlington and Fred Beckman
3. Austin Bros. 3 Ring Circus and Real Wild West (1945)
4. Barrett Shows and Oklahoma Bill's Wild West (1920)
5. Bee Ho Gray's Wild West (ca. 1919–32)
6. Bronco John, Famous Western Horseman and His Corps of Expert Horsemen (1906)—J. H. Sullivan
7. Buckskin Ben's Wild West and Dog and Pony Show (1908)—Benjamin Stalker
8. Buckskin Bill's Wild West (1900)
9. Buffalo Bill's Wild West (1883–1900s)

10. Buffalo Bill's Wild West and Pawnee Bill's Far East (the "Two Bills" show) (1908–1913)
11. California Frank's All-Star Wild West (1911)—Frank Hafley
12. Colonel Cummins' Wild West Indian Congress and Rough Riders of the World—Frederick T. Cummins (early 1900s)
13. Diamond Dick's Wild West (ca. 1895–1905)
14. Fred Akins Real Wild West and Far East Show (1909–10)
15. Gene Autry's Flying A Ranch Stampede (1942)
16. Irwin & Hirsig Wild West (1910)
17. Irwin Brothers Cheyenne Frontier Days Wild West Show (1913–17)
18. Jones Bros.' Buffalo Ranch Wild West (1910)
19. Miller Bros. 101 Ranch Real Wild West (1907–31)
20. Pawnee Bill's Wild West Show (1888–1907)
21. Texas Jack's Wild West (ca. 1900)

Sixteen Movies about Buffalo Bill

1. *The Life of Buffalo Bill* (1912)
2. *The Indian Wars* (1913)
3. *Adventures of Buffalo Bill* (1917)
4. *Battling with Buffalo Bill* (1931)
5. *Annie Oakley* (1935)
6. *The Plainsman* (1936)
7. *Young Buffalo Bill* (1940)
8. *Buffalo Bill* (1944)
9. *Buffalo Bill in Tomahawk Territory* (1952)
10. *Buffalo Bill and the Wild West* (1955)
11. *Buffalo Bill and the Indians, or Sitting Bull's History Lesson* (1976)
12. *Wild Bill* (1995)
13. *Buffalo Bill: Showman of the West* (1996)
14. *Cody!—An Evening with Buffalo Bill* (2005)
15. *Carson & Cody—The Hunter Heroes* (2006)
16. *American Experience: Buffalo Bill* (2008)

The Program for the First Season of Buffalo Bill's Wild West

Buffalo Bill's Wild West, an internationally famous show that toured North America and Europe from the 1880s into the twentieth century, was produced by Indian scout, buffalo hunter, and stage performer William Frederick "Buffalo Bill" Cody. Cody's first show, which was held in Omaha, Nebraska, in 1883, included the participation of Pawnee scouts under the leadership of Army scout Major Frank North.

1. Grand Introductory March
2. Bareback Pony Race
3. Pony Express
4. Attack on the Deadwood Mail Coach
5. 100-Yard Race between an Indian on foot and an Indian on horseback
6. Capt. A. H. Bogardus—shooting exhibition
7. Cody and Carver—shooting exhibition
8. Race between Cowboys
9. Cowboy's Fun
10. Riding Wild Texas Steers
11. Roping and Riding Wild Bison
12. Grand Hunt—including a battle with the Indians

Sitting Bull (Tatanka Iyotake) in Buffalo Bill's Wild West

Sitting Bull, Hunkpapa Lakota leader and holy man from Dakota Territory, participated in William Frederick "Buffalo Bill" Cody's Wild West show in 1885, proving to be a huge draw for audiences riveted by his association with the defeat of Lt. Col. George Armstrong Custer by Lakota and Cheyenne forces at the Battle of the Little Big Horn in 1876. During the season the Lakota leader was on tour, Cody and his company appeared in over forty cities in the United States and Canada, playing to approximately one million people and earning a profit estimated at over $100,000.

For Sitting Bull, touring with the Wild West show offered a measure of freedom from conditions on Dakota Territory's Standing Rock Reservation, where he and his people had come under increasingly repressive government control. The Lakota leader was able to interact with a wide range of audiences, including government officials, and speak on behalf of his people. Sitting Bull's contract with Cody's show, which included the sole rights to sell his own photographs and autographs, enabled him to earn money to send home.

When the tour ended on October 11, 1885, in St. Louis, Missouri, Sitting Bull was weary, "sick of the houses and the noises and the multitude of men." He returned home with gifts from Buffalo Bill, who gave him a trained gray circus horse and a white sombrero.

Five Native American Outdoor Dramas and Reenactments

1. *The Big Cypress Shootout*, Big Cypress Reservation, Florida
   http://www.bigcypressshootout.com/
   A reenactment of the Second Seminole War, presented by the Seminole Tribe of Florida, Big Cypress Reservation, Florida.

2. *Chinook Nation—U.S.A.: International Trading Partners, 1792–2010*
   Held on October 3, 2010 at Fort Columbia State Park in Chinook, Washington, this living history event commemorated the first meeting between Chinookan people and sea Captain Robert Gray.
3. Six Nations Forest Theatre, Ohsweken, Ontario, Canada
   http://www3.sympatico.ca/foresttheatre/about_us.html
   This theater presents theatrical productions in an outdoor amphitheatre that promote pride in Native history and work to erase stereotypical images of Native people.
4. *Under the Cherokee Moon*, Cherokee Heritage Center, Tahlequah, Oklahoma
   http://underthecherokeemoon.com
   This outdoor historical drama depicts Cherokee history during the 1700s and 1880s.
5. *Unto These Hills*, Outdoor Drama, Eastern Band of Cherokee Indians, Cherokee, North Carolina
   http://www.cherokee-nc.com/index.php?page=9
   Operated by the Cherokee Historical Association in Cherokee, North Carolina, the outdoor drama *Unto These Hills* began in 1950 and tells the story of the Cherokee Nation from European contact to the Trail of Tears.

Fourteen Major Rodeos

1. Calgary Stampede, Calgary, Alberta, Canada, July
2. Cheyenne Frontier Days, Cheyenne, Wyoming, July
3. Crazy Horse Stampede Rodeo, Crazy Horse Memorial, South Dakota, June
4. Crow Fair Rodeo, Crow Agency, Montana, annually third week in August
5. Fort McDowell Yavapai Nation, Fountain Hills, Arizona, November
6. Gallup Inter-Tribal Indian Ceremonial Rodeo, Red Rock Park, Churchrock, New Mexico, August
7. Indian National Finals Rodeo, Browning, Montana (headquarters)
8. Navajo Nation Fair, Window Rock, Arizona, annually in September (after Labor Day)
9. Omak Stampede, Omak, Washington, annually second week in August
10. Pendleton Round-Up Rodeo, Pendleton, Oregon, September
11. Sarcee (Tsuu T'ina) Indian Rodeo, Bragg Creek, Alberta, Canada, July
12. Shoshone-Bannock Indian Festival Rodeo, Fort Hall, Idaho, August
13. White Swan Treaty Days All IndianRodeo, White Swan, Washington, June
14. Wild Card Rodeo, various locations and dates

FILMS

American Cowboys (USA, 1998, 26 min.), directed by Tania Wildbill and Cedric Wildbill (Umatilla).

Documentary about the rodeo careers in the early 1900s of the first Native rodeo star, Jackson Sundown (Flathead/Nez Perce), and George Fletcher, an African American man who grew up on the Umatilla Reservation in Oregon.

Bares, Broncs and Bulls in the Navajo Nation (USA, 2010, 17 min.), a production of VBS TV.

http://www.vbs.tv/watch/we-are-all-workers--3/bares-broncs-and-bulls-full-length-2
Filmed on location in the Navajo Nation, this online documentary tells the story of young Diné (Navajo) rodeo competitors, among them bareback rider Earl Tsosie Jr., barrel racer Cory Rose Chee, and bull rider Bert Jones. It features action sequences, commentary by the athletes, and a glimpse of their lives at home and in the rodeo ring.

Columbus Day Legacy (USA, 2011, 27 min.), directed by Bennie Klain (Navajo).
This film explores issues of free speech and ethnic pride associated with the Columbus Day parade celebrated by the Italian-American community in Denver, Colorado. The documentary examines the controversy over the annual event, which sparks protests by Native Americans, raising questions about history and identity in America.

Miss Navajo (USA, 2006, 60 min.), directed by William Luther.
This film tells the story of the Miss Navajo Nation competition, which requires a range of knowledge and skills, including the ability to answer difficult questions in the Navajo language and demonstrate proficiency in traditional skills. The filmmaker, whose mother was crowned Miss Navajo 1966, documents one contestant's journey and interviews past winners to reveal the varying roles associated with the title.

Pendleton Round-Up: The Wild West Way (USA, 2010, 59 min.), produced by Nadine Jelsing and Eric Cain.

http://www.opb.org/programs/oregonexperience/programs/player/31-The-Wild-West-Way
A co-production of Oregon Public Broadcasting and the Oregon Historical Society, this film explores the one-hundred-year history of the Pendleton Round-Up, an annual rodeo extravaganza held in Pendleton, Oregon. It draws from archival footage of early Round-Ups to document the origins of the event, including ongoing Native American participation from the local Umatilla Reservation and beyond. The film, which can be viewed online, also illustrates the Indian village at the Round-Up, "the largest encampment on the professional rodeo circuit."

Summer Sun Winter Moon (USA, 2009, 57 min.), directed by Hugo Perez.
Summer Sun Winter Moon, which premiered on PBS in 2009, presents American Indian perspectives about Lewis and Clark's "Corps of Discovery" expedition. The film features the collaboration between classical music conductor and composer Rob Kapilow and Blackfeet poet and educator Darrell Robes Kipp to create a symphony for the Lewis and Clark Bicentennial.

RESOURCES

Baillargeon, Morgan, and Leslie Tepper. *Legends of Our Times: Native Cowboy Life.* Vancouver: UBC Press, and Seattle: University of Washington Press, published in association with the Canadian Museum of Civilization, 1998.

Bales, Michael, and Ann Terry Hill. *Pendleton Round-Up at 100: Oregon's Legendary Rodeo.* Salem, OR: East Oregonian Publishing Co., 2009.

Beard-Moose, Christina Taylor. *Public Indians, Private Cherokees: Tourism and Tradition on Tribal Ground.* Tuscaloosa: University of Alabama Press, 2009.

Brownell, Susan, ed. *The 1904 Anthropology Days and Olympic Games: Sport, Race, and American Imperialism.* Lincoln: University of Nebraska Press, 2008.

Carpenter, Charles H. *Portraits of Native Americans: Photographs from the 1904 Louisiana Purchase Exposition.* New York: New Press, 1994.

Gentry, Carole M., and Donald A. Grinde Jr., eds. *The Unheard Voices: American Indian Responses to the Columbian Quincentenary 1492–1992.* Los Angeles: American Indian Studies Center, University of California, 1994.

Huhndorf, Shari M. *Going Native: Indians in the American Cultural Imagination.* Ithaca, NY: Cornell University Press, 2001.

Iverson, Peter, and Linda MacCannell. *Riders of the West: Portraits from Indian Rodeo.* Seattle: University of Washington Press, 1999.

Kasson, Joy S. *Buffalo Bill's Wild West: Celebrity, Memory, and Popular History.* New York: Hill and Wang, 2000.

Maddox, Lucy. *Citizen Indians: Native American Intellectuals, Race and Reform.* Ithaca, NY: Cornell University Press, 2005.

McNamara, Brooks. *Step Right Up: An Illustrated History of the American Medicine Show.* Garden City, NY: Doubleday, 1976.

Mellis, Allison Fuss. *Riding Buffaloes and Broncos: Rodeo and Native Traditions in the Northern Great Plains.* Norman: University of Oklahoma Press, 2003.

Moses, Daniel David. *The Indian Medicine Shows: Two One-Act Plays.* Toronto, Ontario: Exile Editions, 1995, 2002.

Moses, L. G. *Wild West Shows and the Images of American Indians, 1883–1933.* Albuquerque: University of New Mexico Press, 1996.

Parezo, Nancy J., and Don D. Fowler. *Anthropology Goes to the Fair: The 1904 Louisiana Purchase Exposition.* Lincoln: University of Nebraska Press, 2007.

Peers, Laura. *Playing Ourselves: Interpreting Native Histories at Historic Reconstructions.* Lanham, MD: AltaMira Press, 2007.

Perdue, Theda. *Race and the Atlanta Cotton States Exposition of 1895.* Athens: University of Georgia Press, 2010.

Rydell, Robert W. *All the World's a Fair: Visions of Empire at American International Expositions, 1876–1916.* Chicago: University of Chicago Press, 1984.

Standing Bear, Luther. *My People the Sioux.* Lincoln: University of Nebraska Press, 1975 (originally published in 1928).

Supernaw, Susan. *Muscogee Daughter: My Sojourn to the Miss America Pageant.* Lincoln: University of Nebraska Press, 2010.

Tapahonso, Luci. *Songs of Shiprock Fair.* Walnut, CA: Kiva Publishing, 1999.

Viola, Herman J., and Carolyn Margolis. *Seeds of Change: A Quincentennial Commemoration.* Washington, DC: Smithsonian Institution Press, 1991.

Wallis, Michael. *The Real Wild West: The 101 Ranch and the Creation of the American West.* New York: St. Martin's Griffin, 2000.

White, Richard, and Patricia Limerick. *The Frontier in American Culture.* Edited by James R. Grossman. Berkeley and Los Angeles: University of California Press, 1994.

Web Sites

All Indian Rodeo Cowboys Association: http://www.aircarodeo.com

America's 400th Anniversary Legacy Site: http://www.jamestown2007.org/

Anthropology and the World's Columbian Exposition: http://blogs.nyu.edu/blogs/hg26/amnhphotographs/2009/05/anthropology_and_the_worlds_co.html

The Centennial Exhibition, Philadelphia, PA: http://www.lcpimages.org/centennial/

Indian National Finals Rodeo: http://www.infr.org

Lewis and Clark: The National Bicentennial Exhibition: http://www.lewisandclarkexhibit.org/index_flash.html

Lewis and Clark Expedition: A National Register of Historic Places Travel Itinerary, National Park Service: http://www.nps.gov/nr/travel/lewisandclark/trailtoday.htm

Santa Fe 400: http://www.santafenm.gov/index.aspx?NID=1877

Part Seven

22

Alaska Natives

FIRSTS

1913   Walter Harper (Athabascan) was the first person to reach the 20,320-foot summit of Denali (Mt. McKinley), North America's highest peak.

1924   William L. Paul (Tlingit) was the first Alaska Native to be elected to the Territorial Legislature. The first Native attorney in the state, he helped integrate the Alaska public schools as well as win voting rights for Native people.

1929   The Alaska Native Brotherhood/Alaska Native Sisterhood initiated the first Native claims court suit, the seed of the Alaska Native Claims Settlement Act of 1971.

1945   The United States' first anti-discrimination law was passed by the Alaska Legislature, spurred by the work of civil rights activist Elizabeth Peratrovich (Tlingit).

1957   Constance Harper Paddock (Athabascan) was the first Alaska Native to hold the position of chief clerk of the Alaska House of Representatives.

1962   The premier issue of the *Tundra Times*, the first Alaska Native newspaper, was published. The weekly newspaper was the initial statewide publication to focus exclusively on Alaska Native issues. Howard Rock (Inupiaq) was the paper's first editor.

1971   The first radio broadcast of KYUK-AM took place in May, which made it the first Native-owned and operated radio station in the United States.

     Betty Ivanoff Menard (Inupiaq) became the first Alaska Native woman to reach the summit of Denali (Mt. McKinley), North America's highest peak.

     The first Native Youth Olympics were held in the spring. Twelve schools competed.

1972   Elary Gromoff (Aleut), former CEO of the Aleut Corporation, became the first Alaska Native to graduate from West Point Military Academy.

1974   Eben Hopson (Inuit) was the first mayor of the North Slope Borough, which he helped create. He also became an Alaska state senator.

1975   The First International Conference of Indigenous Peoples opened in British Columbia. It drew Native people from the United States, Canada, Greenland, South America, Australia, and New Zealand. Inupiaq Billy Neakok was the only Alaskan who attended.

1976   Ted Mala (Inupiaq) became the first in his cultural group to receive a Doctor of Medicine and Surgery degree. In 1990, he joined the cabinet of Alaska Governor Walter J. Hickel to become the first Alaska Native commissioner of health and social services.

1977   The First Inuit Circumpolar Conference took place in Barrow, Alaska. It was the first official gathering of Inuit people from Alaska, Canada, and Greenland.

1989   The Alaska State Legislature established the first annual Elizabeth Peratrovich Day in honor of Mrs. Peratrovich (Tlingit), who provided crucial testimony that culminated in Alaska's Anti-Discrimination Bill of 1945.

1993   Georgianna Lincoln (Athabascan) became the first Alaska Native woman in the state's history to serve in the Alaska State Senate.

1995   Glenn G. Godfrey (Alutiiq) was named director in the Division of Alaska State Troopers, the first Alaska Native to rise above the rank of sergeant in the state troopers. In 2000, Governor Tony Knowles named him to the state's highest law enforcement post, public safety commissioner, the first Alaska Native to be chosen for that position.

1997   The Louden Tribal Council of Galena Alaska established the first tribally owned corporation in Alaska when it created the Yukaana Development Corporation (YDC), a for-profit environmental remediation business. YDC worked under the first memorandum of agreement between a tribe and the U.S. Air Force. Louden was also the first tribe to be approved to provide remediation services at a semi-active military base in Alaska.

2010   The Iñupiat Eskimo village of Noorvik, Alaska, became the first place in the United States to be counted in the 2010 census. The village held a Potlatch festival to celebrate the launch of the nation's census.

HISTORY

Five Indigenous National Historic Landmarks in Alaska

In 1962, five sites in Alaska became national historic landmarks.

1. The Birnick Site, near Barrow; AD 500 to the present
2. The Chaluka Site, near Nikolski; 1800 BC to the present
3. The Palugvik, near Cordova; AD 1200 to the present
4. Wales Site, near Wales; archaeological site
5. Yukon Island Mainsite, near Homer; archaeological site

Aleuts and World War II

1942

June 3   Japanese forces dropped bombs on Fort Mears at Dutch Harbor in the Aleutian Chain. Patients at the Bureau of Indian Affairs Hospital in Unalaska were evacuated before the building was bombed and destroyed. The raids led to the evacuation of 886 Aleut civilians to southeast Alaska, where they were placed in deplorable conditions by the federal government until the war ended.

June 6   Japanese troops landed on Kiska, in the Aleutian Chain, 1,400 miles west of Anchorage. Aside from ten men at a weather station, the island is uninhabited. Fourteen months later, Allied forces reclaimed the island.

June 7   The Japanese landed 1,200 troops of the 301st Independent Infantry Battalion under Major Masatoshi Hozumi at Holtz Bay on the northern coast of Attu, the westernmost of the Aleutian Islands. Forty-five Aleuts and two non-Native teachers who lived there were taken prisoner and placed in captivity on Hokkaido. Only twenty-four survived to return to the United States in 1945, where they were relocated on Atka.

June 11   The United States sent aircraft from Atka to bomb Japanese-held positions on Kiska as a response to the Japanese attack on Attu.

June 14   The populations of St. George and St. Paul of the Pribilof Islands were evacuated within twenty-four hours. In many cases, people had two hours to gather up belongings and were limited to one suitcase each. The Navy relocated the St. Paul Aleuts to an abandoned cannery at Funter Bay on Admiralty Island and the St. George Aleuts to an old mine site across the bay from the cannery. Many people died in the unsanitary conditions of the camps. Occupying American forces vandalized Aleut villages.

1943

May 11   The U.S. 7th Infantry Division landed 11,000 infantry on Attu Island. After nineteen days of fighting, the Japanese were defeated at the battle of Chicagof Harbor.

May 30   All organized Japanese resistance ended in the Aleutians.

August 15   American and Canadian troops landed on Kiska Island in the Aleutians and found no Japanese troops. They had fled the island several weeks before the Allied troops landed.

1945

February 4   The Attu battlegrounds and airfields were designated as national historic landmarks.

April 22   Aleuts returned to Unalaska in the Aleutian Chain after being evacuated from their village during World War II.

1988

August 10   President Ronald Reagan signed the Civil Liberties Act, a law making restitution through payments to Aleut residents of the Pribilof and Aleutian islands for loss of personal and community property and village lands during U.S. military occupation of the islands during World War II. The act also apologized for the evacuation, relocation, and internment of Japanese Americans during World War II.

ALASKA NATIVE CULTURAL GROUPS AND REGIONAL CORPORATIONS

Eleven Major Cultural Groups in Alaska

According to the Alaska Native Heritage Center in Anchorage, Alaska Native people belong to eleven cultural groups, which have different homelands, cultures, and languages. Besides residing on the mainland and islands of Alaska, Alaska Native people also live throughout the lower 48 states.

1. Athabascan: traditional homeland in interior Alaska along five major river ways
2. Eyak: traditional homeland in southeastern corner of south central Alaska
3. Yup'ik: traditional homeland in southwest Alaska

4. Cup'ik: traditional homeland in southwest Alaska
5. Unangan: homeland stretches from Prince William Sound to the end of the Aleutian Islands
6. Alutiiq: homeland stretches from Prince William Sound to the end of the Aleutian Islands
7. Inupiaq: homeland in north and northwest Alaska
8. St. Lawrence Island Yup'ik: homeland in north and northwest Alaska
9. Haida: original homeland on Queen Charlotte Islands in British Columbia, Canada; migration north to Prince of Wales Island area within Alaska
10. Tlingit: homeland in southeast Alaska panhandle between Icy Bay in the north and the Dixon Entrance in the south
11. Tsimshian: original homeland between the Nass and Skeena Rivers in British Columbia, Canada; today Tsimshian live mainly on Annette Island in (New) Metlakatla, Alaska (and in settlements in Canada)

Unangan/Aleut

Many Aleut people commonly call themselves Unangan today. The more traditional name is *Unangax̂*, the proper term for Native people of the Aleutian region. The word is pronounced "Unangas" in the western dialect and "Unangan" in the dialect of the eastern Aleutian Islands. Hunters, fishers, and whalers are the original inhabitants of the Aleutian Islands, predating by thousands of years the Russian explorers who arrived in the seventeenth century. People living on the Aleutian Islands received the name *Aleut* from Russians. The meaning is unclear.

Thirteen Alaska Native Regional Corporations

The 1971 Alaska Native Claims Settlement Act (ANCSA), a federal law that addressed Native land claims in Alaska, granted Alaska's sixty thousand Native people title to approximately 44 million acres of their ancient homeland—about 10 percent of the entire land area of Alaska—and $962.5 million to settle conflicts over Native land rights. ANCSA established twelve regional Native corporations, a thirteenth corporation for Natives living outside Alaska, and more than two hundred village corporations to administer the proceeds.

1. Ahtna, Inc., headquartered in Glenallen, http://www.ahtna-inc.com/
2. Aleut Corporation, headquartered in Anchorage, http://www.aleutcorp.com/
3. Arctic Slope Regional Corporation, with offices in Anchorage and Barrow, http://www.asrc.com/Pages/Home.aspx
4. Bering Straits Native Corporation, headquartered in Nome, http://www.beringstraits.com/

5. Bristol Bay Native Corporation, headquartered in Anchorage, http://www
   .bbnc.net/
6. Calista Corporation, headquartered in Anchorage, http://www.calistacorp.com/
7. Chugach Alaska Corporation, headquartered in Anchorage, http://www
   .chugach-ak.com/Pages/splash.aspx
8. Cook Inlet Region, headquartered in Anchorage, http://www.ciri.com/
9. Doyon, Limited, headquartered in Fairbanks, http://www.doyon.com/
10. Koniag, Incorporated, headquartered in Kodiak, http://www.koniag.com/
11. NANA (Northwest Alaska Native Association) Regional Corporation, Inc.,
    headquartered in Kotzebue, http://www.nana.com/
12. Sealaska Corporation, headquartered in Juneau, http://www.sealaska.com/
    page/home
13. Thirteenth Regional Corporation, headquartered in Tukwila, Washington;
    represents Alaska Natives living outside the state, who received funds but no
    lands

Eight Alaska Native Museums and Heritage Centers

1. Alaska Native Heritage Center, Anchorage, Alaska
   http://www.alaskanative.net
   Incorporated in 1989 as an educational and cultural institution for all Alaskans,
   the Alaska Native Heritage Center exhibits the rich heritage of Alaska's major
   cultural groups through interactive, hands-on activities. It provides workshops,
   demonstrations, and guided tours of indoor exhibits and outdoor village sites.
2. Alutiiq Museum and Archaeological Repository, Kodiak, Alaska
   http://www.alutiiqmuseum.org
   Established in 1995, the Alutiiq Museum and Archeological Repository presents
   7,500 years of Alutiiq heritage. Exhibits and heritage programs reflect Alutiiq
   history, arts, and language, as well as their dependence on sea mammals.
3. Ilanka Cultural Center, Cordova, Alaska
   http://www.ilankacenter.org/
   Founded in 2004, the Ilanka Cultural Center honors the heritage, foods,
   languages, arts, clothing, songs, and dances of the Eyak, Alutiiq, Ahtna
   Athabascan, and Tlingit peoples from ancient times to the present day.
4. Iñupiat Heritage Center, Barrow Alaska
   http://www.nps.gov/inup/aboutthecenter.htm
   Dedicated in 1999, the Iñupiat Heritage Center houses exhibits, artifact
   collections, a library, gift shop, and a room where people can demonstrate
   and teach traditional crafts in Elders-in-Residence and Artists-in-Residence
   programs. As an affiliated National Park, the North Slope Borough owns and
   manages the Iñupiat Heritage Center. The Heritage Center is one of several
   partners, associated through New Bedford Whaling National Historical Park
   legislation, who participate in telling the story of commercial whaling in the
   United States.

5. Museum of the Aleutians, Unalaska, Alaska
    http://www.aleutians.org/
    Opened in 1999, the Museum of the Aleutians presents the history and culture of the Aleutians Islands and the Unangan (Aleut) people, who have lived on the islands continually for nine thousand years. Collections and exhibits showcase archaeology, history, ethnography, and masterpieces of Unangan artistry, especially basketry.

6. Sheldon Jackson Museum/Alaska State Museum, Sitka, Alaska
    http://www.museums.state.ak.us/sheldon_jackson/sjhome.html
    The collections of the Sheldon Jackson Museum, founded in 1887, include objects from Tlingit, Haida, Tsimshian, Aleut, Alutiiq, Yup'ik, Iñupiat, and Athabascan. The collections reflect the acquisitions made by founder Sheldon Jackson, missionary and general agent of education for Alaska from 1887 through about 1898. Other objects were subsequently added to the collection, but in 1984 when the museum was purchased by the State of Alaska, the decision was made to add only Alaska Native materials made prior to the early 1930s.

7. University of Alaska Museum of the North, Fairbanks
    http://alaska.org/fairbanks/musuem-of-the-north.jsp
    Opened in 1929, the University of Alaska Museum of the North now features the Gallery of Alaska's thematically grouped exhibits that represent Alaska's major ecological and cultural regions. Highlights include extensive displays of Alaska Native art and artifacts; videos show a whale hunt and Alaska Native dances. The centerpiece of the expanded museum, the Rose Berry Alaska Art Gallery, presents the full spectrum of Alaska art, from ancient Eskimo ivory carvings to contemporary paintings and sculpture, both Native and non-Native.

8. The Yupiit Piciryarait Museum, Bethel, Alaska
    http://www.ypmuseum.org/
    Originally founded by the City of Bethel in 1965 as the Bethel Museum, the Yupiit Piciryarait Museum includes approximately 2,500 pieces of art, photos, and artifacts in galleries displaying exhibits of Yup'ik, Cup'ik, and Athabascan people of the Yukon-Kuskokwim Delta in ancient and contemporary times.

Totem Poles

Totem poles are monumental representations of the history and spirituality of Native lineages carved in wood. The Tlingit and Haida Indians of southeast Alaska commonly carved their works from large trees, mostly red or yellow cedar. Poles may represent ancient times or relatively recent historical events. Totem poles are found all over southeast Alaska, with at least a few in almost every town. The greatest concentrations of totem poles are in Sitka, at the Sitka National Historic Park, and in Ketchikan at Saxman Village and Totem Bight State Historic Park.

RADIO AND FILM

Eleven Alaska Native Radio Stations

Alaska Native radio, which brings a contemporary voice, often in Alaska Native languages, evokes the oral traditions of Alaska's indigenous cultures. Native radio reaches into village homes and urban apartments and condos twenty-four hours a day, seven days a week, informing, educating, and mobilizing listeners with news about matters of public safety, community, and sports events.

 1. Anchorage, Alaska: KNBA 90.3 FM
 2. Barrow, Alaska: KBRW 680 AM
 3. Bethel, Alaska: KYUK 640 AM
 4. Chevak, Alaska: KCUK 88.1 FM
 5. Ft. Yukon, Alaska: KZPA 900 AM
 6. Galena, Alaska: KIYU 97.1 FM
 7. Kotzebue, Alaska: KOTZ 720 AM and 89.9 FM
 8. Sand Point, Alaska: KSDP 830 AM
 9. St. Paul Island, Alaska: KUHB 91.9 FM
10. Unalakleet, Alaska: KNSA 930 AM
11. Unalaska, Alaska: KUCB 89.7 FM

Tribal Voice Radio

In 2010, Tribal Voice Radio began broadcasting from Juneau, Alaska. The Central Council of Tlingit and Haida Indian Tribes launched the online radio station to give voice to the Tlingit, Haida, and Tsimshian tribes of Southeast Alaska.

Ten Early Commercial Films about Alaska and the North, 1922–26

 1. *Carnegie Museum Alaska-Siberian Expedition*, 1912
 2. *The Frozen North*, 1922
 3. *Nanook of the North*, 1922
 4. *Adventures in the Far North*, 1923
 5. *The Eskimo*, 1923
 6. *The Alaskan*, 1924
 7. *Kivalina of the Ice Lands*, 1925
 8. *Alaskan Adventures*, 1926
 9. *Justice of the Far North*, 1925
10. *Primitive Love*, 1926

Nanook of the North, 1922

During 1919–20, American filmmaker Robert Flaherty filmed the story of Nanook, an Inuit (Eskimo). He presented several staged events as reality, although staging certain actions for the camera was the norm of documentary filmmakers of the times. Flaherty encouraged Nanook to hunt walrus and seal with spears in the manner of his ancestors, in order to capture the way the Inuit lived before they acquired guns from Europeans.

When *Nanook of the North* was released in 1922, the public and film critics, who proclaimed it a realistic portrayal of Eskimos, made it a success. The contrived quality of the film, however, drew criticism from the beginning. According to explorer Vilhjalmur Stefansson, *Nanook* was "harmful" because it confirmed most of the ordinary misconceptions people held about Eskimos and it added "new misconceptions more numerous than those which it removes" (Fienup-Riordan 1995, 49). Although Flaherty never worked in Alaska, his film images have influenced how Alaska Yup'ik and Iñupiat Eskimos have been presented in U.S. popular culture.

The *Fast Runner* Trilogy

The *Fast Runner* trilogy, which can be viewed for free online, is a window into a way of life that few are truly aware of beyond "Eskimo" stereotypes. The three films express the dramatic history of one of the world's oldest oral cultures from its own point of view. The trilogy has had an enormous impact on U.S. audiences and revolutionized Native images around the world.

Zacharias Kunuk (Inuit) directed and produced, with collaborator Norman Cohn, *Atanarjuat/The Fast Runner* (2001), the first film in the trilogy. A groundbreaking film, it was the first Native language feature to be produced, written, directed, and acted by Inuit. *Atanarjuat*, which portrays a traditional epic myth spoken entirely in Inuktitut, won the 2001 Camera d'Or for Best First Feature at the Cannes International Film Festival, the first such award for a Canadian director. In 2004, Kunuk won the first Sun Hill Award for Excellence in Native American Filmmaking, a new annual honor from the Harvard Film Archive.

Kunuk and Cohn's second feature film, *The Journals of Knud Rasmussen* (2006) portrays a 1922 contact between Rasmussen and people whose shamanism was being undercut by missionaries. Their third production, *Before Tomorrow* (2009), directed by Marie-Hélène Cousineau, is set in 1840, a time when Inuit had not yet met non-Inuit people.

LEGISLATION

Timeline of Alaska Natives Legislation

1867   The United States and Russia signed the Treaty of Cession, by which the United States purchased Alaska from Russia at a cost of $7.2 million. Article III stated: "The uncivilized tribes will be subject to such laws and regulations as the United States may, from time to time, adopt in regard to aboriginal tribes of that country." Alaska Native people were not consulted regarding the change in "ownership."

1884   President Chester Alan Arthur signed into law an Alaska Organic Act, which created civil government (a "civil and judicial district") in Alaska. The discovery of gold near Juneau prompted the legislative action. The law stated: "The Indians or other persons in said district shall not be disturbed in the possession of any lands actually in their use or occupation or now claimed by them."

1891   Congress created the Metlakatla Reservation on Annette Island, the only reservation in Alaska. Known as the Metlakatla Indian Community, it was founded by Tsimshian Indians in 1887. The reservation is not subject to state jurisdiction.

1905   Congress set up a dual education system for Alaska. Alaska Native schools, maintained under the Department of the Interior, were separate from schools for non-Natives.

1912   Alaska officially became a territory with the passage of legislation that provided for a territorial legislature.

1915   Alaska Territorial Governor John Strong signed into law the Native citizenship bill. Any member of a Native group who reached the age of twenty-one could be granted citizenship only if the person gave up "habits and customs of the old communal life which were hostile to American citizenship" and learned to read and write English.

1924   All Alaska Natives became citizens of the United States with the passage of the Indian Citizenship Act of 1924. The act expressly included Eskimos, Aleuts, and Indians of the Alaska Territory.

1936   The Act of May 1, 1936, extended the Indian Reorganization Act of 1934 to Alaska. Many Native village governments throughout Alaska organized and adopted constitutions under the auspices of the act. Some Native businesses were chartered or financed as well.

1937   Congress passed the Reindeer Act. It provided federal funds and property to Alaska Natives for sustaining the economic use of reindeer. Only Alaska Natives, organizations of Alaska Natives, or the United States for the benefit of these Natives, can own Alaskan reindeer.

1959 On January 3, Alaska became the forty-ninth state in the Union. Under the Statehood Act of 1958, the state selected 104 million acres of federal public domain land for itself. Alaska Natives protested state selections that threatened lands that belonged to them. Federal land withdrawals also threatened Native lands.

1971 President Richard M. Nixon signed into law the Alaska Native Claims Settlement Act (ANCSA), giving Alaska's Native people title to 44 million acres of their ancient homeland and $962.5 million in settlement of the century-old question of Native land rights. The money was paid into thirteen regional corporations that ANCSA created to invest the money. Individual Natives were enrolled in the corporations and received shares of stock restricted to Natives and heirs until 1991. The 1988 Amendments corrected problems in ANSCA.

1976 President Gerald R. Ford signed into law the Omnibus Amendments Act. Besides amending the Alaska Native Claims Settlement Act (ANCSA) of 1971, it permitted the supplemental enrollment of Alaska Natives and extended the deadline for filing claims for benefits under ANCSA until January 2, 1977. The act ratified a decision by Alaska Natives to create a thirteenth regional corporation for those living outside the state.

1980 President Jimmy Carter signed into law the Alaska National Interest Lands Conservation Act (ANILCA). It set aside 90 million acres of public lands in Alaska for parks, forests, and refuges. The act addressed subsistence uses of fish and game by Alaska Natives only as "rural residents." ANILCA has been viewed as an amendment to the Alaska Native Claims Settlement Act.

1988 President Ronald Reagan signed into law the Alaska Native Claims Settlement Act Amendments. The passage culminated the work of fifteen congressional hearings, seven Alaska Federation of Natives conventions, and five Native leadership retreats to correct problems that emerged from implementing the 1971 Alaska Native Claims Settlement Act. Known as "1991 amendments" because they allowed for continuation of Native ownership of Native corporations after December 18, 1991, they gifted and issued stock to Alaska Natives born after that date. The law provided automatic protections for land and Native corporate stock.

AWARDS

Six Award-Winning Alaska Natives

2002 Sarah James, Norma Kassi, and Jonathon Solomon (Gwich'in Athabascan) won the Goldman Environmental Prize. The three activists were instrumental in winning a battle to block oil drilling in the Arctic National Wildlife Refuge in Alaska. The Goldman prize is given each year to "grassroots environmental heroes, who demonstrate conviction, commitment, and courage for their sustained and important environmental achievements."

2004   Katherine Gottlieb (Aleut) became Alaska's first Native recipient of the MacArthur Fellows Program Award, also known as the "Genius Award." She was honored for her exceptional creativity and innovative accomplishments in building Southcentral Foundation, the medical arm of Cook Inlet Region, Inc., into a quality-driven, patient-centered organization tailored to the health needs of Alaska Natives.

2007   Sven Haakanson (Alutiiq), an anthropologist and mask maker, was Alaska's second recipient of the MacArthur "Genius Award." He has been a driving force behind the revitalization of Alutiiq language, culture, and customs. He is executive director of the Alutiiq Museum in Kodiak.

2008   Rosita Worl (Tlingit), president of Sealaska Heritage Institute (SHI), won the prestigious Solon T. Kimball Award for Public and Applied Anthropology. The award honors the outstanding recent achievements of exemplary anthropologists who have contributed to the development of anthropology as an applied science and have had important impacts on public policy.

BOOKS

Ten Books with Writings by Alaska Natives

1. *Alaska's Daughter: An Eskimo Memoir of the Early Twentieth Century*, by Elizabeth Bernhardt Pinson (2004).
2. *Authentic Alaska: Voices of Its Native Writers*, by Susan B. Andrews and John Creed (1998).
3. *Fifty Miles from Tomorrow: A Memoir of Alaska and the Real People*, by William L. Iggiagruk Hensley (Inupiaq) (2008).
4. *Give or Take a Century: An Eskimo Chronicle*, by Joseph E. Senungetuk (Inupiaq) (1971).
5. *Growing Up Native in Alaska*, edited by Alexandra J. McClanahan (2000).
6. *I Am Eskimo: Aknik My Name*, by Aknik (1959).
7. *Sadie Brower Neakok: An Inupiaq Woman*, by Margaret B. Blackman (1989).
8. *The Life I've Been Living*, by Moses Cruikshank (Athabascan) (1986).
9. *On the Edge of Nowhere: A Thrilling True Story of Life in the Big Land—Alaska*, by James Huntington (Athabascan) (1966).
10. *Raven Tells Stories: An Anthology of Alaskan Native Writing*, edited by Joseph Bruchac (Abenaki) (1991).

FILMS

Aleut Story (USA, 2005, 90 min.), directed by Marla Williams.

> The documentary deals with the story of the forced relocation in 1942 of nine hundred Aleutian Americans from their homes in the Aleutian and Pribilof Islands to isolated camps in southeast Alaska, ostensibly for their protection during World War II. The documentary also treats the Aleutians' forced internment and decades-long fight for civil rights.

For the Rights of All: Ending Jim Crow in Alaska (USA, 2009, 57 min.), co-directed by Phil Lucas (Choctaw) and Jeffry Lloyd Silverman.

> The documentary looks at Alaska Native community members and leaders who fought discrimination, tracing the story of the state's civil rights movement and Tlingit activist Elizabeth Peratrovich, renowned for her role in the struggle. The film uses archival materials, interviews, and historical reenactments.

The Land Is Ours (USA, 1996, 57 min.), directed by Laurence Goldin.

> The historical documentary about the Tlingits and Haidas of southeast Alaska is also the story of William Paul Sr., a Tlingit attorney and the first Native elected to the territorial legislature, who helped launch the land claims suit that changed Alaska forever.

A Matter of Respect (USA, 1992, 29 min.), directed by Ellen Frankenstein.

> *A Matter of Respect* is a stereotype-breaking documentary about the meaning of tradition and change. Portraits of four Alaska Natives show them expressing and passing on their culture and identity.

On the Ice (USA, 2011, 96 min.), directed by Andrew Okpeaha MacLean (Iñupiaq).

> *On the Ice* is a drama about two teenage boys who are best friends in Barrow, an isolated Alaska town. A killing involving a third boy force the two teens to explore the limits of friendship. The film has an entirely Inuit cast.

The 21st Annual World Eskimo-Indian Olympics (USA, 1983, 27 min.), directed by Skip Blumberg.

> The World Eskimo-Indian Olympics have been held as an organized event in Fairbanks, Alaska, since 1961. The documentary shows highlights of ancient sports such as the blanket toss, knuckle hop, high kicks, four-man carry, whale blubber eating, and other contests.

ORGANIZATIONS

Alaska Federation of Natives (AFN)
http://www.nativefederation.org

> The Alaska Federation of Natives (AFN), headquartered in Anchorage, Alaska, is the largest statewide Native organization in Alaska. AFN advocates

Alaska Native Brotherhood and Sisterhood

Alaska Native Brotherhood (ANB), a nonprofit organization founded in 1912, is believed to be the oldest state Indian organization in the United States. For the first half of the twentieth century, it was the only organization fighting for and protecting the rights of Eskimos, Aleuts, and Athabascans in Alaska. In 1987, the ANB Hall, located in Sitka, was designated a National Historic Landmark.

Alaska Native Sisterhood (ANS), reported to have been established in 1913, is one of the oldest Native organizations that advocated for civil rights and land claims for Alaska Native people. Along with its partner organization, the ANB, the ANS initiated the struggle for land rights that ended in 1971 with the passage of the Alaska Native Claims Settlement Act. It lobbied Congress for tribal governments in Alaska and ended segregated schools in the state.

for Alaska Native people, their governments, and organizations with respect to federal, state, and local laws. Its membership includes 178 villages (both federally recognized tribes and village corporations), thirteen regional Native corporations, and twelve regional nonprofit and tribal consortiums that contract and run federal and state programs. The AFN was formed in October 1966 when hundreds of Alaska Natives gathered for a conference to address their land rights. From 1966 to 1971, AFN played a key role in the passage of the 1971 Alaska Native Claims Settlement Act (ANCSA).

Alaska Inter-Tribal Council
http://www.ancsa.net/node/176

The Anchorage-based Alaska Inter-Tribal Council is a statewide, tribally governed nonprofit organization that advocates in support of tribal governments throughout the state. The council promotes indigenous self-determination by providing technical assistance to tribal governments, facilitating intergovernmental and interagency communication and collaboration, offering public education regarding Alaska indigenous cultures and tribal governments, and advocating on behalf of tribal initiatives and self-governance.

Alaska Native Arts Foundation (ANAF)
http://alaskanativearts.org

Founded in 2002, the Alaska Native Arts Foundation, a nonprofit organization, works to improve the economic well-being of Alaska Native artists by stimulating demand for and establishing fair market pricing for works of Alaska Native art, educating and training the next generation of Alaska Native artists, increasing awareness of Alaska Native cultures, and creating opportunities to inform about the diverse cultural expressions of Alaska's indigenous peoples.

Alaska Native Health Board

http://www.anhb.org

The Alaska Native Health Board (ANHB), established in 1968, is a statewide voice on Alaska Native health issues. ANHB, located in Anchorage, Alaska, promotes the spiritual, physical, mental, social, and cultural well-being and pride of Alaska Native people. It advises the director of the Alaska Area Native Health Service (AANHS), the U.S. Senate Committee on Indian Affairs, and the House Committee on Natural Resources on federal legislation and appropriations affecting Alaska Native health programs.

Aleutian/Pribilof Islands Association

http://www.apiai.com

Chartered in 1976, the Aleutian/Pribilof Islands Association is the federally recognized nonprofit tribal organization of the Aleut people in Alaska. Located in Anchorage, APIA was created by the merger of two predecessor organizations: the Aleut League, formed in 1966, and the Aleutian Planning Commission, formed a few years later. APIA contracts with federal, state, and local governments, as well as securing private funding to provide a broad spectrum of services throughout the region. These services include health, education, social, psychological, employment and vocational training, and public safety services.

Arctic Slope Native Association

Incorporated in 1972 and headquartered in Barrow, Alaska, the Arctic Slope Regional Corporation (ASRC), a not-for-profit corporation, controls dozens of subsidiaries involved in aerospace, construction, manufacturing, engineering, communications, oilfield services, capital financing, and petroleum-refining and distribution businesses. The northernmost and the largest of the regional corporations, ASRC obtains 40 percent of its revenues from oilfield services, a business managed by the company's subsidiary, Natchiq Inc., the largest oilfield service contractor in Alaska.

Association of Village Council Presidents

http://www.avcp.org

The Association of Village Council Presidents (AVCP), created in 1964, was established to work for the benefit of the people of tribal governments and the people of the Yukon Kuskokwim Delta. AVCP is a tribal nonprofit organization based in Bethel (southwest) Alaska, the regional hub for fifty-six federally recognized tribes, all of whom are members of AVCP. AVCP's member tribes, who reside in small isolated villages in an area approximately the size of Oregon, receive a variety of social service, human development, and culturally relevant programs that promote tribal self-determination and self-governance and work to protect tribal culture and traditions.

Bristol Bay Native Association, Inc.

http://www.bbna.com

Incorporated in 1973, Bristol Bay Native Association, headquartered in Dillingham, Alaska, is a tribal consortium made up of thirty-one tribes, and is organized as a nonprofit corporation to provide a variety of educational, social, economic, and related services to the Native people of the Bristol Bay region of Alaska.

Central Council of the Tlingit and Haida Indian Tribes of Alaska

http://www.ccthita.org

The Central Council of the Tlingit and Haida Tribes of Alaska, a nonprofit organization, was founded in 1935. Headquartered in Juneau, Alaska, the council serves approximately twenty-six thousand Tlingit and Haida people worldwide. It works to preserve sovereignty, enhance economic and cultural resources, and promote self-sufficiency and self-governance through collaboration, service, and advocacy.

Chugachmiut

http://www.chugachmiut.org

Chugachmiut, headquartered in Anchorage, Alaska, is the tribal consortium created to promote self-determination among the seven Native communities of the Chugach Region. It provides health and social services, education and training, and technical assistance to the Chugach Native people.

Cook Inlet Tribal Council

http://www.citci.com

Cook Inlet Tribal Council, headquartered in Anchorage, Alaska, serves the needs of Native people throughout the Cook Inlet Region and beyond, using thousands of years of Native heritage, culture, knowledge, and values to guide its work. The council welcomes all Alaska Natives and American Indians who have made greater Anchorage area their home.

Council of Athabascan Tribal Governments

http://www.catg.org

The Council of Athabascan Tribal Governments (CATG) is a grassroots organization founded in 1985 on the principal of tribal self-governance. The council works to empower and build the capacity of local member tribal governments to assume management responsibility of programs within their villages. Headquartered in Fort Yukon, Alaska, CATG conserves and protects tribal land and other resources, encourages and supports the exercise of tribal powers of self-government, aids and supports economic development.

Dena'nena' Henash Tanana Chiefs Conference (TCC)

http://www.tananachiefs.org

Dena'nena' Henash (Our Land Speaks) Tanana Chiefs Conference was incorporated in 1971. TCC, a nonprofit organization headquartered in Fairbanks, Alaska, has a membership of Native governments from forty-two interior Alaska communities. TCC advocates for land rights, self-determination, and the subsistence rights of rural Alaskans. It works to meet the health and social service needs of more than ten thousand Alaska Natives spread across a region of 235,000 square miles in interior Alaska.

First Alaskans Institute
http://www.firstalaskans.org

First Alaskans Institute, formerly known as First Alaskans Foundation, a nonprofit organization founded in 2000 and headquartered in Anchorage, helps develop the capacities of Alaska Native people and their communities to meet the social, economic, and educational challenges of the future. The institute works through community engagement, information and research, collaboration, and leadership development.

Goldbelt, Inc.
http://www.goldbelt.com

Goldbelt, Inc., was organized in 1974 under the Alaska Native Claims Settlement Act (ANCSA) and has now been in operation for over thirty-five years. It is an urban, Alaska Native, not-for-profit corporation located in Juneau, Alaska. Its primary purpose is to manage assets and to conduct business for the benefit of its shareholders, approximately 3,200 people, almost all of Alaska Native heritage.

Inuit Circumpolar Conference
http://www.inuit.org

The Inuit Circumpolar Conference (ICC), an organization of the Inuit people of Alaska, Canada, Greenland, and Russia, was founded in 1977. Its work involves environmental and social initiatives. In 1983, ICC was granted nongovernmental organization (NGO) status at the United Nations. The ICC Alaska office is located in Anchorage.

Kawerak
http://www.kawerak.org

Kawerak was formed in 1967 as an association of Native villages in the Bering Straits region. Today, Kawerak, located in Nome, Alaska, contracts with the state and federal governments to provide services to residents of the region, 75 percent of whom are Eskimo, Aleut, or of American Indian descent. With programs ranging from education to housing, and natural resource management to economic development, Kawerak seeks to improve the region's social, economic, educational, cultural, and political conditions.

Kodiak Area Native Association
http://www.kanaweb.org/html/profile.php

Kodiak Area Native Association (KANA), formed in 1966 as a nonprofit corporation, provides health and social services for the Alaska Natives of the Koniag region. KANA's service area includes the Kodiak and six Alaska Native villages: Akhiok, Karluk, Old Harbor, Ouzinkie, Port Lions, and Larsen Bay.

Maniilaq Association

http://www.maniilaq.org/flash.html

Formerly called the Northwest Alaska Native Association, Maniilaq was founded in 1966. Located in Kotzebue, Alaska, it represents twelve federally recognized tribes located in Northwest Alaska, providing people with extensive health, tribal, and social services. It advocates for all Native issues, including health, housing, and political rights.

Sealaska Heritage Institute

http://www.sealaskaheritage.org

Sealaska Heritage Institute (SHI) is a regional Native nonprofit organization, founded in 1981 for the Tlingit, Haida, and Tsimshian people of southeast Alaska. In 1997 SHI adopted language restoration as its foremost priority. Besides sponsoring numerous language and culture programs across Southeast Alaska, the institute, headquartered in Juneau, Alaska, also sponsors archival projects, historical research, and new publications.

RESOURCES

Angilirq, Paul Apak, Norman Cohn, and Bernard Saladin d'Anglure. *Atanarjuat, the Fast Runner*. Toronto, Canada: Coach House Books/Isuma Publishing, 2002.

Berger, Thomas R. *Village Journey: The Report of the Alaska Native Review Commission*. New York: Hill & Wang, 1985.

Case, David. *Alaska Natives and American Laws*. Fairbanks: University of Alaska Press, 1984.

Corral, Roy, and Will Mayo. *Alaska Native Ways: What the Elders Have Taught Us*. Portland, OR: Graphic Arts Books, 2002.

Crowell, Aron A., Rosita Worl, Paul C. Ongtooguk, and Dawn D. Biddison, eds. *Living Our Cultures, Sharing Our Heritage, The First Peoples of Alaska*. Washington, DC: Smithsonian Books, 2010.

Evans, Michael Robert. *The Fast Runner: Filming the Legend of Atanarjuat*. Lincoln: University of Nebraska Press, 2010.

Fienup-Riordan, Ann. *Freeze Frame: Alaska Eskimos in the Movies*. Seattle: University of Washington Press, 1995.

Garfield, Brian. *Thousand-Mile War: World War II in Alaska and the Aleutians*. Chicago: University of Chicago Press, 1969; reprint 1995.

Kohlhff, Dean. *When the Wind Was a River: Aleut Evacuation in World War II*. Seattle: University of Washington Press, 1995.

McClanahan, Alexandra J., ed. *A Reference in Time: Alaska Native History Day by Day.* Anchorage: The CIRI Foundation, 2001.

Mitchell, Donald Craig. *Sold American: The Story of Alaska Natives and Their Land, 1867–1959.* Fairbanks: University of Alaska Press, 2003.

———. *Take My Land, Take My Life: The Story of Congress's Historic Settlement of Alaska Native Land Claims, 1960–1971.* Fairbanks: University of Alaska Press, 2001.

Morgan, Lael. *Art and Eskimo Power: The Life and Times of Alaskan Howard Rock.* Kenmore, WA: Epicenter Press, 1988; reprint 2008.

Pratt, Kenneth L., ed., *Chasing the Dark: Perspectives on Place, History, and Alaska Native Land Claims.* Anchorage: U.S. Bureau of Indian Affairs, Alaska Region, ANCSA Office, 2009.

Roderick, Libby. *Alaska Native Cultures and Issues: Responses to Frequently Asked Questions.* Fairbanks: University of Alaska Press, 2010.

Williams, Maria Sháa Tláa, ed. *The Alaska Native Reader: History, Culture, Politics.* Durham, NC: Duke University Press, 2009.

Web Sites

Alaska Native Heritage Center, Anchorage, Alaska: http://www.alaskanative.net

Alaska Native History, Education, Languages, and Cultures Online Materials: http://www.alaskool.org

Alaska Native Science Commission: http://www.nativescience.org

Aleutian World War II National Historic Area and Visitor Center, National Park Service, Amaknak Island, Aleutians: http://www.nps.gov/aleu/index.htm

KYUK, Bethel, Alaska: http://kyuk.org/

Russian Orthodox Diocese of Alaska: http://dioceseofalaska.org

University of Alaska Anchorage Justice Center. Alaska Native Tribal Government: http://justice.uaa.alaska.edu/directory/t/tribal_governments_ak.html

The Iditarod Trail Sled Dog Race

The Iditarod Trail Sled Dog Race ("The Last Great Race"), which began in 1973, is an annual sled dog team race. The race from Anchorage to Nome, Alaska, covers more than 1,150 miles of "the roughest, most beautiful terrain Mother Nature has to offer" (http://www.iditarod.com/learn/). Four Alaska Natives have won this popular state sporting event.

1974	Carl Huntington (Athabascan): 20 days, 15 hours, 2 minutes, and 7 seconds (the slowest winning time recorded)
1975	Emmitt Peters (Athabascan): 14 days, 14 hours, 43 minutes, 45 seconds
1976	Gerald Riley (Athabascan): 18 days, 22 hours, 58 minutes, 17 seconds
2011	John Baker (Iñupiaq): 8 days, 18 hours, 46 minutes, 39 seconds (the fastest winning time ever recorded since 1973)

23

Native Hawaiians

by Yvonne Wakim Dennis

FIRSTS

1831   Lahainaluna School, operated by Protestant missionaries for Native Hawaiians, was the first school established by Americans west of the Rocky Mountains.

1834   Newspapers *Ka Lama Hawaii* and *Ke Kumu Hawaii* were the first publications in the Hawaiian language.

1881   David La'amea Kamanakapu'u Mahinulani Nalaiaehuokalani Lumialani Kalākaua became the first king to ever sail around the world when he left Hawaii to study the issue of immigration and to improve foreign relations. He was also the first king to travel to the United States; he visited President Ulysses S. Grant. King Kalākaua, a patron of the arts, composed the official state song, "Hawai'i Pono'i" ("Hawaii's Own People").

1882   The 'Iolanki Palace was built as the Hawaiian monarchy's official residence and had electricity years before the White House. It was the headquarters of the Hawaiian Kingdom until Queen Lili'uokalani was overthrown in 1893. Today it is the only royal palace in the United States.
    Dr. Matthew Manuia Makalua became the first Native Hawaiian to study for a medical degree in Western medicine, having been sent by King David Kalākaua to study in England. However, he could not return home after graduation because of the overthrow of the Hawaiian Kingdom and ended up working with Sir Joseph Lister in England, helping to develop modern surgical methods.

1900   Robert William Kalanihiapo Wilcox was the first Native Hawaiian elected the first delegate to the United States Congress for the Territory of Hawaii.

1903   Prince Jonah Kūhiō Kalaniana'ole, the "People's Prince," was elected Hawaii's territorial delegate to the U.S. Congress, serving until 1922. He was the first and only person ever elected to that body who was born a royal. Hawaiian representation in the U.S. House of Representatives was limited to a single, non-voting delegate. The prince's birthday, March 26, is an official annual holiday in the state of Hawaii.

1912   Duke Paoa Kahinu Mokoe Hulikohola Kahanamoku became the first Native Hawaiian Olympian to win a gold medal in the 100-meter free-style and a silver medal with the relay team.

1950   Isabella Aiona Abbott was the first Native Hawaiian woman to receive a PhD in science; she became the leading expert on Pacific algae.

1959   Dr. Claire Ku'uleilani Hughes, public health nutritionist, became the first registered Native Hawaiian dietician. In 2011, she was honored as a Living Treasure by Honpa Hongwanji Mission of Hawaii.

1962   Green Beret James Gabriel Jr. was the first Native Hawaiian killed in the Vietnam War. The 1966 #1 song, "The Green Beret," written by Sgt. Barry Sandler, honors Gabriel.

1968   For the first time in the history of the United States, a law school was named after an indigenous person. The William S. Richardson School of Law at the University of Hawai'i at Manoa, Hawaii's only law school, was named after the chief justice of the Supreme Court of Hawaii, Native Hawaiian William S. Richardson. The Richardson court recognized previously ignored claims of the indigenous Hawaiian people.

1970   Dr. Benjamin B. C. Young, who graduated from Howard University Medical School, became the first psychiatrist of Native Hawaiian ancestry.

1972   Momi Cazimero (Native Hawaiian) opened Honolulu's first graphic design firm owned by a woman.

1976   The Polynesian Voyaging Society sailed the double-hulled canoe *Hōkūle'a* to Tahiti. The craft was constructed in a traditional way and navigated with centuries-old technology, proving the proficiency and expertise of Native Hawaiian ancestors.

1978   Hawaii became the first state to declare a native language (Hawaiian) along with English as its official languages.

1982   Rell Kapolioka'ehukai Sunn won first place in the International Professional Surfing ratings. Her success propelled women into the sport.

1984   Public Hawaiian-language immersion preschools (Pūnana Leo) first opened.

1986   John David Waihe'e III became the first Native Hawaiian elected to the office of Governor of Hawaii; he was the first indigenous person ever to be elected governor of any state.

1990   Daniel Kahikina Akaka was appointed U.S. senator, finishing out the term of deceased Senator Spark Matsunaga, making him the first Native Hawaiian to serve in the Senate. He has won every election since 1990; Senator Akaka was first elected to the U.S. House of Representatives in 1976.

1994   *Light in the Crevice Never Seen* by Haunani-Kay Trask was the first book of poetry by an indigenous Hawaiian to be published in North America.

1997   Beloved musician Israel "Iz" Ka'ano'i Kamakawiwo'ole became the first non-government person and only the third person to lie in state at the Capitol building in Honolulu. Thousands of fans attended his funeral; he was one of the few Native Hawaiian musicians to gain worldwide recognition. His medley of "Over the Rainbow" and "What a Wonderful World" was featured in several films, television programs, and commercials. Through his ukulele playing and integration of other music genres into his songs, he remains one of the major influences in Hawaiian music.

1999   Ikua Purdy was voted into the Rodeo Hall of Fame in Oklahoma, the first Hawaiian to be nominated. In 1908, Purdy became the first Hawaiian cowboy to win a Cheyenne, Wyoming, championship with a roping and steer-tying time of one minute, six seconds.

2000   Jay Dee "B. J." Penn became the first non-Brazilian, as well as the first indigenous Hawaiian, to win the black-belt division of the World Jiu-Jitsu Championship.

Logan Maile Lei Tom became the youngest woman and the first indigenous Hawaiian to be selected for the United States Olympic volleyball team.

2003   Dr. Chiyome Leinaala Fukino was appointed director of the Hawaii State Department of Health, making her the first Native Hawaiian and the first woman to hold the position.

2005   The Native Hawaiian Education Act of 2004 created the Center for Excellence in Native Hawaiian Law at the William S. Richardson School of Law (the University of Hawaii at Manoa), now known as Ka Huli Ao: Center for Excellence in Native Hawaiian Law. Its first director was Melody Kapilialoha MacKenzie, chief editor of the *Native Hawaiian Rights Handbook*, which describes Native Hawaiian law.

2006   The University of Hawaii at Hilo established a doctoral (PhD) program in the Hawaiian language. In addition to being the first doctoral program for the study of Hawaiian, it is the first doctoral program established for the study of any native language in the United States. Both the master's (established 2002) and doctoral programs are considered by global scholars as pioneering in the revival of native languages.

2010   'Oiwi Film Festival was the first festival to feature only indigenous Hawaiian filmmakers—telling their stories in their own voices and through their own eyes.

University of Hawaii at Hilo's Ka Haka 'Ula O Ke'elikōlani College of Hawaiian Language presented the first doctorate in Hawaiian and Indigenous Language and Culture Revitalization to a Native Hawaiian student, Kauanoe Kamana.

Nicole Prescovia Elikolani Valiente Scherzinger of the Pussycat Dolls became the first Native Hawaiian and the first indigenous person to win *Dancing with the Stars.*

HAWAIIAN ISLANDS

Eight Hawaiian Islands

Altogether, Ka Pae'Aina O Hawai'i Nei (Hawaiian Archipelago) is made up of 132 islands, reefs, and shoals, stretching 1,523 miles southeast to northwest across the Tropic of Cancer, from longitude 154°40' to 178°25' W and from latitude 18°54' to 28°15' N, a total land area of approximately 6,425 square miles. There are eight big islands, seven of them inhabited.

1. The Big Island (Hawai'i)
2. Maui
3. Kaho'olawe
4. Lanai
5. Moloka'i
6. O'ahu
7. Kaua'i
8. Ni'ihau

Ancient Hawaii

Centuries before Europeans imagined constructing seaworthy crafts, early Hawaiians systematically sailed through sixteen million square miles of the dangerous Pacific Ocean in their double-hulled canoes, using innovative navigation skills of wave patterns, bird flight paths, and cloud formations, as well as the more commonly known aids of the stars and sun. From 700 to 1000 BC, the ancestors of Hawaii's contemporary indigenous peoples came at different times from western Melanesia, southeast Asia, and other places to settle in "Ka Pae 'Aina O Hawai'i Nei" (the

Hawaiian Archipelago). Their sturdy double-hulled outrigger canoes could carry many people, domesticated animals, and supplies, and travel great distances. Their navigational skills were so superb that not only could they engage in far-flung migration efforts, they could also make round-trips among new and old communities. They also perfected the horticultural, hunting, and fishing technologies needed to maintain new populations on uninhabited islands.

For centuries, Hawaiian governments were similar to those of medieval Europe, Asia, and other Polynesian nations. The islands were divided into kingdoms, often compared to a feudal system. *Kapu* is the name of the ancient laws, which translates to "sacred" or "holy." The *kapu* system was connected to the natural world; laws regulated the conservation of resources and considered the future of the people, lands, waters, and all life forms that shared the islands. The philosophy of *Aloha Aina* ("love of the land") made *kapu* one of the earliest examples of environmentalism. As the end of the migration period ended, each island developed its particular culture. Ka Pae 'Aina O Hawai'i Nei remained isolated from the outside world for hundreds of years.

Ni'ihau: Traditional Hawaiian Island

Centuries-old Hawaiian chants recount how Pele, the Volcano Goddess, made Ni'ihau her first home. Ni'ihau is the smallest inhabited island in Hawaii.

Ni'ihau's history is filled with heroic deeds of great leaders *(ali'i)*; their names are reflected in the places and arts of the island. The people were extremely independent and were the last group to be united under King Kamehameha I's rule. Prior to the unification of the Kingdom of Hawaii, Ni'ihau was ruled by Ali'i Kahelelani. His name is now used to refer to the *Ni'ihau kahelelani*, the *puka* shell of the wart turbans (*Leptothyra verruca*), used to make exquisite Ni'ihau shell jewelry. In the 1800s, Kamehameha V deeded most of the island to a New Zealander ranching family, whose descendants still own it. Visitation is restricted: guests are not allowed to remain on the island overnight, which has helped preserve and protect Native Hawaiian values and traditions.

Ni'ihau has no electricity (except for limited solar power), paved roads, cars, stores, indoor plumbing, restaurants, hotels, police, or fire department. Most residents are Native Hawaiians whose families worked the ranch for over a century. However, the ranch closed in 1999, and except for a few jobs at the school, there is no longer any full-time employment on Ni'ihau. Families keep small gardens and make and sell traditional crafts such as the sought-after Ni'ihau shell lei. Hawaiian is spoken, and children attend the only solar-powered school in Hawaii, which makes computer access possible. Families often spend more time with relatives on Kaua'i, especially as homesteading lands become available closer to jobs.

The Niʻihau Cultural Heritage Foundation, created in 2006, assists the people of Niʻihau in retaining their culture and language, as well as in developing economic self-sufficiency. The organization is located in Kalaheo, Hawaii. http://www.niihauheritage.org/index.html

Native Hawaiian and Other Pacific Islander Population

The 2010 census indicates that a total of 540,013 Americans reported being Native Hawaiian and other Pacific Islander (0.2 percent of the U.S. population).

Hawaiian Homelands

The Department of Hawaiian Home Lands manages the trust created by Congress under the Hawaiian Homes Commission Act of 1921, which set aside 200,000 acres as a land trust for homesteading to help "rehabilitate" impoverished Native Hawaiians. The act specifically refers to the devastation of the Hawaiian population, the loss of the land, and the need for Native people to be able to grow traditional crops such as *kalo* (taro). There are three types of leases: residential, agricultural for farming, and pastoral for ranching; one can build a house on an agricultural or farming site. Often the homesteads are not close to employment, and it is difficult to obtain a mortgage for home construction. The waiting list of homestead applicants has 20,000 names, over half of which are residential applicants, yet only about 7,200 leases have been granted in DHHL's ninety-year history.

TIMELINE

Timeline of Native Hawaiian Laws, Policies, and Actions

700 BC?   Like every culture in the world, Hawaiian culture has seen many changes and developments through the centuries. The islands were settled at different times and by different people from Polynesia. At the time of European contact, there were a number of small kingdoms that divided the islands; the structure has often been compared to European kingdoms and the caste system in India. The social system had strict laws, called *kapu*, which were based on religion and governed by a ruling class.

1778	Englishman James Cook headed three expeditions to the South Pacific, searching unsuccessfully for a sea passage between the Atlantic and Pacific Oceans. On January 18, during the third expedition the crews of Captain Cook's two ships sighted the O'ahu, Kaua'i, and Ni'ihau Islands.
1779	The first relations between Hawaiians and British were sociable. However, Cook's men disrespected *kapu* in many ways, including killing a chief and trying to capture Hawaiian leader Ali'i Kalani'opu'u as a hostage. Cook was surrounded and killed.
1780–90	Kamehameha, who later became the first king of Hawaii and was referred to as Kamehameha the Great, organized the different kingdoms under one government. He needed one unified system that could maintain control and sovereignty as foreigners began to arrive in greater numbers. A skilled diplomat, he employed the help of Englishman John Young and Welshman Isaac Davis, the first white men to live in Hawaii.
1807	Kamehameha developed his own navy, consisting of a large ship (an American vessel), several large three-masted schooners, and about twenty-five smaller crafts of twenty to fifty tons. He hired Euro-Americans both to build his ships and to serve in the military.
1810	Kamehameha the Great became the first King of Hawaii. By developing a monarchy, he was able to preserve Hawaii's independence. He employed many foreigners in a variety of occupations and insisted they follow the *kapu* (laws of Hawaii) system. Over the years, he deported people who did not follow *kapu* and rewarded those who did.
1819	Kamehameha the Great died and was succeeded by his son, Kamehameha II. Civil war broke out as the new king aligned himself with those who wanted to destroy traditional laws. The traditionalists were defeated and *kapu* was overturned, weakening the strong government and legacy that Kamehameha the Great had built. Unaware that the traditional religion had suffered a devastating blow, the American Board of Commissioners for Foreign Missions sent missionaries to Hawaii to convert and "civilize" Native peoples by introducing churches, schools, and the press.
1840	The first fully written constitution of the Kingdom of Hawaii, titled *Ke Kumukānāwai a me nā Kānāwai o ko Hawai'i Pae 'Āina*, was written.
1875	The Reciprocity Treaty of 1875, a free trade agreement, was ratified between the Kingdom of Hawaii and the United States. The treaty gave free access to U.S. markets for sugar and other products grown in the Kingdom of Hawaii. Americans and Europeans had been raising sugar crops in Hawaii since 1835.
1884	Bernice Pauahi Bishop, the last living member of the Kamehameha dynasty and one of the wealthiest landowners in Hawaii, died. Her non-

Hawaiian husband, Charles Reed Bishop, honored her dying wishes to preserve the culture of the Hawaiian peoples by ensuring that the lands and monies be placed in trust for them.

1887	King Kalākaua, also known as the Merrie Monarch, sought to strengthen the monarchy and traveled the world making diplomatic visits. Many Euro-Americans living in Hawaii were alarmed by his strategy and campaigned to reduce the power of the monarchy. The king was forced to sign a constitution written by American and European anti-monarchists or lose his throne by threat of a well-armed militia. The "Bayonet Constitution" severely diminished Native Hawaiian voice in government.

Robert William Kalanihiapo Wilcox organized a rebellion to revive the powers of the monarchy and return rights to Native Hawaiians. The army of 150 Hawaiians, Europeans, and Chinese failed to unseat the new government. Seven insurgents were killed, a dozen more wounded, and many captured. A jury of his peers refused to convict Wilcox for treason.

1891	Lili'uokalani inherited the Hawaiian throne after the death of her brother, King Kalākaua, making her the only woman ruler, as well as the last monarch, of the Kingdom of Hawaii.
1893	John L. Stevens, the United States minister assigned to the sovereign and independent Kingdom of Hawaii, conspired with non-Hawaiian residents of the kingdom, including citizens of the United States, to overthrow Hawaii's lawful government. He ordered the U.S. Navy to invade Hawaii and imprison Hawaiian Queen Lili'uokalani. Stevens then extended diplomatic recognition to a provisional government formed by the conspirators.

In a message to Congress on December 18, President Grover Cleveland reported that the government of Hawaii was overthrown, concluding that a "substantial wrong has thus been done which a due regard for our national character as well as the rights of the injured people required that we should endeavor to repair."

1893–95	With aid from President Cleveland, Queen Lili'uokalani created the Kingdom of Hawaii in exile and lobbied for the restoration of her government, threatening military force to return her to power. War broke out, and the monarchists were forced into the mountains. The queen formally abdicated her throne to prevent further bloodshed.
1896	The Republic of Hawaii passed laws banning the Hawaiian language from being spoken or taught in public schools.
1898	The United States annexed Hawaii without the consent of or compensation to the Kingdom of Hawaii or its people. Hawaiian citizens no longer could govern themselves or their lands and ocean resources.

1900   The U.S. Congress passed the Organic Act, which provided a government for the territory of Hawaii. The United States took over 1.75 million acres of lands formerly owned by the Hawaiian Kingdom and mandated that revenue from these lands be "used solely for the benefit of the inhabitants of the Hawaiian Islands for education and other public purposes." The act established a trust relationship between the United States and the inhabitants of Hawaii.

   The Home Rule Party of Hawaii, formed by Robert William Kalanihiapo Wilcox following the annexation of Hawaii, dominated the territorial legislature for two years. It disbanded in 1912.

   The Democratic Party of Hawaii was established to gain sponsorship from the American Democratic Party. It attempted to represent Native Hawaiians in the territorial government.

1921   Congress enacted the Hawaiian Homes Commission Act, which designated 200,000 acres of the ceded public lands for exclusive homesteading by Native Hawaiians, affirming the trust relationship between the United States and the Native Hawaiians.

1938   The U.S. Congress recognized the unique status of Native Hawaiians by passing the Act of June 20, 1938, that included a provision to lease lands within the National Parks extension to Native Hawaiians and a provision for fishing areas for Native Hawaiians.

1959   Congress admitted Hawaii to the United States as a state. Administration of Hawaiian Home Lands was transferred to the State of Hawaii, but the federal government kept power to enforce the trust, including the power to approve land exchanges and legislative amendments affecting the rights of beneficiaries under the act.

ca. 1972   ALOHA (Aboriginal Lands of Hawaiian Ancestry) was organized to seek reparations from the U.S. government for crown lands claimed by the Republic of Hawaii in 1894, transferred to the U.S. government in 1900, and transferred back to the State of Hawaii in 1959.

1974   The Native American Programs Act was amended to include Native Hawaiians. This made it possible for Native Hawaiians to become eligible for some, but not all, federal assistance programs originally intended for Native Americans. The act defined a Native Hawaiian as "an individual any of whose ancestors were natives of the area which consists of the Hawaiian Islands prior to 1778."

1978   The Office of Hawaiian Affairs was created to correct Native Hawaiian problems caused by the overthrow of the Kingdom of Hawaii. The

Hawaiian language, along with English, became the official state language of Hawaii for the first time since the overthrow.

1983   The Native Hawaiians Study Commission published a final report on the needs and concerns of Native Hawaiians. It was submitted to the U.S. Senate Committee on Energy and Natural Resources and the U.S. House of Representatives Committee on Interior and Insular Affairs.

'Aaha Pūnana Leo ("language nest"), a nonprofit organization, was established with federal support to begin the process of restoring and revitalizing the Native Hawaiian language, beginning with a Native Hawaiian language preschool immersion program. Today, Native Hawaiian children can obtain their entire K–12 education in Hawaiian.

1987   Ka Lahui Hawai'i was formed as a grassroots initiative for Hawaiian sovereignty. Native Hawaiian activist/attorney and United Nations representative Mililani Trask, elected as the first *kia'aina* (governor), and her sister, University of Hawaii professor Haunani-Kay Trask, were key in organizing efforts. Both Native Hawaiians and non-Native Hawaiians were welcomed as citizens of Ka Lahui.

1988   The Native Hawaiian Health Care Act mandated that the health concerns of Native Hawaiians be addressed. The organization Papa Ola Lokahi was created to address the physical, spiritual, and mental health needs of Native Hawaiians with culturally appropriate modalities.

The Native Hawaiian Education Act authorized the development of innovative Native Hawaiian educational programs, with maximum participation by Native Hawaiians in planning and managing them.

1989   The organization Nation of Hawai'i was formed and led many protests against the occupation of Hawaii. It holds a seat on the International Indian Treaty Council.

1993   Ka Pakaukau, an organization under the leadership of founder Richard Kekuni Akana Blaisdell, MD, convened the *Ka Ho'okolokolonui Kanaka Maoli*, the "People's International Tribunal," which brought indigenous leaders from around the world to Hawaii to put the United States government on trial for the theft of Hawaii's sovereignty. The tribunal found the U.S. guilty.

In November, U.S. President Bill Clinton signed the Apology Resolution passed by Congress. This resolution "apologizes to Native Hawaiians on behalf of the people of the United States for the overthrow of the Kingdom of Hawai'i." The bill was coauthored by Hawaiian Senators Daniel Inouye and Daniel Akaka.

2005   The U.S. Department of Housing and Urban Development made home ownership possible for eleven Hawaiian families thanks to a

HUD mortgage loan guarantee program created in 2001 specifically to provide affordable housing for Native Hawaiians living on Hawaiian Home Lands.

2010   Dr. David Sai, a national of the Hawaiian Kingdom, filed a complaint in U.S. District Court against President Obama and other federal officials for violating an 1893 Executive Agreement known as the Lili'uokalani assignment, legally binding President Cleveland and his successors to administer Hawaiian Kingdom law, not U.S. law.

2011   On April 7, 2011, the Native Hawaiian Government Reorganization Act of 2011 was ordered to be reported out of the Senate Committee on Indian Affairs, favorably and without amendment.

Hawai'i Governor Neil Abercrombie signed into law Act 195, which recognizes Native Hawaiians as the indigenous people of Hawaii. This measure became an important step for the future of Native Hawaiian self-determination.

Kamehameha Schools

Founded in 1887, Kamehameha Schools is a statewide educational system for Native Hawaiians supported by an endowment from Princess Bernice Pauahi Bishop, which was established in 1883. Kamehameha K–12 campuses on O'ahu, Hawaii, and Maui and twenty-one statewide preschools serve almost seven thousand students. Although the schools have faced lawsuits by non-Native Hawaiians who want to be enrolled, they remain an institution for those of Native Hawaiian descent and strive to preserve Native Hawaiian culture and values. The Kamehameha Schools system boasts several notable alumni and is believed to have the largest endowment of any private or secondary school in the nation.

http://www.ksbe.edu/

Federal Recognition of Native Hawaiian Government

Better known as the Akaka bill, because it was sponsored by Senator Daniel Akaka, the Native Hawaiian Government Reorganization Act of 2011 would provide Native Hawaiians with a government-to-government relationship with the United States. The proposed bill would give Native Hawaiians a status comparable to that of the 565 federally recognized tribes in the United States. Since 2000, Senator Akaka has proposed various bills, including different versions of the "Akaka Bill," to support the rights of Native Hawaiians. In 2011, Senator Alaka became chairman of the U.S. Senate Committee on Indian Affairs.

CULTURAL AWARDS, HONORS, AND FESTIVALS

Thirteen Hawaiian Music Hall of Fame Honorees

The Hawaiian Music Hall of Fame, located in Honolulu, was founded in 1994 to "promote, preserve, and perpetuate Hawaiian music and hula by celebrating the achievements of significant individuals and groups."

1995	Joseph Kekuku is credited with inventing the steel guitar. His group, Kekuku's Hawaiian Quintet, toured the world for thirty years; he was inducted into the Steel Guitar Hall of Fame in 1993.
1996	Haunani Kahalewai is known as "Hawaii's First Lady of Song"; she was widely recognized for her incredible vocal range.
1998	John Kameaaloha Almeida composed three hundred songs, many of them Hawaiian standards. Although he was blind, he had his own band and was a leading ukulele and steel guitar musician. He is thought to be the last master of the Hawaiian mandolin.
2000	Keaulumoku was the first and probably the oldest-known chanter to be inducted. Known throughout the islands, he was considered a prophet.
2001	The Haili Church Choir of Hilo, Hawaii, is one of the oldest church choirs in Hawaii and is credited with perpetuating Hawaiian music tradition and culture.
2002	Charles Philip "Gabby" or "Pops" Pahinui was the first slack-key guitarist to make a recording and played an important part in the 1970s Hawaiian Cultural Renaissance.
2004	Kahauanu Lake was a beloved ukulele musician, as well as an arranger of hula music.
2005	Bill Ali'iloa Lincoln performed internationally for over sixty years. Remembered for his high falsetto range, he also played the ukulele, guitar, bass, and piano, plus danced and taught hula.
2006	The Brothers Cazimero is a musical duo made up of bass player Robert Cazimero and twelve-string guitar musician Roland Cazimero, who also teach hula. For over thirty years, they have performed on Lei Day, Hawaii's spin on May Day and a celebration of Native Hawaiian culture.
2007	Marlene Sai was discovered by the legendary musician Don Ho and is an award-winning singer and actress. She received the 1986 Female Vocalist of the Year Na Hoku Hanohano Award.
2008	Alice Angeline Johnson, "Song Bird of Maui," was a singer, composer, and member of the Royal Hawaiian Band.

| 2009 | Dennis David Kahekilimamaoikalanikeha Kamakahi is a Grammy-winning slack-key guitar musician and composer. |
| 2010 | Ernest Ka'ai was often cited as Hawaii's greatest ukulele player. He was considered to be the first musician to play a complete melody with chords. |

Twenty-One Maoli Arts Month Awardees

The Maoli Arts Month (MAMo) is to visual artists what the Merrie Monarch Festival is to Hula cultural practitioners. The annual festival celebrates those contemporary artists whose works keep Native Hawaiian culture alive. Each year, a few participating artists are chosen to receive a MAMo Award for their commitment to preserving Hawaiian traditions and teaching their art.

2006	Rocky Jensen—Internationally known master carver, illustrator, and author Imaikalani Kalahele—Poet, painter, fibrous sculptor Herb Kawainui Kāne—Art historian, painter, sculptor, author, designer of the *Hōkūle'a*, traditional voyaging canoe "Aunty Mary Lou" Kekuewa—Ancient Hawaiian featherwork artist Marie McDonald—Lei-maker, *kapa* (traditional fabric) and *ipu* (gourd instrument) designer Ipō Nihipali—Water sculptor, painter, tattoo artist
2007	Sean Kekamakupa'a Ka'onohiokalani Lee Loy Browne—Sculptor, stone carver Joseph Hau'oli Dowson Sr.—Land- and seascape painter Sam Ka'ai—Master woodcarver, sculptor, artist, sailor, storyteller Jo-Anne Kahanmoku-Sterling—Featherwork artist Leialoha Kanahele—Painter of traditional Hawaiian landscapes Pua Van Dorpe—*Kapa* cloth artist
2008	Elizabeth Maluihi Lee—*Lauhala* weaver (leaves of the pandanus tree are woven into mats, hats, etc.) Al Lagunero—Internationally known painter and illustrator David P. Parker—Painter, author, historian Henry "Hanale" Kila Hopfe—Cultural practitioner, artist, sculptor
2009	Gussie Bento—Quilter, feather lei maker Alapa'i Hanapi—Sculptor
2010	Gladys Kukana Grace—*Lauhala* weaver Bob Freitas—Sculptor
2011	Hiko' Ula Hanapi—the late artist-teacher and creator of HOEA, the Native Hawaiian Arts School in Waimea (Big Island)

Twelve Native Hawaiian "Living Treasures of Hawai'i"

In 1976, Buddhist temple Honpa Hongwanji Mission of Hawaii Honolulu created the Living Treasures of Hawaii program to recognize and honor individuals who have demonstrated excellence in their fields and who have made lifelong and significant contributions toward creating a more humane society.

1977	Iolani Luahine: kumu hula, dancer, chanter, and teacher; was considered the high priestess of the ancient hula. The 'Iolani Luahine Hula Festival was established in her memory and awards an annual scholarship award to a hula student.
1979	Charles Philip "Gabby" or "Pops" Pahinui: award winning slack-key guitarist. Abraham Kahikina Akaka: Akaka was *Kahu* (shepherd) of Kawaiaha'o Church in Honolulu, Hawaii, and delivered his messages in both the Hawaiian and English languages.
1983	Rubellite Kawena Johnson: historian, professor emerita of Hawaiian language and literature, and member of the Advisory Committee to the United States Commission on Civil Rights for Hawaiian sovereignty issues. Morrnah Nalamaku Simeona: *kahuna lapa'au* (healer) in Hawaii; taught her updated version of *ho'oponopono* throughout the United States, Asia, and Europe.
1984	Herb Kawainui Kāne: artist, historian, author, and founder of the Pacific Voyaging Society. Designer and builder of the traditional sailing canoe *Hōkūle'a*, he served as its first captain.
1985	Gladys Kamakakuokalani 'Ainoa Brandt: educator and civic leader.
2002	Myron Bennett "Pinky" Thompson: social worker and community leader in Hawaii and a cultural leader among Native Hawaiians.
2004	"Aunty" Genoa Leilani Adolpho Keawe-Aiko: Native Hawaiian music icon.
2005	Isabella Aiona Abbott: educator, ethnobotanist, and the first native Hawaiian woman to receive a PhD in science.
2010	Elizabeth Kawohiokalani Ellis Jenkins: master educator who developed a culturally appropriate Native Hawaiian method of instruction that stressed the importance of Hawaiian language, traditions, history, and values through teaching and mentorship.
2011	Josephine Kaukali Fergerstrom: *kumu lauhala* artist and teacher who has helped to preserve the Hawaiian weaving tradition.

Five Native Hawaiian Cultural Festivals

Merrie Monarch Hula Festival
http://www.merriemonarch.com
> Founded in 1964, this annual festival takes place in Hilo, Hawaii, during April.

Prince Lot Hula Festival
http://www.mgf-hawaii.org/HTML/Hula/princelothulafestival.htm
> Founded in 1967, the festival takes place in Honolulu, O'ahu, in July.

Maoli Arts Month
http://www.maoliartsmonth.org/index.html
> Founded in 2006, the month-long festival takes place at different venues throughout O'ahu beginning in April.

Mary Kawena Pukui Arts Festival:
http://www.bishopmuseum.org
> Founded in 2000, the festival takes place in Honolulu, O'ahu, in February.

Na Hula Festival
http://www1.honolulu.gov/parks/programs/index.htm
> Hawaii's oldest non-competitive Hula Festival (founded in 1941) is held every August in Honolulu, O'ahu.

Hawaiian Music

Traditional Hawaiian music is characterized by two types of chants and songs that recount historical and/or spiritual events. *Mele oli* are ceremonial solo chants performed without accompaniment, while *mele hula* include dancing and musical instruments such as the drum (*pahu*), double gourd (*ipu heke*), gourd rattle (*uliuli*), and nose flute (*'ohe hano ihu*), plus slapping of hands on the chest (*pai umauma*).

After contact with foreign cultures, other instruments were added that are now Native Hawaiian music icons. In the mid-1800s, Mexican cowboys (*paniolo*) brought along their guitar traditions borrowed from Spain, but soon Native Hawaiians adapted their own technique by loosening the guitar strings, called "slacking." This unique sound complements traditional music; musicians are able to provide rhythm on the loosened bass strings and melody on the treble strings. In the late 1800s, the Portuguese brought the *braguinha*, which later became synonymous with Hawaiian music. Native Hawaiians called the instrument *ukulele*—combining the word "flea" (*uku*) with "to jump" (*lele*)—which literally means "jumping flea" and describes the fast-moving fingers of a ukulele player.

Native Hawaiian musicians are also credited with the invention of the steel guitar, a staple of American country music. World famous contemporary Hawaiian music is a dynamic combination of the distinctive ancient traditions and foreign influences. There has been a resurgence of traditional pre-contact Hawaiian music which helps retain the indigenous language and culture.

CELEBRITIES

Fifteen Popular Celebrities of Native Hawaiian Descent

1. Tia Carrere: actress/singer
2. Lance Hahn: vocalist for punk band, J Church
3. Douglas Farthing Hatlelid (Chip Douglas): musician and producer of singing group, The Monkees
4. Don Ho: entertainer/singer
5. Hôku Christian Ho: singer/actress/composer
6. Maren Kawehilani Jensen: actress
7. Gilbert Francis Lani Damian Kauhi: actor/comedian
8. Jason Scott Lee: actor
9. Agnes Nalani Lum: actress/model
10. Jason Momoa: actor
11. Kelly Preston: actress
12. Keanu Reeves: actor
13. Shannon (Shannyn) Marie Kahololani Sossamon: actress
14. Brendon Boyd Urie: musician
15. Pete Wentz: musician and songwriter for the band Fall Out Boy

Seven Native Hawaiian Athletes

Native Hawaiian athletes excel in a variety of athletics, from their traditional sport of surfing to the very Japanese sport of sumo wrestling.

Edward Ryan Makua Hanai Aikau
Renowned surfer famous for his courageous rescue feats; he died trying to save the capsized *Hokule'a* on its second journey. He won the 1977 Duke Kahanamoku Invitational Surfing Championship.

Akebono
First non-Japanese born competitor to reach *yokozuna*, the highest rank in sumo wrestling (1993).

Jesse James Wailani Kuhaulua Takamiyama Daigorō
First non-Japanese born competitor to win the sumo wrestling top division championship (1972).

Duke Paoa Kahanamoku
Won five medals in four Olympics (1912, 1920, 1924, and 1932) in swimming and water polo. Introduced the Native Hawaiian sport of surfing to the world and was nicknamed the "World Ambassador of Surfing."

Logan Maile Lei Tom
Youngest woman (age nineteen) and the first indigenous Hawaiian to be selected for the U.S. Olympic volleyball team (2000).

Shane Victorino
Plays for the Philadelphia Phillies baseball team (since 2006). He received the Lou Gehrig Memorial Award (2008) and the Tug McGraw "Good Guy Award" (2010).

Kailee Wong
Played professional football (linebacker) from 1998 to 2006. During his career he played for the Minnesota Vikings and the Houston Texans.

BOOKS

Fourteen Books of Native Hawaiian Writings

These fourteen books were written by a cross section of Native Hawaiian authors in diverse genres from children's books to poetry.

1. *Ancient Hawaii,* by Herb Kawainui Kane (1997).
2. *Between the Deep Blue Sea and Me: A Novel,* by Lurline Wailana McGregor (2008).
3. *Emma: Hawaii's Remarkable Queen,* by George S. Kanahele (1999).
4. *Hawaiian Family Album,* by Matthew Kaopio (2008).
5. *Heart of Being Hawaiian,* by Sally-Jo Keala-o-Anuenue Bowman (2008).
6. *Ho'okupu: An Offering of Literature by Native Hawaiian Women,* by Miyoko Sugano and Jackie Pualani (2009).
7. *Kalahele: Poetry and Art,* by Imaikalani Kalahele (2002).
8. *Light in the Crevice Never Seen,* by Haunani-Kay Trask (1999).
9. *Moloka'i Nui Ahina,* by Kirby Wright (2007).
10. *No Footprints in the Sand: A Memoir of Kalaupapa,* by Henry Kalalahilimoku Nalaielua and Sally-Jo Keala-o-Anuenue Bowman (2006).
11. *The Rise of a King: Kamehameha Set, Books 1–6,* by David Kawika Eyre (2009).

12. *The Salt-Wind Ka Makani Pa'akai*, by Brandy Nālani McDougall (2008).
13. *Sista Tongue*, by Lisa Linn Kanae (2008).
14. *Song of the Exile*, by Kiana Davenport (2000).

FILMS

Happy Birthday, Tutu Ruth (USA, 1996, 27 min.), directed by Ann Marie Kirk (Native Hawaiian).

    A documentary about the life of 91-year-old Ruth Makaila Nakagawa Kaholoa'a, who is half Hawaiian and half Japanese, from Hawaii Island.

Homealani (USA, 2010, 60 min.), directed by Ann Marie Kirk (Native Hawaiian).

    Homealani is the story of Oliver Homealani, the filmmaker's grandfather. Kirk takes viewers on a journey of discovering who her grandfather was as an indigenous man, and also deals with his legacy.

Keepers of the Flame (USA, 2005, 60 min.), directed by Eddie Kamae (Native Hawaiian).

    Filmmaker Kamae chronicles the lives of three indigenous Hawaiian women, Mary Kawena Pukui, 'Iolani Luahine, and Edith Kanaka'ole, who helped save the indigenous language that was in peril. The stories are told through interviews with people who were influenced by the women.

Kekohi (USA, 2008, 30 min.), directed by Kaniela Joy, Ed Joy, Quddus Ajimine (Native Hawaiian).

    The film is about the son of a warrior king, selected to be the royal court's message runner during the early- to mid-seventeenth century. The young man feels insulted by the appointment until he learns about the dangers, prestige, and accolades of being a royal messenger.

King Kamehameha: A Legacy Renewed (USA, 2002, 27 min.), directed by Tuti Baker (Native Hawaiian).

    The film follows the journey of a worldly art conservator into the heart of North Kohala, a rural community at the end of the road on the northern tip of Hawaii Island. The film is a portrait of the people of Kohala and explores how the conservator's life was changed by the community and its people.

Malama Haloa: Protecting the Taro (USA, 2010, 39 min.), directed by Puhipau (Native Hawaiian) and Joan Lander of Na Maka o ka 'Aina (an independent video production company).

    The film deals with Taro grower Jerry Konanui, who shares a lifetime of his work to propagate and save from extinction varieties of Hawaiian taro, a plant honored as the elder sibling of the first people of Hawaii. His work involved protecting the food from the risks of genetic engineering.

Na Kamalei: The Men of Hula (USA, 2006, 57 min.), directed by Lisette Marie Flanary.

    Beyond deep-rooted stereotypes of "grass-skirt girls," *Na Kamalei: The Men of Hula* captures the journey of legendary master hula teacher Robert Cazimero and the only all-male school in Hawaii as they prepare to compete in the world's largest hula festival.

Noho Hewa: The Wrongful Occupation of Hawaii (USA, 2008, 80 min), directed by Anne Keala Kelly (Native Hawaiian).

A contemporary look at indigenous Hawaiian people, politics, and resistance in the face of systematic erasure under U.S. laws, economy, militarism, and real estate speculation. Told from Hawaiian points of view, people address the legal and political relevance of the Hawaiian sovereignty struggle.

Release Our Water (USA, 2010, 30 min.), directed by Kelly Arlos Pauole (Native Hawaiian).

Interviews with people from the community of East Maui discuss the diversion of water from East Maui Stream to Upcountry and Central Maui. The film reveals that the displacement of East Maui's Native peoples, cultural loss, and decline in health of the land and its people can be directly related to the water diversion.

Stolen Waters (USA, 1996, 27 min.), directed by Puhipau (Native Hawaiian) and Joan Lander.

This film documents the battle over the water in Waiahole Ditch on the island of O'ahu, where taro farmers and long-time residents seek to reclaim the natural stream waters that were taken in the early 1900s by sugar plantations.

The Voyage Home: Hawai'iloa's Northwest Voyage (USA, 1996, 56 min.), directed by Karin Williams.

In a renaissance of traditional Hawaiian sea voyaging, the first Hawaiian double-hulled wooden canoe to be made in centuries sails to the Pacific Northwest Coast.

ORGANIZATIONS

'Aha Pūnana Leo ('APL)
http://www.ahapunanaleo.org

Incorporated in January 1983, the 'Aha Pūnana Leo ("nest of voices"), headquartered in Hilo, Hawaii, was created to save the Hawaiian language from extinction. The Pūnana Leo preschools, the foundation of the 'APL, are located throughout the islands.

Association of Hawaiian Civic Clubs (AOHCC)
http://aohcc.org

AOHCC is the oldest Hawaiian community-based grassroots organization and was founded in 1918 by Prince Jonah Kuhio Kalaniana'ole, delegate to the U.S. House of Representatives. AOHCC, comprising over fifty Hawaiian civic clubs throughout the United States as well as Hawaii, advocates for indigenous Hawaiians with *pono* (righteousness) in the areas of culture, health, economic development, education, social welfare, and nationhood.

Bishop Museum

http://www.bishopmuseum.org

> Founded in 1889, the Bishop Museum in Honolulu is the largest museum in the state and houses a vast collection of Hawaiian artifacts, as well as the family heirlooms of Princess Bernice Pauahi Bishop, the last descendant of the royal Kamehameha family. The museum also hosts festivals and events.

Council for Native Hawaiian Advancement (CNHA)

http://www.hawaiiancouncil.org/

> Founded in 2001, the CNHA, a statewide and national network of over one hundred Native Hawaiian organizations, strives to affect public policy, operate a community loan fund, deliver capacity-building and leadership-development services, unify all aspects of the Native Hawaiian community, preserve cultural knowledge, and promote community-owned enterprises. CNHA is headquartered in Honolulu, Hawaii.

Friends of Moku'ula

http://www.mokuula.com

> Founded in 1990, the Friends of Moku'ula, located in Lahaina, Maui, Hawaii, educates the Hawaiian and non-Hawaiian community on the significance of historical sites in a non-exploitative way and develops economic opportunities through historic preservation.

Hawaiian Cultural Center (Utah)

http://www.hawaiianculturalcenter.org/history.html

> The Hawaiian Cultural Center in Midvale, Utah, is a cultural and social center for Native Hawaiians in Utah. It offers classes and workshops in Native Hawaiian culture and arts.

Hawaiian Kingdom

http://www.hawaiiankingdom.org/

> The Hawaiian Kingdom is a Native Hawaiian sovereignty organization whose purpose is to expose the occupation of Hawaii within the framework of the 1907 Hague Conventions IV and V and domestic statutes, and to provide a foundation for the ultimate end of the occupation of the Hawaiian Kingdom. The kingdom is located in Honolulu, Hawaii.

KAHEA

http://kahea.org

> KAHEA, founded in 2000, is an environmental alliance of cultural practitioners and conservation advocates who work to improve the quality of life for Hawaii's people and future generations through the revitalization and protection of the state's unique natural and cultural resources. The alliance promotes proper stewardship of resources as well as social responsibility by working for

multicultural understanding and environmental justice. KAHEA, an acronym for Ka (the) Hawaiian-Environmental Alliance, translates from Hawaiian as "the call." It is headquartered in Honolulu, Hawaii.

Kapa Hawaii

http://www.kapahawaii.com

Kapa Hawaii preserves and teaches about the many types of Polynesian bark cloth collectively known as "tapa," with a special emphasis on *kapa*, the tapa made in the Hawaiian Islands. Kapa Hawaii, founded in 2008, is headquartered in Makaha, O'ahu.

Native Hawaiian Education Association (NHEA)

http://www.nhea.net/

Founded in 1998, NHEA advocates for Native Hawaiian viewpoints in education. Its members are Native Hawaiian educators who address issues relevant to their community. NHEA is located in Kahului, Hawaii.

PA'I Foundation

http://www.paifoundation.org

The PA'I Foundation, organized in 2001, preserves and perpetuates Hawaiian cultural traditions for future generations. Its headquarters are in Honolulu, Hawaii.

Polynesian Voyaging Society (PVS)

http://pvs.kcc.hawaii.edu

The Polynesian Voyaging Society was founded in 1973 to test the ancient navigation skills of the indigenous peoples of Hawaii. Traditional sailing vessels have been built and sailed using indigenous techniques. The PVS, located in Honolulu, also uses traditional knowledge and wisdom to maintain the health of the planet.

RESOURCES

Chun, Malcolm Nāea. *Na Kukui Pio 'Ole; The Inextinguishable Torches: The Biographies of Three Early Native Hawaiian Scholars: Davida Malo, S. N. Hale'ole and S. M. Kamakau.* Honolulu: First People's Productions, 1993.

Coffman, Tom. *Nation Within: The History of the American Occupation of Hawai'i.* Kihei, HI: Koa Books, 2009.

Daws, Gavan. *Shoal of Time: A History of the Hawaiian Islands.* Honolulu: University of Hawaii Press, 1989 (originally published in 1968).

Halualani, Rona Tamiko. *In the Name of Hawaiians: Native Identities and Cultural Politics.* Minneapolis: University of Minnesota Press, 2002.

Holt, John Dominis. *On Being Hawaiian.* Honolulu: Ku Pa'a, 1995.

Johnson, Rubellite Kawena. *Essays in Hawaiian Literature.* Honolulu: R. K. Johnson, 2001.

Kame'eleihiwa, Lilikala. *Na Wahine Kapu: Divine Hawaiian Women.* Honolulu: 'Ai Pōhaku Press, 1999.

Kanahele, Elama, Kimo Armitage, and Keao NeSmith. *Aloha Niihau.* Waipahu, HI: Island Heritage Publishing, 2007.

Kinzer, Stephen. *Overthrow: America's Century of Regime Change from Hawaii to Iraq.* New York: Times Books, 2006.

Malo, Davida. *Ka Moolelo Hawaii: Hawaiian Traditions.* Translated by Malcolm Nāea Chun. Honolulu: First People's Press, 1996.

Mander, Jerry, and Koohan Paik. *The Superferry Chronicles: Hawaii's Uprising Against Militarism, Commercialism, and the Desecration of the Earth.* Kihei, HI: Koa Books, 2009.

McLynn, Frank. *Captain Cook: Master of the Seas.* New Haven: Yale University Press, 2011.

McGregor, Davianna. *Na Kua'aina: Living Hawaiian Culture.* Honolulu: University of Hawaii Press, 2007.

Silva, Noenoe K. *Aloha Betrayed: Native Hawaiian Resistance to American Colonialism.* Durham, NC: Duke University Press, 2004.

Vowell, Sarah. *Unfamiliar Fishes.* New York: Riverhead Books, 2011.

Web Sites

'Aha Pūnana Leo: http://www.ahapunanaleo.org

Council for Native Hawaiian Advancement: http://www.hawaiiancouncil.org

Friends of Moku'ula: http://www.mokuula.com

Kamehameha Publishing: http://www.kamehamehapublishing.org/index.php

Kapa Hawaii: http://www.kapahawaii.com/

Nation of Hawai'i: http://www.hawaii-nation.org/index.html

Ni'ihau Cultural Heritage Foundation: http://www.niihauheritage.org/index.html

Office of Hawaiian Affairs: http://www.oha.org

'Ōiwi: A Native Hawaiian Journal: http://www.hawaii.edu/oiwi/

Wiki

The word *wiki* means "quick," and *wiki wiki* implies "very quick" in the Hawaiian language. Wikipedia creator Ward Cunningham was inspired by the name of the Wiki Wiki Shuttle bus system at the Honolulu International Airport, learned its meaning, and called his new Web site "WikiWikiWeb," now known as Wikipedia.

24

Urban Life

FIRSTS

1926   New York's Native community founded the American Indian Club, the first urban Indian association in the United States. Located in Greenwich Village, the club welcomed newcomers to the city, built a network of professional connections, and provided youth scholarship programs.

1947   The Phoenix (Arizona) Indian Center became the first urban American Indian center to open in the United States.

1991   The Hotel Santa Fe in Santa Fe, New Mexico, opened. Owned by the people of the Picuris Pueblo of New Mexico, the hotel is the only venture of its kind in the United States. The Picuris Pueblo became the first tribe in the United States to partner with nontribal, local business people to build and operate an off-reservation hotel.

2005   The grand opening of the Residence Inn by Marriott, the first tribally owned enterprise in Washington, DC, took place. The hotel project was also the first intertribal partnership of its kind, bringing together the San Manuel Band of Serrano Mission Indians and the Viejas Band of Kumeyaay, both of California, and the Forest County Potawatomi Community and the Oneida Tribe of Indians, both of Wisconsin.

2010   President Barack Obama addressed the twenty-seventh annual powwow, Gathering of Nations, the first address to the group from a United States president. Obama's message was broadcast on the "LoboVision" video screen at the University of New Mexico's basketball arena, the event site. One of the largest urban powwows in the world, the Gathering of Nations takes place annually in Albuquerque, New Mexico.

Ancient Native American Urbanization

Contrary to popular belief, American Indians have lived in cities in what is now the United States since ancient times. Cahokia, a vast urban center on the banks of the Mississippi River in Illinois, was home to more than twenty thousand people in the city center and ten thousand in the outskirts. Built roughly between 900 and 1400, Cahokia is considered the largest ancient site within the United States.

After 900, urbanization increased in Arizona, New Mexico, and Colorado, when large towns of compact masses of contiguous rooms were constructed. Yellowjacket in southwest Colorado, built roughly between 950 and 1300, was believed to house some thirty thousand people in the mid-1200s.

In addition to their own urban communities, Indians often lived in colonial cities built by European colonizers. Nineteenth-century federal policies, however, restricted Native populations to isolated reservations in order to distance them from rapidly growing non-Indian communities. As a result, by 1900, the Indian population was concentrated in rural areas.

Franklin Avenue, Minneapolis, Minnesota

In 2010, Franklin Avenue in south Minneapolis, Minnesota, became the first urban American Indian destination corridor in the United States. Franklin Avenue has played a central role in modern American Indian urban history. Since the days of relocation in the 1950s, it has been home to one of the densest populations of urban Indians in the United States. The first urban Indian Health Board and the first American Indian-preference U.S. housing project were created on Franklin Avenue, as well as the founding of the American Indian Movement (AIM).

AMERICAN INDIAN PLACE NAMES

Twenty-One U.S. Cities with American Indian Place Names

Many cities, towns, and other geographical locations have Indian place names. Some of these names are English spellings of Native words. Others are Indian tribal names or personal names of individuals. Still others are named after events. Native peoples also gave descriptive names to places that helped travelers to recognize the sites.

Because the first colonists often mispronounced many Native words they heard, linguists today cannot always identify the original tribal language or meaning of numerous Indian place names. Original Indian names for geographical features have also been altered over the centuries of use. Sometimes the original Indian word, phrase, or name, and its translation, are known. Sometimes translations of Indian place names reflect best guesses by linguistic scholars as to their meanings.

Alabama: Mobile, from the Muskogean (Creek) language, name for a group of Indians from the Alabama Tribe

Alaska: Ketchikan, from the Na-Dene language, which may mean "the river belonging to Kitschk"; other accounts claim it means "thundering wings of an eagle"

Arizona: Tucson took its name from an O'odham Indian village, Stookzone, which stood at the base of Stjukshon Mountain, later known as Sentinel Peak

California: Tahoe City, possibly from the Hokan language, meaning "edge of the lake"

Florida: Tallahassee, from the Muskogean (Creek) language, meaning "abandoned town" or "old town"

Illinois: Chicago, from the Algonquian language, which may mean "wild onion," "garlic field," "skunk," or possibly "great"

Kansas: Wichita, from the Caddoan language, meaning a tribe of Indians living in the region between the Arkansas and Red rivers

Maine: Saco, from the Algonquian language, meaning "flowing out" or "outlet"

Michigan: Kalamazoo, from the Algonquian language, meaning "otter tail"

Minnesota: Shakopee, from the Siouan language, meaning "six"

Mississippi: Biloxi, from the Siouan language, meaning "first people," the name of a local Indian tribe

Nebraska: Omaha, from the Siouan language, meaning "dwellers on the bluff" or "upstream"

New Jersey: Paramus, from an Algonquian language, meaning "place of water" or "place of wild turkeys"

New York: Manhattan, from the Algonquian language, meaning "island of many hills" or "where one gathers bows"

Ohio: Miami, from the Algonquian language, derives from the tribe's name for itself

Pennsylvania: Susquehanna, from the Iroquoian language, may have been the name of a confederacy of tribes, rather than a single tribe; meaning is unknown

Rhode Island: Narragansett, from the Algonquian language, derives from the tribe's name for itself

Tennessee: Chattanooga, from the Muskogean (Creek) word for "rock"

Utah: Kanab, from the Uto-Aztecan language, meaning "willow tree"

Washington: Walla Walla, from the Penutian language, possibly meaning "down below"

Wisconsin: Milwaukee, from the Algonquian language, meaning "the good land," "gathering place by the water," or "beautiful or pleasant lands"

NATIVE AMERICANS IN URBAN AREAS

Urban Percentage of American Indian Population in the United States, 1900–2010

Over the decades, census takers have used different procedures to identify Native people; therefore it is difficult to estimate precisely how much, in percentage terms, the urban/metropolitan Native population has grown over the decades. Nevertheless, the figures show that the percentage of Native people moving to cities and metropolitan areas has been steadily growing.

1900	0.4
1910	4.5
1920	6.1
1930	9.9
1940	9.2
1950	13.4
1960	27.9
1970	44.5
1980	49.0
1990	51.0
2000	66.0

Twelve Urban Areas with the Largest Native American Populations in 2000

1.	New York, New York	87,241
2.	Los Angeles, California	53,092
3.	Phoenix, Arizona	35,093
4.	Tulsa, Oklahoma	30,227
5.	Oklahoma City, Oklahoma	29,001
6.	Anchorage, Alaska	26,995
7.	Albuquerque, New Mexico	22,047
8.	Chicago, Illinois	20,898
9.	San Diego, California	16,178
10.	Houston, Texas	15,743

11. Tucson, Arizona	15,658
12. San Antonio, Texas	15,224

The Bureau of Indian Affairs Relocation Program, 1951–79

Although there was some migration to urban areas by American Indians during the first half of the nineteenth century, World War II and the voluntary relocation program of the Bureau of Indian Affairs (BIA) were major factors in tens of thousands of Native people leaving economically troubled reservations and rural areas to move to cities.

World War II created an exodus of many Indian men and women from reservations into the armed forces and jobs in war-related industries. Many veterans returning from war chose to go to cities to find work instead of returning to reservation homelands.

During 1951, the BIA extended an unofficial small-scale relocation program, which assisted Navajos and Hopis, to serve all American Indians who needed work. The BIA established job placement offices in Denver, Colorado; Salt Lake City, Utah; Los Angeles, California; and Chicago, Illinois. Later it opened offices in Oakland, San Francisco, and San Jose, California; St. Louis, Missouri; Dallas, Texas; Cleveland, Ohio; Oklahoma City and Tulsa, Oklahoma; and Seattle, Washington.

Field offices provided one-way paid transportation to an urban area, job placement, subsistence funds until the first paycheck, and counseling. Job training was added later. By the early 1970s, an estimated one hundred thousand Native people had left their reservation homes, with BIA assistance, in search of economic opportunities in cities.

Opinions vary in regard to the program's successes and failures, its official objectives, and goals. Official policy did not prevent anyone from returning to reservation, but BIA figures indicate high return rates. Nonetheless, many of those who relocated found economic opportunity in cities.

Twenty-Six Urban American Indian Community Centers

Community centers in cities were among the organizations that developed with the increasing urbanization of Indians. The centers, which vary in size, provide a wide range of multipurpose programs to diverse clientele, including social, economic, and educational services. Some also maintain gift shops, art galleries, theaters, and other public outreach programs.

Alaska

Alaska Native Heritage Center
http://www.alaskanative.net
8800 Heritage Center Drive
Anchorage, AK 99504
(907) 330-8000

Founded: 1989

Central Council of Tlingit and Haida Indian Tribes of Alaska
http://www.ccthita.org
320 West Willoughby Ave., Suite 300
Juneau, AK 99801
(907) 586-1432
Founded: 1935

Arizona

Native Americans for Community Action, Inc.
http://www.nacainc.org
2717 North Steves Blvd., Suite 11
Flagstaff, AZ 86004
(928) 526-2968
Founded: 1971

Phoenix Indian Center
http://www.phxindcenter.org
4520 North Central Ave., Suite 250
Phoenix, AZ 85012
(602) 264-6768
Founded: 1947

Tucson Indian Center
http://www.ticenter.org
Suite 101 97 East Congress
Tucson, AZ 85701
(520) 884-7131
Founded: 1963

Arkansas

American Indian Center of Arkansas
http://www.arindlanctr.org
1100 North University, Suite 143
Little Rock, AR 72207
(501) 666-9032
Founded: 1977

California

Friendship House: Association of American Indians, of San Francisco Inc., CA
http://www.friendshiphousesf.org
56 Julian Avenue

San Francisco, CA 94103-3547
(415) 865-0964
Founded: 1973

Southern California American Indian Resource Center
http://www.scair.org
2218 Alpine Boulevard
Alpine, CA 91901
(619) 445-9236
Founded: 1997

United American Indian Involvement, Inc.
http://uaii.org
1125 West 6th Street, #103
Los Angeles, CA 90017
(213) 202-3970
Founded: 1974

Colorado

Denver Indian Center
http://www.denverindiancenter.org
4407 Morrison Road
Denver, CO 80219
(303) 936-2688
Founded: 1983

Illinois

American Indian Center of Chicago
http://www.aic-chicago.org
1630 West Wilson Ave.
Chicago, IL 60640
(773) 275-5871
Founded: 1953

Maryland

Baltimore American Indian Center
http://baic.org
113 South Broadway
Baltimore, MD 21231
(410) 675-3535
Founded: 1968

Massachusetts

North American Indian Center of Boston
http://www.naicob.org
105 Huntington Avenue
Jamaica Plain, MA 02130
(617) 232-0343
Founded: 1991

Michigan

North American Indian Association of Detroit
http://www.naiadetroit.org
22720 Plymouth Road
Detroit, MI 48239
(313) 535-2966
Founded: 1940

Minnesota

American Indian Family Center
http://www.aifc.net
579 Wells Street
St. Paul, MN 55101
(651) 793-3803
Founded: 1997

Minneapolis American Indian Center
http://www.maicnet.org
1530 East Franklin Avenue
Minneapolis, MN 55404
(612) 879-4555
Founded: 1975

New Mexico

Albuquerque Indian Center
105 Texas Street Southeast
Albuquerque, NM 87108
(505) 268-4418
Founded: 1990

New York

American Indian Community House
http://www.aich.org

11 Broadway, 2nd Floor
New York, NY 10004
(212) 598-0100
Founded: 1969

Native American Community Services of Erie and Niagara Counties, Inc.
http://www.nacswny.org
1005 Grant Street
Buffalo, NY 14207
(716) 874-4460
Founded: 1975

Ohio

Native American Indian Center of Central Ohio
http://www.naicco.org
67 E. Innis Avenue
Columbus, OH 43207
(614) 443-6120
Founded: 1975

Oregon

Native American Youth and Family Center
http://www.nayapdx.org
5135 NE Columbia Boulevard
Portland, OR 97218
(503) 288-8177
Founded: 1994

Pennsylvania

Council of Three Rivers American Indian Center
http://www.cotraic.org
120 Charles Street
Pittsburgh, PA 15238
(412) 782-4457
Founded: 1972

Tennessee

Native American Indian Association of Tennessee
http://www.naiatn.org

230 Spence Lane
Nashville, TN 37210
(615) 232-9179
Founded: 1983

Texas

American Indians in Texas at the Spanish Colonial Missions
http://aitscm.org
1313 Guadalupe Street, Suite 104
San Antonio, TX 78207
(210) 227-4940
Founded: 1994

Utah

Indian Walk-In Center
http://www.iwic.org
120 W. 1300 South
Salt Lake City, UT 84115
(801) 486-4877
Founded: 1974

Washington

Seattle Indian Center
http://www.seattleindiancenter.us
611 Twelfth Avenue South, Suite 300
Seattle, WA 98144
(206) 329-8700
Founded: 1972

Nine Urban American Indian Businesses, 2010

Arizona: Phoenix
Spirit Electronics, Inc.
http://www.spiritelectronics.com
Provides supply-chain solutions and electronic components distribution for global technology leaders in aerospace, defense, and communications industries. The company has been a Native American, woman-owned business since 1979.

Minnesota: Champlin
Deco Security Services
http://www.deco-inc.com

A privately held, Native American–owned company provides security services, including guards, systems monitoring, and electrical contracting work to federal, tribal, and corporate clients since 1986. Deco has primary branch locations in cities in thirteen states and Washington, DC.

Minnesota: Minneapolis
Birch Bark Books
http://birchbarkbooks.com
Independent bookstore owned by Louise Erdrich (Turtle Mountain Chippewa) that specializes in children's books, with an emphasis on Native American titles. The store, founded in 2000, sells Native art and jewelry and hosts community events.

Minnesota: Minneapolis
Mashkiki Waakaaigan Pharmacy
Created by the Fond du Lac Band of Ojibwe and the U.S. Indian Health Service, the Mashkiki (medicine) Waakaaigan (house) (MW) Pharmacy provides prescriptions with no copayments to federally recognized Natives with private or public health benefits. MW also provides assistance to people without health benefits.

New Mexico: Santa Fe
Hotel Santa Fe
http://www.hotelsantafe.com
The 163-room Hotel Santa Fe, the Hacienda, and Spa, a Pueblo-style complex, is a partnership between Picuris Pueblo of New Mexico and nontribal investors. It opened in 1991.

New York: Ithaca
Ongweoweh Corporation
http://www.ongweoweh.com
A pallet industry, distributing, managing, recovering, and recycling more than seventeen million pallets yearly throughout North America. It was founded in 1978 by Frank C. Bonamie (Cayuga Nation).

Texas: Dallas
BRENCO Industrial Services, LLC
http://www.brenco-llc.com
Commercial construction company specializing in interior and exterior renovations, additions, environmental services, and more. It was founded in 2001 by Steve Cardwell (Cheyenne/Arapaho Tribes of Oklahoma).
Virginia: Reston

TeraThink
http://terathink.com
Technology and management consulting firm to the federal government. It is a Native American owned, 8(a) certified business founded in 2002.

Washington, DC
Residence Inn by Marriott
http://www.marriott.com/hotels/travel/wascp-resdence-inn-washington-dc-capitol
The thirteen-story hotel in Washington, DC, which broke ground in 2003, is an economic partnership of the Four Fires: the San Manuel Band of Serrano Mission Indians of California, the Forest County Potawatomi Community of Wisconsin, the Oneida Tribe of Wisconsin, and the Viejas Band of Kumeyaay Indians of California.

Honoring Nations Honoree

Menominee Community Center of Chicago, 2003
Menominee Indian Tribe of Wisconsin
Keshena, Wisconsin, and Chicago, Illinois

A partnership between an urban Indian center and a tribal government, the tribally funded Community Center (now an officially recognized off-reservation community of the Menominee Indian Tribe), serves nearly five hundred Menominee tribal citizens in the greater Chicago area. The partners work together to ensure that all members stay involved in tribal affairs by organizing trips to the Wisconsin reservation 250 miles away, providing full electoral rights for off-reservation citizens, and holding official tribal legislative meetings at the center.

NEW YORK CITY AND SKYWALKERS

Fifteen New York City Buildings and Bridges Built by Skywalkers

For over one hundred years, Mohawk ironworkers (called "skywalkers") from upper New York State and southern Quebec, Canada, have been building tall bridges, skyscrapers, power plants, arenas, and stadiums across North America. They are legendary for "walking the steel" in New York City. According to one ironworker, "Almost all of New York above the twenty-story level has been built by Mohawks."

1. AOL Time Warner Building, completed in 2004
2. Bear Stearns Building, completed in 2001
3. Chase Manhattan Bank, completed in 1960
4. Chrysler Building, completed in 1930
5. Empire State Building, completed in 1931
6. French Building, completed in 1927
7. Graybar Building, completed in 1927
8. Hell Gate Bridge, completed in 1916
9. Madison Square Garden, completed in 1968
10. Rockefeller Center, completed in 1939
11. United Nations Headquarters, completed in 1952
12. George Washington Bridge, completed in 1931
13. World Trade Center North Tower, completed in 1970
14. World Trade Center South Tower, completed in 1971
15. Verrazano-Narrows Bridge, completed in 1964

Twin Towers, New York City, and September 11, 2001

From 1966 to 1974, hundreds of Mohawk ironworkers helped build the World Trade Center's Twin Towers in New York City. On September 11, 2001, terrorist hijackers intentionally crashed two airliners into the Twin Towers, killing everyone on board and many others working in the buildings. Both towers collapsed within two hours, destroying nearby buildings and damaging others. In the fall of 2001, a younger generation of Mohawk ironworkers traveled to New York to help clear twisted metal from the World Trade Center site.

POEMS AND BOOKS

Fourteen Poems about City Life by Native Poets

1. "Autobiography, Chapter XLII: Three Days in Louisville," by Jim Barnes (Choctaw). In *Harper's Anthology of 20th Century Native American Indian Poetry*, edited by Duane Niatum (1988).
2. "City," by Joseph Bruchac (Abenaki). In *Carriers of the Dream Wheel*, edited by Duane Niatum (1975).
3. "City Games of Life and Death: Walking the Mission District [San Francisco]," by Elizabeth Cook-Lynn (Crow/Creek/Sioux). In *Returning the Gift: Poetry and Prose from the First North American Native Writers' Festival*, edited by Joseph Bruchac (1994).

4. "Dream Song I: Indian Hills . . . Oklahoma City, Okla. '49," by Richard Ray Whitman (Yuchi). In *The Clouds Threw this Light: Contemporary Native American Poetry*, edited by Phillip Foss (1983).

5. "Harlem, MT: Just Off the Reservation," by James Welch (Blackfeet/Gros Ventre). In *Riding the Earthboy 40* (1976).

6. "Los Angeles, 1980," by Paula Gunn Allen (Laguna Pueblo/Sioux). In *American Indian Writings*, edited by Joseph Bruchac (1981).

7. "The New Apartment, Minneapolis," by Linda Hogan (Chickasaw). In *Harper's Anthology of 20th Century Native American Poetry*, edited by Duane Niatum (1988).

8. "Anchorage," by Joy Harjo (Muskogee/Creek). In *That's What She Said*, edited by Rayna Green (1984).

9. "Norman, Oklahoma, 07:VII:92," by Earle Thompson (Yakama). In *Returning the Gift*, edited by Joseph Bruchac (1994).

10. "A San Diego Poem: January-February 1973," by Simon J. Ortiz (Acoma Pueblo). In *The Remembered Earth*, edited by Geary Hobson (1979).

11. "A Song to the Chicago Indian Village [Wrigley Field], U.S.A.," by Marion "Tumbleweed" Beach (Creek). In *From the Belly of the Shark*, edited by Walter Lowenfels (1973).

12. "Sunday Morning: Iowa City," by Wendy Rose (Hopi/Miwok). In *What Happened When the Hopi Hit New York* (1982).

13. "Things (for an Indian) to Do in New York City," by Sherman Alexie (Spokane/Coeur d'Alene). In *The Summer of Black Widows* (1996).

14. "Winter Camp at Berkeley," by Gerald Vizenor (Chippewa). In *The Clouds Threw this Light: Contemporary Native American Poetry*, edited by Phillip Foss (1983).

Twelve Novels about City Life by Native Authors

1. *The Antelope Wife*, by Louise Erdrich (Turtle Mountain Chippewa) (1999). Minneapolis, Minnesota.

2. *Bone Game*, by Louis Owens (Choctaw/Cherokee) (1996). Santa Cruz, California.

3. *Ceremony*, by Leslie Marmon Silko (Laguna Pueblo) (1977). Gallup, New Mexico.

4. *Dead Voices: Natural Agonies in the New World*, by Gerald Vizenor (White Earth Chippewa) (1992). Oakland, California.

5. *House Made of Dawn*, by N. Scott Momaday (Kiowa) (1968). Los Angeles, California.

6. *The Indian Lawyer*, by James Welch (Blackfeet/Gros Ventre) (1990). Helena, Montana.

7. *The Jailing of Cecelia Capture*, by Janet Campbell Hale (Coeur d'Alene/Kootenai) (1985). San Francisco, California.

8. *Night Flying Woman: An Objibway Narrative*, by Ignatia Broker (Ojibway) (1983). Minneapolis, Minnesota.
9. *Roofwalker*, by Susan Power (Dakota) (2002). Chicago, Illinois.
10. *Survivor's Medicine: Short Stories*, by E. Donald Two-Rivers (Ojibwe) (1998). Chicago, Illinois.
11. *The Toughest Indian in the World*, by Sherman Alexie (Spokane/Coeur d'Alene) (2000). Spokane, Washington.
12. *The Woman Who Owned the Shadows*, by Paula Gunn Allen (Laguna Pueblo/Sioux) (1983). San Francisco, California.

FILMS

The Exiles (USA, 1961, 72 min.), directed by Kent Mackenzie.
> A docudrama (the performers play themselves) shows twelve hours in the life of a group of Indians living and suffering in Los Angeles, California. *The Exiles* has been hailed as one of the greatest films ever made by and about contemporary Native people.

Grand Avenue (USA, 1996, 165 min.), directed by Daniel Sackheim.
> An HBO miniseries based on a 1995 collection of short stories of the same name, written by Greg Sarris (Pomo/Miwok). *Grand Avenue* offers an unsparing depiction of contemporary urban life set in a Santa Rosa, California, neighborhood in which three families struggle to survive in American society.

High Horse (USA, 1995, 40 min.), directed by Randy Redroad (Cherokee).
> *High Horse* is a provocative narrative about the concept of "home" for Native Americans. The film opens in what the filmmaker calls "the artificial world of the colonizers"—the streets of a modern American city (New York City). From a cop to a young bike messenger, dislocated Native people search for and sometimes find their figurative and literal homes. They reclaim what has been stolen from the past in different journeys of love, loss, and identity.

High Steel (Canada, 1965, 13 min.), directed by Don Owen.
http://www.nfb.ca/film/high_steel
> This short documentary offers a dizzying view of the Mohawk Indians of Kahnawake who work in Manhattan erecting the steel frames of skyscrapers. Famed for their skill in working with steel, the Mohawks demonstrate their nimble abilities in the sky. Viewers also see community life on the Kahnawake Reserve, in Quebec, Canada.

House Made of Dawn (USA, 1977, 88 min.), directed by Richardson Morse.
> Adapted from Kiowa author N. Scott Momaday's Pulitzer Prize–winning novel of the same name, the film tells the story of Abel, a man who must deal with two distinct but conflicting worlds: Los Angeles, California, and his southwestern reservation.

La Mission (USA, 2009, 117 min.), directed by Peter Bratt (Quechua).

San Francisco, California's Mission District is the setting for an exploration of a neighborhood in transition and the people who call it home. The story deals with the healing of a broken man, of a father's relationship with his gay son, and of a neighborhood struggling to break the chains of violence.

To Brooklyn and Back: A Mohawk Journey (Canada/USA, 2008, 57 min.), directed by Reaghan Tarbell (Kahnawake Mohawk).

The filmmaker explores her roots and traces the connections of her family from the Kahnawake Reserve outside Montreal, Canada, to the ten-square block area in Brooklyn known as Little Caughnawaga. There, while the Mohawk iron-workers were building Manhattan's iconic skyscrapers, the women sustained a vibrant community far from home in the mid-1990s.

Urban Indians and Seattle's Civil Rights History (Seattle Civil Rights and Labor History Project, University of Washington)

http://depts.washington.edu/civilr/UrbanIndians.htm

The video includes excerpts from oral history interviews with activists Ramona Bennett (Puyallup), Willard Bill (Muckleshoot), Randy Lewis (Colville), Blair Paul (Tlingit), Jeanne Raymond (Confederated Tribes of the Umatilla), and Lawney Reyes (Colville).

The Urban Relocation Program (USA, 2005, few min.), coproduced by Native American Public Telecommunications and Adanvdo Vision.

http://www.pbs.org/indiancountry/history/relocate.html

Randy Edmonds (Caddo/Kiowa), a Los Angeles, California, powwow announcer who grew up in Anadarko, Oklahoma, remembers how the Bureau of Indian Affairs agent recruited him to relocate. He and Paula Starr (Cheyenne/Arapaho) discuss their experiences in an online excerpt from *Indian Country Diaries*, a two-part series of documentaries that explores the challenges facing Native Americans in the twenty-first century, in both urban and reservation settings.

ORGANIZATIONS

National Council of Urban Indian Health (NCUIH)

http://www.ncuih.org

The National Council of Urban Indian Health, a membership-based organization headquartered in Washington, DC, is devoted to supporting and developing quality, accessible, and culturally sensitive health care programs for American Indians and Alaska Natives living in urban communities. NCUIH is also a resource center providing advocacy, education, training, and leadership for urban Indian health care providers.

United American Indian Involvement, Inc.

http://www.uaii.org/index.php?title=United_American_Indian_Involvement

Founded in 1974, the United American Indian Involvement, Inc., headquartered in Los Angeles, California, is a comprehensive multidisciplinary service center that has expanded its scope to meet the needs of urban American Indian communities in California.

American Indian Movement (AIM)

In 1968, Dennis Banks, Clyde Bellecourt, and other Chippewa people living in Minneapolis and St. Paul, Minnesota, created the American Indian Movement (AIM). They spoke out against high unemployment, slum housing, and racist treatment in cities and fought for treaty rights and the reclamation of tribal land. Dressed in signature red jackets, AIM members carried two-way radios, tape recorders, and cameras. Using CB radio and police scanners, they got to the scenes of alleged crimes involving Native people before or as police arrived, to document or prevent police brutality. In 1970, John Trudell (Santee Dakota), Russell Means (Oglala Lakota), and others joined AIM, which orchestrated many protests and gave the organization great visibility during the 1970s.

AIM opened the K–12 Heart of the Earth Survival School in Minneapolis in 1971, and, in 1972, mounted the Trail of Broken Treaties march on Washington, DC, where members took over the Bureau of Indian Affairs (BIA), protesting its policies and demanding reform.

AIM chapters continue to advocate for indigenous rights, cultural renewal, and urban and reservation employment programs. AIM members (and others) oppose the use of caricatures of Indian people as mascots for professional and collegiate sports teams.

RESOURCES

Amerman, Stephen Kent. *Urban Indians in Phoenix Schools, 1940–2000.* Lincoln: University of Nebraska Press, 2010.

Carpio, Myla Vincent. *Indigenous Albuquerque.* Lubbock: Texas Tech University Press, 2011.

Doxtator, Antonio J., and Renee J. Zakhar. *The American Indians of Milwaukee.* Arcadia, 2011.

Fixico, Donald L. *Termination and Relocation: Federal Indian Policy, 1945–1960.* Albuquerque: University of New Mexico Press, 1986.

———. *The Urban Indian Experience in America.* Albuquerque: University of New Mexico Press, 2000.

Hilden, Patricia Penn. *When Nickels Were Indians: An Urban, Mixed-Blood Story.* Herndon, VA: Smithsonian Institution, 1995.

Inseminger, William. *Cahokia Mounds: America's First City.* Charleston, SC: The History Press, 2010.

Jackson, Deborah Davis. *Our Elders Lived It: American Indian Identity in the City.* DeKalb, IL: Northern Illinois University Press, 2001.

Johnson, Troy R. *The American Indian Occupation of Alcatraz Island: Red Power and Self-Determination.* Lincoln: University of Nebraska Press, 2008.

Krouse, Susan Applegate, and Heather A. Howard, eds. *Keeping the Campfires Going: Native Women's Activism in Urban Communities.* Lincoln: University of Nebraska Press, 2009.

LaGrand, James B. *Indian Metropolis: Native Americans in Chicago, 1945–1975.* Urbana: University of Illinois Press, 2005.

Lobo, Susan, ed. *Urban Voices: The Bay Area American Indian Community, Community History Project, Intertribal Friendship House, Oakland, California.* Tucson: University of Arizona Press, 2002.

———, and Kurt Peters. *American Indians and the Urban Experience.* Walnut Creek, CA: AltaMira Press, 2001.

Nestor, Sandy. *Indian Placenames in America: Volume 1: Cities, Towns, and Villages.* London: McFarland and Co., 2003.

Reyes, Lawney L. *Bernie Whitebear: An Urban Indian's Quest for Justice.* Tucson: University of Arizona Press, 2008.

Riney, Scott. *The Rapid City Indian School.* Norman: University of Oklahoma Press, 1999.

Thrush, Coll. *Native Seattle: Histories from the Crossing-Over Place.* Seattle: University of Washington Press, 2008.

Weibel-Orlando, Joan. *Indian Country, L.A.: Maintaining Ethnic Community in Complex Society.* Urbana: University of Illinois Press, 1999.

Weitzman, David. *Skywalkers: Mohawk Ironworkers Build the City.* New York: Macmillan, 2010.

Young, Biloine Whiting. *Cahokia: The Great Native American Metropolis.* Urbana: University of Illinois Press, 1999.

Web Sites

Harvard Project's Nations Directory Programs, 1999–2006: http://hpaied.org/images/resources/general/Dir_web.pdf

National Council of Urban Indian Health (NCUIH): http://www.ncuih.org/index

Native American Business Development: http://www.nativeedge.org

Urban Indian Health Institute (UIHI): http://www.uihi.org

Urban Indians and Seattle's Civil Rights History: http://depts.washington.edu/civilr/UrbanIndians.htm

Index

About the Authors

Arlene Hirschfelder is author or editor of numerous books on Native Americans, including *Native Americans: A History in Pictures* and *Rising Voices: The Writings of Young Native Americans*. She has been a consultant to the Smithsonian's National Museum of the American Indian.

Paulette F. Molin, a member of the Minnesota Chippewa Tribe from the White Earth Reservation, is the author of *American Indian Themes in Young Adult Literature* (Scarecrow, 2005). She has worked in educational administration and cocurated exhibitions on American Indian boarding school history.

Yvonne Wakim Dennis (Cherokee/Sand Hill/Arab), the author of *Children of Native America Today* and other books for children and adults, serves as education director of the Children's Cultural Center of Native America. She is a multicultural consultant for businesses, schools, and organizations.

Hirschfelder, Molin, and Dennis coauthored the award-winning book, *American Indian Stereotypes in the World of Children: A Reader and Bibliography*, published by Scarecrow Press in 1982 and 1999. For more than twenty-five years, it has continued to be a seminal work on the topic.

CPSIA information can be obtained at www.ICGtesting.com
Printed in the USA
BVOW081849190312

285320BV00003BA/2/P